THE REFORMA

D1338937

John Calvin developed arresting new teachings on rights and liberties, church and state, and religion and politics that shaped the law of Protestant lands. Calvin's original teachings, which spread rapidly throughout the West, were periodically challenged by major crises – the French Wars of Religion, the Dutch Revolt, the English Civil War, American colonization, and the American Revolution. In each such crisis moment, a major Calvinist figure emerged – Theodore Beza, Johannes Althusius, John Milton, John Winthrop, John Adams, and others – who modernized Calvin's teachings and translated them into dramatic new legal and political reforms. This rendered early modern Calvinism one of the driving engines of Western constitutionalism. A number of basic Western legal ideas of religious and political rights, social and confessional pluralism, federalism and social contract, and more owe a great deal to this religious movement.

This book is essential reading for scholars and students of history, law, religion, politics, ethics, human rights, and the Protestant Reformation.

JOHN WITTE, JR. is Jonas Robitscher Professor of Law and Director of the Center for the Study of Law and Religion at Emory University, Atlanta. His many publications include *Law and Protestantism: The Legal Teachings of the Lutheran Reformation* (2002) and *To Have and to Hold: Marrying and its Documentation in Western Christendom, 400–1600* (2006).

THE REFORMATION OF RIGHTS

Law, Religion, and Human Rights in Early Modern Calvinism

JOHN WITTE, JR.

Emory University

CAMBRIDGE UNIVERSITY PRESS

CAMBRIDGE UNIVERSITY PRESS

Cambridge, New York, Melbourne, Madrid, Cape Town, Singapore, São Paulo,
Delhi, Dubai, Tokyo

Cambridge University Press
The Edinburgh Building, Cambridge CB2 8RU, UK

Published in the United States of America by Cambridge University Press, New York

www.cambridge.org
Information on this title: www.cambridge.org/9780521521611

First published 2007
Reprinted 2010

Printed in the United Kingdom at the University Press, Cambridge

A catalogue record for this publication is available from the British Library

ISBN 978-0-521-81842-1 hardback
ISBN 978-0-521-52161-1 paperback

To Ria, Gertie, and Jane
My sisters, my friends

Contents

Illustrations

Preface and acknowledgments

Over the past three decades, a veritable cottage industry of important new scholarship has emerged dedicated to the history of rights talk in the Western tradition prior to the Enlightenment. We now know a great deal more about classical Roman understandings of rights (*iura*), liberties (*libertates*), capacities (*facultates*), powers (*potestates*), and related concepts, and their elaboration by medieval and early modern civilians. We can now pore over an intricate latticework of arguments about individual and group rights and liberties developed by medieval Catholic canonists, philosophers, and theologians, and the ample expansion of this medieval handiwork by neo-scholastic writers in early modern Spain and Portugal. And we now know a good deal more about classical republican theories of liberty developed in Greece and Rome, and their transformative influence on early modern common lawyers and political theorists, eventually on both sides of the Atlantic.

This volume tracks the development of rights talk in those parts of the Western tradition inspired by the teachings of the Genevan Reformer, John Calvin (1509–1564). Building in part on classical and Christian prototypes, Calvin developed arresting new teachings on authority and liberty, duties and rights, and church and state that have had an enduring influence on Protestant lands. Calvin's original teachings were periodically challenged by major crises in the West – the French Wars of Religion, the Dutch Revolt, the English Revolution, American colonization, and the American Revolution. In each such crisis moment, a major Calvinist figure emerged – Theodore Beza, Johannes Althusius, John Milton, John Winthrop, John Adams, and others – who modernized Calvin's teachings and converted them into dramatic new legal and political reforms. This rendered early modern Calvinism one of the driving engines of Western constitutionalism. A number of our bedrock Western understandings of civil and political rights, social and confessional pluralism, federalism and social contract, and more owe a great deal to Calvinist theological and political reforms. This is the main argument of this volume.

Some of this argument will be familiar to some readers, especially to specialists on the history of Calvinism. A century ago, great European scholars like Otto von Gierke, Max Weber, Emile Doumergue, Abraham Kuyper, Georg Jellinek, Josef Bohatec, Charles Borgeaud, and others drew direct and easy lines from Geneva to Philadelphia, from Calvin to Rousseau. In the past half century, whole societies of specialists have emerged to study some of the individual titans who appear in these pages – Calvin, Beza, Althusius, Milton, and Winthrop especially. The classic overviews of Calvinism, however, were focused largely on large political patterns, and paid rather little mind to the emerging rights talk and legal nuances of the tradition. And the more recent case studies of individual titans, however excellent, do not track the gradual development of a distinctly Calvinist doctrine of law, religion, and rights over time and across cultures. This volume tells this story of the development of Calvinist rights doctrines to complement the many fine studies on the development of Catholic rights doctrine already in hand.

I would like to express my warmest appreciation to Dr. Craig Dykstra and his colleagues at the Lilly Endowment, Inc. in Indianapolis for their extraordinarily generous grant that provided me with research support and time to work on this and related volumes on law, religion, and the Protestant tradition. I would also like to offer my profound thanks to Dr. Alonzo McDonald and his colleagues in the Alonzo L. McDonald Family Agape Foundation for lending further generous support and wise counsel.

I would also like to express my gratitude to several scholars who were kind enough to offer me their criticisms and counsel. These include my Emory colleagues, Frank S. Alexander, Harold J. Berman, Timothy P. Jackson, Michael J. Perry, Philip L. Reynolds, and Steven M. Tipton, as well as several colleagues and friends at other universities, notably Patrick M. Brennan, Don S. Browning, Charles Donahue, Daniel L. Dreisbach, R. H. Helmholz, Wolfgang Huber, Robert M. Kingdon, David Little, Martin E. Marty, David Novak, Joan Lockwood O'Donovan, Steven Ozment, Charles J. Reid, Jr., David VanDrunen, Johan van der Vyver, and Nicholas P. Wolterstorff.

I would like to recognize several joint degree graduates of our Center for the Study of Law and Religion at Emory University who furnished valuable research assistance on this and related volumes, notably Amos Davis, Laurie Ann Fallon, Christy Green, Charles Hooker, Anne Jacobs, Joel Nichols, Sarah Pentz, Jimmy Rock, and Judd Treeman, and also three other young scholars, Collin Freer, Wallace McDonald, and Gregory Williams. I owe special thanks to my Center colleagues, April Bogle, Anita Mann, Amy Wheeler, and Janice Wiggins for their expert services in support of the Lilly and McDonald projects of which this volume is part and product. And I owe a mountain of debt to my wife Eliza for enduring so many conversations about the themes of this volume, and for sharpening so many passages herein with her keen editorial eye.

My warm thanks to the curators and librarians at the following institutions who were kind enough to open their marvelous collections to me – the British Library in London, the Max Planck Institute in Frankfurt am Main, the Newberry Library in Chicago, the Robbins Collection at the University of California at Berkeley, and various libraries at Cambridge University, Edinburgh University, Harvard University, Heidelberg University, Oxford University, Princeton University, and the University of Chicago.

Finally, I would like to express my deep appreciation to Kate Brett and Kevin Taylor at Cambridge University Press for taking on this volume and for working so assiduously to see to its timely publication, despite my unconscionably tardy delivery of the manuscript.

This volume is dedicated to my three sisters, Ria, Gertie, and Jane, who in their own unique ways have taught me the true meanings of "liberty" and "reformation."

John Witte, Jr.

Abbreviations and references

Adams   *The Works of John Adams, Second President of the United States, with a Life of the Author, Notes, and Illustrations,* ed. C. F. Adams, 10 vols. (Boston, 1850–1856)

AFR   *Archiv für Reformationsgeschichte*

Calvin, *Seneca*   *Calvin's Commentary on Seneca's De Clementia,* trans. Ford Lewis Battles and A. M. Hugo (Leiden, 1969)

CO   *Ioannis Calvini opera quae supersunt omnia,* ed. G. Baum, *et al.,* 59 vols. (Brunswick, 1863–1900). References throughout to Calvin's Sermons (Serm.), Commentaries (Comm.), and Lectures (Lect.) are to this edition of his works unless otherwise indicated; all translations from this source are by the author.

CPW   *Complete Prose Works of John Milton,* 7 vols., Don M. Wolfe gen. ed. (New Haven, CT, 1953–1980)

Dic.   Johannes Althusius, *Dicaeologicae libri tres, totum et universum jus, quo utimur, methodice complectentes* (Frankfurt, 1618)

Ehler and Morrall   Sidney Z. Ehler and John B. Morrall, eds., *Church and State Through the Centuries: A Collection of Historic Documents with Commentaries* (Newman, MD, 1954)

Institutes (1536)   *Ioannis Calvini Institutio Religionis Christianae* (Basel, 1536), translated as John Calvin, *Institution of the Christian Religion,* trans. Ford Lewis Battles (Atlanta, GA, 1975)

Institutes (1559)   *Ioannis Calvini Institutio Religionis Christianae* (Basel, 1559), translated as *Institutes of the Christian Religion,* ed. John T. McNeill, trans. Ford Lewis Battles (Philadelphia, PA, 1960)

LW   Jaroslav Pelikan and Helmut T. Lehmann, eds., *Luther's Works,* 55 vols. (Philadelphia, PA, 1955–1968)

MC   *Confessio et apologia pastorum & reliquorum ministrorum Ecclesiae Magdeburgensis* (Magdeburg, 1550)

NTAnn   Theodore Beza, *Iesu Christi D. N. Novum Testamentum, sive novum foedus,* 2 vols. (Geneva, 1565)

xiv

Pol. Johannes Althusius, *Politica methodice digesta atque exemplis sacris & profanis illustrata*, 3rd edn. (Herborn, 1614), reprinted as *Politica Methodice Digesta of Johannes Althusius (Althaus)*, ed. Carl J. Friedrich (Cambridge, MA, 1932)

Stephenson and Markham   Carl Stephenson and Frederick George Marcham, *Sources of English Constitutional History*, rev. edn., 2 vols. (New York, 1972)

Thorpe   Francis Thorpe, ed., *The Federal and State Constitutions, Colonial Charters, and Other Organic Laws*, 7 vols. (Washington, DC, 1909)

TT Theodore Beza, *Tractationum Theologicarum*, 3 vols., 2nd edn. (Geneva, 1582)

WA   *D. Martin Luthers Werke: Kritische Gesamtausgabe*, repr. edn., 78 vols. (Weimar, 1883–1987)

ZSS (KA)   *Zeitschrift der Savigny-Stiftung für Rechtsgeschichte: Kanonistische Abteilung*

All Bible quotations are taken from the Revised Standard Edition unless clearly indicated.

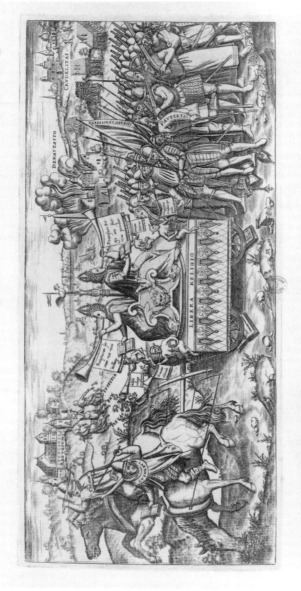

LIBERAE RELIGIONIS TYPVS.

LIBERA RELLIGIO CVM PRIMVM INTRAVIT IN ORBEM,
PELLVNTVR SVBITO PAX PIETASQVE SIMVL.

LIBERA RELLIGIO NI MOX EXCESSERIT ORBE,
ASPERIVS MISEROS HORRIDA BELLA PREMVNT.

Fig. 1. "Liberae Religionis Typus", allegory on the Reformation depicting John Calvin (1509–1564) and Martin Luther (1483–1546)

Introduction

In his *Origins of Totalitarian Democracy* (1952), J. L. Talmon described the French Revolution as the harbinger of modern forms of both liberal democracy and totalitarian fascism. The political ideas of the French Revolution, said Talmon, were sufficiently "protean" and "provocative" to guide these juxtaposed political movements along paths that the *philosophes* could never have anticipated. A Lincoln and a Marx, a Roosevelt and a Mussolini could all take inspiration from the core teachings of the French Revolution.[1]

An analogous claim can be made about the Calvinist Reformation. This Protestant movement first broke out in Geneva under the leadership of the French theologian and jurist, John Calvin (1509–1564), and then swept over large parts of France, Scotland, the Netherlands, Germany, England, and North America in the next 250 years. Calvin's original political ideas were also sufficiently "protean" and "provocative" to inspire a wide range of both totalitarian and democratic tendencies. It is easy enough to expose the totalitarian tendencies of many leading Calvinists – Calvin himself, Theodore Beza, Oliver Cromwell, Samuel Rutherford, John Winthrop, Cotton Mather, and their ample modern progeny. It is easy enough to compile an ample list of victims who were reviled, censored, imprisoned, tortured, banished, and even executed by Calvinists for their religious beliefs – Michael Servetus, Jean Morély, Jacob Arminius, Hugo Grotius, Richard Overton, John Lilburne, Roger Williams, and Anne Hutchinson, to name a few. It is easy enough to find early modern Calvinist tracts and sermons, on both sides of the Atlantic, earnestly defending all manner of monarchy, slavery, chauvinism, racism, bigotry, elitism, persecution, and other shameful forms of pathos and injustice. Any honest appraisal of the Calvinist tradition of law, religion, and human rights must acknowledge these brute and brutal facts.

---

[1] Jacob Leib Talmon, *The Origins of Totalitarian Democracy* (Boston, 1952).

This volume tells the human rights side of the Calvinist story, while also acknowledging its grimmer side. It shows how Calvin and his followers developed a distinct theology and jurisprudence of human rights and gradually cast these rights teachings into enduring institutional and constitutional forms in early modern Europe and America. The first and most essential rights for early modern Calvinists were religious rights – the rights of the individual believer to enjoy liberty of conscience and free exercise of religion, and the rights of the religious group to enjoy freedom of worship and autonomy of governance. Already in Calvin's day, the reformers discovered that proper protection of religious rights required protection of several correlative rights as well, particularly as Calvinists found themselves repressed and persecuted as minorities. The rights of the individual to religious conscience and exercise required attendant rights to assemble, speak, worship, evangelize, educate, parent, travel, and more on the basis of their beliefs. The rights of the religious group to worship and govern itself as an ecclesiastical polity required attendant rights to legal personality, corporate property, collective worship, organized charity, parochial education, freedom of press, freedom of contract, freedom of association, and more. For early modern Calvinists, religious rights thus became, in Georg Jellinek's words, the "mother" of many other human rights.[2]

Religious rights also became the "midwife" of many constitutional laws in the early modern period. Calvinists discovered through hard experience that religious and other human rights have little salience in societies that lack basic constitutional structures and procedures that give them meaning and measure. Human rights have little value for parties who lack basic rights to security, succor, and sanctuary. Human rights have little pertinence for victims who lack legal standing in courts or procedural rights to pursue apt remedies against political officials or fellow citizens who have abused their rights. Human rights have little cogency in communities that lack the ethos and ethic to render rights violations a source of shame and regret, restraint and respect. And so, over time, early modern Calvinists worked with others slowly to develop a human rights culture and a set of constitutional structures dedicated to the rule of law and to the protection of the essential rights and liberties of all peaceable believers.

Calvinists took the lead in producing a number of landmark constitutional documents that gradually expanded the Western regime of

---

[2] Georg Jellinek, *Die Erklärung der Menschen- und Bürgerrechte: Ein Beitrag zur modernen Verfassungsgeschichte* (Leipzig, 1895), 42.

human rights in the early modern period. These documents included the Ecclesiastical Ordinance (1541/61) and the Civil Edict (1568) of Geneva; in the Netherlands, the Union of Utrecht (1579) and the Act of Abjuration (1581); in France, the Edict of Nantes (1598); in Scotland, the Solemn League and Covenant (1643); in England, the Petition of Right (1628), the Bill of Rights (1689), and the Toleration Act (1689); in New England, sundry documents from the Body of Liberties (1641) to the Massachusetts Constitution (1780). Supporting these and other legal texts on point were thousands of Calvinist pamphlets, sermons, declarations, briefs, and learned tracts that defined and defended an ever greater roll and role of rights in church, state, and society.

Chapter 1 herein shows how John Calvin laid many of the foundations for this development of rights in his work in Geneva. Calvin began his reformation movement there in 1536, freshly armed with the first edition of his *Institutes of the Christian Religion*. In his early years, Calvin echoed the Protestant calls for liberty already made famous by Martin Luther a generation before – liberty of the individual conscience from canon laws and clerical controls, liberty of political officials from ecclesiastical power and privilege, liberty of the local clergy from central papal rule, liberty of the young Protestant churches from oppression by church and state alike. Initially, Calvin tinkered with this Protestant inheritance more than he transformed it. He spent time rooting these Protestant claims for liberty in the Bible and in selected classical and Catholic sources, and showing how spiritual and political liberty are both different than and essential to republican constitutionalism. In these early years, Calvin also called for general toleration of Catholics, Protestants, Orthodox, Jews, and Muslims alike.

In his mature writings, Calvin worked out a much fuller theory of law, religion, and human rights. His mature theory became more parochial in its focus, and it rendered Calvin and the Genevan authorities more hostile to moral indiscipline and religious dissent within their community. But this theory also became foundational for the later development of Calvinist theories of rights, particularly religious rights. Calvin developed a strong theory of the liberty of Christian conscience, which provided the eventual cornerstone for the constitutional protections of religious liberty advocated by Calvinists. He developed a detailed theory of moral laws and duties that foreshadowed a whole range of later Calvinist natural law and natural rights theories. He called for protection of "the common rights of mankind" which spurred the development of a number of later Calvinist theories of public, private, and procedural rights.

Calvin charted a deft course between Lutherans of his day, who tended to subordinate the church to the state, and Anabaptists, who tended to withdraw the church from the state and society altogether. Like Lutherans, Calvin insisted that each local polity (like Geneva) be a uniform Christian commonwealth that adhered to the general principles of the Bible and natural law and that translated them into detailed positive laws of religious worship, Sabbath observance, public morality, marriage and family life, social welfare, public education, and more. Like Anabaptists, Calvin insisted on the basic separation of the offices and operations of church and state, leaving the church to govern its own doctrine and liturgy, polity and property, without state interference. But, unlike both groups, Calvin insisted that both church and state officials were to play complementary legal roles in the creation of the local Christian commonwealth and in the cultivation of the Christian citizen.

Calvin emphasized the uses of the law and the collaboration of church and state in achieving the same within the local community. Both natural laws and positive laws, he believed, are useful in creating two tracks of morals – "civil norms" which are common to all persons and "spiritual norms" which are distinctly Christian. These two sets of norms, in turn, give rise to two tracks of morality – a simple "morality of duty" demanded of all persons regardless of their faith, and a higher "morality of aspiration" demanded of believers in reflection of their faith. This two-track system of morality corresponded roughly to the proper division of jurisdiction between church and state, as Calvin saw it. It was the church's responsibility to teach aspirational spiritual norms. It was the state's responsibility to enforce mandatory civil norms. This division of responsibility was reflected in the procedural divisions between the Consistory and the Council in Calvin's Geneva. In most cases that did not involve serious crimes, the Consistory would first call parties to their higher spiritual duties, backing their recommendations with (threats of) spiritual discipline. If such spiritual counsel failed, the parties were referred to the Council to compel them, using civil and criminal sanctions, to honor at least their basic civil duties.

Calvin's most original contribution to the Western rights tradition lay in his restructuring of the liberty and order of the church. This he accomplished by combining the principles of rule of law, democratic government, and spiritual liberty into a coherent ecclesiology. First, Calvin urged respect for the rule of law within the church. He devised detailed laws that defined the church's doctrines and disciplinary standards, the rights and duties of their officers and parishioners, the procedures and methods of the Consistory courts. The church was thereby protected from the intrusions of state law and the vicissitudes of its members. Church officials were limited in their discretion. Parishioners understood their spiritual duties. When new rules were issued, they were discussed, promulgated, and made well known. Issues that were ripe for review were resolved by the Consistory. Parties that had cases to be heard exhausted their remedies at church law before turning to state authorities. To be sure, this principle of the rule of law was an ideal that was often breached, from Calvin's day forward. Yet this principle eventually helped to guarantee order, organization, and orthodoxy within the widely dispersed Calvinist churches of early modern Europe and North America.

Second, Calvin urged respect for the democratic process within the church. Church officers were to be elected by the congregation and delegates to church synods were to be elected by their peers. Churches were to hold periodic congregational meetings and to give standing to communicant members to air their concerns and press their claims. Implicit in this democratic process was a willingness to entertain changes in doctrine, liturgy, and polity, to accommodate new visions and insights, to remedy clerical missteps and abuses, to spurn ideas and institutions whose utility and veracity were no longer tenable. To be sure, this principle did not always insulate Calvinist churches from a belligerent dogmatism. Just ask Michael Servetus or Jean Morély. But this principle of democracy helped to guarantee constant reflection, renewal, and reform within the church – *semper reformanda ecclesiae* (always reforming the church), in Calvin's signature phrase.

Third, Calvin urged respect for liberty within the church. Christian believers were to be free to enter and leave the church, free to partake of the church without fear of bodily coercion and persecution, free to assemble, worship, pray, and partake of the sacraments without fear of political reprisal, free to elect their church officers, free to debate and deliberate matters of faith and discipline, free to pursue discretionary matters of faith, the *adiaphora*, without undue laws and structures. To be sure, this principle, too, was an ideal that Calvin already compromised in his unusual empowerment of the Consistory in his later years; some New England Calvinists breached this ideal even further in their theocratic experiments. Yet this principle of liberty helped to guarantee constant action, adherence, and agitation for reform by individual church members.

It was Calvin's genius to integrate these three cardinal principles of ecclesiology. Democratic processes prevented the rule-of-law principle from promoting an ossified and outmoded orthodoxy. The rule of law prevented the democratic principle from promoting a faith swayed by fleeting fashions and public opinions. Individual liberty kept both corporate rule and democratic principles from tyrannizing spiritual minorities. Together, these principles allowed the church to strike a perpetual balance between law and liberty, structure and spirit, order and innovation, dogma and *adiaphora*. They also helped widely dispersed Calvinist congregations to adapt and adjust themselves to a variety of locales, and to absorb and accommodate local spiritual and cultural flavors without losing their core religious identity.[3]

This integrated theory of the church had obvious implications for the theory of the state. Calvin hinted that a similar combination of rule of law, democratic process, and individual liberty might serve the state equally well, though he did not work a detailed political theory. What Calvin adumbrated, his followers elaborated in a variety of ways.

Chapter 2 recounts that, shortly after his death in 1564, Calvin's original theory of law and liberty, and church and state faced its first major crisis. The crisis was the St. Bartholomew's Day Massacre of 1572, in which some 10,000 to 100,000 French Calvinists were slaughtered in a month of barbarism instigated by French Catholic authorities. Calvin's teachings provided little guidance to respond to a crisis of this magnitude. Calvin assumed that each local community would have a single faith. How could Calvinists countenance religious pluralism and demand toleration as a religious minority in a majority Catholic community? Calvin assumed that church and state would cooperate in the governance of a godly polity. What if church and state came into collision, or even worse into collusion against Calvinists? Calvin assumed that Christian subjects should obey political authorities up to the limits of Christian conscience, and bear persecution with penitence, patience, and prayer in hopes that a better magistrate would come. But what if the persecution escalated to outright pogrom? Were prayer, flight, and martyrdom the only options for conscientious Christians? Was there no place for resistance and revolt, even regicide and revolution in extreme cases? These challenges had faced Calvinists in various places throughout the 1540s to 1560s. They became stark life-and-death issues for French Calvinists after 1572.

It was Calvin's hand-picked successor in Geneva, Theodore Beza (1519–1605), who responded most decisively to this crisis. Echoing in part several German Lutherans and several English and Scottish Calvinists of the 1550s

---

[3] This feature of early modern Calvinist churches bears some resemblance to the classic Jewish law principle of *dina d'malkhuta dina*, which allowed Jewish communities in the diaspora to adapt to local legal cultures without losing their core devotion to Halacha. See Elliot N. Dorff and Arthur Rossett, *The Living Tree: The Roots and Growth of Jewish Law* (Albany, NY, 1988), 265–275.

and 1560s, Beza reconstructed some of Calvin's original teachings, which Beza had initially defended fiercely. Every political government, Beza now argued, is formed by a tacit or explicit covenant or contract sworn between the rulers and their subjects before God as third party and judge. In this covenant, God agrees to protect and bless the community in return for their proper obedience of the laws of God and nature, particularly as set out in the Decalogue. The rulers agree to exercise God's political authority in the community, and to honor these higher laws and protect the people's rights. The people agree to exercise God's political will for the community by electing and petitioning their rulers and by honoring and obeying them so long as they remain faithful to the political covenant. If the people violate the terms of this political covenant and become criminals, Beza argued, God empowers rulers to prosecute and punish them – and sentence them to death in extreme cases. But if the rulers violate the terms of the political covenant and become tyrants, God empowers the people to resist and to remove them from office – and sentence them to death in extreme cases. The power to remove tyrants, however, lies not directly with the people, but with their representatives, the lower magistrates, who are constitutionally called to organize and direct the people in orderly resistance – in all out warfare and revolution if needed.

For Beza, tyrants were rulers who violated the terms of the political covenant – particularly its foundational requirement that all must honor the rights of God to be worshiped and the rights of God's people to discharge the duties of the faith in conformity with God's law. Beza made the rights of the people the foundation and condition of good government. "The people are not made for rulers, but rulers for the people," he wrote famously. If the magistrate rules properly, the people must obey him. But if the magistrate exceeds his authority in violation of the political covenant, the people, through their representatives, have not just the right but the duty to resist him as a tyrant.

The issue that remained for Beza was how to ground his doctrine of rights and to determine which rights were so fundamental that, if breached by a tyrant, triggered the right to organized resistance. Here Beza cleverly reworked Calvin's main arguments, taking his cues from Calvin's own late-life statements on the need to protect the subjective rights of the individual. The first and most important rights, Beza reasoned, had to be religious rights – "liberty of conscience" and "free exercise of religion." Persons are, after all, first and foremost the subjects of the Creator God and called to honor and worship God above all else. If the magistrate breaches these religious rights, then nothing can be sacred and secure any longer. What is essential to the protection of the liberty of conscience and free exercise of religion? Beza continued catechetically: the ability to live in full conformity with the law of God. What is the law of God? First and foremost the Decalogue, which sets out the core duties of right Christian living. What do these Ten Commandments entail? The rights to worship God, to obey the Sabbath, to avoid foreign idols and false oaths in accordance with the First Table of the Decalogue, and the rights to marriage, parentage, and a household, and to life, property, and reputation protected by the Second Table. Is the Decalogue the only law of God? No, the natural law that God has written on the hearts of all people teaches other rights that are essential to the protection of a person and a people. Beza touched on several of these broader natural rights: freedom of religious mission and education, freedom of church government and emigration, freedoms of speech, assembly, and petition, and freedom of marriage, divorce, and private contract. Beza did not do much to ground and systematize these natural rights, nor did he make clear which of them was so fundamental that their breach could trigger organized resistance. But he put in place much of the logic of a fundamental rights calculus that later Calvinists would refine and expand.

Chapter 3 shows how Beza's main argument about political covenants and fundamental rights came in for endless variations and expansions over the next two centuries, particularly among later Calvinists who fought against tyrants in the Netherlands, Scotland, England, and eventually America. These types of arguments had immediate application in the revolt of the Dutch Calvinists against the tyranny of Spain. Much like America two centuries later, the Netherlands was ruled by a foreign monarch, the Spanish emperor, Philip II, who became abusive. In the 1560s, Philip imposed a series of increasingly onerous restrictions on the Netherlands – heavy taxes, commercial regulations, military conscriptions, forced quartering of soldiers, and more – in breach of many ancient charters of rights and liberties. Even worse, Philip set up the terrifying Spanish Inquisition in the Netherlands, slaughtering Calvinists and others by the thousands and confiscating massive amounts of private property in a determined effort to root out Protestant heresy and to impose on the Netherlands the sweeping new decrees of the Catholic Council of Trent. In the later 1560s and 1570s, under the inspired leadership of William of Orange and others, the Dutch put into action the early Calvinist principles of resistance and revolution. Whipped up by thunderous preaching and thousands of pamphlets, Calvinists and other Dutchmen eventually threw off their Spanish oppressors. They issued a declaration of independence, justifying their revolt from Spain on the strength of "clear truths" about "the laws and liberties of nature." They established a confederate government featuring seven sovereign provinces and a national government, each with its own constitution and its own bill of rights. Some of these provincial constitutions embraced the most advanced rights protections of the day, rendering the Netherlands a haven for many, though not all, cultural and religious dissenters from throughout Europe.

The Dutch Revolt drew to itself a number of powerful Calvinist theorists. The most original work came from the prolific pen of the German-born Calvinist jurist, Johannes Althusius (1557–1638). Drawing on a vast array of biblical, classical, Catholic, and Protestant sources, Althusius systematized and greatly expanded many of the core political and legal teachings of Calvin, Beza, and other co-religionists – that the republic is formed by a covenant between the rulers and the people before God, that the foundation of this covenant is the law of God and nature, that the Decalogue is the best expression of this higher law, that church and state are separate in form but conjoined in function, that families, churches, and states alike must protect the rights and liberties of the people, and that violations of these rights and liberties, or of the divine and natural laws that inform and empower them, are instances of tyranny that must trigger organized constitutional resistance.

Althusius added a number of other core ideas to this Calvinist inheritance. He developed a natural law theory that still treated the Decalogue as the best source and summary of natural law but layered its Commandments with all manner of new biblical, classical, and Christian teachings. He developed a theory of positive law that judged the validity and utility of any human law, including the positive laws of Moses and the canon laws of the church, against both the natural law of Scripture and tradition and the fundamental law of the state. He called for a detailed written constitution as the fundamental law of the community and called for perennial protection of "the rule of law" and "rule of rights." He developed an expansive theory of popular sovereignty as an expression of the divine sovereignty that each person reflects as an image bearer of God. He developed a detailed and refined theory of natural rights – religious and social, public and private, substantive and procedural, contractual and proprietary. He demonstrated at great length how each of these rights was predicated on the Decalogue and other forms of natural law, and how each was to be protected by public, private, and criminal laws and procedures promulgated by the state. Particularly striking was his call for religious toleration and absolute liberty of conscience for all as a natural corollary and consequence of the Calvinist teaching of the absolute sovereignty of God whose relationship with his creatures could not be trespassed.

More striking still was Althusius's "symbiotic theory" of human nature and "covenantal theory" of society and politics. While acknowledging the traditional Calvinist teaching of the total depravity of persons, Althusius emphasized that God has created all persons as moral, loving, communicative, and social beings, whose lives are most completely fulfilled through symbiotic relationships with others in which they can appropriately share their bodies and souls, their lives and spirits, their belongings and rights. Thus, while persons are born free, equal, and individual, they are by nature and necessity inclined to form associations – marriages and families, clubs and corporations, cities and provinces, nation-states and empires. Each of these associations, from the tiniest household to the vastest empire, is formed by a mutually consensual covenant or contract sworn by all members of that association before each other and God. Each association is a locus of authority and liberty that binds both rulers and subjects to the terms of their founding contract and to the commands of the foundational laws of God and nature. Each association confirms and protects the sovereignty and identity of its constituent members as well as their natural rights and liberties.

Althusius applied this Christian social contract theory most fully in his description of the state. Using the political history of ancient Israel as his best example, he showed historically and philosophically how nation-states develop gradually from families to tribes to cities to provinces to nations to empires. Each new layer of political sovereignty is formed by covenants sworn before God by representatives of the smaller units, and these covenants eventually become the written constitutions of the polity. The constitutions define and divide the executive, legislative, and judicial offices within that polity, and govern the relations of its rulers and subjects, clerics and magistrates, associations and individuals. They determine the relations between and among nations, provinces, and cities, and between and among private and public associations – all of which Althusius called a form of "federalism" (from *foedus*, the Latin term for covenant). The constitutions also make clear the political acts and omissions that constitute tyranny and the procedures and remedies available to those who are abused. Althusius produced the most comprehensive Calvinist theory of law, religion, and human rights in the early modern period, and many of his insights anticipated teachings that would become axiomatic for Western constitutionalism and human rights.

Chapter 4 recounts what John Milton (1608–1674) called "the reformation of the Reformation" of rights in seventeenth-century England. The catalyst for this new reformation of rights was, again, tyranny – this time, by the English monarchy against the people of England, not least the swelling population of English Calvinists. In 1640, these Calvinists joined many others in rebellion against the excesses of the Crown. The causes for the English Revolution were multiple and complex. The landed aristocracy and merchants chafed under oppressive royal taxes and fees raised to support the unpopular wars and lavish living of King Charles. Many believers suffered under harsh new Anglican establishment laws that drove Calvinists and other religious nonconformists by the thousands first out of their families and churches, then out of England altogether. The whole country resented the increasingly belligerent enforcement of royal measures by the newly empowered royal and ecclesiastical courts. When Parliament was finally called into session in 1640, after an eleven-year hiatus, its leaders seized power by force of arms. Civil war erupted between the supporters of Parliament and the supporters of the King. The Parliamentary party eventually prevailed, and passed an Act in 1649 "declaring and constituting the People of England to be a Commonwealth and Free State." Parliament abolished the kingship, and, remarkably, King Charles was tried by a special tribunal, convicted for treason, and executed by public beheading. Parliament also abolished the aristocratic House of Lords and declared that "supreme authority" resided in the people and their representatives. Anglicanism was formally disestablished, and episcopal structures were replaced with Calvinist church forms. "Equal and proportional representation" were guaranteed in the election of local representatives to Parliament. England was now to be under "the democratic rule" of Parliament and the Protectorate of Oliver Cromwell.

After Cromwell died in 1658, however, the Commonwealth government collapsed. King Charles II, son of Charles I, returned to England, reclaimed the throne in 1660, and restored traditional monarchical government, Anglican establishment, and pre-revolutionary law. This Restoration era was short-lived, however. When his successor King James II, the other son of Charles I, began to abuse his royal prerogatives as his father had done, Parliament forced him to abdicate the throne in 1688 in favor of the new dynasty of William and Mary. This was the Glorious Revolution. It established permanently government by the King in Parliament and introduced a host of new guarantees to English subjects, notably those set out in the Bill of Rights and the Toleration Act of 1689.

The English Revolution unleashed a massive torrent of writings and legislation calling for the enhancement and enforcement of the rights and liberties of Englishmen. Part of the effort was to extend the traditional rights of life, liberty, and property in the Magna Carta (1215) to apply to all churches and citizens, not just Anglicans and aristocratic freemen. Part of the effort was to build on the Petition of Right (1628) that had set out several public, private, and procedural rights for the people and their representatives in Parliament. But the most radical and memorable efforts of the English Revolution were the many petitions and platforms issued in the 1640s and 1650s calling for the establishment of a democratic government dedicated to protection of a full panoply of rights and liberties of the people. These included freedoms of religion, speech, press, and assembly, the right to conscientious objection to oaths, tithes, and military service, freedom from forced quartering of soldiers and sailors, freedom of private property and from unjust takings, freedom from excessive taxation and regulation, freedom of private contract, inheritance, marriage, and divorce, the right to civil and criminal jury trial, and all manner of criminal procedural protections – no *ex post facto* legislation and bills of attainder, no warrantless arrests, no illegal searches and seizures, the right to bail, the right to a fair and speedy trial, the right to face one's accusers, the right to representation in court, the privilege against self-incrimination, freedom from cruel investigation and punishment, the right to appeal. While most of these rights proposals were quashed – partly by Cromwell's Protectorate and altogether by the Restoration government of 1660 – they provided a normative totem for the later common law to make real. Already in the Glorious Revolution of 1689, freedoms of religion, speech, and assembly were partly realized, as were several criminal procedure protections. And many more of these rights proposals came to vivid expression and experimentation among the English colonists in North America.

While scores of sturdy English Calvinist rights theorists emerged in seventeenth-century England, it was the great poet and political philosopher John Milton who provided the most interesting integrative theory of rights and liberties. While some of Milton's ideas strayed beyond Calvinist conventions, most of his political ideas remained within the tradition and indeed extended it. Citing Calvin, Beza, and an array of Dutch, Scottish, and English Calvinists, Milton argued that each person is created in the image of God with "a perennial craving" to love God, neighbor, and self. Each person has the law of God written on his and her heart, mind, and conscience, and rewritten in Scripture, most notably in the Decalogue. Each person is a fallen and fallible creature in perpetual need of divine

Milton

grace and forgiveness, which is given freely to all who ask for it. Each person is a communal creature, naturally inclined to form private, domestic, ecclesiastical, and political associations. Each such association is created by a consensual covenant or contract that defines its form and function and the rights and powers of its members, all subject to the limits of natural law. Each association is headed by an authority who rules for the sake of his subjects and who must be resisted if he becomes abusive or tyrannical. All such resistance must be as moderate, orderly, and peaceable as possible, but it may rise to revolt and regicide if necessary in the political sphere.

In devising his own reformation of rights, Milton seized on what he thought to be the Calvinist reformers' most important lesson – namely, that the Reformation must always go on, *semper reformanda*. England must not idolize or idealize any Protestant teachings, Milton insisted, even those of Calvin and the Genevan fathers. England must rather develop and deepen, apply and amend these teachings in a continuous effort to reform church, state, and society anew. There can be "no excuse for our delay in reforming," Milton wrote already in 1642. Milton further seized on what he took as a cardinal teaching of Calvinism – that God calls each and every person to be a prophet, priest, and king, and vests them with natural rights and duties to speak, worship, and rule in church and state, family and society at once. For Milton, the driving forces of England's perpetual reformation, therefore, were not only clerics or magistrates, scholars or aristocrats. The true reformers were just as much the commoners and householders, craftsmen and farmers of every peaceable type. Every person was created by God with freedom of conscience, reason, and will. Every person was called by God to discharge both their private Christian vocations and their public social responsibilities in expression of their love of God, neighbor, and self. This was a form of Christian populism and popular sovereignty that the Calvinist tradition had not put quite so strongly before.

Milton went even further beyond traditional Calvinist teachings in defining the religious, domestic, and civil rights and liberties that each person must enjoy in discharging these offices of prophet, priest, and king. Among religious liberties, he defended liberty of conscience, freedom of religious exercise, worship, association, and publication, equality of multiple biblical faiths before the law, separation of church and state, and disestablishment of a national religion. Among domestic liberties, he stressed urgently the right to marry and divorce in accordance with the explicit teachings of Scripture alone as well as attendant rights to nurture, discipline, and educate one's children and to have one's private home free from unwanted searches and seizures of papers and possessions. Among civil liberties, he offered a

brilliant defense of the freedoms of speech and press, and also defended
earnestly the rights to democratic election, representation, petition, and
dissent, as well as the rights to private contract and association and to jury
trial.

Milton premised his logic of liberty on a fervent belief in Truth, with a
capital T – The Truth of God and Scripture, the Truth of reason and nature,
all to be discovered by free and robust education and inquiry, experiment
and debate. Only when freed from the tyranny of prelates and monarchs,
of tradition and custom, of ignorance and error, of censors and licensors,
he believed, could divine, natural, and human Truth finally be discovered
and developed. Milton also premised his logic of freedom on a fervent faith
in the inherent goodness and potential of every English man and woman.
Once freed from the tyrannies of church and state and of mind and heart,
once steeped in the virtues of Scripture and nature and of learning and literature, he believed, every Englishman would seize the Truth with alacrity and
soar to splendid new heights of understanding and accomplishment. What
England needed to accomplish all this was a "second Reformation" that
built on but went beyond the successes of the sixteenth-century Calvinist
Reformation. This was to be an "outer reformation" that purged the core
institutions of family, church, and state from all remaining sources and
species of tyranny and brought true domestic, spiritual, and civil liberty.
It was also to be an "inner reformation" that purified the heart, mind, and
conscience of the tyranny of tried and tired traditions and unleashed a lively
spirit of inquiry and learning, a true love of virtue and goodness, a native
talent for self-rule and self-direction. These powerful sentiments became
the core ingredients of many Calvinist theories of democracy and popular
sovereignty in succeeding decades.

Chapter 5 shows how some of the ideas of the English reformation of
law, religion, and human rights came to vivid expression and expansion
in the American colonies, particularly in Puritan Massachusetts and other
New England colonies from 1620 to 1780. The Puritan American colonists
were given freedom in their founding charters to experiment locally with
many of the most radical proposals and ideals that the English Calvinist revolutionaries had propounded. The colonists seized with particular
alacrity on the proposals for the protection of rights and liberties within
a democratic government. In his famous *Body of Liberties* (1641), Calvinist
jurist and theologian Nathaniel Ward set forth a twenty-five-page bill of
rights for the colony of Massachusetts Bay, which captured every one of the
rights and liberties proposed by Calvin, Beza, Althusius, Milton, and the
Puritan pamphleteers, and added many more rights and liberties besides,

particularly in protection of women, children, and animals. The *Body of Liberties* was an anchor text for New England colonial constitutionalism and anticipated many of the rights provisions of the 1780 Massachusetts Constitution and other New England state constitutions. While these legal instruments were often breached and ignored by autocratic and theocratic colonial leaders, they provided an essential legal substratum of rights that proved enduring.

A number of New England Puritans – most notably John Winthrop (1588–1649), John Cotton (1584–1652), Thomas Hooker (1586–1647), Samuel Willard (1640–1707), and the three Mathers, Richard (1596–1669), Increase (1639–1723), and Cotton (1663–1728) – distilled prevailing Calvinist views of the person into a basic theory of authority and liberty, society and politics. On the one hand, they argued, every person is created in the image of God and justified by faith in God. Every person is called to a distinct vocation, which stands equal in dignity and sanctity to all others. Every person is a prophet, priest, and king, and responsible to exhort, minister, and rule in the community. Every person thus stands equal before God and before his or her neighbor. Every person is vested with a natural liberty to live, to believe, to love and serve God and neighbor. Every person is entitled to the vernacular Scripture, to education, to work in a vocation. On the other hand, every person is sinful and prone to evil and egoism. Every person needs the restraint of the law to deter him from evil, and to drive him to repentance. Every person needs the association of others to exhort, minister, and rule him with law and with love. Every person, therefore, is inherently a communal creature. Every person belongs to a family, a church, and a political community.

The New England Puritans, echoing some of their European co-religionists, cast these theological doctrines into democratic forms designed, *inter alia*, to protect human rights. On the one hand, they cast the doctrines of the person and society into democratic social forms. Since all persons stand equal before God, they must stand equal before God's political agents in the state. Since God has vested all persons with natural liberties of life and belief, the state must ensure them of similar civil liberties. Since God has called all persons to be prophets, priests, and kings, the state must protect their freedoms to speak, to preach, and to rule in the community. Since God has created persons as social creatures, the state must promote and protect a plurality of social institutions, particularly the church and the family. On the other hand, the New England Puritans cast the doctrines of sin into democratic political forms. The political office must be protected against the sinfulness of the political official. Political power, like ecclesiastical power, must be distributed among self-checking executive, legislative, and judicial branches. Officials must be elected to limited terms of office. Laws must be clearly codified, and discretion closely guarded. If officials abuse their office, they must be disobeyed. If they persist in their abuse, they must be removed, even if by revolutionary force and regicide.

The New England divines added to this distillation of traditional Calvinist teachings their own distinctive theory of covenant. They used the biblical idea of covenant in both theological and sociological terms. The covenant described not only the relationships between persons and God, but also the multiple relationships among persons in church, state, and society. The covenant of grace defined the relationship between each person and God. Initially, the Puritans viewed this covenant as something of a "divine adhesion contract," with God setting all the terms and even dictating through predestination who could enter the contract and enjoy its promise of salvation. When early colonists, such as Anne Hutchinson and Roger Williams, challenged this understanding, they were summarily banished from the colony. By the eighteenth century, however, the Puritans described the covenant of grace more as a bargained exchange about salvation – each person choosing to reach his or her own conclusions about the duties owed to God, neighbor, and self, based on reason, conscience, experience, and biblical meditation. This understanding of private religious liberty figured prominently in the first New England constitutions forged in the 1770s to 1790s.

The New England Puritans used the doctrine of covenant to describe not only the relationship between God and humanity, but also the relationships among persons. They distinguished among (1) social covenants, the Mayflower Compact (1620) and its scores of colonial progeny; (2) political covenants and oaths for political office that eventually became constitutional texts; and (3) ecclesiastical covenants, the famous Charleston Church Covenant (1630) and its dozens of progeny. The social covenant created the society or commonwealth as a whole. It defined each community as God's elect people and set a high moral standard so that the community could be a "city on a hill," a "light to the nations." The political and ecclesiastical covenants created the two chief seats of authority within that community, the church and the state. The Puritans emphasized that church and state were two independent covenantal associations within a broader covenantal community. Each was called to discharge discrete covenantal duties, as adumbrated in the laws of God and nature, and elaborated in the covenant by which the church and state were formed. Each was to be separate from the other in their forms and functions, offices and officers, but mutually responsible to see that all served the common good in accordance with the terms of the social covenant.

While the offices of church and state are divinely ordained, the officials who occupy them are sinful creatures, the Puritans emphasized. Left to their own devices, they will invariably convert these offices into instruments of self-gain and tyranny. Such official arbitrariness and abuse will inevitably lead to both popular insurrection and divine sanction. The Puritans thus advocated and adopted a variety of constitutional safeguards against autocracy and abuse within both church and state. Both church and state officials were to have as "godly a character" as possible – models of spirituality and morality for the community who swore oaths of allegiance to God and the Bible. Both church and state officials were to occupy their offices only for limited tenures with rotation of office; life tenures were simply too dangerous. Both church and state were to have democratic election of officers, and periodic congregational and town meetings between these officers and their subjects. Both church and state were to have self-limiting "republican" forms of government, with separate forms or branches of authority, each with power to check the sinful excesses of the other. Both church and state were to have "federalist" structures of government: the church was to be divided into independent congregations, each with its own internal structures of pastoral, pedagogical, and diaconal authority and discipline but loosely conjoined in a broader synod; the state was to be divided into independent townships, each with its own internal structures of executive, legislative, and judicial authority, but loosely conjoined in a broader provincial government.

These Puritan theological and political ideas and practices provided a fertile seedbed from which grew a good bit of later American constitutionalism. Many of the basic ideas and institutions of the social, ecclesiastical, and political covenants were written directly into the original New England constitutions of 1780 onward, and openly advocated for the nation by a variety of Puritan sermonizers and political conservatives in the early republic – most prominent among them, the great Massachusetts lawyer and statesmen, John Adams (1735–1826), a cradle Calvinist. Several fundamental Puritan ideas survived among both the "liberal" and the "republican" schools of later eighteenth- and nineteenth-century America. "Liberal" writers found in Puritan ideas of natural man and natural law important sources for their ideas of the state of nature and natural liberty. They found in Puritan ideas of a social covenant and a political covenant prototypes for their theories of a social contract and a governmental contract. They found in the doctrine of church covenants and separation of church and state a foundation for their ideas of disestablishment of religion and free exercise for both religious individuals and religious groups. "Republican" writers, in turn, transformed the Puritan idea of the elect nation into a revolutionary theory of American nationalism. They recast the Puritan ideal of the covenant community into a theory of public virtue, discipline, and order. They translated the Puritans' insistence on spiritual rebirth and reformation into a general call for "moral reformation" and "republican regeneration."

Basic Puritan constitutional institutions survived within the new federal and state constitutions of the young American republic as well. Political rulers were required to manifest a moral, virtuous, and godly character and take oaths to attest to the same. Most officials were required to stand for democratic elections to their offices. Political offices usually had limited tenures. Political authority was distributed among executive, legislative, and judicial branches, each with authority to check the others. Federalism was constitutionally prescribed. Liberties of citizens were copiously enumerated. Church and state were separated, yet allowed to cooperate.

Such is the main story of this volume. I make no pretense that the dozen or so figures analyzed closely herein are the only representatives of the Calvinist tradition of law, religion, and human rights, or that these early modern figures gave the final word of "Calvinist" or "Reformed" rights talk.[4] A brief review of John T. McNeill's old classic, *The History and Character of Calvinism*,[5] or the new masterwork by Philip Benedict, *Christ's Churches*

---

[4] I shall be using the terms "Calvinist" and "Reformed" interchangeably throughout this volume, knowing that these terms are somewhat slippery and controversial. Today, most scholars seem to prefer the label "Reformed" – in part because earlier scholars had used the term "Calvinist" pejoratively to describe "pietistic" or "scholastic" theologians who stood opposed to or departed from Calvin; in part because a distinctive mark of this tradition is the call for perpetual reformation; in part because many sixteenth-century contemporaries of Calvin, such as Ulrich Zwingli, Martin Bucer, Guillaume Farel, Pierre Viret, Jacques Lefèvre, Heinrich Bullinger, and Theodore Beza, were also influential in formulating the distinctive theological doctrines and accents of the miscalled "Calvinist" tradition. See esp. Richard A. Muller, *After Calvin: Studies in the Development of a Theological Tradition* (Oxford, 2003); Donald R. McKim, *Introducing the Reformed Faith* (Louisville, KY, 2001).

  While I see the wisdom of all this, my interest in this volume is to show how a distinct tradition of rights talk developed out of John Calvin's own foundational insights and how that tradition was transmitted and transmuted in the next two centuries. The older term "Calvinist tradition," despite its deficiencies, strikes me as the best short-hand way to express this interest. My story would have a different accent and title if I were to follow the traditions of rights talk rooted in sixteenth-century contemporaries of Calvin. Moreover, while "Reformed" might be a recognizable term today for Protestant insiders, it is not so self-evident to scholars outside the Protestant tradition, particularly non-Christians who also use the terms "reformed" to describe movements within their traditions. But all that said, I carry no stronger brief for either term, and thus use them interchangeably, with apologies to those deeply invested in one term or the other.

[5] John T. McNeill, *The History and Character of Calvinism* (Oxford and New York, 1954).

Purely Reformed,[6] makes clear that hundreds of strong Calvinist voices in the early modern tradition – American, Austrian, Canadian, Dutch, English, French, German, Hungarian, Scottish, South African, Swiss and others – have spoken to these fundamental themes of law, religion, and human rights. And today, Calvinists of many denominations around the world have developed more themes, especially since the rise of the international human rights movement. A comprehensive study of all these Calvinist figures, each pursued in the detail of the individual case studies herein, could easily fill several long bookshelves. And a close account of how all their work influenced legal, political, and social institutions and practices at the local and daily level could easily fill several dozen more long shelves. Truncation and selection have been necessary evils in preparing a manageably sized and (I hope) reasonably coherent account.

I have chosen to truncate the analysis by focusing on the early modern story, from the sixteenth to the eighteenth centuries, leaving the modern and postmodern stories of Calvinist rights to a later volume or two. The early modern Calvinist tradition features a level of continuity, coherence, and concentration of thought about rights that is harder to find in various modern and postmodern Calvinist traditions that I have (admittedly only) sampled. The early modern Calvinist tradition also features a level of definite and deliberated development of rights ideas and institutions that is harder to trace today in the more fragmentary and episodic expressions of Calvinist rights talk of the past two centuries.

I have chosen to select a few key figures for close analysis rather than prepare a survey that devotes a few paragraphs to each of the few hundred figures worthy of analysis. I tried to write such a survey, but it quickly became a narrative of one Calvinist saying one thing, and then another saying another thing; that fat manuscript is now lying in large heaps of discarded pages on the cutting floor. Instead, I have selected those figures who stood tallest in times of crisis and challenge, and who self-consciously retrieved and reconstructed traditional Calvinist teachings on law, religion, and human rights to meet these new exigencies. This methodology will inevitably rankle some readers whose favorite Calvinist heroes might well be slighted herein. But, in my view, we have enough fine surveys of the tradition of Calvinist political thought, and have collected enough good samples to know where some of the deep veins of insight lie buried. In my view, we would be better served to mine some of these veins more

---

[6] Philip Benedict, *Christ's Churches Purely Reformed: A Social History of Calvinism* (New Haven and London, 2002).

carefully, to dig deeper beneath the surface and to refine better what we bring out. The greatest compliment that could be made to this book is that it stimulates the production of many other and better studies of the scores of other Reformed rights thinkers who also deserve close analysis, from the sixteenth century to our day.

TOWARD A NEW HISTORY OF WESTERN RIGHTS

The story of this book might well surprise, even shock, scholars and students of human rights and of Calvinism. Our schoolboy texts have long taught us that the history of human rights began in the later seventeenth and eighteenth centuries. Human rights, we often hear, were products of the Western Enlightenment – creations of Grotius and Pufendorf, Locke and Rousseau, Montesquieu and Voltaire, Hume and Smith, Jefferson and Madison. Human rights were the mighty new weapons forged by American and French revolutionaries who fought in the name of political democracy, personal autonomy, and religious freedom against outmoded Christian conceptions of absolute monarchy, aristocratic privilege, and religious establishment. Human rights were the keys that Western liberals finally forged to unlock themselves from the shackles of a millennium of Christian oppression and Constantinian hegemony. Human rights were the core ingredients of the new democratic constitutional experiments of the later eighteenth century forward. The only Christians to have much influence on this development, we are told, were a few early Church Fathers who decried pagan Roman persecution, a few brave medievalists who defied papal tyranny, and a few early modern Anabaptists who debunked Catholic and Protestant persecution.[7]

Proponents of this conventional historiography have recognized that Western writers since classical Greek and Roman times often used the terms "right" or "rights" (*ius* and *iura* in Latin). But the conventional argument is that, before the dawn of the Enlightenment, the term "right" was usually used in an "objective" rather than a "subjective" sense. "Objective right" (or "rightness") means that something is the objectively right thing or action in the circumstances. Objective right obtains when something is rightly ordered, is just or proper, is considered to be right or appropriate when judged against some objective or external standard. "Right" is being used here as an adjective, not as a noun: it is what is correct or proper – "due and meet" in Victorian English. Thus when pre-seventeenth century writers

---

[7] See recent representative literature analyzed in Victoria Kahn, "Early Modern Rights Talk," *Yale Journal of Law and the Humanities* 13 (2001): 391.

spoke of the "natural rights" of a person they were really referring to the "natural duties" of a person – the right thing for the person to do when judged by an external standard posed by nature or by natural reason. As the great University of Chicago don, Leo Strauss, put it:

> Natural right in its classic form is connected with a teleological view of the universe. All natural beings have a natural end, a natural destiny, which determines what kind of operation is good for them. In the case of men, reason is required for discerning these operations: reason determines what is by nature right with regard to man's natural end.[8]

Enlightenment philosophers, beginning with Hobbes and Locke, Strauss continued, first began to use the term "natural right" in a subjective rather than an objective sense. For the first time in the later seventeenth century, the term "right" was regularly used as a noun not as an adjective. A "subjective right" was viewed as a claim, power, or freedom which nature vests in a subject, in a person. The subject can claim this right against another subject or sovereign, and can have that right vindicated before an appropriate authority when the right is threatened, violated, or disrespected. The establishment of this subjective understanding of rights is the start to the modern discourse of human rights, we are told. When early Enlightenment figures spoke of "natural rights" or the "rights of man according to natural law," they now meant what we usually mean by "rights" today – the inherent claims that the individual subject has to various natural goods like life, liberty, and property. This was "an entirely new political doctrine," writes Strauss.

> The premodern natural law doctrines taught the duties of man; if they paid any attention at all to his rights, they conceived them as essentially derivative from his duties. As has been frequently observed, in the course of the seventeenth and eighteenth centuries a much greater emphasis was put on rights than ever had been before. One may speak of a shift of emphasis from natural duties to natural rights.[9]

Strauss's historical account of rights is much more nuanced than this, as are the later historical accounts of some of his best students who have found some place for early modern Christian theories.[10] Moreover, it must

---

[8] Leo Strauss, *Natural Right and History* (Chicago, 1953), 7.

[9] *Ibid.*, 182. See further Strauss, *The Political Philosophy of Hobbes: Its Basis and its Genesis*, trans. Elsa Sinclair (Chicago, 1952); Strauss, *What is Political Philosophy? And Other Studies* (Glencoe, IL, 1959), esp. 197ff.

[10] See, esp. Michael P. Zuckert, *The Natural Rights Republic: Studies in the Foundation of the American Political Tradition* (Notre Dame, IN, 1996); Zuckert, *Natural Rights and the New Republicanism* (Princeton, 1994); Zuckert, *Launching Liberalism: On Lockean Political Philosophy* (Lawrence, KS, 2002). I am grateful to John Perry of the University of Notre Dame for directing me on various schools of Straussian thought.

be remembered that Strauss himself (and some of his students) wrote their histories of rights in part to decry the unhinging of objective and subjective rights, and the consequent decay of modern rights talk into a long subjective wish list of goods that have no objective basis. And Strauss himself in some of his writings spent a good deal of time mining the rich theologies and philosophies of his own tradition of Judaism.[11] But, particularly when cast into popular secular form, as it often is, this basic "Straussian" account of the Enlightenment origins of Western rights has persisted, with numerous variations, in many circles of discourse to this day.

One of those circles, ironically, is that of conservative Protestantism. Many conservative Calvinists and other Protestants today still view human rights with suspicion, if not derision. Some view human rights as a part and product of dangerous Catholic natural law theories that Calvinists have always purportedly rejected. More view human rights as a dangerous invention of the Enlightenment, predicated on a celebration of reason over revelation, of greed over charity, of nature over Scripture, of the individual over the community, of the pretended sovereignty of man over the absolute sovereignty of God.[12] These critics view the occasional discussions of natural law and rights in Calvin and other early reformers as a scholastic hangover that a clearer-eyed reading of Scripture by later Calvinists happily expunged from the tradition.[13] At a certain level of abstraction, this conservative Protestant critique of human rights coincides with certain streaks

---

[11] Leo Strauss, *Jewish Philosophy and the Crisis of Modernity: Essays and Lectures in Modern Jewish Thought*, ed. Kenneth H. Green (Albany, NY, 1997). See also Catherine H. Zuckert and Michael P. Zuckert, *The Truth About Leo Strauss: Political Philosophy and American Democracy* (Chicago, 2006).

[12] This is the position often associated with the great Swiss Reformed theologian, Karl Barth. See detailed sources in the recent study by Stephen J. Grabill, *Rediscovering the Natural Law in Reformed Theological Ethics* (Grand Rapids, MI, 2006), 21–53. While Barth was certainly opposed to much natural theology, natural law, and natural rights talk, he was not so adverse to human rights as he is often made out to be. For example, as a pastor in Safenwil he worked hard to secure the rights of workers and unions, the right to secure better wages and working conditions, the right to secure a job that satisfied one's calling and that confirmed one's "human dignity." As a Christian socialist, he was a fierce advocate for the rights of the poor, the widow, the orphan, the sojourner. As he put it: "God always stands on this and only on this side, always against the exalted and for the lowly, always against those who already have rights and for those from whom they are robbed and taken away." And as principal author of the courageous 1934 Barmen Declaration against Nazism, Barth gave vivid new expression to the founding rights of the Calvinist tradition – the right to religious liberty and the right of religious leaders prophetically to condemn tyrants who abridge these first rights to religion. See sources quoted and analyzed in George Hunsinger, "Karl Barth," in *Modern Christian Teachings on Law, Politics, and Human Nature*, ed. John Witte, Jr. and Frank S. Alexander, 2 vols. (New York and London, 2005), I:352–380, II:280–306.

[13] See sources and further discussion in my "A Dickensian Era of Religious Rights," *William and Mary Law Review* 42 (2000): 707, 719–724, 768–770. Allen D. Hertzke has recently argued that conservative American Protestant Evangelicals are beginning to warm to modern rights talk. *Freeing God's Children: The Unlikely Alliance for Global Human Rights* (Lanham, MD, 2004).

of "Straussian" historiography about the Enlightenment origin of rights. Various Straussians dismiss premodern Christian rights talk as a betrayal of the Enlightenment. Various Protestants dismiss modern Enlightenment rights talk as a betrayal of Christianity.

Whatever the philosophical and theological merits of these respective positions might be, the historical readings and narratives that support them can no longer be sustained. Not just by my account. A whole cottage industry of important new scholarship has now emerged to demonstrate that there was ample "liberty before liberalism,"[14] and that there were many human rights in place before there were modern democratic revolutions fought in their name. Indeed, it is now quite clear that the Enlightenment was not so much a wellspring of Western rights as a watershed in a long stream of rights thinking that began more than a millennium before. A comprehensive history of Western rights is still very much a work in progress today, with serious scholars still discovering and disputing in earnest the basic roots and routes of development. But a broad outline of the story of the development of Western rights is becoming clearer. In that emerging story, both the Reformation and the Enlightenment have an important place, but only in later chapters. Both these two movements presupposed and built on critical rights developments in classical Rome and in medieval Catholic Europe. Indeed, leaders of both the Reformation and the Enlightenment inherited many more rights and liberties than they invented. While they certainly made their own original and critical rights contributions, too, what Protestant theologians and Enlightenment philosophers contributed more than anything were new theoretical frameworks that eventually widened these traditional rights formulations into a set of universal claims that were universally applicable to all.

A thumbnail sketch of the main watershed periods in the history of Western rights is worth risking to help situate and appreciate what the Calvinist tradition, in particular, contributed. The first major watershed period in the history of Western rights came with the development of classical Roman law, both before and after the Christian conversion of Emperor Constantine in the fourth century CE.[15] The classical Roman jurists used the Latin term *ius* to identify a "right" in both its objective and

---

[14] Quentin Skinner, *Liberty Before Liberalism* (Cambridge, 1998). See further Virpi Mäkinen and Petter Korkman, eds., *Transformations in Medieval and Early-Modern Rights Discourse* (Dordrecht, 2006); R. W. Davis, ed., *The Origins of Modern Freedom in the West* (Stanford, CA, 1995); J. C. D. Clarke, *The Language of Liberty 1660–1832: Political Discourse and Social Dynamics in the Anglo-American World* (Cambridge, 1994).

[15] See sources and discussion in Charles A. Donahue, "*Ius* in the Subjective Sense in Roman Law: Reflections on Villey and Tierney," in *A Ennio Cortese*, ed. D. Maffei, 2 vols. (Rome, 2001), 1:506–535;

subjective senses. (*Ius* also meant law or legal order more generally.) The objective sense of *ius* – to be in proper order, to perform what is right and required, "to give to each his due" (*ius suum cuiuque tribuere*) – dominated the Roman law texts. But these texts also occasionally used *ius* subjectively, in the sense of a person "having a right" (*ius habere*) that could be defended and vindicated. Many of the subjective rights recognized at classical Roman law involved property: the right to own or co-own property, the right to possess, lease, or use property, the right to build or prevent building on one's land, the right to gain access to water, the right to be free from interference with or invasion of one's property, the right or capacity to alienate property, the right to bury one's dead, and more. Several texts dealt with personal rights: the rights of testators and heirs, the rights of patrons and guardians, the rights of fathers and mothers over children, the rights of masters over slaves. Other texts dealt with public rights: the right of an official to punish or deal with his subjects in a certain way, the right to delegate power, the right to appoint and supervise lower officials. Others dealt with procedural rights in criminal and civil cases. Charles Donahue has recently identified 191 texts on subjective rights in the *Digest* alone (one of the four books of Justinian's sixth-century *Corpus Iuris Civilis*) and speculates that hundreds if not thousands more such texts can be found in other books of classical Roman law.[16]

The classical Roman law also referred to subjective rights using the Latin term *libertas*, which roughly translates as liberty, freedom, privilege, or independence. At its most basic level, *libertas* was, as Justinian put it, "the natural ability (*facultas*) to do anything one pleases, unless it is prohibited by force or law."[17] One's *libertas* at Roman law turned in part on one's status in Roman society: men had more *libertas* than women, married women more than concubines, adults more than children, free persons more than slaves, and so on. But each person at Roman law had a basic *libertas* inherent in his or her social status. This included a basic right to be free from subjection or undue restraint from others who had no right (*ius*) to or possessory claim (*dominium*) over them. Thus the wife had *libertas* from sexual relations with all others besides her husband. The child had *libertas* from the direction of all others save the paterfamilias or his delegates. Even the slave had *libertas*

Max Kaser, *Ius Gentium* (Cologne, 1993); Kaser, *Ausgewählte Schriften*, 2 vols. (Naples, 1976–1977); Kaser, "Zum 'Ius' Begriff der Römer," Acta *Juridica* 19 (1977): 63; Tony Honoré, *Ulpian: Pioneer of Human Rights*, 2nd edn. (Oxford, 2002); C. Wirszubski, *Libertas as a Political Idea at Rome During the Late Republic and Early Principate* (Cambridge, 1950).

[16] Donahue, "*Ius* in the Subjective Sense in Roman Law."

[17] *The Institutes of Justinian: Text, Translation, and Commentary*, ed. and trans. J.A.C. Thomas (Cape Town, 1975), I. III.

from the discipline of others besides his or her master. And those rights could be vindicated by filing actions against the offender before a judge or other licensed official, directly or, as was more typical for those in lower social stations, through a representative.

Some *libertas* interests recognized at Roman law were cast more generally, and were not necessarily conditioned on the correlative duties of others. A good example was the freedom of religion guaranteed to Christians and others under the Edict of Milan (313) passed by Emperor Constantine. This included "the freedom (*libertas*) to follow whatever religion each one wished"; "a public and free liberty to practice their religion or cult"; and a "free capacity (*facultas*) to follow their own religion and worship as befits the peacefulness of our times."[18]

The rediscovery and new study of the ancient texts of Roman law in the late eleventh and twelfth centuries helped to trigger a renaissance of subjective rights talk in the West. Brian Tierney has shown that, already in the twelfth century, medieval canonists (the jurists who worked on the church's laws, which were called canon laws) differentiated all manner of rights (*iura*) and liberties (*libertates*).[19] They grounded these rights and liberties in the law of nature (*lex naturae*) or natural law (*ius naturale*), and associated them variously with a power (*facultas*) inhering in rational human nature and with the property (*dominium*) of a person or the power (*potestas*) of an office of authority (*officium*). The early canonists repeated and glossed many of the subjective rights and liberties set out in Roman law – especially the public rights and powers of rulers, the private rights and liberties of property, and what the great canonist Gratian in *c.* 1140 called the "rights of liberty" (*iura libertatis*) enjoyed by persons in various stations in life and offices of authority.[20] The canonists also began to weave these early Roman law texts into a whole complex latticework of what we now call rights, freedoms, powers, immunities, protections, and capacities for different groups and persons.

Most important to the medieval canonists were the rights needed to protect the "freedom of the Church" (*libertas ecclesiae*). "Freedom of the Church" from civil and feudal control and corruption had been the rallying cry of Pope Gregory VII which had inaugurated the Papal Revolution

---

[18] In Ehler and Morrall, 4–6, with original in Lactantius, *De Mortibus Persecutorum [c. 315]*, 48.2–12, ed. and trans. J. L. Creed (Oxford, 1984), 71–73.
[19] Brian Tierney, *The Idea of Natural Rights: Studies on Natural Rights, Natural Law, and Church Law, 1150–1625* (Grand Rapids, MI, 1997); see further Peter Landau, "Zum Ursprung des 'Ius ad Rem' in der Kanonistik," in *Proceedings of the Third International Congress of Medieval Canon Law* (1971): 81–102.
[20] C. 16, q. 3, dictum post c. 15, quoted in Tierney, *Idea of Natural Rights*, 57.

of 1075.[21] In defense of this revolution, medieval canonists specified in great detail the rights of the church to make its own laws, to maintain its own courts, to define its own doctrines and liturgies, to elect and remove its own clergy. They also stipulated the exemptions of church property from civil taxation and takings, and the right of the clergy to control and use church property without interference or encumbrance from secular or feudal authorities. They also guaranteed the immunity of the clergy from civil prosecution, military service, and compulsory testimony, and the rights of church entities like parishes, monasteries, charities, and guilds to form and dissolve, to accept and reject members, and to establish order and discipline. In later twelfth- and thirteenth-century decrees, the canon law defined the rights of church councils and synods to participate in the election and discipline of bishops, abbots, and other clergy. It defined the rights of the lower clergy vis-à-vis their superiors. It defined the rights of the laity to worship, evangelize, maintain religious symbols, participate in the sacraments, travel on religious pilgrimages, and educate their children. It defined the rights of the poor, widows, and needy to seek solace, succor, and sanctuary within the church. It defined the rights of husbands and wives, parents and children, masters and servants within the household. The canon law even defined the (truncated) rights that Orthodox Christians, Jews, Muslims, and heretics had in Christian society.[22]

These medieval canon law rights were enforced by a hierarchy of church courts and other administrative church offices, each with distinctive and complex rules of litigation, evidence, and judgment, and each providing the right to appeal, ultimately to Rome and the papal rota. These rights formulations were rendered increasingly sophisticated and systematic in the fourteenth through sixteenth centuries through the work of

---

[21] Harold J. Berman, *Law and Revolution: The Formation of the Western Legal Tradition* (Cambridge, MA, 1983).

[22] Tierney, *Idea of Natural Rights*; Tierney, *Rights, Law, and Infallibility in Medieval Thought* (Aldershot, Hampshire, 1997); Tierney, *Religion, Law, and the Growth of Constitutional Thought, 1150–1650* (Cambridge, 1982); M. J. Roca, "Der Toleranzbegriff im Kanonischen Recht," *ZSS* (*KA*) 121 (2004): 548; Udo Wolter, "Amt und Officium in mittelalterlichen Quellen vom 13. bis 15. Jahrhundert: Ein begriffsgeschichtliche Untersuchung," *ZSS* (*KA*) 78 (1988): 246; Charles J. Reid, Jr., "Rights in Thirteenth Century Canon Law: An Historical Investigation" (Ph.D. Diss. Cornell, 1994); Reid, Jr., "Thirteenth Century Canon Law and Rights: The Word *ius* and its Range of Subjective Meanings," *Studia Canonica* 30 (1996): 295; Reid, Jr., "Roots of a Democratic Church Polity in the History of the Canon Law," *Canon Law Society of America Proceedings* 60 (1998): 150; Reid, Jr., *Power Over the Body, Equality in the Family: Rights and Domestic Relations in Medieval Canon Law* (Grand Rapids, MI, 2004); James Muldoon, "The Great Commission and the Canon Law," in *Sharing the Book: Religious Perspectives on the Rights and Wrongs of Proselytism*, ed. John Witte, Jr. and Richard C. Martin (Maryknoll, NY, 1999), 158.

such scholars as William of Ockham, John Wycliffe, Conrad Summenhart, Richard Fitzralph, Jean Gerson, Francisco de Vitoria, Fernando Vázquez, Francisco Suarez, and others.[23]

The medieval canon law formulations of rights and liberties had parallels in medieval common law and civil law. Particularly notable sources were the thousands of eleventh- to sixteenth-century treaties, concordats, charters, and other constitutional texts that were issued by various religious and secular authorities. These were often detailed, and sometimes very flowery, statements of the rights and liberties to be enjoyed by various groups of clergy, nobles, barons, knights, urban councils, citizens, universities, monasteries, and others. These were often highly localized instruments, but occasionally they applied to whole territories and nations. A familiar example of the latter type of instrument was the Magna Carta (1215), the great charter issued by the English Crown at the behest of the church and barons of England. The Magna Carta guaranteed that "the Church of England shall be free (*libera*) and shall have all her whole rights (*iura*) and liberties (*libertates*) inviolable" and that all "free-men" (*liberis hominibus*) were to enjoy their various "liberties" (*libertates*).[24] These liberties included sundry rights to property, marriage, and inheritance, to freedom from undue military service, and to freedom to pay one's debts and taxes from the property of one's own choosing. The Magna Carta also set out various rights and powers of towns and of local justices and their tribunals, various rights and prerogatives of the king and of the royal courts, and various procedural rights in these courts (including the right to jury trial). These medieval charters of rights became important prototypes on which later revolutionaries would call to justify their revolts against arbitrary and tyrannical authorities. Among others, early modern Calvinist revolutionaries in France, Scotland, the Netherlands, England, and America all reached back to these chartered rights to justify their revolutions against tyrants, and eventually reached beneath these charters to the natural laws and rights on which they were founded.

The sixteenth-century Protestant Reformation grounded its revolt not only in ancient charters of rights, however, but also in biblical calls for

---

[23] A. S. Brett, *Liberty, Right, and Nature: Individual Rights in Later Scholastic Thought* (Cambridge and New York, 1997); Davis, ed., *The Origins of Modern Freedom in the West*; Richard Tuck, *Natural Rights Theories: Their Origins and Development* (Cambridge/New York, 1979); Michel Villey, *La Formation de la pensée juridique moderne* (Paris, 1968); Villey, *Le Droit et les droits de l'homme* (Paris, 1983); Vielly, *Leçons d'histoire de la philosophie du droit*, new edn. (Paris, 1977).

[24] *The Statutes at Large of the United Kingdom of Great Britain and Ireland*, 45 vols. (London, 1786–1869), I:1.

freedom. Particularly the New Testament was amply peppered with all manner of aphorisms on freedom: "For freedom, Christ has set us free." "You were called to freedom." "Where the Spirit of the Lord is, there is freedom." "You will know the truth, and the truth will make you free." "You will be free indeed." You have been given "the glorious liberty of the children of God."[25] These and other biblical passages inspired Martin Luther to unleash the Reformation in Germany in 1517 in the name of freedom (*libertas, Freiheit*) – freedom of the church from the tyranny of the pope, freedom of the laity from the hegemony of the clergy, freedom of the conscience from the strictures of canon law, freedom of the state from the rule of the church. "Freedom of the Christian" was the rallying cry of the early Protestant Reformation. It drove theologians and jurists, clergy and laity, princes and peasants alike to denounce medieval church authorities and canon law structures with unprecedented alacrity. The church's canon law books were burned. Church courts were closed. Monastic institutions were confiscated. Endowed benefices were dissolved. Church lands were seized. Clerical privileges were stripped. Mandatory celibacy was suspended. Indulgence trafficking was condemned. Annates to Rome were outlawed. Ties to the pope were severed. Appeals to the papal rota were barred. Each nation, each church, and each Christian was to be free.

Left in such raw and radical forms, this early Protestant call for freedom was a recipe for lawlessness and license, as Luther learned the hard way during the Peasants' Revolt of 1525. Luther and other Protestants soon came to realize that structures of law and authority were essential to protecting order and peace, even as guarantees of liberties and rights were essential to preserving the message and momentum of the Reformation. The challenge for early Protestants was to strike new balances between authority and liberty, order and rights on the strength of cardinal biblical teachings.

One important Protestant contribution to Western rights talk, which was common to early Lutherans, Calvinists, Anglicans, and Anabaptists, was to comb through the Bible in order to redefine the nature and authority of the family, the church, and the state vis-à-vis each other and their constituents. Most Protestant Reformers regarded these three institutions of family, church, and state as fundamental orders of creation, equal before God and each other, and vested with certain natural duties and qualities that the other authorities could not trespass. To define these respective offices clearly not only served to check the natural appetite of the *paterfamilias, patertheologicus,* and *paterpoliticus* for tyranny and abuse. It also helped to

---

[25] Gal. 5:1,13; 2 Cor. 3:17; John 8:32,36; Rom. 8:21.

clarify the rights and liberties of those subject to their authority, and to specify the grounds on which they could protest or disobey.[26]

A second major contribution was the Protestant Reformers' habit of grounding rights in the duties of the Decalogue and other biblical moral teachings. The First Table of the Decalogue prescribes duties of love that each person owes to God – to honor God and God's name, to observe the Sabbath day and to worship, to avoid false gods and false swearing. The Second Table prescribes duties of love that each person owes to neighbors – to honor one's parents and other authorities, not to kill, not to commit adultery, not to steal, not to bear false witness, not to covet. The Reformers cast the person's duties toward God as a set of rights that others could not obstruct – the right to religious exercise: the right to honor God and God's name, the right to rest and worship on one's Sabbath, the right to be free from false gods and false oaths. They cast a person's duties towards a neighbor, in turn, as the neighbor's right to have that duty discharged. One person's duties not to kill, to commit adultery, to steal, or to bear false witness thus gives rise to another person's rights to life, property, fidelity, and reputation.

These biblical formulations of rights were common among all four branches of the Reformation. On this common Protestant foundation, Calvinists developed a whole series of distinctive rights contributions that featured their doctrinal accents on the covenant, the three uses of the law, total depravity, the priesthood, prophethood, and kingship of all believers, and more, as we shall see in more detail in the chapters that follow.

While medieval canonists grounded rights in natural law and ancient charters, and while Protestant Reformers grounded them in biblical texts and theological anthropology, Enlightenment writers in Europe and North America grounded rights in human nature and the social contract. Building in part on the ancient ideas of Cicero, Seneca, and other Stoics of a pre-political state of nature, as well as on Calvinist ideas of social, political, ecclesiastical, and marital covenants, John Locke, Jean Jacques Rousseau, Thomas Jefferson, and others argued for a new contractarian theory of human rights and political order. Each individual person, they argued, was created equal in virtue and dignity, and vested with inherent and unalienable rights of life, liberty, and property. Each person was naturally capable of choosing his or her own means and measures of happiness without necessary external references or Commandments. In their natural state, or in "the state

[26] John Witte, Jr., *Law and Protestantism: The Legal Teachings of the Lutheran Reformation* (Cambridge and New York, 2002).

of nature," all persons were free to exercise their natural rights fully. But life in this state of nature was at minimum "inconvenient," as Locke put it – if not "nasty, brutish, and short," as Thomas Hobbes put it. For there was no means to balance and broker disputes between one person's rights against all others, no incentive to invest or create property or conclude contracts when one's title was not sure, no mechanism for dealing with the needs of children, the weak, the disabled, the vulnerable. As a consequence, rational persons chose to move from the state of nature to a society with stable governments. They did so by entering into social contracts and ratifying constitutions to govern their newly created societies. By these instruments, persons agreed to sacrifice or limit some of their natural rights for the sake of creating a measure of social order and peace. They also agreed to delegate their natural rights of self-rule to elected officials who would represent and exercise executive, legislative, and judicial authority on their behalf. But, at the same time, these social and political contracts enumerated the various "inalienable" rights that all persons were to enjoy without derogation, and the conditions of "due process of law" under which "alienable" rights could be abridged or taken away. And these contracts also stipulated the right of the people to elect and change their representatives in government, and to be tried in all cases by a jury of their peers.

Particularly the American and French constitutions reflected these new Enlightenment views, in part. The Virginia Declaration of Rights (1776), for example, provided in Article 1: "That all men are by nature equally free and independent, and have certain inherent rights, of which, when they enter into a state of society, they cannot, by any compact, deprive or divest their posterity; namely, the enjoyment of life and liberty, with the means of acquiring and possessing property, and pursuing and obtaining happiness and safety." The Declaration went on to specify the rights of the people to vote and to run for office, their "indubitable, unalienable, and indefeasible right to reform, alter or abolish" their government if necessary, various traditional criminal procedural protections, the right to jury trial in civil and criminal cases, freedom of press, and various freedoms of religion. But the Declaration also reflected traditional Christian sentiments in Articles 15 and 16: "[N]o free government, or the blessings of liberty, can be preserved to any people but by a firm adherence to justice, moderation, temperance, frugality, and virtue and by frequent recurrence to fundamental principles." And "it is the mutual duty of all to practice Christian forbearance, love, and charity towards each other."[27] Even stronger such traditional

---

[27] In Thorpe, VII:3813.

Christian formulations stood alongside new Enlightenment views in the 1780 Massachusetts Constitution.

The 1791 Bill of Rights, amended to the 1787 United States Constitution, provided a new set of rights of national citizenship to be enforced by the new federal courts. While the Constitution itself had spoken generically of the "blessings of liberty" and specified a few discrete "privileges and immunities" in Articles I and IV, it was left to the Bill of Rights to enumerate the rights of American citizens. The Bill of Rights guaranteed the freedoms of religion, speech, assembly, and press, the right to bear arms, freedom from forced quartering of soldiers, freedom from illegal searches and seizures, various criminal procedural protections (the right to grand jury indictment and trial by jury, the right to a fair and speedy trial, the right to face accusers and have them compelled to appear, freedom from double jeopardy, the privilege against self incrimination, freedom from excessive bail and cruel and unusual punishment), the right to jury trial in civil cases, the guarantee not to be deprived of life, liberty, or property without due process of law, and the right not to have private property taken for public use without just compensation. This original Bill of Rights was later augmented by several other amendments, the most important of which were the right to be free from slavery, the right to equal protection and due process of law, and the right for all adults, male and female, to vote.[28]

The Bill of Rights to the United States Constitution was defended in its day on a variety of grounds – with Enlightenment arguments among the most well known. It is no small commentary for this volume, however, that every one of the guarantees in the 1791 Bill of Rights had already been formulated in the prior two centuries – by Calvinist theologians and jurists among others. Some of these rights were already formulated by Theodore Beza and the French and Scottish resistance fighters of the later sixteenth century, more by Johannes Althusius and the Dutch constitutionalists at the turn of the seventeenth century, still more by John Milton and the English Puritans in the middle of the seventeenth century, and more yet by the New England Puritans from John Winthrop and Nathaniel Ward in the seventeenth century to Elisha Williams and John Adams in the eighteenth. Moreover, a number of the core ideas of American constitutionalism – popular sovereignty, federalism, separation of powers, checks and balances, church and state, and more – were also quite fully formulated by Calvinists in the prior two centuries, especially in the Netherlands,

---

[28] US Constitution, preamble; Arts. 1.9, 1.10, IV; Amendments 1–8, 13–15, 19, 24, 26, reprinted with many prototypes and defenses in Philip B. Kurland and Ralph S. Lerner, eds., *The Founders' Constitution*, 5 vols. (Chicago, 1987).

England, and New England. This is not to say, of course, that Calvinists had a monopoly on the American constitutional loom. But it is to say that Calvinists wove many strong theological threads into the fabric of early American constitutionalism.

Enlightenment arguments proved more singularly decisive in shaping the French Declaration of the Rights of Man and Citizen (1791). This signature instrument, which revolutionized a good deal of Western Europe, enumerated various "natural, unalienable, and sacred rights," including liberty, property, security, and resistance to oppression, "the freedom to do everything which injures no one else," the right to participate in the foundation and formulation of law, a guarantee that all citizens are equal before the law and equally eligible to all dignities and to all public positions and occupations, according to their abilities. The Declaration also included basic criminal procedural protections, freedom of (religious) opinions, freedoms of speech and press, and rights to property.[29] Both the French and American constitutions and declarations were essential prototypes for a whole raft of constitutional and international documents on rights that were forged in the next two centuries.

While traditional Enlightenment foundations and formulations of rights have remained prominent among some theorists, a concept of universal rights predicated on "human dignity" has become increasingly common today – in the West and well beyond. In the mid-twentieth century, the world stared in horror into Hitler's death camps and Stalin's gulags, where all sense of humanity and dignity had been brutally sacrificed. In response, the world seized anew on the ancient concept of human dignity, claiming this as the "Ur-principle" of a new world order.[30] The Universal Declaration of Human Rights of 1948 opened its preamble with what would become classic words: "recognition in the inherent dignity and of the equal and inalienable rights of all members of the human family is the foundation of freedom, justice, and peace in the world."[31]

The United Nations and several nation-states issued a number of landmark documents on human rights thereafter. Foremost among these were the two great international covenants on rights promulgated by the United Nations in 1966. Both these covenants took as their starting point the

---

[29] In Léon Duguit, *Les Constitutions et les principales lois politiques de la France depuis 1789* (Paris, 1952), 1; my translation.

[30] The term "Ur-principle" is from Louis Henkin, *et al.*, *Human Rights* (New York, 1999), 80. See further Michael J. Perry, *Toward a Theory of Human Rights: Religion, Law, Courts* (Cambridge, 2007), ch. 1.

[31] Ian Brownlie, ed., *Basic Documents on Human Rights*, 3rd edn. (Oxford, 1992), 21.

"inherent dignity" and "the equal and inalienable rights of all members of the human family," and the belief that all such "rights derive from the inherent dignity of the human person."[32] The International Covenant on Economic, Social, and Cultural Rights (1966) posed as essential to human dignity the rights to self-determination, subsistence, work, welfare, security, education, and various other forms of participation in cultural life. The International Covenant on Civil and Political Rights (1966) set out a long catalogue of rights to life and to security of person and property, freedom from slavery and cruelty, basic civil and criminal procedural protections, rights to travel and pilgrimage, freedoms of religion, expression, and assembly, rights to marriage and family life, and freedom from discrimination on grounds of race, color, sex, language, and national origin. A number of other international and domestic instruments took particular aim at racial, religious, and gender discrimination in education, employment, social welfare programs, and other forms and forums of public life, and the protection of children, migrants, workers, and indigenous peoples.[33] Later instruments, like the 1981 UN Declaration on the Elimination of All Forms of Intolerance and Discrimination Based on Religion or Belief, the 1989 Vienna Concluding Documents, and the 1992 UN Declaration on Minorities provided important foundations for the protection of religious rights for individuals and groups.[34]

Today, rights talk has become a dominant mode of political, legal, and moral discourse in the modern West and well beyond – sometimes too dominant when it drowns out other critical forms of moral and political discourse.[35] Various classes of rights are now commonly distinguished by Western jurists and philosophers.[36] One common distinction is between public or constitutional rights (those which operate vis-à-vis the state) and private or personal rights (those which operate vis-à-vis other private parties). A second distinction is between the rights of individuals and the rights of associations or groups (whether private groups, like businesses or churches, or public groups, like municipalities or political parties). A third is between natural rights (those that are based on natural law or human nature)

---

[32] See the preambles to both documents in *ibid.*, 114, 125.

[33] See representative documents in *ibid.*, 148, 162, 169.

[34] Natan Lerner, *Religion, Secular Beliefs, and Human Rights: 25 Years After the 1981 Declaration* (Leiden, 2006).

[35] Mary Ann Glendon, *Rights Talk: The Impoverishment of Political Discourse* (New York, 1991).

[36] See, among many others, W. N. Hohfeld, *Fundamental Legal Conceptions* (New Haven, 1919); Carl Wellman, *An Approach to Rights* (The Hague and Boston, 1997): Michael J. Perry, *The Idea of Human Rights: Four Inquiries* (New York and Oxford, 1998); Joel Feinberg, *Rights, Justice, and the Bounds of Liberty* (Princeton, 1980).

and positive rights (those that are based in the positive law of the state). A fourth is between substantive rights (those that create or confirm goods or entitlements) and procedural rights (those that guarantee subjects certain types of treatment by government officials). A fifth is between human rights (those that inhere in a human qua human) and civil rights (those that inhere in citizens or civil subjects). A sixth is between unalienable or nonderogable rights (those that cannot be given or taken away) and alienable or derogable rights (those that can be voluntarily given away or can be taken away under specified legal conditions like due process of law). A seventh is between will theories of rights (that emphasize the individual's rational choices and desires) and interest theories of rights (that focus on individual's needs and society's duties to meet those needs). International human rights jurists now also bundle these binary pairs differently into "first generation" civil and political rights, "second generation" social, cultural, and economic rights, and "third generation" rights to peace, environmental protection, and orderly development.

Different types of legal claims and jural relationships are inherent in these various classifications of rights. Some scholars distinguish rights (something that triggers a correlative duty in others) from privileges (something that no one has a right to interfere with). Others distinguish active rights (the power or capacity to do or assert something oneself) and passive rights (the entitlement or claim to be given or allowed something by someone or something else). Others distinguish rights or privileges (claims or entitlements to something) from liberties or immunities (freedoms or protections from interference). This latter distinction is also sometimes rendered as positive liberty or freedom (the right to do something) versus negative liberty or freedom (the right to be left alone). In all these foregoing formulations, however, the term "right" and its various synonyms and analogues is being used in a subjective sense – what is called a "subjective right."

The chapters that follow analyze how the early modern Calvinist tradition did its part to help build this emerging Western edifice of human rights ideas and institutions – drawing in part on classical and medieval Catholic rights prototypes, and working in part with humanists, neo-scholastics, and early Enlightenment philosophers of their day. Calvin and the early modern Calvinists analyzed herein all used the term "right" in both its objective and subjective senses. They measured objective rightness variously by the norms of Scripture and tradition, reason and conscience, natural law and common law. They focused their subjective rights talk on what Calvin called "the common rights of mankind," "the rights of a common nature," and "the equal rights and liberties" of all. Early modern Calvinists did not develop a consistent taxonomy and nomenclature of rights: they tended to dump into one big linguistic heap terms and concepts like "rights," "liberties," "freedoms," "privileges," "immunities," "powers," "capacities," and others, and often used these terms and concepts variously and interchangeably. It was only in the twentieth century that Calvinist jurists like Herman Dooyeweerd and Johan van der Vyver began to sort out these various terms carefully and to develop a more linguistically precise and systematic Calvinist architecture of rights.[37]

Of the seven binary pairs of rights listed above, early modern Calvinists focused on the first three – public and private rights, individual and group rights, natural and positive rights. Early modern Calvinists were particularly ardent champions of the rights of life, liberty, property, and the pursuit of happiness, rights of democratic election and representation, rights to political dissent and civil resistance, freedoms of religion, speech, press, petition, and assembly, freedoms of contract and association, rights to marriage, family, divorce, and inheritance, rights to form and dissolve corporations, partnerships, and other voluntary associations. Early modern Calvinists were equally ardent champions of group rights – particularly the rights of the church, the family, and the school, three institutions that they considered to be essential to maintaining the faith and order of the commonwealth and to buffering the state's proclivities to tyranny over individuals. Early modern Calvinists generally viewed these individual and group rights as at once natural and positive, personal and civil in character. For them, these rights were rooted in the natural order and human nature, but they had to be formulated and vindicated as positive rights at state law. They were also anchored in covenant relationships between persons and God. In the sixteenth and early seventeenth centuries, Calvinists tended to assert Decalogue-based rights as the inalienable rights whose abridgement could lead to resistance and revolt. In the seventeenth and eighteenth centuries, they used both theological anthropology and covenant theology to sort out a number of hard questions of what rights were alienable and inalienable, and what social and political conditions were necessary for their enduring protection and vindication.

Of the "three generations" of rights, early modern Calvinists focused on what international lawyers now call "first generation" civil and political

---

[37] See Johan D. van der Vyver, *Seven Lectures on Human Rights* (Cape Town, Wynberg, and Johannesburg, 1976); van der Vyver, "The Doctrine of Private-Law Rights," in *Huldigingsbundel vir W. A. Joubert*, ed. S. Strauss (Durban, 1988), 201; van der Vyver, *Leuven Lectures on Religious Institutions, Religious Communities and Rights* (Leuven, 2004). On Dooyeweerd, see detailed sources in my "The Development of Herman Dooyeweerd's Concept of Rights," *South African Law Journal* 110 (1993): 543–562.

rights. But not all "first generation" rights captured the imagination or industry of Calvinists. For example, while they talked generally and generously about "due process" rights, early modern Calvinists did not do much to advance a distinct theory and law of due process, civil and criminal procedure, or evidence. On these legal subjects, Calvinists were generally content to adopt and nurture rights and liberties that had already been born and raised elsewhere – in Greek philosophy and classical Roman law, and in medieval civil law, canon law, and common law. It is a telling anecdote that in the opening dedication to his 1536 *Institutes*, Calvin took a whole series of due process rights for granted in making a plea to Francis I for toleration of the new Protestant faith.

Though they emphasized "first generation" civil and political rights, early modern Calvinists were not averse to many of the values inherent in what are now called "second generation" social, cultural, and economic rights (or "interest rights") and "third generation" rights to peace, orderly development, and environmental protection. Care for the poor and the needy, provision of work and welfare, concern for sustenance and education, and similar values that are at the heart of modern-day second generation rights were also at the heart of early modern Calvinist teaching and practice. While early modern Calvinists were notorious for their officious inquiries into the intimacies of bed and board to ensure religious discipline and order, they were just as famous for the comprehensive networks and safety nets of diaconal care, child education, and social welfare that they instituted in each community. Likewise, concerns for the environment and for peaceful, orderly, and disciplined development in the community that are so widely championed today were important values for early modern Calvinists, too. While Calvinists have, since Max Weber's day, been associated with the rise of modern capitalism and vulgar industrialization, their emphasis on the creation order and on the original mandate to "dress *and keep* the Garden" (Gen. 2:15) made them reflexive environmentalists long before green became fashionable.

But few Calvinists before the twentieth century cast these values in the form and language of rights. Poor relief, social welfare, education, and the like were generally viewed as duties imposed on the church, state, family, and individual more than as second generation rights that could be claimed by the intended beneficiaries. To be sure, even in Calvin's day, the Genevan Consistory gave procedural rights to parties who were unjustly foreclosed from hospitals, schools, diaconal funds, and more. And the records of Consistory and county courts in Calvinist communities throughout Europe and North America are chock full of examples of successful petitions to have these duties of caring and sharing enforced. But neither the historical Calvinist Consistory records that I have sampled nor the theoretical reflections on poor relief, social welfare, and education by early modern Calvinist writers used a systematic discourse of rights. Second generation rights talk in Calvinism would have to wait until the twentieth century – for scholars like Walter Rauschenbusch, Emil Brunner, Nicholas Wolterstorff, and others.[38]

Even more remote to the experience of historical Calvinism is any discussion of third generation rights of peace, development, and environmental protection. Again, Calvinists prized these social values and goods as much as most others in their day, but they did not generally press these considerations in rights terms. Calvin and a number of early modern Calvinist jurists, most notably Althusius, included among the rights to property, the right to enjoy one's property without nuisance or interference by another, and the right to reparations and restitution in the event of willful damage or destruction of one's land, animals, crops, and forests. But this was decidedly a discourse of private property rights of the owner, not the environmental rights of nature herself. No early modern Calvinist that I know of spoke of a subjective right of nature, animals, or plants. Given the thick theological anthropology that came to inform later Calvinist notions of rights, a subjective right of nature would have required a wholly different rights framework. That is a worthy enterprise to pursue, and one that I plan to take up among other themes in a sequel volume on modern Calvinist rights theory. But this volume is about the foundations of Calvinist rights talk in the sixteenth through eighteenth century. And to that subject we now turn, beginning with Calvin's original rights experiment in Geneva.

---

[38] See, e.g., Emil Brunner, *Justice and the Social Order*, trans. Mary Hottinger (New York, 1945); Walter Rauschenbusch, *Selected Writings*, ed. Winthrop S. Hudson (New York, 1984); Nicholas P. Wolterstorff, *Until Justice and Peace Embrace* (Grand Rapids, MI, 1983).

2. "Imaginary Meeting of Reformist Leaders Lighting the Candle of the Gospel." Calvin and Luther (engraving) by Dutch School (seventeenth century)

CHAPTER I

Moderate (religious) liberty in the theology of John Calvin: The original Genevan experiment

[T]here is no kind of government more salutary than one in which liberty is properly exercised with becoming moderation and properly constituted on a durable basis.

John Calvin, *Institutes of the Christian Religion* (1543)[1]

John Calvin is a controversial candidate for the honor roll of religious liberty in the West. He is at once valorized and villainized both for his theology and for his politics of religious liberty, particularly his participation in the execution of Michael Servetus. Calvin's champions can be found in many quarters. John Adams urged: "Let not Geneva be forgotten or despised. Religious liberty owes it much respect, Servetus notwithstanding."[2] Jean-Jacques Rousseau, for all his anti-religious sentiment, had only praise for his compatriot: "Those who consider Calvin only as a theologian fail to recognize the breadth of his genius. The editing of our wise laws, in which he had a large share, does him as much credit as his *Institutes* . . . [S]o long as the love of country and liberty is not extinct among us, the memory of this great man will be held in reverence."[3] Charles Borgeaud judged Calvin's Geneva to be "the first stronghold" of religious and political liberty in modern times.[4] Both Emile Doumergue and Walter Köhler described Calvin as the "pioneer of the freedom of conscience and human rights" that were finally constitutionalized after the eighteenth-century American and French Revolutions.[5] Abraham Kuyper declared that "[e]very competent historian will without exception confirm the words of [American historian

---

References throughout to Calvin's Sermons (Serm.), Commentaries (Comm.), and Lectures (Lect.), are to G. Baum's edition of his works (*CO*) unless otherwise indicated; all translations from this source are by the author.

[1] *CO* I:1105.   [2] Adams, VI:313n.
[3] *Du contrat social* (1762), 2, 7n., in Jean Jacques Rousseau, *The Social Contract and the Discourse on the Origin of Inequality*, ed. Lester G. Crocker (New York, 1967), 44n.
[4] Quoted by McNeill, *History and Character of Calvinism*, 196.
[5] Walter Köhler, "Book Review," *Theologische Jahrbericht* 24 (1904): 579; Emile Doumergue, *Jean Calvin. Les hommes et les choses de son temps*, 7 vols. (Lausanne, 1899–1927) V:465–569.

George] Bancroft: 'The fanatic for Calvinism was a fanatic for liberty; and, in the moral warfare for freedom, his creed was his most faithful counselor and his never-failing support.'"[6]

Many competent historians, however, have categorically denied such assertions. Ernst Troeltsch described Calvin as "notoriously rigid" and his "personal view as undemocratic and authoritarian as possible."[7] George Sabine believed that Calvinism "lacked all leaning towards liberalism, constitutionalism, or representative principles [and] . . . was, in general, illiberal, oppressive, and reactionary."[8] Stefan Zweig charged Calvin with "fanatical dogmatism" and with "slaughtering freedom of conscience under the Reformation."[9] Perez Zagorin described Calvin as a "man of severe and inflexible character" who was "manifestly intolerant" of all forms and formulations of faith besides his own.[10] Roland Bainton declared that "the Reformation at the outset brought no gain for religious liberty. Rather the reverse,"[11] particularly under Calvin, "the arch-inquisitor of Protestantism" and "dictator of Geneva."[12] "If Calvin ever wrote anything in favor of religious liberty," said Bainton, "it was a typographical error."[13]

Both these judgments depend on too tendentious a reading of Calvin's writings and too ready a conflation of his views with those of his followers. On questions of religious liberty, Calvin must be read as a theologian and pastor, not as a political theorist and jurist. To be sure, as a youth in France, he had studied law and the political classics, and this early training is reflected in the style and substance of some of his works.[14] And, to be sure, during his work as pastor and member of the Consistory in Geneva from 1541 till his death in 1564, Calvin frequently addressed legal and political questions – both in Geneva and in many other places in Europe. But Calvin

---

[6] Abraham Kuyper, *Lectures on Calvinism* [1898], repr. edn. (Grand Rapids, MI, 1981), 78, quoting George Bancroft, *History of the United States of America*, 15th edn., 2 vols. (Boston, 1853), 1:319.

[7] Ernst Troeltsch, *The Social Teaching of the Churches*, trans. O. Wyon, 2nd. impr., 2 vols. (London, 1949), II:628.

[8] Quoted by Robert M. Kingdon and Robert D. Linder, *Calvin and Calvinism: Sources of Democracy?* (Lexington, MA, 1970), xiii.

[9] Stefan Zweig, *Strijd rond een brandstapel. Castellio tegen Calvijn* (Amsterdam, 1936), 6.

[10] Perez Zagorin, *How the Idea of Religious Toleration Came to the West* (Princeton, 2003), 77–82.

[11] Roland H. Bainton, "The Struggle for Religious Liberty," *Church History* 10 (1941): 96.

[12] Roland H. Bainton, *The Travail of Religious Liberty* (London, 1953), 53.

[13] Roland H. Bainton, *Concerning Heretics. . . . An Anonymous Work Attributed to Sebastian Castellio* (New York, 1935), 74.

[14] Calvin, *Seneca*. On Calvin's humanism, see Gisbert Beyerhaus, *Studien zur Staatsanschauung Calvins mit besonderer Berücksichtigung seines Souveränitätsbegriffs*, repr. edn. (Aalen, 1973), 26–47; Josef Bohatec, *Budé und Calvin: Studien zur Gedankenwelt des französischen Frühhumanismus* (Graz, 1950), 127–148; Quirinius Breen, *John Calvin: A Study in French Humanism* (Grand Rapids, MI, 1931), 40–66, 86–99.

wrote no summa on political theory, no systematic work on religious liberty, no civil code on church–state relations, no letter on religious toleration. His writings on religious and civil liberty were principally theological in character, addressed to the cardinal Christian topics of God and man, sin and salvation, law and Gospel. His discussions of liberty were left scattered widely throughout the multiple editions of his *Institutes of the Christian Religion* as well as in his biblical commentaries, sermons, lectures, letters, and consilia.

It is easy to select from these scattered sentiments quotations to support both positive and negative impressions of Calvin's views of religious liberty and human rights. Calvin often wrote with a strong rhetorical flourish, and in unguarded moments or on particularly heated subjects, he partook readily of the bombast and hyperbole that typified sixteenth-century humanist literature.[15] Calvin's champions can find many strong statements in his writings on separation of church and state, liberty of conscience, free exercise of religion, and religious toleration, and make Calvin out to be the father of modern religious liberty and political democracy. Calvin's critics can assemble an equally high pile of quotations on religious bigotry, chauvinism, prejudice, repression, and officiousness that make Calvin out to be a rigid and unbending theocrat.

Neither of these interpretations does justice to Calvin. Viewed as a whole and in sixteenth-century theological terms, Calvin's scattered sentiments on religious liberty fall into two distinct phases. In his early writings of the 1530s and 1540s, Calvin focused on the spiritual liberty of the individual believer vis-à-vis God's spiritual law and his political liberty vis-à-vis the magistrate's civil law. His principal concern was to distinguish these two forms of religious liberty from each other, and to define the appropriate limitations that the church and the state could impose on them. As his thinking matured in the later 1540s till his death in 1564, and he confronted the hard realities of Genevan ecclesiastical and political life, Calvin modified his position considerably. His focus was less on the liberty of the individual, and more on the respective jurisdictions and duties of the church and the state. By the time he had finished dividing up the respective callings and claims of church and state, Calvin had created ample room for corporate religious liberty, but less room for individual religious liberty – particularly for one so stridently heretical and dangerous to the church as Michael Servetus.

---

[15] Quirinius Breen, "John Calvin and the Rhetorical Tradition," *Church History* 26 (1957): 14; Bohatec, *Budé und Calvin*, 257–263.

A perennial theme in both phases of Calvin's discussion is that, whatever its form, religious liberty must always be exercised with "becoming moderation."[16] Liberty and law, freedom and order, toleration and discipline are created and constituted together, Calvin believed, and must constantly balance each other to achieve the ideal of "moderate liberty."

CALVIN'S EARLY FORMULATIONS

John Calvin was born in 1509 in Noyon, France into a devout, minor aristocratic Catholic family. His father, Gerard, served as a canon lawyer and secretary to the local bishop and cathedral chapter. Around 1521, Calvin's father sent him to a *collège* in Paris where he followed a typical course of humanist studies, including theology, classics, and languages. His father then directed him to study law at the Universities of Bourges and Orléans, where he worked with such legal masters as Andreas Alciatus and Pierre L'Estoile. He took his licentiate in law (roughly the equivalent of a modern master's degree) and then returned to Paris for further legal studies, now with the noted legal humanist Guillaume Budé. In 1531, Calvin's father Gerard died – as an excommunicant from the church, owing to an earlier dispute with the bishop and cathedral chapter. Calvin and his family tried in vain to have Gerard buried in a consecrated cemetery, precipitating an angry dispute with local religious authorities that helped to alienate Calvin from the Catholic church. Sometime in the following year or two, Calvin was, as he put it, "suddenly converted" to Protestantism. In 1533, either shortly before or after his conversion, Calvin had to flee Paris, along with his friend Nicholas Cop, the rector of the University of Paris, who was exiled for expressing his new Protestant sympathies. Calvin remained an exile from France for the rest of his life.[17] Over the course of the next two years, while in Basel, he prepared the first edition of his *Institutes of the Christian Religion*, which he published in 1536, just before his arrival in Geneva.

As a young Protestant neophyte, Calvin naturally came under the influence of the first generation of Protestant leaders. He read several writings of Martin Luther, Philip Melanchthon, Martin Bucer, and other Protestants,

---

[16] "Moderation" (*moderatio*) is, for Calvin, a cardinal virtue that he first celebrated in Calvin, *Seneca*, 1.2.

[17] See Calvin's account in his preface to his *Commentary on Psalms* (1557), *CO* xxxi:22ff. Among numerous modern biographies, see William J. Bouwsma, *John Calvin: A Sixteenth Century Portrait* (New York and Oxford, 1988); Bernard Cottret, *Calvin: A Biography*, trans. M. Wallace McDonald (Grand Rapids, MI, 2000).

together with a number of Protestant catechisms, confessions, and church laws and their many apostolic and patristic antecedents.[18] His early writings on religious liberty – most notably his long discussion in the 1536 *Institutes* – reflect a particular affinity for Lutheran lore.

Two kingdoms

Like his Lutheran brethren, Calvin sought to formulate a theory of religious liberty that would avoid the extremes of both radical Anabaptist antinomianism and radical Catholic legalism. He sought to counter the claims of certain Anabaptists that Christian believers are set free from all law and authority.[19] He sought to counter the claims of certain Catholics that Christian believers can be free only through submission to law and authority. Nowadays, Calvin wrote, "as soon as the term 'Christian liberty' is mentioned, either passions boil or wild tumults rise . . . On the pretext of this freedom, some men shake off all obedience toward God and break into unbridled license, while others disdain it, thinking such freedom cancels all moderation, order, and choice of things . . . [T]hese wanton spirits, who otherwise most wickedly corrupt the best things, must be opposed in time."[20]

Calvin sought to reconcile this dialectic of liberalism and legalism through use of the Lutheran theory of the two kingdoms. According to Lutheran lore, God has ordained two kingdoms or realms in which humanity is destined to live, the earthly or political kingdom and the heavenly or spiritual kingdom. The earthly kingdom is the realm of creation, of natural and civic life, where a person operates primarily by reason, law, and passion. The heavenly kingdom is the realm of redemption, of spiritual and eternal life, where a person operates primarily by faith, hope, and charity. These two kingdoms embrace parallel temporal and spiritual forms of justice and morality, truth and knowledge, order and law, but they remain separate and distinct. The earthly kingdom is fallen, and distorted by sin. The heavenly kingdom is saved, and renewed by grace – and foreshadows the perfect kingdom of Christ to come. A Christian is a citizen of both kingdoms at once, and invariably comes under the structures and strictures of each.[21]

---

[18] Cottrett, *Calvin*, 3–24, 53–106; A. Ganoczy, *Le jeune Calvin. Genése et evolution de la vocation réformatrice* (Wiesbaden, 1966).

[19] Willem Balke, *Calvin and the Anabaptist Radicals*, trans. William Heynen (Grand Rapids, MI, 1981).

[20] *Institutes* (1536), 6.1; 6.14; see also *ibid.*, 1.30; 6.35; Comm. Rom. 13:1; Josef Bohatec, *Calvins Lehre von Staat und Kirche mit besonderer Berücksichtigung des Organismusgedankens*, repr. edn. (Aalen, 1961), 581–633 (hereafter Bohatec, *CLSK*).

[21] Witte, *Law and Protestantism*, 87–118.

Calvin recited this two kingdoms theory several times in his writings of the 1530s, each time with a breeziness that reflects comfortable acceptance of the doctrine.[22]

[T]here is a twofold government in man: one aspect is spiritual, whereby the conscience is instructed in piety and in reverencing God; the second is political, whereby man is educated for the duties of humanity and civil life that must be maintained among men. These are usually called the "spiritual" and the "temporal" jurisdictions (not improper terms) by which is meant that the former sort of government pertains to the life of the soul, while the latter has to do with the concerns of the present life – not only with food and clothing but with laying down laws whereby a man may live his life among other men honorably and temperately. For the former resides in the mind within, while the latter regulates only outward behavior. The one we may call the spiritual kingdom, the other the political kingdom . . . There are in man, so to speak, two worlds, over which different kings and different laws have authority.[23]

In a few passages in this early period, Calvin seemed to equate the heavenly kingdom with the church and the earthly kingdom with the state. He stated flatly, for example, that "the church is Christ's kingdom" and that the earthly kingdom is "the political order of laws and lawgivers."[24] But such passages must be read in context. Calvin's early two kingdoms theory was not simply a political theory of institutions, but a theological framework designed to distinguish the realms not only of church and state, but also of soul and body, spirit and flesh, inner life and outer life, conscience and reason, redemption and creation.

Calvin's early views on religious liberty were part of this theological framework. Calvin distinguished: (1) the "spiritual liberty" or "liberty of conscience" of the believer in the heavenly kingdom; and (2) the "political liberty" or "civil freedom" of the believer in the earthly kingdom. Such terms were commonplace in Catholic and Protestant circles of the day, but Calvin cast them in a distinctive mold. He insisted that these two forms

---

[22] See, e.g., *Institutes* (1536), 6.13–14; 6.35. Calvin used multiple terms to describe these two kingdoms: the heavenly kingdom, the kingdom of Christ, the spiritual kingdom, the spiritual jurisdiction versus the earthly kingdom, the kingdom of this world, the political kingdom, the civil realm, the temporal jurisdiction. In his later writings, Calvin also described these two kingdoms in more traditional Catholic terms as the inner forum and outer forum, which is a much narrower anthropological conception. See, e.g., *Institutes* (1559), 3.19.15. For the significance of this narrowing of the two kingdoms for Calvin's understanding of religious liberty, see below pages 74–76. See further David VanDrunen, "The Two Kingdoms: A Reassessment of the Transformationist Calvin," *Calvin Theological Journal* 40 (2005): 248–266; and for comparisons with the views of Strasbourg reformer, Martin Bucer, see Willem van 't Spijker, "The Kingdom of Christ According to Bucer and Calvin," in *Calvin and the State*, ed. Peter de Klerk (Grand Rapids, MI 1993), 121–122.

[23] *Institutes* (1536), 6.13.   [24] *Ibid.*, 6.14, 20.

of liberty, like other features of the two kingdoms, are completely separate. He also insisted that these two forms of liberty are perpetually limited by and counterpoised to the prevailing laws and orders of the two kingdoms. For Calvin, freedom and order, liberty and law always belong together.

Spiritual liberty

In the heavenly kingdom, spiritual law and spiritual liberty stand counterpoised. God has ordained a "spiritual law" or "law of conscience" to govern citizens of the heavenly kingdom. This law teaches "those things that God either requires of us or forbids us to do, both toward [ourselves] and towards others." Its provisions are written on the heart and conscience of each person, rewritten in the pages of Scripture, and summarized in the Ten Commandments. To obey this spiritual law leads to eternal blessings and beatitude in the life hereafter. To disobey leads to eternal curses and condemnation. Since the fall into sin, Calvin argued, no person has been capable of perfectly obeying this law. The scourge of original sin infects all persons, even the most devout saints. By itself, therefore, the spiritual law becomes "a great accuser, condemning us in our conscience, cursing us to eternal damnation."[25]

Through his grace, God liberates the conscience from such curses and condemnation; he bestows "spiritual liberty" on believers, on citizens of the heavenly kingdom. This liberty has two dimensions. On the one hand, by accepting God's grace in faith, believers are freed from the requirement to earn their salvation by perfect obedience of the law. Faith and grace provide them with an alternative pathway to blessing and beatitude. Believers are made righteous and just despite their inability to obey the law. On the other hand, believers are freed to live by the law, without fear of its condemnation. Although God has canceled the condemnation of the law, he has not canceled its commandments. The law remains in place "as an exhortation to believers" to lead a godly life. It is "not something to bind their consciences with a curse," but it is a means for them "to learn more thoroughly each day what the Lord's will is like." With the sting of the law removed, believers have the liberty of conscience to follow its commandments, albeit imperfectly.[26]

Liberty of conscience stands counterpoised not only to God's spiritual law, but also to the Catholic church's canon law. Like other early Protestants, the early Calvin had little faith in the vast system of canon law rules

---

[25] *Ibid.*, 1.4; 1.7–24; 1.33; 6.47; 6.49.   [26] *Ibid.*, 1.30; 1.33; 6.2–3.

and structures by which the medieval church had come to govern spiritual life and much of temporal life in Western Christendom. He issued a bitter broadside against the arguments from Scripture, tradition, and the sacraments that the church had used to support its canon law system. "[T]he power to frame laws was both unknown to the apostles, and many times denied the ministers of the church by God's Word," he argued. And, again, "it is not a church which, passing the bounds of God's Word, wantons and disports itself to frame new laws and dream up new things" for spiritual life.[27]

The church must respect the God-given liberty of conscience of Christian believers. To be sure, said Calvin quoting St. Paul, "all things [must] be done decently and in order." Certain rules and structures "are necessary for internal discipline [and] the maintenance of peace, honesty, and good order in the assembly of Christians." But the church has no authority to impose laws "upon consciences in those matters in which they have been freed by Christ," in the so-called *adiaphora* – "the outward things of themselves 'indifferent'" to salvation. Though Calvin did not spell them out systematically, for him such matters included habits of food, drink, dress, holy days, confessions, pilgrimages, marital relations, and the like, which the Catholic church traditionally governed in copious detail through the penitential rules of the internal forum and the canon laws of the external forum. Canon laws that govern such matters, Calvin regarded as illegitimate "human traditions" that improperly "establish another service of God than that which he demands [in his spiritual law], thus tending to destroy Christian liberty." Such canon laws "tyrannize," "ensnare," confuse," and "destroy the repose" of conscience by all manner of "traps and superstitions." In essential matters of faith and spiritual conduct, of course, Christians are bound to comply with God's spiritual law. But in discretionary matters of spiritual living (the *adiaphora*), Christian consciences "must be held in no bondage, and bound by no bounds." Christians might voluntarily bind themselves in such discretionary matters, especially to protect the frail consciences of other believers. But such restraint is neither necessary nor subject to the church's regulations.[28]

The church must also respect the liberty of conscience of Jews, Turks, Muslims, heretics, and others. Church leaders may certainly bar such "enemies of religion" from the communion; church members may

---

[27] *Ibid.*, dedicatory epistle; 6.14–32.
[28] *Ibid.*, 6.4; 6.6–8; 6.13–14; 6.32; Geneva Confession (1536), item 17, "Human Traditions," in Arthur C. Cochrane, ed., *Reformed Confessions of the Sixteenth Century* (Philadelphia, 1966; repr. edn., Louisville, 2003), 117ff. On Calvin's evolving concept of *adiaphora*, see John Lee Thompson, *John Calvin and the Daughters of Sarah* (Geneva, 1992), 227ff.

likewise spurn such persons from their civic and economic circles. But no church leader or member may subject religious outsiders to forced baptisms, persecutions, inquisitions, crusades, and other forms of religious coercion practiced in the past. Christians must instead practice "clemency and moderation" in their treatment of religious outsiders, "lest we soon descend from [religious] discipline to butchery."[29] As Calvin put it in his 1536 *Institutes*:

[W]e ought to strive by whatever means we can, whether by exhortation and teaching or by mercy and gentleness, or by our own prayers to God, that they may turn to a more virtuous life and may return to the society and unity of the church. And not only are excommunicants to be so treated, but also Turks and Saracens, and other enemies of religion. Far be it from us to approve those methods by which many until now have tried to force them to our faith, when they forbid them the use of fire and water and the common elements, when they deny them to all offices of humanity, when they pursue them with sword and arms.[30]

Through such benign means, religious outsiders might eventually be inspired to embrace the life, law, and liberty of the Christian faith.

The early Calvin thus regarded liberty of conscience in quite narrow theological terms. Liberty of conscience is, "in all its parts, a spiritual thing," he wrote, a liberty to obey the commandments of God with a free conscience. God defines the duties of man through divine commandments. Persons have the liberty to choose to obey these commandments. The "whole force" of liberty of conscience, "consists in quieting frightened consciences before God whether they are disturbed or troubled over forgiveness of sins; or anxious whether unfinished works, corrupted by the faults of the flesh, are pleasing to God; or tormented about the use of things indifferent."[31]

Political liberty

While God ordained spiritual liberty to balance the spiritual law of the heavenly kingdom, God ordained political liberty to balance the political law of the earthly kingdom. These twin forms of spiritual and political

---

[29] *Institutes* (1539), in *Joannis Calvini opera selecta*, ed. Peter Barth, Wilhelm Niesel, and Dora Scheuner, 5 vols. (Munich, 1926–52), V:221–222.

[30] *Institutes* (1536), 2.28. In subsequent editions of the *Institutes*, Calvin dropped the last two sentences of this text – thereby neither extending such "clemency" to "Turks and Saracens" nor condemning outright traditional forms of religious coercion. See *Institutes* (1559), 4.12.10; but cf. this same text in the 1560 French edition of the *Institutes*, which restores the language of the 1536 text quoted above. Calvin's critic Sebastian Castellio highlighted this textual shift, in his condemnation of Calvin's participation in the execution of Michael Servetus, arguing that Calvin had effectively betrayed his own premises. See *De haereticis an sint persequendi* (1553; fasc. edn. Geneva, 1954), 108 and discussion below pages 69–70.

[31] *Institutes* (1536), 6.5.

liberty and law cannot be conflated, Calvin insisted. "[C]ertain men, when they hear that the Gospel promises liberty . . . think they cannot benefit by their liberty so long as they see any power set up over them . . . But whoever knows how to distinguish between body and soul, between this present fleeting life and that future eternal life, will without difficulty know that Christ's spiritual kingdom and the civil jurisdiction are things completely distinct." "Spiritual liberty can perfectly well exist along with political bondage." Spiritual bondage can perfectly well exist along with political liberty.[32]

Calvin described the political rulers and laws of the earthly kingdom in largely general and homiletic terms in this early period. God has appointed political rulers to be his "vice-regents," "vicars," and "ministers" in the earthly kingdom. Indeed, wrote Calvin, citing Psalm 82:6, "those who serve as magistrates are called 'gods'." They are vested with God's authority and majesty. They are "called" to an office that is "not only holy and lawful before God, but also the most sacred and by far the most honorable of all callings in the whole life of mortal men." They are commanded to embrace and exemplify clemency, integrity, honesty, mercy, humanity, humility, grace, innocence, continence, and a host of other Godly virtues.[33]

Political rulers must govern the earthly kingdom by written political laws, not by personal fiat. Their laws must encompass the biblical principles of love of God and neighbor, but they must not embrace biblical laws per se. Instead, "equity alone must be the goal and rule and limit of all laws," a term which Calvin used both in the classic Aristotelian sense of correcting defects in individual rules if they work injustice in a particular case, and in his own sense of adjusting each legal system to the changing circumstances and needs of the local community. Through such written, equitable laws, political rulers must serve to promote peace and order in the earthly kingdom, to punish crime and civil wrongdoing, to protect persons in their lives and properties, "to ensure that men may carry on blameless intercourse among themselves" in the spirit of "civil righteousness." Such political laws must also, Calvin said in a pregnant but undelivered aside, "prevent idolatry, sacrilege against God's name, blasphemies against his truth, and other public offenses against religion." But he hastened to add

---

[32] *Ibid.*, 6.35.
[33] *Ibid.*, 6.33–35; 6.39; Geneva Catechism (1536), in *Tracts and Treaties in Defense of the Reformed Faith*, trans. Henry Beveridge, ed. T.F. Torrance, 3 vols. (Grand Rapids, MI, 1958), item 21 on "Magistrates." See further John T. McNeill, "John Calvin on Civil Government," in *Calvinism and Political Order*, ed. George L. Hunt (Philadelphia, 1965), 30ff.; Harro Höpfl, *The Christian Polity of John Calvin* (Cambridge, 1982), 43ff.

that he did not wish to "commit to civil government the duty of rightly establishing religion, which I put . . . beyond human decision." The political law, said Calvin in summary of his position, serves only to ensure "that a public manifestation of religion may exist among Christians, and that humanity may be maintained among men."[34]

These God-given duties and limits define not only the political office but also the political liberty of Christian believers in the earthly kingdom. Political liberty and political authority "are constituted together," said Calvin. The political liberty of believers is not so much a subjective right as a function of the political office.[35] When political officials respect the duties and limits of their office, believers enjoy ample political liberty to give "public manifestation of their faith." When political officials betray their office, however, through negligence, injustice, overreaching, or outright tyranny, the political liberty of the believer is abridged or even destroyed. As a consequence, said Calvin, "those who desire that every individual should preserve his rights, and that all men may live free from injury, must defend the political order to the utmost of their ability."[36]

Calvin insisted that "private individuals" have a Godly duty to obey tyrannical political officials up to the limits of Christian conscience.[37] Calvin rehearsed the familiar biblical texts. "The powers that be are ordained by God," and the Bible repeatedly enjoins our obedience to them. Political subjects must obey magistrates (Rom. 13:1–7, Titus 3:1, 1 Pet. 2:13). Children must honor their parents (Ex. 20:12, Lev. 19:5, Deut. 5:16; Matt. 15:4, Mark 7:10, Eph. 6:1–2). Wives must be subject to their husbands (1 Cor. 14:34–36; Eph. 5:21–33; Col. 3:18). Servants must obey their masters (1 Chr. 29:17, Eph. 6:5, Col. 3:22, 1 Tim. 6:1, Phil. 2:12). Congregants must respect their ministers (Acts 5:1–11).

these arguments have a different spin in the colonies

These obligations of obedience continue even when these authorities become abusive and arbitrary, Calvin insisted. This is particularly true in the political sphere, which provides order and stability for individual persons as well as for families, churches, businesses, and other social

---

[34] *Institutes* (1536), 1.33; 6.36–37; 6.48–49. On the classic Aristotelian view of equity as a corrective in the individual case, see Aristotle, *Ethics*, 1, 5; Aristotle, *The Art of Rhetoric*, 1, 12; both in *The Basic Works of Aristotle*, ed. Richard McKeon (New York, 1941). See also Calvin, *Seneca* (Latin text, 111; Battles and Hugo trans., 371). On Calvin's view of equity as the adjustment of general norms of love to the legal system of particular communities, see *Institutes* (1536), 6.49. See also Günther Haas, *The Concept of Equity in John Calvin's Ethics* (Waterloo, Ontario, 1997).

[35] Calvin discussed subjective rights mostly in the last decade of his writing. See below pages 57–59 and chapter 2, pages 139–140. On subjective versus objective rights, see above pages 20–21.

[36] *Institutes* (1536), 6.54; Comm. Rom 13:10; see also Bohatec, *CLSK*, 109–116; Josef Bohatec, *Calvin und das Recht* (Graz, 1934), 81–82 (hereafter Bohatec, *CR*).

[37] *Institutes* (1536), 6.55–56.

structures to flourish. Some political order is better than no order at all, and private disobedience usually brings greater disorder. Some justice and equity prevail even in the worst tyrannies, and even that is jeopardized when individuals take the law into their own hands. Sometimes tyrannies are God's test of our faith or punishment for our sin, and we insult God further by resisting his instruments. Individuals must thus obey and endure patiently and prayerfully, and leave vengeance and retribution to God. Better for a conscientious Christian to "turn the other cheek," than to slap their leaders in the face. Better to pray patiently than to sin boldly.[38]

But to honor earthly authorities cannot be to dishonor God, Calvin continued. When earthly authorities command their individual subjects to disobey God, to disregard Scripture, or to violate conscience, their political citizens and subjects not only may disobey – they must disobey. Our "obedience is never to lead us away from obedience to Him, to whose will the desires of all kings ought to be subject, to whose decrees their commands ought to yield," Calvin wrote in his 1536 *Institutes*. "If they command anything against Him, let it go unesteemed."[39] For to love and honor God is the first and greatest commandment.

This was true with respect to authorities in households, churches, and states alike. Children could disobey parents who taught them false doctrine, coerced them into unwanted marriages, or disinherited them in violation of God's law and liberty. Wives could leave husbands who imperiled their souls or divorce those who fell from the faith and then deserted them. Servants could leave masters who commanded them to commit sin or committed grievous sin against them. Parishioners could leave churches that taught false doctrine. And just the same, political subjects could disobey the authorities who violated God's law and authority.[40]

All such authorities who betray their office to the detriment or defamation of God are reduced to private persons, Calvin argued. They no longer hold an office of authority, but are mere "brigands" and "criminals."[41] "Dictatorships and unjust authorities are not governments ordained by God," Calvin wrote in his 1540 Commentary on Romans 13. "Those who

---

[38] *Ibid.*; Comm. Rom. 12:17–19; 13:1–10. See also his later Comm. Titus 3:1; Comm. 1 Pet. 2:13; Comm. Harm. Gosp. Matt. 5:38–41, Luke 6:29–30, repeated in *Institutes* (1559), 4.20.31–32; see further Comm. 1 Cor. 7:14–15; Serm. Deut. 5:16; Comm. Harm. Law Deut. 5:16.

[39] *Institutes* (1536) 6.56.

[40] See John Witte, Jr., *From Sacrament to Contract: Marriage, Religion, and Law in the Western Tradition* (Louisville, KY, 1997), 75ff. (on leaving tyrannical abusers in the household); *CO* 6:537–588 (on leaving abusers in the church).

[41] See Dedicatory Letter to Institutes (1536) and Comm. Rom. 13:1.

practice blasphemous tyranny" are no longer "God's ministers."[42] Calvin later expanded on this in his Commentary on Acts, arguing that both public and private authorities who disobey God effectively forfeit their office:

As soon as rulers lead us away from the obedience of God, and strive against God with sacrilegious boldness, their pride must be abated, so that God may remain in authority above them. Then every hint of honor vanishes. For God did not entrust men with honorable titles in order to overshadow His own glory. So, if a father, who is not content with his own position, tries to steal the chief honor of God the father, he becomes a mere man. If a king, ruler, or magistrate, becomes so lofty that he diminishes the honor and authority of God, he becomes a mere man. Likewise a pastor who exceeds his office, by setting himself against God must be stripped of his honor, lest his pretense deceives us further.[43]

A bit later in this same Commentary on Acts, Calvin wrote against his Catholic detractors:

[T]here is absolutely no foundation to the charge that they make against us, that we overthrow the political order, put an end to laws and judicial investigations, and subvert the power of kings . . . [But] if religion ever forces us to resist tyrannical edicts, which forbid giving due honor to Christ, and due worship to God, then we too may rightly testify that we do not violate the authority of kings. For they have not been lifted to such an exalted position, that, like giants, they may endeavor to pull God from his throne. Daniel's defense was true. "I have done nothing wrong against the king," although he had nevertheless not obeyed the impious edict, for he had done no injury to a mortal man, because he has preferred God to him (Dan. 6:22). So let us, in good faith, pay to princes their proper dues, but let us be ready for civil disobedience of all kinds, for if they [the authorities] are not content with their own station, and wish to take away from us the fear and worship of God, there is no reason for anyone to say that they are despised by us, because the authority and majesty of God are of more importance to us.[44]

[The question that remained for Calvin was how such abusive or tyrannical authorities should be disobeyed, and what remedies were available for their victims.] Calvin made clear that, in emergencies, private parties could practice self-defense when they were attacked by other private parties (including presumably authorities who had exceeded and thus forfeited their political offices and had now become mere private persons). The key, said Calvin, was that victims should practice "moderation and equity" in such contexts. They should not escalate the assault by fighting more than was needed to "turn aside the undeserved attack," and they should certainly not later attack in revenge. Outside of emergency contexts, Calvin

---

[42] Comm. Rom. 13:1, 5.   [43] Comm. Acts 5:29.   [44] Comm. Acts 17:7.

preferred litigation and prosecution as the best procedure to deal with abusive or tyrannical parents, spouses, masters, or ministers. He spent a great
deal of time working out the rules of civil and criminal procedure that
should apply in these cases. And he spent even more time adjudicating
these cases for the Consistory in Geneva and making recommendations to
the city council to order restitution between bickering parties or to sever
relationships as needed. But here, too, "moderation and equity" were to
be the watchwords, Calvin warned. Even those who properly decide to
forgo private retaliation and instead to file lawsuits in a just cause must
not succumb to a "frenzied desire for revenge." "The man who seeks the
aid of a magistrate with a heart that is malevolent and desirous of revenge
is no more to be excused than if he devises means for taking revenge by
himself."[45]

When it was the high magistrate himself who was doing the abusing,
Calvin again urged a "moderate and equitable" solution – this time involving both lower magistrates and church ministers. Calvin knew enough
about the insurrection and rioting triggered by the Anabaptist radicals of
his day and had read enough in classical history about the dangers of simply
unleashing the crowd against tyrants.[46] Given his penchant for orderliness
and moderation, he wanted no part of this. So, he sought a more structured and constructive response both by the state and church authorities.
No political regime is governed by "one person alone," Calvin argued.
Even monarchs have a whole coterie of lower officials – counselors, judges,
chancellors, and lieutenants – charged with implementation of the law.
Moreover, many communities have "magistrates of the people, appointed
to restrain the willfulness of kings (as in ancient times the ephors were set
against the Spartan kings, or the tribunes of the people against the Roman
consuls or the demarchs against the senate of the Athenians; and perhaps,
as now are, such power as the three estates exercise in every realm when they
hold their chief assemblies)." These lower magistrates, especially the elected

---

[45] See Serm. Deut. 22:25–30; Comm. Gen. 14:1–9; 16:12; 22:9; 32:34; 34:1–3; Comm. Harm. Gosp.
Matt. 5:39; Comm. Rom. 12:19. See the rules of procedure set out in his Ecclesiastical Ordinances
(1541), Edict of Officers (1543), and Marriage Ordinance (1546), in John Witte, Jr. and Robert M.
Kingdon, *Sex, Marriage and Family in John Calvin's Geneva*, 3 vols. (Grand Rapids, MI, 2005–),
1:51–61, 80–93 (hereafter Witte and Kingdon, *SMF*). Calvin had also drafted, or at least intended to
draft, detailed codes of civil and criminal procedure in Geneva. What survives of his effort is in *CO*
x/1:125–146. See analysis in Bohatec, *CR*, ch. 1
[46] See esp. Calvin, *Seneca*, 1.13.2 where Calvin seemed to condone popular resistance against a foreign
"tyrant who breaks in upon public liberty and tumultuously disturbs the peace of the city; then, to
keep possession once taken, he is compelled to remove all who are of any rank in the city, who can
arouse the people to recoup their liberty. When he has committed these deeds, he sees to it that no
avengers or champions stand up."

members that sit in city councils and in territorial or national parliaments, must protect the people if higher magistrates become abusive or tyrannical – doubly so if these higher magistrates impugn God's authority and law. As Calvin put it in his 1536 *Institutes*:

I am far from forbidding them to withstand, in accordance with their duty, the fierce licentiousness of kings, that, if they wink at kings who violently fall upon and assault the lowly common folk, I declare that their dissimulation involves nefarious perfidy, for by it they dishonestly betray the freedom of the people, of which they know they have been appointed protectors by God's ordinance.[47]

Church leaders, in turn, must preach and prophesy loudly against the injustice of tyranny and petition tyrannical magistrates to repent of their abuse, to return to their political duties, and to restore the political freedom of religious believers. Calvin opened his 1536 edition of the *Institutes* with precisely such a petition to King Francis I of France, on behalf of the persecuted Protestants in France.[48] In his dedicatory epistle to Francis, he stated that, as a believer, he was compelled to "defend the church against [political] furies," to "embrace the common cause of all believers."[49] Against "overbearing tyranny," Calvin later put it, a Christian must "venture boldly to groan for freedom."[50]

Calvin set forth no declaration of liberty in his dedicatory epistle to King Francis. This would have been suicide given the political climate of the day. Instead, he cleverly singled out those abuses of Protestants that defied widely recognized rights and freedoms of his day, particularly criminal procedural rights. Calvin protested the widespread and unchecked instances of "perjury," "lying slanders" "wicked accusations," and the "fury of evil

---

[47] *Institutes* (1536), 6.55.

[48] According to some interpreters, this may also have been one of his goals in drafting his *Commentary on Seneca's De Clementia*. See Gisbert Beyerhaus, *Studien zur Staatsanschauung Calvins mit besonderer Berücksichtigung seines Souveränitätsbegriffs*, repr. edn. (Aalen, 1973), 29 (calling the tract a "*Tendenzschrift*" addressed to the pressing problems of persecution and political abuse in Calvin's day); Doumergue, *Jean Calvin*, 1:211ff. (arguing that Calvin's commentary was a protest against religious persecution, an appeal for royal clemency and restraint, and, as such "a magnificent manifesto on liberty" for persecuted Protestants). But cf. criticisms in Quirinius Breen, *John Calvin: A Study in French Humanism* (Grand Rapids, MI, 1931), 80ff. Whatever Calvin's actual intent in 1532, he certainly adopted much of the same style of argumentation for political liberty of Christians in his dedicatory letter in the 1536 *Institutes*. Moreover, many of the passages in his *Commentary on Seneca's De Clementia* counseling political magistrates to respect their offices and thereby to protect the liberty of their political subjects have close parallels in various editions of Calvin's *Institutes*. See the convenient table in Calvin, *Seneca*, app. 4, 393–395.

[49] [Dedicatory Epistle] to the Most Mighty and Most Illustrious Monarch Francis, Most Christian King of the French, His Esteemed Prince and Lord, in *Institutes* (1536).

[50] Letter to Melanchthon (June 28, 1545), *CO* XII:98–100. In his preface to his Commentary on the Psalms (1557), Calvin made clear that he had written his dedication to Francis as a protest against the religious persecution of Protestants. *CO* XXXI:24.

men" that conspired to incite "public hatred" and "open violence" against believers. He protested that "the case" of the Protestants "has been handled with no order of law and with violent heat rather than judicial gravity." He protested various forms of false imprisonment and abuses of prisoners. "Some of us are shackled with irons, some beaten with rods, some led about as laughing stocks, some proscribed, some most savagely tortured, some forced to flee." He protested the many procedural inequities. Protestants are "fraudulently and undeservedly charged with treason and villainy." They are convicted for capital offenses, "without confession or sure testimony." "[B]loody sentences are meted out against this doctrine without a hearing." He protested the bias of judges and the partiality of judicial proceedings. "Those who sit in judgment . . . pronounce as sentences the prejudices which they have brought from home." He protested the intrusions on the church's freedoms of assembly and speech. "The poor little church has either been wasted with cruel slaughter or banished into exile, or so overwhelmed by threats and fears that it dare not even open its mouth." All these offenses stood diametrically opposed to basic political freedoms and criminal procedures recognized at the time both in the Empire and in France. "[A] very great question is at stake," Calvin declared to King Francis: "how God's glory may be kept safe on earth, how God's truth may retain its place of honor, how Christ's kingdom may be kept in good repair among us."[51]

Calvin sought no absolute political liberty for religious believers. He was fully aware of fraudulent and excessive religious exercises. He urged his fellow believers "to keep within its own limits all that liberty which is promised and offered to us in Christ." He likewise urged King Francis and other political officials to root out the impious imposter: "[I]f any persons raise a tumult under the pretext of the Gospel . . . if any depict the license of their own vices as the liberty of God's grace, there are laws and legal penalties by which they may be severely restrained according to their deserts. Only let not the Gospel of God be blasphemed," nor those who adhere to it be defamed.[52]

Calvin's early formulations on liberty revealed a bold and brilliant young mind at work. Calvin had mastered the intricacies of the Lutheran two kingdoms theory, and converted it to his own use. He had charted a course

---

[51] *Institutes* (1536), dedicatory epistle. On prevailing criminal procedural rights, see John H. Langbein, *Prosecuting Crime in the Renaissance: England, Germany, France* (Cambridge, MA, 1974); Adhemar Esmein, *A History of Continental Criminal Procedure with Special Reference to France*, repr. edn. (South Hackensack, NJ, 1968).

[52] *Ibid.*; *Institutes* (1536), 6.35.

between radical antinomianism and radical legalism. He had crafted a theory that balanced freedom and order, liberty and law both within the church and within the state. He had provided a lean and learned apologia for religious liberty and related freedoms that would inspire fellow Protestants for generations, indeed centuries, to come. This was no small achievement for a man newly converted to the Protestant cause and still in his early twenties.

Calvin's early formulations on liberty did betray considerable casuistry, however. Calvin may have reconciled the dialectic of law and liberty, of legalism and antinomianism in his early writings. But to reconcile one dialectic he introduced many others. He drew clear and easy lines between the heavenly and earthly kingdoms, the spiritual and the political life, the coercion and counsel of the law, the essential and indifferent matters of faith, the pious and impious canons of the church, the equitable and inequitable statutes of the state, the governance of the "manifestation" but not of the "manner" of religion, the duty to obey versus the right to petition the magistrate, among many other dualities. To be sure, such line-drawing followed the prevailing humanist methodology used by the leading theologians and jurists of the time.[53] And Calvin was convinced that his "readers, assisted by the very clarity of the arrangement, will better understand" the subject.[54] But such line-drawing did little to produce the authoritative synthesis on religious liberty to which Calvin aspired. Why should young Calvin's line-drawing be any more authoritative than a millennium of line-drawing by the Catholic church? How should the pious believer, cleric, or magistrate, untutored in humanist dialectics, parse and police these fine distinctions in their private and professional lives? Calvin did not say.

Calvin's early formulations on religious liberty were not only casuistic, they were also incomplete. Catholic and Protestant writers of the day viewed religious liberty in both individual and institutional terms. Calvin focused principally on the individual and his or her spiritual liberty vis-à-vis the church and political liberty vis-à-vis the state. He had relatively little to say about the relationships per se of church and state, clergy and magistracy, prelate and prince. Calvin's treatment of church–state relations was derivative of his theory of individual religious liberty in this early period. He seemed content to shorten the legal arm of the church and to lengthen the legal arm of the state. He also seemed content to assign the church to

---

[53] See generally Neal W. Gilbert, *Renaissance Concepts of Method* (New York, 1960). Calvin's contemporary Peter Ramus (1515–1572), who had a strong influence on later Calvinists, had developed this line-drawing methodology to such a level of refinement that much of human knowledge was being pressed into an endless series of binary opposites. See below page 153.

[54] *Institutes* (1536), 6.38.

the heavenly kingdom and the state to the earthly kingdom, and to assume that the ontological distinctions between these two kingdoms would provide ample direction and division for ecclesiastical and political officials.

CALVIN'S MATURE FORMULATIONS

Calvin's later formulations on religious liberty had the opposite tendency. As his thinking matured, and he took up his pastoral and political advisory duties in Geneva, Calvin began to think in more integrated and more institutional terms. He blurred the lines between the earthly kingdom and heavenly kingdom, between spiritual and political life, law, and liberty. He also focused more closely and concretely on the institutional responsibilities and relationships of church and state. Whereas the religious liberty of the individual had been a principal concern of Calvin in the 1530s, religious liberty of the church took priority and precedence thereafter – to the point where the individual's religious freedom would have to yield to the church's in the event of conflict. This new priority was no more clearly demonstrated than in Calvin's actions toward Servetus.

It must be emphasized that in his later writings Calvin faithfully repeated his early formulations on the religious and political liberties of the individual. He continued to insist on the cardinal distinction between the "spiritual kingdom" and the "political kingdom."[55] He continued to insist on the spiritual liberty of believers from the coercion of the spiritual law and from superstitious human traditions, and indeed bolstered his earlier arguments with ample new biblical support. He continued to insist on the political liberty of the believer vis-à-vis the political official and civil law. In fact, he peppered his later sermons and commentaries with general endorsements of political liberty for believers and non-believers alike. "There is nothing more desirable than liberty." Liberty is "an inestimable good," "a singular benefit and treasure that cannot be prized enough," something that is worth "more than half of life." "How great a benefit liberty is, when God has bestowed it on someone." Calvin emphasized the importance of political suffrage and the franchise in the political community. The "right to vote," he once said, is the "best way to preserve liberty." "Let those whom God has given liberty and the franchise use it." "[T]he reason why

---

[55] *Institutes* (1559), 3.19.15; 4.20.1. But note that Calvin now tended to view the two kingdoms theory simply as an expression of the traditional Catholic concept of the inner forum (governed by penitential rules) versus external forum (governed by canon law rules). See above note 22. For Catholic antecedents, see Winfried Trusen, "Forum internum und gelehrtes Recht im Spätmittelalter," *ZSS* (*KA*) 57 (1971): 83.

tyrannies have come into the world, why people everywhere have lost their liberty . . . is that people who had elections abused the privilege." "I freely admit," Calvin wrote in summary of his position, "that there is no kind of government more salutary than one in which liberty is properly exercised with becoming moderation and properly constituted on a durable basis."[56] Many such passages occur in Calvin's later writings, both formal and informal. Calvin never lost his appetite for the spiritual and political liberty of the individual.

Moreover, Calvin, in his later years, also began to speak at times about the subjective "rights" (*iura, droits*) of individuals, in addition to their "liberties" or "freedoms" (*libertates, libertés*).[57] Sometimes, he used such general phrases as "the common rights of mankind" (*iura commune hominum*), the "natural rights" (*iura naturali*) of persons, the "rights of a common nature" (*communis naturae iura*), or "the equal rights and liberties" (*pari iura et libertates*) of all.[58] Usually, he referenced more specific rights. He spoke, for example, about the "rights of Christian liberty," the "rights of citizenship" in the Kingdom of God or in heavenly Jerusalem, and, one of his favorite expressions, the "right of adoption" that Christians enjoy as new sons and daughters of God and brothers and sisters in Christ.[59] He referenced "the right to inhabit," "the right to dwell in," and "the right and privilege to claim the territory" that Yahweh gave to the chosen people of Israel.[60] He mentioned "Paul's rights of Roman citizenship."[61] He spoke frequently, as a student of Roman law would, about property rights: "the right to land," and other property, "the right to enjoy and use what one possesses," the "right to recover" and the "right to have restored" lost or stolen property; the "right to

---

[56] *Institutes* (1559), 3.19.1–8, 14; Serm. Gen. 39:11; Serm. 1 Sam. 8, 17; Comm. Harm. Law Deut. 15:1–11; 17:14–18; 24:7; Serm. Deut. 16:18–19; 18:14–18; *Institutes* (1543), 20.7. See additional such passages in Höpfl, *Christian Polity*, 156–160; John T. McNeill, "The Democratic Element in Calvin's Thought," *Church History* 18 (1949): 153.

[57] I want to say a special word of thanks to my friend, David Little, who properly criticized me for failing in my earlier writings to recognize the many references to subjective rights in Calvin's later writings. Professor Little has developed his reading of the Calvinist and other Protestant teachings on law, politics, and human rights in a brilliant new title *Protestantism and World Order* (forthcoming). See also David Little, "Reformed Faith and Religious Liberty," in *Major Themes in the Reformed Tradition*, ed. Donald R. Mckim (Grand Rapids, MI, 1992), 196. A few of the relevant passages discussed in this paragraph are also listed in Bohatec, *CLSK*, 91–118.

[58] Comm. Gen. 4:13; Comm. Harm. Law Numb. 3:5–10, 18–22, Deut. 5:19; Comm. Ps. 7:6–8; Lect. Jer. 22:1–3, 22:13–14; Lect. Ezek. 8:17; Comm. I Cor. 7:37.

[59] Comm. Ps. 87:6; Comm. I Cor. 10:23; Comm. Harm. Law Ex. 19:9–15; Comm. John 1:12; Comm. John 3:16; 8:33; Comm. Acts 9:16; Comm. Rom. 3:30, 5:17; Comm. Gal. 5:21; Comm. Heb. 2:5, 17, 6:12; Comm. James 1:18.

[60] Comm. Gen. 45:5; Comm. Harm. Law Deut. 3:12–20, 34:1–29; Comm. Josh. 14:13; Lect. Is. 22:1–25; Lect. Dan. 11:41–42; Comm. Heb. 7:10.

[61] Comm. Rom. 1:1; Philemon 9, 13, 17.

compensation" for work; the right "to sell," "to bequeath," and to "inherit" property, particularly in accordance with the "natural rights of primogeniture."[62] He spoke of the "right to bury" one's parents or relatives.[63] He also spoke frequently of the "marital" or "conjugal" rights of husband and wife, and the "sacred," "natural," and "common" rights of parents over their children – in particular, the "right" and "authority" of a father to "name his child," "to raise the child," and to set the child up in marriage.[64] He spoke in passing about the "sacred right of hospitality" of the sojourner, the "right of asylum" or of "sanctuary" for those in flight, the "right of redemption" during the year of Jubilee, and the "natural rights" and "just rights" of the poor, the needy, the orphans, and the widows.[65]

Calvin's discussions of individual rights and liberties, however, were left scattered and unsystematized in his later writings, serving only as occasional minor keys in his loud new orchestrations on law and order. He still insisted that liberty and law, freedom and order – and now rights and rules – belong together. But the law and order side of the equation took prominence in his later writings as he struggled to define the functions and interrelationships of moral, political, and ecclesiastical laws and structures within both the heavenly and the earthly kingdoms. By the time of his 1559 *Institutes*, Calvin in effect superimposed on the Lutheran two kingdoms theory his own variant of the Catholic two swords theory. He assigned the church a legal role in the governance of the earthly kingdom, and the state a moral role in the governance of the heavenly kingdom. At the same time, he rendered obedience to church officials and law both a spiritual and a civic duty, and obedience to political officials and law both a civic and spiritual duty. Such new sentiments left his familiar views on individual religious liberty both scattered and somewhat indeterminate. The following sections gather and systematize Calvin's scattered discussions of liberty vis-à-vis (1) the moral law; (2) the positive laws of the state; and (3) the positive laws of the church.

---

[62] Comm. Gen. 6:5, 9:3, 27:1, 33:3, 49:8; Serm. Gen. 27:3–9; Comm. Harm. Law Ex. 1:15–22, Ex. 17:8–16, 20:3, 22:1–4, 29–30, 23:20–23, 23:25–31, Lev. 25:44, 27:8, Numb. 36:1–5; Deut. 5:19, 20:5–8, 21:14–17, 25:17–19, Serm. Deut. 25:1–4; Comm. Josh. 16:1; Serm. 1 Sam. 8:11–22; Comm. Ps. 47:7, 68:9, 69:36, 74:2, 81:5, 89:19, 105:6–11, 44; Lect. Is. 2:5, 54:17; Lect. Jer. 24:10; Lect. Hos. 13:15; Comm. John 8:11; Comm. Acts 13:46; Comm. Rom. 9:12–13; Comm. 2 Thess. 3:6.

[63] Comm. Harm. Law Ex. 21:18–32; Lect. Amos 8:3–4.

[64] Comm. Gen. 16:1, 20:9, 21:14, 20, 34:4; Comm. Harm. Law Ex. 20:9, 12, 21:7–11, 15, 17, Lev. 20:9, Numb. 30:1–16, Deut. 5:16; Lect. Is. 7:1–25; Comm. Harm. Gosp. Luke 15:20; Comm. John 3:29; Comm. 1 Cor. 7:10, 11, 37.

[65] Comm. Gen. 18:2, 19:6; Comm. Harm. Law Ex. 23:10–11, Lev. 25:23–34; Comm. Ps. 72:4, 82:3, Lect. Is. 30:1, 58:7; Lect. Jer. 22:1–3, 41:1–3; Lect. Amos 5:12.

Liberty and moral law

At the foundation of Calvin's later formulations was a newly expanded theory of the moral law, which God uses to govern both the heavenly and earthly kingdoms. Calvin described the "moral law" much as he had described the "spiritual law" before – as moral commandments, engraved on the conscience, repeated in Scripture, and summarized in the Decalogue. He used widely varying terminology to describe this moral law – "the voice of nature," the "engraven law," "the law of nature," "the natural law," the "inner mind," the "rule of equity," the "natural sense," "the sense of divine judgment," "the testimony of the heart," the "inner voice," among other terms. Calvin generally used these terms synonymously to describe the norms created and communicated by God for the governance of humanity, for the right ordering of individual and social lives. He considered the commandments of the Decalogue to be the fullest expression of the moral law,[66] but he grounded many other human customs and habits in this moral law as well.

God makes "three uses of the moral law" in governing humanity, said Calvin – invoking the classic Protestant doctrine of the "uses of the law," which he had mentioned in passing in his earlier writings.[67] First, God uses the moral law theologically – to condemn all persons in their conscience and to compel them to seek his liberating grace. Here Calvin expanded on his earlier discussion of the dialectic between spiritual law and spiritual liberty. By setting forth a model of perfect righteousness, the moral law "warns, informs, convicts, and lastly condemns every man of his own unrighteousness." The moral law thereby punctures his vanity, diminishes his pride, and drives him to despair. Such despair, Calvin believed, is a necessary

---

[66] *Institutes* (1559), 2.7.1; 2.8.1; 4.20.15; *CO* xxiv:262–724; *CO* xxvi:236–432. See Erik Wolf, "Theologie und Sozialordnung bei Calvin," in Erik Wolf, *Rechtstheologische Studien* (Frankfurt am Main, 1972), 3, 12–15; I. John Hesselink, *Calvin's Concept of the Law* (Allison Park, PA, 1992), 18–24, 51–85; Höpfl, *Christian Polity*, 179–180; Jürgen Baur, *Gott, Recht und weltliches Regiment im Werke Calvins* (Bonn, 1965), 26–75; John T. McNeill, "Natural Law and the Teaching of the Reformers," *Journal of Religion* 26 (1946): 168.

[67] *Institutes* (1536), 1.33; Calvin, *Seneca*, 1.2.2 (Latin text, 24–25, Battles and Hugo trans., 73–77); 1.22.1 (Latin text, 124–126, Battles and Hugo trans., 301–307). The latter text suggests that Calvin derived his theology of the uses of the moral law not only from his biblical and theological studies but also from his earlier legal and political studies. In this 1532 work, Calvin endorsed classic Greek and Roman doctrines of the purposes, aims, or uses of criminal law and punishment. Both Plato and Seneca had defined these as "retribution," "deterrence," and "rehabilitation," which correspond roughly to Calvin's understanding of the "theological," "civil," and "educational" uses of the moral law. See Plato *Laws*, 9.6 862E, 11.11 932C; Plato *Gorgias*, 81, 525B in Plato, *The Collected Dialogues, Including The Letters*, ed. Edith Hamilton and Huntington Cairns (Princeton, NJ, 1961); Calvin, *Seneca* 1.22.1 (Latin text, 124–126, Battles and Hugo trans. 301–307). See also the translator's notes in Calvin, *Seneca*, 137.

precondition for the sinner to seek God's help and to have faith in God's grace. "[I]t is as if someone's face were all marked up so that everybody who saw him might laugh at him. Yet he himself is completely unaware of his condition. But if they bring him a mirror, he will be ashamed of himself, and will hide and wash himself when he sees how filthy he is." The moral law is that mirror. It drives persons to seek the cleansing "spiritual liberty" that is available to them through faith in God's grace – the liberty of conscience from the condemnation of the moral law.[68]

Second, God uses the moral law civilly – to restrain the sinfulness of non-believers, those who have not accepted his grace. "[T]he law is like a halter," Calvin wrote, "to check the raging and otherwise limitlessly ranging lusts of the flesh . . . Hindered by fright or shame, sinners dare neither execute what they have conceived in their minds, nor openly breathe forth the rage of their lust." The moral law imposes upon them a "constrained and forced righteousness" or a "civil righteousness." Though their consciences are "untouched by any care for what is just and right," the very threat of divine punishment compels sinners to obey the basic duties of the moral law – to fear God, to rest on the Sabbath, to avoid blasphemy, idolatry, and profanity, to obey authorities, to respect their neighbor's person, property, and relationships, to remain sexually continent, to speak truthfully of themselves and their neighbors.[69]

God coerces sinful consciences to adopt such "civil righteousness" in order to preserve a measure of order and liberty in the sin-ridden earthly kingdom. "Unless there is some restraint, the condition of wild beasts would be better and more desirable than ours," Calvin wrote. Persons need the God-given constraints of conscience in order to survive in "a public community." "Liberty would always bring ruin with it, if it were not bridled by the moderation" born of the moral law. And again: "We can be truly and genuinely happy not only when liberty is granted to us, but also when God prescribes a certain rule and arranges for a certain public order among us so that there may be no confusion."[70]

Third, God uses the moral law educationally – to teach believers, those who have accepted his grace, the means and measures of sanctification, of spiritual development. "We are not our own," says Calvin, quoting St. Paul. "[T]he faithful are not given liberty to do whatever seems good to

---

[68] *Institutes* (1559), 2.7.6–9; 3.19.3–6; *CO* XXIV:725–727; Comm. Gal. 5:13; Comm. Gal. 3:19; *Institutes* (1559), 2.7.8. Calvin also used the image of the sinner as debtor, incapable of discharging his debt. See, e.g., Serm. Deut. 5:23–27.

[69] *Institutes* (1559), 2.7.10; 2.8.6–10; 4.20.3; see also *CO* XXIV:725–727; *CO* XXVI:236ff.

[70] Lect. Jer. 30:9; *Institutes* (1559), 2.7.10

them and that each one follow his own appetite." Even the most devout saints, though free from the condemnation of the moral law, still need to follow the commandments "to learn more thoroughly . . . the Lord's will [and] to be aroused to obedience." The law teaches them not only the "civil righteousness" that is common to all persons, but also the "spiritual righteousness" that is becoming of sanctified Christians. As a teacher, the law not only coerces them against violence and violation, but also cultivates in them charity and love. It not only punishes harmful acts of murder, theft, and fornication, but also prohibits evil thoughts of hatred, covetousness, and lust. Such habits of "spiritual righteousness" are not to be exercised in the heavenly kingdom alone. They are to imbue all aspects of the life of the believer – spiritual and temporal, ecclesiastical and political, private and public. Calvin stressed that Christians must take their faith and conscience directly into the political, public, and external life of the earthly kingdom, "as ambassadors and stewards of the treasure of salvation, of the covenant of God . . . of the secrets of God." By so doing, they not only allow God's glory and image to shine in the earthly kingdom, but they also induce its sinful citizens to seek God's grace.[71]

Calvin's expanded theory of the uses of the moral law of human conscience laid important groundwork for the expansion of political liberty and civil rights. In his earlier writings, Calvin had argued that God imposes various duties on the political office, and that these duties also "constitute" the political liberties of their subjects in the earthly kingdom. When political officials respect the God-given duties of their office, the political liberties of their subjects are amply protected. Now, Calvin argued that God imposes various duties not just on political officials, but on all persons in the earthly kingdom. These include the moral duties, set out in the Decalogue, to respect the person, property, reputation, and relationships of their neighbors. When members of the earthly kingdom respect these God-given duties of communal living, the civil freedoms of their neighbors are amply protected.

It was only a short step from this theory of political and civil duties to a theory of subjective civil rights and political freedoms. A person's duty to his neighbor could be easily cast as the neighbor's right to have that duty discharged. A political official's duty to rule citizens justly could be easily cast as the citizen's freedom from unjust rule. Calvin began to talk in these terms in the last years of his life, particularly in his discussion of the "right to Christian liberty," and the "natural" or "common" "rights" of

---

[71] Serm. Deut. 5:4–7, 22; *Institutes* (1559), 2.7.12; 2.8.6; 2.8.51; 3.3.9; 3.6.1; 3.17.5–6; Comm. I Peter 1:14.

property, marriage, parenthood, and personal integrity.[72] These tentative references of Calvin became important starting points for the development of a Reformed theory of subjective rights. Beginning with his immediate successor, Theodore Beza, Calvin's followers used his theology of the moral law as a foundation on which to build a whole edifice of civil rights and political liberties – at first for Christians alone, and eventually for all peaceable parties.

Calvin's expanded theory of the moral law also laid the groundwork for the expansion of spiritual liberty and religious rights. Earlier, Calvin had been largely content to view the dialectic of spiritual law and spiritual liberty as a matter of the heavenly kingdom alone. As a consequence, he insisted that liberty of conscience was "a wholly spiritual thing" and could not be construed as a political freedom. Now, with his new emphasis on the omnicompetence of God's sovereignty, Calvin drew the spiritual dialectic of law and liberty into the earthly kingdom as well. God's moral law governs both the heavenly and the earthly kingdoms. Christians are given liberty of conscience to follow this moral law as citizens of both kingdoms alike. As Calvin put it: "We obtain liberty in order that we may more promptly and more readily obey God in all things," spiritual and temporal. These premises could lead easily to the conclusion that liberty of conscience must be an absolute guarantee in both the heavenly and earthly kingdoms for all persons, or at least for Christians. Calvin dithered on this point – in part constrained by his own strong rhetoric against the antinomianism of the Anabaptists and for the exclusively spiritual character of Christian liberty.[73] His followers struggled with this question, too, but eventually developed a theory of religious freedom for all peaceable faiths.

Liberty and state law

In his later writings, Calvin expanded the place and purpose not only of the moral law but also of the positive law in the two kingdoms. Earlier, Calvin had recognized as positive law only the "political laws" of the state, whose authority is rooted in the moral law, and whose jurisdiction is strictly limited to the earthly kingdom. Now, Calvin recognized as positive law both the political laws of the state and the ecclesiastical laws of the church. Both the state and the church are legal entities, Calvin argued. Each institution

---

[72] See references above pages 57–59.
[73] Comm. I Peter 2:16; see also *Institutes* (1559), 3.17.1–2; cf. *Institutes* (1559), 3.19.14–16 with *Institutes* (1559), 4.10.5.

has its own forms of organization and order, and its own norms of discipline and rule. Each is called to play a distinct role in the enforcement of Godly government and discipline in the community. Each provides "external means or aids through which God invites us into communion with Christ, and keeps us there."[74] Each institution participates in the elaboration of Godly moral law and the enforcement of its inherent "uses." Each helps to define, and to delimit, the province of religious liberty.

God has vested in the state "the temporal power of the sword," said Calvin. As before, Calvin insisted that the magistrate is the vice-regent of God; that he must rule with written positive laws rooted in tradition and morality and guided by equity and justice; that citizens must obey him and his law up to the limits of Christian conscience.[75] But now Calvin offered some refinements both to the structure and to the purpose of political government and state law. These refinements, though they did not yield a comprehensive political theory, were pregnant with political implications, which later Protestants helped to deliver.

The structure of political governments must be "self-limiting," Calvin said, so that "rulers are check-mated by their own officers" and offices. Such inherent political restraints rarely exist in a monarchy, Calvin believed, for monarchs too often lack self-discipline and self-control, and betray too little appetite for justice, prudence, and Christian virtue. "If one could uncover the hearts of monarchs," Calvin wrote late in his life, "he would hardly find one in a hundred who does not likewise despise everything divine." Thus, "it is safer and more tolerable that government be in the hands of a number of persons who help each other," such as prevails in an aristocracy, or even better in "a [mixed] system comprised of aristocracy, tempered by democracy." What Calvin had in mind was rule by the "best characters," by the spiritual and moral elite, who were elected to their offices by the people. Mere division of political authority, however, was an insufficient safeguard against political tyranny. Calvin thus encouraged all magistrates to govern through local agencies, to adhere to precedent and written rules, to divide

---

[74] *Institutes* (1559), subtitle of book 4 ("*de externis mediis vel adminiculuis quibus deus in Christi societatem nos invitat et in ea retinet*"). It was only in this final edition of the *Institutes* that Calvin clearly defined church and state, together, "as external means" of grace, thereby effectively eclipsing the two-kingdoms theory. In the 1536 edition, he had treated in one chapter the topics of "Christian Liberty," "Ecclesiastical Power," and "Political Administration," with strong emphasis on the organic connections among the topics. See *Institutes* (1536), ch. 6. In subsequent editions of his *Institutes*, he broke up these three topics into separate chapters – taking up "Christian Freedom" in the context of soteriology, "Ecclesiastical Power" in the context of the sacraments, "Political Administration" in the context of the Christian life. See the 1539, 1543, 1545, 1550, 1553, and 1554 editions in *CO* 1:252–1151.

[75] See generally *Institutes* (1559), 4.20.

their power among various self-checking branches and officials, to stand periodically for elections, to hold regular popular meetings in order to give account of themselves and to give air to popular concerns.[76] Though Calvin never synthesized these various "democratic elements" of political theory,[77] his followers in France, the Netherlands, England, and New England wove them into a comprehensive theory of political democracy, as we shall see in later chapters.

The purpose of political government and law is, in essence, to help God achieve the civil use of the moral law – to cultivate civil restraint and civil righteousness in all persons, if necessary through the coercive power of the sword. Calvin described this function in various ways. Magistrates are "ordained protectors and vindicators of public innocence, modesty, decency, and tranquility; their sole endeavor should be to provide for the common safety and peace of all." Magistrates have as their "appointed end" "to adjust our life to the society of men, to form our social behavior to civil righteousness, to reconcile us one with another, and to promote general peace and tranquility."[78]

Calvin made clear that the magistrate's cultivation of the civil use of the law was inherently limited.

It is true that when magistrates create laws, their manner is different from God's. But then their purpose has to do only with the way we govern ourselves with respect to the external civil order to the end that no one might be violated, and each might have his rights [protected] and have peace and concord among men. That is their intention when they create laws. And why? [Because] they are mortal men; they cannot reform inner and hidden affections. That belongs to God.[79]

The best means for the magistrate to help cultivate the civil use of the moral law, said Calvin, is through direct enforcement of the provisions and principles of the Decalogue. The magistrate is the "custodian of both tables" of the Decalogue, said Calvin.[80] He is responsible to govern both the relationships between persons and God, based on the First Table of the Decalogue,

---

[76] Serm. 2 Sam. 1–4; Serm. Job 10:16–17; 19:26–29; 34:138; Serm. Deut. 17:16–20; 18:14–18; *Institutes* (1559), 4.20.9–11, 31; Comm. Rom. 13:1–10. See also Bohatec, *CLSK*, 116ff., 619ff.; Höpfl, *Christian Polity*, 160ff.; McNeill, "John Calvin on Civil Government," 24ff.; M.E. Chenevière, *La pensee politique de Calvin*, repr. edn. (Geneva, 1970), 181ff.

[77] See McNeill, "The Democratic Element" and Robert M. Kingdon, "Calvinism and Democracy," in *The Heritage of John Calvin*, ed. John H. Bratt (Grand Rapids, MI 1973), 177.

[78] *Institutes* (1559), 4.20.2, 9.   [79] Serm. Deut. 5:17.

[80] *Institutes*, 4.20.9. See also *ibid.*, 2.8.11–12; Comm. Harm. Law Deut. 10:12–13, Deut. 6:5, 19:18. For a comparison of Calvin's division of the Commandments between these tables, and that of other Christian and Jewish writers, see Bo Reicke, *Die zehn Worte in Geschichte und Gegenwart* (Tübingen, 1973), 9–42.

and the multiple relationships among persons, based on the Second Table. Thus the magistrate is to promulgate laws against Sabbath-breaking, blasphemy, heresy, "idolatry, sacrilege against God's name, against his truth, and other public offenses against religion" that violate the principles of the First Table. He is "to defend the worship of God, and to execute vengeance upon those who profanely despise it, and on those who endeavor . . . to adulterate the true doctrine by their errors." The magistrate is also to promulgate laws against homicide, theft, adultery, perjury, inchoate crimes, and other forms of immorality that violate the principles of the Second Table. By so doing, the magistrate coerces all persons, regardless of their faith, to respect and maintain the "civil righteousness" or "public morality" dictated by God's moral law.[81]

Calvin was convinced that, through this exercise of Godly moral authority, the state magistrate enhances the ambit of religious liberty. By teaching each person the rudiments of Christian morality, even if by force, the magistrate enables those who later accept Christ to be "partially broken in . . . not utterly untutored and uninitiated in Christian discipline" and discipleship. By upholding minimal standards of Christian morality, the magistrate protects the "public manifestation of religion" and provides a public and peaceful space for Christianity and the church to flourish. By purging the community of overt heretics, idolaters, and blasphemers, the magistrate protects the Godly character of the community and the sanctity of the church and its members. Individual Christians and the church as a whole thus enjoy greater freedom to exercise the Christian faith.[82]

Calvin did not enhance the magistrate's civil jurisdiction over religious and moral matters without establishing safeguards. First, magistrates were not "to make laws . . . concerning religion and the worship of God."[83] They were only to enforce God's law on religion and worship, especially as it was set forth in the First Table of the Decalogue and interpreted by the church. This principle stood in marked contrast to both Lutherans and Anglicans, who at the time vested in the magistrate the power to promulgate all manner of civil laws respecting religious worship, liturgies, prayers, and other cultic activities. Calvin countenanced no such legal religious establishment.

Second, Christian subjects were to resist magistrates who prescribed religious and moral duties that directly contravened the Bible, particularly the First Table of the Decalogue. "Earthly princes lay aside all their power when they rise up against God," Calvin wrote. "We ought rather to spit

---

[81] *Institutes* (1559), 4.20.3; Lect. Dan. 4:1–3.   [82] *Institutes* (1559)., 2.8.10; 4.20.3.   [83] *Ibid.*, 4.20.3.

on their heads than to obey them when they are so restive and wish to rob God of his rights."[84] To be sure, said Calvin,

we must obey our princes who are set over us. Even though they torture us bodily and use tyranny and cruelty toward us, it is necessary to bear all this, as St. Paul says. But when they rise against God they must be put down, and held of no more account than worn-out shoes . . . When princes forbid the service and worship of God, when they command their subjects to pollute themselves with idolatry and want them to consent to and participate in all the abominations that are contrary to the service of God, they are not worthy to be regarded as princes or to have any authority attributed to them. And why? Because there is only one foundation of all the power of princes – that God has set them in their places. When they wish to tear God from his throne, can they be respected?[85]

"While we are commanded to be obedient to our superiors," Calvin declared from his Genevan pulpit, "the exception still remains that this must not detract from any of those prerogatives which belong to God, which have already been treated in the First Table [of the Decalogue]. For we know that the service by which God is worshipped must precede everything else." For a Christian in good conscience "to resist tyrannical edicts and commandments which forbid us to give due honor to Christ and due worship to God" is not to be "rebellious against kings, for they be not so exalted, that they may go about like giants to pull God out of his seat and throne."[86]

Third, magistrates were not to trespass or abridge the God-given rights and liberties of their subjects. To the contrary, said Calvin, "God empowered the magistrate to protect the rights of everyone" and called him to "pass uniform and consistent laws" to ensure that "no one suffered violations of

---

[84] Lect. Dan. 6:22. Particularly in his later life writings, Calvin often talked about the "rights of God" (in addition to God's power, authority, sovereignty, and more). Human disobedience, idolatry, and sin "rob, steal, defraud, despoil, and betray" God of his rights, said Calvin, and God will vindicate his rights by judgment, and if necessary by punishment. Calvin also made clear that, even in appointing his priests and prophets in the Old Testament or his ministers and magistrates in the New Testament, God never "abandons, abdicates, relinquishes, or betrays" his rights to humans but always reserves final rights and authority to himself. See Comm. Harm. Law Ex. 1:15–22, 10:21–29, 12:4–14, 20:1–6, 23:13, 20–23, 25–31, 28:1–43, 33:1–23; Numb. 31:1–54; Deut. 5:8–10, 13:12–17, 17:12–13, 21:23, 23:9–14; Comm. Ps. 2:12, 16:2–3; Lect. Is. 10:1–34, 26:1–21, 41:1–29, 44:1–28, 45:1–25, 57:1–21, 58:5, 60:1–23; Lect. Jer. 12:14, 18:18, 25:7, 28:4, 34:17; Lect. Ezek. 1:3, 5:11, 13:17–18, 16:21, 18:5–9, 20:18–19, 27–28, 34, 37, 39; Lect. Dan. Dedicatory Epistle, 4:17, 6:16, 21–22, 8:11, 9:27; Lect. Hos. 13:4–5; Lect. Amos 7:16; Lect. Jonah 2:8–9; Lect. Micah 2:7; Lect. Habb. 2:3, 19; Lect. Zeph. 1:5; Lect. Mal. 2:1–6, 9; Comm. John 2:4, 5:22, 18:11; Comm. Rom. 12:19; Comm. Acts 15:4, 22:1; Comm. I Cor. 4:15; Comm. Eph. 5:6; Comm. Phil. 2:6; Comm. Heb. 2:5, 17. See further below ch. 2, pages 115–117.

[85] Lect. Dan. 6:22.

[86] Comm. Harm. Law Deut. 5:16; Comm. Acts 17:7. See also Comm. Acts 5:29 (resisting tyrants who seek to destroy the Gospel); Serm. 1 Sam. 26:22–25 (resisting foreigners who seek to destroy the church). See further below pages 115–117.

his persons or property." It was "nefarious perfidy," Calvin repeated in his 1559 *Institutes*, for magistrates "to violently fall upon and assault the lowly common folk" and "dishonestly betray the freedom of the people, of which they know that they have been appointed protectors by God's ordinance."[87]

Fourth, magistrates were not to enforce God's laws indiscriminately. "We must not always reckon as contentious the man who does not acquiesce in our decisions, or who ventures to contradict us," said Calvin. "We must exercise moderation; so as not instantly to declare every man to be a 'heretic' who does not agree with our opinion. There are some matters on which Christians may differ from each other, without being divided into sects."[88]

Finally, magistrates were always to enforce God's laws equitably. They must seek to adjust their punishments to the capacities of each subject and the dangers of that person's crime. "All teachers have . . . a rule here which they are to follow . . . modestly and kindly to accommodate themselves to the capacities of the ignorant and the unlearned."[89]

This is what he [Isaiah] means by the metaphor of the bruised reed, that he does not wish to break off and altogether crush these who are half-broken, but, on the contrary, to lift up and support them, so as to maintain and strengthen all that is good in them. We must neither crush the minds of the weak by excessive severity, nor encourage by our smooth language anything that is evil. But those who boldly and obstinately resist . . . must be broken and crushed.[90]

One person whom Calvin helped the magistrate to "crush" was Michael Servetus – unleashing what has been called "one of the most famous controversies of modern times about religious freedom."[91] The facts of the Servetus case are not contested. Servetus, an accomplished Spanish scientist and theologian, was best known in his day for two unrelated acts – the discovery of the circulation of blood in the lungs, and the publication of a 1531 tract, *Concerning the Errors of the Trinity*.[92] The latter act was the more controversial, for in his tract Servetus charged the church with all manner of distortion and confusion in developing its doctrine of God as Father, Son, and Holy Spirit. The book was widely condemned, in Catholic and Protestant circles alike. When Servetus sent a copy to the Bishop of Saragossa, the

[87] Serm. Deut. 25:1–4; Calvin, *Institutes* (1559), 4.20.31; see also Serm. I Sam. 8:11–22 and discussion in Bohatec, *CLSK*, 94–97; Little, *Protestantism and World Order*.
[88] Serm. 1 Cor. 11:6; Comm. Titus 3:10.   [89] Comm. Rom. 1:14.   [90] Lect. Isa. 42:3.
[91] Josef Lecler, *Toleration and the Reformation* (London, 1960), 1:325. On Servetus, see Roland H. Bainton, *Hunted Heretic: The Life and Death of Michael Servetus* (Boston, 1953); Bainton, *Travail*, 72ff.; Richard Nürnberger, "Calvin und Servet: Eine Begegnung zwischen reformatorischem Glauben und modernem Unglauben im 16. Jahrhundert," *AFR* 49 (1958): 196; Jerome Friedman, *Michael Servetus. A Case Study in Total Heresy* (Geneva, 1978).
[92] Roland H. Bainton, "Documenta Servetiana," *AFR* 44 (1953): 223; *ibid.*, 45 (1954): 99.

bishop referred him to the Inquisition, which ordered him to appear. Servetus disappeared, surfacing again in 1545, when he sent Calvin a letter posing several queries about the Trinity. Calvin answered his queries, and sent him a copy of the *Institutes* in an effort to persuade him of his errors. Servetus promptly returned the volume to Calvin, having annotated numerous corrections and insulting comments in the margins.[93] Calvin broke off the correspondence, confiding ominously to a friend in 1546, that if Servetus "takes it upon himself to come" to Geneva, "I shall never permit him to depart alive."[94]

In 1553, Servetus published a *Restitutio* of his volume on the Trinity, which Protestants and Catholics again swiftly condemned. This time Servetus was arrested by Catholic authorities, and brought before the Inquisition. Calvin, among others, furnished the inquisitorial court with documentary evidence of Servetus's heresy and blasphemy, including the copy of his *Institutes* that Servetus had annotated. He also urged pastors and book dealers in Geneva and abroad to burn this *Restitutio*.[95] Servetus managed to escape his inquisitors. During his flight, Servetus stopped in Geneva – one, but certainly not the only, convenient stopping point along his way. On Sunday morning, he attended worship services at a local Genevan church where Calvin was preaching. He was pointed out to Calvin, who had him arrested by the city authorities. Servetus was indicted before the Geneva Council for "horrible, shocking, scandalous, and infectious" heresy, in violation of prevailing local law as well as general civil law. Calvin served as his first accuser and testified among several others against him. Servetus, unrepresented by counsel in the case, answered his accusers, both openly in court and through annotations on the record compiled against him. He was ordered to recant and repent. He refused. He was then sentenced to death by slow fire at the stake. Calvin supported Servetus's plea for a more merciful means of execution. The magistrate refused, burning Servetus at the stake on October 27, 1553.[96]

Executions for heresy were hardly a novelty in the mid-sixteenth century, let alone in the centuries before. In the same decade of Servetus's execution, Queen Mary of England executed some 273 Protestants who resisted her return to Catholicism. The following decade, the Duke of Alva

---

[93] *CO* VIII:645–720.   [94] Letter to Farel (February, 1546), *CO* XII:282–284.

[95] Letter to Pastors of the Church of Frankfurt (September 6, 1553), *CO* XIV:599–600; Letter to Sulzer (September 5, 1553), *CO* XIV:614–616.

[96] For the proceedings, see *CO* VIII:721–832 and *The Register of the Company of Pastors of Geneva in the Time of Calvin*, trans. Philip E. Hughes (Grand Rapids, MI 1966), 223–284 (hereafter *RCP* (Hughes trans.)).

executed untold thousands of Dutch Protestants in an (ultimately futile) attempt to quiet the ferment for reformation in the Netherlands. In 1572, at least 10,000 French Calvinists were killed in a month of fanatical religious genocide called the St. Bartholomew's Day Massacre. But executions for heresy were not known in Protestant Geneva, which in Calvin's day had become something of a haven for Protestant nonconformists from throughout Europe.[97] Of the 139 convicted felons known to have been executed in Geneva between 1542 and 1564, Servetus was apparently the only one executed for heresy.[98] It was difficult to justify such executions using the strict biblical logic on which Calvin generally insisted. Banishment and other non-capital punishment of heretics could be grounded easily in Scripture; execution could not be.[99]

Calvin's critics, most notably Sebastian Castellio, saw Servetus's execution as the inevitable consequence of Calvin's improper enhancement of the state's power over "the public manifestation of religion." How is the magistrate to distinguish between God's law for religion, which he must enforce, and man's law for religion, which he may not? How is the magistrate to decide whether a doctrinal teaching is blasphemous, idolatrous, or heretical? How is the magistrate to be protected against undue influence by a theologian and pastor as formidable as Calvin? What purpose does civil discipline of such a person serve? "I hate heretics, too," Castellio wrote, as well as blasphemers, idolaters, and other apostates.

But . . . I see two great dangers. And the first is that he be held for a heretic who is not a heretic. This happened in former times, for Christ and his disciples were put to death as heretics, and there is grave reason to fear a recurrence of this in this century . . . Great care must be exercised to distinguish those who are really seditious from Christians. Outwardly they do the same thing and are adjudged guilty of the same crimes by those who do not understand. Christ was crucified among thieves. The other danger is that he who is really a heretic be punished more severely or in a manner other than that required by Christian discipline.[100]

Castellio condemned with particular vehemence Calvin's endorsement of Servetus's execution for espousing heretical doctrine. "[T]o kill a man is not to defend a doctrine, it is to kill a man . . . Religious doctrine is not the

---

97 See William C. Innes, *Social Concern in Calvin's Geneva* (Allison Park, PA, 1983), 205–219 (on religious refugees in Geneva).
98 E. W. Monter, "Crime and Punishment in Calvin's Geneva, 1562," *AFR* 64 (1973): 281.
99 Höpfl, *Christian Polity*, 172ff., 201ff.
100 Sebastian Castellio, *Concerning Heretics* (1554), ed. Roland H. Bainton (New York, 1935), 126 (quoting from "Dedication by Martin Bellius to Duke Christoph of Württemberg").

affair of the magistrate, but of the doctor. What has the sword to do with doctrine?"[101]

Calvin found little convincing in such criticisms, and in his later years – as his critics multiplied and insurrection in Geneva mounted[102] – he defended his views with ever more bitter vitriol. It is here where Calvin's critics can find some of his most intemperate statements against religious liberty, and where Calvin casts a dark shadow on his otherwise carefully nuanced treatment of religious liberty. Calvin's interpretation of a passage about stoning false prophets illustrates his new bombast:

This law at first appears to be too severe. For merely having spoken should one be so punished? But if anybody slanders a mortal man he is punished and shall we permit a blasphemer of the living God to go unscathed? If a prince is injured, death appears to be insufficient for vengeance. And now when God, the sovereign emperor, is reviled by a word, is nothing to be done? God's glory and our salvation are so conjoined that a traitor to God is also an enemy of the human race and worse than a murderer because he brings poor souls to perdition. Some object that since the offense consists only in words, there is no need for such severity. But we muzzle dogs, and shall we leave men free to open their mouths as they please? Those who object are like dogs and swine. They murmur that they will go to America where nobody will bother them. God makes plain that the false prophet is to be stoned without mercy. We are to crush beneath our heel all affections of nature when his honor is involved. The father should not spare the child, nor the brother his sister, nor the brother his brother, nor the husband his own wife or the friend who is dearer to him than life. No human relationship is more than animal unless it be grounded in God.[103]

Similar vitriol courses through Calvin's 1554 manifesto *Defense of the Ortho-dox Christian Faith . . . Against the Manifold Errors of Michael Servetus.*[104] These later utterances catch Calvin in a very dark and defensive mood, and can be used to cast him and his views on religious liberty in a very dark and sinister profile.

Liberty and church law

While God has vested in the state the coercive power of the sword, Calvin argued, God has vested in the church the spiritual power of the Word. God calls the members of the church to be his priests and prophets – to

---

[101] Quoted by Roland H. Bainton, *Sebastian Castellio: Champion of Religious Liberty* (New York, 1951), 75.

[102] See, e.g., *RCP* (Hughes trans.), 295–304; Letter from the Pastors of Geneva to their Colleagues in Berne (October 4, 1554), *CO* xv:250–252; Letter to Farel (May 25, 1554), *CO* xv:140–141.

[103] Quoted by Bainton, *Travail*, 68–69.   [104] *CO* viii:453–644.

preach the Gospel, to administer the sacraments, to teach the young, to gather the saints, to care for the needy, to communicate God's Word and will throughout the world. The church is to be a beacon of light and truth, a bastion of ministry and mission. Just as pious Christians must take their faith into the world to reflect God's image and glory, so the church must take its ministry into the world to project God's message and majesty for all persons to behold.[105]

God has established his church with a distinct and independent polity, Calvin argued. The church's responsibilities must be divided among multiple offices and officers. Ministers are to preach the word and administer the sacraments. Doctors are to catechize the young and to educate the parishioners. Elders are to maintain discipline and order and adjudicate disputes. Deacons are to control church finances and to coordinate the church's care for the poor and needy.[106] Each of these church officials, Calvin believed, is to be elected to his office by fellow communicant members of the congregation. Each is subject to the limitation of his own office, and the supervision of his fellow officers. Each is to participate in periodic congregational meetings that allow members to assess their performance and to debate matters of doctrine and discipline. This form of ecclesiastical polity, whose inner workings Calvin discussed in copious detail, would be described by later Calvinists as an "ecclesiastical democracy."[107]

God has vested in this church polity three forms of legal power (*potestas*), said Calvin. First, the church holds doctrinal power, the "authority to lay down articles of faith, and the authority to explain them." Included herein is the power to set forth its own confessions, creeds, catechisms, and other authoritative distillations of the Christian faith, and to expound them freely from the pulpit and the lectern. Second, the church holds legislative power, the power to promulgate for itself "a well-ordered constitution" that ensures (1) "proper order and organization," "safety and security" in the church's administration of its affairs; and (2) "proper decency" and "becoming dignity" in the church's worship, liturgy, and ritual. "When churches are deprived of . . . the laws that conduce to these things," said Calvin, "their very sinews disintegrate, and they are wholly deformed and scattered. Paul's injunction that 'all things must be done decently and in good order' can be met only if order itself and decorum are established

---

[105] *Institutes* (1559), 4.1.1–17; Serm. Deut. 5:22.
[106] *Institutes* (1559), 4.3; Ecclesiastical Ordinances (1541), in *CO* x/1:15–30.
[107] Cambridge Synod and Platform (1648), 8, in Williston Walker, ed., *The Creeds and Platforms of Congregationalism* (New York, 1960), 217–218.

through the addition of observances that form a bond of union." Third, and "most importantly," said Calvin, the church has jurisdictional power, the power to enforce laws that help to maintain discipline and to prevent scandal among its members.[108]

The church's jurisdiction, which is rooted in the power of the keys, must remain "wholly spiritual" in character, Calvin insisted. Its disciplinary rules must be "founded upon God's authority, drawn from Scripture, and, therefore, wholly divine." Its sanctions must be limited to admonition, instruction, and, in severe cases, banning and excommunication – with civil and criminal penalties left for the magistrate to consider and deliver. Its administration must always be "moderate and mild," and left "not to the decision of one man but to a lawful assembly" – ideally a consistory court, with proper procedures and proper deference to the rule of law.[109]

In his writings in the 1540s, Calvin conceived of this ecclesiastical jurisdiction in rather modest terms, simply as a way of purging the church of manifest sin and sinners and of policing the purity of the Lord's Supper or Eucharist.[110] By the end of his life, however, these disciplinary codes resurrected a good deal of the traditional Catholic canon law and restored to the church consistory courts a good deal of the traditional authority that Calvin and other early Protestants had so hotly criticized three decades before. For example, in a 1560 amendment to the ecclesiastical ordinances, which Calvin endorsed, we read:

The matters and cases which come most commonly before the consistories are cases of idolatry and other kinds of superstition, disrespect towards God, heresy, defiance of father and mother, or of the magistrate, sedition, mutiny, assault, adultery, fornication, larceny, avarice, abduction, rape, fraud, perjury, false witness, tavern-going, gambling, disorderly feasting, and other scandalous vices: and because the magistrate usually does not favor such gatherings, the consistory will use the ordinary reprimands, namely, brotherly admonition, as sharp and as vehement as the

---

[108] *Institutes* (1559), 4.1.5; 4.8.1; 4.10.27–38; 4.11.1; see further *De Scandalis*, in *CO* VIII:1–84.

[109] *Institutes* (1559), 4.10.5, 30; 4.11.1–6; 4.12.1–4, 8–11. See also Calvin's consilia, in *CO* X/1:207–208, 210–211 (urging the Consistory "to keep to its own boundaries and limits" and that "excessive strictness should be kept within bounds"); Ecclesiastical Ordinances (1541), *CO* X/1:15–30 (urging that discipline "should be done with such moderation, and with no force that someone might be injured; or even these corrections are simply remedies to return sinners to the Lord").

[110] *CO* X/1:15–30 lists "the persons whom the elders ought to admonish" – "those who dogmatize against received doctrine," "anyone who is negligent in church attendance in a way that evinces contempt of the communion of the faithful," secret sinners who are to be privately admonished, and notorious sinners who are to be censured, if necessary excommunicated, and turned over to the civil authorities. The ordinances state such limitations are imposed so that "the ministers have no civil jurisdiction, nor use anything but the spiritual sword of the Word of God, as Paul commands them; nor is the Consistory to derogate from the [Genevan City] Council or ordinary justice; the civil power is to remain unimpaired."

case demands, suspension from the Lord's Supper, deprivation of the Lord's Supper for a stated period of time; and persistent offenders will be publicly named, so that people will know who they are.[111]

This was no idle directive. Studies of Genevan life during Calvin's tenure show that the Genevan Consistory played an increasingly active role in the maintenance of spiritual and moral discipline for all Genevan subjects. The Consistory worked hand-in-hand with the Genevan Small Council and served, effectively, as a grand jury and preliminary hearings court for a variety of spiritual and moral offenses. It participated in the enforcement of laws governing not only blasphemy, heresy, sacrilege, and other spiritual lapses but also marriage, divorce, and child care, education, charity and poor relief among other civil causes and concerns.[112]

While the state's law helped God to achieve the civil use of the moral law, the church's law helped God to achieve all three uses of the moral law. By maintaining a pure Godly doctrine and law, the church upheld the theological use of the law to induce sinners to behold their depravity and to seek God's grace. By maintaining structural order and decorum, the church upheld the civil use of the law to deter sinful conduct and to preserve a measure of public righteousness and liberty among its members. By maintaining spiritual discipline, the church upheld the educational use of the law to teach the saints the meaning and measure of sanctification and spiritual righteousness.

Moreover, the church's enforcement of spiritual discipline achieved within the church the same goals of retribution, deterrence, and rehabilitation that the state's criminal law achieved within civil society.[113] Through its spiritual discipline, the church exacted retribution against the sinner, so that God's honor, law, and sacraments could be preserved. It deterred both the sinner and others in the church from violations of God's word and will. It corrected and rehabilitated the sinner and brought him back into community with his fellow believers.[114] Calvin saw no difficulty in

---

[111] Emile Rivoire and Victor van Berchem, eds., *Les Sources du droit du canton de Genève*, 4 vols. (Aarau, 1927–1935), III, item no. 992 (hereafter *SD*).

[112] Bohatec, *CR*, 94–131; Walter Köhler, *Zürcher Ehegericht und Genfer Konsistorium*, 2 vols. (Leipzig, 1942); Robert M. Kingdon, *Adultery and Divorce in Calvin's Geneva* (Cambridge, MA and London, 1995); Witte and Kingdon, *SMF*.

[113] See *Institutes* (1559), 4.11.1:
[T]he whole jurisdiction of the church pertains to the discipline of morals . . . For as no city or township can function without magistrate and polity, so the church of God . . . needs a spiritual polity. This is, however, quite distinct from the civil polity, yet does not hinder or threaten it but rather greatly helps and furthers it. Therefore, this power of jurisdiction will be nothing, in short, but an order framed for the preservation of the spiritual polity.

[114] *Ibid.*, 4.11.3–5; 4.12.

imposing upon Christian believers both civil and ecclesiastical discipline, and would hear nothing of a double jeopardy defense. Multiple forms and purposes of discipline were inherent in God's moral law, and punishment by the state cannot preclude discipline by the church, or vice versa.[115]

Calvin's radical expansion of the law and authority of the visible church in his later writings and actions served at once to contract and to expand the province of religious liberty. On the one hand, Calvin contracted the exercise of the individual's spiritual liberty within the church. To be sure, Calvin repeated verbatim his early panegyrics about liberty of conscience from the condemnation of the moral law and from superstitious human traditions.[116] He repeated his condemnations of the "innumerable human traditions of the Romanists – so many nets to ensnare miserable souls . . . and to bind the conscience which Christ has set free."[117] But what Calvin gave with one hand, he took with the other. Though Christians might have ample liberty of conscience, they certainly do not have much freedom of exercise as members of the church. They must "freely" bind themselves to obey the church's "well-ordered constitution" and comprehensive code of spiritual discipline. They must "gladly" submit to the mandated forms and habits of worship, ritual, and liturgy so that the church's decorum, discipline, and dignity will not be compromised.[118] They must "voluntarily" restrict their spiritual freedom even in discretionary matters of spiritual living so that weaker members of the church will not be offended and misled. Within the church, individual religious liberty and discretion must give way to corporate religious order and organization. Those who could not submit to the church's strictures were, of course, free to leave the church – a local application of the "right of emigration" provided in the 1555 Religious Peace of Augsburg.[119] But in a small community such as Geneva, lack of communicant status within one local congregation often led to various civil deprivations in the city as a whole. Banned or excommunicated parties could not act as godparents, get married, or receive poor

---

[115] See, e.g., *ibid.*, 4.11.3 (illustrating how a drunk or a fornicator would need to be subject to both laws and punishments). See numerous examples in Witte and Kingdon, *SMF*. See also Johannes Althusius's expansion of this point to include private law suits below, pages 180–181.

[116] *Institutes* (1559), 3.19.1–16.   [117] *Ibid.*, 4.10.1–2.

[118] *Ibid.*, 4.10.27–31. See, e.g., the strained logic of *ibid.*, 4.10.31:

Now it is the duty of Christian people to keep the [church] ordinances that have been established according to this rule with a free conscience, indeed, without superstition, yet with a pious and ready inclination to obey; not to despise them, not to pass over them in careless negligence. We must be far from openly violating them through pride and obstinacy.

[119] In Ehler and Morrall, 164.

relief, and were subject to various forms of unofficial social shunning.[120] "What sort of freedom of conscience could there be with such caution and excessive attention to detail?" Calvin once asked himself rhetorically.[121] Not much, thought his critics, despite Calvin's lengthy ratiocinations to the contrary.

While Calvin contracted the religious liberty of individuals, he expanded considerably the religious liberty – the rights and powers – of the church.[122] Indeed, Calvin argued strongly for a measure of ecclesiastical autonomy and a basic separation of the institutions and offices of church and state. "There is a great difference and unlikeness between the ecclesiastical and civil power" of the church and state, said Calvin. "A distinction should always be observed between these two clearly distinct areas of responsibility, the civil and the ecclesiastical." The church has no authority to punish crime, to remedy civil wrongs, to collect taxes, to make war, or to meddle in the internal affairs of the state. The state, in turn, has no authority to preach the Word, to administer the sacraments, to enforce spiritual discipline, to collect tithes, to interfere with church property, to appoint or remove clergy, to obstruct bans or excommunications, or to meddle in the internal affairs of a congregation. When church officials operate as members of civil society, they must submit to the civil and criminal law of the state; they cannot claim civil immunities, tax exemptions, or privileges of forum. When state officials operate as members of the church, they must submit to the constitution and discipline of the church: they cannot insist on royal prerogatives or sovereign immunities. To permit any such interference or immunity between church and state, said Calvin, would "unwisely mingle these two [institutions] which have a completely different nature."[123]

---

[120] Thomas A. Lambert, "Preaching, Praying, and Policing in Sixteenth-Century Geneva" (Ph.D. Diss. Wisconsin, 1998), 255–263; Köhler, *Zürcher Ehegericht*, II:504ff.

[121] *Institutes* (1559), 4.10.31.

[122] In his later-life writings, Calvin began to talk more regularly of the "rights" (*iura; droits*) of the church – the "rights" and "privileges" of priestly office, the rights to preach, prophesy, and teach the Word, the right to administer the sacraments, the right to care for the poor and needy, the right of the Old Testament Levites to make sacrifices and burnt offerings, to enter the temple sanctuary, the right to make sacred oblations, the right to collect and use tithes. See Comm. Gen. 14:19; Comm. Harm. Law Ex. 6:16–18, 7:1–7, 13:1–59, Lev. 27:30–33, Numb. 5:8, 8:6, 11:1–35, 13:1–30, 18:20–24, 28:8–19, Deut. 12:19, 18:1–8; Comm. Ps. 24:1–4; Comm. I Tim. 2:12; Comm. Titus 1:5–6, 3:10; Comm. Heb. 7:5–12; Comm. Jude 1–2.

[123] Institutes (1559), 4.11.3–16; 4.20.1–4; Consilia, *CO* x/1:215–217, 223–224; Ecclesiastical Ordinances (1541), *CO* x/1:15–30. See also *Institutes* (1559), 3.19.15, where Calvin urges that the "political kingdom" and "spiritual kingdom" "must always be considered separately; while one is being examined, the other we must call away and turn aside the mind from thinking about the other." In the next paragraph, Calvin seems to equate these two kingdoms with "civil government" and "church laws."

Calvin's principle of separation of church and state bore little resemblance, however, to modern American understandings of "a high and impregnable wall between church and state."[124] Despite his early flirtations with radical political implications of the two kingdoms theory, Calvin ultimately did not contemplate a "secular society" with a plurality of absolutely separated religious and political officials within them. Nor did he contemplate a neutral state, which showed no preference among competing concepts of the spiritual and moral good. For Calvin, each community is to be a unitary Christian society, a miniature *corpus Christianum* under God's sovereignty and law.[125] Within this unitary society, the church and the state stand as coordinate powers. Both are ordained by God to help achieve a Godly order and discipline in the community, a successful realization of all three uses of the moral law. Such conjoined responsibilities inevitably require church and state, clergy and magistracy to aid and accommodate each other on a variety of levels. These institutions and officials, said Calvin, "are not contraries, like water and fire, but things conjoined."[126] "[T]he spiritual polity, though distinct from the civil polity does not hinder or threaten it but rather greatly helps and furthers it."[127] In turn, "the civil government has as its appointed end . . . to cherish and protect the outward worship of God, to defend sound doctrine of piety and the position of the church . . . and a public manifestation of religion."[128]

Calvin's principles were as much reminiscent of medieval forms of church–state relations as prescient of modern forms. To be sure, Calvin anticipated a number of modern concepts of separation, accommodation, and cooperation of church and state that later would come to dominate Western constitutionalism. But Calvin also appropriated many of the cardinal insights of both the "two-powers" theory of Pope Gelasius and the "two-swords" theory of the Papal Revolution. Particularly like his medieval predecessors, Calvin saw that to maintain its liberty, the church had to organize itself into its own legal and political entity, and to preserve for itself its own jurisdiction and responsibility. It had to wield its own "sword," maintain its own "power." Calvin differed from his medieval predecessors, however, in insisting on a more democratic form of ecclesiastical and civil polity, a more limited ecclesiastical jurisdiction, and an equality of church and state before God.

---

[124] *Everson v. Bd. of Education*, 330 US 1, 16 (1947).
[125] Herbert Butterfield, "Toleration in Early Modern Times," *Journal of the History of Ideas* 38 (1977): 573, 576.
[126] Serm. 1 Sam. 11:6–10, *CO* xxix:659.   [127] *Institutes* (1559), 4.11.1.   [128] *Ibid.*, 4.20.2–3.

SUMMARY AND CONCLUSIONS

The Protestant Reformation was, at its core, a fight for freedom – freedom of the individual conscience from intrusive canon laws and clerical controls, freedom of political officials from ecclesiastical power and privilege, freedom of the local clergy from central papal rule and oppressive princely controls. "Freedom of the Christian" was the rallying cry of the early Reformation. Catalyzed by Martin Luther's posting of the 95 Theses in 1517 and his burning of the Catholic canon law books in 1520, Reformation leaders denounced Catholic church laws and authorities with unprecedented alacrity and urged radical political reforms on the strength of the new Protestant theology.

The Reformation ultimately settled into Lutheran, Calvinist, and Anabaptist movements on the Continent, with Anglicanism striking something of a via media amongst them and Catholicism in Great Britain. Together, these four Reformation movements broke the unity of Western Christendom and thereby laid the foundation for the modern Western system of political and religious pluralism. They broke the superiority of clerical authority and canon law and thereby vested new power in civil authorities and civil law. They broke the primacy of corporate Christianity, and thereby laid new emphasis upon the role of the individual in the economy of salvation and the individual rights that should attach thereto.

John Calvin made major contributions to this transformation of Western theology and law. His theory of the Christian conscience provided the cornerstone for the constitutional protections of liberty of conscience and free exercise of religion advocated by later Protestants in France, the Netherlands, England, Scotland, and America. His theory of moral laws and duties inspired a whole range of later Calvinist natural law and natural rights theories. His references to "the common rights of mankind," "the rights of a common nature," and "the equal rights and liberties" of all provided normative traction for the later development of a robust Calvinist theory and law of public, private, and procedural rights for individuals and groups. His theory of a congregationalist church polity broke the power of synodical and episcopal centralization, and eventually was used to support concepts of confessional or religious pluralism within the state. His theory of a coequal and cooperative clergy and magistracy provided a strong foundation for later constitutional protections of both separation and accommodation of church and state. His theory of the moral responsibilities of both church and state to the community lay at the heart of later Christian theories of social pluralism and civic republicanism.

Calvin charted a course between the Erastianism of Lutherans that subordinated the church to the state, and the asceticism of Anabaptists that withdrew the church from the state and society. Like Lutherans, Calvin and his followers insisted that each local polity be an overtly Christian commonwealth that adhered to the general principles of natural law and that translated them into detailed positive laws of religious worship, Sabbath observance, public morality, marriage and family life, social welfare, public education, and more. Like Anabaptists, Calvin and his followers insisted on the basic separation of the offices and operations of church and state, leaving the church to govern its own doctrine and liturgy, polity and property, without interference from the state. But, unlike both groups, Calvin insisted that both church and state officials were to play complementary legal roles in the creation of the local Christian commonwealth and in the cultivation of the Christian citizen.

Calvin emphasized the uses of the law in the Christian commonwealth, and the collaboration of church and state in achieving the same. Natural laws and positive laws provide two tracks of morals, he argued – "civil norms" which are common to all persons, and "spiritual norms" which are distinctly Christian. These norms, in turn, give rise to two tracks of morality – a simple "morality of duty" demanded of all persons regardless of their faith, and a higher "morality of aspiration" demanded of believers in order to reflect their faith. In Calvin's mind, commandments and counsels, musts and shoulds, absolutes and adiaphoras can thereby be distinguished.

This two-track system of morality corresponded roughly to the proper division of jurisdiction between church and state, as Calvin saw it. It was the church's responsibility to teach aspirational spiritual norms. It was the state's responsibility to enforce mandatory civil norms. This division of responsibility fit rather neatly into the procedural divisions between the Consistory and the Council in Calvin's Geneva. In most cases that did not involve serious crimes, the Consistory would first call parties to their higher spiritual duties, backing their recommendations with (threats of) spiritual discipline. If such spiritual counsel failed, the parties were referred to the Council to compel them, using civil and criminal sanctions, to honor at least their basic civil duties.

One of Calvin's most original and lasting contributions to the Western rights tradition lay in his restructuring of the liberty and order of the church. Calvin combined ingeniously within his ecclesiology the principles of rule of law, democracy, and liberty. First, Calvin urged respect for the rule of law within the church. He devised laws that defined the church's doctrines and disciplinary standards, the rights and duties of their officers and parishioners, the procedures for legislation and adjudication. The church was thereby protected from the intrusions of state law and the sinful vicissitudes of their members. Church officials were limited in their discretion. Parishioners understood their spiritual duties. When new rules were issued, they were discussed, promulgated, and well known. Issues that were ripe for review were resolved by proper tribunals. Parties that had cases to be heard exhausted their remedies at church law. Disgruntled individuals and families that departed from the church left their private pews and personal properties behind them. Dissenting congregations that seceded from the fold left their properties in the hands of the corporate body. To be sure, this principle of the rule of law within the church was an ideal that too often was breached, in Calvin's day and in succeeding generations. Yet this principle helped to guarantee order, organization, and orthodoxy within the Reformed church.

Second, Calvin urged respect for the democratic process within the church. Pastors, elders, teachers, and deacons were to be elected to their offices by communicant members of the congregation. Congregations periodically held collective meetings to assess the performance of their church officers, to discuss new initiatives within their bodies, to debate controversies that had arisen. Delegates to church synods and councils were to be elected by their peers. Council meetings were to be open to the public and to give standing to parishioners to press their claims. Implicit in this democratic process was a willingness to entertain changes in doctrine, liturgy, and polity, to accommodate new visions and insights, to spurn ideas and institutions whose utility and veracity were no longer tenable.[129] To be sure, this principle did not always insulate the church from a belligerent dogmatism in Calvin's day or in the generations to follow. Yet this principle helped to guarantee constant reflection, renewal, and reform within the church – *semper reformanda ecclesiae*, a church dedicated to perpetual reformation.

Third, Calvin urged respect for liberty within the church. Christian believers were to be free to enter and leave the church, free to partake of the church's offices and services without fear of bodily coercion and persecution, free to assemble, worship, pray, and partake of the sacraments without fear of political reprisal, free to elect their ministers, elders, deacons, and teachers, free to debate and deliberate matters of faith and discipline, free to pursue discretionary matters of faith, the adiaphora, without undue laws and structures. To be sure, this principle, too, was an ideal that Calvin

---

[129] See, e.g., Consilium *CO* x/1:220 (urging "constant reform and renewal," but warning against "rash changes and constant innovations").

and his followers compromised, particularly in his actions toward Servetus and in his undue empowerment of the consistory courts in his later years. Yet this principle helped to guarantee constant action, adherence, and agitation for reform by individual members of the church.

It was Calvin's genius to integrate these three cardinal principles into a new ecclesiology. Democratic processes prevented the rule-of-law principle from promoting an ossified and outmoded orthodoxy. The rule of law prevented the democratic principle from promoting a faith swayed by fleeting fashions and public opinions. Individual liberty kept both corporate rule and democratic principles from tyrannizing ecclesiastical minorities. Together, these principles allowed the church to strike a unique perpetual balance between law and liberty, structure and spirit, order and innovation, dogma and adiaphora. This delicate ecclesiastical machinery did not inoculate Calvinist churches against dissent and schism. Calvinist churches, like all others, have known schism, intolerance, and abuse from Calvin's day forward. But this ecclesiastical machinery did help to render the pluriform Calvinist church remarkably resilient over the centuries in numerous countries and cultures.

This integrated theory of the church had obvious implications for the theory of the state. Calvin hinted broadly in his writings that a similar combination of rule of law, democratic process, and individual liberty might serve the state equally well. Such a combination, he believed, would provide the best protection for the liberty of the church and its individual members. What Calvin adumbrated, his followers elaborated. In the course of the next two centuries, European and American Calvinists wove Calvin's core insights into the nature of corporate rule into a robust constitutional theory of republican government, which rested on the pillars of rule of law, democratic processes, and individual liberty.

CHAPTER 2

The duties of conscience and the free exercise of Christian liberty: Theodore Beza and the rise of Calvinist rights and resistance theory

Once the free exercise of the true religion has been granted . . . the ruler is so much more bound to have it observed [that] if he acts otherwise, I declare that he is practicing manifest tyranny, and [his subjects] will be all the more free to oppose him. For we are bound to set greater store and value in the salvation of our souls and the freedom of our conscience than in any other matters, however desirable.

Theodore Beza (1574)[1]

THE ST. BARTHOLOMEW'S DAY MASSACRE

In the early morning of August 24, 1572, armed soldiers, acting on royal orders, broke into the Paris bedroom of French Calvinist leader, Admiral Gaspard de Coligny, and stabbed him to death. The soldiers heaved his corpse from the window into the courtyard below where a mob was gathering. They slashed and mutilated the corpse further and then began dragging it, now bereft of head, hands, and genitals, through the streets of Paris. Church bells peeled from the monastery of St. Germain l'Auxerrois signaling the start to a pogrom. On cue, soldiers and a growing mob of Catholic supporters began to break into the homes and shops of Calvinists, slaughtering them and pillaging their goods with growing abandon. Waves of popular violence and savagery broke out in the following weeks not only in Paris but also in several other French cities and towns. Within two months, thousands of French Calvinists had been slaughtered, including a number of their intellectual, political, and military leaders – from 10,000 to

---

[1] Theodore Beza, *De Iure Magistratum*, translated as Theodore Beza, *Concerning the Rights of Rulers Over Their Subjects and the Duties of Subjects Toward Their Rulers*, trans. Henri-Louis Gonin (Cape Town and Pretoria, 1956), 85 (hereafter *Rights of Rulers*).

3. "Maccabean Revolt," from Nicholas Fontaine, *L'histoire du vieux et du noveau Testament* (Paris 1699).

100,000 according to contemporaries. Untold thousands more were exiled from France or coerced into re-communion with Rome.[2]

This pogrom, known as the St. Bartholomew's Day Massacre, was a defining moment in the Calvinist tradition. A mere decade before, Calvinism had seemed ready to contest Catholicism for the heart and soul of France. By 1562, some two million French souls had converted to Calvinism, gathered in more than two thousand new churches throughout France. The number of Calvinist converts and churches was growing rapidly in all ranks of French society, but especially among the aristocracy. This growth was due in no small part to the disciplined campaigns of missionary work, book publication, church planting, school building, and charity work offered by the Calvinists. It was also due in part to the ready exportation of Geneva's sturdy system of local city-state rule and spiritual discipline that was ideally suited for many of the small French cities and towns that converted to Calvinism.[3]

After 1560, the spread of French Calvinism was also due to the growing military prowess of French Calvinists, led by such new converts as Admiral de Coligny. That year, despite strong protests from Geneva, a group of Calvinists attempted a *coup d'état* against the young French King Henry II. This brought harsh reprisals on various Calvinist communities and the establishment of a French inquisitorial court targeting Calvinists. But those royal retaliations only steeled the resolve of Calvinists and enhanced the attractiveness of this faith to new converts disenchanted with the laxness of the French church and weakness of the French monarchy. In 1561, the Queen Mother Catherine de Medici sought to halt further religious strife by calling together Catholic leaders and Protestant leaders in the Colloquy of Poissy and urging them to reconcile their theological differences. Little came of it. In 1562, French Catholic forces slaughtered a Calvinist congregation gathered for worship in the town of Vassy. That triggered a decade of massive blood feuds between Catholic and Calvinist forces in many parts of France.

---

[2] Donald R. Kelley, *François Hotman: A Revolutionary's Ideal* (Princeton, 1973), 213ff.; Scott M. Manetsch, *Theodore Beza and the Quest for Peace in France, 1572–1598* (Leiden, 2000), 30ff. See detailed accounts in Barbara Diefendorf, *Beneath the Cross: Catholics and Huguenots in Sixteenth-Century Paris* (New York and Oxford, 1991); Janine Garrison-Estèbe, *Tocsin pour un massacre, la saison des Saint-Barthélemy* (Paris, 1968).

[3] Robert M. Kingdon, *Geneva and the Coming of the Wars of Religion in France 1555–1563* (Geneva, 1956); Philip S. Gorski, *The Disciplinary Revolution: Calvinism and the Rise of the State in Early Modern Europe* (Chicago, 2003); Henry Heller, *The Conquest of Poverty: The Calvinist Revolt in Sixteenth-Century France* (Leiden, 1986).

By 1572, both sides were worn out by a decade of savage but inconclusive religious war. Peace finally seemed at hand, if only by grudging resignation. After a quiet summer of 1572, many French Calvinist aristocrats gathered in Paris to celebrate the August wedding of their Protestant Prince, Henry of Navarre, to the sister of the new French Catholic King Charles IX. This wedding should have helped to solidify the religious peace. Admiral de Coligny, who had come to Paris for the wedding, sought to solidify the peace further by urging Charles to take up war with Spain, a cause that might have united warring French Catholic and Calvinist forces against France's old and hated rival. Catherine de Medici, suspecting that Coligny was indirectly seeking to aid Dutch Calvinists suffering under Spanish persecution, would have none of it. Catherine or one of her advisors persuaded the King that Admiral Coligny was plotting another *coup d'état*, and that the many Calvinist wedding guests gathered in Paris were in fact a secret army poised to overthrow him. Charles (or someone acting on his authority) then ordered the massacre.

Theodore Beza, Calvin's successor in Geneva, feared that the St. Bartholomew's Day Massacre was "the unfolding of a universal conspiracy" to effectuate the "anathema" that the Catholic Council of Trent had pronounced on Protestantism and to eliminate Calvinism from France root and branch.[4] Beza's fears were compounded when reports reached him that the Pope and Catholic rulers throughout Europe had cheered the news of the massacre, and that the Pope had struck a medal in honor of the occasion. His fears were compounded still further when propagandists for the French crown and Catholic church began to lay the blame squarely on the Calvinist leadership in Geneva for instigating all this religious violence and warfare. After enduring fifteen years of bloody campaigns of Calvinist insurrection orchestrated from Geneva, the propagandists claimed, it was necessary for the French crown and church finally to stand up and defend themselves decisively. This triggered a furious campaign of counter-propaganda by Calvinist apologists and sympathizers throughout France and well beyond.[5]

But more than counter-propaganda was needed to respond to the St. Bartholomew's Day Massacre. The massacre permanently broke the wave of Calvinist expansion into France and forced Calvinist leaders to rethink

---

[4] Letter to Bullinger (September. 1, 1572), *Correspondance de Théodore de Bèze*, ed. Hippolyte Aubert, *et al.*, 21 vols. (Geneva, 1960–1999), XIII:179. See also his earlier letters to Bullinger and others relating fears of persecution born of the Council of Trent. *Ibid.*, V:96, VI:255, VII:328–329, VIII:170 and analysis in Manetsch, *Theodore Beza*, 118–120.

[5] Robert M. Kingdon, *Myths About the St. Bartholomew's Day Massacres, 1572–1576* (Cambridge, MA, 1988).

their strategies of mission and expansion.[6] More importantly, the massacre demanded a fundamental rethinking of Calvinist theories of law, religion, and politics. Calvin's own teachings assumed that each local community would have a single faith. How could Calvinists countenance religious pluralism and demand toleration as a religious minority? Calvin assumed that church and state would cooperate in the governance of a godly polity. What if church and state came into collision, or even worse into collusion against Calvinists? Calvin assumed that Christian subjects should obey political authorities up to the limits of Christian conscience, and bear persecution with penitence, patience, and prayer in hopes that a better magistrate would come. What if the persecution escalated to outright pogrom? Were prayer, flight, and martyrdom the only options for conscientious Christians? Was there no place for resistance and revolt, even regicide in extreme cases? These challenges faced Calvinists throughout the 1540s to 1560s. They became stark life-and-death issues after 1572.

In response, French Calvinist leaders unleashed a massive wave of writings that ultimately brought forth a reconstructed Calvinist theory of law and religion, authority and liberty, rights and resistance. The political government of each community, Calvinists now argued, was formed by a three-way covenant between God, the rulers, and the people. By this covenant, God agreed to protect and bless the rulers and the people in return for their proper obedience to the laws of God and nature, particularly the Decalogue. The rulers agreed to honor these higher laws and protect the people's essential rights, particularly those rights anchored in the Decalogue. The people agreed to exercise God's political will for the community by electing and petitioning their rulers and by honoring and obeying them so long as the rulers honored God's law and protected the people's rights. If the people violated the terms of this political covenant and became criminals, the magistrate could properly prosecute and punish them – and sentence them to death in extreme cases. If the rulers, in turn, violated the terms of the political covenant and became tyrants, they could be properly resisted and removed from office – and sentenced to death in extreme cases. The power to resist and remove tyrants, however, lay not directly with the people, but with their representatives, the lower magistrates, who were constitutionally called to organize and direct the people in orderly resistance to tyrants – in all out warfare and revolution if needed.

From a later political perspective, the rise of French Calvinist resistance theory was a critical step in the development of the Western theory

---

[6] Benedict, *Christ's Church Purely Reformed*, 127ff.

of democratic revolutions and constitutional government.[7] Revolutionary movements in Scotland, the Netherlands, England, America, and even Jacobin France[8] would take inspiration and instruction from some of these early French Calvinist political tracts. From the theological perspective of the day, however, the rise of resistance theory was also a critical step in the development of a Calvinist theory of rights. Later sixteenth-century Calvinists saw the right to resist tyrants first and foremost as a religious right – the right of the individual to obey the duties of conscience and to enjoy the free exercise of religion, the right of the community to be free from heresy, apostasy, and untrue religion, the right of God Himself to be worshiped properly and fully in accordance with the law and the Gospel. Resistance theory, in this sense, was an expression of the fundamental rights of the individual and community to discharge the fundamental religious duties imposed on them by God.

Once cast in these terms, it became possible to extend the logic of resistance theory to embrace other fundamental rights and duties. After all, the duty to worship God was set out in the First Table of the Decalogue, whose Commandments about worship, idolatry, blasphemy, and the Sabbath the magistrate was called to respect and protect. When the magistrate failed in his duty to respect and protect these Commandments, Christians had a right and duty to resist him. The Decalogue also had a Second Table, whose Commandments against violations of family, life, property, marriage, and reputation the magistrate was also called to respect and protect. When a magistrate violated these Second Table duties and rights, Christians had a fundamental religious right and duty to resist as well.

This new logic made French Calvinist resistance theory both more concrete and more potent. It had been a commonplace of earlier Christian thought that Christians were to obey the powers that be up to the limits of Christian conscience, and to resist and revolt against those who usurped the throne. Now, those limits of Christian conscience were more clearly defined and grounded in a theory of fundamental rights and liberties that citizens and subjects could claim as God's representatives and image-bearers on earth. It had also been a commonplace of the tradition

---

[7] See Doumergue, *Jean Calvin*, v:465ff.; Michael Walzer, *The Revolution of the Saints: A Study in the Origins of Radical Politics* (Cambridge, MA, 1965); R. R. Palmer, *The Age of the Democratic Revolution*, 2 vols. (Princeton, 1959–1964); John W. Sap, *Paving the Way for Revolution: Calvinism and the Struggle for a Democratic Constitutional State* (Amsterdam, 2001); David W. Hall, *The Genevan Reformation and the American Founding* (Lexington, MA, 2003); David T. Ball, *The Historical Origins of Judicial Review, 1536–1803: The Duty to Resist Tyranny* (Lewiston, NY, 2005).

[8] See Dale van Kley, *The Religious Origins of the French Revolution: From Calvin to the Civil Constitution, 1560–1791* (New Haven, 1996).

to think of resistance to tyrants mostly in passive terms: the Christian had the freedom to disobey quietly or to leave the community with a clear conscience. Now, resistance was cast in more active terms: each Christian believer had the right and the duty to disobey and to fight tyranny with a clear conscience so long as he or she followed the terms and procedures of the political covenant and the direction and example of faithful lower magistrates.

Calvin had touched on a number of these legal and political ideas, as had Martin Luther in his later life and some of his more radical followers like the authors of the Magdeburg Confession of 1550. This made it easy for later sixteenth-century French Calvinists to present their ideas and activities as a continuation and expansion of the Protestant Reformation. But there was no mistake that, after the St. Bartholomew's Day Massacre, French Calvinism had transformed Calvin's original understanding of church and state, law and religion, rights and liberties.

BEZA'S EARLY FORMULATIONS

A pivotal figure in this transformation of Calvinist thought was Theodore Beza (Théodore de Bèze) (1519–1605), Calvin's protégé and chosen successor in Geneva.[9] Like Calvin, Beza was a Frenchman, of minor aristocratic stock. He, too, was trained in law at the University of Orléans. After a severe illness that nearly cost him his life, Beza converted to the Protestant faith. Upon his conversion, the French Parlement outlawed him, confiscated his ample property and benefices, and burned him in effigy. Beza came as a refugee to Geneva in 1548. He moved to nearby Lausanne in 1550 and for the next eight years taught Greek in the Lausanne Academy, and wrote poetry, drama, and an early work on predestination. In 1558, he returned to Geneva and the following year became rector of the new Genevan Academy, a position which he retained for the next three years. He was also appointed as professor of theology, a post from which he continued to have a decisive influence on the Genevan Academy and broader Calvinist world until his retirement in 1599.

Beza also became one of the pastors of the Genevan church. After Calvin's death in 1564, he was elected as Moderator of the Company of Pastors,

---

[9] See Manetsch, *Theodore Beza*; Paul Geisendorf, *Théodore de Bèze* (Geneva, 1967); Eugène Choisy, *L'État chrétien calviniste a Genève au temps de Théodore de Bèze* (Geneva, 1902); Henry Martin Baird, *Theodore Beza: The Counselor of the French Reformation, 1519–1605* (New York, 1899); Werner Klingenheben, "Der demokratisierte Staat und die herrschaftsfreie Kirche bei Theodor Beza" (Ph.D. Diss. Göttingen, 1974).

making him the leading clerical voice on the Genevan Consistory. He was
reelected to this position every year until 1580 when he stepped down for
reasons of health. Beza was also an effective legal and political advisor
and diplomat for Geneva. Like Calvin, he drafted a number of important
statutes and legal consilia for the city authorities, and authored a critical pair of volumes that systematized the new Reformed law of marriage,
annulment, and divorce. He was in regular contact with the political and
military leaders of the French Protestant movement and often traveled to
other countries to meet them. He was the leading voice for the French
Reformed churches at the Colloquy of Poissy in 1561. In the religious wars
that followed, Beza marched with the Calvinist troops, serving as military chaplain. Beza also participated in several important synods and other
church gatherings, including service as Moderator of the National Synod
of the French Reformed Church at La Rochelle in 1571.

Beza was blessed with long life and a lively pen. He wrote decisively
on several controversial theological doctrines – heresy, predestination, the
sacraments, marriage, polygamy, excommunication, and ecclesiology most
fully and forcefully. He published sermons and commentaries on several
books of the Bible, a pithy summary of the Reformed faith, a French psalter,
a massive pile of letters, several speeches, an authoritative biography of
Calvin, a famous confession of faith, and an annotated translation of the
New Testament. Several of his writings were still in print in the seventeenth
century in all the main European languages of the day, and played a critical
role in defining and defending Reformed dogma.[10]

While he sprinkled legal and political themes throughout many of these
tracts, Beza's main contributions to the Calvinist tradition of law, religion,
and human rights came in two major tracts: (1) *The Punishment of Heretics by
Civil Authorities* (1554)[11] that set out much of his early thought on church and
state, liberty and law; and (2) *On the Rights of Rulers Over Their Subjects and
the Duty of Subjects Toward Their Rulers* (1574),[12] an influential formulation
of Calvinist resistance theory, predicated in part on emerging theories of

---

[10] Most of Beza's major works are collected in *TT* (my translations throughout); the most important
works for our purposes, besides those listed in the next note, are: *Confessio christiane fidei, & eiusdem
collatio cum Papisticis haeresibus* (1559/60), *TT* I:1–84; *De Pace Christianarum ecclesiarum consilium*
(1566), *TT* II:138–151; *De veris et visibilus Ecclesiae Catholicae notis Tractatio* (1575), *TT* III:132–148.

[11] *De haereticis a civili magistratu puniendis, adversus martini belli farraginem, & novorum academicorum
sectam* (1554), in *TT* I:85–169. "Martinus Bellus" was a pseudonym for Sebastian Castellio, whose
teachings on predestination Beza attacked as well in *TT* I:337–506.

[12] See Beza, *Rights of Rulers* and Théodore de Bèze, *Du Droit des Magistrats*, ed. Robert M. Kingdon
(Geneva, 1970). Doubtless owing to its controversial contents, Beza did not include this book in his
collected works.

natural rights and political covenant that Beza helped to adopt into and adapt to the Calvinist tradition.

Beza, of course, did not operate alone. He called on five decades of Protestant and five centuries of Catholic teachings on law, politics, and society as well as a whole arsenal of classical and Patristic sources. He also drew inspiration and instruction from some of his contemporary co-religionists – especially the Marian exiles from England and Scotland, John Ponet, John Knox, and Christopher Goodman, fellow Frenchmen Antoine de Chandieu, Lambert Daneau, Simon Goulart, François Hotman, Hubert Languet, Philippe DuPlessis Mornay, and Peter Martyr Vermigli, the Swiss reformers Heinrich Bullinger and Pierre Viret, several Dutch pamphleteers, and others whose contributions I shall note in passing in this and in later chapters.[13] But my main focus in this chapter will be on Beza and how he, in conversation and contestation with other Protestants, both echoed and altered some of Calvin's fundamental insights into law, religion, and human rights. Because of his stature as Calvin's successor, and because of the cogency of his transformed legal and political ideas, I shall argue, Beza was the leader of a new reformation of rights.

Church and state

Beza began his legal and political reflections where Calvin had ended. Indeed, his first major political tract, *The Punishment of Heretics* (1554), was a robust defense of the execution of Michael Servetus against Sebastian Castellio's criticisms of Calvin and the Genevan authorities.[14] For Beza, the execution of so callous and calculating a heretic and blasphemer as Servetus was not only justified but necessary. And the collaboration between church and state officials in Geneva in carrying out this execution was not only necessary but exemplary of how to maintain proper order and discipline in a local Christian community. To make this case, Beza set forth a rather elaborate apologia for the Genevan model of law, authority, and discipline in his 1554 tract, which he elaborated in several other writings in the 1550s and 1560s.

Like the mature Calvin, the early Beza believed in a unitary Christian society – the "City of God on earth," "the republic of the Christian Church," a "visible form of the invisible body of Christ" (*corpus Christianum*), as he

---

[13] See further Christoph Strohm, *Ethik im frühen Calvinismus* (Berlin and New York, 1996).
[14] See above pages 69–70 and Zagorin, *Religious Toleration*, 93–144.

variously described it.[15] "Our purpose, our desire, and our intention," Beza
declared, "is that the ruins of Jerusalem may be rebuilt; that this spiritual
temple may rise again; that the house of God built on living stones may be
restored in its integrity." In time and with God's help, Beza believed, the
Reformed faith might ultimately embrace all persons and territories united
into a new *corpus Christianum*, a new unified body of Christ and Christian
believers on earth. But for now at least this ideal of a unified and integrated
society could be realized only locally, in individual cities and territories
dedicated to the Reformed cause and modeled on the city of Geneva.[16]

Each such unitary Christian society is governed both by "universal laws"
of Scripture and custom and by "local laws" promulgated by city authorities,
Beza argued. The universal laws of Scripture or divine laws (*iura divina; iura
scriptura*) are set out most forcefully in the Ten Commandments and elaborated in sundry other moral and juridical rules set out in the Old and New
Testaments as well as in the legal teachings of the apostolic church. The universal common or customary law (*ius gentium; ius commune*) is the body of
laws that both church and state rulers have commonly adopted and adapted
over the centuries for the right ordering of Christian society. Beza considered both the civil laws of the Christian Roman Empire and the canon laws
of the Roman Catholic church to be potentially viable expressions of this
"common" or "customary" law. Their rules and procedures could be used in
modern Reformed societies, provided that these laws accorded with the cardinal teachings of Scripture, and were purged of any "pagan" or "papalist"
teachings. Good examples were the numerous discrete rules of Christian
civil law and Catholic canon law that Beza imported to fill out and systematize a comprehensive Reformed law of marriage, annulment, and divorce.[17]

"Local laws" (*iura municipale*) were, by definition, man-made or positive laws. They were posited or promulgated by local city or provincial
authorities under the governance of Scripture and the guidance of customary or common laws. These "local laws" were of two main types: "positive
ecclesiastical laws" and "positive civil laws." Ecclesiastical laws were for the
church, civil laws were for the state to promulgate and enforce. Church
and state were distinct legal authorities within the unitary Christian society, Beza argued. Each institution had a distinct "jurisdiction," a power to

---

[15] Quoted by Robert M. Kingdon, "The First Expression of Theodore Beza's Political Ideas," *AFR* 46
(1955): 88, 90.

[16] Second Harangue at the Colloquy of Poissy (1561), translated in Baird, *Theodore Beza*, 168. See also
Choisy, *L'État chrétien*, 436–450.

[17] *TT* II:1–159 excerpted and analyzed in Witte and Kingdon, *Sex, Marriage and Family*; Kingdon,
Adultery and Divorce, 166–174.

make and enforce law, literally "to speak the law" (*ius dicere*). The church held the "spiritual power" of the Word. The state held the "civil power" of the sword. The church's spiritual power was focused on spiritual matters – religious doctrine and liturgy, church polity and property, Christian piety and discipline. The state's civil power was focused on temporal matters – property and contract, crimes and delicts, taxes and warfare. The church enforced its ecclesiastical laws using spiritual means – preaching and teaching, admonishing and reprimanding, banning and excommunicating. The state enforced its civil laws using temporal means – counseling and fining, imprisoning and flogging, banishing and executing.[18]

Beza spent a good deal of time detailing the polity, power, and prerogatives of the church and their expression in positive ecclesiastical laws. Like Calvin, he divided the powers of the local congregation among ministers, teachers, deacons, and elders, each of which offices he grounded in sundry New Testament texts and apostolic examples. Collectively, these four offices of the church made and maintained the ecclesiastical laws of the local church. These ecclesiastical laws fell into two groups. One group governed the essentials of doctrine, liturgy, and morality based directly on the Bible and the teachings of the apostolic church. These included laws that defined the basic biblical teachings about God and man, sin and salvation, the church and the sacraments. They also included laws that distilled the basic biblical norms of marriage and family, oaths and promises, blasphemy and Sabbath worship, and more. Such laws on the "inner essentials" of the faith had, of necessity, to be uniform from local congregation to congregation and to bind all members of local Reformed churches to each other and to Christ. They were ultimately to be codified in creeds, confessions, and catechisms mutually agreed upon by representatives of local churches that gathered in periodic Reformed synods and councils. Each local church had to "write" these essential laws "on the hearts and consciences" of all its members through its preaching and teaching, through its discipline and diaconal work. Each local consistory had to punish violations of these essential ecclesiastical laws – first through quiet admonition and instruction, if that failed through public reprimand and confession, and if that also failed through banning and excommunication.[19]

---

[18] *TT* 1:50–53, 92–94.

[19] *TT* 1:32–33, 40–41, 50–51, with later elaboration in *TT* III:132–148; *NTAnn.*, s.v. 1 Cor. 3:10, 12:28, Eph. 4:11. Beza had already formulated some of these views in his *Summa totius Christianismi* (1555), *TT* 1:170–205. He elaborated his views in his *Sermons sur les trois premiers chaptres du cantique des Cantiques de Salomon* (Geneva, 1586), 614ff. and *Tractatus pius et moderatus de vera excommunicatione et christiano presbyterio* (Geneva, 1590). See Tadataka Maruyama, *The Ecclesiology of Theodore Beza: The Reform of the True Church* (Geneva, 1978), 20–25, 106–132, 228–242.

A second group of ecclesiastical laws concerned the non-essentials (the adiaphora) of the faith – the number and timing of services, the details of liturgies and ceremonies, the structure and arrangement of the sanctuary, issues of diet, dress, vestments, holiday observance, and more. Ecclesiastical laws governing such "exterior things may vary according to the circumstances of time, place, and person," said Beza. "They can never be perpetual or universal without exception. For what is considered orderly and fashionable in one place, may or may not be used in another place, or may even be . . . dangerous or harmful in another. Thus there is often ample variety among the canons, since it was necessary to respect those things which were expedient" in each place. There is no harm in allowing such local variety from congregation to congregation. For ecclesiastical laws governing such non-essential matters "do not concern the conscience" but only serve for "the edification and quietness of the [local] church." Local consistories have authority to promulgate and enforce such laws to ensure a modicum of peace and order within each congregation. And for the sake of "decorum and decency" all members of the church should oblige them. But these were not the kinds of laws that generally required the heavy spiritual machinery of banning or excommunication.[20]

While local church authorities had jurisdiction over ecclesiastical laws, local state authorities had jurisdiction over civil laws, and worked hand-in-hand with the local church in the maintenance and governance of each unitary local Christian society. In his early years, Beza largely repeated Calvin's view of the magistrate. God had appointed the magistrate to be his representative, to reflect his majesty and authority, to appropriate and apply his law on earth. The magistrate was, in this respect, a "god on earth," said Beza quoting Psalm 82, one who held authority of, by, and for God. His principal task was to pass and enforce civil laws that would restrain and punish public offenses and protect peace, order, and justice in the local community. The magistrate, Beza wrote, must "conserve all things public as well as private, sacred as well as profane, in order that the citizens of the Republic whom he superintends live the happiest life possible."[21]

"Pursuit of happiness" (*beatus; prospérité*) by each individual citizen did not, for Beza, entail the pursuit of self-defined desires or ambitions. *Beatus* meant "spiritual happiness" or "blessedness" in the way that the term is used in the Psalms: "Happy" or "blessed" is "the man that feareth the Lord, that delighteth greatly in his commandments."[22] It was the magistrate's duty to help the local community and each individual within it to pursue "happiness" in this rich biblical sense. The magistrate had to guard "the

[20] *TT* 1:40–42.   [21] *TT* 1:91–92.   [22] Psalm 112:1 (King James Version).

peace and concord of his subjects," said Beza, not as an end in itself, "but principally for this end that the peace and concord may tend to the glory and honor of God." He had to ensure "that all men live not only in a certain civil honesty, but also with piety and true worship of God." By so doing the magistrate would help ensure "that the religion would be perfect and holy, and that the whole church would be ordered according to the Word of God."[23]

Like Calvin, Beza grounded the magistrate's jurisdiction in the Bible. He, too, described the magistrate as the "custodian of both tables of the Decalogue."[24] As he put it in the 1559 *Confession of Faith*:

We believe that God wishes to have the world governed by laws and magistrates, so that some restraint may be put upon its disordered appetites. And as he has established kingdoms, republics, and all sorts of principalities, either hereditary or otherwise, and all that belongs to a just government, and wishes to be considered as their Author, so he has put the sword in the hands of the magistrates to suppress crimes against the First as well as the Second Table of the Commandments of God.[25]

As custodian of the First Table of the Decalogue, the magistrate was to promulgate civil laws governing the relationships between persons and God – laws against "public" expressions of heresy, idolatry, and blasphemy, and laws in support of the Sabbath and the public worship of God and in protection of the church and its ministers and ministry. As custodian of the Second Table of the Decalogue, the magistrate was to promulgate civil laws governing the relationships between persons – laws of marriage and family, persons and properties, reputations and relationships, procedure and evidence in amplification of the Commandments to honor one's parents and not to kill, steal, covet, commit adultery, or bear false witness.

This magisterial responsibility to pass civil laws in application and ampli-fication of the First Table brought the state into close association with the church. Indeed, in his early writings, Beza went so far as to intimate that the magistrate was an "officer" of the church – though he soon rejected this view as too dangerous to the church's freedom.[26] As a supporter, if not officer, of the church, the magistrate was called to patronize and protect

---

[23] *TT* 1:53–54, 84; see further *Sermons sur la Cantique*, 449ff.

[24] *TT* 1:94, 144. See further Theodore Beza, *Lex dei, moralis, ceremonialis et civilis* (Geneva, 1577), 61ff. where Beza adduces all the passages from the Pentateuch that support the magistrate's role as "custodian of both tables of the Decalogue."

[25] *TT* 1:53–54.

[26] Cf. the 1559 Confession in *TT* 1:53–54 (calling magistrates God's "lieutenants and officers, whom He has commissioned to exercise a legitimate and holy authority") with the 1560 Confession in *TT* 1:80–84 where this language is softened. See his mature position in Theodore Beza, *Psalmorum davidis et aliorum prophetarum libri quinque* (London, 1580), s.v. Ps. 82:6.

the church's polity and property and to facilitate and encourage its worship and discipline – in imitation of the great kings of ancient Israel, David, Solomon, and Josiah, and the great emperors of Christian Rome, Constantine, Theodosius, and Justinian.[27]

Beza insisted, however, that the magistrate's positive civil laws were to complement, not to compete with, the church's positive ecclesiastical laws. The magistrate could not make civil laws that governed the church's doctrine or liturgy, regulated its ministers or ministry, or dictated its forms and functions. Even the "non-essentials," the *adiaphora* of church life, were beyond the magistrate's control. These were all "internal" and "private" matters for the church to resolve in accordance with its own ecclesiastical laws. The magistrate could only reach "external" expressions of the faith – "public expressions" or "outward manifestations" of religion that affected the broader Christian community. Blasphemous speech, idolatrous expressions, heretical activities, blatant violations of the Sabbath Day, and other such open, public violations of the First Table of the Decalogue were for the magistrate to police and punish. These were not only sins against God and His church. They were also crimes against God's people in the local Christian community.[28]

Liberty of conscience and heresy

It was on this foundation that Beza defended the collaboration of church and state authorities of Geneva in the indictment, conviction, and execution of Michael Servetus for heresy. Servetus's champion, Sebastian Castellio, had argued that heretics ought not to be punished – ideally not at all, and certainly not by a magistrate's death sentence. Beza summarized Castellio's argument thus: heretics have freedom of conscience like everyone else. They cannot be compelled to believe doctrines of which they are not convinced. We allow many others who reject Christ and Christian doctrines altogether to live with impunity; Reformed Christians are not crusading against Jews, Turks, infidels, and others. Why should heretics be singled out just because they offer a different interpretation of Christian doctrine? Why should they be coerced into a peculiar form of the Christian faith? Why should their views be prejudged by a human tribunal; would it not be better to wait for the Final Judgment of God to separate the wheat and the tares? If heretics must be judged and punished, why should the magistrate and criminal sanctions be involved? After all, heresy concerns religious doctrine. Religious

---

[27] *TT* 1:53, 93–94.   [28] *Ibid.* and *TT* 1:138–140.

doctrine is the exclusive purview of the church alone. And the church, by definition, deals only in spiritual sanctions of admonition and excommunication, not in torture and execution. So, why was a heretic like Servetus burned at the stake by the Genevan civil authorities, stoked by Calvin and other church leaders? Catholic regimes have long engaged in this kind of spiritual belligerence through their crusades, inquisitions, and pogroms; that is why we Protestants left the Catholic Church. Are torture and execution really the way of a Reformed Protestant faith dedicated to the freedom of conscience, Castellio challenged?[29]

Beza met this challenge head on. Heretics are, by definition, those whose consciences have taught them true religious doctrine but who have now voluntarily rejected it. They are not merely religious outsiders like Jews or Muslims who have not seen the light. They are not merely lazy Christians who have not carried their weight. They are not merely private sinners or dimmer lights who have fallen a bit short of God's law. Heretics are those who have made the conscientious choice to destroy the church and the Christian community from within. They have been warned repeatedly of their errors, but have failed to retract their views or to retreat from the church. Instead, they have stayed on, "gnawing at the vitals of the church like a cancer." They have become "instruments of the devil" who work to crumble the skeleton of religious doctrine that gives the church its form, stature, and strength. Such a dangerous cancer must be cut from the body of Christ, even though that causes pain and bloodshed. To allow the cancer of heresy to grow unchecked would be to condemn the body of Christ to a slow and lingering death.[30]

While the church must excommunicate the heretic from the congregation, the state must drive the heretic from the Christian community. The church holds "the power of the Word" to make judgments of doctrine, said Beza, and to separate religious truth from error, orthodoxy from heresy. Only the church has the power to judge a spiritual teaching or practice to be in violation of the Word of God. The state has no original jurisdiction over doctrine and heresy. The state may not proceed against a heretic unless and until the church has rendered its doctrinal judgment and declared a person a heretic. Once the church has found heresy, then the state may act. Indeed it must act. For it is dangerous to leave a heretic excommunicated from the local congregation but free to roam in broader Christian society. The heretic will breed discord and dissent within society. He will prey upon the weak and temperamental and gather a following. Once one

---

[29] See above pages 69–70 for detailed references to Castellio.   [30] *TT* 1:128–167.

heretic succeeds in this, others will follow suit, and still others thereafter. And soon what had once been a unitary and peaceful local Christian society dedicated to the proper worship of God will become a bevy of factions, each defecting from the other, each deflecting from the true and proper worship and teaching of God. This is a recipe for anarchy, Beza concluded. The state's calling is to keep the peace, and to protect the true and proper worship of God in his church. It is the state's responsibility to avoid such a turn of events. And the best way to do so is to punish the heretic.

At minimum, this requires the state to censure, imprison, or ban the heretic and thus protect the local Christian society from any lingering doctrinal confusion or any growing communal defection. But some heretics deserve more severe punishment. After all, the state routinely executes criminals convicted of serious crimes like murder, rape, or theft, Beza argued. The victims in such cases are persons and their property. The crime of heresy is far more serious. Here, the victim is Christ Himself and the whole church community who represent Christ's body on earth. If a magistrate has power to execute a murderer, surely he has power to execute the heretic as well.

For the majesty of God should be held to be of such moment among all men, through the everlasting ages, that whoever scoffs at it, because he scoffs at the very Author of life, most justly deserves to be put to death by violence. This I say, this I cry aloud, relying upon the truth of God and the testimony of conscience.[31]

To punish a heretic is not to violate the heretic's freedom of conscience but to protect the freedom of the church, Beza insisted. The "magistrate cannot coerce faith any more than the minister can." "God alone is the Lord of the conscience," and no human law, whether civil or ecclesiastical, can intrude on God's sovereignty. But a heretic is, by definition, one who not only entertains dangerous beliefs in his conscience, but who acts publicly on his dangerous beliefs to the detriment and endangerment of the church and its members. It is the public expression of the heresy, not the private entertainment of the heretical thoughts that makes the spiritual and civil punishment of a heretic necessary.[32]

Beza returned to this argument several more times in his dealings with purported heretics who claimed freedom of conscience to advance or practice religious teachings contrary to Reformed orthodoxy. A telling

---

[31] *TT* 1:155.
[32] *TT* 1:98–99, 151–161; Theodore Beza, *Sermons sur l'histoire de la passion et sepultre de nostre Seigneur Iesus Christ, descrite par les quatre Evangelistes* (Geneva, 1592), 62 (calling Christ "the sole legislator of our consciences").

early example was Beza's condemnation of the polygamous speculations of Bernard Ochino. Ochino was a distinguished Italian scholar and preacher, and a former leader of the Franciscan order. He had converted to Protestantism in 1542 and had lived in Geneva for a time. Calvin had commended Ochino warmly in a 1545 letter, which allowed him to move freely among various Protestant cities.[33] But, in a late-life title, *Thirty Dialogues* (1563), Ochino offered a series of Socratic musings about the cogency of various standard theological doctrines. Included was a dialogue "whether in some instances an individual man should make his own decision under the inspiration of Almighty God to marry a second wife." Ochino's fictional interlocutors left hanging the suggestion that – because there was no clear biblical commandment against polygamy and because there were many examples of leading polygamists in the Bible – the decision about the propriety of polygamy might be better left to the judgment of an individual Christian conscience instructed by God.[34]

This proved to be perilous speculation. When Ochino's volume reached Geneva, Beza immediately wrote a blistering attack on his views, which he later wove into his *Tract on Polygamy* (1568).[35] It did not help Ochino's cause that it was Sebastian Castellio, the defender of Servetus, who translated the *Thirty Dialogues* into Latin and commended them in a robust preface. After reviewing at length Ochino's biblical exegesis, Beza condemned him as an "apostate" and "heretic." In Beza's view, it was the simple act of publishing his heretical speculations that was sufficient for a finding of heresy; Ochino did not practice or even advocate polygamy. Beza's attack on Ochino's speculations was a key piece of evidence used by the Zurich authorities to prosecute Ochino later that year. The Zurich authorities found Ochino guilty of heresy and banished the frail 76-year-old and his four children in midwinter. He wandered through Germany and Poland in search of refuge, and died the following year in Moravia.

An even more attenuated doctrinal error – now, ominously, about the place of freedom within the local church – led to the excommunication, banishment, and censorship of Jean Morély.[36] Morély was a well-educated

[33] Letter to Oswald Myconius (August 15, 1545), *CO* xii:136–137.

[34] *Bernardini Ochini Senensis Dialogi* xxx (Basel, 1563), 186ff. See Roland Bainton, *Bernardino Ochino* (Florence, 1941); See Witte and Kingdon, *Sex, Marriage and Family*, vol. i, ch. 7.

[35] *TT* ii:1–63. For Calvin's and Beza's views on polygamy, see Kingdon and Witte, *Sex, Marriage and Family*, i:220–261.

[36] See Philippe Denis and Jean Rott, *Jean Morély (ca. 1524 – ca. 1594) et l'utopie d'une démocratie dans l'eglise* (Geneva, 1993); Robert M. Kingdon, *Geneva and the Consolidation of the French Protestant Movement 1564–1572: A Contribution to the History of Congregationalism, Presbyterianism and Calvinist Resistance Theory* (Madison, WI, 1967), 43–137.

French aristocrat who had converted to the Protestant cause and moved to
Geneva in 1554. He was a staunch believer in the new Reformed doctrine,
which he saw as a proper resurrection of the "golden age" of biblical and
apostolic teaching. But Morély developed misgivings about the Consistory's
authority to exercise spiritual discipline in Geneva. In 1562, he published
a lengthy and learned *Tract on Christian Discipline and Polity* which called
for greater freedom and democratic rule within each local church.[37]

Morély made clear that he was all for a unitary local Christian society
under the coordinate rule of church and state authorities – "a holy and
Christian republic," as he put it, echoing Beza. He was all for the maintenance of firm Christian discipline, and for the excommunication and
criminal punishment of brazen heretics – even their execution in extreme
cases when heretics fomented riot or created an ample following. Morély's
real concern, however, centered on the procedure used and the power exercised by the local church in judging and punishing heretics. In Morély's
view, the "heart," "soul," and "living voice" of church government and
authority lay with the local congregation – not with the local consistory
and certainly not with a higher church council or a city council. Judgments about heresy and punishments for heretics should thus be up to the
communicant members of each local congregation.[38]

Christ is the head of the church, its chief "prophet, priest, and king,"
Morély argued. All members of the local congregation are "Christ's priests,"
part of the "priesthood of believers" who serve and care for their neighbors.
All members are "Christ's prophets," who work under the inspiration of the
Holy Spirit to "make disciples of all nations, teaching them to observe all"
that Christ has "commanded" them. And just the same, all members are
"Christ's kings," who should govern the church and maintain its spiritual
discipline, following the example of the apostolic church.[39]

For Morély, this was the true meaning of the power of the "keys"
described in Matthew 16:19: "I give you the keys of the kingdom of heaven,
and whatever you bind on earth shall be bound in heaven, and whatever
you loose on earth shall be loosed in heaven." Christ gave this power "to
bind and to loose" to the congregation as a whole, he insisted, not to the
Consistory alone. This becomes clear, Morély claimed, when we read the
first "keys" passage in Matthew 16:19 together with a second "keys" passage
in Matthew 18:15–18. There Christ says:

---

[37] Jean Morély, *Traicté de la discipline & police chrestienne* (Lyon, 1562), facs. ed. (Geneva, 1968). (My
translations throughout.)
[38] *Ibid.*, 32, 41, 96, 106, 186, 188.   [39] *Ibid.*, 28, 30, 33, 48–49, 60, 270, 277–279.

If your brother sins against you, go and tell him his fault, between you and him alone. If he listens to you, you have gained your brother. But if he does not listen to you, take one or two along with you, that every word may be confirmed by the evidence of two or three witnesses. If he refuses to listen, tell it to the church; and if he refuses to listen even to the church, let him be to you as a Gentile and a tax collector. Truly, I say to you, whatever you bind on earth shall be bound in heaven, and whatever you loose on earth shall be loosed in heaven.

The word "church," in this passage, said Morély, "does not mean a council of elders or a consistory." It means "the congregation of its members, the unity of Christ's body." The commonsense reading of Christ's words is that Christians facing disciplinary issues must move from one-on-one admonition, to small group admonition, to admonition by the whole congregation (not just another small group like the consistory). Thus, for Morély, it was the right and the duty of the whole congregation to exercise the power of the keys to make fundamental judgments about doctrine and discipline under the inspiration of the Holy Spirit. This was especially true in serious cases of heresy that might require the local church to excommunicate one of its fellow members. "The consent of the whole church is the source of excommunication as well as of restoration" of one of its own members, Morély wrote. "This power to throw out of the church, to bar from its communion, to cut off from this body of the Lord, or to receive into this church and replace in this company and community, is a sovereign power, which belongs to each church." "[I]t cannot by right belong to the ministers but to the whole congregation."[40]

Morély called this a "democratic" form of church government, and considered such a polity the best guarantee of "freedom of the church." Local churches dedicated to democracy, he wrote, are ideally positioned "to take up the ancient discipline and to restore the ancient morals." Where there is "democracy," "all things are done more wisely, with greater maturity and consideration, than in another sort of government, whatever it be." A democratic church government ensures that each member of the church is free to participate in the fundamentals of preaching, teaching, and discipline, even while church "officers" are assigned lead responsibility for these functions. It also ensures that the Holy Spirit is free to work through the hearts and minds of all church members and make them more effective agents of Christ, whose body the church as a whole represents.[41]

Morély did not call for direct democracy within the church, featuring deliberations of the whole and plebiscites on all issues. He recognized

---

[40] *Ibid.*, 127, 168–169.   [41] *Ibid.*, 175–177, 183. See also Maruyama, *Ecclesiology*, 91–92.

the need for local consistories to manage daily affairs of church polity, property, and poor relief. He acknowledged the need for periodic regional and national synods to codify cardinal doctrinal and moral positions that affected all local churches. But these church offices and bodies had to practice a form of representative democracy. Church officers who sat on consistories and councils must be elected to their positions by the members of the congregation and accountable to them for their actions thereafter. Those churches that did not have such elections should petition for them, following the practices of the apostolic church. Those churches that chafed under abusive, ignorant, or incompatible ministers, teachers, elders, or deacons should vote them out of office. Those churches that could not abide the mandates of a broader synod or church council should be guaranteed the right to leave.[42]

Morély's 1562 book anticipated several arguments for freedom and democracy that would later become canonical for Calvinist congregationalists on both sides of the Atlantic. But Morély was well before his time – at least in local Reformed circles in Geneva and France. His views were instantly denounced as a calculated assault on the power of the Genevanstyle consistory and of the broader synods and councils of the Reformed churches. The Provincial Synod of Orléans (1562) condemned his book for its "wicked doctrine" that "tends to the confusion and dissipation of the church."[43] Later that same year of 1562, the Geneva Consistory ordered Morély to appear to answer for his "pernicious" and "slanderous" views.[44] Morély fled instead, fearing for his life. He finally appeared some eight months later, after ducking several more subpoenas. The Consistory admonished him for his "scandalous" views and ordered him to recant. Morély stood firm. The Consistory again pressed him to recant. He asked for time to prepare a written reply. The Consistory had heard enough. Because Morély "was heard but did not respond appropriately," the Consistory record reads, and because "he can meanwhile maintain his errors" to the detriment and endangerment of the church, the Consistory excommunicated him. Beza (with Calvin) was given the "honorable duty" to report the case to the city Council and to urge them to impose criminal sanctions on Morély as well.[45] On Beza's recommendation, the Council convicted Morély *in absentia* for heresy and contempt "to set an example to others." They ordered all copies of his books publicly burned, rounded up

---

[42] Kingdon, *Consolidation*, 54–57.   [43] Quoted in *ibid.*, 63.

[44] *Registres du Consistoire de Genève au Temps de Calvin*, gen. ed. Robert M. Kingdon, 21 vols. (Geneva, 2001–), vol. xx (forthcoming), folio 115 (August 26, 1563).

[45] *Ibid.*, vol. xx, folio 120v (August 31, 1563).

all his sympathizers for close questioning and reproof, and banished him permanently from the city. The Consistory also took the unusual step of publishing the detailed record of their proceedings against Morély to deter further the spread of such "schismatic and seditious" ideas.[46]

Morély's ideas of a democratic church polity continued to challenge the leadership of the French Reformed Church for a decade thereafter. His ideas eventually found a champion in the distinguished Calvinist philosopher, Peter Ramus, who pressed the case skillfully with several Protestant leaders in France, Germany, and Switzerland. Though it was fiercely resisted in a torrent of learned books and pamphlets, this democratic agitation might have triggered greater reforms in sixteenth-century Calvinist ecclesiology had not Ramus and many other sympathizers been slaughtered in the St. Bartholomew Day Massacre of 1572.[47]

Beza had little sympathy with these arguments. He repeatedly condemned all such "simple democratic views" of the church as "shameful error."[48] He also led the national synods of La Rochelle (1571) and Nîmes (1572) to condemn the new democratic experimentation and teachings of some local French churches. While he supported the "free and legitimate election" of church officers by the members of the congregation "as far as it is possible, and as God will permit," Beza regarded democracy alone as "the most troublesome and most seditious" form of church government.[49] Ecclesiastical democracy was "troublesome," said Beza, because it left doctrinal and disciplinary decisions to the "whim" of the congregation. Surely, the fundamentals of the faith should not be judged by counting the votes of the untutored. Surely, the honor of Christ and the holiness of his Word cannot depend on shifting majoritarian sentiments alone.[50] Ecclesiastical democracy was "seditious," Beza continued, because it stood foursquare against the teaching of Scripture. The consistory is "not a new kind of institution, contrary to the Word of God."[51] It has always been a part of the church's structure and discipline. In the apostolic church, the consistory or council was the analogue to the Jewish Sanhedrin (Acts 15). From the start, the consistory held the power of excommunication, the power to drive miscreants like Annanias and Sapphira from the church (Acts 5:1–11), just

---

[46] Reprinted in Denis and Rott, *Jean Morély*, 261–265.

[47] See documents in *ibid.*, 266–362; Kingdon, *Consolidation*, 203–219.   [48] *NTAnn.*, 1:83.

[49] Letter to Bullinger (November 13, 1571), reprinted in Kingdon, *Consolidation*, 212; see also *TT* 1:47. The phrase "as far as it is possible, and as God will permit," is from the 1559 Confession of Faith, art. 31.

[50] Letter (*c.* 1571/2), *TT* III:307. See also Maruyama, *Ecclesiology*, 117–125.

[51] *NTAnn.* s.v. Matt. 18:16, Acts 15:22; 1 Tim. 3:1, later elaborated in Theodore Beza, *De veris & visibilus Ecclesia*, *TT* III:132–147.

as Christ had earlier driven the moneychangers from the Temple (Matt. 21:12–17).[52] Thus when Christ delegated to the church the power of the keys "to bind and loose," he gave it to the leadership of the church, the consistory, not to the congregation as a whole. "There is nothing more dangerous and unjust as well as unfitting to the Word of God than either to place the whole congregation under the suffrage of the ministers alone, or to subject the judgments of ministers and elders [in the consistory] to the whim of the crowd."[53]

The consistory is, by definition, an "aristocratic institution," Beza continued, and the church government features a combination of the three classic forms of government.[54] Just as Calvin had called for a state government that was a "mixed regime tending toward aristocracy," so Beza called for church government that brought monarchy, aristocracy, and democracy into a "golden mean" (*aurea mediocratis*), under the principal direction of the aristocratic consistory – a form of balanced rule by the best qualified. As he later put it:

It seems to me that the Christian Church, both in its current form and in its ancient Israelite form, has been divinely constituted in a threefold state. The Church's head is a unique Monarch [Christ Himself], our eternal High Priest who rules over all principalities everywhere. He resides in heaven, though, through His Spirit, He is present with and leads the congregations under His authority. Next is the consistory that is commonly called the most divine aristocratic institution. Finally, there is what is called the universal multitude of the faithful which provides a perfect example of the divine democratic state. Through its consensus, the aristocratic consistory is constituted. The guardians of this multitude are the Christian magistrates who are everywhere ordained by God, and represent God in the entire world.[55]

SOURCES AND DEVELOPMENT OF NEW RIGHTS THEORIES

It is hard to see much promise in all of this for the development of a Reformed theory of rights. Much of what the early Beza offered was an effective apologia for the realities of Genevan church–state relations and an efficient application of Calvin's sternest views about liberty and heresy. His theory presupposed a unitary local Christian society, uniformly dedicated to the Reformed cause. It presupposed the cooperation of local church and

---

[52] *NTAnn.* s.v. Acts 15:22; *TT* III:138ff.; Theodore Beza, *Traicté des vrayes essencielles et visibiles marques de la vraye Eglise Catholique* (Geneva, 1592), 28–33.

[53] *TT* III:306–307.   [54] Letter to Bullinger, reprinted in Kingdon, *Consolidation*, 212.

[55] Beza, *Tractatus pius*, 113.

state authorities, particularly in the maintenance of Christian doctrine and discipline and in the punishment of error and heresy. And it presupposed that the heretic was a wayward member of the local church or society bent on destroying its unity and defying its authority.

Beza's early formulations left little room for individual liberty. Servetus had argued that liberty of conscience should lead to religious pluralism. Ochino had experimented with the edges of free speech. Morély had tested the democratic implications of the Protestant commonplace that all Christians are God's prophets, priests, and kings. Beza would have none of this. Individuals, in his early view, were essentially free to elect their officials and to follow their local rules of religious doctrine and discipline – or to leave, on pain of criminal punishment if they lingered. In private, individuals were certainly free to entertain the counsels of conscience; to do otherwise would be to invade the sovereignty of Christ who is the "Lord of conscience." But in public, individuals had to conform their lives to the laws of the local church and state, whose leaders were responsible "to train the consciences of citizens," and "to keep [their] opinions dutiful," as Beza put it.[56] To utter a suspect opinion in public earned them a hearing before the Consistory. To publish a book experimenting with suspect doctrines earned them excommunication from the church and banishment from the community. To challenge orthodox doctrine directly earned them a conviction for heresy before the council – and execution if they persisted.

But what if the local community was not united by a single faith, but maintained multiple faiths, with the Reformed faith a minority? What if the state did not cooperate with the local churches but left them to their own devices? What if the heretic in question was not an individual citizen but the political leader of that society – the emperor, king, prince, duke, lord, or mayor? What if the heretical leader sought to "train the consciences of citizens" in his heresy and to keep their "opinions dutiful" in support of his or her false teaching? Even worse, what if the political leader declared the Reformed church and its leaders to be heretical and exercised his harsh judgment on them, using exactly the same arguments that Beza had proffered of the need to protect the local society from dangerous sedition and factions? What recourse did a conscientious communicant and Reformed community have in the face of such oppression?

This was precisely the grim dilemma that French Calvinists would face desperately in the aftermath of the St. Bartholomew's Day Massacre of 1572. But even in the early 1550s, when Beza was writing his *Punishment*

---

[56] Translated in Kingdon, "First Expression," 90–91.

of Heretics, these were hardly hypothetical questions. After all, the Catholic authorities in France had declared Beza himself to be a heretic and traitor after his conversion to Protestantism in 1548 and had confiscated his property and burned him in effigy. Other Catholic authorities – the Holy Roman Emperor and various monarchs and dukes of France, Spain, England, Scotland, the Netherlands, and elsewhere – were inflicting all manner of savageries on Protestant heretics, torturing and killing them by the hundreds, and driving them by the thousands into Geneva and other Reformed polities like Lausanne where Beza still lived. Indeed, just as Beza was putting the finishing touches on his *Punishment of Heretics*, a fresh wave of Marian exiles was arriving from England and Scotland, driven out by the bloody pogroms against Protestant heretics that the two Queen Marys had instituted in the early 1550s.

Beza began to take up these questions in the concluding pages of his 1554 *Punishment of Heretics*. Ideally, he wrote, the magistrate is one "who by the public consent of the citizens is declared custodian of peace and tranquility. This peace depends on the observation of laws, which establishes the safety of all the citizens."[57] But sometimes magistrates break their own laws. Sometimes their laws do not conduce to "peace and tranquility" but to "persecution and belligerence." Sometimes magistrates are greedy, reckless, and dangerous, driving their subjects into poverty and harm, raping their subjects' wives and children, summoning their subjects' young men into feckless wars to enhance their territories and expand their coffers. Sometimes "through obvious cruelty or crass ignorance," they "combat the reign of Christ." What should be done in these circumstances?

First, all the Church should take refuge in prayers and tears, and correct its life. For these are the weapons of the faithful for overcoming the ravages of the world. However the inferior magistrate must, as much as possible, with prudence and moderation, yet constantly and wisely, maintain pure religion in the area under his authority. A signal example of this is shown in our times by Magdeburg, that city on the Elbe . . . When then several princes abuse their office, whoever feels it necessary to refuse the Christian magistrates offered by God against external violence by the unfaithful or by heretics, I charge deprives the Church of God of a most useful and (as often as it pleases the Lord) necessary defense.[58]

Beza elaborated on this a bit in his Confession of Faith, which he completed at the same time as the French edition of his *Punishment of Heretics* in Geneva in 1560. He now made the traditional distinction between tyrants who usurped their office and legitimate authorities who became tyrannical.

---

[57] In *ibid.*, 89.   [58] In *ibid.*, 92.

Usurpers were to be resisted fervently, ideally by the authorized lower magistrates. But if these magistrates failed, even private persons, following the example of the ancient Maccabees, could lead the resistance if God opened a way to them. Legitimate authorities who became tyrannical, however, could be resisted only by the lower magistrates, such as the electoral princes in the Holy Roman Empire or the Estates-General in the kingdom of France. Private persons could and should disobey unjust orders and laws, or flee the jurisdiction. But they could not fight or resist on their own.[59] "[W]e do not cease to beg our brothers to arm themselves only with patience, until God comes to their aid, either in another way, or by raising them up a [new] prince."[60]

These early reflections were "an embryonic justification for democratic revolution," writes Robert Kingdon. Beza's argument in a nutshell was this: the political office was "ordained by God and represents God in the world." But the political officers who occupy that office depend for their authority upon "the public consent of the citizens." When the political officer no longer respects his office and no longer represents God in the world, "public consent" can give way to "public dissent." When this dissent is expressed properly though the lower magistrates, the political officer loses his authority and must be resisted, and if necessary forcibly removed from office.[61]

To be sure, this was not yet a revolutionary call to arms. Beza still counseled individual citizens and subjects suffering under political tyranny to take refuge in patience, prayers, and penitence. He still restricted the right of "refusal" and "resistance" to the lower magistrates. He still limited the exercise of this right of resistance to cases where higher magistrates violated "the reign of Christ," the "rule of pure religion in the area." He still insisted that this right of resistance must be exercised "prudently," "moderately," and "under the supervision of" and "for the sake of the Church of God." He did not specify the criteria to be used to judge whether resistance was necessary. He did not specify the procedures to be followed if resistance was

---

[59] *TT* II:53–55. See also the 1559 Confession of Faith, art. XL that Beza and Calvin largely drafted, in Cochrane, ed., *Reformed Confessions*, 158; Beza maintained the same position in his interventions in the 1561 Colloquy of Poissy, quoted at length in Baird, *Theodore Beza*, 164–183 and in his letter to the Dutch Refugee Church in London (June 25, 1568), in J. J. van Toorenenbergen, *Gheschiedenissen ende Handelingen die voornemelick aengaen de nederduystche natie ende gemeynten wonende in Engelant ende uit bysonder tot Londen* (Amsterdam, 1873), 67–77. See Doumergue, *Jean Calvin*, v:532ff.

[60] Beza, Letter to Bullinger (1560), in *CO* XVIII:1–3.

[61] Kingdon, "First Expression," 92–93; Robert M. Kingdon, "Calvinism and Resistance Theory, 1550–1580," in *The Cambridge History of Political Thought, 1450–1700*, ed. J. H. Burns (Cambridge, 1991), 193–218.

judged expedient. He did not specify what kind of resistance was permissible – passive or active, verbal or physical, peaceable or violent. But each of these embryonic arguments would develop into fuller revolutionary forms – slowly over the next two decades, explosively after the St. Bartholomew's Day Massacre of 1572.

The Magdeburg Confession

It is significant that Beza cited the Magdeburg Confession (1550) as his "signal example" of how to respond to political abuse and tyranny. For the Magdeburg Confession was a major distillation of the most advanced Lutheran resistance theories of the day, which the Calvinist tradition absorbed.[62] The leaders of the small Saxon city of Magdeburg had drafted this Confession in response to the order of the Holy Roman Emperor to adopt a new imperial law on religion called the Augsburg Interim. The Augsburg Interim sought to impose by civil law the uniform Catholic doctrines and liturgies being crafted by the Council of Trent. It also sought to stamp out, what the Interim called the "raging Lutheran heresy" that "infected" and "inflamed" the German portions of the Holy Roman Empire. Much like Beza arguing against Servetus, the Interim argued that the Lutheran heresy was "a pernicious disease" that now ravaged and endangered the Catholic Church. Left to grow for three decades, it had caused "popular discord" and "dissension," which led inevitably to "calamity and destruction" of the body of Christ. Despite many peaceable attempts to win them back to the faith, Lutheran heretics continued to live in open violation of "the Statutes and Ceremonies of the Universal Catholic Church" and at grave cost to "Christian concord and moderation" and to "justice, peace, and unity" within the Empire.[63]

The Interim aimed to put an end to this once and for all, and to restore a single unitary Catholic faith in the Empire under the coordinate rule of pope and emperor. Those Lutheran polities that did not accept the Interim

---

[62] *Confessio et apologia pastorum & reliquorum ministrorum Ecclesiae Magdeburgensis* (Magdeburg, 1550) (hereafter *MC*). I am grateful for David M. Whitford for furnishing me with the unpublished manuscript of a working translation of this document, which I have adapted herein based on review of the original German text. See analysis in David M. Whitford, *Tyranny and Resistance: The Magdeburg Confession and the Lutheran Tradition* (St. Louis, MO, 2001). How much direct influence the Magdeburg Confession had on Beza remains disputed. See Cornel Zwierlein, "The Importance of 'Confessio' in Magdebourg (1550) for Calvinism: A Historiographical Myth," *Bibliothèque d'humanisme et renaissance* 68 (2005): 27–46.

[63] Preamble to "The Interim, or Declaration of Religion of His Imperial Majesty Charles V," in *Tracts and Treaties in Defense of the Reformed Faith*, trans. Henry Beveridge, ed. T. F. Torrance, 3 vols. (Grand Rapids, MI 1958), III:190–239, at 190–194.

peaceably would face military conquest and destruction. Several Lutheran polities and leaders had already capitulated. The city of Magdeburg would not. Imperial forces threatened to put the city under siege. The Magdeburg leadership stood firm, and began to write boldly in defense of their actions. The 1550 Confession was the most important of more than a hundred pamphlets and sermons that poured out in defense of their stand. The Confession recited the essential Lutheran doctrines that the ministers held contrary to those newly established by the Interim. The Confession then rehearsed the arguments to justify their refusal to obey the new imperial laws, and to resist their implementation – with force if necessary. Its main conclusion was set out in the preamble:

If the high authority does not refrain from unjustly and forcibly persecuting not only the lives of their subjects but even more their rights under divine and natural law, and if the high authority does not desist from eradicating true doctrine and true worship of God, then the lower magistracy is required by God's divine command to attempt, together with their subjects, to stand up to such superiors as far as possible. The current persecution which we are suffering at the hands of our superiors is primarily persecution by which they attempt to suppress the true Christian religion and the true worship of God and to reestablish the Pope's lies and abominable idolatry. Thus the Council [of Magdeburg] and each and every Christian authority is obliged to protect themselves and their people against this.[64]

In one sense, the Magdeburg Confession simply echoed Martin Luther's loud calls for resistance that had revolutionized Western Christendom three decades before. In his writings in the late 1510s and early 1520s, Luther had again and again railed against the pope as a "spiritual tyrant," indeed the "anti-Christ," "the whore of Babylon," a "werewolf" who stalked the Vineyard of God to the peril of innocent Christians. Through false doctrines and abusive laws, Luther charged, the pope and his clerical retinue had destroyed the Christian Gospel, tyrannized the Christian conscience, and raped the bride of Christ. The pope had pillaged the people's property and stolen them blind through the crass spiritual commercialism he employed to support his rapacious designs. Luther had then called on various lower magistrates – the princes, nobles, dukes, and cities of Germany – to stand up and throw off this spiritual tyrant for the sake of the freedom of the Gospel.[65]

It was one thing, however, to resist and reject the tyranny of the pope and other clergy. After all, the pope had, according to Luther, usurped the God-given authority of the Christian magistrate and invaded the God-given

---

[64] *MC*, A1v.   [65] See Witte, *Law and Protestantism*, 53–65.

freedom of the Christian conscience. It was quite another thing, however, to resist and reject the tyranny of the emperor and other magistrates. After all, one of Christ's most famous statements had been to "render to [the Emperor] Caesar the things that are Caesar's, and to God the things that are God's" (Matt. 22:21; Mark 12:17; Luke 20:25). St. Paul had elaborated:

Let every person be subject to the governing authorities. For there is no authority except from God, and those that exist have been instituted by God. Therefore he who resists the authorities resists what God has appointed, and those who resist will come into judgment. For rulers are not a terror to good conduct, but bad . . . Therefore one must be subject, not only to avoid God's wrath, but for the sake of conscience. (Rom. 13:1–5)

St. Peter was even more pointed:

Be subject for the Lord's sake to every human institution, whether it be to the emperors as supreme, or to governors as sent by him to punish those who do wrong and to praise those who do right . . . Live as free men, yet without using your freedom as a pretext for evil; but live as servants of God. Honor all men. Love the brotherhood. Fear God. Honor the emperor. (1 Peter 2:13–17)

"Honor your father and mother" and by extension all other authorities, the Bible stated repeatedly, "so that your days may be long in the land which the Lord your God has given you" (Ex. 20:12, Lev. 19:5, Deut. 5:16; Matt. 15:4, Mark 7:10, Eph. 6:1–2). All this seemed rather firm and clear biblical authority that a conscientious Christian should respect and obey the authorities, and suffer patiently and prayerfully if the authorities abused their office or became tyrants.

The Magdeburg Confession countered these biblical texts with a barrage of arguments drawn from the Bible, history, and law that called for resistance to political tyranny, particularly state encroachments on the "essential rights of religion." Biblical arguments dominated the Confession. The Magdeburg ministers worked especially hard to counter what they viewed as a misreading of the familiar biblical injunctions to obedience even to the point of martyrdom.[66] Yes, we must honor the authorities "so that our days may be long." But if our days are being cut short, then we should not honor those authorities who shorten them. Yes, political authorities were "appointed by God to do good." But if they are not doing good, then they could not have been appointed by God. Yes, the magistrate is not "a terror to good conduct but to bad." But if he becomes a terror to good conduct, then he must be a bad magistrate. Yes, we must "render to Caesar the things

---

[66] *MC*, G3r-H1r; K1r-K3r, L2r-L4r.

that are Caesar's, and to God the things that are God's." But if Caesar wants or takes what is God's, then we must withhold or retrieve it for God's sake. Yes, "he who resists the authorities resists God." But if the authorities resist God, then surely we must avenge God's honor. Yes, "vengeance is mine," says the Lord. But "we are his instruments" for good, and "God punishes in such a way that those who execute the punishment are not doing wrong but are carrying out God's will and command."[67]

The Bible makes clear that God ordained the authorities in church, state, and family to keep order and peace in this sinful world so that the Gospel can flourish and each person can pursue his or her God-given calling. None of these authorities may get "mixed up with one another," or intrude on each other's created mandate. None may abandon, betray, or exceed their God-given office. And most importantly, none may violate the sovereignty of God. All authorities thus rule conditionally. If any authorities

seek the extermination of religion and decent morals, and persecute true religion and decent living, then they dispose of their own honor, and they can no longer be considered to be authorities or parents either before God or within the conscience of their subjects. They become an ordinance of the devil instead of God, an ordinance which everyone can and ought to resist with a good conscience, each in accordance with his calling.[68]

The Bible makes clear that the calling to resist abusive political authorities lies first and foremost with lower magistrates. God has instituted multiple authorities, not just one. All political authorities are equipped with the power of the sword to do good and to punish evil. That power must be exercised internally within the government as well as externally within the community. When an inferior magistrate does evil, a fellow or superior magistrate must correct or remove him. When a superior magistrate does evil, his fellow or inferior magistrates must, in turn, correct and control him, always within the limits of the honor and respect that the higher magistrate deserves (Ex. 22:28, Acts 23:5). If the higher magistrate commits only a minor or personal offense, lower magistrates should admonish him quietly and gently, following biblical examples (Gen. 9:23). But if he unjustly endangers "life and limb," "wife and child," and the "local liberties of the people," the lower magistrates "may make use of their rights to defend themselves" and their subjects, particularly if those subjects come to the lower magistrates for protection. Even worse, if the higher magistrate commits a premeditated attack on "the highest and most essential rights of the people" – indeed, if he attacks "our Lord himself, the author of these

---

[67] *Ibid.*, M1r, J1r. L4r-M1r.   [68] *Ibid.*, G3r, G4v, L1r.

rights" – then even the most "insignificant and weakest regents" must rise up against him. If necessary, those lower magistrates must call upon "every pious and reasonable Christian" to join them in the resistance "with quiet confidence" that they are all doing the Lord's work. In such circumstances, "we must, ought, and will . . . fight, struggle and battle with our lives and limbs, trusting in divine grace that God is on our side."[69]

The Magdeburg Confession did not define the "local liberties of the people," or "the highest and most essential rights of the people" that could trigger these steps of escalating resistance and revolt. The authors hinted broadly that the threatened establishment of "unnatural" and "unbiblical" Catholic laws of marriage and celibacy might be such an example. They stated more plainly that their "procedural rights" had been abridged: "Divine, natural, and secular laws" alike recognize that criminals have a right to a public hearing and their day in court. But we have been "accused only on hearsay evidence," and have not had a chance to "face our accusers." Just because other Lutheran towns have capitulated, does not mean we should lose "our rights by default." "Our case must be judged in accordance with proper justice."[70]

But the Confession's main concern was that the emperor was violating the people's "essential rights" of religion, and those violations certainly merited a more forceful response. We "seek nothing else but the freedom to remain and be left in the true recognized religion of the holy and only redeeming Gospel." We act peaceably. We educate our children to be good and useful citizens. We pray daily for our rulers. We pay our taxes and tributes. We register our properties. We "desire no one's land and people and covet no one's worth and goods." "Your Imperial Majesty allows both Jews and heathens to follow their religion, and do not force them from their religions to the Papacy." But "we are not even allowed to have the same freedom of religion that is granted to non-Christians." Instead, the Emperor seeks "to reintroduce the Pope's idolatry, to suppress or exterminate the pure doctrine of the Holy Gospel . . . in violation not only of divine law but also of written civil law."[71]

In these circumstances, the Bible requires "a lesser God-fearing magistracy and all those over whom it has been set to give protection against such unjust force and maintain true doctrine and worship, and preserve body and life, soul and honor." Those lower magistrates who fail to discharge their duty are ignoring the admonition of Proverbs 24:10–12: "Rescue those who are being taken away to death; hold back those who are stumbling to

[69] *Ibid.*, J4r-K1r, K2R-L1r, M1r-M2r, P2r-P3r.   [70] *Ibid.*, H2r, K4r.   [71] *Ibid.*, H4r-J2r, K1r.

the slaughter." Others must come to help, too, lest they ignore the lesson of Judges 5:23 where God is said to have cursed a people "because they did not come to the help of the Lord, to the help of the Lord against the mighty." It was God who "ordained force," and he expects it to be used to "advance and defend His word, true divine worship, and appropriate reverence for God."[72]

Not only the Bible, but history makes it abundantly clear that resisting tyrants, particularly those who tread on the religious rights of their people, is not only a right but a duty of the faithful. Biblical history is full of examples: Jonathan and David resisted King Saul, as did Saul's own servants when he became tyrannical. The leaders of Zebulun and Naphtali defied Jabin, the Canaanite King. Elias, Jehu, and Naboth refused to obey King Ahab. Asa deposed his own tyrannical mother, Queen Maacah. Daniel disobeyed King Darius. The Maccabees attacked the Romans. The Confession returned to these examples again and again as illustrations of a person's duties in the face of tyranny. Christian history, too, is full of examples. Think of Ambrosius refusing Justine, Moritz resisting Maximinus, Ambrose admonishing Theodosius, Laurentius refusing the orders of Decius, and more.[73] Even the pagan Roman ruler Trajan handed his deputy a sword with the words: "In so far as I command what is right wield this sword against my foes; but if I do the opposite, then wield it against me."[74]

These examples from religious and secular history, the Confession continued, underscored the "universal" and "natural" validity of the "law of legitimate self-defense."[75] Defense of oneself and of third parties against attack, using force and violence when necessary, was a familiar legal doctrine of the European *ius commune*. When a person is unjustly attacked by another, the victim has the right to defend himself, to resist – passively, by running away, or actively, by staying to fight with proportionate force. Other parties, particularly relatives, guardians, or caretakers of the victim, also have the right to intervene to help the victim – again passively, by assisting escape, or actively, by repelling the assailant with force.

When a magistrate exceeds his authority, the Confession argued by analogy, he forfeits his office and becomes simply like any private person. If he uses force to implement his excessive authority, his victims and third parties may resist him passively or actively, just as if he were any other criminal thug. Furthermore, if the higher magistrate giving the orders has exceeded his authority, then all lower magistrates, ministers, and military

---

[72] *Ibid.*, K1r, L3r, P2v, quoting Judges 5:23.   [73] *Ibid.*, J3r, L1r-L4r, M4r-N1r, O3r-O4r.
[74] *Ibid.*, M4r.   [75] *Ibid.*, K1r, N.

folks implementing his orders have also exceeded their authority. They are accomplices in the crime of the former higher magistrate now private citizen. And they are all themselves now merely private citizens engaged in criminal actions. Both the victim and third parties have the right of passive or active resistance against these assailants, too.

The Confession drew from this law of self-defense several lessons for how to respond to the emperor and his political allies who now sought to coerce the Lutherans to return to Catholicism. First, all those who aided and acted for this tyrant were themselves accomplices to his crime of tyranny, and they were all guilty before God. This included all lower magistrates who implemented his orders. It included soldiers and allies who marched for the tyrant, citizens and subjects who paid taxes in support of the tyrant, Christians who knowingly prayed for the success of the tyrant, and more. All these parties, the Confession warned, are accomplices in the "persecution" and "murder" of Christ and His Gospel, and they will face "horrible punishment on the Day of Judgment." They are the "new crucifiers of our Lord."[76]

Second, all those who are called to care for others must assist their dependents to resist this tyrannical attack. Lower magistrates, judges, and police must protect the local citizens. Pastors, elders, and sextons must protect their local congregants. Fathers, mothers, and masters must protect their children, servants, and wards. Teachers and tutors must protect the students in their schools. If any of these dependents were attacked on the street by a simple criminal their caretakers would have to intervene. Failure to do so would render them an accomplice to the criminal attack. Tyrants are simple criminals, and innocent victims must thus be defended against them, the Confession argued. Those who fail in their defense become criminals themselves. "God will judge guilty not only those who themselves commit unjust killing, but also those who have not helped to protect and save, according to their ability."[77]

Third, invoking the Lutheran doctrine of the priesthood of all believers, the Confession argued, with rising rhetoric, that "all pious Christians should concern themselves with this common emergency and take it as much to heart and treat it as seriously as if it concerned each person individually." All Christians are called to be priests to their peers, Good Samaritans to strangers in peril. All Christians are thus responsible to intervene when a victim is assailed by a common criminal, or when a community is ravaged by a criminal tyrant. This becomes doubly imperative when the victim of this

[76] *Ibid.*, N4r-O1r, P3r-P4r.   [77] *Ibid.*, P1r. See further *ibid.*, P2r-P4r.

criminal attack is ultimately Christ himself, whose people and preaching are being unjustly assailed. "As much as you do it for them, you do it to me," Christ had said.[78]

The Confession stopped short of arguing that each and every Christian member of the community could and should seek the violent overthrow of tyrants. This was a recipe for anarchy, and the Magdeburg ministers worked hard to counter such an insurrectionary conclusion. A more structured response was called for – with the higher magistrates passing instructions down the hierarchy of lower magistrates and ultimately down to the local caretakers on the best means and measures of response. The Confession did allow, at one point, that "in an emergency an individual has to attend to things himself."[79] But without elaboration, this suggestive text must be read as a simple restatement of the traditional self-defense rule in a one-on-one encounter with an assailant. In the face of political tyranny, the main argument insisted, an individual's first reflex should be prayer and patience, then passive disobedience of false authorities and advice to others on how to disobey, then petitions for help from the lower authorities and insistence on the vindication of essential rights that have been violated. Only after exhausting peaceable remedies and receiving orders from a legitimate lower authority to join a just war or rebellion was a private person entitled to violent disobedience. But once so entitled he or she could fight with all due alacrity. None of this was a violation of the individual Christian's duties to God and conscience:

The laws and liberties of our German Empire are such that Christians may use them in [good] conscience, just like they make use of other secular rules that are not against God. Indeed, if Christians do not make use of them, they will lose out to their own eternal shame before the world and to the harm of their successors.[80]

The Magdeburg Confession was a forceful distillation and extension of the most radical Lutheran teachings on resistance to political tyranny. As Quentin Skinner and others have shown, a number of these arguments had already been pressed by Lutheran and other Protestant theologians and jurists – Martin Bucer, Johannes Bugenhagen, Gregory Brück, Andreas Osiander, Lazarus Spengler, Johann Oldendorp, Johannes Eisermann, and others.[81] And Luther himself had moved a long way toward this position in

---

[78] *Ibid.*, N3r-N4r, P1r, P4r   [79] *Ibid.*, G1r.   [80] *Ibid.*, G1r, H2r-J3r, o4r.

[81] Heinz Scheible, *Das Widerstandsrecht als Problem der deutsche Protestanten 1523–1546* (Gütersloh, 1969); Eike Wolgast, *Die Religionsfrage als Problem des Widerstandsrechts im 16. Jahrhundert* (Heidelberg, 1980); Gerald Strauss, *Law, Resistance and the State: The Opposition to Roman Law in Reformation Germany* (Princeton, 1986); Skinner, *Foundations*, ii:195–206.

the 1530s.[82] But the Confession's forceful synthesis of these arguments into a public brief on resistance theory was an impressive intellectual achievement. It was also an impressive political achievement, for it eventually turned popular opinion against the Emperor and his Augsburg Interim. After a year of laying siege to the city of Magdeburg, the Emperor's military ally, Duke Maurice of Saxony, ultimately switched back to the Lutheran side, and the threatened conquest of Magdeburg turned into a stalemate. This, in turn, led to the gradual collapse of other imperial military campaigns against the Lutherans and abandonment of the Emperor's program to enforce the Augsburg Interim law throughout the Empire. Ultimately the Emperor accepted the Peace of Augsburg (1555) that allowed each polity in Germany to have its own religious confession, whether Catholic or Lutheran, under the principle of *cuius regio, eius religio*.[83]

Calvin and the Marian exiles

The 1550 Magdeburg Confession's three main lines of arguments – from the Bible, from history, and from law – became standard tools for Beza and others in the next decades who constructed Calvinist theories of resistance to tyrants. These lines of argument were congenial to Calvinists, in no small part because Calvin himself had argued much the same in his 1536 *Institutes* and in his sermons and commentaries of the 1540s and early 1550s.[84] Calvin, too, had flipped on their heads many of the biblical passages that taught unswerving obedience to authorities, particularly when the rulers assailed the community's true Christian religion. He, too, had shown how biblical and Christian history commends resistance to leaders of church, state, and family who violate Scripture and conscience. And he, too, had called on lower popular magistrates and church ministers to lead "moderate" and "orderly" resistance to tyrants who violate Scripture and conscience – magistrates by wielding the sword, ministers by preaching the Word. Practicing what he preached, Calvin the minister had written his own robust condemnation of the Augsburg Interim in 1548: he called it an "abjuration" and "deformation of true doctrine" designed to consign Christians to "the tyranny of sin and Satan."[85] And he had also lectured

---

[82] See Martin Luther, *Warning to His Dear German People* (1531) and *Disputation Concerning the Right to Resist the Emperor* (1538), in *WA* xxxix/2:60; *LW* xlvii:6.

[83] In Ehler and Morrall, 164–173.

[84] See above pages 50–55. Several of these arguments had also been developed by Martin Bucer, Calvin's supporter in Strasbourg, whose views were also influential in Calvinist circles. See Hans Baron, "Calvinist Republicanism and its Historical Roots," *Church History* 8 (1939): 30.

[85] See his "Antidote" to the Adultero-German Interim (1548), in *CO* vii:545–674.

Luther's successor Philip Melanchthon for his failure to be more resistant to the Emperor in emulation of the Magdeburg ministers.[86]

But Calvin's teachings differed from the Magdeburg Confession at three crucial points. First, Calvin did not ground his resistance arguments in a theory of popular sovereignty or subjective rights of the individual. The Magdeburg Confession spoke of "local liberties of the people," "the highest and most essential rights" of religion, and the people's "rights under divine and natural law," whose trespass could trigger organized resistance. Calvin did not usually speak in such terms – though he did in later life begin to speak occasionally of subjective rights, as we have seen (see pages 57–59). He left his discussion of subjective rights unconnected to his discussion of resistance to tyranny. In discussing resistance, Calvin still preferred to describe the liberty of citizens not so much as a subjective right or a natural claim of the sovereign individual but as a function of the authority of their political rulers. If the authorities abided by the limits of their political office, the liberties of their subjects would be adequately protected. If those authorities exceeded their office to the detriment of the life, limb, and liberty of private subjects, the latter had to disobey quietly, move away quickly, or suffer patiently and prayerfully until directed and protected by lower magistrates.[87]

Second, and related, Calvin narrowed the grounds for resistance to tyranny. From the start, Calvin did allow for active organized resistance, led by the lower magistrates, the "ephors." But on what grounds could these lower magistrates resist? In his 1536 *Institutes* and 1540 *Commentary on Romans*, he counseled resistance when the higher magistrate violated "Scripture and conscience," "the Word and Law of God," "true faith," or "true doctrine and piety." This could easily have become an expansive ground for resistance. For, in Calvin's view, Scripture and conscience and the word and law of God embrace the whole Christian life. But surely Calvin could not have meant that every magisterial act that threatened or violated a Christian's life of faith could trigger organized resistance. In his 1552 *Commentary on Acts* and his 1555 *Sermons on Deuteronomy*, Calvin became more precise. He now called for resistance to authorities who "detract from any of those prerogatives which belong to God . . . addressed by the First Table" of the Decalogue. "We know that the service by which God is worshipped must precede everything else," and that the duties of the First Table

---

[86] Letter to Melanchthon (June 18, 1550), *CO* xiii:593–596.

[87] See above pages 50–55; *Institutes* (1559), bk. 1, ch. 15–18. See also Volker Heise, *Der calvinistische Einfluss auf das humanistische Rechtsdenken exemplarisch dargestellt an den "Commentarii de iure civili" von Hugo Donellus (1527–1591)* (Göttingen, 2004), 274–289.

outline the fundamentals of such divine worship.[88] Calvin elaborated these views in his 1561 *Lectures on Daniel,* now describing the First Table as a recitation not only of man's duties of religious worship but also of "God's rights" to be properly worshiped and obeyed: "Earthly princes lay aside all their power when they rise up against God. We ought rather to spit on their heads than to obey them when they are so restive and wish to rob God of his rights." "When princes forbid the service and worship of God, when they command their subjects to pollute themselves with idolatry and want them to consent to and participate in all the abominations that are contrary to the service of God, they are not worthy to be regarded as princes or to have any authority attributed to them."[89]

This clarified the grounds for resistance of political tyrants. Now resistance was allowed when the authorities commanded their subjects to abide false gods, graven images, blasphemous speech, and Sabbath-breaking – in open violation of the First Table commandments, and thus in violation of "God's rights." But this also narrowed the grounds for resistance considerably. What if the magistrate breached Second Table commandments? What if he broke up marriages and families, and murdered, raped, stole, pillaged, defamed, or falsely accused his subjects mercilessly in flagrant violation of Second Table duties. Could lower magistrates step in here? If they failed, could private persons take up active resistance on the argument that such Second Table violations abridged the "people's rights" just as First Table violations abridged "God's rights"?

No, no, said Calvin repeatedly. Active resistance, even when orchestrated by the lower magistrates, was proper only when the higher magistrate flagrantly violated the rights of God and man's duties to God as set out in the First Table. Even the most flagrant breaches of Second Table duties were not sufficient grounds to justify active resistance. Private persons could certainly disobey such unjust laws quietly and flee the jurisdiction peaceably. But, barring passive resistance or escape, they should face such calamity to their persons, properties, families, and reputations with Christian patience and prayer, in imitation of Christ. Listen, for example, to Calvin's plea to his followers in the preface to his 1561 *Lectures on Daniel*:

I am well aware of how many indignities you have suffered in these last six months – let alone the innumerable fires throughout thirty years. I know that in many places you have often known the violence of rioting mobs, and bombarding with stones, the attacks with naked steel. I know how your enemies have watched and waited

---

[88] Serm. Deut. 5:16, *CO* XXVI:309 (1555).
[89] Lect. Dan. 6:22 (1561). See similarly Serm. 2 Sam. 1:1–4 (1562).

and then suddenly broken up your peaceful meetings with violence. I know how some have been killed in their homes, some in the open streets; dead bodies dragged around for sport; women raped; many men beaten up; even a pregnant woman and unborn baby pierced through; houses broken open and looted. But although far worse atrocities may still await you, you must show that you are Christ's disciples, well trained in his school; you must take care that no raging, intemperate actions of the ungodly shall shake you out of the moderation you have so far shown and which alone has overcome and broken all assaults.[90]

Calvin repeated this counsel to patient and penitent suffering again and again in dozens of private letters in the last decade of his life.[91]

Third, Calvin was more insistent than the Magdeburg ministers in calling lower magistrates to follow proper procedures in judging cases of resistance and to order their troops to operate "moderately" when active resistance was judged to be necessary. In a 1561 letter to Admiral Coligny, for example, Calvin distinguished between the duties of aristocratic and popular magistrates and outlined the necessary procedural safeguards for any resistance. If the King of France, he wrote, were to "practice inhumanity to abolish religion" and if the legitimate "princes of blood" undertook resistance to "protect their rights for the common good," and if "the courts of Parlement joined in their cause," then and only then could all "good subjects lend them armed support" and pay taxes and offer materiel and services to this just military cause.[92] But even after these procedures had been followed, lower magistrates, military leaders, and individual soldiers alike had to fight to ensure that "moderation" was observed by all and "no excesses committed."[93] Calvin was mortified, for example, when he learned of a battle in the city of Lyon in 1562, in which a Calvinist army had avenged the slaughter of the congregation of Vassy. Calvinist forces had not only defeated their Catholic rivals but had also desecrated the city's Catholic cathedral and destroyed and pillaged various Catholic religious properties. This was "a terrible scandal that defamed the Gospel," Calvin excoriated the Protestant captain who had led the troops. The battle was made worse because local Reformed ministers had joined the soldiers. "It is not a decent action for a minister to make himself a soldier or captain, but it is much worse to abandon the pulpit to carry arms."[94]

While in the later 1550s and early 1560s, Beza shared Calvin's reservations about some of the radical logic and implications of the Magdeburg

---

[90] Lect. Dan., preface.

[91] *CO* xv:759; 16:112–113; 17:180, 378, 437, 580–581, 715–716; 18:82, 208, 218, 255, 268, 270, 427–428; 19:121, 409–412. See Doumergue, *Jean Calvin*, v:486–495.

[92] Letter to Coligny (April, 1561), *CO* xviii:425–431.

[93] Letter to the Church of Lyon (May 13, 1562), *CO* xix:409–411.   [94] *Ibid.*, 410.

Confession, a number of their fellow reformers did not. Particularly the Marian exiles, who had been forced out of England and Scotland because of the anti-Protestant persecution of Mary Tudor in England and Mary of Guise in Scotland, embraced this radical logic of resistance, and extended its rights talk.

John Ponet, the former Bishop of Winchester exiled in Strasbourg, vigorously defended a notion of popular sovereignty in a 1556 tract on political power, in which he included a private license to resist tyrants, even to the point of tyrannicide.[95] Ponet agreed with Calvin that a magistrate's "authority and power both to make laws and to execute laws proceeded from God." But God had delegated to his people the authority to elect political officials who should occupy the divinely ordained political office. "Kings, princes and governors have their authority of the people," Ponet argued repeatedly. No ruler "may do anything to the hurt of his people without their consent." Magistrates hold their authority "in trust," on "condition," as a "proxy" for the people. They are "put in trust in courts and parliaments to make laws and statutes to the advancement of God's glory and conservation of the liberties and commonwealth of their country."[96]

Not only magistrates, but all private persons are God's representatives and image bearers on earth, Ponet argued. Like the magistrates, the people must discharge political duties on God's behalf, for which they must give account of themselves "before the throne of the highest" on the Day of Judgment. This includes the right and duty to elect the right person to rule on God's behalf. More importantly, it requires the people to "weigh men's commandments before they be hasty to do them, to see if they be contrary or repugnant to God's commandments and justice." "Men ought not to obey their superiors, that shall command them to do anything against God's word, or the laws of nature . . . or contrary to civil justice, or the hurt of the whole state." "All men ought to have more respect to their country, than to the prince: in the commonwealth, than to any one person . . . Commonwealths and realms may live, when the head is cut off, and may put on a new head."[97]

---

[95] John Ponet, *A Shorte Treatise of Politike Power* (1556), facs. ed. appended to Winthrop S. Hudson, *John Ponet (1515?–1556): Advocate of Limited Monarchy* (Chicago, 1942). Quotations throughout have modernized spelling. For good studies, see Barrett L. Beer, "John Ponet's *Short Treatise of Politike Power* Reassessed," *Sixteenth Century Journal* 21 (1990): 373; Barbara Reardon, "The Politics of Polemic: John Ponet's Short Treatise on Politic Power and Contemporary Circumstances, 1553–1556," *The Journal of British Studies* 22 (1982): 35; Michael Walzer, "Revolutionary Ideology: The Case of the Marian Exiles," *The American Political Science Review* 57 (1963): 643.

[96] Ponet, *A Short Treatise*, 8–11, 18, 27, 61, 67, 106–107, 110, 162.   [97] *Ibid.*, 53–61.

The "deposing of kings and the killing of tyrants" who violate God's laws is "consonant to God's judgment," Ponet wrote without hesitation. Ponet preferred that such correction and punishment of tyrants be done through the Parliament representing the people and imitating the ancient Spartan ephors. But much of his tract was a lament that Parliament had not exercised its responsibilities in the face of the obvious tyranny of Queen Mary of England. Ponet thus called on the leaders of the church to excommunicate rulers "when they spoil, rob, undo, and kill their poor subjects without justice or good laws." At one point, he called every "private man" to resort to the "two weapons" that God had given him "to destroy the greatest tyranny that ever was: that is penance and prayer." But while this was the preferred response to tyranny, Ponet insisted that a "private man [may] have some special inward commandment or surely proved motion of God . . . or be otherwise commanded or permitted by common authority upon just occasion and common necessity to kill."[98]

Ponet left these revolutionary speculations about private regicide hanging, and he died before he had much of a chance to put them into action. John Knox, the fiery father of Scottish Presbyterianism, went further. Knox had been condemned to death as a heretic already in 1546 for his Protestant preaching. While he barely escaped execution, he spent two years as a prisoner rowing in the French galleys. This had hardened him in his resolve to fight against the religious tyranny of Catholic rulers. When the two Queen Marys began to reestablish Catholicism on the British Isles by the point of the sword, Knox insisted that his fellow Protestants must either flee or fight such tyranny and idolatry.[99] To do nothing was to become an accomplice in the tyranny and to render oneself vicariously liable for the idolatrous offense against God. Citing various Old Testament stories where God punished a whole tribe or the whole people of Israel for the sinful actions or omissions of one or two of its members – think of the story of Achan in Joshua 7 – Knox wrote in 1554: "[W]ho can deny but such men as daily do accompany wicked men, and yet never declare themselves offended nor displeased with their wickedness, do consent to their iniquity?" "[T]he prophets of God sometimes may teach treason against kings, and yet neither he, nor such as obeys the word spoken in the Lord's name by him, offends God." "For all those who would draw us from God (be they queens or kings), being of

[98] *Ibid.*, 11–12, 18, 67, 75, 101, 110, 112–113, 117–118, 124, 162.
[99] *The Works of John Knox*, ed. David Laing, 6 vols. (Edinburgh, 1846; repr. edn., New York, 1966), II:453. See further Jasper G. Ridley, *John Knox* (Oxford, 1968); W. Stanford Reid, "John Knox's Theology of Political Government," *Sixteenth Century Journal* 19 (1988): 529.

the devil's nature, are enemies unto God, and therefore will God [judge us] in such cases unless we declare ourselves enemies unto them." "We cannot keep the league between [God] and us inviolate if we favor, follow, or spare idolaters."[100]

Shortly thereafter, Knox came to Geneva, and asked Calvin in person "[w]hether it was necessary to obey a magistrate who enforces idolatry and condemns the true religion? And whether men of position who have castles and towns are entitled to defend themselves and their followers by armed force against this ungodly violence?"[101] Calvin condoned flight, but not fighting. "If any tumult shall arise for the sake of religion," Calvin later reported on the conversation, "I pronounced that to me it seems the better and the safer course, to remain quiet till some peculiar call for interference should clearly appear – that it is our duty rather to ask God for a spirit of moderation and prudence, to stand us in aid in the critical moment, than to agitate idle inquiries."[102]

Knox soon rejected Calvin's calls for moderation – in his *First Blast of the Trumpet Against the Monstrous Regiment of Women*, and in a series of open letters to the Queen, nobles, and common folk of Scotland, all published in Geneva in 1558.[103] Knox now wrote with vicious misogyny against the "unnatural rule," and "shameful gynaecrocy," of the two Queen Marys – arguments that shamed Calvin and Beza, and alienated both Queen Mary Tudor and her successor Queen Elizabeth I against Calvinists, despite Calvin and Beza's efforts to disavow Knox's fulminations.[104] It was not so much Mary's gender, however, but her politics of reestablishing Catholic "idolatry" that moved Knox to call for her removal, even her execution by lower magistrates or private persons. As he put it in a fateful passage:

I fear not to affirm that it had been the duty of the nobility, judges, rulers, and people, not only to have resisted and againststanded Mary, that Jezebel whom they call their Queen, but also to have her punished to the death with all sort of her idolatrous priests, together with all such as should have assisted her, what time that she and they openly began to suppress Christ's Evangel, to shed the blood of the saints of God, and to erect that most devilish idolatry . . . which once most justly by common oath was banished from that realm.[105]

---

[100] Knox, *Works*, III:184, 187.
[101] Bullinger to Calvin (March 26, 1554), *CO* xv:89–93; Calvin to Bullinger, *CO* xv:123–126.
[102] Letter to Bullinger, (April 28, 1554), *CO* xv:123–126.   [103] Knox, *Works*, IV:429–540.
[104] See Calvin, Letter to William Cecil (May, 1559), *CO* xvII:490 disavowing Knox's misogny; Beza's amendment to his Confession of Faith in 1560, TT II:80–84, explicitly stipulating the biblical propriety of female rulers.
[105] Knox, *Works*, IV:507.

While Ponet and Knox emphasized the people's divinely ordained powers and prerogatives to elect and depose their rulers, Christopher Goodman, the former Cambridge don exiled in Geneva, focused on the people's divinely ordained rights and liberties. Goodman did include in his 1558 tract *How Superior Powers Ought to be Obeyd* some of the same misogynistic attacks on female rulers. And he did call for private resistance, even to the point of tyrannicide.[106] But Goodman's more novel argument was that magistrates must strike a mean between granting their subjects "too much liberty" and "too little liberty." Granting too much liberty, he argued, will lead the people to contempt, sedition, "dissoluteness," "carnal liberty," rioting, tumult, and "contempt" for law and order "whether divine or human." But giving them too little liberty will do exactly the same. "[T]he people ought not suffer all power and liberty to be taken from them, and thereby to become brute beasts without judgment and reason, thinking all things lawful, which their rulers do without exception, command them, be they never so far from reason or godliness." God will "not suffer" that "the rights and liberties that he has given to all his people . . . be taken from them."[107]

What are "these rights and liberties that God has given to all his people" that cannot be "taken from them" – literally that cannot be "alienated"? They are the "inalienable" rights set out in the Bible, particularly in the Ten Commandments. As Goodman put it in a crucial passage:

[I]t is an easy matter for all manner of subjects to know what liberty belongs unto them by the word of God, which they may lawfully claim as their own possession, are likewise bound at all times to practice: wherein also appears what things are prohibited unto them, which they may in no case exercise . . . [T]here may be nothing lawful for you by any commandment of man, which your Lord God in any case forbids: and nothing unlawful or forbidden to you which he commands, whether it appertains to the first table or the second [table of the Decalogue]. Which rule if ye observe, you may be assured to please God: like as by doing the contrary you shall purchase his heavy wrath and indignation.[108]

This was Goodman's rights formula: the rights and liberties that God gives to each person as his or her "inalienable" "possession" are set out in the Decalogue. Nothing that God requires in the Decalogue may the magistrate forbid. Nothing that God forbids in the Decalogue may the

---

[106] Christopher Goodman, *How Superior Powers Ought to be Obeyd* (1558), facs. edn., ed. Charles H. McIlwain (New York, 1931), 52–53, 74–76, 97–99, 142 (spelling throughout modernized). See, e.g., David H. Wollman, "The Biblical Justification for Resistance to Authority in Ponet's and Goodman's Polemics," *Sixteenth Century Journal* 13 (1982): 29; Dan G. Danner, "Christopher Goodman and the English Protestant Tradition of Civil Disobedience," *Sixteenth Century Journal* 8 (1977): 60.

[107] Goodman, *Superior Powers*, 147–154.   [108] *Ibid.*, 160–161.

magistrate require. A person thus has the inalienable right to "observe the Sabbath Day and keep it holy" and "to labor six days and to rest on the Sabbath." A person has the inalienable right to "honor [his or her] father and mother so that [their] days may be long in the land which the Lord your God has given [them]." A person has the inalienable right to proper religious worship and speech – to be free from laws commanding him to worship false gods, to maintain graven images, to swear false oaths, or otherwise take the name of God in vain. A person has the inalienable right to life (freedom from killing), to property (freedom from stealing), to marital integrity (freedom from adultery), and to reputation and fair process (freedom from false testimony). A person has the right to be free from having his family, household, and possessions coveted by others. If the magistrate requires or condones conduct contrary to this formula, the magistrate is violating each subject's rights and liberties. To do so is to practice tyranny and to invite resistance for God's sake. This was a considerably more expansive notion of liberties and rights than either Calvin or Beza had countenanced to date.

Goodman referred in passing several times to this understanding of authority and liberty, rule and right as part of a "covenant" or "solemn agreement" made between the rulers and their subjects before God. These covenants, he suggested, were the modern parallels to the ancient biblical covenants in which Moses and the later kings of Israel promised to uphold the laws of God and the liberties of his people. In ancient times, breaches of these covenants by the rulers led to both divine censure and popular resistance. There were lessons in this for our day, Goodman suggested.[109] Calvin included similarly suggestive passages about these political covenants in several of his late-life commentaries, sermons, and lectures.[110] Though neither Calvin nor Goodman worked out the political implications of these speculations about the political covenant, they became the starting point for Theodore Beza's mature political reflections.

BEZA'S MATURE FORMULATIONS ON AUTHORITY AND LIBERTY

Such were some of the scattered new teachings on resistance and rights in the Calvinist tradition in the 1550s and 1560s, many of them forged by exiles and victims of persecution. Beza was already sifting through these arguments in the later 1560s, as he sought to respond to the growing oppression of Calvinists during the French wars of religion. After the St. Bartholomew's

---

[109] *Ibid.*, 72–75, 160, 164–165.
[110] Serm. Deut. 26:16–19, 27:11–15, 29:9–18; Serm. 1 Sam. 10:25, 2 Sam. 1:4.

Day Massacre, he brought his ideas together decisively in his 1574 tract *Concerning the Rights of Rulers Over Their Subjects and the Duty of Subjects Toward Their Rulers*. The tract's title was ironic and strategic. Beza's real topics were the *duties of rulers* and the *rights of their subjects*. But to announce this on the book's cover would only guarantee its instant censure and rebuke. It proved hard enough to get the book published: the Genevan authorities would not approve its publication for fear of royal reprisal, and ultimately the book was published anonymously in Heidelberg. The same circumspection and strategy marked the book's contents. Much of it was an understated and closely reasoned lawyer's brief, chock full of recitations of precedent and careful distinctions and answers to anticipated counter-claims. These judiciously placed digressions cleverly broke up the book's main argument that quietly but cogently countenanced active resistance to tyranny in the context of outlining a revolutionary understanding of constitutional authority and liberty.

Beza did include some of the familiar arguments from the Bible, history, and law that the Magdeburg Confession of 1550 had crafted – so much so that later library catalogers sometimes treated his *Rights of Rulers* as a new edition of the Magdeburg tract.[111] Like the Magdeburg ministers, Beza argued that, when read in full biblical context, the injunctions to "obey authorities," "turn the other cheek," "render to Caesar," and the like were not an invitation to martyrdom in the face of tyranny but an admonition to orderly disobedience in the name of God.[112] He, too, rummaged freely through biblical, classical, and Christian history to demonstrate the proper response of magistrates and subjects to the savageries of tyrants.[113] And he, too, distilled these biblical and historical teachings into a robust legal argument for the right of the people and the lower magistrates to resist tyrants, with force if necessary.

But while the Magdeburg Confession centered its legal argument on a theory of self-defense, Beza centered his legal argument on a theory of political covenant. The law of self-defense, he later said, provided only "an emergency argument," a way of sorting out what people could and should do when a political structure went awry and became tyrannical. The law of political covenant, by contrast, provided a more enduring argument. It

---

[111] See publication history in Introduction to Beza, *Rights of Rulers*, 1–5; Kingdon, Introduction to Beza, *Du droit des Magistrats*. The subtitle of some printings of Beza's tract encouraged this conflation with the Magdeburg Confession: *A Treatise Essential at this Time to Advise Magistrates as well as Subjects About Their Duty, Published by Those of Magdeburg in 1550 and Now Reviewed and Augmented with Many Arguments and Examples.*
[112] Beza, *Rights of Rulers*, 77–85.   [113] *Ibid.*, 25, 27, 41–64, 73, 75.

reformed the political office itself so as to check the rulers and safeguard the people against tyranny and to build in structured responses if tyranny broke out despite these restraints.[114]

Weaving together scattered insights from classical, Catholic, and earlier Protestant sources, Beza argued that each commonwealth is formed by a "covenant," "contract," "compact," or "constitution" – terms which he used variously and interchangeably and did not define clearly.[115] He did make clear, however, that this was a three-party covenant, involving God, the rulers, and the people. God is the "originator" and "guarantor" of the political order and office, Beza argued, echoing his earlier views. At creation, God ordained the office of political authority so that his people could enjoy "not only order, peace and quiet in this life," but also so that they would be induced to live their lives "to the glory of God," their Creator. That is what St. Paul meant in saying that the "powers that be are ordained by God," and that all magistrates are "God's servant[s] for your good" (Rom. 13:1, 4).[116]

While the powers that be are ordained by God, they are elected by the people, who act on God's behalf in choosing or consenting to their rulers. For Beza, the people's right to vote for or consent to their rulers was essential to the legitimacy of the political regime. Throughout history, and throughout our world today, he argued, magistrates are put into their offices by the election or consent of the people. To prove his point, Beza embarked on a twenty-page tour of ancient Israel, Greece, and Rome, of the history of Frankish tribes and French dynasties, and of sundry modern polities from Spain to Poland, Italy to England, to show that the people either elect or consent to their political rulers.[117] This was only a miniature version of the book-length historical argument for popular election or approbation of rulers that Beza's fellow reformer François Hotman had just developed in his book entitled *Franco-Gallia* (1573). Even with dynastic succession, Hotman had argued, kings ultimately "were constituted by the people and not by hereditary right." The people never consented to tyrants, but to "those who were reputed just," those who "did not have boundless, absolute, and unchecked power, but were bound by settled law, so that they were no less under the people's power and authority than the people were under theirs." Throughout the history of France and of many other nations, Hotman argued, "[t]he assembly of the people and the public council of the nation had supreme power not only to confer the kingdom but withdraw it."

---

[114] Letter to Bullinger (December, 1574), *Correspondance de Bèze*, xiv:129.
[115] Beza, *Rights of Rules*, 35, 37, 64, 65, 81, 85.
[116] *Ibid.*, 83–84. See also his later *NTAnn*, s.v. Acts 5:9; Rom. 13:1–9; 1 Pet. 2:13–17.
[117] Beza, *Rights of Rulers*, 41–64.

"This splendid liberty of holding public councils is part of the common law of peoples, and th[e] kings who scheme to suppress this sacred liberty are violators of the law of peoples and enemies of human society, and are regarded not as kings but as tyrants."[118]

Even with hereditary monarchs and emperors past and present, Beza argued echoing Hotman, the people are still required to give their consent to these appointments to office and to have opportunities to consent to the laws the monarchs make for their regimes. "[T]he histories of ancient times recorded by profane writers establish – and indeed Nature herself seems to proclaim this with a loud voice – that rulers receive their authority . . . by the free and lawful consent of the people." This consent is signaled in the oath that rulers swear before the people on assuming their political office. Beza called this oath-swearing ceremony the "liturgy" of the political covenant, an echo of the covenant-swearing ceremonies featured in the coronations of the ancient kings of Israel reported in the Books of Samuel and Kings.[119]

The political covenant establishes not just a single ruler but multiple rulers who serve, in part, to check and balance each other. "[S]ince the origin of the world," Beza wrote,

there has never been a king – even if you were to select the very best – who did not in some measure abuse his authority. It must indeed be conceded, as the philosophers enlightened by natural reason alone have also recognized, that monarchical rule brings ruin and destruction upon the people rather than protection and welfare unless it is curbed by certain reins.

Beza mused in passing that it might be better to have no monarch at all, since "God was from the beginning the sole monarch." But he focused his analysis on the "certain reins" that checked and balanced a monarch's proclivities to abuse and tyranny. Beza called for a "mixed constitution" that balanced monarchical power with the aristocratic and democratic power of the lower magistrates.[120] He had just defended this "mixed constitutional" theory of government in a furious debate with Thomas Erastus, who was pressing for a considerably more expansive view of the monarch's role within both church and state.[121] Beza wanted nothing to do with this "Erastian" form of government. Not only must the church have its own government

---

[118] François Hotman, "Francogallia," in *Constitutionalism and Resistance in the Sixteenth Century: Three Treatises by Hotman, Beza, and Mornay*, ed. Julian Franklin (New York, 1969), 55–70.

[119] *Ibid.*, 31, 34.   [120] *Ibid.*, 49.

[121] Beza's *Tractatus pius et moderatus*, published in 1590, was written in 1569 in response to an attack by Thomas Erastus on Beza's ecclesiology. Beza rejected Erastus's call to follow the example of ancient Israel that consigned final religious and political authority to the monarch, even the authority to excommunicate. Rejecting this as a form of "Roman tyranny," Beza called instead for a "golden mean" between monarchy, democracy, and aristocracy.

separate from the state, but the monarch in the state must be buffered by an array of lower magistrates.

Beza distinguished two main kinds of lower magistrates who, together, provided a buttress against tyranny and a buffer "between the supreme magistrate and the people."[122] One group of magistrates included the aristocratic "officials of the kingdom" – judges, governors, dukes, marquises, counts, viscounts, barons, squires, and similar officials who were appointed with discrete "public duties and tasks." All these lower magistrates derived their authority from the office of the supreme magistrate, though not from the supreme magistrate himself. Like the supreme magistrate, each swore a political oath that bound them to "the protection and defense of the kingdom, each in accordance with his own office."[123] A second group of magistrates was more democratic. They were the popular assemblies of the estates who represented the interests of the people, particularly in times of crisis or tyranny. They were the modern-day "ephors" whom Calvin had mentioned already in his 1536 *Institutes*, representatives of the people who sat periodically in councils, parliaments, and diets with the supreme magistrate and his retinue and "gave their consent" to the new laws. Beza was rather vague about which lower magistrates belonged in this category or precisely what democratic function they served outside of tyrannical emergencies. But it was quite clear that he saw the national and provincial French parlements as prime examples of this popular form of lower magistracy.[124]

Each of these lower magistrates, Beza insisted, was called to help maintain the rule of law and constitutional order within the community. Each was to protect "strenuously the good laws to whose defense they personally have sworn, each in accordance with the station he has obtained in the constitution of the community, and in general all should strive to prevent the laws and conditions upon which that constitution rests from being undermined by any violence from without or from within." And again, it is just "according to all law, divine and human, that by reason of the oath taken by them [that they] ensure the observance to the laws."[125]

The three-way political covenant imposed "mutual obligations" that "benefited" God, the rulers, and the people alike. First, Beza argued, the political covenant bound all political rulers to abide "by the law of God and the law of nature." This was the principal way by which God participated in the political covenant and benefited from it. Thus "it is the principal

---

[122] Beza, *Rights of Rulers*, 38.   [123] *Ibid.*, 39–40.
[124] See Robert M. Kingdon, Introduction to Beza, *Du droit des Magistrats*; Kingdon, "Calvinism and Resistance Theory," 206–212.
[125] Beza, *Rights of Rulers*, 41–43, 74.

duty of a most excellent and pious ruler that he should apply whatever means, authority, and power granted to him by God to the end that God may truly be recognized among his subjects and may, being recognized, be worshipped and adored as the supreme king of all kings."[126]

The best source and summary of the law of God and nature was the Decalogue, whose two tables set the constitutional foundation for every Christian community. Through the Decalogue, God outlawed all positive laws of the state that were considered "impious or unjust." "Impious laws" were those that violated the First Table commandments against false gods, graven images, blasphemy, or Sabbath breaking. "Unjust laws" were those that violated the Second Table commandments that required honor of parents, and prohibited killing, stealing, adultery, perjury, and coveting.[127] Beza put this political obligation to abide by the Decalogue in the very first paragraph of his *Rights of Rulers* and returned to it again and again here and in his later writings. This was consistent with his and Calvin's earlier view that the magistrate is the custodian of both tables of the Decalogue.

The Decalogue was not the only form of higher law that ground and bound the magistrate. Beza called magistrates to adhere to "natural law" and a broader "sense of natural justice" and "natural equity" as well. "[C]ommon principles of nature still linger in man after the fall," Beza insisted, "however corrupt" men might be. "This is so firmly established and enduring that nothing which is openly opposed and repugnant to them should be regarded as just and valid between men." It is thus eminently appropriate, said Beza, to rummage through the histories of classical Greece and pre-Christian Rome, and the customs of the Germanic tribes and feudal lords in search of evidence of natural law principles in action that could not be trespassed. In his *Rights of Rulers*, Beza mentioned only a few such historical examples of natural law violations, such as mandatory ritual slaughter of children or the self-mutilation of the bodies of male citizens.[128] In his just published tracts on polygamy, marriage, and divorce, he listed a whole series of other violations of natural law, justice, and equity – infanticide, incest, sodomy, concubinage, prostitution, and the improper marriages of children, of eunuchs, or of the mentally handicapped. No positive laws could command or countenance such open violations of the laws of nature and the laws of God.[129]

[126] *Ibid.*, 28, 82.   [127] *Ibid.*, 25.   [128] *Ibid.*, 64–65.

[129] See Witte and Kingdon, *Sex, Marriage and Family* vol. 1. Beza elaborated his views of natural law, and its relationships to the Decalogue and other moral distillations in his *Lex dei moralis* and more briefly in his *Propositions and Principles of Divinity, Propounded and Disputed in the University of Geneva*, trans. Robert Waldegrave (Edinburgh, 1591), ch. 34ff.

Second, in addition to requiring obedience to the laws of God and nature, the political covenant required political rulers to protect and promote the "rights and liberties" and "privileges and freedoms" of their subjects. "The people were not created for the sake of the rulers, but the rulers for the sake of the people," Beza proclaimed famously.[130] And, in order to protect the people, rulers were required to protect and respect their basic rights. Like Goodman, Beza looked to the Decalogue as a convenient source and summary of the most basic rights of persons – their rights to religion, life, property, marriage, parentage, and reputation.[131] But he also looked beyond the Decalogue – to "natural law," "common decency," "natural equity," and the common law of nations to fill out the list of natural rights of the people that the political covenant protected.

Beza focused especially on the natural rights that he considered to be of paramount importance to the health and happiness of the commonwealth. Foremost among these were the religious rights of the people. These Beza spelled out in several strong passages scattered throughout his *Rights of Rulers* and amplified in some of his later writings. Among religious rights, Beza emphasized "liberty of conscience," the right of a person to freedom from coercion into an unwanted form of faith, and freedom to change one's faith after being persuaded. He included "freedom of mission," the right to spread the Gospel not by the sword, but "by the influence of the Spirit of God alone," "by teaching, conviction, and exhortation." He spoke of the "free exercise of religion," by which he meant principally the right of Christians to "join in pious gatherings, there to hear the word of God and have communion of the sacraments as Christ ordained it should be done in the church." He alluded to the "freedom of government" of the church, the corporate right of each congregation and religious community to govern itself without state interference, a topic which he defined and defended at length in other writings. He mentioned the "freedom to educate," which he elaborated elsewhere as the right of parents and guardians to bring up their children in their own form of faith, in the home, school, and church. Finally, he noted the "freedom to emigrate," the right of persons to move to another place where their religious rights would be more readily respected. Catholics and Lutherans enjoyed this right under the Peace of Augsburg (1555). Calvinists did not, and Beza argued here and at greater length later that Calvinists, too, should have freedom to emigrate peaceably.[132] These

---

[130] Beza, *Rights of Rulers*, 30, 44.   [131] *Ibid.*, 27–29, 66, 68, 74, 80, 83–85.
[132] *Ibid.*, 28–29, 84–86. See his earlier argument in *De Pace Christianarum* (1566), *TT* II:120–121 and further references on pages 140–141.

latter views ultimately helped to influence the emigration provisions for Calvinists that found their way into the Edict of Nantes (1598) and eventually the Peace of Westphalia (1648).[133]

To be sure, all these religious rights had to be exercised within the limits imposed by the First Table of the Decalogue. For Beza, there was no religious right to worship false gods or graven images or to blaspheme or desecrate the Sabbath, as he thought Jews, Muslims, Anabaptists, and Catholics had done. But there was also no political power to bring these wayward souls into the true faith by the point of a sword. The "teaching, conviction, and exhortation" of the Word of God, not the warfare, bloodshed, and belligerence of the sword of man, were the best ways to win over new believers and to win back wayward ones. Only when a magistrate sought to coerce a people to give up "the free exercise of the true religion" in favor of a false religion could there be resort to the sword and then only in self-defense.[134]

This was a striking departure from Beza's earlier defense of the execution of Michael Servetus for heresy. In his *Punishment of Heretics* (1554), Beza had insisted that a person who had been judged a heretic by the church, could and should be punished by the state, even by execution in extreme cases. The St. Bartholomew's Day Massacre was a spectacular illustration, among many others, of the dangers of empowering the magistrate to punish a person for mere heresy alone. Beza made clear that heretics could still be punished if they acted on their heresy to the physical danger and damage to others or the whole community. There was no free exercise right to crime. No murderer would be spared just because he acted in the name of his heretical belief. No army would be admitted to the city gates just because they marched in the name of God. Heresy coupled with crime was actionable, said Beza. But heresy alone was not a crime.

In addition to religious rights, Beza also took special note of each private person's rights to free speech and political petition: (1) the right of private parties to "rebuke the magistrate for the injustice committed in violation of the laws;" (2) the right of private persons to "lodge complaints with the supreme magistrate concerning the injustice of an inferior;" and (3) the right of private persons to petition lower magistrates about other "affairs touching the constitution of the kingdom." To criticize, petition, or sue a magistrate for his political failings was not to be discourteous, let alone disobedient, Beza insisted. The magistrate "suffers no injustice if he is constrained to do his duty." After all, the political office has been "entrusted to him under specified conditions," and there is no one better to discern a breach of

---

[133] On these developments, see Manetsch, *Theodore Beza*, 308–336.   [134] *Ibid.*, 84–85.

condition than the people for whose benefit and protection the political covenant was created.[135]

In describing his doctrine of the political covenant, Beza also reflected an unusual solicitude for freedom of contract: the right of private parties to enter contracts, pacts, and agreements concerning marriage, commerce, banking, labor, property, and other transactions. Both here and in his earlier books on marriage and in his opinions on the consistory bench, Beza spelled out some of the rules of valid contract formation, reformation, and dissolution, the requirements of capacity and fitness to enter contracts, the limitations on contracts that involved usury, exploitation, price-gouging, sharp dealing, and more.[136]

Beza used his expertise on marital and other private contracts to underscore, by analogy, some of the main features of political covenants and the proper grounds for their formation and dissolution. Both private contracts and political covenants that include terms that violate the basic laws of God and nature are "null and void," and must be formally "annulled," he argued. To enter into a private marital contract, for example, both parties must abide by biblical and natural laws that define marriage as a heterosexual monogamous union entered into presumptively for life and in hopes of the blessing of children. Marital contracts that stipulate unnatural or unconscionable conditions to the contrary, such as permitting each spouse to commit adultery, agreeing to marry while already being married to another, or conspiring together to abort or smother unwanted children, violate these basic conditions of what a marriage is. Such contracts must be involuntarily annulled even if the putative marriage has been consummated and yielded children.[137]

Political covenants are comparable, Beza argued. Like private contracts, political covenants must accord with the basic laws of God and nature for the political office, and must be free from unconscionable or unnatural conditions. Thus a ruler's demands, for example, that his subjects "abjure the true faith for the sake of saving their lives," or "kill their parents or children," or engage in similar open violations of divine and natural law, are precisely the kind of unnatural and unconscionable conditions that can never be countenanced. Even if the rulers and people had voluntarily entered a political covenant on such terms, parties would not and could not be held to these terms. In private law, we annul or dissolve such unconscionable contracts without much issue in order to protect innocent parties

---

[135] *Ibid.*, 28–29, 72–77, 81.
[136] See Theodore Beza, *De repudiis et divortiis* (Geneva, 1569); Choisy, *L'État chrétien*, 442–444.
[137] Beza, *De repudiis et divortiis*, 207–372.

from exploitation. In public law, we should do the same, said Beza. "[E]ven if a people, knowingly and of its own free will, has consented to something that in itself is manifestly irreligious and against natural law, such an obligation is null and void." It would be "so utterly unjust and manifestly sinful" to maintain such political covenants that "everyone not entirely destitute of human insight realizes that it cannot be exacted or performed by anyone with a good conscience."[138]

Also like private contracts, political covenants must be entered into voluntarily and not through force, fear, or fraud. By definition, therefore, magistrates who come to power by conquest, usurpation, or through fraudulent means are presumptively not legitimate authorities. Even if the people have entered into a purported political covenant under such circumstances, the covenant is voidable and the political magistrate is vulnerable to dismissal as a tyrant. Just as an innocent spouse who is coerced or tricked into marriage may choose to continue the marriage or sue for annulment after the wedding, so an innocent people who have been coerced or tricked into obedience may accept this magistrate or annul their relationship with him. "[I]f anyone strives to seize or has already usurped an unjust tyranny over others . . . then shall private citizens before all else approach their legitimate magistrates in order" to remove him. But if the legitimate authority "connives" or "refuses to perform his duty then let each private citizen bestir himself with all his power to defend the lawful constitution of his country to whom after God he owes his entire existence." Even private "tyrannicide" is warranted as a last resort to remove such a usurping tyrant, Beza allowed.[139]

Again, like private contracts of marriage, political covenants that were freely and properly entered into might eventually end through divorce for cause. In a marriage, where one party spiritually and physically deserts the other or betrays the essence of the marriage by committing adultery or inflicting mortal abuse on the other, the innocent party may sue for divorce. Similarly in a political community, Beza continued, where the magistrate deserts his people or betrays the fundamentals of his political office by becoming a tyrant, the people may properly seek to divorce him.[140]

But just as the dissolution of a private marriage contract through annulment or divorce requires orderly procedures, so does the dissolution of a

---

[138] Beza, *Rights of Rulers*, 44–45, 64–65.

[139] *Ibid.*, 33–34. Beza qualified this position in his later *Sermons sur l'histoire de la passion*, 282, 491, 501, where he denounced all private assassinations. See discussion in Robert M. Kingdon, "Beza's Political Ideas as Expressed in His Sermons on the Passion" (unpub. ms.).

[140] Beza, *De repudiis et divortiis*, 299–313.

public political covenant. Disgruntled spouses may not simply walk away from their marriages, and declare themselves divorced or declare on their own that their marriage is annulled. By reason of its consecration by the church and registration by the state, the marriage contract has become a public institution. It transcends the interests of the couple themselves, and implicates the interests of the whole community. The disgruntled spouse must thus file complaints before the appropriate authorities, seek those authorities' intervention and protection if they are being abused, and request a public judgment that the marriage has ended by annulment or divorce, that the guilty spouse must be punished, and that the innocent spouse has been liberated. Until such public judgment has been rendered, the parties are bound by their marital contract, which they had entered into "for better or for worse."[141]

If these complex procedures are due for the dissolution of a private marital contract, Beza argued, surely one can see that they are doubly necessary for the dissolution of the public political covenant. For the political covenant involves far more parties, and the risks of dissolving it improperly are far higher. It can certainly not be left to random private persons to make and execute judgments whether the political covenant is null and void because it had been invalidly entered. Nor can it be left to private persons to judge whether a once-valid political covenant is now broken by reason of the magistrate's tyranny. These are constitutional judgments, not individual judgments. They are to be made only by properly constituted and authorized lower magistrates. And unless and until the lower magistrates make these judgments, individual members of the community are bound by the political covenant.

Beza returned to this argument by analogy again and again in an effort to answer the agitation for popular insurrection and anarchy that was breaking out anew in French Calvinist communities after the St. Bartholomew's Day Massacre. "If we must so far abide by private contracts, pacts, agreements, and understandings that we suffer damage rather than break our word, how much more should private citizens be on their guard lest they in any way refuse to honor an obligation entered into by a solemn and public agreement?" "[I]t is not becoming that men in private station should inquire over-curiously even concerning doubtful matters beyond their comprehension or station in life." And again: "I most strongly approve of Christian patience as laudable beyond all the other virtues [for] rebellions and all disorder I detest as awful abominations."[142]

---

[141] See detailed sources in Witte and Kingdon, *Sex, Marriage and Family*, vols. I, III.
[142] Beza, *Rights of Rulers*, 38, 27, 31.

This did not mean that private citizens had to practice martyrdom in the face of tyranny. They could and should still fully and freely exercise their rights under the political covenant. Using their religious rights, they could still worship and teach the true God, ignoring a magistrate's orders to the contrary. They could disregard laws that violated the laws of God and the Christian conscience. Or they could move away if the magistrate persisted. Exercising their free speech rights, they could still sue the magistrate for his failures, and petition the lower magistrates to protect them and their rights. Private persons, Beza wrote, "can and are even under an obligation to examine (albeit discretely and in a peaceful manner) what elements of reason and justice are to be found in the command" of a tyrant. "When the supreme ruler has become a tyrant, he must be deemed by his own perjury to have freed the people from their oath, and not contrariwise, when the people justly asserts its rights against him."[143]

But unless and until the lower magistrates have acted to restrain a tyrant in accordance with the terms of the political covenant, private citizens are not allowed to take the law into their own hands. "[N]o private citizen is entitled on his own private authority to oppose the tyrant with violence against violence," said Beza. All such private retaliation and revenge leads to "endless disorders," yielding "a thousand tyrants" in place of the one who was removed. Instead, private persons must petition the lower magistrates who are charged with protection of the political covenant. If those lower magistrates fail to intervene, private citizens must either leave or suffer patiently and prayerfully.[144]

Like the Magdeburg ministers, Beza set out a hierarchy of political abuses escalating to tyranny to which the lower magistrates must respond. In cases of modest abuses by the higher magistrate, such as excessive taxes that pay for the magistrate's "wasteful or avaricious vices" or immoral behavior that betrays the majesty of his office, Beza left it largely to the "aristocratic" lower magistrates to offer the offending magistrate private admonition and reproof with no political or popular consequences. In cases of more serious violations of the "divine, natural, and constitutional laws [or rights, "*iura*" is the original term in the text] of their nation," however, both the aristocratic and democratic magistrates must challenge him by "all lawful means available" and coerce him to return to his duties.[145]

The most obvious cases of tyranny for Beza were the magistrate's open and persistent violations of the First and Second Tables of the Decalogue. These were at once violations of the magistrate's duties to obey the laws of God and the people's rights that the law of God gave them. "Once

---

[143] *Ibid.*, 27–28, 76.   [144] *Ibid.*, 27, 36–38, 72–74.   [145] *Ibid.*, 64–65, 72–80.

the free exercise of the true religion has been granted" in a community in accordance with the First Table of the Decalogue, "the ruler is so much more bound to have it observed [that] if he acts otherwise, I declare that he is practicing manifest tyranny, and [his subjects] will be all the more free to oppose him," wrote Beza. "For we are bound to set greater store and value in the salvation of our souls and the freedom of our conscience than in any other matters, however desirable."[146] The same is true when the magistrate betrays the parents, families, persons, properties, and reputations protected by the Second Table. This occurs where a magistrate "plunders his territory," "savagely slays the parents of his subjects, ravishes their wives and daughters, pillages their houses and possessions, and finally murders them as the fancy takes him," "without self-control," "against law and reason" and in "wanton breach of their sworn promises."[147]

If this belligerent and tyrannical conduct persists, and "peaceable remedies" are unavailing, the lower magistrates must "at once unanimously insist on an assembly of the Estates and meanwhile as far as they can and may defend and protect themselves against undisguised tyranny." This democratic body must, in turn, protect the people by organizing the resistance to the tyrant, and exercising their "right to procure support from abroad, especially from the allies and friends of the kingdom." "They are certainly bound, even by means of armed force if they can, to protect against manifest tyranny the safety of those who have been entrusted to their care and honor."[148]

SUMMARY AND CONCLUSIONS

Theodore Beza began as a faithful and forceful defender of John Calvin's mature views on church and state, law and liberty. He ended up embracing theories of rights, liberties, and resistance that Calvin himself had only tentatively tendered. Beza came to his mature position reluctantly, knowing that he was straying beyond the formulations of his Genevan mentor. But he also came to his mature position resolutely, knowing that he was pressing Calvin's teachings to their logical and practical conclusions and knowing that he was following Calvin's admonitions of *semper reformanda ecclesiae* – always reforming the church and its teachings anew in the light of Scripture and the Spirit and in the face of new challenges and crises.

In his early years, Beza insisted that both church and state were legal entities. Both were called to create and maintain a uniform local Christian

---

[146] *Ibid.*, 27–29, 83–85.   [147] *Ibid.*, 66, 68, 74, 80.   [148] *Ibid.*, 27, 41, 72.

commonwealth. Both cooperated in achieving the civil, theological, and educational uses of the moral law, particularly as summarized in the Decalogue. The church held the authority of the Word, the state held the authority of the sword. The church guided the private lives of believers and the internal matters of the faith, the state governed the public lives of citizens and the external expression of faith. The church judged biblical doctrine and Christian discipline. The state judged public crimes and social order. All persons enjoyed private liberty of conscience. But the public exercise of their religion was anything but free, either within the church or within the state. All persons enjoyed the freedom to accept God's grace through faith. But the words and deeds they used to demonstrate and advocate their faith had to follow the strict mandates of morality imposed by church and state authorities. From 1558 onward, Beza worked side-by-side with Calvin in governing the spiritual life of Geneva, and he departed little from his mentor's teachings in the first years after Calvin's death in 1564.

As Calvinism expanded rapidly into France and as Calvinists faced increasing repression as religious minorities, however, Beza and his colleagues struggled to refine and extend the right to resist political tyranny and to insist on religious liberty. While he retained most of his and Calvin's early teachings, Beza began already in the later 1560s to make piecemeal changes to accommodate the realities that the state was sometimes the enemy of the church and that local communities were sometimes anything but unitary Christian commonwealths devoted to the Reformed way. After the St. Bartholomew's Day Massacre in 1572, Beza resolved to expand Calvin's narrow theory of resistance and broaden the ambit of religious freedom and related rights. This ultimately required him to reconstruct some of Calvin's deeper teachings on authority and liberty as well. Absorbing and extending the more radical logic of resistance exemplified by the Magdeburg ministers and the Marian exiles, he set forth a robust covenantal theory of authority and liberty in his 1574 tract on *The Rights of Rulers and the Duties of Subjects.*

Beza's *Rights of Rulers* was something of a patchwork quilt, sewn together from slender strands of argument scattered over all manner of classical, patristic, scholastic, and Protestant sources. Beza was trained as a classicist and a humanist, and he knew his sources and how to read them. He was also a professor in the Genevan Academy for four decades and had a major library to call on there and in other universities that he visited. His main new argument – that there was a covenant, compact, or contract that bound together the people, rulers, and God – built in part on ancient Hebrew and classical Stoic ideas that were echoed by several medieval Catholic writers, especially Marsilius of Padua and Nicholas of Cusa.[149] Calvin himself had tinkered with the political implications of the doctrine of covenant, as had Ulrich Zwingli, Martin Bucer, Heinrich Bullinger, Peter Martyr Vermigli, Pierre Viret, John Knox, Christopher Goodman, and others. Beza's argument that the people had to elect and consent to their rulers also had several ancient and medieval antecedents that propounded what Walter Ullmann famously called the "ascending theory of sovereignty" in the Middle Ages.[150] This idea was newly championed in Beza's day by John Ponet, John Knox, François Hotman, and others who saw popular election or approbation of political rulers as an ancient birthright of all citizens and a natural expression of a person serving as God's image bearer on earth. Beza's insistence that the Decalogue provided a template for defining both the duties of the ruler and the rights of the people was adumbrated especially by Christopher Goodman as well as by some earlier Lutheran jurists.[151] Beza's distinction between the active popular resistance (even tyrannicide) that foreign usurping tyrants deserved and the orderly constitutional resistance that legitimate magistrates demanded even when they became tyrants built on commonplaces of Roman law and medieval legal philosophy, particularly as developed by John of Salisbury, Bartolus, and Baldus. And Beza's argument that lower aristocratic and lower democratic magistrates were conjoined by a "mixed constitution" and worked together to coordinate constitutional resistance to higher magistrates who became tyrannical had already been signaled by Calvin as well as by fellow reformers like Pierre Viret, Peter Martyr Vermigli, and other Protestant interpreters of passages on point by Aristotle and Cicero.[152]

Beza's genius was to sew all these strands of argument together into a more coherent political theory. The Magdeburg Confession of 1550 had marshaled thirty years of scattered Lutheran lore into a memorable manifesto on political resistance that ultimately saved Lutheranism for the city and eventually for a good bit of the Holy Roman Empire. Beza's *Rights of Rulers* of 1574 drew together forty years of Reformed reflections on the rights of resistance into a powerful new construction of the nature

---

[149] See esp. J. W. Gough, *The Social Contract: A Critical Study of its Development*, 2nd edn. (Oxford, 1957).

[150] Walter Ullmann, *Medieval Political Thought*, rev. edn. (Harmondsworth, 1975); Ullmann, *Principles of Government and Politics in the Middle Ages*, 3rd edn. (London, 1974).

[151] See above pages 113–114, 121–122.

[152] See above notes 81 and 84 and more generally Burns, ed., *The Cambridge History of Political Thought*, 159–245; Oscar Jászi and John D. Lewis, *Against the Tyrant: The Tradition and Theory of Tyrannicide* (Glencoe, IL. 1957); Skinner, *Foundations*, II:189–349; A. London Fell, *Origins of Legislative Sovereignty and the Legislative State*, 6 vols. (Königstein and Cambridge, MA, 1983–).

of political authority and personal liberty. To be sure, Beza did not develop a full-blown constitutional theory – with a detailed doctrine of separation of powers and checks and balances or with a lengthy bill of rights. He never worked out in detail the balance of monarchy, aristocracy, and democracy that would fit his "golden mean" – though he eschewed the tendency of some later sixteenth-century Huguenots to embrace pro-monarchical and anti-resistance theories when a Calvinist ruler happened to sit on the throne.[153] Also to be sure, Beza did not offer a full-blown covenantal theory of law, politics, and society that worked out in detail the origin, nature, and purpose of sovereignty and authority, rights and liberties, dignity and equality, and more. But his *Rights of Rulers* helped permanently turn the Calvinist tradition in that direction, and most Calvinist political writers on both sides of the Atlantic remained on this new course in the next two centuries.

Particularly important for the development of Calvinist rights talk was Beza's core theory of the political covenant sworn before God by the people and their rulers to uphold the laws of God and nature and the rights and liberties of citizens. This would become a standard argument for Calvinist theories of law, religion, and human rights that still rings true among some Protestants today. In sixteenth-century France, the most famous formulation and expansion of this argument came from Stephanus Brutus Junius, pen name for Philippe Duplessis-Mornay, the likely author of *Vindicae, Contra Tyrannos: Or Concerning the Legitimate Power of the Prince Over the People, and of the People Over the Prince.*[154] In Scotland, the most powerful exposition, which built on both Beza and Knox, was George Buchanan's *De Jure Regni apud Scotos; A Dialogue Concerning the Rights of the Crown in Scotland* (1601). A bit later came Samuel Rutherford's 1644 tract whose lengthy title says it all: *Lex, Rex, or The Law and the Prince; A Dispute for the Just Prerogative of King and People: Containing the Reasons and Causes of the Most Necessary Defensive Wars of the Kingdom of Scotland.*[155] In the Netherlands, England, and America, as we shall see in subsequent chapters, a whole series of scholars and pamphleteers would build on this basic foundation of a political covenant to develop arguments for political revolution and constitution-making in the name of human rights. And, eventually, this Christian covenant theory of politics and society would be transmuted into increasingly secularized forms in the social and political contract

---

[153] See Michael Wolfe, *The Conversion of Henry IV: Politics, Power, and Religious Beliefs in Early Modern France* (Cambridge, MA, 1993), 31ff. and discussion in Manetsch, *Theodore Beza*, 135ff.

[154] Ed. and trans. George Garnett (Cambridge, 1994).

[155] Reprinted together in fasc. edn. (Harrisonburg, VA, 1982).

arguments of the Enlightenment and post-Enlightenment, most notably in the early years by such cradle Calvinists as John Locke and Jean-Jacques Rousseau.

A second innovation was Beza's use of the marriage covenant as a prototype for the political covenant. Of course, the notion that the marital household was the historical and ontological foundation of the polis was an ancient teaching, most famously developed by Aristotle in his *Politics* and *Ethics*. Other Greeks and Roman Stoics had called marriage "the foundation of the republic" and "the private font of public virtue." The Church Fathers and medieval scholastics had called marital and familial love "the seedbed of the city," "the force that welds society together." Other early Protestants had called the household a "little church," a "little state," a "little seminary," a "little commonwealth."[156] Calvin had made his own contributions to these teachings by calling marriage "the fountainhead of life," "the holiest kind of company in all the world," "the principal and most sacred . . . of all the offices pertaining to human society." "God reigns in a little household, even one in dire poverty, when the husband and the wife dedicate themselves to their duties to each other. Here there is a holiness greater and nearer the kingdom of God than there is even in a cloister."[157] Beza repeated many of these formulations in his influential volumes on annulment, divorce, and polygamy published in the late 1560s.

What was new in Beza's 1574 *Rights of Rulers* was his argument that the marital covenant was not only the ontological foundation but also the methodological prototype of the political contract. Like marital covenants sworn between a husband and a wife before God, Beza argued, political covenants were solemn agreements sworn by rulers and the people before God. Like marital contracts, political covenants required full and free consent by all parties, and the capacity and freedom of all to enter into these covenants. Like marital covenants, political covenants had many of their basic terms preset by God and nature, including the requirement that both the rulers and the people respect the laws of God and the laws of nature, the rights and liberties of citizens, and the faith and order of the commonwealth. Like marital covenants, political covenants could be annulled when these conditions for formation were violated, or one party to the covenant could seek a divorce if the other party breached the faith or violated a fundamental condition of their association. But, like marital covenants, political

---

[156] See detailed sources in John Witte, Jr., *God's Joust, God's Justice: Law and Religion in the Western Legal Tradition* (Grand Rapids, MI, 2006), 295–385.

[157] Comm. Gen. 2:18, 21, 24, 6:2; Serm. Deut. 21:10–14; Comm. Mal. 2:14, 16; Comm. Harm. Gosp. Matt. 19:11; Comm. 1 Cor. 7:14, 9:11; Serm. 2 Tim. 5.

covenants could not be dissolved randomly by just anyone and certainly not by popular rebellion. Because these covenants were public commitments involving all manner of parties, past, present and future, they had to be resolved by formal and public procedures and mechanisms which the parties had to agree to in advance in forming their political covenant. This emphasis on the methodological symmetry and synergy between marriage and state-making and between divorce and political transition would become a standard feature of Calvinist political theory in the seventeenth and eighteenth centuries – figuring perhaps most famously in the evolving social and political contract theory of John Locke in his *Two Treatises of Government*.[158] Similarly, this emphasis on the symmetries between marital and political formation and dissolution would become a common feature of Protestant marital theory – used, on the one hand, to advocate the natural rule of the husband over his wife, and, on the other, to advocate divorce for cause with a right to remarriage thereafter.

A third major innovation was Beza's reformulation of Calvin's theories of political authority and political liberty into a theory of subjective rights. Calvin had insisted that authority and liberty were "constituted together." He had made the rights of political subjects largely a *consequence* of good government. If the magistrate ruled properly, in accordance with the will of God, the rights of the people would be maintained. If the magistrate exceeded his authority, the people were to suffer his tyrannical outrages with Christian dignity and patience, and in humble recognition that God might be scourging them for the sins that they and their fellows may have committed. Beza continued to insist that authority and liberty were "constituted together," and he continued to insist that popular resistance and insurrection were no solutions to political tyranny. But Beza made the rights of political subjects not a *consequence* but a *condition* of good government. "The people are not made for rulers, but rulers for the people," he wrote, echoing the Marian exiles. If the magistrate rules properly, the people must obey him. But if the magistrate exceeds his authority, the people, through their representatives, have not only the right but also the duty of conscience to resist such tyranny. No magistrate should be suffered who has fundamentally breached the covenant he had sworn to God and his people. To suffer such a tyrant would insult God who had called all rulers to represent his divine being and authority on earth and to strive for divine justice and equity for all of God's people.

---

[158] See John Locke, *Two Treatises of Government*, ed. Peter Laslett (Cambridge, 1960), I.9, 47, 98, II.77–83.

The issue that remained for Beza was how to ground his doctrine of subjective rights, and how to decide which of the rights were so inalienable and inviolable that if breached triggered the right to resistance. Here Beza, building on the thought of the Marian exiles, cleverly reworked Calvin's main arguments, taking his cues from Calvin's own late-life tinkering with the doctrine of subjective rights. The first and most important rights, he reasoned, had to be the rights of "liberty of conscience" and "free exercise of religion." Persons are, after all, first and foremost the subjects of the Creator God and called to honor and worship God above all else. If the magistrate, who was also created by this same God and represents God's authority on earth, breaches these religious rights, then nothing can be sacred and secure any longer. What is essential to the protection of the liberty of conscience and free exercise of the people's religion, Beza continued catechetically: the ability to live in full conformity with the law of God. What is the law of God: first and foremost the Ten Commandments, which set out the various duties of right living that a conscientious Christian needs to discharge in effective exercise of the faith. What do these Commandments entail: the rights to worship God, to obey the Sabbath, to avoid foreign idols and false oaths in accordance with the First Table of the Decalogue, and the rights to marriage, parentage, and a household, and to life, property, and reputation protected by the Second Table. Is the Decalogue the only divine law that governs and guides us: no, the natural law that God has written on the hearts of all people teaches other rights that are essential to the protection of a person and a people. Beza touched on several of these broader rights: freedom of religious mission and education, freedom of church government and emigration, freedoms of speech, assembly, and petition, and freedom of contract most pointedly. Beza did not ground these rights adequately, nor did he make clear which of them was so fundamental that their breach could trigger organized resistance. But he put in place a fundamental rights calculus that later Calvinists would refine and expand.

The most striking reversal of thought that this rights calculus occasioned for Beza was in his theory of religious freedom and toleration of the non-orthodox. Early in his career, Beza had stridently defended the cooperation of church and state in the execution of Michael Servetus for heresy. He had also led the repression of Bernard Ochino, Jean Morély, and others for their heretical speculations. His argument was that church and state officials should cooperate to cut such heresy out of the locally unified body of Christ, lest this body succumb to disease, faction, and decay. The St. Bartholomew's Day Massacre convinced Beza that such views were neither right nor expedient. In his mature view, churches were still free to purge heretics and pagans from their congregations. But they could use only spiritual means of censures, bans, and excommunication without enlisting the aid of the state. States were still free to punish religious dissenters who committed crimes in the name of their false faith. But their false faith alone could no longer be viewed as a crime. Peaceable heretics should be tolerated in the community and religious pluralism embraced. Heretics and non-believers should be brought to the true faith only by proper preaching and teaching, not by the sword and the rack. Beza never went so far as to say that "error has rights," or that heretics must have the free exercise of religion as individuals or as groups. But he insisted that all persons, even heretics, must enjoy the liberty of conscience to be left alone in their error if they wished. He later converted these new sentiments into an elegant plea for toleration of Calvinists in hostile Catholic territories. Such views were instrumental in the later religious toleration principles of the Edict of Nantes (1598) and the Religious Peace of Westphalia (1648).

4. "Hezekiah's Reforms, 2 Kings 18," from Nicholas Fontaine, *L' histoire du vieux et du noveau Testament* (Paris, 1699).

CHAPTER 3

Natural rights, popular sovereignty, and covenant politics: Johannes Althusius and the Dutch Revolt and Republic

[I]n accordance with the law of nature and in order to preserve and defend ourselves and our fellow-countrymen, our rights, the privileges and ancient customs and the freedom of our fatherland, and the life and honor of our wives, children, and posterity, so that we may not become the Spaniard's slaves, and forsaking the King of Spain with good right, we have been compelled to devise and practice other means which seem to provide better for the greater safety and preservation of our aforesaid rights, privileges, and liberties.

Dutch Act of Abjuration (1581)[1]

THE DUTCH REVOLT

With these words, the Estates General of the Netherlands declared to the world that Philip II, King of Spain, Duke of Burgundy, and Lord of the Netherlands, was a tyrant whom they could no longer obey. The Act of Abjuration recited the familiar Calvinist resistance arguments. "The prince of a country is established by God as his subjects' sovereign in order to defend and protect them against all injury, force, and violence, just as a shepherd's duty is to keep his sheep safe." He is established "for his subjects' sake," and must "govern them by law and reason and to protect and love them as a father does his children." The Dutch provinces and people have always accepted "their princes and lords under [these] set conditions." They have always required their rulers to swear "contracts and accords" to rule in accordance with "the law and Word of God" and "in conformity with their chartered privileges and ancient customs . . . rights and liberties."[2]

But Philip blatantly betrayed these essential conditions of legitimate rule, the Act of Abjuration recounted. The trouble began already in 1559, when

---

[1] Herbert H. Rowen, ed., *The Low Countries in Early Modern Times: A Documentary History* (New York, 1972), 102.

[2] *Ibid.*, 92–93, 102–103.

143

Philip ordered a sweeping reorganization of the Catholic church hierarchy in the Netherlands. This subjected the seventeen northern and southern provinces to eighteen new bishops – all of them royal appointees and most of them more loyal to Spain than to Rome, more skilled in statecraft than soulcraft. This upset century-long patterns of local religious rule sealed by old concordats and covenants between bishops and princes, archdeacons and aristocrats.[3] Matters got worse when Philip imposed the Inquisition on the Netherlands, and appointed well-practiced Spanish inquisitors to stamp out the Protestant heresies that had been growing there at an alarming pace. This not only alienated the diverse Protestant groups of the Netherlands, but rallied them to face their new enemy en masse. The Inquisition also angered most local Catholics, who wanted none of this savage torture from foreign zealots bent on correcting religious niceties. Matters got still worse when Philip insisted on publishing the new decrees of the Council of Trent in his own name rather than the Pope's and began forcing them upon a reluctant Catholic and Protestant populace in 1565. This outraged Catholics and Protestants alike. Catholics resented this distant foreign lord who had usurped the Pope's role and was now telling them to change their old beliefs and practices on pain of inquisition. Protestants resented these new establishment laws even more, for they branded Protestants as both heretics and traitors and subjected them to bitter new persecution. Calvinist ministers in particular began preaching and publishing hellfire-and-brimstone sermons against this new scourge of spiritual tyranny, calling the people to the purifying faith of the Protestant Reformation. In 1566 their inflamed followers rioted wildly, destroying church windows, altars, and other Catholic spiritual images and buildings in several waves of violent iconoclasm.[4]

Philip resolved to crush this popular uprising. He sent a large army to the Netherlands under the command of the Duke of Alva, who implemented the new royal policies with ruthless efficiency between 1567 and 1571. Particularly galling to locals was the Duke's imposition of fresh rounds of onerous taxes and commercial regulations on the provinces, towns, estates, and guilds; of new campaigns to conscript Dutchmen to fight in Philip's many wars; and of abusive policies to quarter thousands of soldiers in

---

[3] See M. Dierickx, *De oprichting der nieuwe bisdommen in de Nederlanden onder Filips II, 1559–1570* (Antwerp, 1950), with samples in Anne S. De Blecourt and Nicolaas Japiske, eds., *Klein plakkaatboek van Nederland. Verzameling van ordonnantien en plakkaten betreffende regeeringsvorm, kerk en rechtsspraak (14e eeuw tot 1749)* (Groningen, 1919). See also Olav Moorman van Kappen, "Stadtrechts-reformationen des 16. Jahrhunderts in den Niederlanden," in *Recht, Verfassung und Verwaltung in der frühneuzeitlichen Stadt,* ed. Michael Stolleis (Böhlau, 1991), 141.
[4] Martin van Gelderen, *The Political Thought of the Dutch Revolt, 1555–1590* (Cambridge, 1992), 82ff.

already strapped local communities and households.[5] Even worse was the terrifying escalation of the Inquisition that sent untold thousands of Dutch Protestants and scores of dissident Catholics to their deaths and led to massive confiscations of private property.[6] Many of the nobles and princes fled from the Netherlands to England and Germany and began organizing their resistance, particularly under the emerging leadership of Prince William of the House of Orange. In the spring of 1572, a group of resistance fighters, initially dismissed by the Spanish as "sea beggars," led a series of bold commando raids to take over the ports in the provinces of Holland and Zeeland. These resistance fighters gained ample traction when local sympathizers, Catholic and Calvinist alike, joined them to drive the Duke of Alva's armies out of these provinces. The resistance gained even more traction when some of the Duke's mercenary armies began to mutiny as their hardship increased and their wages never came.

As the fighting escalated in the course of the 1570s, Calvinists began to take the lead in the resistance, with help from "Geneva-bred advisors."[7] The Prince of Orange and other apologists used increasingly strident rhetoric, some of it plucked directly from Dutch and French Calvinist resistance tracts, to portray the Dutch Revolt as a *battaile royale* between the forces of Protestant good and Catholic evil, of Christian freedom and spiritual tyranny.[8] These religious and ideological lines soon hardened into territorial lines as well. As Catholics and Protestants targeted more of each other's properties and leaders, many Catholics fled south to the ten provinces that would become Belgium, and many Protestants fled north to the seven provinces that would become the United Provinces of the Netherlands. For a brief time, both sides sought to paper over their religious differences and focus on their common political, social, and economic problems that were mounting exponentially with the Spanish occupation.[9] The Pacification of

---

[5] In the vast literature see esp. Jonathan Israel, *The Dutch Republic: Its Rise, Greatness, and Fall, 1477–1806*, repr. edn. (Oxford, 1998); Geoffrey Parker, *The Dutch Revolt* (Ithaca, NY, 1977); Pieter Geyl, *The Revolt of the Netherlands, 1555–1609*, 2nd edn. (London, 1958).

[6] M. Dierickx, "De lijst der veroordeelden door de Raad van Beroerten," *Revue belge de philologie et d'histoire* 60 (1962): 415; Israel, *The Dutch Republic*, 155–169.

[7] Herbert D. Foster, *Collected Papers of Herbert Darling Foster* (n.p., 1927), 96–98.

[8] Benjamin J. Kaplan, *Calvinists and Libertines: Confession and Community in Utrecht, 1578–1620* (Oxford, 1995), 11. See samples of William's writings in E. H. Kossman and A. Mellink, eds., *Texts Concerning the Revolt of the Netherlands* (Cambridge, 1974), 84, 93, 109, 112, 188, 211.

[9] See generally O. J. De Jong, "Unie en Religie," in *De Unie van Utrecht. Wording en werking van een verbond en van een verbondsacte*, ed. S. Groenveld and H. L. Ph. Leeuwenberg (The Hague, 1979), 155. It remains a controversy how much William of Orange and the other apologists for the Revolt used Calvinist resistance writings versus others, and how much of this thought was of Dutch origin rather than imported from France, England, Scotland, and Germany. See sources and discussion in J. van der Berg and P. G. Hoftijzer, eds., *Church Change and Revolution* (Leiden, 1991); van Gelderen, *Political Thought*, 260–287; Sap, *Paving the Way for Revolution*, 114–128.

Ghent (1576), for example, prohibited "all attacks on the Roman Catholic religion and its exercise," restored to the prelates their "abbeys, dioceses, foundations, and residences," and made restitution to other Catholic clerics whose properties had been confiscated and destroyed. But the Pacification galled many Calvinists, for it granted them only freedom of conscience and said nothing about restitution of their properties.[10] Matters were made worse when the Religious Peace of Antwerp (1578) guaranteed the Catholic clergy their traditional spiritual jurisdiction and ordered the civil courts to defer to Catholic church courts on issues of marriage, inheritance, charity, and public morality.[11] Whatever religious rapprochement might have been possible was quashed when Pope Gregory XIII issued an encyclical in 1578 that praised the heroism of King Philip and the Duke of Alva and threatened excommunication to any Catholic who supported the Dutch Revolt. When, in response, some Catholic resistance fighters and leaders in the Netherlands began to abandon their posts to the Spanish, the lines of opposition became indelibly clear: it was now Dutchman versus Spaniard, Protestant versus Catholic, patriot versus traitor, freeman versus tyrant.[12]

In 1579, Philip's able new general, the Duke of Parma, confederated the ten southern Belgian provinces in the Union of Arras, and declared their loyalty to Spain and faithfulness to Rome. In response, the seven northern Dutch provinces of Holland, Zeeland, Gelderland, Utrecht, Overijssel, Friesland, and Groningen confederated in the Union of Utrecht. The Union of Utrecht consolidated and coordinated the military, diplomatic, commercial, taxation, and related efforts of the Dutch provinces, and put in place the rudiments of a confederate government under the Estates-General and House of Orange.[13] The Union, however, preserved the political and legal sovereignty of each province. It guaranteed respect for "the special and particular privileges, freedoms, exemptions, laws, statutes, laudable and traditional customs, usages, and all other rights of each province and of each town, member, and inhabitant of these provinces" and pledged that any violation of them "shall be decided by ordinary courts of justice, arbiters,

---

[10] Pacification of Ghent, Arts. 3–5, 20–21 (November 8, 1576), in De Blecourt and Japiske, *Klein plakkaatboek*, 113. See sample reactions by Peter Beutterich and the French Calvinist Philip du Plessis Mornay, in Kossman and Mellink, eds., *Texts Concerning the Revolt*, 159, 163.

[11] Religious Peace of Antwerp, Arts. 2–3, 8–10, 15–18 (July 22, 1578), in E. van Meteren, *Historien de Nederlanden* VIII (Amsterdam, 1647), 141–142.

[12] As one pamphleteer put it: "True liberty and the maintenance of the one and only Roman Catholic religion are incompatible. Maintenance of the Roman Catholic religion and restoration of the Spanish tyranny amounts to the same thing." Peter Beutterich, *The True Patriot to the Good Patriots* (1578), in Kossman and Mellink, *Texts Concerning the Revolt*, 159, 161.

[13] P. F. M. Fontaine, *De raad van state. Zijn taak, organisatie en werkzaamheden in de jaren 1588–1590* (Groningen, 1954); Israel, *The Dutch Republic*, 169–240.

or amicable settlement." The Union also guaranteed each of the seven Dutch provinces independent authority over religion and the church, insisting only that they preserve the freedom of conscience of all peaceable parties.[14]

As they were drawn to Calvinism, the Dutch provinces turned against Catholicism. Placards against public Catholic worship appeared first in Zeeland and Holland and eventually in the other five provinces as well. Harsher measures soon followed. Most remaining Catholic clergy were eventually banished or killed, and most of their corporate properties were confiscated by Calvinist leaders in church and state. Strong populations of Catholic laity still remained in the Netherlands after the Revolt, particularly in the cities of Middleburg, Haarlem, Utrecht, and Delft, where they commanded a substantial majority. Strong populations of Mennonites and other Anabaptists also remained in some of the provinces as did scattered smaller groups of Lutherans and various Swiss and German Pietists.[15] But the Calvinists, despite their relatively small numbers, now controlled the religious and political leadership of the Netherlands. The Declaration of 1581 announced that "Philip the Second had forfeited his lordship, principality and inheritance of these countries," and that the Dutch "have decided not to recognize him hereafter."[16] Though war continued intermittently for the next decade, eventually at the cost of William of Orange's life, the Dutch provinces and nation had won their independence.

The Dutch Revolt catalyzed a fantastic array of supporting pamphlets, sermons, briefs, and learned tracts.[17] Initially, many apologists saw the Revolt as a proper vindication of the people's ancient rights, liberties, and privileges that had been set out in hundreds of medieval law codes and charters that still governed them. The most important of these documents

---

[14] Treaty of the Union (January 29, 1579), Arts. 1, 13, in Kossman and Mellink, *Texts Concerning the Revolt*, 165. More precisely, Article 13 authorized the provinces of Holland and Zeeland to deal with religion "according to their discretions" and the remaining provinces to follow the Religious Peace of Antwerp (1578) or to devise their own policy, which would require ratification by the confederation. See discussion in De Jong, "Unie et Religie," 157ff.

[15] See generally L. Rogier, *Geschiedenis van het katholicisme in Noord-Nederland in de zestiende en zeventiende eeuw*, 3 vols. (Amsterdam, 1945–1947); Willem P. C. Knuttel, *De toestand der nederlandsche katholieken ten tijde der republiek*, 2 vols. (The Hague, 1892–1894).

[16] Rowen, *The Low Countries*, 102. See detailed legal study in Robert Feenstra, "A quelle époque les Provinces-Unies sont-elles devenues indépendantes en droit à l'égard du Saint-Empire," *Tijdschrift voor Rechtsgeschiedenis* 20 (1952): 30–63, 182–218.

[17] See Willem P. C. Knuttel, *Catalogus van de pamflettenverzameling berustende in de Koninkje Bibliothek*, 9 vols. (The Hague, 1889–1920), excerpted in English translation in Rowen, *The Low Countries* and Kossman and Mellink, *Texts Concerning the Revolt*. See analysis in van Gelderen, *Political Thought* and P. A. M. Geurts, *De Nederlandse Opstand in de Pamfletten, 1566–1584* (Nijmegen and Utrecht, 1956), 25–45, 190–228.

were the so-called Joyous Entry of 1356 and the Grand Privilege of 1477, both of which came in for endless recitation and discussion. These old treaties, though perennially amended, provided something of a digest of the rulers' duties and the people's rights, including their right to civil disobedience and organized self-defense in the event of tyranny.[18] William of Orange, among others, often recited these documents in lamenting "the innumerable cruelties, unjust decisions, brutalities, and other outrages perpetuated contrary" to "all the freedoms, oaths, contracts and privileges of the country."[19] We demand the "privileges, rights, and freedoms that have been handed down to us" be restored.[20] "[W]e must protect ourselves and avoid being finally overwhelmed and ruined completely and placed forever in intolerable servitude, and made slaves of a master who tyrannizes over our bodies, possessions, and consciences."[21] We call upon ourselves and our countrymen to rise to "necessary, reasonable, Christian, permitted, and inevitable defense and self-defense."[22]

By the mid 1570s, apologists for the Revolt stood not only on their chartered liberties and "written rights," but also on what William called their "divine and natural rights."[23] One anonymous pamphleteer declared in 1581: "God has created men free and wants them to be governed justly and righteously and not willfully and tyrannically."

[T]he people of a country charge and entrust the king or lord with his power, on such conditions as are usual according to the constitution of the country; but in all countries, whatever their nature, the king is always charged to administer right and justice and to be submissive to God's law and the rights of the country. If he becomes instead of a father a murderer, instead of a shepherd a butcher, instead of a prince a tyrant, the provinces are no longer bound to obey him.[24]

Echoing the French Calvinist resistance tracts of Beza, Hotman, and Mornay, another pamphleteer, Francis Coornhert, recounted the religious and "secular rights and reasons which make it possible to oppose and resist a king, prince, or lord of the country, if, contrary to the oath he has sworn

---

[18] van Gelderen, *Political Thought*, 25–30, 110–133. But see the caveats in J. J. Woltjer, "Dutch Privileges: Real or Imaginary," in *Britain and the Netherlands*, ed. J. S. Bromley and E. H. Kossman (London, 1975), 19.

[19] Letter to Philip Marnix, Delft (November 28, 1573), in Kossman and Mellink, *Texts Concerning the Revolt*, 109, 111; van Gelderen, *Political Thought*, 121.

[20] Response to Pacification of Ghent (February 19, 1577), in Kossman and Mellink, *Texts Concerning the Revolt*, 135.

[21] Letter to Philip Marnix, Delft (November 28, 1573), in *ibid.*, 109, 111.

[22] Quoted in van Gelderen, *Political Thought*, 121.   [23] Quoted in *ibid.*, 121.

[24] *A True Warning to All Worthy Men of Antwerp* (1581), in Kossman and Mellink, *Texts Concerning the Revolt*, 228–229.

to the provinces and subjects, he wants to rob them of all their possessions and deprive them of their rights and privileges." No king rules alone,
Coornhert argued, but with co-rulers and lesser magistrates who must
control and contain him. "He may not violate, importune, or molest any
one, nor take his life or possessions on his own authority and at his own
will" but only in accordance with "the sacred law and under the judgment" of these lower officials. If these lower officials "discover that the
king or lord of the province is exceeding his power and that consequently
the provinces are damaged, subjects oppressed, or the privileges and rights
of the provinces violated, they must prevent this with all diligence and
stand up against him" as "all written and natural laws" dictate. "[L]ife is
hardly worth living" if we allow a tyrant to "take from us our rights and
freedoms."[25]

Another pamphleteer focused on the need to protect the free exercise
of religion, rather than just the liberty of conscience, as the Pacification
of Ghent and other provisional measures had done. With arguments that
still ring strikingly true today, the pamphleteer argued that true religious
freedom requires freedom of worship, speech, association, and education.
Liberty of conscience without freedom of exercise is a ruse.

I know that they promise freedom of conscience provided there is no public worship and no offence is given, but this is only to trap and ensnare us. For it is well
known that conscience, which resides in people's minds, is always free and cannot
be examined by other men and still less be put under their control or command.
And in fact, no one has ever been executed or harassed merely on grounds of
conscience, but always for having committed some public act or demonstration,
either in words, which are said to be an offence, or in acts which are described
as exercise of religion. There is no difference between so-called freedom of conscience without public worship, and the old rigour of the edicts and inquisition of
Spain . . .

How is it possible to grant freedom of conscience without exercise of religion?
For what are the consequences for people who wish to enjoy the benefit of this
freedom? If they have no ceremonies at all and do not invoke God to testify to
the piety and reverence they bear Him, they are in fact left without any religion and without fear of God . . . And I have not even mentioned that one
will not of course be allowed to state what one thinks; any one who says any
word detrimental to the dignity of the ecclesiastical state or the Roman religion will be accused of acting scandalously or of desecrating human and divine

---

[25] Francis Coornhert, *A Short Instruction . . . that is Lawful to Resist a King or Lord of the Country* (March
28, 1586), in Kossman and Mellink, *Texts Concerning the Revolt*, 267–269. See similar views in Francis
Vranck, *A Short Exposition of the Rights Exercised by the Knights, Nobles, and Towns of Holland and
West Friesland from Time Immemorial for the Maintenance of the Freedoms, Rights, Privileges and
Laudable Customs of the Country* (1587), in *ibid.*, 274–281.

majesty. But this is only the start. The authorities will go further and search books and cabinets and coffers, they will eavesdrop on private conversation, a father will not be allowed to teach his children how to call on God, nor will we be allowed to use our mother-tongue in our prayers. Soon, as I have said before, it will be necessary to restore the edicts and the inquisition in their full severity everywhere.[26]

By the turn of the seventeenth century, apologists for the Dutch Revolt began to give way to architects of the young Dutch Republic. Only a few of the names of the leading architects are known today outside of Dutch specialist circles. But they include a number of formidable legal and political minds in the later sixteenth and seventeenth centuries, whose writings were well known in their day and were critical to the development of sturdy new ideas and institutions of Dutch law, politics, and society: C. P. Hooft, Hugo Grotius, Peter Bertius, Paul Buis, Daniel Berckringer, Gisbertus Voetius, Paulus Voetius, Johannes Voetius, William Apollonius, Jacob Triglandus, Antonius Walaeus, Johannes Althusius, William McDowell, Martinus Schookius, R. H. Schele, Lambert van Velthuyzen, Arnold Vinnius, Simon van der Made, Simon van Leeuwen, Antonius Matthaeus I, II, and III, Ulrich Huber, Johan and Pieter de la Court, and others. Many of these were law professors at the Dutch universities of Leiden, Utrecht, Groningen, and Frankener. Their writings together fill several long shelves of books that are still considered the anchor texts of modern Roman–Dutch law.[27]

One of the earliest and most original of these scholars was the distinguished German-born jurist, Johannes Althusius (1557–1638). His work not only helped to integrate the Dutch legal, political, and social teachings of his day; it also served to elaborate an emerging Calvinist theory of natural law, popular sovereignty, and the rights and liberties of individuals and associations. While he certainly did not speak for every Dutch Calvinist of his day, let alone every Dutchman, Althusius's deep and profound writings had a monumental and enduring influence on Dutch and Calvinist thought. I present him here as the leader of a new reformation of rights.

---

[26] Marnix of St. Aldegonde?, *Discourse of a Nobleman* (1584), in Kossman and Mellink, *Texts Concerning the Revolt*, 264–266. See similar views in *A Brief Discourse Upon the Peace Negotiations* (1579), in *ibid.*, 182–187.

[27] See, among others, E. H. Kossman, *Political Thought in the Dutch Republic: Three Studies* (Amsterdam, 2000), 25–84; P. van Heijsbergen, *Geschiedenis der Rechtswetenschap in Nederland* (Amsterdam, 1925), 35–119; J. Wessels, *History of Roman Dutch Law* (Cape Town, 1908), 294–354; D. Nobbs, *Theocracy and Toleration: A Study of the Disputes in Dutch Calvinism from 1600–1650* (Cambridge, 1938).

THE WORK OF JOHANNES ALTHUSIUS

Johannes Althusius has been called "the clearest and most profound thinker which Calvinism has produced in the realm of political science and jurisprudence."[28] He studied law, theology, philosophy, and the classics at the universities of Cologne, Geneva, Heidelberg, and Basel, working intermittently with such Calvinist worthies as François Hotman and Denis Godefroy. He took his doctorate in canon law and civil law (*doctor juris utriusque*) from the University of Basel. His first appointment came in 1586 as lecturer in Roman law and philosophy at the Herborn Academy, a new Calvinist college established by William of Orange's brother that was attracting faculty and students from throughout Europe. Among his new colleagues at Herborn was Caspar Olevianus, co-author of the Heidelberg Catechism (1568), a Calvinist creedal landmark. Althusius also served as a lawyer in the local courts and was called upon more than once to defend the Academy's rights against the encroachments of local nobles and officials. This experience helped to shape his lifelong interest in defining and defending the rights of private associations. In 1594, Althusius was promoted to professor of law at Herborn, and served twice as rector of the Academy in 1597 and 1602. His later years there, however, were marked by repeated internal controversy. Particularly notable for our purposes was Althusius's debate with his colleagues about the modern uses of biblical law, a theme that would occupy him deeply in his later writings.

In 1604, Althusius moved to Emden, an important seaport city in eastern Frisia, near the border of the Holy Roman Empire and the newly united Netherlands. Emden was a major center for Calvinist refugees from throughout Europe, and an emerging intellectual and missionary center for

---

[28] Carl J. Friedrich, "Introductory Remarks," to Johannes Althusius, *Politica methodice digesta atque exemplis sacris & profanis illustrata*, 3rd edn. (Herborn, 1614), reprinted as *Politica Methodice Digesta of Johannes Althusius (Althaus)*, ed. Carl J. Friedrich (Cambridge, MA, 1932), xviii. For Althusius's writings and reputation, see Hans Ulrich Scupin *et al.*, eds., *Althusius-Bibliographie. Bibliographie zur politischen Ideengeschichte und Staatslehre, zum Staatsrecht und zur Verfassungsgeschichte des 16. bis 18. Jahrhundert* (Berlin, 1973), updated in Dieter Wyduckel, "Einleitung, Literaturverzeichnis," in Johannes Althusius, *Politik*, trans. Heinrich Janssen, ed. Dieter Wyduckel (Berlin, 2003), vii–lxxxii. Among numerous studies, see Friedrich, "Introductory Remarks," xv–xcix; Frederick S. Carney, "Translator's Introduction," *Politica Johannes Althusius*, ed. and trans. F. S. Carney (Indianapolis, IN, 1995), ix–xxxiii; Thomas O. Hueglin, *Early Modern Concepts for a Late Modern World: Althusius on Community and Federalism* (Waterloo, Ontario, 1999); Otto von Gierke, *The Development of Political Theory*, trans. Bernard Freyd (New York, 1966); Karl-Wilhelm Dahm, Werner Krawietz and Dieter Wyduckdel, eds., *Politische Theorie des Johannes Althusius* (Berlin, 1988); Frederick S. Carney, Heinz Schilling and Dieter Wyduckel, eds., *Jurisprudenz, Politische Theorie und Politische Theologie* (Berlin, 2004); Erik Wolf, *Grosse Rechtsdenker der deutschen Geistesgeschichte*, 4th edn. (Tübingen, 1963), 177–219; Christoph Strohm, "Recht und Jurisprudenz im reformierten Protestantismus 1550–1650," *ZSS (KA)* 123 (2006): 453–493.

the spread of Calvinism. Althusius was appointed as legal counsel for the city (*Stadtsyndicus*) and became deeply involved in the city's multiple legal, commercial, and diplomatic negotiations.[29] He played a leading role in helping Emden wrest greater independence from the local territorial count and nobles, an accomplishment that made him something of a local hero.[30] Though he continued to give lectures, he did not hold a formal university position thereafter and turned down attractive professorships in Leiden and Frankener. Althusius was also elected as an elder of the Reformed church of Emden in 1617, and served on the local consistory, hearing cases on spiritual, moral, and family questions much like Calvin and Beza had done on the Genevan Consistory.[31]

While these local achievements in church and state were notable in their day, Althusius's more enduring contributions to the Calvinist tradition of law, religion, and human rights came through his writings. Though he left a score of books,[32] it was especially his trilogy of works on ethics, politics, and law that made signature contributions. His two-volume *Civil Conversations* of 1601 (expanded in 1611), worked out a system of "ethical habits and techniques" of "speaking and listening," "proclamation and silence," to guide rhetoric, dialogue, and persuasion in various social institutions, most notably in the church and the state.[33] His massive *Politics* of 1603 (revised in 1610 and again in 1614), set forth a comprehensive theory of social, political, and legal order and activity, and the forms and norms of sovereignty, authority, and liberty that obtain within each sphere.[34] His

---

[29] See, e.g., *Recess vnd Accord-buch, das ist, Zusamen Verfassung aller Ordnung[en], Decreten, Recessen, Accorden, und Verträgen, so zwischen . . . Herrn Edtzarden vnd Herrn Johan . . . Herrn vnd Graffen zu Ostfrieszlandt* (Emden, 1612, 1656).

[30] See, e.g., an early pamphlet that Althusius evidently co-authored with his friend Ubbo Emmius, entitled *Vindicae juris populi contra usurpationem iniquam Comitis usque ad annum* 1608, protesting election fraud. I have not found a copy of this tract to review and depend for this description on Friedrich, "Introductory Remarks," xxii.

[31] Heinz Antholz, *Die politische Wirksamkeit des Johannes Althusius in Emden* (Aurich, 1955).

[32] See esp. his *Jurisprudentiae Romanae libri duo ad leges methodi Rameae conformati et tabellis illustrati* (Basel, 1586), which provided a dialectic presentation of civil law, and his more technical legal writing in *Centuria conclusionum de pignoribus et hypothecis* (Herborn, 1591); *Assertiones juridicae* (Herborn, 1604); *De injuriis et famosis libellis* (Basel, 1601); *Theses miscellaneae* (Herborn, 1604); *Tractatus tres de poenis, de rebus fungibilibus ac de jure retentionis* (Kassel, 1611); and a later collection of excerpted texts in *Jo. Althusius aphorismi universi juris civilis vel repertorium* (Basel, 1630).

[33] Johannes Althusius, *Civilis conversationis libri duo recogniti et aucti. Methodice digesti et exemplis sacris et profanis passim illustrati* (Hanover, 1601, 1611). I have used the 1601 edition (hereafter *Civ. conv.*). (My translations throughout.)

[34] Johannes Althusius, *Politica methodice digesta atque exemplis sacris & profanis illustrata*, 3rd edn. (Herborn, 1614), reprinted as *Politica Methodice Digesta*, ed. Carl J. Friedrich (Cambridge, MA, 1932). See an abridged English translation, *Politica Johannes Althusius*, trans. and ed. Frederick S. Carney, German excerpts from the 1603 edition in Erik Wolf, ed., *Quellenbuch zur Geschichte der*

three-volume *Theory of Justice* (1617) laid the groundwork for a comprehensive theory of law and justice, with attention to the rights and liberties of private persons and the various private and public associations that they formed.[35]

Althusius presented these three big tracts as "comprehensive," "total," and "universal" accounts of the disciplines of ethics, politics, and law respectively. Each tract was amply illustrated by "sacred and profane examples." Each tract used the dialectical method of the French Calvinist logician Peter Ramus, by which Althusius defined the first principles of these three disciplines, and then divided their constituent precepts and practices into a series of ever more particular binary opposites.[36] Each tract drew on hundreds of scholarly sources – sundry ancient Greeks and Romans, various apostolic and patristic writers, numerous medieval theologians, philosophers, and civilians, a few canonists, various Protestant jurists, all manner of contemporary Catholic and Protestant political writers, and several collections of civil, imperial, feudal, and urban law. Important for our purposes was Althusius's use of various Reformed writers. John Calvin, Theodore Beza, Martin Bucer, Heinrich Bullinger, Lambert Daneau, Hugo Donellus, Denis Godefroy, François Hotman, Francis Junius, William Perkins, Jerome Zanchius, and others each came in for frequent citation and discussion – though Althusius also made heavy use of contemporaneous Catholic writers like Jean Bodin, Peter Gregory Tolosanus, Fernando Vázquez, and other scholars at the neo-scholastic school of Salamanca.[37] Important, too, was Althusius's heavy reliance on the Bible, which as a good Calvinist he cited endlessly in support of his arguments.[38] And important were his

deutschen Rechtswissenschaft (Frankfurt am Main, 1949), 102–144, an abridged German text of the 1614 edition in Althusius, *Politik*, ed. Wyduckel, and a Latin and English version of the preface to the 1610 edition in John Christian Laursen, ed., *New Essays on the Political Thought of the Huguenots of the Refuge* (Leiden, 1995), 193–201. I have used the 1614 Friedrich edition of this tract unless otherwise noted, and have adapted the English translation by F. S. Carney in *Politica* (hereafter *Pol.*)

[35] Johannes Althusius, *Dicaeologicae libri tres, totum et universum jus, quo utimur, methodice complectentes* (Herborn, 1617; Frankfurt 1618); I have used the 1618 edition throughout (hereafter *Dic.*). (My translations throughout.)

[36] See esp. the analytical tables that Althusius put at the head of each of his main volumes and often at the head of each separate section or book therein. See further Walter Ong, *Ramus and the Decay of Dialogue: From the Art of Discourse to the Art of Reason* (Chicago, 2004) and Carney, "Translator's Introduction," in *Politica*, xiiff.

[37] See the lists compiled by Wyduckel in *Politik*, liii–lxviii, and those in *Dic.* preface, 3–5. See further Robert M. Kingdon, "Althusius' Use of Calvinist Sources," *Rechtstheorie* 16 (1997): 19; Ernst Reibstein, *Johannes Althusius als Fortsetzer der Schule von Salamanca* (Karlsruhe, 1955). On neo-scholastic sources see Introduction above at note 23.

[38] See Friedrich, "Introductory Remarks," xlvii-lii; Heinrich Janssen, *Die Bibel als Grundlage der politischen Theorie des Johannes Althusius* (Frankfurt am Main, 1992). Althusius also made some use of the Apocrypha, which was more unusual in the Calvinist circles of his day.

repeated references to local Dutch laws and political experiences, including the Dutch Revolt. Indeed, Althusius is credited for writing "the only theory of the Dutch Revolt ever written."[39]

Althusius's theory of resistance and revolt against tyrants was, in fact, textbook Calvinism. Like Calvin, Althusius called for "moderate," "structured," and "orderly" resistance to tyranny, without popular insurrection or private regicide which could only lead to anarchy. Like Beza, he defined tyrants as magistrates who violated the terms of their political compact or covenant with God and the people – particularly the foundational laws of God and nature and the fundamental rights of persons and peoples. Like most Calvinist resistance writers, Althusius distinguished between tyrannical usurpers of power and legitimate rulers who became tyrannical. Usurpers were merely private persons who could be resisted by anyone in exercise of the right of self-defense. Legitimate rulers who became tyrants, however, could be resisted only through the organized efforts of representative ephors who were called to remove tyrants by as orderly a means as possible – but with all-out warfare if necessary, as in the "signature example" of the Dutch Revolt against Spanish tyranny. The ephors were "the protectors of the covenant entered into between the supreme magistrate and the people," Althusius argued. They were called to "establish the law, or God, as the [true] lord and emperor" of the commonwealth, and to vindicate "the rights of the people" and "the rights of the nation itself" against any and all tyrants. For "the people have not transferred these rights to the supreme magistrate but reserved them to themselves" and "entrusted to the ephors the care and defense of these rights against all violators, disturbers, or plunderers, even if that is the supreme magistrate himself."[40]

But resistance theory was only a small part of Althusius's work – and a rather late addition. Althusius analyzed tyranny and resistance systematically only in the final 1614 edition of his *Politics*, and a bit more in his 1617 *Theory of Justice*. And his analysis mostly stitched together Calvinist

---

[39] E. H. Kossman, "The Development of Dutch Political Theory in the Seventeenth Century," in *Britain and the Netherlands*, ed. J. S. Bromley and E. H. Kossman (The Hague, 1971), 92–93. See further Hueglin, *Early Modern Concepts*, 25ff.; O. Moorman van Kappen, "Die Niederlande in der 'Politica' des Johannes Althusius," in *Politische Theorie des Johannes Althusius*, ed. Werner Krawietz and Dieter Wyduckdel (Berlin, 1988), 123–146.

[40] *Pol.* xviii.48–55, 73–102; *Pol.* xxxviii.1–123; *Dic.* i.113; *Civ. conv.* 1.7–9, ii.1. See further below pages 200–203 and Peter J. Winters, "Das Widerstandrecht bei Althusius," in Krawietz and Wyduckdel, *Politische Theorie*, 543–556; Patricio Carvajal Aravena, "Human Rights in Althusius' Political Theory: The Right of Resistance," in *Jurisprudenz, Politische Theorie und Politische Theologie*, ed. Frederick S. Carney, Heinz Schilling, and Dieter Wyduckel (Berlin, 2004), 227–242.

commonplaces drawn from sundry sources, not least the ample pamphlet literature born of the Dutch Revolt. Althusius's broader interest was to cast these commonplaces on the right to resistance into a more comprehensive theory of rights and liberties, law and order, society and politics that would make tyranny much easier to define, deter, and denounce. His work was not just an apology for the Dutch Revolt but a recipe for the good society, not just a vindication of the right to resist but a validation of the rights of persons and peoples altogether. Much like John Locke and John Adams writing in the context of the English and American Revolutions, Althusius used the Dutch Revolt as an occasion to explore deeply the foundations and fundamentals of law, politics, and society. He was writing for the ages, not just for his own age. By copiously combing and combining the insights of sundry Jewish, Greek, Roman, and Christian sources, he sought to create a "total" and "universal" theory that would appeal not only to fellow Calvinists and countrymen but to anyone in his world of Christendom who was serious about faith and order, authority and liberty.

Althusius offered: (1) a "demonstrative theory" of natural law that focused on the concordance between Christian and classical, biblical and rational teachings of law and authority;[41] and (2) "a symbiotic theory of human nature" that focused on the natural and necessary attachments of the person to God, neighbor, and society.[42] His rights theory was part and product of this legal and sociological framework. In his *Politics*, Althusius focused on the "sovereign rights of the people," which he called "the vital spirit, soul, heart, and life" of any legitimate commonwealth. Though contractually delegated to the "oversight and stewardship" of the political office, these "rights of sovereignty" belong fully and "inalienably" to "the people as a whole." In his *Theory of Justice*, he focused on the "rights of persons," the particular "rights that arise from these sources of sovereignty." Included were

---

[41] I take this phrase from the Danish Protestant Nicolaus Hemming, whose work straddled the Lutheran and Calvinist worlds of law. Writing in the later sixteenth century, Hemming developed what he called a "demonstrative method of natural law," which aimed to demonstrate the natural universality and superiority of the Decalogue as a source and summary of natural law. He adduced hundreds of ancient Greek and Roman passages that he saw to be consistent with conventional Protestant interpretations of the Commandments. See esp. Nicolaus Hemming, *De lege naturae apodicta methodus* (Wittenberg, 1563), and other sources in Witte, *Law and Protestantism*, 139–140. Althusius cited Hemming sparingly, but seems to have been inspired by his methodology. This was also something of the method used by the Calvinist jurist Hugo Donnellus and Calvinist theologian Jerome Zanchius, both of whom influenced Althusius greatly. On these two figures, see respectively, Christoph Strohm, "Althusius' Rechtslehre im Kontext des reformierten Protestantismus," in *Juriprudenz, Politische Theorie*, 71–102; Grabill, *Rediscovering the Natural Law*, 132–148.

[42] For this term, see esp. Huegelin, *Early Modern Concepts*, 85–108; Wyduckel, "Introduction," Althusius, *Politik*, xviiiff.

the rights of conscience and mind, life and body, property and contract, procedure and evidence.[43] In brief, Althusius's *Politics* was primarily about the rights of people, his *Theory of Justice* primarily about the rights of persons.[44]

NATURAL LAW, COMMON LAW, AND POSITIVE LAW

In working out his legal theory, Althusius sought to demonstrate the ultimate concordance between biblical and rational, Christian and classical teachings on the nature and purpose of law. His mature legal theory effectively merged the hierarchies of law developed by fellow jurists and theologians of his day, both Catholic and Protestant. Civil law and canon law jurists distinguished three main types of law: (1) the natural law or law of nature *(ius naturale, lex naturae)*, the set of immutable principles of reason and conscience that are supreme in authority and divinity; (2) the law of nations or common law *(ius gentium, ius commune, lex communis)*, the legal principles and procedures that are common to multiple political communities and often the basis for treaties and other diplomatic conventions; and (3) the civil law or positive law *(ius civile, ius positivum)*, the statutes, customs, and cases of various states, churches, fiefdoms, manors, and other local political communities.[45] Theologians and moralists, in turn, generally distinguished three main types of biblical law: (1) moral law *(lex moralis)*, the enduring moral teachings of the Decalogue and the New Testament; (2) juridical or forensic law *(lex juridicales, ius forensi)*, the rules and procedures by which ancient Israelites and apostolic Christians governed their religious and civil communities; and (3) ceremonial law *(lex ceremonialis)*, the Mosaic laws of personal diet, ritual sacrifice, priestly life, and the like that governed the religious life of the ancient Israelites. Some theologians saw parallels between these three ancient types of biblical law and the three layers of modern Catholic and Protestant church law that governed, respectively, the essentials of doctrine and morality, the commonplaces of ecclesiastical

---

[43] See esp. *Pol.* (Preface 1610 and 1614 edns.); *Dic.* 1.25–26.

[44] This distinction between the rights of persons as individuals and the rights of the people as a whole through their representatives was not altogether clear in Althusius, particularly when Althusius discussed the notion of "popular sovereignty." Most scholars have focused on Althusius's *Politics*, where the rights of the people are emphasized, and have concluded that Althusius had no theory of the subjective rights of the person. See sources and discussion in E. H. Kossman, "Popular Sovereignty at the Beginning of the Dutch Ancien Regime," *The Low Countries History Yearbook* 14 (1981): 1–28; Kossmann, "Development of Dutch Political Theory," 92–93. But Althusius did touch on the subjective rights of the person in his *Politics*, and analyzed these rights at length in his *Theory of Justice*.

[45] *Dic.* 1.13.6, 10. See his earlier formulations in Althusius, *Jurisprudentiae Romanae*, ch. 1.

polity and property, and the discretionary aspects (the adiaphora) of local church life.[46]

In his early writings, notably in his 1586 *Roman Law*, Althusius repeated these traditional hierarchies of law. In his later writings, however, most fully in his 1617 *Theory of Justice*, he collapsed these traditional legal terms and hierarchies into two main types of law: natural laws and positive laws. And he subsumed most of the other traditional types of law within these two categories. He treated the moral laws of the Bible and the common laws of nations as two visible forms of the same invisible natural law hidden within each person's reason and conscience. And he regarded the laws of ancient Israelites and of modern churches as two types of positive law that stood alongside the positive laws of historical and modern states. The modern validity of all these positive laws turned on their concordance with natural law. Their modern utility for the state turned on their compliance with the fundamental law (*lex fundamentalis*) of the community.[47]

Natural law is "the will of God for men," Althusius argued. God has "written this natural law" on the hearts, souls, minds, and consciences of all persons, as Romans 2:15 and sundry other biblical and classical sources make clear. Everyone, by his or her very nature, thus has the "ideas [*notitiae*] and inclinations [*inclinationes*] of this natural law" born within them. Some of these "natural inclinations" are common to humans and animals. Like animals, humans by nature are inclined to "preserve their lives and to procure the necessities to remain alive." They are inclined to defend themselves against force and *force majeure*. They are inclined to ally themselves with others and to rally around natural leaders to aid them in their self-defense. They are inclined to "procreate by the union of male and female and to educate their natural-born children." They are inclined to care for themselves and for their loved ones when they are sick, hurt, or ailing. Self-preservation, self-protection, and self-perpetuation are "natural inclinations" that the natural law teaches to persons and animals alike.[48]

The natural law also teaches persons higher ideas that appeal uniquely to human reason and conscience. By them, "a man understands what justice is, and is impelled by this hidden natural instinct to do what is just and to avoid what is unjust." Through the natural law, God commands all persons to "live a life that is at once pious and holy, just and proper." He teaches them the natural "duties of love that are to be performed toward

[46] *Pol.* xxi.35–40; *Pol.* xxii.1–12. See also *Pol.*, Preface (1603, 1610, and 1614 edns.) for Althusius's discussion of the relationships among the disciplines of theology, law, ethics, and political science.

[47] On his understanding of fundamental law, see below pages 190–192.

[48] *Dic.* 1.13.10–18; *Pol.* 1.32–39; *Pol.* ix.21; *Pol.* xviii.22; *Pol.* xxi.16–19; *Pol.* xxxviii.37.

God and one's neighbor." He sets out the basic "rules of living, obeying, and administering" that must govern all persons and associations. He sets forth "general principles of goodness and equity, evil and sinfulness" that every man must know in order to live with himself and with others. He teaches the "actions and omissions that are appropriate to maintaining the public good of human society" as well as the private good of households and families. By the natural law, Althusius wrote in final summary of his position, God

> teaches and writes on human hearts the general principles of goodness, equity, evil, and sin, and He instructs, induces, and incites all persons to do good and avoid evil. He likewise condemns the conscience of those who ignore these things and excuses those who do them. He thereby directs them to goodness and dissuades them from evil. If they follow the path of goodness, he excuses them. If they do not, he condemns them.[49]

This natural law has had many names in the classical and Christian traditions, Althusius recognized – Godly law, divine law, moral law, natural law, natural justice, natural equity, the law of conscience, the law of the mind, the law of reason or right reason, the law inside people, the immutable law, the supreme law, the general law, the common law, and others. Parsing the names for the natural law was not so important to Althusius. He regarded them mostly as synonyms and used them interchangeably.[50]

Knowing the norms that the natural law teaches was the more important and the more difficult task. Althusius knew the traditional formula taught by the medieval scholastics and by the neo-scholastics of his day: that the natural law gives all persons an innate or natural knowledge of good and evil (called *synderesis*), that by exercising their reason persons can come to understand the norms of this natural law, and that by exercising their conscience they can learn to apply these norms equitably to concrete circumstances. But Althusius also recognized that, throughout history, persons and peoples have reached different formulations and applications of the natural law. Even in avowed Christian societies today, persons have "different degrees of this [natural] knowledge and inclination. This law is not evidently inscribed equally on the hearts of all. The knowledge of it is communicated more abundantly to some and more sparingly to others, according to the will and judgment of God." So, given this reality, how can

---

[49] *Dic.* 1.13.1, 14–15; *Pol.* xxx.16, 19–20.
[50] *Dic.* 1.13.13–18; *Dic.* 1.14; *Pol.* xxi.1–20. In his 1586 *Jurisprudentiae Romanae*, ch. 1, Althusius did differentiate these categories more clearly, following conventional Roman law jurisprudence, but he largely abandoned this effort in his 1614 *Politics* and 1617 *Theory of Justice*.

we really know "the nature of the norms of the law that are implanted in us by nature?" How can we be absolutely certain that we as individuals, or as the leaders of our communities, have "a true perception" of the contents of the natural law? How can we even know which person's or community's formulations of the natural law are better than another's? Persons are fallible creatures who perceive natural law only "indirectly," "circumstantially," "through a glass darkly," through "flickering shadows" emitting from distant caves of light. Communities have widely variant "customs, natures, attitudes, and viewpoints" that are affected by the "age, condition, circumstances, and education" of their members. There is no universal code of written natural law to consult. So, how can we be sure of the natural law's norms and contents?[51]

We can know the norms of the natural law if we study both Scripture and tradition, revelation and reason very carefully, Althusius argued. We know that God has given a fuller revelation of his law in the Bible, particularly in the Ten Commandments and in the moral teachings of Moses and the Prophets, Christ and St. Paul. This cannot be a new form of natural law, for God would not and could not contradict the natural law that he already revealed to us in and through our human nature. Biblical moral law is rather a more perfect conformation and elaboration of the natural law ideas and inclinations that are already inscribed on the hearts and minds of everyone, believers and non-believers alike. Through Moses, God rewrote on stone what was already written on our hearts. Through Christ, God rewrote this law anew by fulfilling its commandments and promises and by teaching his followers how to discern its "weightier matters." To be sure, Althusius acknowledged, biblical moral law has clearer precepts and higher purposes than any other form of natural law. It provides a more certain knowledge of the will of God for our lives. It sets out a pathway to salvation for those who can abide by its letter and a pathway to sanctification for those who can live by its spirit. But the Bible's moral law only rewrites more copiously the natural law that is already written cryptically on the hearts of everyone.[52]

While God and Scripture have rewritten the natural law for believers to discern, reason and experience have rewritten this natural law for non-believers to discover. In every major civilization, Althusius argued, enlightened leaders and magistrates have emerged who have used their natural reason to translate the general principles of natural law in their minds into specific positive or proper laws (*leges positivum, leges propriae*) for their

[51] *Dic.* 1.6.4–6, 26; *Dic.* 1.13.16–18; *Pol.* XXI.20–21; *Pol.* XXIII.1–20.
[52] *Pol.* VII.7–12; *Pol.* X.3–12; *Pol.* XVIII. 32–44; *Pol.* XXI.22–29.

communities. These enlightened leaders have inevitably tailored these positive laws to "the customs, nature, needs, attitudes, conditions, and other special circumstances" of the people ruling and being ruled. This has produced widely variant positive laws over time and across cultures, particularly when these local laws are viewed in their details. But these enlightened leaders have also inevitably positioned these laws to reflect some of the natural light within their hearts, and have maintained these laws because they have proved to be both right and useful. This has produced laws that are common to many peoples and polities, even those that have had no interaction with each other. Every major civilization, said Althusius, has developed comparable sets of law to govern religious worship and observance, to honor marriage and the family, to obey authorities and to respect traditions, to protect human lives, properties, and reputations, to care for relatives, widows, orphans, and the poor, to speak respectfully to others, to testify truthfully, to honor promises, contracts, and agreements, to vindicate wrongs and to punish wrongdoers, to fight wars and repel attacks, to give to each and everyone what is due. These common laws, independently developed by different peoples and polities over time and across cultures, must be regarded as "visible expressions of the same invisible natural law" within all persons, Althusius argued. They must be taken as reflections of "the natural and divine immutable equity that is mixed into them," as indications "of the common practice of natural law."[53]

These common laws (*iura commune)* or laws of nations (*iura gentium*) – gathered from the commonplaces of sundry positive laws and the common practices of sundry legal communities – stand alongside biblical moral laws as a second form and forum of natural law. Indeed, at a certain level of abstraction, the moral laws of the Bible and common laws of the nations converge, even though they have very different origins, ends, and languages. "A law is both natural and common," Althusius wrote, "if the common use of right reason produces it for the necessity and utility of human social life. It, too, can then be called natural law." "While some distinguish among common law [*ius commune*], natural law [*ius naturale*], and the law of nations [*ius gentium*], others more properly call each of them forms of the [same] natural law . . . Christ himself often called natural law things that are usually called the law of nations."[54]

This belief in the ultimate concordance, if not confluence, of biblical law, natural law, and common law helps to explain Althusius's somewhat

---

[53] *Dic.* 1.13.4–18; *Dic.* 1.14.1–14; *Dic.* 1.35.22–23; *Pol.* vii.7–12; *Pol.* ix.20–21; *Pol.* x.3–12; *Pol.* xviii.32–44; *Pol.* xxi.22–29; *Pol.* xxii throughout.
[54] *Dic.* 1.13.11, 18–19.

baffling style of argumentation in his *Politics* and *Theory of Justice*. In both tracts, Althusius piled citation upon citation, from all manner of seemingly unrelated sources, in demonstration of each simple assertion about what the natural law contained and commanded. Some of this no doubt was the pedantic puffery of a legal humanist – the flashy displays of unnecessary erudition that still mark some law review articles today. But, for Althusius, all this dense citation to sundry sources evidently had a larger purpose. He seemed convinced that the more frequently a legal teaching and practice appeared in diverse legal, theological, and philosophical texts, the more readily it could be taken as proof of the content of the natural law. If the ancient Israelites directed from Sinai and the ancient Greeks and Romans directed from Olympus independently embraced the same legal teaching, that had to speak volumes about the natural foundations and qualities of this teaching. If Aristotle and Moses, Cicero and Christ, Plato and Paul all concurred on a given principle of right living and proper ruling, that had to give this principle a special priority in discerning the content of natural law. And if modern-day Catholics and Protestants, who have been slaughtering and slandering each other with a vengeance, still come to the same conclusions about the cogency and utility of these classical and Christian legal teachings, that had to commend these teachings even more strongly as natural universals. Althusius thus scoured the sources for any and every proof text that he could find to support each step of his argument. This made his writing more of a legal brief than a philosophical argument, more of an historical demonstration of natural law precepts in action than a logical deduction from *a priori* first principles.[55]

Althusius rested his case on the contents of the natural law most firmly on the confluence between the Commandments of the Decalogue and the moral teachings of sundry classical traditions. For him, the Decalogue was the clearest and most comprehensive confirmation and codification of the natural law, of every person's inner natural inclinations to piety and justice, to faith and order, to love of God and love of neighbor. As such, "the Decalogue has been prescribed for all people to the extent that it agrees with and explains the common law of nature for all peoples." "The precepts

---

[55] *Dic.* 1.14.1–14; *Pol.* XXI.30–40; *Pol.* XXII.1–3, 10. Some readers will recognize this argument demonstrating the commonalities of natural, Judaic, Hebraic, classical, and common law in the writings of Althusius's English contemporary, John Selden (1584–1654). See John Selden, *Opera Omnia tam edita quam inedita in tribus voluminibus*, 3 vols. (London, 1726), particularly "De jure naturali et gentium juxta disciplinan Erbraeorum," 1:66–759; "De synderesis & praefecturis juridiis veterum Ebraeorum," 1:766–1891; "De successionibus in bona defunctorum; & de successionibus in pontificatum Erbaeorum," 11:1–201; "Uxor Ebraica," 11:529–860. While Selden's writings were published too late to influence Althusius, Selden made ample use of Althusius.

of the Decalogue . . . infuse a vital spirit into the association and symbiotic life that we teach."

They carry a torch to guide the kind of social life that we desire; they prescribe and constitute a way, rule, guiding star, and boundary for human society. If anyone would take them out of politics, he would destroy it; indeed, he would destroy all symbiosis and social life among men. For what would human life be without the piety of the First Table and the justice of the Second [Table of the Decalogue]? What would a commonwealth be without the communion and communication of things useful and necessary to human life?[56]

Several times Althusius worked through each of the Commandments to show their enduring natural law teachings. His formulation in the 1614 *Politics* reads thus:

The first commandment of the first table is about truly cherishing and choosing God through the knowledge of him handed down in his word, and through unity with him accompanied by a disposition of trust, love, and fear . . . The second commandment is about maintaining in spirit and in truth a genuine worship of God through prayers and the use of the means of grace . . . The third commandment is about rendering glory to God in all things through the proper use of the names of God, oaths of allegiance to him, respect for what has been created by the Word of God and intercessory prayers . . . The fourth commandment is about sanctifying the Sabbath in holy services through hearing, reading, and meditating upon the Word of God . . . The fifth commandment is about those things that inferiors are expected to perform toward superiors and vice versa . . . The sixth [commandment] requires the defense, protection, and conservation of one's own life and that of one's neighbor. The conservation of one's own life comes first, and consists in defense, conservation, and propagation of oneself . . . Conservation of the neighbor's life is his protection through friendship and other duties of charity, such as provision for food, clothes, anything he else needs to be sustained . . . The seventh commandment concerns the conservation of one's own mind and body and that of one's neighbor through sobriety, good manners, modesty, discretion, and any other appropriate means . . . The eighth commandment concerns the defense and conservation of one's goods and those of one's neighbor, and their proper employment in commerce, contracts, and one's vocation . . . The ninth commandment concerns the defense and conservation of the good name and reputation of oneself and one's neighbor through honest testimony, just report, and good deeds . . . The tenth commandment concerns concupiscence, and exerts influence on each of the precepts of the second table. [As Cicero wrote:] "We are taught by the authority and bidding of laws to control our passions, to bridle our

---

[56] *Pol.*, Preface (1610 and 1614 edns.); *Pol.* XXI.29. See sustained discussions of the Decalogue in *Pol.* VII.7–12; *Pol.* X.3–12; *Pol.* XVIII.32–44; *Pol.* XXI.22–29, 41; *Dic.* 1.13.10–18; *Dic.* 1.14.1–3; and further brief references in *Pol.* XVIII.66; *Pol.* XIX.14, 31, 59, 69; *Pol.* XXVII.18; *Pol.* XXIX.1; *Pol.* XXVIII.32, 38, 77, 100.

every lust, to defend what is ours, and to keep our minds, eyes, and hands from whatever belongs to another."[57]

These moral teachings of the Decalogue are echoed and elaborated elsewhere in the Bible, said Althusius – particularly in the Gospel's repeated explications of the spirit of the Decalogue, and in the many moral lessons set out by the Old Testament prophets and New Testament apostles. These enduring moral laws of the Bible must lie at the foundation of the positive law of any modern Christian polity.

But not all biblical law should be taken as natural law, nor considered mandatory or even useful for our day. Many of the Mosaic laws recorded in the Pentateuch are simply the positive laws of the ancient Jewish people. Many of the legal actions and admonitions of the patriarchs, judges, and kings of ancient Israel are simply evidence of one positive law system in action. Particularly the Mosaic "ceremonial" laws and customs respecting diet, dress, sacrifice, ritual, levitical life, temple rules, and more, even though authored by God, were specific to the time and place of this ancient wandering tribal people.[58] Christ explicitly rejected the letter of this Mosaic ceremonial law in favor of its general moral spirit. Remember his statement about the complex laws of the Sabbath: "The Sabbath was made for man, not man for the Sabbath" (Mark 2:23–28; Luke 6:1–5). Mosaic ceremonial laws, let alone the later rabbinic accretions upon them, have no place in modern communities – save as an illustration of how one legally sophisticated ancient community exercised its natural inclinations and obligations to religious worship and ritual life. While a modern-day Christian magistrate would do well to develop a comparable set of ceremonial laws tailored to the needs of the local community, and perhaps even emulate some of the ancient biblical prototypes, he cannot simply "impose these Jewish positive laws, which by their nature are changeable and obsolete." That would be to "destroy the Christian liberty" that Christ gave us and to "entangle himself and others in a yoke of slavery."[59]

More useful, for Christian and non-Christian polities alike, are the "juridical laws" of Moses. These are the many detailed laws and procedures set out in the Bible to govern crime and tort, marriage and family,

---

[57] Pol. xxi.25–27, quoting in part from Cicero, *The Orator*, 1.43.

[58] Althusius anticipated Montesquieu in giving an ethnographic account of how the "nature of a people" and of their positive laws are shaped by "nature and location of a region . . . whether it is east, north, west, or whatever in relation to the rising and setting of the sun, and whether it is flat, mountainous, windy, or calm."*Pol.* xxiii.1–14.

[59] *Pol.* xxi.33–40; *Pol* xxii.3–4; *Dic.* 1.14.5–11; *Dic.* 1.16.9–10; *Dic.* 1.101.43; *Dic.* 1.115.1–36. See further below pages 196–199 on the religious laws of modern polities.

property and commerce, procedure and evidence, and more. These provisions are more useful and probative because they give more specific content, context, and coherence to the Decalogue and other statements of natural law. "[T]he moral commandments of the Decalogue are general," Althusius wrote. "They have no certain, special, and fixed punishment attached to them," let alone procedural mechanisms for how they should be justly and equitably interpreted and applied. The juridical law of Moses "makes more specific determinations, which it relates to the circumstances of the act." So, while the natural law commands "that evildoers ought to be punished," it "proposes nothing concerning the punishment," save the bald commandment, "thou shalt not kill," which does not seem to be just in all circumstances. The juridical law "works out specifically that adulterers, murderers, and the like are to be punished by death, unless the punishment should be mitigated on account of other circumstances. The Mosaic law has various punishments for these crimes," and prescribes a number of useful procedures to weigh the evidence of the crime and to determine a just punishment.[60] Similarly, the Mosaic juridical law offers a number of useful legal rules and procedures for the acquisition, use, and maintenance of public and private property, for the litigation and settlement of private disputes, and for the proper interactions between husband and wife, parent and child, master and servant, creditor and debtor, seller and buyer. None of these juridical positive laws of Moses should be considered binding upon modern-day Christians just because they happen to be in the Bible. But insofar as they are parts and products of the natural law, these juridical laws are edifying for our day, and can be appropriated as apt in the construction of modern positive laws.[61]

What underscored the natural validity and modern utility of the juridical laws of Moses was that they often had parallels in other legal systems, most notably in classical Roman law. "Virtually all Europeans still use" the classical Roman law, wrote Althusius, because its detailed laws have also proved to be "both right and useful."[62] To be sure, some ancient Roman law provisions betrayed the natural law more than illustrated it. Think of the many old laws celebrating the pagan imperial cult, the domestic laws that permitted infanticide, concubinage, and prostitution, the commercial laws that countenanced exploitation of orphans, captives, and slaves, and others. Such laws that openly contradict the Decalogue and other natural law principles cannot be viewed as binding on anyone – as the early apostles

---

[60] Pol. XXI.33; *Dic.* 1.14.5; *Dic.* 1.16.9–18.
[61] *Pol.* VIII.72–91; *Pol.* XXI.32–33; *Dic.* 1.14.20; *Dic.* 1.15.18–21.
[62] *Dic.* 1.14.1–14; *Pol.* VIII.72–86; *Pol.* XXI.30–40; *Pol.* XXII.1–3, 10.

and Church Fathers already made clear in their call for legal reforms of Roman society. But the classical Roman law texts also hold numerous more enlightened legal teachings, many parallel to those in Mosaic juridical law, that are "consistent with the natural law and that cater to public utility and the common good." Some of these Roman laws have also been adopted and adapted into the canon laws of the medieval church and the civil laws of early modern European nations. When these ancient Roman law texts and their later legal adaptations are interpreted and applied "naturally, equitably, and justly," they, too, can be taken as reflections and illustrations of the natural law in action.[63]

This was the method that Althusius used to work out an elaborate system of public, private, criminal, and procedural law for his day. He started with the natural law principles of Scripture and tradition. He then cited the elaboration of these principles in the precepts and procedures of various legal systems with an eye to discovering and demonstrating what they held in common. He combed very carefully through biblical law and classical Roman law. He rummaged more freely and selectively through medieval and early modern civil law, canon law, feudal law, manorial law, and urban law. Althusius's method was not always so neat or cogent. Sometimes he repeated his discussion of the same natural law principle or precept in different chapters and books, with each discussion somewhat different from the last. Sometimes, he just dumped into one long string citation all kinds of passages whose intersection with each other, let alone integration with the natural law principle in question, was not obvious. Sometimes he would pluck out one ancient passage as normative, even when many other passages in the same source qualified or contradicted the one he singled out. Sometimes he would just arbitrarily pick a provision from Mosaic, civil, or canon law and declare it to be a provision of the common law of nations, without showing its analogues in other legal systems. There was more *a priori* reasoning at work in Althusius's theory than he let on. But, these caveats aside, his demonstrative method of argument produced an astonishingly comprehensive and complex jurisprudence.

The most salient part of his work, for our immediate purposes, is how Althusius used his demonstrative method of natural law to construct a theory of rights and liberties. Before working through his theory of rights in the next section, allow me to illustrate how he defined and defended one such natural right – the "freedom and rights of the body" *(libertas et iura corporis)*. Both in his *Politics* and in his *Theory of Justice*, Althusius

---

[63] *Dic.* 1.14.16–20; *Dic.* 1.15.1–21; *Dic.* 1.16.8.

anchored this natural right in the Commandment, "Thou shalt not kill," and its echoes in a number of Greek and Roman legal and philosophical texts.[64] In his *Theory of Justice*, he went on to "demonstrate" what this bodily freedom entailed. His most thorough discussion came in two chapters on "freedom and its characteristics." These chapters were wedged between long chapters on the legal power of a master over his slaves and of a paterfamilias over his household. Althusius seemed to position his freedom discussion to underscore the natural limits that even a master and father had to respect, despite the repeated admonitions of natural, biblical, and Roman law alike that these authorities be "honored, respected, and obeyed."

Althusius's opening passage on the right to bodily freedom reads thus: "There is a freedom of the body by which the civil law allows a person to use his bodily members to do or conduct anything in a way that is both agreeable and permissible. This is given to us as a natural right, unless obvious exceptions are made."[65]

Althusius cited six texts from Justinian's *Corpus Iuris Civilis* to support this proposition. He started with a text from Justinian's *Institutes*, which gave an expansive definition of the rights of "freedmen" in ancient Rome. "Freedom, from which the expression freedmen is derived, is the natural ability to do anything one wishes, unless it is prohibited by force or by law."[66] He next cited a text from the *Digest* that gave the same definition of liberty, but now without restricting it to "freedmen" and while condemning slavery as "an institution of the *ius gentium*, whereby someone, contrary to nature, is made subject to the ownership of another."[67] A couple of sentences later Althusius lifted up several other Roman law texts that countenanced the emancipation of slaves, servants, captives, and children, and expanded the category and liberties of "freedmen" and free-born citizens.[68] The upshot of these texts was that freedom is a natural and native quality of all men, and those who are not free should be made free so as far as possible. As he later put it: "Today, all freedmen have become completely free."[69] But lest the reader think that Roman law countenanced outright hedonism in its call for "freedom of each to do whatever he wishes" up to

---

[64] Pol. VII.9–10; *Pol.* X.5–6; *Pol.* XXI.27; *Dic.* 1.25.7; *Dic.* 106.1–4; *Dic.* 1.117.1–2, 6, 17–24.

[65] *Dic.* 1.25.7. See also *Dic.* 1.117.6.

[66] Justinian, *Institutes* 1.3; see also Althusius, *Pol.* XXXVIII.8. I am grateful to Charles J. Reid for helping me decipher Althusius's cryptic Roman law references in his discussion of bodily freedom in the *Theory of Justice.*

[67] *The Digest of Justinian*, Latin edn. ed. Theodore Mommsen and Paul Krueger, English. trans. Alan Watson (Philadelphia, 1985), 1.54.

[68] Justinian, *Institutes* 1.3, 1.5, 2.1, 2.12, 2.15.   [69] Althusius, *Dic.* 1.25.30

the limits of the law, Althusius pointed to two other texts from the *Digest* that counseled virtuous exercise of freedom: "Not everything which is lawful is honorable." And with respect to freedom of the body in marriage: "In such unions, one must always consider not only what is lawful but what is honorable."[70]

Alongside these classical Roman law texts, Althusius lined up a dozen biblical passages that made similar points. He contrasted the natural freedom that all should enjoy with the unnatural slavery imposed by enemies or family members. Ignoring the many other Old Testament passages on slavery, he pointed to Deuteronomy 20:11 as a warning against slavery and servitude: "If they accept and open their gates, all the people in it shall be subject to forced labor and shall work for you." He also cited the Apocryphal book Sirach 33:20 that extended this call for freedom to the household: "Let neither son nor wife, neither brother nor friend, have power over you as long as you live." Again to avoid the seeming hedonism of these passages, he pointed to several passages from St. Paul that echoed the Roman law texts in their calls for prudence. He included 1 Corinthians 6:12: "Everything is permissible for me, but not everything is beneficial." Also 1 Corinthians 8:9: "Be careful, however, that the exercise of your freedom does not become a stumbling block to the weak."

Althusius went on to describe the bodily freedom taught by the natural law as follows:

It is the power to make law or to disregard it, to choose to release one's own business when it is in need of management. It is [to have] bodily freedom, or the very uninhibited use of one's body, a freedom of nature or of action, the opposite of which is imprisonment, confinement, bondage and chains. [It is freedom] to use one's own, or another's, as appropriate.[71]

In support of these propositions, Althusius cited two dozen passages from the *Corpus Iuris Civilis* and from a modern commentary thereon by Antoine Favre. He included several titles in the *Institutes* and *Digest* on "the rights of persons" (*iura personae*) in general, and the rights of "free born persons," "freedmen," and "manumitted" and "emancipated" slaves, servants, and children. He also included a number of passages on specific rights and freedoms respecting marriage and family life, the acquisition and use of property and business interests, and their alienation by contract, gift, or testament. He again made clear, citing Justinian's *Code*, that the "status

---

[70] Justinian, *Digest* 50.17.144, 197.
[71] Althusius, *Dic.* 1.25.7. For crimes and torts against this bodily freedom, see *Dic.* 1.117.

of freedman," while highly coveted, does "not afford an exemption from civil duties," nor release a person from his or her "natural obligations."[72]

Althusius intermixed with these Roman law texts ten biblical passages that added further nuance and balance. For example, he supported the natural freedom "to make one's own law or to disregard it" and to have "uninhibited use of one's body" with a citation to the cautions of 1 Corinthians 7:4–6: "The wife's body does not belong to her alone but also to her husband. In the same way, the husband's body does not belong to him alone but also to his wife. Do not deprive each other except by mutual consent." He added to the list Ephesians 5:29, which underscored St. Paul's teaching that one's body is to be preserved as a "temple of the Lord": "After all, no one ever hated his own body, but he feeds and cares for it, just as Christ does the Church." Likewise, he supported the proposition that the person has the natural right to make use of his own or another's property with citations to Genesis 50:5–6 and Jeremiah 40:1–3, among others, which taught that all such property uses need to respect the basic natural law duties to love God, neighbor, and self. The lesson in this cluster of passages was clear: freedom of the body and its support is a natural good, but it must be exercised with due moderation and respect for virtue and for the interests of others.

A few pages later in the *Theory of Justice*, Althusius returned to his exposition of freedom of the body, now with attention to the doctrine of self-defense and defense of others:

The protection of one's body and life is how nature makes a man's body free. This is within his power and character. He has the freedom to use and care for his own limbs, and this is invaluable. For this reason, the law allows any man the protection, defense, and preservation of his body and life from harm. Thus he is allowed to carry weapons. He is to be free and immune from murder, assault, beating, whipping, wounds, punishment, mutilation, lashing, attack, branding, and any other sort of abuse, punishment, imprisonment, repression or detainment. He is to be free from all injustice, cruelty, and improper coercion.

The protection of one's life and body are natural human properties. This is considered the most important thing. Accordingly, a man is given the right to protect himself against force and injury, and he is similarly allowed to use harshness and force against those injuring him or bringing force to bear against him. This defense extends first to one's person and life, and then to everything that serves the interests of the human body and life, such as the value of his reputation, goods, and relatives.

---

[72] Justinian, *Institutes* 1.3–6, 1.9; *ibid.* II.1; *ibid.* III.8–9; Justinian, *Digest* 1.5, 7; *ibid.* 28.1–31; *ibid.* 50.16.10–11; *ibid.* 50.17.4–15, 118, 144, 197; "The Code of Justinian" in *The Civil Law*, ed. S. P. Scott, 7 vols. (New York, 1973), VI.37.

While one is permitted to repel and turn aside force, this cannot be done by killing when one is inflicted only by a light wound or when there is only a slight danger to one's life given the type of weapon, assailant, struggle, or blow. But a man may certainly resist with deadly force an attack inflicted upon his body. And he may defend a strong attack against him with equal strength . . . so long as the defensive force is not greater or fiercer than the attacking force. The protection of one's dignity and reputation against harm or provocation, however, should not be made with force but only with words.

The features and benefits of this protection are that it is permitted to resist a thief or an attacker or anyone using force to ensure one's own safety. The protection of family members and domestic servants is also allowed.[73]

Embedded in this discussion were citations to nearly 100 texts from the Bible and Apocrypha, many of them specific provisions and examples of proper protection of one's life, liberty, property and family drawn from the Mosaic law of crime and tort and the glosses thereon by Christ and St. Paul – though Althusius ducked the hard Gospel passages where Christ called his followers "to turn the other cheek" (Matt. 5:39, Luke 6:29). Interwoven with these biblical passages were nearly fifty passages from the classical Roman law, particularly the *lex Aquilia*, and various glosses and commentaries on these Roman law texts by Catholic and Protestant jurists – Benedict Aretius, Julius Clarus, Diego Covarruvias, Andreas Gail, Joseph Mascardus, Jacob Menochius, Fernando Vázquez, and Matthaeus Wesembecke.

And so Althusius went on – piling passage upon passage, proof text upon proof text to demonstrate the concordance that he saw between biblical and rational, classical and Christian, Catholic and Protestant forms and formulations of natural law principles. One can almost see him sitting in the library for months on end poring over huge piles of legal and theological texts and compiling massive lists of each and every passage that he could find that bore on a given topic. Once he completed his reading, he must have just divided and subdivided these lists into ever more discrete categories, following his favorite Ramist techniques, and then inserted these lists of citations at apt points throughout his own text. It is an utterly fascinating and utterly exhausting display of erudition.

RELIGIOUS AND SOCIAL RIGHTS AND LIBERTIES

This demonstrative method allowed Althusius to define and defend a whole series of rights. The most important were a person's natural rights and liberties (*iura et libertates naturali*). In their most elementary form, these

---

[73] Althusius, *Dic.* 1.26.21–27. See further *ibid.* 1.106.1–4.

natural rights were either affirmative or negative claims that a party could make on the basis of natural law – the right, freedom, or power to act by and for oneself (*ius, libertas, et potestas suiipsius*) and the right, freedom, or power to be free from or to forgo acting – or more simply the "right to freedoms" (*iura libertates*) of various sorts.[74]

Since he regarded the Decalogue as the best source and summary of the natural law, Althusius used its two tables to divide these natural rights into two main classes: (1) spiritual or religious rights and liberties (*iura et libertates religionis*); and (2) temporal or civil rights and liberties (*iura et libertates civile*). He sometimes called these the "rights of the soul" (*iura animae*) and the "rights of society" (*iura societatis*) as well, corresponding to the duties owed to God under the First Table of the Decalogue and the duties owed to neighbors under the Second. Althusius regarded both these sets of natural rights as "fundamental rights" – indispensable to the survival of a person and polity and foundational to any more specific rights formulations in positive law.

Religious rights and liberties

Althusius recited only briefly the natural religious rights that were anchored in individual commandments of the First Table of the Decalogue. "[E]ach and everyone in the whole realm should worship freely and fully without any fear or peril," he wrote. A person has the right to discharge the duties of his or her faith, and must be free from any coercion to worship false gods, to maintain graven images, to swear false oaths, or to take the name of God in vain. A person must be free to "enjoy" and "to observe the Sabbath Day," and "to labor six days and to rest on the seventh." If state authorities violate these natural rights of religion, they are engaging in tyranny and should be resisted. If other persons or associations (including the church) violate these rights, they are engaging in crime and should be prosecuted.[75]

The First Table of the Decalogue spoke not in the language of religious rights, however, but in the language of religious duties. And it used strong language at that: "Thou shalt have no other gods before me!" "Thou shalt not take the name of the Lord thy God in vain!" "Observe the Sabbath and keep it holy!" The hard question was how to balance these religious rights

---

74 *Dic.* 1.25.1–8; *Pol.* XXI.22–24.

75 *Pol.* XX.12–13, 20–22; *Pol.* XXXVII.21–22, 33–34, 36; *Pol.* XXVIII.14, 53–66; *Pol.* XXXVIII.10–14, 77–78; *Dic.* 1.101.32–33, 42–43; *Dic.* 1.113.8–9, 12. See also *Dic.* 1.115.10–36 on the "profanation of divine things" which Althusius presented more as a crime against God and the state than a violation of the rights of the individual or of the church. See further below pages 180–181.

and duties. Did a private person have the religious right to alter, amend, or even abandon these First Table religious duties, say on the strength of an alternative formulation of natural law besides the Decalogue? Did state officials have the power to propound, prescribe, or least prefer one formulation of religious duties over another? Could the state establish a single religion alone, and insist that its subjects comply with it or at least support it? Could the state tolerate religious nonconformists, and if so, which groups and on what grounds? While these were the perennial questions of religious liberty in the West, for a Dutch community that had just been racked by religious warfare, persecution, and inquisition, and was now struggling to define the legal place of Calvinism and other faiths, these were intensely pressing questions.

Althusius resolved these questions by defending the absolute liberty of conscience (*libertas conscientiae*) but insisting on only a qualified right of religious exercise (*ius religionis exercitium*).[76] Althusius saw the absolute liberty of conscience as the natural corollary to the absolute sovereignty of God, a doctrinal staple of Calvinism. Sovereignty is a legal term, said Althusius, a right and power to command and control. Through the opening words of the Decalogue, "I am the Lord, thy God," the Bible makes clear that "God alone can command the conscience." God alone can bring a person "out of the house of sinful bondage" and into the "promised land" – whether in this life or in the next. God alone can change the hearts and charge the souls of men. No human person or authority may thus require a person "to believe against his will. Faith must be persuaded, not commanded; it must be taught, not ordered." For the magistrate or anyone else to invade the sanctuary of conscience is to impugn the sovereignty of God. For the magistrate "to impose a penalty on the thoughts of men" is to obstruct the work of the Holy Spirit. "The natural law imparts to all men a freedom of the soul or mind [*libertas animi*]," Althusius wrote in later summary of his position. "This is an unfettered power to want and to choose . . . to evaluate, to desire, and to make choices," "to have the unfettered use of one's own will and judgment." "The exercise of this right cannot be hindered by a command or order, by fear or compulsion."[77]

For the state to guarantee this natural freedom of the heart, soul, and mind to all persons is not to threaten Christianity, but to testify to faith in its cogency. It is not to insult God but to invite God to do his handiwork in the hearts of each person. Althusius grounded this view in several Bible

[76] The terms are in *Dic.* 1.25.8; *Pol.* xxviii.62.
[77] *Pol.* vii.4–7; *Pol.* xi.33–45; *Pol.* xxviii.14, 37–73, 62–66; *Dic.* 1.25.8–10.

verses. We know from the Gospel of St. John, for example, that "the truth
will set you free" and that "if the Son sets you free, you will be free indeed"
(John 8:32–36). We also can claim with St. Paul: "Am I not free? Am I not
an apostle?" "We would endure anything rather than put anything in the
way of the Gospel of Christ" (I Cor. 9:1–12). These passages underscore
that the conscience, soul, and mind of a person must be left entirely free
from constraint and compulsion so that the triune God is left entirely free
to do the work of salvation in each person. Althusius thus stood foursquare
against the traditional practice of inflicting persecutions, pogroms, and
inquisitions upon the religiously wayward and suspect. Such invasions of
the soul and body were an offense against God, and could only lead to
social tumult and turmoil and to false confessions and hardened hearts. It
is a far better and safer course to grant to all parties absolute freedom in
the internal matters of faith.[78]

While all parties must enjoy absolute freedom of conscience lest the
sovereignty of God be invaded, no one can enjoy absolute "freedom of
religious exercise" lest the integrity of society be eroded. The ideal is that all
will see the same divine light and come to the "one true orthodox Christian
religion" – by which Althusius meant Calvinism. But, given human sinfulness, no such religious uniformity has ever existed in history, and no such
uniformity obtains in any nation today. Individual households and congregations, sometimes even small villages and towns may practice a uniform
faith, but this uniformity rarely exists beyond the local level. At the provincial, national, and imperial levels, religious pluralism is inevitable. The great
question that every higher magistrate must judge is how much religious
diversity and nonconformity to tolerate within his or her domain without
fraying the bonds of civil community. How much autonomy should be
granted to churches and townships that maintain distinct local faiths based
on a different interpretation of the Word of God and natural law? How
much toleration should be granted to individual churches and believers
who choose no faith, or a faith based on a wholly different religious word?
Althusius's answer: the magistrate must tolerate all forms of faiths whose
presence does not offend God, threaten the integrity of the true established
church, or endanger the common good of society as whole.[79]

[May] the magistrate who embraces the opinion of one party persecute the other
dissenters by force or arms and the sword when certain cities or estates in a realm
embrace different opinions in their creeds, for the defense of which each alleges
the word of God[?] We say that the magistrate who cannot, without peril to

---

[78] *Dic.* I.25.8–10; *Pol.* xxviii.14, 62–66.   [79] *Pol.* xi.33–45; *Pol.* xxviii.60–66.

the republic, change or overcome the discrepancy in religion and creed ought to tolerate the dissenters for the sake of public peace and tranquility, averting his gaze and permitting the exercise of unapproved religion, so long as God illuminates the rest, lest the entire realm, and with it the welcome lodging of the church, be overthrown . . . He shall therefore tolerate the exercise of diverse religions.[80]

Althusius was all for the state establishment of Calvinism, as we shall see in the next section of this chapter.[81] This gave Calvinist churches special political protection and patronage and gave Calvinist ministers special privileges and prerogatives in the community. He saw this as the only way for the community to abide responsibly by the religious duties of the First Table of the Decalogue. But he also counseled toleration of various other Protestants, Jews, Catholics, and some "heretics" in the community who had a different interpretation of the First Table. Though tolerated, these dissenters had limited free exercise rights. Jews were tolerated so long as they built no synagogues, lived in segregated quarters, wore clear identification, and desisted from intermarriage and common worship with Christians. This was better than the medieval policies of pogroms, forced baptisms, ritual banishments and killings of Jews, but not much better. Catholics fared only a little better in his account: while they were not to be ghettoized or marked with badges, they could not have their own church buildings, and could not worship, intermarry, or interact with non-Catholics. "Heretics," who make only "errors" in doctrine, liturgy, or religious practice, or "impious or profane men in whom there is hope of correction" should be openly tolerated in the community, protected from private ridicule and violence, and free to interact with other believers in the hopes that they will see the light. Heretics can be disciplined, even excommunicated by local congregations and consistories. But "so long as the foundation of true religion is retained," their "heretical" constructions of the faith should be tolerated within the political community. For the Bible makes clear that God's church will always be filled with "weak, sinful, crude, inexperienced, and erratic believers." The wide fields of religion will always yield both "wheat and tares," which only God can finally separate on the Day of Judgment. It makes no sense for the state to demand uniformity in all the minute particulars of the faith, for "no mode of thought has ever come forth as so perfect that the judgment of all learned men would subscribe to it."[82]

---

[80] *Pol.* XXVIII.66, adapting the translation in Jesse Chupp and Cary J. Nederman, "The Calvinist Background to Johannes Althusius's Idea of Religious Toleration," in Carney, Schilling, and Wyduckel, *Jurisprudenz, Politische Theorie*, 243, 252.

[81] See below pages 196–199 and further John Witte, Jr., "The Plight of Canon Law in the Dutch Republic," in R. H. Helmholz, ed., *Canon Law in Protestant Lands* (Berlin, 1992), 135–164.

[82] *Pol.* IX.41–45; *Pol.* XXVIII.50–58; *Dic.* I.101.11–19.

The heavy hand of the law should come down only on those who are "open and notorious" heretics, apostates, blasphemers, atheists, epicurians, libertines, infidels, Arminians,[83] sectarians, alchemists, occultists, and other impious men who promote treason and warfare in the name of a false god, who "terrorize the public" with their evil, who "tear up the foundation of faith," seduce the weak, profane the Sabbath, "scorn God and his church," and "deny, break, or call into doubt the articles necessary for salvation." All these are at once enemies of the true church and traitors of Christian society and can be subjected to "severe punishment." At minimum, they can be barred from forming associations, holding property, publishing literature, and propagating their views in public – though if they are peaceable and "learned" they might be able to have "private contact" with orthodox theologians in hopes they can be persuaded of their errors. Members of such groups must be banned from political and ecclesiastical offices. If these enemies of religion make their views public and begin to act on them to the endangerment and division of church, state, and society, they can be subject to exile, imprisonment, and "the sword." This is not a judgment on their faith, Althusius insisted, but a condemnation of their crime.[84]

Judged by the standards of our day, Althusius's theory of religious rights and liberties was decidedly churlish, despite his promising opening admonition that "each and everyone in the whole realm should worship freely and fully without any fear or peril."[85] He tolerated Protestants of various sorts, including Lutherans, Mennonites, Spiritualists, and other Free Church groups, though they received no support from the government. He tolerated Jews and Catholics but only so far as they stayed to themselves and had no sanctuaries for worship. He tolerated peaceable heretics and non-believers in the community so long as they remained unorganized and unpublished. But by the time he had listed all the heretical groups that he thought to be too dangerous and seditious to tolerate, rather few heretics were left who could claim even this limited protection.

Judged not by our standards but by the standards of his own day, however, Althusius's theory of religious liberty and toleration was rather generous. This was a day of firm religious establishments by law, where government

---

[83] Althusius's opposition to Arminianism preceded the condemnations of the Synod of Dordt of 1618. He called Arminianism a heresy that "tears up the foundation of faith." He was particularly offended that fellow Dutch jurist Hugo Grotius lent his support to Arminians. He called him a "lurking wolf" whose "diabolic" teachings on religion and politics would only destroy the "liberty of the church." Letter to Sibrandus Lubbertus (January 9, 1614), reprinted in Friederich, ed., *Politica Methodice Digesta* cxxix.

[84] *Pol.* IX.41–45; *Pol.* XXVIII.56–58, 68–72; *Pol.* XXX.1–6; *Pol.* XXXI.1–6; *Dic.* I.101.20–35; *Dic.* I.115.10–36.

[85] *Pol.* XXVIII.14.

officials gave little place to religious dissenters and had little pause about slaughtering or banishing the religiously wayward or impure. Spain and Portugal were establishing the Catholic decrees of the Council of Trent on all parties by the point of the sword. The Peace of Augsburg (1555) empowered magistrates to establish either Catholicism or Lutheranism in the Holy Roman Empire, with religious dissenters (including Calvinists) granted only the rights to leave peaceably and quickly. Calvinists gained equal standing with Catholics and Lutherans in the Empire by the Peace of Westphalia (1648), but all other Christians and non-Christians retained only the right to leave, and again quickly at that. The Edict of Nantes (1598) reestablished Catholicism in France, and granted toleration only to Calvinists and only so long as they remained in designated territories. Even these restricted rights were melting away in Althusius's day on their way to being dissolved entirely by the Edict of Fontainebleau (1685). Both Elizabeth I and James I in England had passed a whole series of severely repressive acts against "papists," "sectaries," and others who dissented from the Church of England, and these laws triggered bitter persecutions of non-Anglicans in the later 1620s and 1630s.[86] The Netherlands, by comparison, was something of a haven for religious dissenters and nonconformists, even though it maintained a Calvinist establishment in most of its provinces, and even though the National Synod of Dordt (1618) dealt notoriously with the Arminians, including their legal champion Hugo Grotius, who was imprisoned for heresy.

Althusius regarded the twin policies of religious establishment and modest religious toleration in the Netherlands as "the best example" of how a community could follow both the general principles and the individual commandments of the First Table at once. He based this theory of modest religious toleration on Calvin's cardinal doctrine of the absolute sovereignty of God, his theory of religious establishment on an emerging Calvinist doctrine of religious covenant, as we shall see. While other Protestants and Catholics of his day were defending toleration theories that were both more and less generous,[87] Althusius's views were more progressive than many. It is an instructive anecdote that John Locke's famous *Letter on Toleration* of 1689, much of it drafted while Locke sat in the liberal Dutch

---

[86] See sources in John Witte, Jr., *Religion and the American Constitutional Experiment*, 2nd edn. (Boulder, CO and London, 2005), 9–21.

[87] See, e.g., R. Po-Chia Hsai and Henk van Nierop, eds. *Calvinism and Religious Toleration in the Dutch Golden Age* (Cambridge, 2002); C. Berkvens-Stevelink, J. Israel, and G. H. M. Posthumus Meyjes, eds., *The Emergence of Tolerance in the Dutch Republic* (Leiden, 1997); Nobbs, *Theocracy and Toleration*.

coffee houses, was considerably more restrictive than Althusius's *Politics*
published seventy-five years earlier. For Locke, Catholics, Muslims, and
other believers "who deliver themselves up to the service and protection of
another prince" have no place in the community. Jews hardly figured in his
toleration scheme, and "those are not at all tolerated who deny the being
of a God" – for "promises, covenants, and oaths which are the bonds of
human society, can have no hold upon an atheist."[88]

Social rights and liberties

While the First Table of the Decalogue anchored each person's religious
rights, the Second Table anchored each person's social rights. As in his
discussion of religious rights, Althusius first set out the basic natural rights
taught by the Second Table and parallel natural law statements, and then
summarized some of the positive rights that elaborated these natural rights.

The Second Table has five sets of natural rights of a person in society
and five corresponding duties that other persons and groups, including the
church and state, owe to the rights holder. First, as we just saw, everyone
has the right to "natural life" and "bodily liberty and protection." This
Althusius called "the most important" and basic right of the person. He
included within it the freedom to nourish, protect, and care for one's own
life and limb, the right to carry arms for protection, the right to proportionate defense of oneself and one's possessions that are needed for life, freedom
from murder, assault, and personal injury, and freedom from unjust punishment, imprisonment, repression, or detainment. The commandment
"thou shalt not kill" imposes the corresponding duties on everyone not to
"hurt, strike, or treat his body in any inhumane way," or to "diminish or
take away the use of his body." And, among family members this commandment imposes on each the duty to protect and care for their parents,
siblings, children, as well as their kin if they are able. Second, everyone has
the "right to purity and chastity" (*ius castitus et pudicitia*) – the right to keep
oneself holy, chaste, and pure in mind and body, and to restrict and resist the
actions of others who threaten or violate the same. The commandments
against adultery and coveting one's neighbor impose the corresponding
duties on all to desist from fornication and lust, and to deal with their
neighbor "free from the passion of our concupiscence and perverse desire."
Third, everyone has the right to property (*ius dominium*), to the "fruit of

---

[88] John Locke, *Letter Concerning Toleration* (1689), in *The Works of John Locke*, 12th edn., 9 vols.
(London, 1824), v:47. See further pages 274–275 below and Jeremy Waldron, *God, Locke, and
Equality: Christian Foundations of John Locke's Political Thought* (Cambridge, 2002).

his labors," and "to goods that he uses and enjoys." The commandment against stealing requires others to respect and conserve a neighbor's "title, possession, and use" of his or her property and not to injure, diminish, or remove these property interests. Fourth, everyone has the right to a good reputation – the right to enjoy the "honor," "good name," "standing, excellence, dignity, fame, authority, esteem, and prominence" that become his or her status and station in society as accorded by nature, custom, law, and circumstance. Althusius called this bundle of reputation rights a person's "second self," his "civil personality." A person's honor, word, and integrity were vital to their social survival and flourishing. The commandment "thou shalt not bear false witness" imposes the corresponding duty on everyone to protect the reputation and good name of their neighbors and desist from insults, lies, defamation, and slander. Fifth, everyone has the "right to a family" (*ius familiae*) – the right to marry, to procreate, nurture, and educate their children, to have their marriage, family, and household respected and protected. The commandments about honoring parents, not committing adultery, and not coveting a neighbor's wife, in turn, impose on everyone else the duty to respect the "honor, authority, dignity, and preeminence, and indeed the right of the family."[89]

These five basic natural rights of social life, anchored in the Second Table of the Decalogue, undergirded various public, private, and procedural rights that were to be "constituted" by the positive law of the state. In Althusius's world, public rights were constitutional claims that a person or group could make against the state or one of its officials. Private rights were claims that one private party could make against another private party, based on contract, marriage, tort, property, last will and testament, and the like. Procedural rights were the rules that governed courts and other government offices in treating parties involved in private suits or criminal prosecutions; these were sometimes called civil and criminal procedural rights respectively. Althusius expounded each of these collections of rights in turn – with emphasis on private and procedural rights and with attention to the commonplaces among various positive laws that helped to define the common law of nations.

Althusius gave only passing attention to "public" rights – beyond the religious rights just covered, which were a form of public rights. He did touch briefly on public rights of domicile, voting, representation, and fair treatment. Each person who is born in a city or properly emigrates thereto, he wrote, has the "rights and powers of dwelling in the city, of setting

---

[89] *Dic.* 1.25–26; *Dic.* 1.117–122; *Pol.* x.5–7; *Civ. conv.* 11.1.

up a residence and household, of transferring one's family and possessions thereto, of having a workshop in the same place, of being a member of the private association that fits their vocation and profession, and of engaging in commercial activity." Each person also has "the power of using and enjoying all rights, advantages, and benefits that the whole city has established for all citizens, and approved by common consent." The most important of these is the "right to vote [*ius suffragii*] in the common business and actions of managing and administering the city, and the form and manner which the city is ruled and governed according to laws it approves and a magistrate that it constitutes with the consent of the citizens." Each person also has the right to have his or her interests represented in and by the government. And each person has a general right to "fair treatment" by the authorities: "Peace is cultivated and fairness is protected when right, liberty, and honor are extended to each citizen according to the order and distinction of his worth or status."[90]

This last phrase – "according to the order and distinction of his worth and status" – underscored the reality that, for Althusius, public rights had to be balanced with social realities. While he sometimes talked loosely about the equality of all persons before the law, Althusius was no egalitarian. He regarded differences between persons based on birth and gender, wealth and ability, status and office, opportunity and achievement to be important for maintaining social coherence. In his 1601 *Civil Conversations*, he spent a good deal of time setting out the proper norms and habits of interaction and communication between persons in different stations and offices of social life, and he highlighted the "special dignity" of ministers and magistrates, nobles and aristocrats.[91] He repeated these distinctions in his *Politics* and the need for any legal and political order to accommodate them. "Fairness" (*aequabilitas*) for all citizens, he wrote, is not the same as "equality" (*aequalitas*) of all citizens. To "level all individual citizens" without regard for their abilities, achievements, offices, or obligations is not only "unfair" and "unjust," and it will only bring manifest "disorder."[92]

While he was cryptic in his discussion of public rights, Althusius was expansive in his discussion of private rights. Private rights were an essential "possession" and "protection" of the individual, he argued, and it was vital that the state's private laws protect these private rights in detail.[93] At its

---

[90] *Pol.* vi.43–44; *Pol.* ix.5–9; *Dic.* 1.81.8–15.
[91] See esp. *Civ. conv.* 1.1, 7–9; *Civ. conv.* ii.1–2, 5–7.   [92] *Pol.* vi.47; *Dic.* xxvi.10–19, 33; *Dic.* 1.81.7–18.
[93] *Dic.* 1.25.10. For Protestant antecedents of this division of private law, particularly among Lutheran Wittenberg jurists, see Harold J. Berman, *Law and Revolution ii: The Impact of the Protestant Reformations on the Western Legal Tradition* (Cambridge, MA, 2003), 111–126.

most elementary level, Althusius argued, all private law can be reduced to three basic loci: (1) property or things – whether universal or particular, real or personal, corporal or incorporeal, movable or immovable; (2) persons – whether single or in natural, voluntary, or contractual groups, whether acting on their own or on behalf of their group or office; and (3) the acts that persons commit, perform, or forgo – voluntarily or involuntarily, intentionally or unintentionally – respecting things, persons, or various combinations of things and persons. Private rights fall into two main classes that straddle these three loci of private law. These rights are rooted in either (1) property or things (*dominium*), or (2) voluntary or involuntary obligations (*obligatio*). The law of private rights concerns: (1) how these rights of property and obligation are acquired, distributed, or alienated (what Althusius called *dicaeodotica*), and (2) how they can be met, discharged, or vindicated by proper legal actions or procedures (what he called *dicaeocritica*).[94]

Althusius's intricate and lengthy discussion of the rights rooted in property (*dominium*) gave full testimony to his deep training in Roman law. He differentiated the rights of title and possession, acquisition and use, alienation and devise, and the like that attach to various real and personal, tangible and intangible property interests. Each of these property interests, he showed, can be acquired temporarily or permanently, in whole or in part, and by various legitimate means: by tradition and custom, by contract or gift, by occupation and use, by purchase or loan, by testate or intestate succession, each of which has a whole complex set of rules governing them. He then showed how each of these property interests creates various powers and liberties that are vested in individual persons or in voluntary groups of persons – those bound by marriages, families, partnerships, corporations, churches, schools, guilds, and more.[95]

Private rights are grounded not only in property but also in obligations between and among persons (*obligationes*). Althusius differentiated natural and contractual obligations. Natural obligations are generally those that are based on "natural associations" that are chosen for us more by nature or by circumstance, than by contract or consent – such as between parent and child, brother and sister, neighbor and neighbor, and the like. These natural associations create mutual rights and duties of care, support, loyalty, and others in faithful discharge and adherence to the essential tasks and dispositions for that natural relationship.[96] For example, parents have the

---

[94] See the detailed table at the head of Book 1 in *Dic.*
[95] *Dic.* 1.18–24, 27–33, 36–63, 78–81, 130; *Dic.* 11.12–23.   [96] *Dic.* 1.81.4, 7, 18.

natural obligation to nurture and educate their children and the right to preclude others from violating their children or interfering in the same without cause. The husband and wife, in turn, have a right to their spouse's performance of these child-rearing duties.[97]

Contractual obligations are those that a person voluntarily promises or undertakes to discharge, which, in turn, trigger rights of reliance or expectation in obligees and beneficiaries of those contractual promises. Althusius distinguished all manner of contracts – private and public, written and oral, nominate and innominate, mediated and unmediated, bilateral and multilateral, present and future, gratuitous or commercial, guaranteed and contingent, and others which parties enter into for all manner of personal, commercial, banking, labor, service, and other reasons. Althusius championed "freedom of contract," which he called a "founding principle of the commonwealth," and he dwelt at length on the requirements of consent, capacity, and competence that make this freedom of contract real. Once a fit and competent party fully and freely consents to a contract, he argued, this triggers a right in others to have those contractual duties discharged.[98]

Althusius did not present these private rights of property and obligation as abstract claims. For him, all of these were rights that could and should be vindicated and remedied if threatened, abridged, or violated by other persons or groups. This task fell to tort law and criminal law, bodies of law in which a person's procedural rights were also elaborated. Through a private suit in tort (called a delict at civil law), the person or group can seek restitution, damages, or equitable relief for the rights violation by the defendant. Through criminal prosecution, the state can impose fines, imprisonment, or more severe impositions on the same defendant. And, sometimes through ecclesiastical discipline, the church can impose spiritual sanctions on that same defendant as well. A single violation of a private right can thus give rise to multiple procedures and sanctions. A man who fornicates with his neighbor's wife, for example, risks payment of damages for the tort to her husband and family, whipping or banishment (execution in extreme cases) for the crime of adultery, and spiritual sanctions of confession or banning (excommunication in extreme cases) for his sin of fornication if he is a member of the church. Each of these is a separate body of laws, procedures, and sanctions designed to protect rights and to

---

[97] *Dic.* 1.5, 7, 9–10, 13, 25, 28–30. See also *Dic.* 1.80 and *Dic.* III.9.38–44 on rights of and over adopted children and *Pol.* III.37–41. See also below pages 184–186 the Christian household.
[98] *Dic.* 1.64–97; *Dic.* II.11–22.

punish wrongs, said Althusius, and he would hear nothing of a double (or triple) jeopardy defense by the wrongdoer.[99]

Much of Althusius's system of torts or private offenses mirrored his system of private rights.[100] He distinguished torts committed by individuals or groups that result in threat, damage, destruction, misuse or abuse of another person or group's (1) property interests; (2) personal rights to body, mind, reputation, and chastity; or (3) natural or contractual relations and obligations. He added a fourth category of offenses against the integrity, operations, and power of various natural and private contractual associations in society, not least the family, church, and business. Each of these torts gave the victim the procedural right to sue the party who had committed these offenses and seek appropriate remedies. Althusius worked through some of the complex issues of fault, causation, liability, damages, and the like that the law of torts occasioned, and the law of actions, procedures, evidence, proof, and appeal before various courts and officials that were required for a successful tort suit.[101]

A number of torts were not just private offenses against the rights of a victim but also public offenses against the rights of sovereignty (*iura majestatis*) of the community. Althusius regarded only more serious torts against a person's natural rights of marriage, life, liberty, property, and reputation as crimes worthy of parallel state prosecution. For these were open violations of the Second Table of the Decalogue and its elaboration in other natural laws.[102] The criminal law also punished violations of the First Table which Althusius called "attacks on the majesty of God" (*laesae majestatis divinae*). They included the crimes of heresy, apostasy, idolatry, superstition, blasphemy, and Sabbath breaking, which he called "primary violations," and demonology, sorcery, witchcraft, and others, which he called "secondary violations."[103] Also included were attacks on the community as a whole through treason, rebellion, fraud, or by chronic abuse of one's political or military office or power, or embezzlement of the public funds and property that one held on the community's behalf.[104]

SOCIETY AND POLITICS

Althusius's theory of society and politics helped to actualize and implement his theory of law and rights. In our discussion so far, we have seen Althusius refer often to the positive and fundamental laws of the state, to formal

---

[99] *Dic.* 1.98–100, 126, 142.   [100] See the table at the head of *Dic.* 1.98.
[101] *Dic.* 1.111–130, 135–146; *Dic.* III.1–57; *Pol.* XXIX.29–60.
[102] *Dic.* 1.104–106.   [103] *Dic.* 1.101–103.   [104] *Dic.* 1.81, 101–106, 113, 131–134.

structures and procedures of legislation and adjudication, to private and public associations, communities, and societies, and more. This was not loose talk. He gave full and systematic attention to these concepts, notably in his *Politics* but also in a few chapters in his *Theory of Justice* and *Civil Conversations.*

Althusius started his theory of society and politics with an account of the state of nature – now human nature, and more particularly the nature of persons as creatures and image bearers of God. God created humans as moral creatures, Althusius argued, with a natural law written on their hearts and consciences and "an innate inclination," "hidden impulse," and "natural instinct" to be "just and law abiding." God created persons as rights holders, vested with a natural sovereignty rooted in the supernatural sovereignty of God, whose image each person bears upon birth. God created persons as resilient creatures, with a natural capacity to preserve, protect, and reproduce themselves. God created humans as "virtuous" and "rational creatures," who are called to pursue a "holy, just, comfortable, and happy" life. God created persons as social creatures with a "symbiotic impulse for community," "an instinct to live together with others and to establish civil society." God created persons as loving creatures, who naturally need to give and to receive love in order to be fully human and to abide fully by the most primal command of the natural law: to love God, neighbor, and self. And God created persons as "language-bearers," as "creatures of communication," equipped to learn, teach, and develop the complex norms, habits, and gestures of proper communication and interaction in the home, church, state, school, business, and other associations.[105]

While all persons are created with these natural qualities and inclinations, each is born naked, fragile, and utterly dependent on the care of parents and guardians. As a person weans and grows, he gradually learns that he needs the association, skill, and labor of others to "awaken" his reason and conscience, to procure the necessities of life, to be fulfilled as a loving, interactive, and communicative being. He gradually learns that persons have "different degrees of knowledge and inclination" of the moral law and different levels of "excitement to obey" its particulars – and even worse that some have become altogether depraved and lawless to the danger and detriment of those around them. He learns that persons have diverse gifts and strengths, which can complement and complete those of others when conjoined and coordinated. He learns that "when brought together and united, some men can aid others, many together can provide the necessities

---

[105] *Pol.* 1.1–35; Pol. xx.19–28; *Dic.* 1.7; *Civ. conv.* 1.1, 7–11; *Civ. conv.* 11.2–6, 9–10.

of life more easily than each alone, and all can live more safely from attack by wild beasts and enemies." He learns the ultimate lesson of being created as a symbiotic creature – that "no man is able to live well and happily by and for himself." Thus, upon maturation, each person "consents" to join various other associations in order to realize his full character, capacity, and calling, to secure the integrity of his person, property, and reputation, to obtain the things necessary and useful for natural, civil, and moral life.[106]

Althusius distinguished three main types of associations that exist in most advanced civilizations: (1) private natural associations anchored in marriage and family ties; (2) private voluntary associations (*collegia*), formed by related or unrelated parties; and (3) public or political associations – whether local (villages, towns, and cities), regional (duchies, provinces, and territories), or "universal" (nations or empires). Each of these associations, he argued, is formed by a "tacit or explicit" contract or covenant – a "bond of association and common agreement" about the "property, work, and rights in common" among the members of each association. By this "bond," "contract," or "covenant," the members agree to "communicate and share" a portion of their property, work, and rights with other members of that association, "each fairly and properly according to his ability." By so doing, each person's multiple and unique needs are met so far as possible in the context of creating a community and common life. Althusius called these voluntary social contracts the "founding charters" or "consensual constitutions" of the natural, voluntary, and political associations that together form a commonwealth.[107]

Each of these founding charters, contracts, or covenants is governed by a "general law of community, association, or symbiosis" (*lex communis, lex consociationis, lex symbiosis*), which Althusius regarded as a common provision of the natural law, ultimately rooted in the Commandment to "honor thy father and mother."[108] This law of community teaches that in any such contractual association, some must be ruling authorities, others must be obedient subjects. The "right to rule" (*ius majestatis*) is assigned according to natural and intellectual ability: the duty to obey is accepted in accordance with individual and social need. Structures of authority and obedience are "unnatural," Althusius believed, but they are "necessary" for personal flourishing and social order. "By the natural law all men are equal and subject to the jurisdiction of no one, unless they subject themselves to another's authority by their own consent and voluntary act, and transfer to

---

[106] *Pol.*, Preface (1610 and 1614 edn.); *Pol.* 1.1–10; *Pol.* XXI.16–21; *Dic.* 1.81.1–7.
[107] *Pol.* 1.1–10, 19, 25, 27, 29–35; *Pol.* II.1–6; *Dic.* 1.7, 90.   [108] *Pol.* XXI.19; *Dic.* 1.14.

another their rights." Most people agree, however, to transfer their rights
and subject themselves to these "unnatural" structures and strictures of
authority, for they realize that without them even their most elementary
associations will not long survive, and even their most basic rights will mean
little.[109]

The general law of association, however, puts basic limits on the activities
of every authority – whether in the home, church, state, or other voluntary
association. Every authority must rule "for the sake" of his or her subjects –
for the purpose of allowing them to seek their ultimate end of attaining a
"holy, just, comfortable, and happy" life. Every authority must care for the
soul and the body of his or her subjects – educating and "filling their souls"
with right doctrine and "knowledge of things useful for this life," providing
their bodies with nurture, protection, security, and relief. Every authority
must ensure that the "moral law" is applied "equitably and justly" within
that association, always striving to balance firmness and fairness, rule and
right, justice and mercy in accordance with the teachings of "natural equity"
(*aequitas naturalis*). Every authority must develop a body of proper internal
laws (*leges propriae*) of the association tailored to "the nature, utility, condition, and other special circumstances" of the association and its members.
Every authority must put into "practice the common natural law" which
governs all persons, and must "indicate how individual members of that
association are able to seek and attain the natural equity" to which they are
entitled.[110] For Althusius, familial, private, and political associations alike
were distinct spheres of law and love, justice and equity. Each association
was grounded in the natural law and governed by the general law of associations. Each association, in turn, was a source of positive or proper law.
Each made specific laws for the sake of achieving justice and equity for that
association and protecting the rights and liberties of its members.[111]

Private associations

The most elementary and most essential association of any commonwealth
is the marital household – husband and wife, parents and children, who
are sometimes joined by servants, grandparents, grandchildren, and other
relatives. This "domestic commonwealth," wrote Althusius citing Aristotle,
is the "seedbed of all private and public associational life," the "cornerstone"

---

[109] *Pol.* 1.10–18; *Pol.* XVIII.18.   [110] *Pol.* 1.3, 10–18; *Pol.* IX.1–8; *Pol.* XX.24–30; *Dic.* 1.13.
[111] This notion of "spheres" was given fuller exposition by later Dutch Calvinist writers like Abraham
Kuyper and Herman Dooyeweerd. See below pages 323–324.

of all other commonwealths and common causes.[112] The family is at once natural and voluntary in character. Already in Paradise, God had brought the first man and the first woman together, and commanded them to "be fruitful and multiply." God had created them as social creatures, naturally inclined and attracted to each other. God had given them the physical capacity to join together and to beget children. God had commanded them to love, help, and nurture each other and to inculcate in each other and in their children the love of God, neighbor, and self. While grounded in the natural order, however, marriage is formed by a voluntary marital contract between a fit man and fit woman of the age of consent and with the capacity to contract. Children are born into this unit without volition or consent, but they gradually develop the right to stay or to leave the family unit when they reach the age of consent. Though formed by a bilateral contract between a man and woman, who have equal rights to consent to or dissent from the union, this first association is structured as a hierarchical order under the gentle authority of the *paterfamilias*:

Husband and wife, who are bound to each other, communicate the advantages and responsibilities of married life. The director and governor of the common affairs of the marital association is the husband. The wife and family are obedient, and do what he commands. The advantages and responsibilities are either proper to one of the spouses, or common to both. Proper advantages and duties are either those the husband communicates to his wife, or those the wife communicates to her husband. The husband communicates to his wife his name, family, reputation, station in life, and economic condition. He also provides her with guidance, legal protection, and defense against violence and injury [and] supplies her with all other necessities, such as management, solicitude, food, and clothing . . . The wife extends to her husband obedience, subjection, trust, compliance, services, aid, honor, reverence, modesty, and respect. She brings forth children for him, and nurses and trains them. She joins and consoles him in misery and calamity. She accommodates herself to his customs, and without his counsel and consent she does nothing. And thus she renders to her husband an agreeable and peaceful life.

There are common advantages and responsibilities that are provided and communicated by both spouses, such as kindness, use of the body for avoiding harlotry and for procreating children, mutual habitation except when absence may be necessary, intimate and familiar companionship, mutual love, fidelity, patience, mutual service, communication of all goods and right . . . management of the family, administration of household duties, education of children in the true religion, protection against and liberation from perils, and mourning of the dead . . . [Together,] the parents should educate their children, instruct them in the true knowledge of God, govern and defend them, even lay up treasures for them, make

---

[112] *Pol.* 11.14, 42; *Dic.* 1.79.

them participants in everything they themselves have, including their family and station in life, provide a suitable marriage for them at the right time, and upon departing from life make them their heirs and provide optimally for them.

The marital household is the bedrock of law, politics, and society, Althusius believed. It provides society with the first and best example of authority and discipline, of love and support, care and nurture of the bodies and souls of its members. It is the first school of justice and mercy, piety and charity, virtue and citizenship.[113]

The marital household lies at the heart of a whole network of natural relatives, clans, sibs, tribes, and others who are conjoined by blood and marriage. The head of this extended family network is usually the oldest paterfamilias from the most distinguished family, who enjoys the distinct "right to coerce" or discipline (*ius coercendi*) his relatives into cooperating together and discharging their family duties. All the members, in turn, share in the "rights of blood or family" (*iura sanguinis*) – the right to enjoy the "affection, love, and good will" of their family, and to be assured of their succor, support, and sanctuary if and when needed.[114]

While private natural associations are rooted in blood and marital ties, private voluntary associations (*collegia*) are generally formed by contracts between related or unrelated parties. Guilds, partnerships, businesses, banks, shops, farms, corporations, schools, universities, societies, clubs, "synagogues"[115] – all manner of voluntary associations can be formed by mutual consent among two or more persons. Through these voluntary contracts, the members of these associations mutually agree to share their "property, work, and rights" for a common purpose, whether secular or religious, commercial or charitable, temporary or permanent. They agree

---

[113] *Pol.* II.38–49; *Pol.* III.37; *Pol.* XVIII.105; *Pol.* XXXVIII.84; *Dic.* 1.7, 27–30, 79, 142. See also Johannes Althusius?, *De Matrimonio contrahendo et dissolvendo* (Basel, 1593).

[114] *Pol.* I.16–36; *Pol.* III.1–36; *Dic.* 1.7; *Dic.* 1.78.

[115] *Pol.* IV.4. But see below pages 196–199 where Althusius calls for no synagogues. Althusius was ambiguous about the political status and standing of churches and other religious associations. He treated them variously as natural associations, private contractual associations, and public political associations. Some of these issues were resolved decisively in the next generation in the ecclesiological masterwork of Gisbertus Voetius, *Politica Ecclesiastica*, 4 vols. (Leiden, 1663–1676), abridged as *Gisberti Voetii, Tractatus selecti de Politica Ecclesiastica*, ed. F. L. Rutgers (Amsterdam, 1885). In this work, Voetius laid out a comprehensive covenantal theory of the church that showed it to be at once public and private, voluntary and natural in character. See esp. Part I, bks. I and IV and Part II, bk. I. This ecclesiological formulation, which compares in sophistication to Anglican divine Richard Hooker's *Laws of Ecclesiastical Polity*, would become standard among later seventeenth- and eighteenth-century Dutch Calvinists. See further Emil Conring, *Kirche und Staat nach der Lehre der niederländischen Calvinisten in der ersten Hälfte des 17. Jahrhundert* (Berlin, 1965); Josef Bohatec, "Das Territorial- und Kollegialsystem in der holländischen Publizistik des XVII. Jahrhunderts," *ZSS* (*KA*) 66 (1948): 1; Nobbs, *Theocracy and Toleration*, 130–212.

to an internal system of government, whether formal or informal, written or customary, chartered or negotiated. They work out their own systems and procedures of authority and rule, property and contract, liberty and privilege for their voluntary members. So long as they abide by the natural law and its elaboration in the state's criminal and private law, these voluntary associations enjoy a general freedom of contract.[116]

Once properly formed, these voluntary associations take on their own legal personality and identity, which transcends the legal personality and identity of any individual member. Individuals are now defined by their membership in this association. They have duties and rights, powers and freedoms not simply as individuals, but now as authorities or subjects, officers or members of that association. As individuals, they retain "the right to leave" (*ius emigrandi*) that voluntary association – albeit on the conditions for exit defined in the contract of association (such as rules defining whether they can take back their property or be reimbursed for their lost labor). But if they remain as voluntary members of that association, individuals must yield to its internal norms and habits and must follow whatever internal processes and procedures may exist for changing them. The association as a whole has rights to hold property and make contracts, the capacity to sue and be sued, the obligation to pay taxes and obey regulations imposed by appropriate authorities. Particularly in his *Theory of Justice*, Althusius set out the intricate laws and structures of partnerships, corporations, and some other private voluntary associations in eye-glazing detail.[117] His efforts to provide a conceptual legal map of the vast jungles of associations that had grown up in medieval and early modern Europe, using the founding principle of consensual contract, would later catch the appreciative eye of Otto von Gierke, Max Weber, and other modern social theorists.[118]

Political associations

In the development of civilizations, Althusius argued, groups of private (natural or voluntary) associations covenant together to form public (political) associations. The simplest such public political associations, and the earliest to develop, are hamlets and villages, then larger towns, counties, and cities. These small local associations eventually covenant together to form larger public associations – duchies, provinces, territories, or bishoprics.

---

[116] *Dic.* 1.78.3–10.   [117] Pol. IV.1–30; *Dic.* 1.8, 78, 81.
[118] See Hueglin, *Early Modern Concepts*, 15–28, 197–232.

Not uncommonly, these intermediate public associations conjoin to forms commonwealths, nations, or empires – "universal public associations," as Althusius called them.[119]

While this political evolution from private to public political associations can be seen in the history of many peoples, for Althusius the "earliest," "best," "wisest," and "most perfect example" was recorded in the political history of biblical Israel.[120] The Israelite people moved from the marital household of Abraham and Sarah to the extended families of Isaac and Jacob, then to the twelve tribes founded by Jacob's twelve children, then to the towns and cities led by Joshua and the later Judges, and finally to a single nation of Israel ruled by kings. As Althusius read the Bible, each step in this political evolution of Israel was forged by a "consensual covenant" between the rulers and the people, with God presiding as third-party governor and guarantor. When the people and their families and tribes needed judges to govern their new cities, God commanded them: "You shall establish judges and moderators in all your gates that the Lord gave you through your tribes, who shall judge the people with righteous judgment" (Deuteronomy 16:18). When the tribes later came together to form the nation of Israel, they entered into covenant with King David. The Bible recorded this critical final step of Israel's political evolution as follows:

Then all the tribes of Israel came to David at Hebron, and said, "Behold, we are your flesh and bone. In times past, when Saul was king over us, it was you that led out and brought in Israel; and the Lord said to you, 'You shall be shepherd of my people Israel, and you shall be prince over Israel.'" So all the elders of Israel came to the king at Hebron; and King David made a covenant with them at Hebron before the Lord, and they anointed David king over Israel (II Samuel 5:1–3).[121]

These same political covenant ceremonies were repeated anew with King Solomon, King Rehoboam, and others (I Kings 1:34–40, 12:1–20).

Althusius drew several lessons from this political history of ancient Israel – and from parallel histories of other peoples to which he frequently

---

[119] *Pol.* VI.1; *Pol.* XVIII; *Pol.* XXXVIII.84–86; *Dic.* 1.32, 81.

[120] *Pol.* Preface (1610 and 1614 edn.); *Pol.* XVIII.18–40; *Pol.* XIX.79; *Pol.* XXII.15–19. For context, see Miriam Bodian, "The Biblical 'Jewish Republic' and the Dutch 'New Israel' in Seventeenth-Century Dutch Thought," *Hebraic Political Studies* 1 (2006): 186–202.

[121] See also Deuteronomy 17:14–15, which Althusius also quoted repeatedly:
When you come to the land which the Lord your God gives you, and you possess it and dwell in it, and then say, "I will set a king over me, like all the nations that are around me"; and you may indeed set as king over you him whom the lord your God will choose. One from among your brethren you shall set as king over you; you may not put a foreigner over you, who is not your brother.

adverted. One lesson was that both biblical and natural law condone the doctrine of popular sovereignty, which he defined as the natural right and power of the people to rule themselves or to elect representatives to rule on their behalf. "God has formed in all peoples by the natural law itself the free power to constitute princes, kings, and magistrates for themselves," he wrote. "This means that, insofar as any commonwealth that is divinely instructed by the law of nature has civil power, it can transfer this power to another or others, who, under the title of kings, princes, consuls, or other magistrates, assume the direction of its common life." This natural right to self-rule is so powerful and universal that even God Himself respected this right when the ancient Israelites insisted on its vindication. "God marvelously governed this people for about four hundred years as if he himself were their king," wrote Althusius. And God had the perfect natural right, as the Creator of the law of nature, to rule the Israelites permanently as their king. But "the people requested their own king. God was at first indignant and gave them Saul, whom God designated and immediately chose himself" and whom he crowned through the services of his prophet Samuel. But the people did not welcome Saul. They wanted another king, David, to serve in his stead. God yielded to their choice. "By his word, he established the descendents of David in the control of the realm. But God performed these actions in such a way that the people were not excluded from giving their consent and approval." While God helped to coronate these earthly kings to rule in his stead, "the kings were considered to be chosen by the people as well, and to receive from them the right to rule as king [*ius regis*]" on behalf of the people.[122]

If even God yielded to the natural right of the people to select their own political rulers, then surely every earthly ruler must yield to this natural right as well. "Rulers are made for the people, not people for the rulers," Althusius wrote, quoting Beza and other earlier Calvinists. "The people can exist without the ruler, but the ruler cannot exist without the people." "By nature and circumstance the people are prior to, and more important than, and superior to their rulers." The people elect rulers for the sake of delegating to them the administration of laws that they cannot manage easily on their own. These rulers must act on the people's behalf, and with the interest of the people in mind. They can exercise no more authority over the people than the people can exercise over themselves, and no more authority than the people have explicitly delegated to these rulers. In particular, rulers may not trespass natural laws or natural rights any more than the people

---

[122] *Pol.* Preface (1603 edn.); *Pol.* IX.3–4; *Pol.* XVIII.8, 18–20, 58–59; *Pol.* XIX.8–10, 15–18, 73; *Dic.* I.32.15–19.

can. And they may never convert their political office into an instrument for "their personal and private benefit rather than for the common utility and welfare." As a precaution against such abuse, Althusius insisted that no atheist, heretic, or bastard, and nobody who was impious, impish, or immoral be allowed to serve in political office.[123]

A second lesson that Althusius drew from the political history of ancient Israel was that political associations, like natural and private associations, are formed by voluntary covenants or contracts sworn by the people and their rulers before God. Althusius described these political covenants much like Beza had done half a century before – as mutual promises by the people and their rulers to uphold the laws of God and nature, the rights and liberties of the people, and the faith and order of the community. The rulers swear an oath of office before the people and before God to "administer the realm or commonwealth according to laws prescribed by God, right reason, and the body of the commonwealth." They swear to "bear and represent the person of the entire realm, of all subjects thereof, and of God from whom all power derives." They swear to maintain the soul and body, piety and justice, faith and order of the people and the community – in accordance with the spiritual and temporal Commandments of the Decalogue. The people, in turn, by "common consent," promise to "bind themselves to obey and comply with the supreme magistrate who administers the commonwealth according to prescribed laws" so long as those positive laws "do not conflict with the law of God and the right of the realm." They further promise to accord legitimate magistrates their "trust, compliance, service, aid, and counsel," to pray for the magistrates' survival, wisdom, flourishing, and happiness, to pay their taxes, to register their properties, to answer their conscriptions, and to oblige all other just laws and orders that cater to the peace, order, and happiness of the commonwealth.[124]

Particularly at the national level, the political covenant was in part a religious covenant (*pactum religiosum*) – in emulation of the covenant that the ancient Israelite people and their rulers swore before Yahweh (Deut. 4–6, 29–30). As in ancient Israel, so in our day, Althusius argued, the magistrate and the people promise that "all in the realm" will worship God truly and fully and will acknowledge God as "the ultimate Lord" of the nation. They promise to put in place a "godly republic," dedicated to the glory of God, the honor of his name, the rule of his law. God, in turn, promises to bless and protect the people if they honor their covenantal

---

[123] See above pages 172–175.
[124] *Pol.* VI.30–31; *Pol.* VII.4–12; *Pol.* XVIII.18; *Pol.* XIX.6–7, 14, 98; *Pol.* XX.1–2; *Pol.* XXVIII.30–32.

duties – and threatens to curse and punish them severely if they fail. God is the "creditor" under this covenant, Althusius argued; the people are the "debtors." The covenant imposes upon the people both individual and communal rights and responsibilities, and joint and several liability on all. "One debtor is held responsible for the fault of another and shares his sin if he does not hold the violator of the covenant to his duty, and resist and impede [his sinfulness] so far as he is able." It was thus of paramount importance that each and every member of the community, not least the magistrates themselves, adhere to the letter and spirit of the covenant, and counsel their neighbors to do the same.[125]

Althusius distinguished various types, phases, or dimensions of the political covenant. The first was the agreement among the people themselves who, directly or through their representatives, chose to form a political association regardless of its type of government. The second was between the rulers and the people, by which each side defined the forms and norms of government of the political association, and their respective duties and rights, powers and privileges therein. The third agreement was between the ruler and God to maintain a Godly commonwealth that served to the glory of God and secured the blessings of liberty for the people and their associations. The fourth was between the chief magistrate and the lower magistrates, by which each side agreed to check and balance the other as a safeguard against tyranny. Althusius did not make clear whether these were all forms and functions of the same political covenant or were separate political covenants that were ultimately conjoined. But he did make clear that all these agreements together served as the "fundamental law," "founding constitution," and "contractual mandate" of the political community.[126]

Althusius regarded political covenants – at the urban, provincial, and national levels alike – as the best guarantee of the "ultimate rule of laws [*leges*] and rights [*iura*] in human society." "Rule by law" and "rules of law" grounded in the law of nature and bounded by the political covenant, he thought, provided the commonwealth with "a guiding light of civil life, a scale of justice, a preserver of liberty, a bulwark of public peace and discipline, a refuge for the weak, a bridle for the powerful, a norm and straightener of rulership." For Althusius, these political covenants were not just mythical, metaphysical, or metaphorical constructs. They were written charters and constitutions, to which the rulers and the people solemnly swore their allegiance before God. They specified in detail the mutual

[125] *Pol.* XXVIII.22; *Pol.* XXXVIII.31–35, 40. For expansion of this theory by New England Puritans, see pages 288–294 below.

[126] *Pol.* X.4; *Pol.* XIX.6, 15, 23, 29, 49; *Pol.* XX.18; *Pol.* XXVIII.30–32; *Dic.* 1.13.3, 6–8.

rights and duties, powers and prerogatives of the rulers and the people, and the principles and procedures for the creation and enforcement of positive laws. "Written constitutions," he wrote, provide the best "fences, walls, guards, or boundaries of our life, guiding us along the appointed way for achieving wisdom, happiness, and peace in human society."[127]

A third lesson that Althusius drew from the political history of ancient Israel was that, upon execution of the political covenant, a new legal and political entity is formed. Each political association, be it a city, province, or nation, becomes a distinct legal entity, an independent living body politic with its own legal and political personality, its own life and spirit. The formal head of each political association is the chief magistrate – the city mayor, the provincial governor, the national king. The members are those lower associations whose leaders joined in covenant to create this higher association – the families and voluntary associations that covenanted together to form the cities; the guilds, estates, orders, and cities that covenanted together to form the provinces; the cities and provinces that covenanted together to form the nation. At the provincial and national levels, Althusius made clear, the members of the political association are no longer "the individual men, families, or private associations themselves," but rather the lower political associations of which they are a part and who represent the people and their interests. "Individual persons from these groups of members are now called natives, inhabitants of the realm, and sons and daughters of the realm." "They are to be distinguished from foreigners and strangers, who have no claim upon the right of the realm. It can be said that individual citizens, families, and [private voluntary] associations are not members of a realm just as boards, nails, and pegs are not considered parts of a ship." Of course, without these persons and private associations, the ship of state would fall apart. But just as a ship is known for its larger parts – its bow, stern, rudder, and deck – so the ship of state is known for its collections of individuals gathered in various political groups and offices.[128]

This does not mean that the people lose their sovereignty and rights once the political association is formed. At every level of government, the people remain sovereign and supreme; they retain their fundamental rights as persons and as members of private associations. Even the "right of national sovereignty" belongs ultimately to the people as a whole, not to any person within it – especially not to any king or other supreme magistrate who happens to be at the head of the nation. All the people who constitute the nation are literally, said Althusius, the "owners of the nation's

---

[127] *Dic.* I. 13.3, 6–8.   [128] *Pol.* v.5–11; *Pol.* IX.4–6; *Dic.* I.81.8–9, 17–18.

rights of sovereignty." Through the creation of the national covenant, or constitution, the people as a whole agree to delegate the administration of their power to the king. Because of this delegation, "the king represents the people, not the people the king." The king must be responsible to the people, represented in their various associations.

> The right of a king consists in the faithful and diligent care and administration of the commonwealth entrusted to him by the people . . . The king holds, uses, and enjoys these riches . . . as a usufructuary [a leaseholder]. When the king dies, or is denied the royal throne by legitimate means, these rights of the king return to the people, the owner [of these rights]. The people then reassign them as it thinks best for the good of the commonwealth. Therefore the right of the king is one thing, the right of the people another. The former is temporary and personal; the latter is permanent. The former is lesser, the latter greater. The former is a loan given by contract to the authorized king, the latter is an indivisible property [owned by the people].[129]

Not only do the people retain their fundamental sovereignty and rights; the lower political associations also retain their fundamental identity and sovereignty as parts of these broader political structures. Each local political association retains it own "right of sovereignty" (*ius majestatis*), its own "rights, privileges, benefits, and prerogatives" that the people have delegated to them. This is the political power to exercise personal and subject matter jurisdiction within that political association, to undertake legal actions on behalf of and for the sake of the members, to "dispose, prescribe, ordain, administer everything necessary and useful" for the maintenance and flourishing of the political association and the people. Of course, a city's right of sovereignty is subject to that of the higher provinces and nation, just as a province's right of sovereignty is subject to the highest sovereignty of the nation. But these local political rights of sovereignty remain in place and must be respected so far as possible, Althusius argued. For the more local the administration of authority, the more "individualized the care that is given to the individuals and groups." The agreement of a city to join a province, or of a city and province to join a larger national republic, does not end their political identity or sovereignty, but confirms it. It guarantees representation of their local interests in higher politics and assures them of protection and support in the event of attack or emergency. It further confirms that the higher political associations are created by and composed of these smaller associations, and ultimately dependent upon them

---

[129] *Pol.* Preface (1603 and 1610 edn.); *Pol.* IX.4, 15–24; *Pol.* XVIII.102–104; *Pol.* XXIV.29–50; *Pol.* XXXVIII.31, 39–40.

for their survival. Lower political associations are the essential foundations of higher political associations, without which a province or nation-state would crumble.[130]

Althusius's insistence on preserving local political sovereignty, even while defending the rights and powers of a sovereign nation-state, was a critical argument in the defense of the Dutch constitutionalism of his day, and eventually in the development of the modern theory of political federalism as well. It also had strong implications for sorting out the complex political relationships of various polities in the Holy Roman Empire of his day, not least the city of Emden. His views stood in marked contrast with the theories of royal absolutism and nationalist sovereignty propounded by Jean Bodin, James I, and others, for whom Althusius reserved some of his harshest critique. For Althusius, sovereignty was a universal blessing vested in all the people in their particular associations, not an indivisible prerogative vested exclusively in a hereditary monarch. Federalism was an essential guarantee of the sovereignty of the people, and the lower private and political associations that they inhabited, a buffer against the inevitable tendencies of higher magistrates toward political tyranny and nationalist absolutism.[131]

Federalism was not the only such safeguard. Separation and cooperation of powers served that function as well. Althusius called for a "mixed government" that combined monarchical, aristocratic, and democratic elements but that separated executive, legislative, and judicial powers. Each power should enjoy a measure of control over and dependence on the other, said Althusius, and all powers are subordinate to the law of the state itself, particularly the fundamental law that brings these powers into being. All powers and authorities should exercise "moderation" "so that the right of each member of the commonwealth is conserved, and neither diminished nor increased to the detriment of another." It is especially important to ensure "that the power of the king is not so enhanced that the liberty of the people is suppressed."[132] Althusius worked out in detail the layers of urban, provincial, and national offices that discharged these powers, and the particular procedures, purposes, and prerogatives that attached to each. He devoted a good deal of his *Politics* to this huge analytical task, focusing

[130] *Pol.* VI.39–44; *Pol.* VIII.3, 40, 50–67; *Pol.* XVII.24–31; *Dic.* 1.33.1–8, 24, 31–35
[131] See Huegelin, *Early Modern Concepts*, 109–135; Gierke, *Development*, 266–276; Carl J. Friedrich and Robert G. McCloskey, eds., *From the Declaration to the Constitution: The Roots of American Constitutionalism* (New York, 1954), xxiiiff.; Fabrizio Lomonaco, "Huguenot Critical Theory and 'Ius Maiestatis' in Huber and Althusius," in Laursen, *New Essays*, 171–192.
[132] *Pol.* XXIX.2; *Pol.* XXXVIII.1–16; *Dic.* 1.32.20–22.

especially on the respective powers of the executive and legislative offices over religion and morality, rights and liberties, education and welfare, war and crime, property and contracts, taxation and commerce, money and titles, diplomacy and negotiation, and more.[133] His *Theory of Justice* added several long chapters on the judicial power and the rules of evidence and procedure, pleading and appeal, representation and advocacy that obtain therein.[134]

Althusius's summary of the power of the provincial governor illustrates both the detail of his enumeration of powers at each level of government, and the level of authority that he assumed that individual provinces should retain within the broader national state:

The provincial governors wield complete jurisdiction and power in the land of their provinces, in which they also are also called royal. Excepting all the things that are reserved for the high [national] magistrate, he enjoys: I. Superiority, preeminence and general jurisdiction in each and every matter of the governance of the province, II. A universal law to strengthen and further the entire kingdom and each province, III. A law for announcing general assemblies and councils, IV. A law for waging war and making peace, V. A law for general learning and founding schools, VI. A law for appointing princes, dukes, marquises, counts, barons, nobles, secretaries and for releasing kings, VII. A law for establishing taxes, VIII. A law for establishing and condoning annual market days, IX. A law for establishing a sequence of public offices, X. A law for founding communities, XI. A law for legitimizing and restoring children, XII. A law for recovering reputation and honor, XIII. A law for granting lifetime pardon, XIV. A law for granting immunity and privileges, XV. Laws for public safety, XVI. A law for striking coinage, XVII. A law for challenging foreigners and avoiding problems, XVIII. A tribunal for dukes and counts and other disputes among other people of rank, XIX. A law for making proclamations and general announcements. Each and every one of these things is reserved for the highest prince and cannot be shared or become subject to provincial power, nor can it be usurped or used by anyone else. To all the things that have been enumerated here I add the law of investigation and punishment, which can be exercised by the highest magistrate in a province.[135]

Lest his reader think this to be a recipe for princely absolutism within local provinces, Althusius provided just as much detail in enumerating the coordinate and balancing powers of other branches of government at the provincial and national levels. Particularly noteworthy were the heightened powers and roles that he assigned to the "ephors" in ensuring the separation and cooperation of powers and the effective and efficient administration of the republic. The ephors were no longer the vaguely defined "inferior

---

[133] *Pol.* VII–XXXVII. [134] *Dic.* 1.33.7; *Dic.* 1.81–82; *Dic.* III.1–5. [135] *Dic.* 1.33.6–7.

magistrates" and "emergency officers" that Calvin and Beza had introduced into Reformed political teaching. Althusius's ephors were critical officers called to exercise a range of legislative and executive powers at the urban, provincial, and national levels of government. Reflecting some of the political complexities of the Holy Roman Empire in his day, Althusius distinguished among various types of ephors and the responsibilities of each. Some ephors were hereditary and permanent, some elected and temporary. Some were clerical appointees with assigned ecclesiastical roles, others lay delegates with assigned temporal roles. Some ephors had general power over the whole national realm, others had power only over local provinces and cities. The most important common task of the ephors was to "administer, govern, and conserve the body and rights" of the individual provinces and of the individual cities, guilds, estates, and private associations that constituted the provinces. Althusius thus called ephors the "rectors, governors, directors, administrators, regents, pastors, leaders, deliverers, and fathers" of the realm. The ephors with national jurisdiction were also called to elect and constitute the nation's supreme magistrate. They were to advise the supreme magistrate and give their consent to all his general laws. They were to stand in for him if and as needed. They were to defend him when he was unjustly attacked. They were to contain and control him – "restraining and impeding his freedom in undertakings that are wicked and ruinous to the commonwealth, in containing him within the limits of his office, and finally in fully providing and caring for the commonwealth." They were to resist and depose him if he became a tyrant.[136]

Church and state

Also noteworthy was the role that Althusius assigned to ministers and other clergy in ensuring the separation and cooperation of political powers. Althusius left conflicting images of the church and its relationship to the state. One image was that of the church as a private voluntary association, whose members elect their own authorities and maintain their own internal doctrine and discipline, polity and property without state interference or support. This was the image that Althusius offered while counseling the toleration of religious minorities – Lutherans, Spiritualists, Mennonites, Catholics, Jews, and other peaceable religious groups.[137]

A second, equally prominent image, however, was that of the church as an arm of the state, subject to its patronage, protection, and prerogative.

---

[136] *Pol.* XVIII.2–9, 48–49, 63–91, 107–110.   [137] See above pages 184–187.

This image came through in Althusius's repeated descriptions of the chief magistrates of the provinces and nation who bore "ultimate responsibility" to "establish and conserve the true Christian religion and uncorrupted worship of God" within their realms and attend to "the ecclesiastical administration and communication" of their people. Much like the ancient kings of Israel and the Christian emperors of Rome, he wrote, the chief magistrate of the province and nation is called by God "to judge concerning the knowledge, discernment, direction, definition, and promulgation of the doctrine of faith" in accordance with the Scripture. He must "establish and permit only one religion" in his realm. He must pass criminal laws for the whole realm to maintain right worship and punish false worship. He must "validate" orthodox canons, confessions, and catechisms and see that they are rightly taught and maintained. He must "constitute regular ecclesiastical jurisdictions, presbyteries, synods, and consistories," and to "legislate through them" the basic requirements for clergy and polity at the provincial, city, and congregational levels. He must see that ministers are legitimately called, elected, and confirmed, discharge their tasks properly, and are disciplined or removed if they become "mischievous and useless". He must establish universities for the cultivation and transmission of true religion, art, and science. He must see that local consistories and presbyteries are regularly convened and generally competent. He must, if necessary, call his own synods and ecclesiastical gatherings to deliberate more serious issues of doctrine or church administration, to ensure that the religious affairs of his regime are in order, and that proper religious personnel and publications are at hand. He must send out inspectors and superintendents regularly to ensure compliance with the letter and spirit of the law. He must send out inquisitors and censors to "chastise" and "stigmatize" those who maintain "morals and luxuries that are not prevented or punished by law, but which corrupt the souls of subjects or squander their goods unproductively." He must seek out and cut out "heresy, error, schisms, and other forms of gangrene that . . . creep into, occupy and destroy the body" of Christ.[138] In these passages Althusius appears to be an exponent of a rigid religious establishment and regimented territorial church that brooked no dissent and tolerated no dissenters.

Althusius softened this view with a third image of the church as a separate seat of law and authority, which cooperated with the magistrate in governing the spiritual and religious affairs of the commonwealth. This was a role he evidently reserved to the "true" and "orthodox" Reformed churches alone;

---

[138] *Pol.* VIII.39; *Pol.* XXVIII.27–49, 51; *Pol.* XXIX.9; *Pol.* XXX.1–30; *Dic.* 1.32.6.

other peaceable religious communities, in this third picture of the church, were tolerated but had to remain private associations with no public or political role to play.[139] By contrast, the Reformed churches were both private and public associations, with both spiritual and temporal, ecclesiastical and political duties to discharge. On the one hand, these churches should follow the rules laid down in Calvin's 1541 Ecclesiastical Ordinance: their ministers, elders, deacons, and teachers should be elected to their offices by their own congregations. These officers should serve in a hierarchy of representative church bodies – local consistories, regional presbyteries or classes, and national synods – that worked together to maintain religious doctrine and moral discipline for the local and broader church membership. They should exercise spiritual power by preaching the Word, administering the sacraments, tendering diaconal care, catechizing the young, educating the community, admonishing the sinful, and imposing bans and excommunication on the recalcitrant.

On the other hand, Althusius argued, Reformed ministers should act in effect as "spiritual ephors"[140] who serve the spiritual, moral, and educational needs of the broader commonwealth – much like other ephors serve its political, military, and material needs. In describing this public religious function, Althusius assigned the Reformed ministers many of the very same duties he had already assigned to the chief magistrate – establishing right worship, liturgy, doctrine, and discipline and creating schools, libraries, welfare agencies, censorship boards, and the like. Althusius later explained that, while the supreme magistrate bore ultimate responsibility to God for the spiritual lives of all his subjects, he had to be "very careful in this activity not to apply his own hands to these matters, but commit and entrust them to the clergy." For the daily "care and administration of ecclesiastical things and functions belong not to the secular magistrate but to the private association [*collegium*] of presbyteries."[141]

There is a two-fold administration of ecclesiastical matters. One part pertains to the magistrate, and the other to the clergy. Each directs and obeys the other, and

---

[139] But cf. *Dic.* III.1.26; *Dic.* III.3.14, 18, 26, where he discusses the jurisdiction of Catholic church courts and the traditional canon law rules of privilege of forum, which provided that Catholic clergy could be prosecuted or sued only in church courts, not secular courts. In *Dic.* 1.81.28, he wrote generically: "The priests' tasks include attending to the law, including answering all requests for judgment, encouraging education, serving as guardians of morals, caring for the poor, for prisoners, for those unjustly persecuted, and supervising orphans, newborn children, foreign children, and those from other towns, and [caring for] the elderly and others like them."

[140] I have not found a passage where Althusius says this directly, but he does say a community needs ecclesiastical ephors and he does heap a great deal of political responsibility on Reformed clergy.

[141] *Pol.* VIII.31–33; *Pol.* XXVIII.5–7, 48; *Dic.* 1.81.27–28.

each helps the other in the distinct administration entrusted to it, according to the example of Moses and Aaron. The administration of the chief magistrate directs the clergy as long as he enjoins them to perform the parts of their office according to the Word of God, and orders and arranges for other things that are necessary for establishing, conserving, and transmitting to posterity the true worship of God. On the other hand, the supreme magistrate is subject to the administration and power of the clergy with respect to censures, admonitions, and whatever concerns eternal life and salvation. In the administration of ecclesiastical matters, the magistrate does nothing without the counsel and consent of the clergy based on the Word of God. This administration is imposed upon the magistrate by the mandate of God . . . and is supported by examples of pious men and by arguments from reason.[142]

This left Althusius with a rather traditional Calvinist view of a unitary Christian commonwealth, subject to the spiritual authority of the clergy and the temporal authority of the magistracy. This view stood in some tension with Althusius's other statements on church–state relations. It also left hanging many hard questions: how did this view of a unitary Christian commonwealth square with his views of freedom of conscience and free exercise of all peaceable religions? What rights, roles, and rules were given to non-Reformed believers in the community, and how did their natural rights of liberty of conscience square with the political duties of maintaining a single religion? What power did Reformed ministers have over these religious dissenters, and what justified giving ministers such political power? How did magistrates and ministers divide their spiritual responsibilities, and how and by whom would inevitable disputes between these authorities be resolved? What quid pro quo did the magistrate extract for protecting and patronizing the Reformed faith and clergy over all others: did the magistrate effect clerical appointments, enact clerical discipline, extract clerical endorsements, control church properties, dictate church polities, define church doctrine, affect church discipline, and more?

These were not abstract questions about religious toleration and church–state relations. They divided churches and provinces bitterly in the decades following the Dutch Revolt. And they must have come up regularly in Althusius's work as a city counselor and eventually as a Consistory elder in Emden. While much of Althusius's legal, political, and social theory was deep and detailed, his account of church–state relations remained incomplete and partly incoherent.

---

[142] *Pol.* XXVIII.5–7.

Tyranny

This last caveat aside, Althusius's detailed account of law, rights, society, and politics made the definition of tyranny rather straightforward to him. A tyrant, he said, is one who "violates, changes, overthrows, or destroys" "the fundamental law and rights" (*lex et jura fundamentalis*) of the commonwealth or "the natural laws and rights" (*leges et iura naturali*) on which the fundamental laws and rights are based.[143] This formula itself was by now commonplace in Calvinist and other Christian circles. But having spelled out in so much more detail than earlier Calvinists had done what these fundamental and natural laws and rights are, Althusius now had a much more refined grid by which to judge a political action or actor to be tyrannical.

Althusius did dutifully tick off the shopworn arguments for resistance to tyranny that earlier Calvinist writers had offered. The Bible's calls to obey "the powers ordained by God" always presuppose that these rulers are legitimate representatives of God. Tyrants who offend God and defy true religion are no longer God's agents, and must be removed both for God's sake and for the people's sake. Tyrants forfeit their political offices and become private persons against whom the natural rights of self-defense can apply. The people must always consent to their rulers, and they would not and could not consent to a tyrant. Tyrants are those who violate the people's ancient charters and privileges, which charters sometimes condition a ruler's legitimacy on compliance with its terms and stipulate a right to resist if those conditions are breached. No tyrant can be tolerated who threatens to smash the ship of state on the rocks. History is full of examples of courageous leaders who have stood up to tyrants. Althusius also recited the traditional rules and rationales for leaving the judgment and execution of resistance to designated ephors and other officers rather than to the crowd. Wild insurrection will ensue if private persons are left free to judge and resist tyrants on their own. We must leave these judgments to constitutional authorities who can judge both whether an official has become tyrannical and what remedies are apt for a ruler judged to be tyrannical – reprimand, restriction, removal, revolt, or regicide. All these and other arguments were well known in contemporary Protestant and Catholic circles, and Althusius peppered his account with citations to all manner of authorities in support.[144]

---

[143] *Pol.* IX.21; *Pol.* XXXVIII.5–7, 37; *Dic.* I.113.1–3.

[144] *Pol.* VIII.91–92; *Pol.* XVIII.69–86; *Pol.* XIX.35–37; *Pol.* XX.12–21; *Pol.* XXXVIII.30, 36–40, 43–76; *Dic.* I.113.25.

Althusius's more distinct contribution was to show that tyranny is in its essence a "constitutional violation" – a violation of the political covenant by which the polity itself was constituted, a violation of the constitutional duties of the rulers and the fundamental rights of the people as set out in this political covenant, and even more fundamentally a violation of the natural law and natural rights that undergird and empower all constitutions and covenants. For Althusius, a tyrant was a magistrate who acted "illegally and unnaturally" (*contra legem et naturam*) in breach of the contractual and covenantal duties that he or she swore to God and to the people. Any "egregious," "chronic," "persistent," "pervasive," "willful," "intentional," and "widespread" breach of a ruler's constitutional duties, abuse of his constitutional powers, neglect of his constitutional offices, usurpation of another's constitutional office, or violation of the people's constitutional rights and liberties was, for Althusius, a prima facie case of tyranny. Of course, "not every such misdeed by a magistrate deprives him of his scepter," Althusius cautioned. Citing Beza's analogy between marital and political contracts, he wrote: "A marriage is not dissolved by a misdeed committed by one mate against another – unless it is a misdeed like adultery, which runs directly contrary to the very nature of marriage." Likewise, a political association is not dissolved just by any official misstep, but when the magistrate's tyrannical conduct runs "contrary to the fundamentals and essence of the human association," "begins to shake the foundation and loosen the bonds of the associated body of the commonwealth," or "destroys civil or political life . . . and the most important goods of the commonwealth, such as its peace, order, virtue, law, and nobility." "Is there not equal reason for conceding divorce between a king and a commonwealth because of the intolerable and incurable cruelty of a king by which all honest cohabitation and association with him are destroyed?"[145]

With that formula in hand, Althusius worked through all the essential constitutional powers and duties that each executive, legislative, and judicial authority at each level of government had to discharge. He focused especially on government powers relating to peace and order, war and diplomacy, crime and delicts, taxation and commerce, property and money, banking and business, religion and morality, education and welfare. Egregious, chronic, persistent, pervasive, and intentional abuse, misuse, or neglect of these powers to the "grave detriment" of the commonwealth were all potential cases of tyranny to Althusius. Such magisterial conduct must, at minimum, empower private subjects to engage in non-violent disobedience

---

[145] *Dic.* 1.113.9–17; *Pol.* xviii.105; Pol. xxxviii.3–27.

and public ephors to institute constitutional remedies.[146] In more serious cases, it allowed for sanctions, restrictions, or removal of the offending magistrates, even revolutionary revamping of the government as a whole.

Another egregious form of tyranny was the systematic "violation or abridgement of the rights of the members of the community and their associations." Althusius singled out for special emphasis governmental conduct that violated the people's natural rights – that "impeded orthodox religious exercise," that abolished schools and education, that "chronically neglected the sick, poor, and innocent," or that "consistently abused private individuals" in their lives and bodies, their lands and goods, their standing and reputations, their homes and relatives, their contracts and associations. All of these "rights and duties given by God are older and more powerful" than any of those set out in the constitution or political covenant. "Even if they are not made explicit in the constitution," or given adequate interpretation, these natural rights "must be understood to be in effect. God is superior to and master of both the rulers and the people," and the rights and duties set out in the natural law must take precedence over all others. Moreover, the political covenant "between the people and their ruler does not create duties that are superior to those which exist between . . . a wife and a husband, children and parents, master and servant, patron and client," and other such natural associations. With respect to these private associations, the law of the state serves only to "deter and punish dishonest, immoral, or unholy people . . . who subvert these existing structures of authority or [legitimate] holders of power within them." When state authorities themselves subvert these social structures, resistance is both natural and necessary.[147]

Althusius also focused on violations of the procedural rights of the people. He listed violations of a number of important criminal procedural rights – false arrests, accusations, indictments, and sentences of innocent parties, false imprisonment or protracted pre-trial incarceration, torture, starvation, or enslavement of prisoners, use of anonymous indictments and untested evidence, denial of rights to defend oneself, to have counsel, to examine hostile witness, to introduce exculpatory evidence, or even to have one's day in court following prescribed procedures, imposition of extraordinary tribunals or *ex post facto* laws, use of biased, bribed, or incompetent judges, imposition of unjust, inequitable, or widely variant punishments, failure to grant appeals of motions, judgments, or sentences, excessive fines, cruel punishments, and more. Each of these abuses and violations of

[146] *Pol.* xxxviii.10–28; *Dic.* 1.36.38, *Dic.* 1.113.17–21.
[147] *Dic.* 1.113.8–9 12, 18; *Pol.* x.5–10; *Pol.* xxxvii.21–22, 33–34, 36.

procedural rights should give individual victims constitutional redress, Althusius argued, and a persistent pattern of such abuses to several victims at once is prima facie evidence of judicial tyranny that requires a more systemic response.[148]

SUMMARY AND CONCLUSIONS

"I hold that the revolt of the Netherlands and the success of Holland are the beginning of modern political science and of modern civilization . . . To the true lover of liberty, Holland is the holy land of modern Europe."[149] So wrote an overly exuberant American historian in 1894. His enthusiasm was shared by a number of other American writers of his day, who praised the early modern Netherlands as a haven of religious toleration, a sanctuary for America's colonists, and a seedbed of Western constitutionalism. Some writers took special note of the remarkable analogies between the Dutch Revolt and the American Revolution, between the 1581 Act of Abjuration and the 1776 Declaration of Independence, between the 1579 Union of Utrecht and the 1781 Articles of Confederation. Still others saw striking parallels between Prince William's "clear truths" about "rights, liberties, and privileges" grounded in "natural and divine laws" and Thomas Jefferson's "self-evident truths" about "life, liberty, and the pursuit of happiness" founded on "the laws of nature and nature's God."[150]

A century and more of careful historical scholarship has both substantiated and qualified such exuberant claims. The analogies between the Dutch Revolt and American Revolution still remain striking to historians today, and it remains undeniable that the Dutch experience was inspirational to a number of American founders. John Adams, for example, wrote: "The originals of the two republics are so much alike, that the history of one seems but a transcript of that of the other."[151] Thomas Jefferson praised the Dutch freedom fighters: "In love of liberty, and bravery in defense of it, she has been our great example."[152] James Madison argued that "the example of Holland proved that a toleration of sects dissenting from the established sect was

---

[148] *Dic.* 1.113.20–83; *Pol.* xxix.47–60.

[149] Thorold Rogers, "Review of William E. Griffis, *Brave Little Holland,*" *The New England Magazine* (n.s.) 10 (1894): 517, 520.

[150] See, e.g., John Lothrop Motley, *The Rise of the Dutch Republic: A History*, 3 vols. (New York, 1877); George A. Henty, *By Pike and Dyke: A Tale of the Rise of the Dutch Republic* (New York, 1894). See further sources and analysis in J. W. Nordholt Schulte, *The Dutch Republic and American Independence*, trans. H. H. Rowen (Chapel Hill, NC, 1982).

[151] Quoted in *The New England Magazine* (n.s.) 10 (1894): 517, 521.   [152] Quoted in *ibid.*, 518.

safe, and even useful."[153] Moreover, a number of cardinal legal and political ideas and institutions developed in the early Dutch Republic – confederacy and federalism, enumerated powers and rights, separation of powers and privileges – had striking analogues in both the state and federal constitutions of the young American republic.

But the distinctly Dutch pedigree of these American constitutional ideas and institutions has proved harder to document. The eighteenth-century American founders were intensely eclectic, and regularly adduced all manner of classical, biblical, and early modern sources in support of their views.[154] While they cited the Dutch example repeatedly, most founders had only limited access to a few poorly translated Dutch political tracts and displayed only a hazy knowledge of the inner workings of early modern Dutch constitutionalism. Those who knew more, like Adams, Madison, and Alexander Hamilton, expressed concern about the monarchical institutions, religious establishments, social hierarchies, and unrepresentative institutions that remained in place in the Dutch Republic of their day.[155] Moreover, a number of the more provocative and enduring Dutch revolutionary ideas – popular sovereignty, natural rights, social contract, written constitutions, fundamental laws, constitutional liberties, and others – took on quite different accents and applications in revolutionary America.[156] The sixteenth-century Dutch Revolt was certainly generative of a number of enduring legal and political ideas and institutions. But there were ample developments of all these doctrines in the two-century interval, and there were many other sources of influence on the American founders besides those of the Dutch Revolt and republic.

This same circumspection should be used in assessing the enduring legacy of Johannes Althusius for the Western tradition of law, politics, and society. Since his work was rediscovered a century ago, Althusius has been claimed as the father of all manner of modern ideas and institutions. Otto von Gierke, for example, in his pathbreaking study that resurrected Althusius from obscurity, saw him as a pivotal Protestant social contract theorist, whose views were eventually championed by Jean-Jacques Rousseau and the French *philosophes*. Carl Friedrich saw Althusius's theory of political

---

[153] Quoted by Anson P. Stokes, *Church and State in the United States*, 3 vols. (New York, 1950), 1:120.

[154] See Donald S. Lutz, *The Origins of American Constitutionalism* (Baton Rouge, LA, 1988).

[155] See detailed sources in William H. Riker, "Dutch and American Federalism," *Journal of History of Ideas* 18 (1957): 495; William H. Riker, *Federalism: Origin, Operation, Significance* (Boston, 1964) and a list of Dutch legal treatises available to the American founders in Herbert A. Johnson, *Imported Eighteenth Century Law Treatises in American Libraries, 1700–1799* (Knoxville, TN, 1978).

[156] Kossman, "Development of Dutch Political Theory," in Bromley and Kossman, *Britain and the Netherlands*, 1–25, 99–100.

pluralism and divided sovereignty as critical to the development of modern-day confederacy and federalism. Heinz Antholz treated Althusius's concerns for the political effects of geography and climate as prescient of the insights of Baron Montesquieu. Peter Winters regarded Althusius's sturdy Calvinist republicanism as a foretaste of the political philosophy of Edmund Burke. Abraham Kuyper saw him as an early prophet of a distinct theory of sphere sovereignty. Robert Nisbet and Daniel Elazar saw him as one of the fathers of modern-day consociationalism. And all manner of scholars have begun to look to him as a father of covenantal politics and a prophet of European political union.[157] Such a rich and varied legacy is perhaps inevitable for a theorist as prolific and original as Althusius, who was living at the edge of the Netherlands on the eve of its influential golden age. And, with due regard for the development of his doctrines and the diversity of intervening sources of influence, Althusius's teachings were certainly influential on, if not generative of, many later movements in Western law, politics, and society.

The further question for this volume concerns not the influence that Althusius had on Western politics but the reformation that he led for Western Calvinism. Althusius was an ardent Calvinist throughout his life – a student at the Genevan Academy, a professor of the Calvinist academy in Herborn, an elder of the Calvinist church, a member of the Calvinist Consistory court in Emden. He knew the Calvinist tradition intimately, and cited profusely to scores of Calvinist writers, not least John Calvin and Theodore Beza. He followed the early Calvinist method of grounding his legal and political arguments in the Bible as well as the later Calvinist habit of channeling his arguments with Ramist dialectics. And he repeated faithfully several key political insights developed by Swiss, French, Scottish, Dutch, and German Calvinists before him – that the republic is formed by a covenant between the rulers and the people before God, that the foundation of this covenant is the law of God and nature, that the Decalogue is the best expression of this higher law, that marriage is the cornerstone of the commonwealth, that church and state are separate in form but conjoined in function, that families, churches, and states alike must protect the rights and liberties of the people, and that violations of these rights and liberties, or of the divine and natural laws that inform and empower them, are instances of tyranny that must trigger organized constitutional resistance.

---

[157] See sources and examples in Gerhard Menk, "Johannes Althusius und die Reichsstaatsrechlehre," in *Politische Theorie des Johannes Althusius*, ed. Werner Krawietz and Dieter Wyduckdel (Berlin, 1988), 255–300; Hueglin, *Early Modern Concepts*, 15–28, 197–232; Kossman, "Popular Sovereignty." See further below page 287.

Althusius developed and deepened a number of these inherited Calvinist teachings and added several others. He developed a demonstrative natural law theory that still treated the Decalogue as the best source and summary of natural law but layered its Commandments with all manner of new biblical, classical, and Christian teachings. He developed a theory of positive law that judged the validity and utility of any human law, including the positive laws of Moses and the canon laws of the church, against both the natural law of Scripture and tradition and the fundamental law of the state. He called for a detailed written constitution and for perennial protection of "the rule of law" and "rule of rights" within each commonwealth. He developed an expansive theory of popular sovereignty and political election and representation. He developed a refined theory of natural rights – religious and social, public and private, substantive and procedural, contractual and proprietary – and demonstrated how these rights were to be given concrete positive form in public, private, and criminal law and procedure. Particularly striking was his call for religious toleration and absolute liberty of conscience as a natural corollary and consequence of the Calvinist teaching of the absolute sovereignty of God, whose relationship with his creatures could not be trespassed.

More striking still was Althusius's symbiotic theory of human nature and covenantal theory of society and politics. While acknowledging the traditional Calvinist teaching of the total depravity of persons, Althusius emphasized that God has created all human beings as moral, loving, communicative, and social beings, whose lives are most completely fulfilled through rich symbiotic relationships with others in which they can appropriately share their bodies and souls, their lives and spirits, their belongings and rights. Thus, while persons are born free, equal, and individual, they are by nature and necessity inclined to form associations – marriages and families, clubs and corporations, cities and provinces, nation-states and empires. Each of these associations, from the tiniest household to the vastest empire, is formed by a mutually consensual covenant or contract sworn by all members of that association before each other and God. Each association is a locus of authority and liberty that binds both rulers and subjects to the terms of their founding contract and to the commands of the foundational laws of God and nature. Each association confirms and protects the sovereignty and identity of its constituent members and their natural rights and liberties.

Althusius applied this Christian social contract theory most fully in his description of the state. Adducing especially the biblical example of the political formation of ancient Israel, he showed how nation-states develop gradually from families to tribes to cities to provinces to nations. Each new layer of political sovereignty is formed by covenants sworn before God by representatives of the smaller units, and these covenants eventually become the written constitutions of the polity. The constitutions define and divide the executive, legislative, and judicial offices within that polity, and govern the relations of its rulers and subjects, clerics and magistrates, associations and individuals. They also make clear the acts and omissions that constitute tyranny and the procedures and remedies available to those who are abused.

This was a comprehensive Christian contract theory of law, society, and politics – drawn together from all manner of biblical, classical, patristic, scholastic, and modern-day Protestant and Catholic lore. Like Calvin and Beza before him, Althusius read very widely and deeply in the Western tradition. He was more concerned about the cogency of the ideas that he read than the pedigree of the author who wrote them. Natural law teaches all persons the ways of God, Althusius believed, and that made him less prone to denominational snobbery than some of his co-religionists in his selection of sources. Althusius aspired to create from Calvinist premises a universal legal, political, and social theory that would appeal not just to fellow Calvinists but to all people of good faith and good will.

Althusius had no use for those whom he judged to be of bad faith or ill will. His list of suspects was long: it included absolute monarchists, Machiavellians, nationalists, heretics, apostates, blasphemers, atheists, epicurians, libertines, infidels, Arminians, sectarians, alchemists, occultists, and other impious men who promote treason, insurrection, and disorder in the community and who defy the most elementary and essential teachings of the Decalogue. He called for censorship of their writings, disruptions of their assemblies, dissolutions of their corporate properties, exclusion of their members from political office and elections, and banishment of their leaders from society. These were deprivations and abridgements of rights that later Calvinists would find shocking, even though they embraced and developed much of the rest of his theory of law, religion, and human rights.

5. Oliver Cromwell (1599–1658) preaching to a Puritan congregation (engraving) by English School (seventeenth century)

CHAPTER 4

Prophets, priests, and kings of liberty: John Milton and the rights and liberties of Englishmen

For by natural birth, all men are equally alike born to like property, liberty, and freedom, and as we are delivered of God by the hand of nature into this world, everyone with a natural, innate freedom and property (as it were writ in the table of every man's heart, never to be obliterated) even so we are to live, everyone equally and alike to enjoy his birthright and privilege; even all where God by nature hath made him free ... Every man by nature being a King, Priest, and Prophet in his own natural circuit and compass, whereof no second may partake, but by deputation, commission, and free consent from him whose right and freedom it is.

Richard Overton (1646)[1]

God is decreeing to begin some new and great period in his Church, even to the reforming of [the] Reformation itself, [in order] to make a knowing people, a Nation of Prophets, of Sages, and of Worthies.

John Milton (1644)[2]

We now under Christ [are] a royal priesthood, 1 Pet. 2:9, as we are co-heirs, kings and priests with him.

John Milton (1659)[3]

In 1640, the English "world turned upside down."[4] For the first time in eleven years, King Charles called Parliament into session, and the members erupted in unprecedented fury against two decades of belligerent royal policies that had left the nation in disarray. Some of Parliament's fury was directed at Charles's religious policies. Upon his succession to the throne in 1625, Charles had stepped up his father's already stern Anglican

---

[1] Richard Overton, *An Arrow Against All Tyrants and Tyranny* (1646), 3–4, in William Haller, *Tracts on Liberty in the Puritan Revolution, 1638–1647*, 3 vols. (New York, 1934), I:113. Throughout this chapter, I have modernized the spelling of quotes from early modern English sources, but have retained the original spelling of the titles.

[2] *CPW* II:553–554. [3] *CPW* VII:286.

[4] Acts 17:6. See Christopher Hill, *The World Turned Upside Down: Radical Ideas During the English Revolution*, repr. edn. (New York, 1988).

establishment laws and began persecuting Calvinists (often called Puritans) and other religious dissenters with a vengeance, driving them by the boatload to the Netherlands and to America – some 20,000 people in 1632 alone. In 1633, he appointed William Laud as Archbishop of Canterbury, who began purging English pulpits of Calvinist sympathizers and packing them with conservative clerics who were loyal to the Crown and to the textbooks of established Anglicanism – the Book of Common Prayer, the Thirty-Nine Articles of the Faith, and the Authorized or King James Version of the Bible. Charles and Laud strengthened considerably the power and prerogatives of the Anglican bishops and the ecclesiastical courts. They also tried to impose Anglican bishops and establishment laws on Scotland, triggering an expensive and ultimately futile war with the Scottish Presbyterians. English dissenters who criticized these religious policies were pilloried, whipped, and imprisoned, and a few had their ears cut off and were tortured. When the Parliament was finally called in 1640, it let loose a massive torrent of protests, including the famous Root and Branch Petition and The Grand Remonstrance that called for the abolition of much that was considered sound and sacred in the Church of England.[5]

Some of Parliament's fury was directed at the Crown's repressive political and economic policies. Continuing in his father James I's footsteps, Charles regarded the Parliament not so much as a representative of the people as a functionary of the Crown, to be called or suspended at the monarch's discretion. After 1629, he suspended the Parliament in retaliation for its uncooperativeness, and began imposing fiscal and economic policies that traditionally called for Parliamentary involvement, if not consent. These policies were implemented by a series of new royal officers, notably the widely hated Earl Thomas Strafford. Needing money for his unpopular wars and lavish living, Charles levied crushing taxes on the people without their consent. He feigned a national military emergency that strengthened his royal prerogative and allowed him to institute military tribunals to mete out rough justice against rebels and to fabricate a form of national taxation on all people. He fined the gentry for their failure to become knights and for their purported trespasses on the royal forests. He quadrupled inheritance taxes and receipts from wardships. He sold commercial monopolies to the highest bidders, creating oligarchies that inflicted massive abuses on workers and high prices on consumers. He confiscated private properties and compelled farmers and small businessmen to make loans that were

---

[5] See representative documents on both sides in CPW 1:954–998; Joyce Lee Malcolm, ed., *The Struggle for Sovereignty: Seventeenth-Century English Political Tracts*, 2 vols. (Indianapolis, IN, 1999), 1:21–144.

never repaid. He forced tradesmen and craftsmen into guilds that were subject to strict controls, heavy bureaucracies, and sundry fees. To make all these onerous restrictions work, Charles enhanced the power of the royal prerogative courts and administrators – Star Chamber, Admiralty, High Commission, Requests, Privy Council and more – that enforced royal policies ruthlessly, and stripped away many of the procedural protections and conventions maintained by lawyers in the Inns of Court. Charles's royal officers also interfered deeply in city and rural county governments that had governed local affairs for centuries without much royal involvement. An already weakened economy was made worse by a series of poor harvests and the collapse of the lucrative cloth trade, and by spiraling inflation.[6]

When Parliament was finally called into session in 1640, an unlikely assemblage of aristocrats, gentry, lawyers, artisans, financiers, and religious dissenters united in seizing power with a vengeance. Whipped up by Calvinist preachers who thundered fire-and-brimstone sermons denouncing the tyranny of the English church and state, Parliament worked hard to dismantle Charles's policies.[7] In a series of Acts from 1640 to 1642, Parliament abolished the Star Chamber, the Court of High Commission, and other royal prerogative courts. It also shifted civil and criminal jurisdiction to the common law courts. Parliament limited ship money, forced loans, and other hated taxes and claimed exclusive jurisdiction over all future taxation. It removed many of the new encumbrances on the aristocracy and gentry, restored the traditional uses of the royal forests, and removed some of the monopolies and guilds. It severely truncated the temporal power of the Anglican bishops and removed the clergy from the House of Lords. It tried both Strafford and Laud for their belligerence, sending Strafford to the gallows and Laud to the Tower. And it passed a law that required the King to call Parliament thereafter at least triennially and ideally every year.[8]

When, in response, Charles sought to abolish the Parliament and to arrest some of its leaders for treason, civil war broke out. Royal and Parliamentary forces locked in battle from 1642 to 1646 and again in 1648. Most Calvinist

---

[6] See Lawrence Stone, *The Causes of the English Revolution, 1629–1642* (San Francisco, 1972), 135–144; Christopher Hill, *The Century of Revolution, 1603–1714* (London, 1974). For excerpts and analysis of these royal policies, see J. P. Kenyon, ed., *The Stuart Constitution* (Cambridge, 1986).

[7] See William R. Haller, *The Rise of Puritanism, Or, the Way to the New Jerusalem as Set Forth in Pulpit and Press from Thomas Cartwright to John Lilburne and John Milton, 1570–1643*, 4th printing (New York, 1965); Christopher Hill, *Puritanism and Revolution: Studies in Interpretation of the English Revolution of the Seventeenth Century* (London, 1965).

[8] Berman, *Law and Revolution* II, 201–224, with documents in S. R. Gardiner, *The Constitutional Documents of the Puritan Revolution, 1625–1660*, 3rd rev. edn. (Oxford, 1906), 137–261; Christopher Hill and Edmund Dell, eds., *The Good Old Cause: The English Revolution of 1640–1660, Its Causes, Course, and Consequences. Extracts from Contemporary Sources* (London, 1940).

forces lined up in support of Parliament. Many Anglicans remained loyal to Charles. Charles did not help his cause, however, when it was discovered that he sought secretly to enlist the aid of the Scots, promising them special patronage and protection for Presbyterianism in exchange for their military support. Charles also did not help his cause when he proved powerless to put down the Irish Rebellion of 1641, a bloody uprising of Irish Catholics against Protestant settlers in Ireland.[9] Charles's own fecklessness in dealing with these Irish Catholics, his marriage to a Catholic, and his attempts to ally with Catholic French and Spanish forces compounded the many rumors already circulating that he was moving to restore a Catholic establishment in England. This enraged the Parliamentary forces even more, and provided no end of fodder for Protestant propagandists. They ultimately defeated the royal armies, and took Charles into custody in 1647.

While the Long Parliament, as it came to be called, continued to meet regularly throughout the 1640s, it was stymied by the increased radicality of some of its members, and the sectarian divisions among Separatist, Independent, and Leveller parties. Only in 1649, with the more radical elements finally and forcibly purged, did the Rump Parliament, as the purged body was now called, return to more concerted leadership of the nation. That year, the Rump Parliament passed an Act "declaring and constituting the People of England to be a commonwealth and free state." It abolished the kingship and the aristocratic House of Lords and declared that "supreme authority" resided in the people and their representatives. It formally and finally disestablished Anglicanism and its episcopal ecclesiastical structures, and confiscated large portions of the Anglican Church's property. And most momentous of all, a Parliamentary committee tried the deposed King Charles in a sensational trial, convicted him for treason, and executed him by public beheading. England was now to be a Commonwealth, free from hereditary monarchy, free from an aristocratic House of Lords, free from an established Anglican Church, and subject to "the democratic rule" of Parliament.[10]

This democratic experiment was short-lived. From 1649 to 1653, much political power shifted to a forty-one member aristocratic Council of State, which served alongside the Rump Parliament. This new government did pass several laws that liberalized marriage and divorce laws and that opened large tracts of property held by the church and the Crown. But it also passed severe laws repressing adultery, blasphemy, Quakers, and unlicensed

[9] Crawford Gribben, *The Irish Puritans: James Ussher and the Reformation of the Church* (Darlington, 2003).

[10] Gardiner, *Constitutional Documents*, 262–417; Malcolm, *Struggle*, 1:367–390.

evangelical preaching, and it imposed a number of unpopular taxes on the people. In 1653, Oliver Cromwell, fresh from military victories over the rebellious Irish Catholics and the Scottish Presbyterians who had recognized Charles II as their king, abolished the Rump Parliament and called for new elections. The new Barebones Parliament, as it came to be called, created a new Protectorate government under Cromwell's leadership. This Protectorate government proved even more repressive than the last, and Cromwell's stern moral, military and economic policies were singularly ineffective. After Cromwell died in 1658, his son Richard took over, but he proved too weak to sustain the Commonwealth government, and it collapsed.[11]

In 1660, King Charles II, son of Charles I, returned to England and restored the traditional monarchical government and the traditional Anglican establishment. This Restoration era, too, was short-lived. When his successor, King James II, the other son of Charles I, began to abuse his royal prerogatives as his father had done and to betray his growing Catholic sympathies, Parliament forced him to abdicate the throne in 1688 in favor of the new dynasty of William and Mary. This was called the Glorious Revolution. It established government by the King in Parliament and brought forth the Bill of Rights and the Toleration Act of 1689, two critical constitutional documents that included a number of the rights guarantees initially proposed by the revolutionaries in the 1640s and 1650s.[12]

Just as the St. Bartholomew's Day Massacre and the Dutch Revolt had done, so the English Revolution of 1640–1660 triggered an avalanche of popular writing by Calvinists. More than 22,000 pamphlets, sermons, and tracts were published in these twenty years, denouncing the tyranny of the prior regime, justifying the removal and eventual execution of the monarch, and calling for more robust protections of the "people's rights and liberties."[13] And just as earlier Calvinists had done, English Calvinists pointed first to their historically "chartered rights and liberties" that had been

---

[11] S. R. Gardiner, *History of the Commonwealth and Protectorate, 1649–1656*, 4 vols., repr. edn. (Adelstrope, Gloucestershire, 1988–1989); Blair Worden, *The Rump Parliament 1648–1653* (Cambridge, 1974); J. C. Davis, *Oliver Cromwell* (Oxford, 2001).

[12] In Stephenson and Markham, 599–605, 607–608.

[13] See *Catalogue of the Thomason Tracts in the British Museum* (London, 1906), and samples in Haller, *Tracts*; Don M. Wolfe, ed., *Leveller Manifestoes of the Puritan Revolution* (New York, 1944); A. S. P. Woodhouse, *Puritanism and Liberty Being the Army Debates (1647–9)*, 2nd edn. (Chicago, 1951); Malcolm, *Struggle*. See discussion in William R. Haller, *Liberty and the Reformation in the Puritan Revolution* (New York, 1955); George Yule, *Independents in the English Civil War* (Cambridge, 1958); H. N. Brailsford, *The Levellers of the English Revolution*, ed. Christopher Hill (London, 1961) and analysis of more recent scholarship in David Wooton, "Leveller Democracy and the Puritan Revolution," in Burns ed., *Cambridge History of Political Thought*, 412–442.

tyrannically abridged. For them, the Ur text was the Magna Carta of 1215 that had been issued by the Crown at the behest of the church and barons of England. The Magna Carta guaranteed that "the church of England shall be free and shall have all her whole rights and liberties inviolable." It also guaranteed that all "free-men" were to enjoy their "liberties" – notably various discrete rights to property, marriage, and inheritance, to freedom from undue military service, to jury trial in criminal cases, and to freedom to pay their debts and taxes from property of their own choosing.[14] Some seventeenth-century pamphlets sought simply to broaden these ancient chartered rights and liberties so that they applied to all peaceable churches, not just the Church of England, and to all English citizens and subjects, not just the narrow class of aristocratic "freemen."[15] This argument was not utopian. Sir Edward Coke, the greatest legal mind of England until his death in 1634, had brilliantly documented four centuries of cases and statutes that had slowly expanded some of the guarantees of the Magna Carta since 1215. His 1628 *Institutes of the Lawes of England*, which put these precedents together, became an anchor text of the pamphleteers in the 1640s and 1650s.[16]

Also important to these pamphleteers was the Petition of Right of 1628, which Coke, too, had largely drafted. This document set forth "the diverse rights and liberties" of Englishmen in and beyond the Magna Carta. Parliament had pressed this document on a very reluctant King Charles in exchange for their consent to new taxes to support his unpopular wars. The Petition sought to prevent any further royal abuses of power. It called for no taxation without "the good will" and "common consent" of Parliament; no forced loans from the people; no taking of a man's life or liberty "but by the lawful judgment of his peers, or by the law of the land"; no taking of a man's land, no imprisonment, and no disinheritance without "due process of law"; no suspension of the writ of habeas corpus; no forced quartering of soldiers or mariners in private homes; no criminal prosecution or punishment save for actions that were expressly outlawed by Parliamentary legislation; and no further use of martial law save in true emergencies. All these "rights and liberties," the Petition declared, were to be maintained and enforced "according to the laws and statutes of this realm," without "prejudice" to the people or to their Parliament.[17]

---

[14] In Stephenson and Markham, 115–126.
[15] See discussion in Haller, *Tracts*, I:102–107, III–113, 177–178, 182, with good examples in *ibid.*, II:170ff., III:263–265, 305, 311–315, 365–366.
[16] In *The Selected Writings of Sir Edward Coke*, ed. Steve Sheppard, 3 vols. (Indianapolis, IN, 2003), vol. II, with analysis in Berman, *Law and Revolution II*, 214–216, 238–245, 257–260, 263–269.
[17] In Stephenson and Markham, 450–453.

But despite this further enumeration, the royal government trampled on the people's rights and liberties and suspended Parliament for the next eleven years. The challenge that the pamphleteers faced in the 1640s and 1650s became this: how to restore the people's rights and to reform their government on the strength of more than dusty old charters and precedents that the King could cavalierly disregard. Their answer: England must establish a strong new democratic constitution dedicated to the rule of law and respect for rights.

Some of the most articulate proposals came from the pens of a trio of powerful Puritan pamphleteers – John Lilburne, Richard Overton, and William Walwyn.[18] Each of these figures wrote a large number of pamphlets on his own and bore the scars of the whips, pillories, and harsh imprisonment he endured for his writings and speeches.[19] The three of them collaborated, along with Thomas Prince, on *An Agreement of the Free People of England* (1649), a proposed new constitution for England. In the preamble, the authors lamented the "long and tedious prosecution of a most unnatural cruel, homebred war," occasioned by "the exercise of unlimited or arbitrary power." They also lamented the "multitudes of grievances and intolerable oppressions" inflicted on the people. Invoking the Gospel teaching, "Blessed are the peacemakers" (Matt. 5:9), they called on their countrymen "to make a right use of that opportunity God hath given us to make this nation free and happy, to reconcile our differences, and beget a perfect amity and friendship once more amongst us, that we may stand clear in our consciences before Almighty God [as] the free people of England."[20]

The 1649 Agreement focused carefully on the forms and functions of government. The heart of the government, they insisted, should be a representative Parliament, with annual election of members, and no member serving consecutive annual terms. All persons were eligible to run for office, save Catholics and foreigners. Interference in elections by anyone was a serious crime. Parliament was to stick to its clearly enumerated powers, including importantly the power over foreign policy and diplomacy and the power to impose taxes at an "equal rate" "upon every real and personal estate." Parliament could not interfere with the judiciary or executive at

[18] See Pauline Gregg, *Free-Born John: The Biography of John Lilburne*, repr. edn. (London, 2000); Joseph Frank, *The Levellers: A History of the Writings of Three Seventeenth-Century Social Democrats, John Lilburne, Richard Overton, and William Walwyn* (New York, 1969); H. N. Brailsford, *The Levellers of the English Revolution*, ed. Christopher Hill (London, 1961), esp. 49–142; D. B. Robertson, *The Religious Foundations of Leveller Democracy* (New York, 1951); Jack R. McMichael and Barbara Taft, eds., *The Writings of William Walwyn* (Athens, GA, 1989).

[19] See samples in Haller, *Tracts*; Wolfe, *Leveller Manifestoes*. See also the major collection in the Union Theological Seminary library in New York City, indexed in Charles R. Gillett, *Catalogue of the McAlpin Collection of British History and Theology: Index* (New York, 1930).

[20] In Wolfe, *Leveller Manifestoes*, 400–410. See also prototypes in *ibid.*, 223–234 and 291–303.

the national or local levels, all of which were answerable to the people. Nor could Parliament interfere in military matters, beyond appointment of generals and raising military revenues when needed; other military matters were left to local governments in the areas where the troops were raised. Though the 1649 Agreement was silent on the subject, this trio of authors had earlier called for a comprehensive revision and codification of English law, and for the crafting of new statutes published in plain English and made easily accessible to the people.[21] They had also urged that both the House of Lords and the monarchy be expunged. Other pamphlets offered much more detailed plans for democratic government after the Rump Parliament formally abolished the House of Lords and executed the monarch in 1649.[22]

The 1649 Agreement further called for "the preservation of those safeguards, and securities of our lives, limbs, liberties, properties, and estates" already set out in the 1628 Petition of Right. To these guarantees, the Agreement added several others. It added a strong religious freedom clause that prohibited "any laws, oaths, or covenants, whereby to compel by penalties or otherwise any person to anything in or about matters of faith, religion or God's worship or to restrain any person from the profession of his faith, or to exercise of religion according to his conscience." Also included was a guarantee of freedom from compulsory tithes and appointed clergy and freedom for members of each parish to elect and contract with their own ministers. In earlier pamphlets, the authors had also called for freedom from compulsory oath-swearing and military service for the conscientiously opposed, freedom from "a single form of church government" enforced by excommunication, and a guarantee that no one could "be punished or persecuted as heretical" "for preaching or publishing his opinion in religion in a peaceable way."[23] Also in earlier documents, this same trio had called for a more general freedom of "speaking, writing, printing, and publishing" and freedom of the people for "contriving, promoting, or presenting any petitions" to Parliament concerning their "grievances or liberties."[24]

In addition to freedom of religion (and speech), the Agreement elaborated several criminal procedural guarantees: no prosecution or punishment for crimes in cases "where no law hath been before provided"; a guarantee of the privilege against self-incrimination; the right to call witnesses in criminal defense; the right to jury trial; no capital punishment "except for

---

[21] *Ibid.*, 139, 317.   [22] Malcolm, *Struggle*, 1: 369ff.

[23] Wolfe, *Leveller Manifestoes*, 122–123, 139. For this and the next five footnotes, see also the detailed examples in Haller, *Tracts*, following the entries on point in the index in vol. III.

[24] Wolfe, *Leveller Manifestoes*, 195, 329.

murder" or other "like heinous offences" notably treason; punishments in non-capital cases that were "equal to the offence"; and no imprisonment for private debts. In earlier pamphlets, the three authors had also called for "just, speedy, plain, and unburdensome" resolution of "controversies and suits in law," at least two witnesses "of honest conversation" for capital conviction, and no detention or imprisonment without a warrant.[25]

Finally, the Agreement protected commerce, business, and private property. It included guarantees of tax- and excise-free domestic and foreign trade as well as freedom from government-sponsored business monopolies, a subject of frequent complaint in earlier pamphlets. It forbad any government actions designed to "level men's estates, destroy property, or make all things common," and required officials to make provision for the poor and restore to the families the private estates of criminals, save those who had been executed for treason. This was a truncated version of the authors' wider calls for a comprehensive system of state schools, hospitals, common recreational places, and well-funded poor relief programs.[26]

This was a quite typical list of the rights and liberties that were being pressed by the Puritan pamphleteers in the mid-seventeenth century. They pressed them not merely as positive rights created by the state, but as "natural rights" created by God and to be confirmed by a state constitution. Every person by his or her very nature, the pamphleteers insisted, has equal and natural rights to life, liberty, and property. Every person is equally called by God to be a "prophet, priest, and king" with a natural right and duty to speak, preach, and rule in the community. Richard Overton put it typically in 1646:

For by natural birth, all men are equally alike born to like property, liberty, and freedom, and as we are delivered of God by the hand of nature into this world, everyone with a natural, innate freedom and property (as it were writ in the table of every man's heart, never to be obliterated) even so we are to live, everyone equally and alike to enjoy his birthright and privilege; even all where God by nature hath made him free.

[E]very man by nature [is also] a King, Priest, and Prophet in his own natural circuit and compass, whereof no second [person] may partake, but by deputation, commission, and free consent from him whose right and freedom it is.[27]

The signature phrase – that every person is a "prophet, priest, and king" with natural rights and duties to speak, preach, and rule in the

---

[25] *Ibid.*, 139–140.   [26] *Ibid.*, 268–270, 288–289.

[27] See note 1. See comparable views, e.g., of the Englishman, Robert Browne, a student of Thomas Cartwright and later father of English Independency and Congregationalism, discussed in G. P. Gooch, *English Democratic Ideas in the 17th Century*, 2nd edn. (New York, 1959), 43.

community – became the organizing idiom of a distinctly Calvinist theory of rights and liberties in mid-seventeenth-century England. It served both to integrate many of the rights and liberties inherited from the common law tradition and to cultivate new rights and liberties that the English Calvinists considered essential to democratic constitutionalism. The English pamphleteers did not invent the phrase. It was made famous a century before by Martin Luther in his 1520 manifesto, *Freedom of a Christian*.[28] This tract, Luther's bestseller, was a frontal assault on medieval hierarchical views of society, particularly the Catholic church's claim that the clergy were by nature and calling superior to the laity. Luther thought this claim unbiblical. Building on 1 Peter 2:9, Revelations 5:10, 20:6 and other biblical texts, he argued for the priesthood, prophethood, and kingship of all believers – that everyone in Christendom must be a priest and servant to his peers, that everyone must preach and prophesy God's truth and justice to his neighbor, that everyone must do his part to help rule and govern the affairs of this earthly kingdom. This was a revolutionary idea in sixteenth-century Europe. It challenged not only the traditional authority of the clergy over laity, but eventually all traditional authority structures – rulers over subjects, husbands over wives, parents over children, masters over servants, and more. While Luther's idea ended clerical hegemony in the Protestant world, it soon became a recipe for anarchy and antinomianism, as each new Protestant convert claimed to be a law unto himself, free from the rule of church, state, and family. Chastened especially by the rioting of the 1525 Peasants' Revolt, Lutherans buffered the radical implications of this idea by emphasizing the natural authority of the heads of family, church, and state over their subjects, and the need for all persons to exercise their natural rights and gifts strictly within the limits of their own unique Christian vocations.[29] The Calvinist reformers took over this more limited teaching of prophet, priest, and king.[30] Thus, when in 1562, the Genevan man of letters Jean Morély used the idea of prophet, priest, and king to call for a more democratic form of local church government free from the heavy hand of the Consistory, he was excommunicated and banished for his "pernicious," "slanderous," "scandalous," "schismatic," and "seditious" views. His books were publicly censored and burned, and those who printed or used them were viewed as accessories to heresy (see pages 97–102).

---

[28] *De Libertate Christiana* (1520), in *WA* VII:49–73, translated in *LW* 31:327–377. A shorter German edition, *Die Freiheit eines Christenmenschen*, appears in *WA* VII:20–38.
[29] See Witte, *Law and Protestantism*, 87–117; Witte, *God's Joust, God's Justice*, 49–62.
[30] See *Institutes* (1559), 4.18.16–17; 4.19.28; Comm. 1 Thess. 4:3.

What had been Calvinist theological heresy in the sixteenth century, however, became Calvinist political orthodoxy in the seventeenth. As English Calvinists chafed under increasingly onerous restrictions on their ability to publish, preach, and participate in Parliament and public, they began to seize anew on this signature Protestant phrase of "prophet, priest, and king" to ground their opposition. These royal restrictions, they argued, were compromising their rights to discharge faithfully the duties of prophet-hood, priesthood, and kingship to which God called all Christians. A few radical Calvinist groups, like the Diggers and Ranters, pressed these argu-ments to anti-establishment extremes.[31] But most English Calvinists used the teaching that each person is prophet, priest, and king to press for the natural and constitutional rights of free speech, religious exercise, and democratic participation in the churches and commonwealth of England.

The most articulate and inventive advocate for this theory was the great English poet and philosopher John Milton (1608–1674). In this chapter, I present him as the leader of a new Calvinist reformation of rights in seventeenth-century England. To be sure, Milton was sometimes more individualistic and idiosyncratic in his views than a number of his fellow reformers.[32] Moreover, he eschewed the fierce denominational loyalty that was expected of a Calvinist in England – flitting easily in and out of warring Independent, Presbyterian, Separatist, Leveller, and other Calvinist camps, and consorting readily with Arminians, Baptists, and other "sectaries" in search of new ideas. But Milton was a fair and forceful summarizer and synthesizer of some of the best inherited Calvinist teachings on rights, revolution, and regicide, and he cast these teachings into enduring English forms, especially in his defense of Parliament's execution of Charles. He repeatedly called England to embrace the Calvinist reformation, and to extend its theological teachings into the political and legal sphere. He grounded his own novel arguments about law, religion, and human rights, as a good Calvinist should, first and foremost in the Bible, whose sundry teachings on point were, in his view, underused by his fellow reformers.[33] And he anchored his theory of liberty in the teaching that each and every Christian in the commonwealth is at once a prophet, priest, and king with

[31] Hill, *The World Turned Upside Down*; Nicholas McDowell, *The English Radical Imagination: Culture, Religion, and Revolution, 1630–1660* (Oxford, 2003).

[32] Bernard E. Meland, "John Milton: Puritan or Liberal?" *Encounter* 33 (1972): 129–140; E. M. W. Tillyard, *The Miltonic Setting Past and Present* (Cambridge, 1938).

[33] Elizabeth Tuttle, "Biblical References in the Political Pamphlets of the Levellers and Milton," in *Milton and Republicanism*, ed. David Armitage, Armand Himy and Quentin Skinner (Cambridge, 1995), 63–81.

inherent rights that attach to these three offices. This teaching provided him with a sturdy theological anthropology to support the freedoms of speech, religion, and association that he championed especially. It also inclined him toward more radical democratic reforms of church, state, and family – though he later retreated toward more aristocratic views of government and more patronizing views of the individual.[34]

Milton did not, of course, work alone or represent the views of every English Calvinist, let alone every Englishman. The honor roll of prophets of liberty in seventeenth-century England is long – William Ball, John Bastwick, Richard Baxter, John Bunyan, Henry Burton, Oliver Cromwell, Thomas Edwards, John Goodwin, Thomas Goodwin, Robert Greville, Henry Ireton, John Owen, Henry Parker, Isaac Pennington, William Prynne, John Pym, Henry Robinson, Samuel Rutherford, John Saltmarsh, Roger Williams, Henry Vane, Henry Vane the Younger, John Wildman, Gerrard Winstanley, among many others. Milton did not help his reputation among some of these figures by serving as Secretary for Foreign Languages in Cromwell's increasingly repressive regime, or by escaping persecution even from the Restoration government of 1660. Lacking these badges of courage, many suspected him of duplicity and political trimming. Even Milton's brilliant poems, *Paradise Lost* and *Paradise Regained*, remained for a time under the shadow of James Harrington's utopian *Oceana* (1656), a more stridently democratic tract that earned Harrington a long stay in prison and eventual exile for treason.[35] But, longer term, Milton could not be matched in the power of his rhetoric or the prescience of his teachings. He anticipated and articulated a number of important Calvinist theories of law, religion, and human rights that would become axiomatic for the later common law, and indeed for the Western legal tradition altogether.

JOHN MILTON AND THE ENGLISH REVOLUTION

Milton was at first reluctant to enter the fray of the English Revolution.[36] His father, an Anglican convert from Catholicism, had sent him to

---

[34] Particularly in his *Readie and Easie Way*, *CPW* VII:340–388, 396–463. See context in *CPW* VII:118–228.

[35] See, e.g., H. F. Russell-Smith, *Harrington and his Oceana: A Study of a 17th Century Utopia and its Influence in America* (Cambridge, 1914); Nicholas Phillipson and Quentin Skinner, eds., *Political Discourse in Early Modern Britain* (Cambridge, 1993); Arihiro Fukuda, *Sovereignty and the Sword: Harrington, Hobbes, and Mixed Government in the English Civil Wars* (Oxford, 1997).

[36] Among countless studies on Milton, see Sharon Achinstein, *Milton and the Revolutionary Reader* (Princeton, 1994); Josef Bohatec, *England und die Geschichte der Menschen- und Bürgerrecht*, 3rd edn., ed. Otto Weber (Graz, 1956), 58–116; Robert T. Fallon, *Divided Empire: Milton's Political Imagery* (University Park, PA, 1995); Robert T. Fallon, *Milton in Government* (University Park, PA, 1993);

Cambridge University to study for the Anglican priesthood. After absorbing the sentiments of his Puritan teachers and observing the practices of the established Anglican clergy, however, Milton concluded that "tyranny had invaded the church," and he "thought it better to prefer a blameless silence before the sacred office."[37] He resolved instead, upon earning his master's degree in 1632, to remain a layman and to pursue the quiet life of a scholar and poet. It proved impossible for him to stay out of the political discussion for long. Especially when the Long Parliament began its heated deliberations in 1640, the country was dividing sharply between royal apologists and revolutionary agitators. In early 1641, Milton stepped into the fray, firmly on the side of revolution. He described his motivations as follows:

As long as liberty of speech was no longer subject to control, all mouths began to be opened against the bishops; some complained of the vices of the individuals, others of those of the order. They said it was unjust that they alone should differ from the model of the other reformed churches; that the government of the church should be according to the pattern of other churches, and particularly of the word of God. This awakened all my attention and my zeal. I saw that a way was opening for establishment of real liberty; that the foundation was laying for the deliverance of man from the yoke of slavery and superstition; that the principles of religion, which were the first objects of our care, would exert a salutary influence on the manners and constitution of the republic; and as I had from my youth studied the distinction between religious and civil rights, I perceived that if I ever wished to be of use, I ought at least not to be wanting to my country, to the church, and to so many of my fellow-Christians, in a crisis of so much danger.[38]

In the course of the next twenty years, Milton published some forty major tracts. The most important for our purposes were five tracts against the Anglican establishment,[39] four more calling for the reformation of marriage,[40] a brief tract on education,[41] a comprehensive book of Christian

---

Christopher Hill, *Milton and the English Revolution* (New York, 1977); Merritt Y. Hughes, *Ten Perspectives on Milton* (New Haven, CT, 1965); Denis Saurat, *Milton: Man and Thinker* (London, 1944); Don M. Wolfe, *Milton in the Puritan Revolution* (New York, 1941). See also the detailed introductions and appendices in each volume in *CPW*.

[37] *CPW* I:823.

[38] John Milton, *Second Defense of the People of England*, using translation in *CPW* I:107–108.

[39] *Of Reformation Touching Church-Discipline in England* (1641), in *CPW* I:514–617; *Of Prelatical Episcopacy* (1641) in *CPW* I:618–652: *Animadversions Upon the Remonstrants Defence Against Smectymnuus* (1641), in *CPW* I:653–735; *The Reason of Church-Government* (1642), in *CPW* I:736–861; *An Apology Against a Pamphlet* (1642), in *CPW* I:862–953.

[40] *The Doctrine and Discipline of Divorce* (1643), in *CPW* II:217–356; *The Judgement of Martin Bucer Concerning Divorce* (1644), in *CPW* I:416–479; *Tetrachordon: Expositions Upon the Four Chief Places in Scripture which Treat of Mariage, or Nullities in Mariage* (1645), in *CPW* II:571–718; *Colasterion: A Reply to a Nameless Answer Against the Doctrine and Discipline of Divorce* (1645), in *CPW* II:719–758.

[41] *Of Education* (1644), in *CPW* II:357–415.

doctrine,[42] five tracts on church, state, and tyranny,[43] a famous manifesto on freedom of speech,[44] and two more defenses of the rights and liberties of the English people.[45] All these tracts, save his *Christian Doctrine*, were published between 1641 and 1660. Thereafter, Milton published revised editions of several of them, as well as some brushed-up versions of his student papers. But he devoted most of his last years to completing his two poetic masterpieces, *Paradise Lost* and *Paradise Regained*.[46] While both these poems echoed his favorite legal and political themes, Milton now cloaked his more strident views in allegory to escape the new Restoration censors.

Many of Milton's writings were chock-full of familiar Calvinist teachings, and studded with generous references to Calvin and the Genevan Reformation and to Theodore Beza, Martin Bucer, George Buchanan, François Hotman, Peter Martyr, William Perkins, Pierre Viret, and other Calvinists.[47] Milton lauded the insights and sacrifices of the early English reformer, John Wycliffe, and the Marian exiles, Christopher Goodman, John Knox, and John Ponet – all "fathers in the faith we hold."[48] He also found inspiring the resistance theology and revolutionary politics of fellow

---

[42] *Two Books of Investigations into Christian Doctrine Drawn from the Sacred Scriptures Alone* (c. 1658–c. 1660), in *CPW* VI:117–807.

[43] *The Tenure of Kings and Magistrates* (1649) in *CPW* III:184–258; *Eikonoklastes* (1649), in *CPW* III:335–601; *A Treatise of Civil Power in Ecclesiastical Causes Showing that it is not Lawfull for any Power on Earth to Compel in Matters of Religion* (1659), in *CPW* VII:229–272; *Considerations Touching the Likeliest Means to Remove Hirelings out of the Church* (1659), in *CPW* VII:273–321; *The Readie and Easie Way to Establish a Free Commonwealth* (1660), in *CPW* VII:340–388, 2nd edn., 396–463.

[44] *Areopagitica; A Speech of John Milton for the Liberty of Unlicensed Printing to the Parliament of England* (1644), in *CPW* II:480–570.

[45] *A Defence of the People of England* (1651), in *CPW* IV:285–537; *A Second Defence of the English People* (1654), in *CPW* IV:538–686. A convenient collection of these and other tracts, is provided in the Liberty Fund edition, *Areopagatica and Other Political Writings of John Milton* (Indianapolis, IN, 1999), and I have occasionally used the translations in this collection as noted by LF.

[46] See Barbara Kiefer Lewalski, " 'To try and teach the erring Soul': Milton's Last Seven Years," in *Milton and the Terms of Liberty*, ed. Graham Parry and Joad Raymond (Cambridge, 2002), 175–190; Lewalski, "*Paradise Lost* and Milton's Politics," in *John Milton: Twentieth-Century Perspectives, Volume 4: Paradise Lost*, ed. J. Martin Evans (New York, 2003), 213–240. For analysis of the political themes of his poetry, which lie beyond the scope of this chapter, see in addition to the foregoing, Joan S. Bennett, *Reviving Liberty: Radical Christian Humanism in Milton's Great Poems* (Cambridge, MA, 1989); Laura Lunger Knoppers, "*Paradise Regained* and the Politics of Martyrdom," *Modern Philology* 90 (1992): 200–219.

[47] See, e.g., *CPW* III:240–258; *Commonplace Book*, in *CPW* I:452–462, 477, 484, 506–507 and notes 163–164 below. See also Hughes, *Ten Perspectives*, 220–239; Hughes, "Milton's Treatment of Reformation History in *The Tenure of Kings and Magistrates*," *The Seventeenth Century: Studies in the History of English Thought and Literature from Bacon to Pope*, ed. Richard F. Jones et al. (Stanford, 1951), 247–263.

[48] *CPW* III:251; see further LF 72–77, 87–95, 123–124, 177, 200–201, 258.

reformers in France, Scotland, and the Netherlands, to which he adverted frequently.

Following Calvinist conventions, Milton believed that each person is created in the image of God with "a perennial craving" to love God, neighbor, and self. Each person has the law of God written on his or her heart, mind, and conscience, and rewritten in Scripture, most notably in the Decalogue. Each person is a fallen and fallible creature in perpetual need of divine grace and forgiveness which is given freely to all who ask for it. Each person is a communal animal, naturally inclined to form private, domestic, ecclesiastical, and political associations. Each such association is created by a consensual covenant or contract that defines its form and function and the rights and powers of its members, subject to the limits of natural law. Each association is headed by an authority who rules for the sake of his subjects and who must be resisted if he becomes abusive or tyrannical. All such resistance must be as moderate, orderly, and peaceable as possible, but it may rise to revolt and regicide if necessary in the political sphere. Milton summarized these familiar Calvinist teachings crisply in a famous passage in *The Tenure of Kings and Magistrates* (1649), the first in a series of his tracts that justified the deposition and eventual execution of King Charles:

[A]ll men naturally were born free, being in the image of and resemblance of God himself, and were by privilege above all the creatures, born to command and not to obey: and that they lived so. Till from the root of Adam's transgression, falling among themselves to do wrong and violence, and foreseeing that such courses must needs tend to the destruction of them all, they agreed by common league to bind each other from mutual injury, and jointly to defend themselves against any that gave disturbance or opposition to such agreement. Hence came cities, towns, and commonwealths. And because no faith in all was found sufficiently binding, they saw it needful to ordain some authority, that might restrain by force and punishment what was violated against peace and common right. This authority and power of self-defense and preservation being originally and naturally in every one of them, and unitedly in them all, for ease, for order, and lest each man should be his own partial judge, they communicated and derived either to one, whom for the eminence of his wisdom and integrity they chose above the rest, or to more than one who they thought of equal deserving . . .

The power of kings and magistrates is nothing else, but what is only derivative, transferred and committed to them in trust from the people, to the common good of them all, in whom the power yet remains fundamentally, and cannot be taken from them, without a violation of their natural birthright . . . Since the king or magistrate holds his authority of the people, both originally and naturally for their good in the first place, and not his own, then may the people as often as they shall judge it for the best, either to choose him or reject him, retain or depose though no tyrant, merely by the liberty and right of free born men, to be governed as seems to them best.[49]

These familiar themes were widely espoused in Milton's own day by fellow English and Scottish reformers as politically and theologically diverse as Samuel Rutherford, Henry Parker, John Lilburne, and others. Milton added further biblical proof texts, historical examples, and colorful rhetorical embroidery to these arguments. Particularly his two long and caustic *Defences of the English People* in their regicide of Charles, both tracts directed against the famous Dutch apologist for monarchy named Salmasius, became a classic formulation and made Milton famous on the Continent. But Milton's main arguments were all Calvinist commonplaces.

More original, and more controversial, was Milton's theory of the "real and substantial liberty" that must prevail in a commonwealth sincerely devoted to a "true and holy reformation."[50] Milton developed his theory of liberty in three overlapping phases – almost in a rolling process of logical discovery and rhetorical calculus. His first major concern, articulated in his five anti-clerical tracts of 1641 and 1642, was religious liberty – particularly the need to protect the individual's liberty of conscience and freedom of worship from the "greedy idols" of legally established Anglicanism and the "spiritual tyranny" of idle ceremonies, corrosive customs, and erroneous beliefs. He returned to these religious liberty themes in several of his later writings, culminating in *A Treatise on Civil Power in Ecclesiastical Causes* (1659) and *The Likeliest Means to Remove Hirelings out of the Church* (1659). Each time, he called more loudly for greater freedom of conscience and faith, greater toleration for all peaceable biblical religions, and greater separation of church and state.

Milton's second concern, set out in his four marriage tracts of 1644 and 1645, was domestic or private liberty – principally, at first, the unilateral right of a man to divorce his wife without proof of a traditional fault or impediment. He returned to this theme a few more times, too, and eventually widened his argument into a more general call for "domestic liberty" or "privacy" – the right of a fit man and fit woman to marry, separate, and divorce in accordance with the simple rules of Scripture and

---

[49] *CPW* III:198–206. Milton elaborated his theory of resistance and regicide in *Eikonoklastes*, *CPW* III:335–601 and in *First Defence*, LF 98–313. See further pages 251–252, 270–271 below and Achinstein, *Milton and the Revolutionary Reader*; Wolfe, *Milton in the Puritan Revolution*, 208–248; Hill, *Milton and the English Revolution*, 160–188.

[50] LF, 365. See detailed references on the need for a "second reformation" in his early writings in *CPW* I:524–525, 535–536, 568–569, 601–602, 703–704, 707, 723, 795–799; LF 178–80; see further pages 235–248.

nature alone, the right of parents and teachers to nurture and educate their children in their own beliefs and values, the right of householders to be free from illegal searches and seizures by censors and police, all of which he considered to be essential rights of private domestic association.

When church and state authorities of the day rebuked him for his radical views, Milton folded his arguments for religious and domestic liberty into a more general theory of civil and political liberty. He sketched some of this argument already in his *Areopagatica* (1644), and then expanded it in his *First* and *Second Defence of the People of England* in 1650 and 1654. Now he advocated not just freedom of religious conscience, but freedom of the mind and of opinion altogether; not just freedom of religious worship, but freedom of all speech and public expression; not just freedom to petition God in prayer but freedom to petition authorities in public; not just freedom to enter and exit marriages without interference, but freedom to participate and rule in all associations, including those of church and state. By the time he was finished, Milton had sketched a good bit of the theory supporting the freedoms of religion, speech, and association that would become central to later English and American constitutionalism.

Milton premised his logic of liberty on a fervent belief in Truth, with a capital T – The Truth of God and Scripture, the Truth of reason and nature, all to be discovered by free and robust education and inquiry, experiment and debate. Only when freed from the tyranny of prelates and monarchs, of tradition and custom, of ignorance and error, of censors and licensors, he believed, could divine, natural, and human Truth finally be discovered and developed. Milton also premised his logic of freedom on a fervent faith in the inherent goodness and potential of every English man and woman. Once freed from the tyrannies of church and state and of mind and heart, once steeped in the virtues of Scripture and nature and of learning and literature, every Englishman would seize the Truth with alacrity and soar to splendid new heights of understanding and accomplishment. What England needed to accomplish all this was a "second Reformation" that built on but went beyond the successes of the sixteenth-century Protestant Reformation. This was to be an "outer reformation" that purged the core institutions of family, church, and state from all remaining sources and species of tyranny and brought true domestic, spiritual, and civil liberty. It was also to be an "inner reformation" that purified the heart, mind, and conscience of the tyranny of tried and tired traditions and unleashed a lively spirit of inquiry and learning, a true love of virtue and goodness, a native talent for self-rule and self-direction.

The laws and liberties of conscience

Milton regarded religious liberty as a God-given and God-directed natural right. By being created in God's image, Milton argued, each person has something of the "mind of God" within him, a "conscience or right reason" that gives him access to divine truth and direction and a will and capacity to act on that knowledge. Each person has the law of God written into his or her conscience, heart, and mind. By this law, each person knows the duties owed to God, neighbor, and self. He knows what is right and wrong, good and bad, holy and evil. He knows the cardinal virtues of justice and charity, wisdom and prudence, sincerity and industry. He knows the differences between humility and pride, generosity and greed, envy and love, anger and kindness, lust and continence, gluttony and temperance, sloth and zeal, and other virtues and vices.[51]

Each person, however, has been created with a natural freedom to choose how to act on the knowledge taught by this natural law of conscience. God did not make persons as blind automatons who loved him out of reflex or servile subjects who obeyed him out of fear. Rather than constrain each person under "a perpetual childhood of prescription," Milton wrote, God "trusts him with the gift of reason to be his own chooser." Animals and plants are created simply to obey the laws of nature around them. Persons are created with the freedom to accept or reject the natural laws of conscience or adopt a wide range of conduct in between. That is what it means to be created as an image-bearer of God, with a natural reason and will that reflect something of the reason and will of their Creator.

Many there be that complain of divine Providence for suffering Adam to transgress, foolish tongues! When God gave him reason, he gave him freedom to choose, for reason is but choosing; he had been else a mere artificial Adam, such an Adam as he is in the motions. We ourselves esteem not of that obedience, or love, or gift, which is of force: God therefore left him free, set before him a provoking object, ever almost in his eyes, herein consist his merit, herein the right of his reward, the praise of his abstinence.[52]

None of this changed with Adam's fall into sin. The natural law of conscience remains inscribed on the conscience of each person, and the natural freedom to act in response to these commandments likewise remains in place. "A kind of gleam or glimmering" of the natural law "remains in

---

[51] *CPW* II:128–133; VI:351–354, 514–528; VII:241–244.   [52] *CPW* II:514–521, 527; III:198–206.

the hearts of all mankind," Milton wrote, and it provides them with some light to shine even in their "darkest darkness." But, because of human sinfulness, this natural light and law of conscience by itself is too dim and diffuse to provide much direction for the earnest pursuit of truth and goodness. To find their way to true virtue, to true love of God, neighbor, and self, persons need the fuller spiritual light of God's Word. To exercise their natural freedom meaningfully, they need supernatural direction. "If there were no God," Milton wrote in rebuke of purely rationalist theories of natural law,

there would be no real dividing line between right and wrong. What was to be called virtue, and what vice, would depend upon mere arbitrary opinion. No one would try to be virtuous, no one would refrain from sin because he was ashamed or feared the law, if the voice of conscience or right reason did not speak from time to time in the heart of every man, reminding him . . . that a God does exist, and that everyone must render to him an account of his actions, good and bad alike."[53]

As both the Bible and other ancient sources make clear, God "reminded" persons of the natural law of conscience in different ways over time and across cultures. In the time of Noah and his progeny, God largely left persons to live by the natural law of conscience alone – though He occasionally sent angels and oracles, plagues and miracles to drive home His most important commandments. Some ancients, notably the great biblical patriarchs, Noah, Abraham, Isaac, and Jacob, showed that they understood this natural law and could act on it responsibly, especially when God or an angel paid them a visit. But left to their own devices and desires, even these great patriarchs often lived in open violation of the natural law, much to the consternation of God.[54]

In the time of Moses, therefore, God elected to give his chosen people of Israel a much fuller "reminder" and revelation of His law. On Mount Sinai, God gave the Jews detailed ceremonial, juridical, and moral laws to govern their relations with God, neighbor, and self, to guide their every step on the way to virtue. By the ceremonial law, He taught them how to dress and eat, what rituals and sacrifices to make, how to build their temples and altars. By the juridical law, He taught them the basic rules of how to organize their domestic, political, and spiritual lives. And by the moral law, He taught them a series of "thou shalts" and "thou shalt nots" to guide them in their duties of love to God, neighbor, and self. God entered into a covenant of works with the Jews, promising them eternal blessings if they obeyed this law, eternal curses if they disobeyed. When the people disobeyed, God in

[53] *CPW* VI:382–398, 514–516; VII:241–246. [54] *CPW* I:761–768; VI:351–381, 515–520.

his mercy sent them prophets to remind them of the law, to drive them to repentance, and to assure them of forgiveness if they returned to the law. When they disobeyed again, he sent them for a time into exile in Babylon. But he later returned a faithful remnant to the promised land and restored to them the ancient law of Moses and renewed the covenant of works.[55]

The Mosaic law, while detailed, was only a partial and temporary revelation of God's law, however, Milton argued. The Mosaic law was binding on the Jews alone, and not on other nations. It was tailored to the time and place of the ancient Israelites – first in their exodus, then in their promised land. It was calibrated to break the hardness of heart and habits of sin that the people had repeatedly betrayed when they lived under the law of nature alone. The Mosaic law served, in the words of Galatians 3:24, as a temporary "schoolmaster until Christ came," a form of elementary instruction and discipline, with detailed rules, procedures, and ceremonies designed to teach the Jews step-by-step how to love God, neighbor, and self, and thus prepare themselves and all people for the coming of Christ. As Milton put it in his *Christian Doctrine*:

The Mosaic law was a written code, consisting of many stipulations, and intended for the Israelites alone. It held a promise of life for the obedient . . . Its aim was to make the Israelites have recourse to the righteousness of the promised Christ, through a recognition of mankind's and therefore of their own depravity. Its aim, also, was that all we other nations should afterwards be educated from this elementary, childish, and servile discipline to the adult stature of a new creature, and to a manly freedom under the Gospel, worthy of God's sons.[56]

Now that the "manly freedom" of the Gospel of Christ has come, Milton argued, the Mosaic law has been rendered obsolete. Christ fulfilled the Mosaic law in all its particulars, so that no one would be forced to try to fulfill it again. He absorbed the punishment that the Mosaic covenant of works threatened for the disobedient, so that no one would have to suffer its condemnation any longer. And he offered salvation freely to all who have faith, so that no one would be forced to the humility and futility of a salvation by works. The Gospel of Christ teaches the same fundamental lessons of virtue taught by the law of Moses and by the law of nature – that we must love God, neighbor, and self in all that we do. But the Gospel, and the further exposition of its teachings in the Epistles, instructs us in a very different way than the Mosaic law. The Gospel guides by general principle; it does not govern by specific precept. It sets forth examples and illustrations of how to live by the spirit of the law; it does not set down

---

[55] *CPW* vi:517–519, 666–715; vii:273–321.   [56] *CPW* vi:517.

rules and procedures of how to observe its every letter. It offers the perfect example of Christ to be imitated, but leaves Christ's followers with freedom to follow that example in various peaceable ways under the guidance of the Holy Spirit.[57]

Christ's teaching is "much more excellent and perfect than the law" of Moses, Milton argued. It is a pulsing, breathing law, "written in the hearts of believers through the Holy Spirit," not a stiff, formal law, written on "tablets of stone" by the "finger of God." It is a universal norm intended for all persons, not just a local rule directed to the instruction of a single people. It is an eternal norm that "will last until the end of the world," not just a temporary law assigned in the time of our schooling. It is a law of freedom, not a law of bondage, a covenant of grace, not a covenant of works. The teaching of Christ provides everyone with a better way to understand more clearly the meaning of virtue and love originally taught by the natural law of conscience. It dispels the shadow of sin that obscures proper understanding of this natural law. It restores in all who accept Christ the free exercise of their natural freedom that was lost in the fall into sin.[58]

Milton returned again and again to this theme of the freedom that is available to all who have faith in Christ.

Christian liberty means that Christ our liberator frees us from the slavery of sin and thus from the rule of the law and of men, as if we were emancipated slaves. He does this so that, being made sons instead of servants, and grown men instead of boys, we may serve God in charity through the guidance of the spirit of truth.[59]

To be sure, said Milton, there is a place for detailed rules for actual youngsters who are being educated to understand the "manly freedom" of Christ to be enjoyed when they become adults. Like the ancient Jews, these budding Christians need rules to prepare them for their mature life in Christ. But the goal of this rule-bound schooling is not to enslave them in sin or shackle them to a life of works righteousness. It is rather "to repair the ruins of our first parents [Adam and Eve] by regaining to know God aright, and out of that knowledge to love him, to imitate him, to be like him, as we may the nearest by possessing our souls of true virtue, which being united to the heavenly grace of faith makes up the highest perfection."[60]

Milton piled up sundry New Testament verses to support his thesis about Christian freedom. "For freedom, Christ has set us free." "You were called to freedom." "Where the Spirit of the Lord is, there is freedom." "For the law of the Spirit of life in Christ has set [you] free from the law of sin and

[57] *CPW* VI:415–484. [58] *CPW* VI:521–562; VII:258–261.
[59] *CPW* VI:537. [60] *Ibid.* and *CPW* II:366–367.

death." "You will know the truth, and the truth will make you free." "You will be free indeed." You all have been given "the law of freedom" in Christ, "the glorious liberty of the children of God." You must all now "live as free men."[61]

For Milton, the upshot of all these biblical passages was that "the whole Mosaic law is abolished by the Gospel, [for] its purpose is attained in that love of God and of our neighbor which is born of faith and through the spirit." The Gospel abolishes not only the ceremonial and juridical laws of Moses. After all, these laws prescribe routine actions that any disciplined person can follow if he tries. The Gospel also abolishes the moral laws of Moses, particularly as set forth in the Decalogue. These moral laws are much harder to follow, for they prescribe a way of life that runs directly contrary to our sinful nature. It is the moral law of Moses, not the ceremonial or juridical law, that "disturbs believers and makes them waver." It is the moral law that even the most disciplined and devout soul cannot fulfill in every particular. It is the moral law that "enslaves," "curses," and "shames" everyone, traps them in their sinfulness, and drives them to despair. If there is any part of the Mosaic law that Christ fulfills on our behalf, Milton thus concluded, it is the moral law. Why would Christ lift only the lighter yoke of the ceremonial and juridical laws that some of us can carry, but leave the heavier yoke of the moral law that will eventually crush all of us in our depravity? That is "a false, a nonsensical redemption," said Milton. "It must have been the entire Mosaic law from which Christ redeemed us."[62]

This was a more radical understanding of Christian freedom from law than was traditional among Calvinists. All Calvinists agreed that the ceremonial laws of Moses dealing with sacrifice, diet, ritual, dress, and the like were entirely abolished by Christ. Most further agreed that the juridical laws of Moses dealing with domestic, political, and religious life were also not per se binding – although perhaps they could still be useful guides for modern life and law. But every true Calvinist insisted that the moral law of Moses remains valid and valuable for Christians.[63] Particularly the Decalogue, Calvinists taught, is the best summary of the natural law of conscience and the clearest source of principles of how to love God, neighbor, and self. As such, the moral law has important "uses" in setting a minimal

---

[61] John 8:32, 36; Rom. 6:18, 22, 8:2, 14:4, 5, 10; 1 Cor. 7:23, 8:13; 2 Cor. 3:17; Gal. 3:10, 4:7, 5:1, 13; Heb. 2:15; James 1:25, 2:12; 1 Pet. 2:16 all quoted and discussed in *CPW* VI:529–539; VII:265–272.

[62] *CPW* VI:525–541, 704–715; VII:252–256.

[63] Milton claimed that the Calvinist theologian, Jerome Zanchius, held similar views to his. See *CPW* VI:533, but this is based on a fundamental misreading of Zanchius's views as I understand them from Grabill, *Rediscovering the Natural Law*, 132–149.

morality of duty for all persons and a higher morality of aspiration for true believers. Christ thus preserved the moral law and exemplified its spirit. Christ freed Christians from its curses so that they could be free to try to live by its commandments without fear of condemnation when they inevitably stumbled. The Westminster Confession (1647), drawn up by an assembly of leading Calvinist divines from Scotland and England, put these familiar Calvinist teachings in authoritative form in Milton's day:

The moral law does forever bind all, as well justified persons as others, to the obedience thereof; and that, not only in regard of the matter contained in it, but also in respect of the authority of God the Creator, who gave it. Neither does Christ, in the Gospel, any way dissolve, but much strengthen this obligation.

Although true believers be not under the law, as a covenant of works, to be thereby justified, or condemned; yet is it of great use to them, as well as to others; in that, as a rule of life informing them of the will of God, and their duty, it directs and binds them to walk accordingly; discovering also the sinful pollutions of their nature, hearts and lives; so as, examining themselves thereby, they may come to further conviction of, humiliation for, and hatred against sin, together with a clearer sight of the need they have of Christ, and the perfection of His obedience. It is likewise of use to the regenerate, to restrain their corruptions, in that it forbids sin: and the threatenings of it serve to show what even their sins deserve; and what afflictions, in this life, they may expect for them, although freed from the curse thereof threatened in the law. The promises of it, in like manner, show them God's approbation of obedience, and what blessings they may expect upon the performance thereof.[64]

Milton rejected this familiar Calvinist teaching of the uses of moral law. He called it the false teaching of "converted Pharisees" who "believe that the law should be observed even in Gospel times." No person needs the law to be forced to grace or to confess his sin, Milton argued. God's grace is irresistible, and his forgiveness is complete; law has no value in this new economy of salvation. It makes no sense to say that Christians are freed from the curse of the law but still must live under its strictures. For law by its nature, and especially the moral law, condemns the disobedient and their children. Remember God's words in the Decalogue: "For I, the Lord your God am a jealous God, visiting the iniquity of the fathers upon the children unto the third and fourth generation of those who hate me" (Ex. 20:5–6). And the moral law is not a voluntary regimen: "Moses imposed the literal or external law even on those who were unwilling to receive

---

[64] Westminster Confession (1647), "Article xx. Of the Law of God," in Joel R. Beeke and Sinclair B. Ferguson, *Reformed Confessions Harmonized* (Grand Rapids, MI, 1999), 131–135.

it: whereas Christ writes the internal law of God on the hearts of believers through his Spirit, and leads them as willing followers."[65]

Such sentiments led many critics to regard Milton as a radical antinomian.[66] The Westminster Divines likely had Milton and like-minded "libertines" in mind when they warned solemnly that the spiritual liberty of the Gospel does not give Christians a license for sin or an exemption from authority.[67] In their 1647 Confession, the Divines agreed wholeheartedly that "God alone is the Lord of conscience, and hath left it free from the doctrines and commandments of men, which are, if anything, contrary to his word." But, then they went on to warn:

They who, upon pretence of Christian liberty, do practice any sin, or cherish any lust, do thereby destroy the end of Christian liberty, which is, that being delivered out of the hands of our enemies, we might serve the Lord without fear, in holiness and righteousness before Him, all the days of our life.

And because the powers which God has ordained, and the liberty which Christ has purchased are not intended by God to destroy, but mutually to uphold and preserve one another, they who, upon pretence of Christian liberty, shall oppose any lawful power, or the lawful exercise of it, whether it be civil or ecclesiastical, resist the ordinance of God.[68]

Milton was no antinomian, however, despite his rantings against the "external" moral law. Indeed, he ranted just as loudly against the "licentious" and the "libertines" who sought to live by no law at all on the pretext of Christian liberty.[69] For Milton, Christian liberty is not a freedom to do as one pleases. It is liberty to do one's duties of love to God, neighbor, and self – the original natural duties written into human conscience, now amplified and elaborated by the spiritual duties set out in Scripture. The "first and foremost right and duty" of every free Christian, therefore, Milton wrote, is to read and "interpret the Scriptures; and by that I mean interpret them

---

[65] *CPW* vi:533–536.   [66] See esp. Woodhouse, *Puritanism and Liberty*, 60ff.

[67] Indeed, one of the Westminster Divines, Samuel Rutherford, was the author of *A Free Disputation Against Pretended Liberty of Conscience Tending to Resolve Doubts Moved by Mr. John Goodwin, Dr. Jeremy Taylor . . . Arminians, Socinians . . . Contending for Lawless Liberty, or Licentious Toleration of Sects and Heresies* (London, 1649), a 410 page diatribe against such views. I have not been able to secure a copy of this tract, and am relying on the quotes and analysis of it in John Coffey, *Politics, Religion, and the British Revolutions: The Mind of Samuel Rutherford* (Cambridge, 1997), 53, 135, 153, 214–215, 224, 247. See also Samuel Rutherford, *Lex, Rex, or the Law and the Prince* (1644), facs. edn. (Harrisonburg, VA, 1982); Rutherford, *The Divine Right of Church-Government and Excommunication* (London, 1646). Similar views were offered by another Westminster Divine, Thomas Case, *Spiritual Whoredom Discovered* (London, 1647), a sermon preached before the House of Commons, excerpted in Woodhouse, *Puritanism and Liberty*, 51–52.

[68] Westminster Confession (1647), "Article xx. Of Christian Liberty, and Liberty of Conscience," in Beeke and Ferguson, *Reformed Confessions*, 170–173.

[69] *CPW* i:579–580.

for himself" in order to discern "the mind of Christ." For "the Scripture only can be the final judge or rule in matters of religion, and that only in the conscience of every Christian to himself." This right and duty to study Scripture is not reserved to "the wise and learned," to preachers and theologians who keep the Bible encased in impossible foreign languages and claim a monopoly on what it means. No, it is just as important that "the simple, the poor, the babes [of] every age and sex" have access to the Scripture in their own language and study it on their own terms. For God is "requiring from them the ability of searching, trying, examining all things, and by the Spirit discerning that which is good."[70]

The second right and duty of the free Christian is, in fact, to do "that which is good" – to lead a virtuous life, as those virtues are expounded in Scripture, exemplified by Christ, and explicated by the Holy Spirit. The precise ethics of virtue are for each person to discern and develop on their own, Milton insisted. But the broad outlines of Christian virtue are clear enough to anyone who reads the Scripture or the classic texts of the tradition.[71] These Christian virtues are set out most clearly in the Decalogue and in other moral norms and habits taught by Scripture. Without pausing a moment to say how all this squared with his loud call for "the abolition of the moral law," or with his insistence that each person read and interpret Scripture for himself, Milton poured out nearly 200 pages of "good works" and "virtuous ethics" that a free Christian could and should freely adopt. He worked his way first through the two tables of the Decalogue – setting out in detail, and with a whole tangle of accompanying biblical texts, "the virtues which are related to God," "the duties to be performed towards neighbors and the virtues connected with this," and "virtues connected with a man's duty toward himself."[72] He then worked his way, one by one, through the Commandments to show the principles and practices of virtue that could be found therein and in related passages. His exegesis was sometimes strained, occasionally scandalous. For example, Milton saw no justification for a Sabbath day of worship or rest among Christians, for this was to him an obsolete ritual of the Old Testament Jews that was canceled by Christ's law of love. He saw no justification for monogamous marriage alone, since polygamy and concubinage were customary in the Old

---

[70] *CPW* 1:566–567, 579, 585; 6:537–539, 574–592, 583–584; VII:243–245, 265–267; LF 439.

[71] In *On Education*, Milton set out the classical Greek and Roman texts alongside the Bible that taught, *inter alia*, the virtuous life on the strength of the natural law. See *CPW* II:357–415 and discussion in Jonathan Scott, *Commonwealth Principles: Republican Writing of the English Revolution* (Cambridge, 2004), 170–190.

[72] *CPW* VI:637–807. The quotations are from the main chapter titles in his *Christian Doctrine*. See also many entries on point in his *Commonplace Book*, 1:344–516.

Testament and there was nothing in the Bible to condemn them.[73] In these and other passages, Milton revealed no consistent biblical hermeneutic, and he constantly violated his own first (and frankly silly) rule of interpretation that "each passage of Scripture has only a single sense."[74] But that said, it must also be said that a good bit of his exegesis of the Decalogue and exposition of virtuous Christian living squared easily with the Westminster Catechisms and other conventional English Calvinist handbooks of morality and dogma.[75]

The third right and duty of the free Christian is to imitate Christ in discharging the "three-fold office" of prophet, priest, and king. Christ is a prophet, Milton wrote, in that he was appointed by his father to "educate his church in heavenly truth and to teach the whole will of his father." Christ is a priest in that he "offered himself to God the father as a sacrifice for sinners, and has always made . . . intercession for us." Christ is a king in that he "rules and preserves, principally by internal law and spiritual power, the church which he has bought for himself."[76] Christians, who are followers and imitators of Christ and who live with the mind of Christ, have the right and duty to discharge these same three offices. Christians, too, as prophets, must educate the church and the whole world about "heavenly truth," and "the whole will" and Word of God. They, too, as priests, must sacrifice for others, pray for them, and care for them as loving neighbors. They, too, as kings, must rule themselves by the same "internal law" and so share in the ruling and preservation of Christ's church. "God is decreeing to begin some new and great period in his church," wrote Milton. "We now under Christ [are] a royal priesthood, as we are co-heirs, kings and priests with him."[77]

Ultimately, Milton came closer to traditional Calvinist formulations of the laws and liberties of conscience than his occasional antinomian rantings might suggest. Like Calvinists, he believed in the radicality of human sin and the need for redemption in Christ. He believed in the division between Law and Gospel, between the life of the flesh and the life of the spirit. He believed in stock doctrines like justification by faith alone, the supreme

---

[73] *CPW* VI:351–381, 704–715 and further pages 257–259 below.   [74] *CPW* VI:581.

[75] The Westminster Shorter and Larger Catechisms were standard Calvinist texts in seventeenth-century England and America; see their discussion of the Decalogue in Beeke and Ferguson, *Reformed Confessions*, 130–170. Milton's discussion follows much of the style and substance of the standard text of the Calvinist theologian, John Wollebius, *Compendium Theologiae Christiniae: The Abridgement of Christian Divinity* (London, 1650).

[76] *CPW* VI:430–437.

[77] CPW I:838–839, 844; 2:253–254; VI:570–573; VII:284–286, 301–303, 319–320, citing Gen. 20:7, Ex. 15:20, 19:6; 2 Tim. 2.2; I Pet. 2:5–9, 5:3, Rev. 1:6.

authority of the Bible, the Christian vocation of all believers, the perennial call to imitate Christ, and the absolute sovereignty of God over all things including the human conscience. While he rejected the moral law as an "external law" of slavery, he embraced it as an "internal law" of virtue, which left him with a distinction without much difference. While he rejected the doctrine of the civil, theological, and pedagogical uses of the moral law, he in fact used the moral law in civil, theological, and pedagogical terms to work out his system of virtue ethics for Christians. While he dismissed the Old Testament as a record of slavery from which Christians were free, he in fact parsed every verse of the Old Testament for lessons and examples of virtuous Christian living. On many fundamental questions of the laws and liberties of conscience, Milton differed from the Calvinist tradition more in form than in substance.

Church and state

One question over which Milton had real substantive differences with Calvinists of his day, and even more with Anglicans, concerned the role of church and state, separately and together, in governing religious life. Just because he had such a robust view of individual religious liberty and private biblical judgment, he looked askance on many traditional forms of religious life and religious establishment that were imposed on individual Christians. Just because he embraced the doctrine of the prophethood, priesthood, and kingship of all Christians, he viewed with skepticism any laws that abridged the Christian's right and duty to speak, to worship, and to rule within the church. As he translated these arguments about individual religious liberty and Christian office-bearing into strong reforms of church and state, it became clear that these arguments applied to other areas of life beyond church–state relations and to other types of rights besides religious rights. What began as a difference in accent with conventional Calvinists, eventually became a real difference of ideas about the reformation of society, politics, and rights, as we shall in the next two sections. But his arguments started with the church – first the established Anglican Church and eventually the established Presbyterian church, as well.

Milton's attack on the established Church of England came in five early rhetorically violent tracts in 1641 and 1642, whose main themes he elaborated in more sober and general terms in several later writings. Milton first took aim at the legally established Anglican doctrines, liturgies, and morals of his day. Many of these were, in his view, old Catholic traditions that had been absorbed into the "half papalist" Anglican Church created by Henry VIII a century before. Rather than live by "the simple Truth" of Scripture and the "primitive Christianity" of Christ and his apostles, Milton argued, the Anglican Church has fabricated a massive network of "idle and idolatrous doctrines," "false and foolish customs," "erroneous and embellished traditions" all designed to "entangle" and "strangle" the free Christian conscience. Rather than lead Christians in a humble and quiet life of charity, prayer, and Scriptural meditation, the church has adopted all manner of elaborate liturgies, masses, cults, and ceremonies that stink with the "vomited paganism of sensual idolatry." Rather than let individual Christians search the Scripture for themselves under the guidance of the Holy Spirit, the church has bound and tied them to calendars and liturgies, rituals and lectionaries, Sabbath days and holy days that smother every breath of private Christian inspiration, imagination, and innovation. Those teachings of Christianity that should be indifferent are made essential. Those that should be left discretionary are made dogmatic. All this error and idolatry masquerading as Christianity, Milton charged, has caused a mighty "wrenching and spraining of the text" of Scripture and a massive "strangling and choking" of its teachings of Christian liberty.[78]

Milton took even sharper aim at the Anglican clergy who, following their medieval Catholic brethren, lord it over the laity in worldly luxury and moral laxness. "To do the work of the Gospel, Christ our Lord took upon him the form of a servant," Milton wrote with intended irony. "[H]ow can his servant in this ministry take upon him the form of a lord?" But lords the Anglican clergy have certainly become – and not just those high clergy in the House of Lords. In every house of worship, Anglican clergy have become landed aristocrats, with vast properties, powers, and prerogatives at their call. Milton railed in disgust at the Anglican clergy of his day. They are "a tyrannical crew," a "corporation of imposters," "halting and time-serving" "Egyptian taskmasters of ceremonies," a "heap of hard and loathsome uncleanness," a "whip of scorpions," "illiterate and blind guides," "a wasteful band of robbers," "a perpetual havoc and rapine," "a continual hydra of mischief and molestation," "importunate wolves," "wild boars," "locusts and scorpions," "downtrodden vassals of perdition," and on and on.[79]

Milton singled out for special criticism the various clerical privileges and habits that so galled English Calvinists and other dissenters – the Anglican clergy's exemptions from taxation and immunities from prosecution, the

---

[78] *CPW* 1:520–527, 561, 584–585, 592–593. See also notes in *CPW* 1:108–128 and in Wolfe, *Milton in the Puritan Revolution*, 45–49.
[79] *CPW* 1:113–115.

high compulsory tithes and religious taxes that supported their extravagant sanctuaries, sinecures, and cemeteries, their lush clerical gowns, surplices and tippets, their ornate icons, artwork, and altars, all neatly railed off from any touch or use by the laity. He attacked the English church courts, those hated and powerful tribunals that controlled the intimate and interior lives of the laity with their "dreadful works of holy discipline, censure, penance, excommunication, and absolution," to say nothing of their rapacious fees and fines. These clerical "leeches" "suck and suck the kingdom" of its life blood. "What a mass of money is drawn from the veins into the ulcers of the kingdom this way; their extortions, their open corruptions, the multitude of hungry and ravenous harpies." What a "loud stench of avarice, simony, and sacrilege" belches out of these "unctuous and epicurean paunches" purporting to be Christ's humble servants in his church, even while living as lavish lords and preying as greedy thieves. All such clerical exploitation violates not only our religious liberty but "all the right[s] we have to our own bodies, goods, and liberties" guaranteed since the Magna Carta (1215).[80]

What makes all this clerical exploitation even worse, Milton continued, is that the clergy are appointed to office without the consent or control of their congregants. The "primitive church" was a "democratic institution," Milton argued at length, citing very selectively from the ancient sources. Early Christians regarded clergy and laity alike as priests before God, each with different Christian offices and vocations to fulfill in the broader community. Following biblical precedents, they elected them to the offices of priests, deacons, presbyters, or bishops. And these elected clergy were all held accountable to the laity and voted out when they failed in office or became abusive. Indeed, "the voice of the people . . . in episcopal elections" and church governance "was so well known" by the third century that even the pagan Roman emperor "desired to have his governors of provinces chosen in the same manner."[81]

All this changed dramatically in the fourth through sixth centuries, however, when the Roman Emperor Constantine and his imperial successors Romanized the church, even as they Christianized the Empire. Particularly damaging was that the emperors elevated the bishops into "prelatical monarchs" made in their own imperial image. Even more damaging was that they made clerical appointments and removals exclusive "prelatical prerogatives," ending three centuries of clerical elections by and accountability to the people in the pews. "Monarchy and prelatry" were thus brought

[80] *CPW* I:537, 545, 547–548, 554–558, 568–569, 576–577, 589–593, 603, 606, 610–614, 617; *CPW* III:239–241.

[81] *CPW* I:114–115, 539–549, 573–577, 624–652; VI:795–796; VII:319–320.

together into a "most unholy union" whose inevitable progeny would be spiritual tyranny. Soon enough, state-appointed bishops no longer served their flocks in love with "brotherly equality, matchless temperance, frequent fasting, incessant prayer and preaching, continual watchings and labors in [their] ministry." Instead, they "forsook their first love, and set themselves up two gods instead, mammon and their belly, then taking advantage of the spiritual power which they had on men's consciences, they began to cast a longing eye to get the body also, and bodily things into their command."[82]

We still maintain this absolute monarchy and tyranny in the church today, Milton charged, even though the state has since been partly democratized through Parliamentary elections. Why can't church members at least elect local clergy in the same way that they elect local members to the House of Commons? "Should not the piety and conscience of Englishmen as members of the church be trusted in the election of pastors to functions that nothing concern a monarch" – especially since they are already trusted to the election of Parliamentarians whose functions so very much concern the monarch? "[H]aving already a kind of apostolic and ancient church election in our state," should not at least that much local election also prevail in the "state church"?[83]

And, why indeed, should there be a "state church" and "statute-religion" at all, Milton demanded – now widening his attack to include the emerging Presbyterian establishment in England.[84] Why should Christianity of any sort be established by human laws? Why should its clergy be ruled by secular magistrates? After all, Christ's most famous political admonition was to "render to Caesar the things that are Caesar's, and to God the things that are God's" (Matt. 22:21). The early church lived faithfully by this Gospel teaching for three centuries, and thrived and grew despite the bitter persecution of those "separated Caesars." It was the same fourth-century Caesar, Constantine, who upon conversion to Christianity first defied this basic political teaching of Christ, Milton charged. It was Constantine who first took "the things that are God's" and made them "the things that are Caesar's." It was Constantine who prescribed the church's doctrines and liturgies and punished its heretics and enemies. It was Constantine who convened the church's councils and synods and controlled its polity and

---

[82] *CPW* 1:576–577 and quotes in Wolfe, *Milton in the Puritan Revolution*, 48. See further *CPW* 1:823–834.

[83] *CPW* 1:600.

[84] As he put it memorably already in 1646, protesting the state establishment of Presbyterianism: "New Presbyter is but Old Priest writ Large." Quoted in Wolfe, *Milton in the Puritan Revolution*, 82–83. See further his *Observations Upon the Articles of Peace* (1649), in *CPW* III:259–334 and in *The Tenure of Kings and Magistrates* (1649), *CPW* III:238. See notes in *CPW* III:1–9, 92–97, 130–136, 196.

property. It was Constantine who appointed the church's bishops and clerics and collected its tithes and taxes. What Constantine and his successors
first established in ancient Rome, the church has maintained for more than
a millennium, with only a few brave Church Fathers and early Reformers
dissenting. To this day, most Protestants and Catholics alike lie "enthralled"
and "seduced" by Constantine's "lavish superstition" – that the establishment of Christianity by law and that the rule of church by state are essential
to the survival of each.[85]

But Christianity does not need laws to survive, nor does the church need
the state to thrive. The very opposite is true, Milton insisted. Separation
and division – not "conflation and confusion" – of church and state, and
of law and faith, are the proper way of Christ. We "should not suffer the
two powers, the ecclesiastical and the civil, which are so totally distinct, to
commit whoredom together, and, by their intermingled and false riches, to
strengthen indeed in appearance, but in reality to undermine, and at last
to subvert one another." Milton returned to this theme again and again,
calling it "absurd" that Christians have "not learned to distinguish rightly
between civil power and ecclesiastical." The Bible makes clear that "Christ's
kingdom is not of this world," and his church "does not stand by force and
constraint, the constituents of worldly authority." Nor is Christ's church like
some "vine" that "cannot subsist without clasping about the elm of worldly
strength," or some building that cannot support itself "without the props
and buttresses of secular authority." To the contrary, Milton argued, "it is
because the magistracy and the church have confuse[d] their jurisdictions"
that "all Christendom" has reaped a "bitter harvest" of crusades and wars,
inquisitions and pogroms, bloodshed and persecution. It is because church
and state have "conflated" their powers and offices that the church has
become "a pontifical despotism decked out, under pretense of religion,
with the spoils of civil power, which it has seized unto itself contrary to
Christ's own precept."[86]

"Christ's own precept" is that the "main foundation" of the church and
"the complete text" of the Christian faith is the Bible. It is blasphemy for
anyone to add to or subtract from the Bible by human laws and traditions
in their governance of the church and the Christian faith. Christ's further

---

[85] *CPW* 1:551–557, 573–577; 11:257–8; vii:260–268, 279–280, 290–294, 307–308; LF 157–158, 162–165, 197–198.

[86] LF 111–112, 406–407; *CPW* vi:798–799; vii:253, 255, 262–268; 1:554; LF 111–112. In his *Commonplace Book*, Milton, referring to Machiavelli, wrote: "That the combining of ecclesiastical and political government (when, that is to say, the magistrates acts as the minister of the Church, and the minister of the Church acts as magistrate) is equally destructive to both . . . The opinions of men concerning religion should be free in a republic, or indeed under good princes." *CPW* 1:476.

precept is that the ruler of this church is not some mighty magistrate or pompous prelate. The ruler of the church is each and every humble individual Christian who meditates on and lives by the "simple Truth" of the Bible. Every Christian is called by Christ to be not only his prophet and his priest, but also his king, his ruler, within the church. Every Christian has the "Word of God before him," "the mind of Christ within him," and "the Spirit of God" to guide him in his understanding. "No man or body of men in these times can be the infallible judges or determiners in matters of religion to any other men's consciences but their own." This is "God's own birthday gift to us," "the true birth-right of every true believer," the "sovereign prerogative" of every "kingly individual" called to rule in Christ's church.[87]

But the church is more than the sum of its conscientious kingly parishioners just as the state is more than the sum of its sovereign individual subjects. Here Milton converted the familiar contract theory of the state into a contract theory of the church as well. Just as each state is voluntarily created by a consensual covenant among like-interested individuals, so each church is created by "common consent" among "like-minded believers," who have "willingly joined themselves in a covenant of union." Just as state subjects agree to alienate a portion of their natural rights to elected state authorities in order to secure peace, order, and proper rule of law in the community, so church members agree to share a portion of their religious rights with other church members in order to secure proper preaching, discipline, and diaconal care in their communion. Just as citizens of the state may remove elected political officials who betray their office and become tyrants, so parishioners in the church may defrock elected church officials who betray the Scripture and become tyrants or heretics. Just as individuals may choose to enter, leave, or abstain from a local political community without compulsion or deterrence, so individuals may choose to enter, exit, or stay outside the local church without coercion or penalty.[88]

This analogy between the formative contracts of church and state was not perfect, of course. Milton insisted that each church was bound to follow the detailed teachings and examples of the Bible in a way that the state was not. As he read the Bible, this meant that preachers, presbyters, and deacons were fine, but that prelates, bishops, and monks were not. It meant that

---

[87] *CPW* I:844; VI:797–799; VII:242–247, 262; LF 157.
[88] *CPW* III:240–247; VI:563–574; LF III–112. See further Victoria Kahn, *Wayward Contracts: The Crisis of Political Obligation in England, 1640–1674* (Princeton, 2004) and Kahn "The Metaphorical Contract in Milton's *Tenure of Kings and Magistrates*," in Armitage, Himy and Skinner, *Milton and Republicanism*, 82–105.

congregational elections for church offices were required, and that prelatical or political appointments of clergy were barred. It meant that congregational meetings were expedient, but that general councils were unfounded. It meant the voluntary contributions to the church's coffers were encouraged, but that mandatory tithing of parishioners was banned.[89] It meant that clerical marriage was allowed, but that mandatory celibacy was not. It meant that clerical proclamations on justice were fine, but that "clerical disturbance in civil affairs" was not. It meant that church cooperation with the state was licit, but that church dependence on the state was "poison." And it meant that spiritual discipline, even "the horrid sentence" of excommunication, was allowed in the church, but that disciplinary actions against the life or limb, or any worldly possession of church members were strictly forbidden in the church.[90]

In scores of pages, scattered over twenty years of publications, Milton sought to prove one-by-one from Scripture that these were the practices and prohibitions that Christ decreed for his church. But he insisted that the exact combination and elaboration of these biblical teachings be left entirely to each congregation's discretion. He insisted further that each individual Christian be left free to be a church of one so long as he or she lived by the Bible.[91] After all, he reminded his readers, while the organized church is a good institution ordained by Christ, "the church itself cannot, much less the state, settle or impose one title of religion . . . but can only recommend or propound it to our free and conscientious examination." "No man, no synod, no session of men, though called the church, can judge definitively the sense of Scripture to another man's conscience," he wrote in 1659. Milton, the schoolboy Anglican and one-time Presbyterian, was now a committed Congregationalist, with strong preferences for church democracy and Christian pluralism and little patience for hierarchical and conciliar churches – whether Anglican, Presbyterian, or Catholic.[92]

While the church may operate only on the "inner man" and only by "persuasion," Milton continued, the state may act only on the "outer man" and never for religious reasons. The state was ordained by God and is formed by political contract for the sake of protecting external order and peace and preserving "the people's rights and liberties" – including notably their religious rights and liberties. The state deals exclusively with "the body

---

[89] Milton was particularly incensed that the Presbyterian establishment sought to collect tithes from all Englishmen. Though he had already denounced mandatory tithing several times, he devoted a blistering pamphlet against this practice in 1659, in *CPW* VII:273–321.

[90] *CPW* I:835–847; III:240–241; VI:573–613; VII:244–247, 258.

[91] *CPW* VI:568. [92] *CPW* I:761–767; VII:247–248, 258, 522–530.

and the external faculties of man," "his life, limbs, and worldly possessions." The state may set limits on how a man may use his liberty and property so that the "public peace and private rights" of others are respected and protected. State officials may take his goods from him by "just taxes" or by fine or forfeiture following "due" prosecution or lawsuit. They may even use force and violence against the outer man when appropriate and proportionate to punish crimes, to right wrongs, or to wage wars.[93]

But state officials have no power to use force or violence against "the inner man and his religion." No person has "power to give them such a commission" in the political contract, and the religious "conscience is not [their] province." To the contrary, religion is by nature and Scripture the unalienable right of the individual: it cannot be given away or taken away by anyone, especially by a state official. Milton returned to this point repeatedly in the later 1640s and 1650s. "Both our belief and practice, which comprehend our whole religion, flow from faculties of the inward man, free and unconstrained by themselves by nature [and] incapable of force." "[N]either traditions, councils nor canons of any visible church, much less edicts of any magistrate or civil session, but the Scripture only can be the final judge or rule in matters of religion." "If any man," particularly a political official, "shall pretend that the Scripture judges to his conscience for other men, he makes himself greater not only than the church, but also than the Scripture, [which is] a presumption too high for any mortal."[94]

"Christ hath a government of his own," Milton continued, "sufficient of itself to all his ends and purposes in governing his church; but much different from that of the civil magistrate." Christ's government "deals only with the inward man and his actions, which are spiritual and to outward force not liable." Through this spiritual government, Christ and his church "show us the divine excellence of his spiritual kingdom, able without worldly force to subdue all the powers and kingdoms of this world, which are upheld by outward [force] only." In this Christian kingdom and spiritual government, "the Gospel should not be made a matter of compulsion, and faith, liberty, and conscience cannot be." The magistrate has "neither right nor can do right by forcing religious things." If he tries, he will get only "counterfeit performances" and "feigned exercises" of a false faith.[95]

---

[93] *CPW* I:835–836; VI:797–799; VII:242–247, 262; LF 287.
[94] *CPW* I:844; VI:612, 797–799, VII:242–247, 256–262. See also Woodhouse, *Puritanism and Liberty*, 229–230.
[95] *CPW* VI:612–614, 797–99; VII:255, 262–268.

It is no answer to this argument, Milton insisted, to point to the example of Old Testament judges and kings, who did use state law and coercive force to govern biblical Judaism. That was the time of the Law. This is the time of the Gospel. That was a time of "bondage and works," when believers were "children" for whom "force was not unbefitting." This is the time of "grace, manhood, freedom and faith; to all which belongs willingness and reason, not force." That was a time when the king was custodian of the two tables of the Decalogue. This is a time when the two tables of Decalogue are the custodians of us all. That was a time when church and state were united, and when kings had a detailed written law of God to apply and "immediate divine direction" to guide them. This is a time when church and state are separate, and when the law of God lies "unwritten" in each man's conscience to be discovered and applied for himself. "If church and state shall be made one flesh again as under the law," said Milton, "let it be with all considered that God who then joined them hath now severed them."[96]

It is also no answer to cite Romans 13 and other New Testament passages that point out that "the powers that be are ordained by God" and that we must obey them as we obey God. No one doubts that legitimate authorities deserve obedience, Milton allowed, for "without magistrates and civil government there can be no commonwealth, no human society, no living in the world." But nothing in Romans 13 "gives judgment or coercive power to magistrates . . . in matters of religion." Indeed, a whole series of biblical passages state the exact opposite. Just read John 4:21–23, Romans 14:5, 9–10, 1 Corinthians 7:23, 9:19, 2 Corinthians 3:17, Galatians 2:16, 4:3, 9–10, 26, 5:13–14, and Colossians 2:8, 16, 23, among many other texts, Milton urged. The force of all these biblical texts read together is that we must obey magistrates, but only so long as they hold to their political contract and stay within their civil jurisdiction – keeping watch over "taxes," "revenues," "bad conduct," and other civil subjects that the New Testament identifies by name. But if magistrates encroach on the spiritual jurisdiction of God, they must be resisted by those whom God has ordained as sovereigns of the spiritual realm on earth, namely, each and every individual Christian armed with the Gospel and its weapons of freedom.[97]

---

[96] *CPW* VII:251–252, 258–260, 271.

[97] *CPW* VI:611–612; VII:250–252, 262–263; LF 162–168. See also Milton's debunking of the traditional teaching of compulsion grounded in Christ's parable of the master who threw a feast for his son, and when stood up by his invited guests sent out his servants to the highways and the byways to "compel" them to come in. This is "scarce authority" on which to rest government coercion in religion, said Milton, when texts like Is. 55:1, Mark 16:16, John 6:44, 7:37, Rev. 3:18, 22:17, and the like all speak of invitation and persuasion to the faith. See *CPW* VII:260–262.

It is finally no answer to say that each nation must have an established faith, and that the state must work to ensure that the national church remains "schismless." Nothing in the New Testament commands this, Milton insisted, and nothing in history commends it. Indeed, it is far better for the state to tolerate a lively plurality of Christian churches than to impose "a numb and chill stupidity of the soul, an unactive blindness of mind upon the people by their leaden doctrine" and "to persecute all knowing and zealous Christians" who might read Scripture differently. Rather than let "fresh sprouts of new ideas" spring forth under the bright light of the Holy Spirit, national religious establishments keep the national church in "frozen captivity" to a "counterfeit, coerced, and conceited uniformity." This is no way to discover Christian truth or to prevent religious schism in a nation. "The timeliest prevention of schism is to preach the Gospel abundantly and powerfully throughout all the land, to instruct the youth religiously, to endeavor how the Scriptures may be easiest understood by all men." Christian truth will come from "a free and lawful debate at all times by writing, conference or disputation of what opinion soever, disputable by Scripture." If such sincere, honest, and open disputation on Scripture is not only tolerated but encouraged by the state, Milton argued, "I trust God will manifest" what is truth and what is falsehood and heresy. Indeed, God's Truth will eventually come riding triumphantly down "a lane of sects and heresies on each side."[98]

The state has but two tasks in policing this "lane" of Christian truth, said Milton. First, the state must respect and tolerate the religious worship and exercise of each and every sect that is founded and grounded in Scripture – "however erroneous" their Scriptural interpretation may appear to be. Only sects that are not peaceable and that violate "the life, limb, and worldly possessions" of their own members or any other can be subject to state sanction and control.[99] But second, the state must outlaw and "extirpate" heretics, whom Milton variously defined as "enemies of the Gospel," and those who "maintain traditions or opinions not probable by Scripture."[100] In his earlier writings, Milton hinted vaguely that the class of heretics included Jews, "Mahometans," "atheists" and those given to "popery, and open superstition."[101] By 1659, he had narrowed his charge of heresy to one: "the papist only; he is the only heretic," for he "counts all heretics but himself."[102]

---

[98] *CPW* I:779–800; VII:249–250.   [99] *CPW* I:797; VI:611–612; VII:258.
[100] *CPW* VII:246–249.   [101] *CPW* II:565; III:311–313, 326, 574; VII:318–319.
[102] *CPW* VII:249.

Before the Reformation, Milton wrote bitterly, Catholics took "the virgin Truth" of Scripture, and "hewed her lovely form into a thousand pieces, and scattered them to the four winds." Since the Protestant Reformation, and despite its lessons, Catholics continue to "exact" their own beliefs and practices "above Scripture" and "against Scripture" and denounce "anathemas" on any who do not follow the pope and the prelatical councils whom they have put in Christ's place at the head of the church. Catholicism is not so much "a religion, but a Roman principality," "a Catholic heresy against Scripture, supported mainly by a civil, and except in Rome, by a foreign power; justly therefore to be suspected, not tolerated by the magistrate of another country." Indeed,

all men who are true Protestants . . . know not a more immediate and killing subverter of all true religion than Antichrist, whom they generally believe to be the pope and Church of Rome. [H]e who makes peace with this grand enemy and persecutor of the true church, he who joins with him, strengthens him, gives him root to grow and spread his poison.[103]

Milton's theory of religious rights and liberties thus remained very Protestant both in inspiration and in application. His theory was based, in part, on a profound critique of the Catholic tradition, and its vestiges as he saw them in his Anglican and Protestant world. Milton denounced, with as much vehemence as the early Luther, the sacramental idolatry, theological superstitions, human traditions, canon laws, ecclesiastical courts, and prelatical hierarchies that for so long dominated the church. He also denounced Constantinianism, that fourth-century "superstition" that traded the simple truths and democratic structures of the early church for a Latinized and Romanized tyrannical state church wholly abstracted from the Scripture, forcibly imposed on the people, and utterly devoid of anything but greed, corruption, and craven dependence. Since Constantine, the church has suffered "many dark ages, wherein the huge overshadowing train of error had almost swept all the stars out of the firmament."[104]

It was the Protestant Reformation, Milton insisted, that first "struck through the black and settled night of ignorance and anti-Christian tyranny." It was Wycliff, Hus, Zwingli, Luther, Calvin, Bucer, Martyr, Ponet, Knox, Goodman, Gilby, and others who "dared to dissent" and "defame" the religious establishment in order to bring "bright and blissful Reformation (by divine power)." Through their efforts "was the sacred Bible sought out of the dusty corners where profane falsehood and neglect had thrown it, the schools opened, divine and human learning raked out

---

[103] *CPW* II:549; VII:249, 253–254, 429. See notes in *CPW* VII:179.   [104] *CPW* I:524–525, 569.

of the embers of forgotten tongues." It was the Reformers who used the Bible to "set up a standard for the recovery of lost Truth," who blew "the first evangelical trumpet to the nations, holding up, as from a hill, the new lamp of saving light to all Christendom." It was the Reformers who gave the church the vernacular Bible, and who claimed it the fundamental right and duty of each and every Christian to read and interpret the Bible under the inspiration of the Holy Spirit. It was the Reformers who called Christians to find their vocations in the world, to answer God's call to be prophets, priests, and kings in imitation and service of Christ.[105]

While these biblical Protestant teachings have found ready application on the Continent – in Lutheran Germany and Scandinavia and in Calvinist Switzerland, France, and the Netherlands – as well as in Scotland, England has not had "a complete reform" Milton lamented. Henry VIII and his successors ultimately replaced one tyrant for another at the head of the church, and retained too many "tattered rudiments," "rotten principles," and "idolatrous superstitions" of Catholicism. But God has "ever had this island under the special indulgent eye of his providence." And now God, a century later, is calling England to "a second Reformation," a "holy" and "better" Reformation. Its "common rule and touchstone is the Scripture" to be applied with "more conscience, more equity, [and] more Protestantly" than ever before.[106]

The Reformation of religious rights and liberties that Milton envisioned for England, however, was more radical than anything that obtained on the Protestant Continent, and more sweeping than most of his fellow English Calvinists could countenance. For Milton, the achievement of "real and substantial" religious liberty required five major reforms. First, and foremost, religious liberty required liberty of conscience for all peaceable biblical believers, the liberty of each person to search out and act on the natural law within him and the biblical texts before him without coercion, control, or penalty from either church or state. Liberty of conscience, Milton wrote, is our "dearest and most precious" right.[107] Second, religious liberty meant freedom of the individual to worship, dispute, and publish freely on the strength of his faith, and freedom to enter and exit a church and community of his own choice or to forgo church association altogether. Third, religious liberty meant state toleration of every peaceable church that was grounded, however unusually, on a sincere and earnest interpretation of the Bible (Catholics notably excluded). Fourth, religious liberty

---

[105] *CPW* I:523–525, 568–569, 703–704, 723, 878; II:550–553; III:240–258.
[106] *CPW* I:524–541, 600–601, 703–704, 723, 795–799; VII:248–249.   [107] *CPW* VII:456.

meant separation of the offices and operations of church and state, leaving the church free to organize and support itself voluntarily and democratically, and relieving the state of the burden of collecting tithes, operating courts, or maintaining properties on the church's behalf. Finally, religious liberty required that there be no legal establishment of a single national religion, but instead a free and open disputation in the nation of a plurality of religions based on Scripture.

Here, in prototypical Protestant form, Milton had set out the core principles of religious liberty that would come to dominate the common law in the following centuries – liberty of conscience, free exercise of religion, equality of a plurality of faiths before the law, separation of church and state, and (outside of England) disestablishment of a national religion.[108] Each of these five principles of religious liberty set forth by Milton had ardent advocates among other English Calvinists of his day. Some fellow reformers pressed one or two of these principles further than Milton dared, particularly in advocating toleration for Catholics and in criticizing the church's power of excommunication, which Milton still supported. But few Calvinists embraced all five of these religious liberty principles together, or cast them in such stridently individualistic terms as Milton. Most Presbyterians and some Independents, such as Samuel Rutherford, Henry Ireton, and John Goodwin, embraced liberty of conscience and toleration for all Protestants and called for some measure of separation between church and state and democratic election within each. But they also still maintained a religious establishment and insisted on state contributions to religion. Some Levellers and Diggers, like Richard Overton and Gerrard Winstanley went further than Milton in calling for toleration of Catholics, Jews, and various peaceable non-biblical religions. But even these reformers ultimately did not abandon the idea of a legally established religion and state-supported church. Only the most radical reformers of his day, John Lilburne, John Saltmarsh, William Walwyn, and Roger Williams, could stand comfortably on every plank of the platform of religious liberty that Milton had built.[109] None of these Reformers, however, save Roger Williams, anchored this platform of religious liberty as firmly as Milton did. But, ten years before Milton became active, Williams had already left for Puritan New

---

[108] See American formulations in my *Religion and the American Constitutional Experiment*, 41–70.

[109] For comparisons of Milton's view with others in his day, see *CPW* II:53–136; III:1–100; VII:27–57, 77–95; W. K. Jordan, *The Development of Religious Toleration in England*, 4 vols. (Cambridge, MA, 1938), vols. III–IV; Wolfe, *Milton in the Puritan Revolution*, 27–119; Haller, *Tracts*, 1:33–98, III–114 and representative texts in *Tracts* vols. II–III; Wolfe, *Milton in the Puritan Revolution*, Appendix, 355–433; Woodhouse, *Puritanism and Liberty*, 179–316.

England, and, banished from there because of his liberal views, had established his own colony of Providence in 1636. Williams founded Providence as "a lively experiment [for] full liberty in religious concernments" which guaranteed "liberty of conscience" and "the free exercise and enjoyment of all their civil and religious rights" to all peaceable parties. He also in 1643 called for "a wall of separation between the garden of the Church and the wilderness of the world."[110] Parliament would eventually group Milton and Williams together as radicals who deserved censorship, as we shall see in a moment.

Just because of the radicality of these religious liberty principles taken together, and just because of the suspect theological pedigree of some of these principles and their proponents, Milton's views did not carry the day in his lifetime. Indeed, they were often cavalierly ignored by other Puritan reformers.[111] Even Oliver Cromwell, who supported Milton and retained him as his Secretary for Foreign Languages, could not adopt his principles for religious liberty despite Milton's repeated prodding.[112] The Restoration government in 1660 rejected every one of them out of hand, and returned England to a firm Anglican state establishment, featuring vicious repression of dissenters. But three decades later, in the Glorious Revolution, Miltonian religious liberty principles came to constitutional form in the famous Toleration Act of 1689 and to even more vivid expression in John Locke's *Letter Concerning Toleration*.[113]

DOMESTIC RIGHTS AND LIBERTIES

While Milton's call for the reformation of religious liberty proved to be three decades before its time, his call for the reformation of domestic liberty would prove three centuries before its time. But a guarantee of domestic liberty was for Milton a "ready and easy" next step in the struggle for "real and substantial liberty" in England – from the liberty of the private prayer

---

[110] Plantation Agreement of Providence (1640) and Charter of Rhode Island and Providence Plantations (1663), in Thorpe, VI:3205–3206, 3211–3213; Roger Williams, Letter from Roger Williams to John Cotton (1643), in *The Complete Writings of Roger Williams*, 7 vols. (New York, 1963), 1:392. On Williams, see Edmund S. Morgan, *Roger Williams: The Church and State* (New York, 1967); Edwin S. Gaustad, *Liberty of Conscience: Roger Williams in America* (Grand Rapids, MI, 1991); David Little, "Roger Williams and the Separation of Church and State," in *Religion and the State: Essays in Honor of Leo Pfeffer*, ed. James E. Wood, Jr. (Waco, TX, 1985), 1–23.

[111] On Milton's reputation in his day, see Haller, *Tracts*, 1:128–139.

[112] Christopher Hill, *God's Englishman: Oliver Cromwell and the English Revolution* (New York, 1970), 183–190, 212–214.

[113] In Stephenson and Markham, 607–608. See further below pages 274–275.

closet to the liberty of the private home itself, as he later put it.[114] In Milton's view, private households of his day, just like individual consciences, were being oppressed by church and state authorities – and on the basis of the same kind of bad theology, superstitious custom, and unjust law. It made little sense to call for the reformation of public liberties in church and state, he argued, without first having the private liberties of the English household in order. "What are all our public immunities and privileges worth, and how shall it be judged that we fight for them with minds worthy to enjoy them, if we suffer ourselves in the meanwhile not to understand the most important freedom that God and nature hath given us in the family?"[115]

[T]he constitution and reformation of a commonwealth . . . is, like a building, to begin orderly from the foundation thereof, which is marriage and the family, to set right first whatever is amiss therein. How can there else grow up a race of warrantable men, while the house and home that breeds them, is troubled and disquieted under a bondage not of God's constraining . . . but laid upon us imperiously in the worst and weakest ages of knowledge, by a canonical tyranny of stupid and malicious monks: who having rashly vowed themselves to a single life, which they could not undergo, invented new fetters to throw on matrimony, that the world thereby waxing more dissolute, they also in a general looseness might sin with more favor.[116]

This argument had intuitive appeal in Protestant England – and not just because of its popular anti-monasticism. Marriage had been one of the first institutions to be reformed in the sixteenth-century Reformation, and it made good sense to any serious Protestant that a "second reformation" would need to begin there, too.[117] Moreover, it was a commonplace among both Anglicans and Calvinists of Milton's day to regard the marital household as the foundation of church and state and the first school of order, justice, and good citizenship. Already in 1590, William Perkins put it thus: "[M]arriage was made and appointed by God himself to be the foundation and seminary of all sorts and kinds of life in the commonwealth and the church . . . [T]hose families wherein the service of God is performed are, as it were, little churches; yea, even a kind of paradise on earth."[118] Robert Cleaver opened his famous 1598 tract, *A Godly Form of Householde Gouernment*, with an oft-repeated maxim: "A household is as it were a little commonwealth, by the good government whereof, God's glory

---

[114] LF 364–366. [115] *CPW* II:438–439. See also LF 366. [116] *CPW* II:431; I:588.

[117] On the Calvinist reformation of marriage, see Witte and Kingdon, *Sex, Marriage and Family*. This subsection on Milton's marital reforms is adapted from my *From Sacrament to Contract*, 177–186.

[118] William Perkins, *Christian Oeconomy or a Short Survey of the Right Manner of Erecting and Ordering a Family According to the Scriptures* (c. 1590), in *The Work of William Perkins*, ed. Ian Breward, 3 vols. (Abingdon, Berks, 1970), III:418–419.

may be advanced, the commonwealth which standeth of several families, benefited, and all that live in that family, may receive much comfort and commodity."[119] William Gouge premised his massive 1622 tome *Domesticall Duties* on the same belief that "the family is a seminary of the church and the commonwealth," and indeed in its own right, "a little church, and a little commonwealth, whereby a trial may be made of such as are fit for any place of authority, or subjection in church or commonwealth."[120] In 1644, Samuel Rutherford reminded his readers of the first premise of Calvinist political theory laid by Beza in his 1574 tract on *The Rights of Rulers*: that marriage and the family are the "first contract of nature" on which all the covenants and contracts of society, church, and state "ultimately depend."[121]

It was not so much Calvinist logic as personal crisis, however, that drove Milton to pay close attention to domestic liberty and marital reform. In 1642, just as he had completed the last of his five tracts calling for religious liberty, Milton had gotten married. His new bride, however, had left him within a month of their wedding day, and she and her family repeatedly resisted his attempts at reconciliation. Milton, his early biographer reports, "could ill bear the disappointment he met with by her obstinate absenting: And therefore thought upon a divorce, that he might be free to marry another."[122]

English church courts, which had long enjoyed jurisdiction over marriage until the Long Parliament banished them in 1641, maintained the strict medieval canon law that forbade divorce and remarriage. Parties who had been properly married could not divorce on any grounds whatsoever – even in cases of brazen adultery or malicious desertion, which other Protestant nations recognized to be sufficient grounds for divorce and remarriage. Under English law, estranged spouses could separate from bed and board on these grounds. But they could not marry another person during the lifetime of their spouse without courting charges of bigamy, a serious criminal offense. Their only hope for escape was to find an impediment – such as an incestuous blood tie between them – that would support a judgment of annulment. Annulment was a formal declaration that the purported marriage was null and void from the start, in most cases leaving each party free to marry another. None of these options was available to Milton, and he felt unjustly enslaved in and to his marriage.

[119] Robert Cleaver, *A Godly Form of Householde Gouernment* (London, 1598), 1.
[120] William Gouge, *Of Domesticall Duties: Eight Treatises* (London, 1622), 17, 27, Epistle, sig. 2v.
[121] Rutherford, *Lex, Rex*, qq. 2, 13 and above pages 136–139. See other examples in Mary Lynn Shanley, "Marriage Contract and Social Contract in Seventeenth Century English Political Thought," *Western Political Quarterly* 32 (1979): 79–91; Susan Dwyer Amussen, *An Ordered Society: Gender and Class in Early Modern England* (Oxford, 1988), 34–66, 134–179.
[122] *CPW* II:138.

Thus, invoking "the duty and the right of an instructed Christian," Milton took his cause to the Parliament – addressing four books to them between 1643 and 1646 in an effort to convince them that he should be allowed to divorce and remarry in such circumstances. In his Address to Parliament, which opened his first tract, *The Doctrine and Discipline of Divorce*, Milton pressed a contractual argument for the right to divorce that followed the exact lines that Parliament had just used to justify their right to revolt against King Charles.

He who marries, intends as little to conspire his own ruin, as he that swears allegiance [to the Crown]: and as a whole people is in proportion to an ill government, so is one man to an ill marriage. If [Parliament] against any authority, covenant, or statute, may by the sovereign edict of charity, save not only their lives, but honest liberties from unworthy bondage, as well may [the married man] against any private covenant, which he never entered to his mischief, redeem himself from unsupportable disturbances to honest peace, and just contentment: And much the rather, for that to resist the highest magistrate though tyrannizing, God never gave us express allowance, only he gave us reason, charity, nature, and good example to bear us out; but in this domestic misfortune, thus to demean ourselves, besides the warrant of those four great directors, which doth as justly belong hither, we have an express law of God, and such a law, as whereof our Savior with a solemn threat forbid the abrogating. For no effect of tyranny can sit more heavily on the commonwealth, than this household unhappiness on the family. And farewell all hope of true Reformation in the state, while such an evil as this lies undiscerned or unregarded in the house.[123]

This was Milton's argument in a nutshell. The domestic commonwealth, like the political commonwealth, is formed by a contract or covenant between two parties, which may be dissolved if it fails in its fundamental purpose. This is the counsel of the "four great directors" – reason, charity, nature, and experience – in the case of political dissolutions. It is counseled by these same four great directors as well as by the Bible in the case of marital dissolutions. If such counsel is ignored, the whole commonwealth will suffer and each member within it.

The purpose of forming a political commonwealth is to protect liberty, establish order, and secure peace, Milton argued, adumbrating arguments that he would elaborate in his later regicide tracts. When one or more of these purposes is irreconcilably frustrated, either by the tyranny of rulers or by the crime of subjects, the political commonwealth is broken, and either the rulers or the people may dissolve it – by force of arms, if necessary. Thereafter, the parties can reorganize their political polity in a manner more consistent with the ideal purposes of liberty, order, and peace. It

---

[123] *CPW* II:229–230.

makes no difference that the political covenant between the people and their rulers is silent on the subject of dissolution in cases of frustration of the main purpose of the covenant. For both common sense and natural law are implied in the covenant and dictate that parties not be unconscionably held to bargains that were once right but have now gone irretrievably wrong:

No understanding man can be ignorant that covenants are ever made according to the present state of persons and of things; and have ever the more general laws of nature and of reason included in them, though not expressed. If I make a voluntary covenant as with a man, to do him good, and he prove afterward a monster to me, I should conceive a disobligement. If I covenant, not to hurt an enemy, in favor of him and forbearance, and hope of his amendment, and he, after that, shall do me tenfold injury and mischief, to what he had done when I so covenanted, and still be plotting what may tend to my destruction, I question not but that his after actions release me; nor know I [a] covenant so sacred that withholds me from demanding justice on him. Howbeit, had not their distrust in a good cause, and the fast and loose of our prevaricating Divines overswayed, it had been doubtless better not to have inserted in a covenant unnecessary obligations, and words not works of a supererogatory allegiance to their enemy . . . Protestants have done before, and many conscientious men now in these times have more than once besought the Parliament to do, that they might go on upon a sure foundation.[124]

Milton pressed the analogous argument in seeking "a sure foundation" from Parliament to reject those "prevaricating Divines" against divorce and to grant him a "disobligement" of his marital contract because it had failed in its fundamental purpose. The purpose of forming a marriage, Milton argued, is to foster love, create community, deter lust, and procreate children. Of these purposes, marital love is, by far, the most critical. "Marriage is a covenant," he wrote, "the very being whereof consists, not in forced cohabitation, and counterfeit performance of duties, but in unfeigned love and peace . . . a sweet and gladsome society." "[T]he apt and cheerful conversation of man with woman," is the "chief and noblest end of marriage." "Where love cannot be, there can be left of wedlock nothing but the empty husk of an outside matrimony" – dry, shriveled, and dispensable.[125]

Milton underscored this priority of marital love by describing marriage as a threefold society – at once "religious, civil, and corporal" in nature. As a religious society, marriage is "a union of soul, spirit, and mind," between husband and wife – a reflection of the perfect love of Adam and Eve in Paradise, an expression of the perfect love between Christ and his church. As a civil society, marriage is a union "of the couple's person and property," in which each spouse vows to support and protect the other in all things "to

---

[124] This from Milton's *Tenure of Kings*, *CPW* III:231–232.   [125] *CPW* II:235–256.

the death." As a corporal society, marriage is a union of bodies in intercourse which serve to cool their passion and to conceive children if that is God's will.[126]

God appointed the religious society of marriage as "the highest and most excellent," Milton argued, for it dealt with the essential matters of the soul, the spirit, and the mind. He appointed the "corporal society" of marriage as the "least essential," for this dealt with discretionary matters of the body and its passions.

We know that flesh can neither join, nor keep together two bodies of itself; what is it then must make them one flesh, but likeness, but fitness of mind and disposition, which may breed the Spirit of concord, and union between them? . . . For as the unity of mind is nearer and greater than the union of bodies, so doubtless is the dissimilitude greater, and more individual.

Without agape or "soul love," a marriage is dead. Without eros or "carnal love," a marriage can live. Think of the marriage of Mary and Joseph.[127]

Having posited this hierarchy of marital purposes – from the religious to the carnal – Milton thought it preposterous "ignorance and iniquity" that the law of his day should provide remedies "for the right of the body in marriage but nothing for the wrongs and grievances of the mind." Impotence and frigidity could lead to annulment. But frustration of "the superior and nobler ends both of marriage and of the married persons . . . looses no hold" on the persons from marriage. "What courts of concupiscence are these, wherein fleshly appetite is heard before right reason, lust before love or devotion." If impotence, frigidity, and other frustrations of the base carnal society of marriage can lead to dissolution, then surely incompatibility, antagonism, and other frustrations of the higher religious society of marriage should lead to dissolution as well. To hold otherwise is to elevate the needs of the body above those of the soul, to privilege marital sex over marital love.[128]

Milton thus advocated divorce if either the religious or the carnal purposes of marriage were frustrated. Frustration of the religious purposes of marriage because of "irreconcilable incompatibility" provided the more compelling case for divorce, he believed. For the community and concordance of the couple's soul, spirit, and mind was the first and foremost reason God instituted marriage. Adam could not abide isolation, even in the perfection of Paradise; no person can abide it in this vale of tears. And, a person trapped in a marriage with "a mute and spiritless mate" is even lonelier than the unmarried person. The disaffected spouse becomes cold, dark, and sad,

[126] *Ibid.*   [127] *CPW* II:268–269, 605–609.   [128] *CPW* II:239–240, 248–250, 599.

growing "not only in bitterness and wrath, the canker of devotion, but in a desperate and vicious carelessness," falling victim to "dissimulation, suspicion, false colors, false pretenses." In such circumstances, divorce is the better course. Who cannot see "how much more Christian it would be to break by divorce that which is more broken by undue and forcible keeping . . . rather than that the whole worship of a Christian man's life should languish and fade away beneath the weight of an immeasurable grief and discouragement?"[129]

Frustration of the carnal purposes of marriage should likewise lead to divorce, Milton argued. In some instances, spouses willfully "betray their bodies" through adultery, cruelty, desertion, drunkenness, incest, sloth, violent crime, or other pathos that destroy any prospects of intimacy with their spouse. In other instances, one spouse suffers permanent impotence, frigidity, contagion, sterility, or disfigurement that precludes intercourse or conception. Where married parties cannot reconcile themselves to these conditions, they must be allowed to divorce, Milton argued. For, unless the innocent or capable spouse is "heroically virtuous," he or she inevitably will "despair in virtue and mutiny against divine providence" – testing the neighbor's bed, visiting the local brothel, or succumbing to various other "temptations, and occasions to secret adulteries, and unchaste roving." Husbands, eager to perpetuate their family name, might be tempted to concubinage for the sake of having children – a temptation to which even the great patriarch Abraham succumbed, to his own misery as well as that of Sara, Hagar, and Ishmael. And, if the couple already has children, the ills and evils of their marital discord "unavoidably will redound upon the children . . . and the whole family. It degenerates and disorders the best spirits, leaves them to unsettled imaginations, and degraded hopes, careless of themselves, their household and their friends, unactive to all public service, dead to the commonwealth."[130]

"To enjoin the indissoluble keeping of a marriage found unfit against the good of man both soul and body," Milton concluded, "is to make an idol of marriage." To be sure, "divorce is not rashly to be made, but reconcilement to be persuaded and endeavored." But, if such reconciliation cannot be achieved, it is better to take the painful step of divorce, to avoid even worse pain. This is for the good of the couple, their children, and the broader commonwealth. "[P]eace and love, the best subsistence of a Christian family, will return home from whence they are now banished; places of prostitution will be less haunted, the neighbor's bed less attempted,

[129] *CPW* II:251–252, 259–260, 589–591, 630–631.   [130] *CPW* II:254, 631–632.

the yoke of prudent and manly discipline will be generally submitted to, sober and well ordered living will soon spring up in the commonwealth."[131]

Milton did not spell out the legal ramifications of these views on marriage and divorce. He instead reprinted, with his own long preface, the legal discussion of marriage and divorce in the tract *De Regno Christi* written by Strasbourg reformer Martin Bucer in 1550. Milton endorsed Bucer's conflation of annulment and divorce, his insistence on the equal rights of husband and wife to petition for divorce on proof of cause, and his call for civil courts rather than church courts to handle all marriage and divorce litigation. He also assembled a rather untidy heap of liberal divorce laws – from the ancient Judaic to the modern Protestant – to demonstrate the purported anachronism of prevailing English law against divorce.[132] Readers who wanted more, Milton said, should read the systematic legal discussion on the subject just published by the distinguished English jurist John Selden.[133]

Milton directed his main energies to the theological ramifications of these views of marriage and divorce. He spent a good deal of time deconstructing the conventional theological arguments for the indissolubility of marriage – dismissing them all derisively as the kinds of "silly superstition," "devilish doctrine," and "heinous barbarism" that a commonwealth dedicated to true liberty could not countenance.[134]

Catholics first called marriage a sacrament because it is permanent, and then later insisted that it is permanent because it is sacrament, a sign of Christ's union with his Church. But this sacramental symbolism of marriage only proves that it is the spiritual, rather than the corporal, union of marriage that is critical, Milton insisted.

For me I dispute not now whether matrimony be a mystery or no; if it be of Christ and his Church, certainly it is not meant of every ungodly and miswedded marriage, but then only mysterious when it is a holy, happy, and peaceful match ... Since therefore none but a fit and pious matrimony can signify the union of Christ and his Church, there cannot be any hindrance of divorce to that wedlock wherein there can be no good mystery.[135]

Continental Protestants argue that marriage is indissoluble because it is a covenant in which God is a party. But this, again, proves only that the spiritual dimensions of marriage are the more pressing, Milton wrote. If marriage is a true covenant among husband, wife, and God, "so much the

---

[131] *CPW* II:230, 276, 431, 438–439, 680.   [132] *CPW* II:692–718.
[133] *CPW* II:350, referring to Selden, *De iure naturali et gentium*, bk. 5, ch. 7.
[134] *CPW* II:235, 238, 248.   [135] *CPW* II:236–237, 591, 601–602, 607, 630–631, 732.

more it argues the chief society thereof to be in the soul rather than in the body, and the greatest breach thereof to be unfitness of mind rather than defect of body, for the body can have less affinity in a covenant more than human." Moreover, to call marriage a covenant is not to prove its indissolubility; quite the contrary, as is evident from the dissolved political covenants of our time, let alone every private covenant that can be dissolved for cause.

[E]quity is understood in every covenant, even between enemies, though the terms be not expressed. If equity therefore made it, extremity may dissolve it. But marriage, they used to say, is the covenant of God. Undoubted: and so is any covenant frequently called in Scripture, wherein God is called to witness . . . [T]his denomination adds nothing to the covenant of marriage, above any other civil and solemn contract: nor is it more indissoluble for this reason than any other against the end of its own ordination . . . But faith they say must be kept in covenant, though to our damage. I answer that only holds true where the other side performs.[136]

Anglicans are even less convincing, Milton charged, for they "dare not affirm that marriage is either a sacrament or a mystery, though all those sacred things give place to man, and yet they invest it with such an awful sanctity, and give it such Adamantine chains, to bind with, as if it were to be worshipped like some Indian deity." But this is an "irrational" and "silly conformity" to one particular of the Catholic tradition which in many other particulars has been rejected.[137]

Both Catholics and Protestants alike argue that marriage is indissoluble because, as Christ commands in Matthew 19:6, "what God has joined together let not man put asunder." The point of this passage, however, said Milton, is not the prohibition against man's putting asunder. It is the requirement that God must join the couple together.

[W]hen is it that God may be said to join, when the parties and their friends consent? No surely; for that may concur to lewdest ends, or is it when the church rites are finished? Neither; for the efficacy of those depends upon the presupposed fitness of either party. Perhaps after carnal knowledge? least of all: for that may join persons whom neither law nor nature dares join; 'tis left, that only then, when the minds are fitly disposed, and enabled to maintain a cheerful conversation, to the solace and love of each other, according as God intended and promised in the very first foundation of matrimony, I will make a help meet for him.

So when it shall be found by their apparent unfitness, that their continuing to be man and wife is against the glory of God, and their mutual happiness, it may assure them that God never joined them.[138]

---

[136] *CPW* ii:245, 275–276, 624.   [137] *CPW* ii:277.   [138] *CPW* ii:274–277, 328, 650–651.

Having deconstructed traditional Christian arguments about divorce, Milton set out to reconstruct a biblical argument for the right to divorce. The key passage, he insisted, is Deuteronomy 24:1.[139] There God proclaimed through Moses: "When a man hath taken a wife and married her, and it comes to pass that she find no favor in his eyes, because he hath found some uncleanness in her, let him write her a bill of divorcement, and give it in her hand, and send her out of his house" – leaving both parties free to remarry thereafter. "Uncleanness" in this passage, said Milton, means "nakedness or unfitness" of body or of mind. It implicates the whole range of corporal and religious grounds for divorce which he had already listed. Of these, religious grounds were the more important, for "what greater nakedness or unfitness of mind than that which hinders ever the solace and peaceful society of the married couple." The ancient Hebrews had recognized this, and built on this passage a comprehensive doctrine of divorce. Their interpretation was followed by the Greeks, the Romans, the early Christian emperors, and many others. This proves, said Milton, that Deuteronomy 24:1 is no special rule for the Jews. It is a universal moral law, "a grave and prudent Law, full of moral equity, full of due consideration towards nature, that cannot be resisted; a law consenting with the laws of wisest men and civilest nations."[140]

Christ did not abrogate this moral law of divorce in his proclamation in Matthew 19:9: "Whosoever shall put away his wife, except it be for fornication, and shall marry another, committeth adultery; and whosoever marrieth her which is put away doth commit adultery." This passage must be understood in context, Milton argued. Christ had already said in Matthew 5:18: "Till heaven and earth pass, one jot or one tittle shall in no wise pass from the law, till all be fulfilled." Moreover, his divorce proclamation was prompted, as Matthew 19:3 reports, by the Pharisees "tempting him, and saying unto him, Is it lawful for a man to put away his wife for every cause?" Christ was giving a direct response to the scheming Pharisees. You, Pharisees, who might "in the hardness of your hearts" abuse the Mosaic law of divorce through inventive interpretation, you may divorce only on grounds of fornication. But others, less hard of heart and less prone to casuistry, may do so on the fuller grounds allowed by Moses. Christ's "rigid sentence against divorce" was designed "not to cut off all remedy from a good man who finds himself consuming away in a disconsolate and unenjoyed matrimony, but to lay a bridle upon the bold abuses of those

---

[139] In his later *Christian Doctrine*, Milton argued that the Mosaic law was a basis only for private virtue not state policy. See above pages 226–235.
[140] *CPW* II:239–244, 306.

overweening rabbis." Christ's words were not a timeless declaration for the church, but a terse denunciation of the Pharisees.[141]

If Christ's words are so understood, Milton continued, St. Paul's words can also be understood. In 1 Corinthians 7:15, Paul writes: "if the unbelieving [spouse] depart, let him depart. A brother or a sister is not under bondage in such cases, but God hath called us to peace." Paul is not contradicting Christ by adding desertion or disbelief as another ground for marital dissolution, Milton argued. He is simply confirming the traditional Hebrew practice that when the union of spirit between husband and wife is broken by a form of spiritual "uncleanness," the marriage is broken and the parties are freed from its bonds.[142] Indeed, Paul goes beyond Moses by granting to both husband and wife alike this freedom to depart from a spiritually broken marriage – a suitable application of Paul's more general teaching that in Christ there is "neither male nor female."[143]

This was the heart of Milton's argument for domestic liberty. Over the next fifteen years, he embroidered this argument a bit more. He called for the same rights of men and women to enter marriages as to exit them through divorce. He called on husbands and wives to love, support and care for each other, and insisted that each had a right to claim these expanded "conjugal debts" from the other. He called for the rights of parents to nurture, discipline, and educate their children in their own faith but with due regard for each child's nature and gifts. He mentioned in passing the need for greater privacy of the home, including, as we shall see in the next section, freedom from illegal searches of the home and seizure of private papers. And he speculated, at some length and leisure, whether polygamy and concubinage were, in fact, outlawed by God, though he said clearly that "homosexuality, fornication, violation, adultery, incest, rape, prostitution, and offences of a similar kind run counter" to God's law and cannot be countenanced at all.[144]

Unlike his writings on religious liberty, which were often ignored in his day, Milton's writings on domestic liberty found instant readership – and mostly of a very hostile sort. Even before he ventured his scandalous speculations on polygamy and concubinage, his readers denounced his permissive theory of marriage and divorce. While many writers could accept the conventional Protestant doctrine of divorce and remarriage in cases of adultery and desertion, they thought Milton's arguments for the right to divorce on grounds of irreconcilable differences alone proved too much. His books were dismissed for holding the "most dangerous and damnable

---

[141] *CPW* II:283, 621, 636, 661–662.   [142] *CPW* II:681–683.   [143] *CPW* II:339.
[144] LF 363–365; *CPW* II:393–413; VI:351–381, 755–757, 781–788.

tenets." If Milton had his way, his critics charged, "the bonds of marriage [will be] let loose to inordinate lust," and men will inevitably "quit of their wives for slight occasions" to the detriment of the couple, the children, the church, and the commonwealth alike. "[W]hat will all the Christian churches through the world . . . think of our woeful degeneration in these deplored times, that so uncouth a design should be set on foot among us."[145]

The 1644 Parliament not only rejected Milton's fourfold call for divorce reform, but moved to censor and burn his *Doctrine and Discipline of Divorce*, along with Roger Williams's *Bloody Tenent of Persecution* and Richard Overton's *Man's Mortallitie*. These books, critics in Parliament and in pulpits pronounced, have converted religious and domestic liberties into "despicable licenses." These authors want "a liberty of sensual lusts, and fleshly looseness," a freedom for "Popery, Judaism, Turkism, Paganism and all manner of false religions under pretense of liberty of conscience." Their books are chock-full of "Anabaptistical, Antinomian, Heretical, Atheistical opinions, as of the soul's mortality, divorce at pleasure, etc."

> If any plead conscience for the lawfulness of polygamy; (or for divorce for other cause than Christ and His apostles mention; of which a wicked book is abroad and uncensured, though deserving to be burnt, whose author hath been so impudent as to set his name to it, and dedicate it to ourselves) or for liberty to marry incestuously, will you grant toleration for this?[146]

Later English reformers, both theological and legal, would look back to Milton as a prophet, who anticipated many of the reforms of English marriage and divorce law from the Matrimonial Causes Act of 1857 forward.[147] But in his own day, on questions of marriage and divorce, Milton was a prophet with little honor, and no legal influence.

CIVIL RIGHTS AND LIBERTIES

It was the threat in 1644 of Parliamentary censorship of his book on divorce that prompted Milton immediately to widen his reformation program to include other civil liberties, most notably the freedoms of speech and press. These were not entirely new ideas; Milton had already sounded a few of them in his earlier tracts on religious liberty. "Nothing is more sweet to man . . . than liberty of speaking," he wrote in 1641. But for the "free born

---

[145] Quotes in William R. Parker, *Milton's Contemporary Reputation* (Columbus, OH, 1940), 74–79.
[146] Quotes from 1643 and 1644 in Haller, *Liberty and the Reformation*, 78–134, esp. 125–126. See also Hill, *Milton and the English Revolution*, 130–139, 222–230 for later reactions to Milton's views.
[147] See references to Milton in Lawrence Stone, *Road to Divorce: England 1530–1987* (Oxford, 1990), 348–351, 407 and summary of these later legal reforms in *ibid.*, 368–422.

people of England," all speaking and publication have long been "pinched," "girded, and straight laced" by "monkish prohibitions, and expurgatious indexes" kept by "some mercenary, narrow-souled, and illiterate chaplain." Censorship is silly and self-defeating for the church, Milton argued. It is silly because censors have "to thrust themselves under disguise into a popular throng [or] to stand the night long under eaves of houses and low windows that they might hear everywhere the free utterances of private breasts." It is self-defeating because "the honest liberty of free speech" is "so dear a concernment as the church's good." For with it "honest men" can "stand up for the church's defense" and "drive her to reform." Indeed, the church and the nation would do so much better if they welcomed "the struggle of contrarieties," "the fierce encounter of Truth and falsehood." For "the property of Truth is, where she is publicly taught, to unyoke and set free the minds and spirits of a nation first from the thralls of sin and superstition, after which all honest and legal freedom of civil life cannot be long absent."[148]

Milton returned to these arguments in 1643 in his preface to *The Doctrine and Discipline of Divorce.* Even before he had any inkling of the pending censorship of this work, he fumed against those with a "design to envy and cry down the industry of free reasoning . . . and innovation." Why have the censors of church and state "closed up" "the womb of teeming Truth"? It is only because she may "presume to bring forth ought, that sorts not with their unchewed notions and suppositions." "[Y]ou now have in your hands a great and populous nation to reform," Milton wrote to Parliament, "from what corruption and what blindness in religion you know well; in what a degenerate and fallen spirit from the apprehension of native liberty."[149]

Freedom of speech

It takes a bit of historical imagination and explanation to appreciate the object of Milton's complaints and the radicality of his vision of "the fierce encounter of Truth and falsehood" through free speech in public. Before 1640 in England, truth was not so much debated as declared, and public platforms and publications for doing so were reserved to those licensed by the government. To be sure, England knew the classical Greek and Roman teachings on *rhetorica, parrhesia* and *licentia,* and these ancient ideas were given ample ventilation by the scholars of the day.[150] A century before,

---

[148] *CPW* I:125, 450–451, 669–670, 795–796, 805, 863.   [149] *CPW* II:224–227.
[150] David Colclough, *Freedom of Speech in Early Stuart England* (Cambridge, 2005), 12–76.

in the heady days of Henry VIII's reformation, Protestants and humanists alike had exploited these earlier rhetorical traditions as well as the prophetic traditions of the Bible to issue their many sermons and pamphlets. But with the Elizabethan settlement in 1559, and even more with the establishment policies of James I from 1603 on, much of this radical rhetoric was subject to increasing restriction. The dominant legal assumption, though not always the social reality, was that public and published speech required prior government licenses.[151]

The proper place for freedom of speech, petition, and debate was thought to be in Parliament. There, traditions going back to the thirteenth century gave members license to speak freely, frankly, and forcefully within the confidence of their chambers in order to offer their best counsel to the Crown and to craft the best policies for the Commonwealth. Thus, when James I and Charles I suspended Parliament for a time and then tried to curtail the speech of its members when called, Parliament rose up in indignant protest. The members issued several striking documents defending these ancient rights of free Parliamentary speech. The Form of Apology and Satisfaction of 1604, for example, declared to James I that these Parliamentary "privileges and liberties" were not a "mere privilege" that could be restricted or removed by the Crown. "Full and frank speech" was a "fundamental privilege," "our right and due inheritance, no less than our very lands and goods."[152]

When King James I again sought to curtail this freedom of speech, Sir Edward Coke confronted him in an epic speech in the House of Commons in 1621. Members of Parliament, Coke declared, have an "ancient right" and "undoubted inheritance" to a "freedom to speak what we think good for government, either in church or commonwealth and what are the grievances" therein that need be redressed. Citing the Magna Carta of 1215 and several later medieval statutes and cases, Coke argued that Parliament must represent and speak for the whole people, and thus that "the freedom of the House is the freedom of the whole land." "We serve here for thousands and ten thousands."[153] Such views, which landed Coke and other members in prison, figured prominently in the formal Commons' Protestation of 1621 and were echoed again in the many speeches surrounding the Petition of

---

[151] C. S. Clegg, *Press Censorship in Elizabethan England* (Cambridge, 1997); Clegg, *Censorship in Jacobean England* (Cambridge, 2001); David Loades, *Politics, Censorship and the English Reformation* (London, 1991); S. Mutchow Towers, *Control of Religious Printing in Early Stuart England* (Woodbridge, Suffolk, 2003).

[152] In Kenyon, *The Stuart Constitution*, 29–35, at 31, with analysis in Colclough, *Freedom of Speech*, 122–123, 138–168.

[153] Quotes in *ibid.*, 172–181. See further *Selected Writings of Sir Edward Coke*, III:1194–1305.

Right of 1628.[154] Anyone who wanted more could read with profit the pages on point in Coke's *Institutes.*

Even as restricted, the laws governing freedom of speech in Parliament were considerably more liberal than those governing public speech, especially publication. For a private person to print a book was akin to minting a coin; it always required a prior government license. Without a license, the publication was presumed a counterfeit, and printing, selling, or possessing it was an actionable crime.[155] King Henry VIII had put such a licensing law in place already in 1530, and this early law was broadened and tightened in a dozen later acts culminating in Charles I's Star Chamber Decree of 1637. Under this latter law, the Crown's Stationers' Company issued the licenses to print, the Bishop of London or Archbishop of Canterbury reviewed and censored the illicit books, and the Court of Star Chamber punished the unlicensed printers and authors, sometimes quite severely. The Stationers' Company had wide jurisdiction to "search what houses and shops (and at what time they shall think fit)" and to seize illegal publications and papers and to seek prosecution of their authors, printers, and distributors before the Star Chamber.[156]

This traditional licensing law, though not revoked, ground to a halt during the first years of the Long Parliament, with the abolition of the Court of Star Chamber in 1641. This resulted in a massive torrent of new publications, Milton's five anti-clerical tracts prominently among them. But on June 14, 1643, the Long Parliament issued a new licensing order in an effort to stamp out the "many false, forged, scandalous, seditious, libelous, and unlicensed Papers, Pamphlets, and Books to the great defamation of Religion and government." The Order left it again to the Stationers' Company to issue the licenses. But now a dozen Protestant ministers, assigned by Parliament, replaced the Bishop of London as the censors of books on religious matters, and Parliament itself replaced the Star Chamber as the final enforcer of the licensing law.[157]

It was this new law that Parliament sought to enforce against Milton's *Doctrine and Discipline of Divorce*, which he had published without a license. Though Milton was apparently never seriously threatened with arrest, he responded in 1644 with his *Areopagatica: A Speech of Mr. John Milton for the Liberty of Unlicensed Printing*, which would become a classic defense of free speech and press in the common law tradition. He wrote this tract, as he later put it,

---

[154] In Stephenson and Markham, 450–453.   [155] Haller, *Liberty and the Reformation*, 134–142.
[156] In *CPW* II:793–796, with analysis of the licensing system in *CPW* II:158–164.
[157] In *CPW* II:797–799.

that the determination of true and false, of what ought to be published and what suppressed, might not be in the hands of the few who may be charged with the inspection of books, men commonly without learning and of vulgar judgment, and by whose license and pleasure, no one is suffered to publish anything which may be above vulgar apprehension.[158]

Milton laid out the argument of the *Areopagatica* in brilliant rhetorical layers. He started with an historical argument that book licensing and censorship were papal tools sharpened by the Inquisition that had no place in Protestant England. Ancient Greece and Rome knew no such system of licensing and censorship, save in cases of outright blasphemy or libel, and the early Church Fathers and Christian emperors held to this policy. It was the medieval Catholic papacy that first introduced the censor and the index of prohibited books – particularly after the invention of the printing press and the publications of early reformers like John Wycliffe and John Hus. This system reached its height when the papacy called on the tyrannous "Spanish Inquisition" to enforce the decrees of the Council of Trent. These hated inquisitors "perfected those catalogues, and expurgating indexes." They "rake[d] through the entrails of many a good author" and invented "new hells" for the many Protestants whom they tortured and killed for their writings.[159]

Surely, no self-respecting English Protestant could think of adopting such a system, Milton intoned gravely, conveniently ignoring a century of English Protestants who did. "I am certain that a state governed by the rules of justice and fortitude, or a church built and founded upon the rock of faith and true knowledge, cannot be so pusillanimous." After all, it was the great leaders of church and state in the Long Parliament who first brought on "all this free writing and free speaking." "You cannot make us now less capable, less knowing, less eagerly pursuing of the truth unless you first make yourselves . . . less the founders of our true liberty." Surely, "freedom of writing" cannot now suddenly "be restrained by a discipline imitated from the prelates and learned by them from the inquisition." Surely we did not all join the Reformation cause against Catholic censorship and superstition only to return censors "into their seats under another name"? Surely, this short "cruise of truth" has not already run its course, leaving "freedom of learning" destined to "groan again" under "old fetters."[160]

Milton's next main argument was that licensing and censorship were impractical to implement and impossible to limit. As the prior experiment of unlicensed printing had made all too clear, censors simply could not

---

[158] LF 366.   [159] *CPW* II:493–505, 529, 537–541, 549–551.   [160] *CPW* II:540–542, 559, 568–569.

keep up with the pace of publication in England, nor stop the flow of illegal foreign books imported in sundry ships and saddlebags. Even if they tried, most licensors had neither the wit nor the wisdom to judge many of the writings that came before them. Nor could they be expected to sustain their interest or attention in the task, given the volume of work. Even if the licensors could do their work, the printers could not. They would be forever waiting on the bureaucrats to make up their minds and approve the texts. They would never really know whether they needed licenses to reprint old books. Would the Bible, for instance, need a license, and could it honestly get one given its rather graphic language about sin, sex, and violence? Would the Bible have to be abridged, leaving out, say, the Song of Songs with its preoccupation with female anatomy or the steamy passages on Samson and Delilah? What if an author revises his work, or makes a change to the approved copy: were new licenses needed or did the old license need amendment? What if the orginal licenser was away or had moved on; was a whole new license needed? How much should the printer charge, especially one forced to sit so long on his other literary wares? The mechanics and economics were just impossible, Milton concluded. And ultimately, why should this system be restricted to the printing of books? Will not Parliament inevitably be moved to require licenses for pamphlets, music, art, and poetry, and eventually for unwritten speech, too – sermons, speeches, songs, plays, board meetings, indeed plain talk altogether and everywhere? There is no stop on this slippery slope of licensing and censorship once the perilous first step is taken.[161]

But the real harm of licensing and censorship is done to the author and even more to the reading public. It is bad enough that the author has to bear the "dishonor and derogation" of having to deal with petty and pecuniary bureaucrats who inevitably will delay and drive up the price of his publications. It is worse that every author, even a great doctor and professor, has to sit "under the correction of his patriarchal licenser." This might well be a "punie" man, half his age and intelligence, who can still tell the author to "blot or alter what precisely accords not with the hidebound humor" that purports to be the censor's "judgment" on behalf of the government and people. Many of the best authors will leave England or fall silent, rather than sit "under the wardship of an overseeing fist" or watch their books "bear the scars" of their "fairest print" and most "cunning thoughts" cut out. Worst of all is that each of these bureaucrats, however incompetent, is made "a judge to sit upon the birth, or death of books." This is tragic, Milton wrote, with obvious self-reference. For a book holds "the breath of

---

[161] *CPW* II:523–526, 532–533.

a man's reason," the "efficacy and extraction" of his "living intellect." It is filled with the "precious life-blood of a master spirit." An author "summons up all his reason and deliberation to assist him; he searches, meditates," and then pours his "life, mind, and soul" into his writing. Books, therefore, "are not absolutely dead things, but do contain a potency of life in them to be as active as that soul was whose progeny they are." It is "as good almost kill a man as kill a good book; who kills a man kills a reasonable creature, God's image; but he who destroys a good book kills reason itself, kills the image of God, as it were in the eye." Censorship is a "kind of homicide," "sometimes a martyrdom," even "a kind of massacre."[162]

Milton used this startling term "massacre" to signal the grave threat that he thought censorship posed to the English Protestant nation as a whole. The very nature of being a Protestant reformer, Milton argued, is to protest, to challenge, to reform, to fight falsehood with truth. The Protestant Reformation was born in this very "struggle of contrarieties" about the most fundamental truths of Scripture and nature. The Protestants' strongest weapons in this struggle were their published books. Their best tactics were their open clashes of ideas with Catholics and with each other. And their wisest conclusion was to call their followers to continue the struggle, to be constantly at work at further discovery and reform – *semper reformanda*, always reforming, as Calvin had put it. "The light which we have gained" from the Reformation, Milton wrote,

was given us, not to be ever staring on, but by it to discover onward things more remote from our knowledge. It is not the unfrocking of a priest, the unmitering of a bishop, and the removing him from off the Presbyterian shoulders that will make us a happy nation, no, if other things as great in the church, and in the rule of life both economical and political be not looked into and reformed, we have looked so long upon the blaze that Zwingli and Calvin hath beaconed up to us, that we are stark blind.[163]

The reformation must go on in the state and society as much as in the church and in the home, Milton insisted. And it must go on with the same methods and insights that earlier Protestants had forged for the reformation of the church – but now writ larger and more generic. The Protestant premises of this new perpetual reformation are these: all have equal access and claim to the Truth. All have vocations and contributions that count. All are prophets, priests, and kings with the freedom and duty to proclaim, to pastor, to participate fully in the Commonwealth. And all must write and speak, all must read and study the books of their fellows, just

---

[162] *CPW* II:492–493, 532–533.   [163] *CPW* II:550, 552–553. See also above page 245.

as they always read and study the Bible separately and together. England is "entering a new and great period," Milton wrote with excitement, "even to reforming of [the] Reformation itself."

> Behold now this vast city; a city of refuge, the mansion house of liberty, encompassed and surrounded with his protection; the shop of war hath not there more anvils and hammers waking, to fashion out the plates and instruments of armed Justice in defense of beleaguered Truth, then there must be pens and heads there, sitting by their studious lamps, musing, searching, revolving new notions wherewith to present, as with their homage and their fealty the approaching Reformation: others as fast reading, trying all things, assenting to the force of reason and convincement. What could a man require more from a nation so pliant and so prone to seek after knowledge. What wants there to such a towardly and pregnant soil, but wise and faithful laborers, to make a knowing people, a nation of prophets, of sages, and of worthies.[164]

This was Milton's ideal – a nation where each and every person is unstintingly engaged in the great struggle and debate between Truth and Falsehood in order to bring greater and better reformation to state and society. This great struggle will perforce feature "much arguing, much writing, many opinions; for opinion in good men is but knowledge in the making." But such factions and differences of opinion in the state and society should be celebrated, much as "sects and schisms" are celebrated in the church. Different private groups and opinions will sharpen and censor each other. Each will reflect new light from above, new angles on truth. So long as we all show "a little generous prudence, a little forbearance of one another, and some grain of charity," we can all "unite into one general and brotherly search after Truth." "[O]ut of the many varieties and brotherly dissimilitudes that are not vastly disproportional arises the goodly and graceful symmetry that commends . . . great reformation."[165]

Freedom of speech, of course, brings not only "goodly and graceful" speech but also at times evil and harmful speech. Bad speech that rises to the level of blasphemy of God, treason against the state, or defamation of another person, Milton insisted, must be subject to "the sharpest justice" against the "malefactors." But none of this can and should be prejudged by a censor; let the reader make these judgments after the fact of publication. So many books – from the classics to modern-day printings – have bad and good speech inextricably intermixed within them. Man is both sinner and saint (*simul iustus et peccator*), and his writings will invariably reflect both qualities. To censor a book is to deny human nature.[166]

---

[164] *CPW* II:553–554. See further LF, 179–180; *CPW* III:496–497, 516, 533–537.
[165] *CPW* II:550–551, 554–555.   [166] *CPW* II:492, 517–521.

To censor a book is also to deny the nature of human judgment. God created all of us as rational creatures, with a reason and conscience to choose a virtuous life, and with a promise of eternal reward for those who make wise choices. Every person, from Adam and Eve forward, has been given "the knowledge of good and evil" and is confronted with sin and temptation. God,

though he command us temperance, justice, continence, yet powers out before us even to a profuseness all desirable things, and gives us minds that can wander beyond all limit and satiety. Why should we then affect a rigor contrary to the manner of God and of nature, by abridging or scanting those means, which books freely permitted are, both to the trial of virtue, and the exercise of truth.

Virtue can be better known and appreciated by seeing its opposite in vice. And the choice of a virtuous life is more genuine and praiseworthy when it is real and not artificial. "If every action which is good or evil in man at ripe years, were to be under pittance, and prescription, and compulsion, what were virtue but a name?"

I cannot praise a fugitive and cloistered virtue, unexercised and unbreathed, that never sallies out and sees her adversary but slinks out of the race, where that immortal garland is to be run for, not without dust and heat. Assuredly, we bring not innocence into the world, we bring impurity much rather: that which purifies us is trial, and trial is by what is contrary.[167]

"Truth and understanding," then, "are not such wares as to be monopolized and traded in by tickets and statutes, and standards" of licensers and censors. Truth comes through revelation not restriction, through persuasion not compulsion, through debate not declaration. Truth comes forth from the individual and collective judgments of each and every private English subject, who discerns and discriminates for him or herself after hearing and reading all opinions on all sides. "A wise man, like a good refiner, can gather gold out of the drossiest volume, and . . . a fool will be a fool with the best book, yea, or without a book." But most Englishmen are not fools. They are a "free and ingenious sort of such as evidently were born to study, and love learning for itself, not for lucre, or any other end, but the service of God and of truth." England is "a Nation not slow and dull, but of a quick, ingenious, and piercing spirit, acute to invent, suttle and sinewy to discourse, not beneath the reach of any point the highest that human capacity can soar to."[168]

---

[167] *CPW* II:514–517, 527–528.
[168] *CPW* II:521, 531, 535–536, 551. See also *CPW* I:125–127, 684–685, 690.

Give Englishmen some real education and real intellectual exercise, said Milton. Let "all the Lord's people become prophets." Let the people take up "the study of highest and most important matters to be reformed" by "disputing, reasoning, reading, inventing, discoursing, even to a rarity, and admiration, things not before discoursed or written of." Give them freedom "to know, to utter, and to argue freely according to conscience, above all liberties." Do all this, said Milton, and "I see in my mind a noble and puissant nation rousing herself like a strong man after sleep, and shaking her invincible locks: Me thinks I see her as an eagle muing her mighty youth, and kindling her undazzled eyes at the full midday beam; purging and unscaling her long abused sight at the fountain itself of heavenly radiance."[169]

Part of the point of all this flowing rhetoric about freedom of speech was to prove just how powerful and edifying real free speech could be. Many of Milton's fellow reformers in his day saw this point exactly, and echoed his views with power and eloquence. William Walwyn, John Goodwin, John Lilburne, Richard Overton, Henry Robinson, Henry Parker, John Robinson, and others offered variations on these arguments for freedom of speech in the 1640s and 1650s, as did an important Leveller petition to Parliament in 1648.[170] All these arguments, with Milton's the most eloquent amongst them, were important precedents for the eventual protections of freedom of speech and press set out in the English Bill of Rights of 1689, and eventually and more fully in American colonial charters and early republican constitutions as well.[171]

Other civil freedoms

Stripped of its ornate rhetoric, Milton's theory of freedom of speech was at heart his theory of freedom of religion writ large. Freedom of the religious and Spirit-filled conscience now became freedom of the rational and inquiring mind. The devout and faithful parishioner in the pew now became the good and solid citizen on the street. The prophet, priest, and king in the church now became the prophet, priest, and king of the state. The tolerated plurality of Scriptural interpretations and applications in private now became the open marketplace of true and false ideas competing in the

---

[169] *CPW* II:556–560.
[170] See sample tracts in Haller, *Tracts*, vols. II–III; Wolfe, *Leveller Manifestoes*, 322–330 and analysis in Haller, *Milton and the Reformation*, 146–149; Achinstein, *Milton and the Revolutionary Reader*, 32–38.
[171] In Stephenson and Markham, 599–605.

public square. The second reformation of the church now became the second reformation of the commonwealth altogether. And Milton predicated all this on the same firm belief that God's truth would triumph once freed from human errors and controls. Just as "all the winds of doctrine were let loose to play upon the earth, so Truth be in the field," Milton wrote;

we do injuriously by licensing and prohibiting to misdoubt her strength. Let her and Falsehood grapple; who ever knew Truth put to the worse in a free and open encounter. Her confuting is the best and surest suppressing. He who hears what praying there is for light and clearer knowledge to be sent down among us, would think of other matters to be constituted beyond the discipline of Geneva, framed and fabricated already to our hands."[172]

Here again was Milton's favorite theme: the Reformation must go on.

Milton's powerful vision of the place of the individual in society and the state could support many other civil liberties besides those of speech and press. Milton did not tend to other civil liberties with nearly the care and passion he devoted to freedom of speech. But here and there in his *Areopagatica*, and more in his later writings, he ticked off other rights and liberties that followed naturally from his view of the individual. Many of these civil rights, too, which were more forcefully articulated by other Puritan pamphleteers in the day, eventually found their way into the 1689 English Bill of Rights and the bills of rights of later American state and federal constitutions.

The most important of these were the right of the people to democratic election of political officials, and the right to petition these officials once elected. What better place for the people to debate truth and falsehood, said Milton, than in the choice of those who should govern them and protect them in "all their rights and liberties." Included in this "right to democratic government" was the right of the people, through their representatives, to consent to the taxes they paid, and to consent to the wars fought and militaries marshaled on their behalf. Also included was the right to Parliamentary oversight of judges and courts to ensure they did not become tyrannical or bastions of privilege. Included, finally, was the most "fundamental right" of the people – the right to dissent from, and if necessary to remove, politicians who no longer served or pleased them. "[T]he right of choosing, yea of changing their own government is by the grant of God himself in the people."[173]

---

[172] *CPW* II:561–562.
[173] LF 63; see also above pages 223–224. See Milton's further endorsement of democratic government and denunciations of hereditary monarchy in LF 60, 70–71, 127–128, 135, 141–143, 148, 154–155, 163–164, 237–238, 244–246, 277, 287, 299–298, 307, 312 as well as his massive screed in *Eikonoklastes*,

Other civil rights naturally followed from this most important right, Milton argued. One was the right to contract and associate with other private persons – not only in marriages and churches, as we have seen, but also in clubs, parties, and other associations organized for political, economic, recreational, or other licit purposes. Another was the right of everyone to proper education and to accessible libraries wherein "to imbue the minds of men with virtue, from which springs that true liberty which is felt within." Yet another important right was the right to jury trial in civil and criminal cases. Here, in the adversarial procedures of the courtroom, the great contests of truth and falsehood were fought out in miniature, with the stakes sometimes very high for the life, liberty, and property of the defendant. This right to be judged by a jury of one's peers, Milton later said, was part of a broader right to a fair trial by "due liberty and proportioned equality" in a duly constituted court.[174]

Milton acknowledged that others had "defended civil freedom more freely" than he had and had spelled out many more essential civil rights, and with greater legal specificity.[175] He often cited with approval the various Puritan proposals crafted by Lilburne, Walywn, Overton and others to give his readers more detail.[176] But Milton's real focus was the theology and anthropology of freedom. And his real wish was to impress on his readers "the weightier matters of the law of liberty," the most important of which were these:

that you should not be afraid to listen either to truth or falsehood, of whatever description that may be; but that you should listen the least of all to those, who never fancy that themselves are free, unless they deprive others of their freedom, who labor at nothing with so much zeal and earnestness, as to enchain not the bodies only, but the consciences of their brethren; and to introduce into church and state the worst of all tyrannies – the tyranny of their own misshapen customs and opinions. May you ever take part with those, who think it just, that not their own sect or faction alone, but all the citizens alike should have an equal right to be free . . .

[Real] liberty be of that kind, which can neither be gotten, nor taken away by arms, and that alone is such, which, springing from piety, justice, temperance, in fine, from real virtue, shall take deep and intimate root in your minds . . . Unless

---

CPW III:335–601. For analysis of the limitations and reversions of Milton's views of democracy and republicanism, see Thomas N. Corns, "Milton and the Characteristics of a Free Commonwealth," in Armitage, Himy and Skinner, eds., *Milton and Republicanism*, 25–42; Wolfe, *Milton in the Puritan Revolution*, 273–297, 325–336; Charles R. Geisst, *The Political Thought of John Milton* (New York, 1984), 71–86.

[174] LF 58–61,79, 262–264, 277, 364–367, 400–412, 421–422, 439–442; *CPW* II:567–568; VII:305, 455–460.

[175] LF 312.   [176] See above pages 215–218.

by real and sincere devotion to God and man, not an idle and wordy, but an efficacious, an operative devotion, you drive from your minds superstition, which originates in an ignorance of true and substantial religion, you will not want [for] those who will sit upon your backs and upon your necks, as if you were beasts of burden . . . Unless you banish avarice, ambition, luxury, from your thoughts, and all excess even from your families, the tyrant, whom you imagined was to be sought abroad, and in the field, you will find at home, you will find within.[177]

SUMMARY AND CONCLUSIONS

John Milton was a great Protestant reformer – a prolific scholar blessed with a longer life and a livelier pen than most of the other great reformers of seventeenth-century England. Unlike many others, Milton fought with his pen, not with his sword, and he suffered the ignominy of being mostly ignored in his day rather than being flogged, tortured, pilloried, or imprisoned like others. Also unlike many others, Milton defied closely guarded denominational labels – Puritan, Presbyterian, Leveller, Independent, Separatist, Brownist, Digger, Ranter, and other fine-grained variations on English Calvinism. Milton was more interested in finding truth than fighting turf wars over the theological and political niceties, as he saw them, that balkanized so much of his English Calvinist world.

This made Milton a controversial Calvinist in his own day, and he remains so in the eyes of many still today. Milton the poet has always been welcome in most Calvinist circles. With all those elegant verses on God and Satan, sin and grace, law and Gospel, heaven and hell: how could he not be welcome? Even hellfire-and-brimstone Calvinists have always found enough in *Paradise Lost* and *Paradise Regained* to give him a place in their pews, albeit usually near the left exit door. But Milton the prose writer, who is the main subject of this chapter: that is a different matter. Yes, the Luther-like clatterings against Catholic superstition, the lovely panegyrics about the Bible, the passionate calls for a new Genevan-style reformation in England, and more have done much to commend Milton to many Calvinists. But even Milton's sympathetic readers, I among them, have always wondered about all that pugnacious and prolix prose – the hundreds of pages of bare-fisted rhetoric raining down on all kinds of delicate subjects, the clever deconstructions and reversals of all kinds of settled texts and traditions, the huge piles of Bible verses and historical sources stacked so seductively to buttress all kinds of counterintuitive propositions – including

---

[177] LF 407–409.

no-fault divorce no less. For many Calvinist readers all this has always looked a bit too suspicious. Such suspicions were underscored when Milton's massive unpublished *Christian Doctrine* came to light for the first time in 1825. For those who read this text closely, its many controversial passages put Milton not only on the far left bank of the Calvinist tradition, but sometimes squarely in the Arminian, Anabaptist, and even anarchist floodplains beyond. It seemed safer to sail him by and stick with steadier and sturdier seventeenth-century Calvinists like Samuel Rutherford and other Westminster Divines.[178]

Whatever the merits of these general theological judgments about Milton's work, they are not apt judgments about his contributions to the Calvinist reformation of law, religion, and human rights. On this subject, Milton captured many of the best teachings of the Calvinist tradition better than his peers did, and he added several other teachings that would become critical to the development of modern rights doctrines on and in Calvinist terms. Milton distilled and instilled many of the best legal and political teachings that Calvin, Beza, Althusius, and other reformers had already laid out. These included teachings about human dignity and divine image bearing, about natural law and the created order, about natural rights and Christian liberties, about subjective rights and social freedoms, about popular sovereignty and political covenants, about rule of law and constitutional order, about political tyranny and the right to resist. On these themes and others, Milton was mostly a faithful and forceful summarizer of the best of the Calvinist tradition. And he cited repeatedly and with genuine admiration the texts on point of the great reformers – Calvin and Bucer, Beza and Hotman, Ponet and Goodman, Knox and Buchanan.

In devising his own reformation of rights, Milton seized on what he thought to be the reformers' most important lesson – namely, that the Reformation must always go on. England must not idolize or idealize any Protestant formulations, Milton insisted, even Calvin's. It must develop and deepen, apply and amend them in a continuous effort to reform church, state, and society anew. "There can be no excuse for our delay in reforming," Milton wrote already in 1642.[179] Milton further seized on what he thought to be a cardinal teaching of Calvinism – namely, that God calls each and every mature person to be a prophet, priest, and king, with natural rights and duties to speak, worship, and rule in church and state, family and society

---

[178] See the range of reactions to him analyzed in Meland, "John Milton: Puritan or Liberal?"
[179] *CPW* 1:795.

at once. For Milton, the driving forces of England's perpetual reformation, therefore, were not only clerics or magistrates, scholars or aristocrats. The reformers were just as much the commoners and householders, craftsmen and farmers of every peaceable type. Every person was created by God with the freedom of conscience, reason, and will. Every person was called by God to discharge both their private Christian vocations and their public social responsibilities in expression of their love of God, neighbor, and self. This was a form of Christian populism and popular sovereignty that the Calvinist tradition had not put quite so strongly before.

Milton went even further beyond traditional Calvinist teachings in defining the religious, domestic, and civil rights and liberties that each person must enjoy in discharging these offices of prophet, priest, and king. Among religious liberties, he defended liberty of conscience, freedom of religious exercise, worship, association, and publication, equality of multiple biblical faiths before the law, separation of church and state, and disestablishment of a national religion. Among domestic liberties, he stressed urgently the right to marry and divorce in accordance with the explicit teachings of Scripture alone as he understood them. He mentioned attendant rights to nurture, discipline, and educate one's children and to have one's private home free from unwanted searches and seizures of private papers and possessions. Among civil liberties, he offered a brilliant defense of the freedoms of speech and press, and also defended earnestly the rights to democratic election, representation, petition, and dissent, as well as the rights to private association and to jury trial. He also endorsed warmly many of the more detailed and expansive rights proposals of the Puritan pamphleteers.

Few of these reforms came to lasting constitutional expression in Milton's day, despite some innovative Parliamentary legislation in the later 1640s. Oliver Cromwell's Protectorate government reversed many of these reforms after 1653, and the Restoration government rejected virtually all of them in 1660. But the Puritan reform pamphlets of the mid-seventeenth century, so elegantly synthesized by Milton, provided a fertile seedbed for the growth of rights and liberties in the common law tradition. In the generation after Milton, the Bill of Rights (1689) and Toleration Act (1689), born of the Glorious Revolution, guaranteed at least a measure of the rights of speech, press, religion, and jury trial that he and others had championed, and these guarantees were strengthened by later Parliamentary legislation. In crafting these reform measures, leaders of the Glorious Revolution looked to Milton and to other Puritan revolutionaries for inspiration.

Even when he was not directly cited or quoted, Milton's ideas of liberty were pervasive, in the air. This was true not just of his famous paean to free speech which became a new Ur text in the common law canon of freedom and was endlessly cited. Another striking example of Milton's indirect influence can be seen in John Locke's *Letter Concerning Toleration* (1689), a document which would have a monumental influence on American founders like Thomas Jefferson.[180] Many of Locke's arguments for religious liberty in this famous letter track closely those made by Milton already in the 1640s and 1650s.[181] Like Milton, Locke aimed to convince the English church and state of his day to end their corrosive alliances and to end their corrupt abridgments of the liberty of conscience. "[A]bove all things," Locke pleaded in his *Letter*, it is "necessary to distinguish exactly the business of civil government from that of religion, and to settle the just bounds that lie between the one and the other." The church, Locke wrote, must be "absolutely separate and distinct from the commonwealth." For the church is simply "a voluntary society of men, joining themselves together of their own accord in order to [engage in] the public worshipping of God, in such manner as they judge acceptable to Him, and effectual to the salvation of their souls." Church members are free to enter and free to exit this society. They are free to determine its order and organization and arrange its discipline and worship in a manner they consider most conducive to eternal life. "Nothing ought, nor can be transacted in this society, relating to the possession of civil and worldly goods. No force is to be made use of upon any occasion whatsoever: for force belongs wholly to the civil magistrate."[182]

State force, in turn, cannot touch religion, Locke continued. The state exists merely to protect persons in their outward lives, in their enjoyment of life, liberty, and property. "True and saving religion consists in the inward persuasion of the mind," which only God can touch and tend. A person cannot be compelled to true belief of anything by outward force – whether through "confiscation of estate, imprisonments, [or] torments" or through mandatory compliance with "articles of faith or forms of worship" established by law. "For laws are of no force without penalties, and penalties in this case are absolutely impertinent, because they are not proper to convince the mind." "It is only light and evidence that can work a change in men's [religious] opinions: which light can in no manner proceed from

---

[180] Sanford Kessler, "Locke's Influence on Jefferson's 'Bill for Establishing Religious Freedom'," *Journal of Church and State* 25 (1983): 231.
[181] See Winthrop S. Hudson, "John Locke: Heir of Puritan Political Theorists," in George L. Hunt, ed., *Calvinism and the Political Order* (Philadelphia, PA, 1965), 108–129; Waldron, *God, Locke, and Equality*.
[182] Locke, *Works* v:9, 13, 16, 21.

corporal sufferings, or any other outward penalties" inflicted by the state. Every person "has the supreme and absolute authority of judging for himself" in matters of faith. But not all are welcome to act on their judgments: Catholics, Muslims, and other believers "who deliver themselves up to the service and protection of another prince," wrote Locke, have no place in this community. Moreover, "those are not at all tolerated who deny the being of a God" – for "promises, covenants, and oaths which are the bonds of human society, can have no hold upon an atheist."[183] Every one of these justly famous statements of Locke could have been written by Milton.

Not only later English reformers, but also American colonists and later American revolutionaries looked to Milton among others for inspiration and instruction in their construction of rights and liberties. In colonial New England, as we shall see in the next chapter, Milton's ideas of religious and civil liberty helped to liberalize and pluralize the earlier Congregationalist establishments, and some of his writings became standard fare for students at Harvard, Yale, and Princeton in the eighteenth century.[184] Both during the American Revolution of 1776, and during the construction of state and federal constitutions over the next twenty-five years, American founders as diverse as John Adams, Thomas Jefferson, James Madison, Thomas Paine, and James Otis cited Milton with reverence, and echoed his political writings – most notably his caustic attack on "Constantinian" constructions of church and state and his defense of revolution against royal tyranny.[185] As John Adams put it in 1776, John Milton was "as honest a man as his nation ever bred, and as great a friend of liberty" that the common law tradition had ever seen.[186]

---

[183] *Ibid.*, v:11, 41, 47.

[184] See Edmund S. Morgan, ed., *Puritan Political Ideas 1558–1794*, repr. edn. (Indianapolis, IN and Cambridge, 2003), 276.

[185] Tony Davies, "Borrowed Language: Milton, Jefferson, Mirabeau," in Armitage, Himy and Skinner, *Milton and Republicanism*, 254–271.

[186] John Adams, *Thoughts Upon Government*, in Adams, IV:466. See also his panegyrics on Milton's genius in *ibid.*, 1:463; II:14; IX:354. But Adams denounced Milton's retreat to rule by an oligarchic national council in his later life. See *ibid.*, IV:464–466, VI:120.

6. "The Reformers' Attack on the Old Rotten Tree, or the Foul Nests of the Cormorants in Danger," satirical cartoon, published by E. Kin

CHAPTER 5

How to govern a city on a hill: Covenant liberty in Puritan New England

[M]en shall say of succeeding plantations: the Lord make it like that of New England: for we must consider that we shall be as a city upon a hill, the eyes of all people are upon us.

John Winthrop (1630)[1]

In his 1765 *Dissertation on the Canon and the Feudal Law*, John Adams, the great Massachusetts lawyer and eventual American President, defended the "sensible" New England Puritans against those "many modern gentlemen" of his day who dismissed them as bigoted, narrow, "enthusiastical, superstitious and republican." Such "ridicule" and "ribaldry" of the Puritans are "grossly injurious and false," Adams retorted. Far from being narrow bigots, the Puritans were for Adams "illustrious patriots," since, in his view, they were the first "to establish a government of the church more consistent with the scriptures, and a government of the state more agreeable to the dignity of human nature than any other seen in Europe: and to transmit such a government down to their posterity."[2]

What impressed Adams most was that the New England Puritans had created a comprehensive system of ordered liberty and orderly pluralism within church, state, and society. While the Puritans drew from a range of Calvinist teachings, the centerpiece of their system was the idea of covenant, which they cast in both theological and sociological terms. For the Puritans,

---

[1] John Winthrop, *A Model of Christian Charity* (1630), quoting Matthew 5:14, in Morgan, *Puritan Political Ideas*, 93. In this chapter, too, I have modernized the spelling and punctuation of the original sources. Recent scholarship suggests that Winthrop delivered this famous sermon in England before leaving for America, rather than aboard the *Arabella* en route. See Francis J. Bremer, *John Winthrop: American's Forgotten Founding Father* (Oxford, 2003), 173–184; Hugh J. Dawson, " 'Christian Charitie' as Colonial Discourse: Rereading Winthrop's Sermon in its English Context," *Early American Literature* 33 (1998): 117.

[2] *Papers of John Adams*, eds. R. Taylor, M. Kline and G. Lint, 2 vols. (Cambridge, MA, 1977), 1:114–116. On Adams, see David McCullough, *John Adams* (New York, 2001); Joseph J. Ellis, *Passionate Sage: The Character and Legacy of John Adams*, 2nd edn. (New York and London, 2001); C. Bradley Thompson, *John Adams and the Spirit of Liberty* (Lincoln, NE, 1998); Catherine Drinker Bowen, *John Adams and the American Revolution* (Boston, 1950).

the idea of covenant described not only the relationships between persons and God, but also the multiple relationships among persons in church, state, and society. These divine and temporal covenants, in turn, defined each person's natural, religious, and civil rights and duties within these various relationships. In his later writings, Adams came to see this Puritan covenantal theory of ordered liberty and orderly pluralism as a critical antecedent, analogue, and alternative to the Enlightenment contractarian theories of individual liberty and religious pluralism that were gaining prominence in eighteenth-century America. Adams eventually worked some of this early Puritan covenantal theory into the 1780 Massachusetts Constitution, which he drafted and defended at great length.

Many historians have slowly come to accept the more sympathetic interpretation of the Puritans reflected in Adams's sentiments. At the turn of the twentieth century, the Puritans were still often depicted as rigid "theonomists" and belligerent "theocrats" who knew neither true law nor true liberty. Their infamous banishment of Anne Hutchinson and Roger Williams in the 1630s, their adoption of Mosaic capital crimes in the 1640s, their hanging of four Quakers in the Boston Common in the 1650s, their savage Salem witch trials in the 1690s seemed proof enough of the Puritans's hostility to liberty.[3] Today, the Puritans are now regularly included among the "leaders of American political thought," whose inspiration and instruction on the fundamentals of law and liberty were indispensable to the success of both the American Revolution and the state and federal constitutional conventions that followed.[4]

In this chapter, I focus on seventeenth-century New England Puritan theories of covenant liberty and liberty of covenant, especially in Massachusetts, and then follow a few of the eighteenth-century lines of development that culminated in the 1780 Massachusetts Constitution, among other founding documents. Unlike the French, Dutch, and English Calvinist movements, the New England Calvinist tradition did not produce a

---

[3] For a good treatment of this earlier historiography, see Gordon S. Wood, "Struggle over the Puritans," *New York Review of Books* 36 (1989): 26; Sidney Ahlstrom, "The Puritan Ethic and the Spirit of American Democracy," in Hunt, *Calvinism and the Political Order*, 88.

[4] See, e.g. Bernard Bailyn, *The Ideological Origins of the American Revolution* (Cambridge, MA, 1967), 32; Clinton Rossiter, *The Political Thought of the American Revolution* (New York, 1963), 8. See the extensive bibliographical essay in David A. Weir, *Early New England: A Covenanted Society* (Grand Rapids, MI, 2005), 304–354; see further Dale S. Kuehne, *Massachusetts Congregationalist Political Thought, 1760–1790* (Columbia, MO, 1996); Darrett B. Rutman, "God's Bridge Falling Down": Another Approach to New England Studies Assayed," *William & Mary Quarterly* (3rd ser.) 19 (1962): 408–421; David D. Hall, "On Common Ground: The Coherence of American Puritan Studies," *William & Mary Quarterly* (3rd ser.) 44 (1987): 193–229; Michael McGiffert, "American Puritan Studies in the 1960's," *William & Mary Quarterly* (3rd ser.) 27 (1970): 36–67.

single towering figure like Theodore Beza, Johannes Althusius, or John Milton on whom to focus the analysis. The leadership of New England Puritanism was, from the start, more pluralistic and diverse, with sundry figures like John Winthrop, John Cotton, Samuel Willard, Richard, Increase, and Cotton Mather, John Wise, Elisha Williams, John Adams, and others all developing diverse insights. The leadership of Puritan New England was also more eclectic, drawing on sundry European theological and political sources for their inspiration, most notably those of Calvinist theology and English jurisprudence.

FOUNDING RIGHTS AND LIBERTIES

The English royal charters that first constituted the New England colonies in the 1620s and 1630s gave the Puritans broad latitude to conceive and create their ideal theology and polity. The charters imposed neither an Anglican nor a royalist establishment. The colonists were free to propound and profess their own religious beliefs, provided that they "win and incite the natives of [the] country, to the knowledge and obedience of . . . the Christian faith" and seek "to advance the enlargement of Christian religion, to the glory of God Almighty." All colonists of good moral and religious standing were free to develop their own political and legal structures, and to elect their own magistrates, provided that this "be not contrary or repugnant to the laws" of England. They were free to sponsor the emigration of like-minded believers to the colony, provided that "none of the said persons be . . . restrained" by the Crown, and that "none be suspected to affect the superstition of the Church of Rome." And they were free to banish any member who planned or attempted "destruction, invasion, detriment or annoyance to the said colony or plantation."[5]

After the Restoration of the Crown and Church of England in 1660, King Charles II and his agents tried repeatedly to impose their will on colonial religion and politics through new forms of legislation and review. They succeeded only partially with the 1691 passage of a new provincial charter for Massachusetts and with the reinforcement of royal control in the other New England colonies. The 1691 Charter reserved to the Crown the power to appoint the Massachusetts governor and deputy-governor,

---

[5] Quotes are from the Charter of New England (1620), Charter of Massachusetts Bay (1629), Grant of New Hampshire to Capt. John Mason (1629), in Thorpe, II:529, 534; III:1846, 1855, 1857; IV:2433, 2436. Unlike other early New England charters, the 1639 Charter of Maine, issued in the last year of King Charles's campaign to reestablish Anglicanism in England, also sought to establish Anglicanism in Maine. Thorpe, III:1625–1637; Weir, *Early New England*, 24–72.

and it gave the king and the governor veto power over any colonial legislation that contradicted prevailing English law. The Charter also mandated compliance with the 1689 English Toleration Act, which gave Anglicans, Baptists, and other Protestant dissenters legal standing in the community, albeit with more limited rights than members of the established Congregationalist churches (as the Calvinist or Puritan churches of the day came to be called).[6] But for much of the seventeenth century and for a couple of decades in the eighteenth despite the 1691 Charter, the New England Calvinists enjoyed both the homogeneity and the hegemony to carry out their theological and political experiments.[7]

The New England Puritans did not create their theology and polity out of whole cloth. Though largely free from the ecclesiastical control of European Calvinists, they maintained the basic convictions of their European brethren. The Geneva Bible and Catechism, the Westminster Confession and Catechisms, the theological treatises of John Calvin and William Perkins, and the various English and Dutch Calvinist pamphlets and tracts that they had brought with them when the colonists emigrated were all important sources of New England colonial theology.[8] Though largely free from the political control of the English Crown, the Puritans respected English "laws and statutes" and "the liberties and immunities of free and natural subjects," as their founding charters required. A number of their early leaders had legal training in England, and for them the treatises of Sir Edward Coke, John Selden, Michael Dalton, and others were standard legal texts, as were various English Puritan political pamphlets and sermons from the 1620s forward.[9]

The Massachusetts Bay colonists, however, did not rely on these English sources alone to guide and govern themselves. Indeed, in 1641, just over a decade after their arrival, they had in place a comprehensive bill of rights and liberties. The 1641 *Body of Liberties*, as the text was called, incorporated the rights guarantees of the Magna Carta (1215) and the Petition of Right (1628), many of the most daring rights proposals of the early Puritan pamphleteers

---

[6] Thorpe, III:1870.

[7] On the demographics of the early colonists, see T. H. Breen, *Puritans and Adventurers: Change and Persistence in Early America* (New York and Oxford, 1980), 46–67; on the fragmentation of New England, see E. Brooks Holifield, *Theology in America: Christian Thought from the Age of the Puritans to the Civil War* (New Haven and London, 2003), 127–158; Mark A. Noll, *America's God: From Jonathan Edwards to Abraham Lincoln* (Oxford and New York, 2002), 31–52.

[8] Perry Miller, *Orthodoxy in Massachusetts 1630–1650: A Genetic Study* (Cambridge, MA, 1933); Randall Stewart, "Puritan Literature and the Flowering of New England," *William & Mary Quarterly* (3rd ser.) 3 (1946): 319.

[9] Morris Cohen, "Legal Literature in Colonial Massachusetts," in *Law in Colonial Massachusetts 1630– 1800*, ed. Daniel Coquillete (Boston and Charlottesville, VA, 1984), 243.

in England, and a number of surprising innovations. The document was drafted by Nathaniel Ward, a distinguished Cambridge-trained lawyer and Calvinist minister, who had come to New England in 1634, with ten years of legal experience as a barrister in England.[10] The *Body of Liberties* fills twenty-five pages in modern edition, and provides a detailed recitation of what Ward called the "first, basic, elemental, and essential" public, private, and procedural rights that were to obtain in the Massachusetts Bay colony.[11]

The preamble to the 1641 *Body of Liberties* makes clear that the Massachusetts colonists regarded the protection of rights and liberties to be essential to the peace and stability of church, state, and society alike:

The free fruition of such liberties, immunities and privileges as humanity, civility, and Christianity call for as due to every man in his place and proportion without impeachment and infringement hath ever been and ever will be the tranquility and stability of churches and commonwealths. And the denial or deprival thereof, the disturbance if not the ruin of both.

We hold it therefore our duty and safety whilst we are about the further establishing of this government to collect and express all such freedoms as for present we foresee may concern us, and our posterity after us, and to ratify them with our solemn consent.

We do therefore this day religiously and unanimously decree and confirm these following rights, liberties and privileges concerning our churches, and civil State to be respectively impartially and inviolably enjoyed and observed throughout our jurisdiction for ever.[12]

The document then opened with strong guarantees of the rights to life, liberty, property, family, and reputation, the core values that Calvinists for a century had imputed to the Second Table of the Decalogue:

No man's life shall be taken away, no man's honor or good name shall be stained, no man's person shall be arrested, restrained, banished, dismembered, nor any ways punished, no man shall be deprived of his wife or children, no man's goods or estate shall be taken away from him, nor any way damaged under color of law or countenance of authority, unless it be by virtue or equity of some express law of the country warranting the same, established by a general court and sufficiently published, or in case of the defect of a law in any particular case by the word of God.

---

[10] On Ward, see Jean Béranger, *Nathaniel Ward (ca. 1578–1652)* (Bordeaux, 1969); Samuel Eliot Morison, *Builders of the Bay Colony* (Boston, 1930), 217–243.

[11] Nathaniel Ward [Theodore de la Gaurd], *The Simple Cobler of Aggawam in America* [1646/7], ed. P. M. Zall (Lincoln, NE, 1969), 46. All subsequent quotations from The *Body of Liberties* are to be found in Morgan, *Puritan Political Ideas*, 177–203, where the *Body of Liberties* is reprinted.

[12] The first paragraph of the *Body of Liberties* is almost identical to the preamble of the Town Orders of Woburn, issued a year before in December 18, 1640, quoted in Weir, *Early New England*, 103.

The *Body of Liberties* fleshed out these basic guarantees with a number of criminal procedural rights and protections. All persons, "whether inhabitant or foreigner," were to "enjoy the same justice" and "equal and impartial" execution of the law. Parties could be charged only for crimes that were explicitly prohibited by statute. Grand juries were to be used to make preliminary findings in cases of suspicious death. Defendants had a right to bail except in cases of capital crime (idolatry, witchcraft, blasphemy, homicide, homosexual sodomy, adultery, kidnapping, treason, or perjury leading to wrongful execution). They could not be punished for failure to appear in court because of unforeseen circumstances. They had a right to a hearing before an impartial judge, and the right to a speedy trial, whether a bench or jury trial. They were guaranteed the privilege against self-incrimination. They could not be subject to double jeopardy for the same offense, and official case records were to be kept by courts to ensure the same. Conviction for crime required proof by "clear and sufficient evidence." Conviction in capital cases required "the testimony of two or three witnesses or that which is equivalent thereunto." A defendant could not be tortured to collect evidence against himself. Every defendant had the right to appeal his case to a higher court and ultimately to the General Council. If the defendant was sentenced to corporal punishment, the *Body of Liberties* provided that "we allow amongst us none that are inhumane, barbarous or cruel." In capital cases, "no man condemned to die shall be put to death within four days next after his condemnation, unless the court see special cause to the contrary, or in case of martial law."

In civil suits, parties could select written or oral pleadings, and could elect a bench or jury trial. In a jury trial, jurors were selected from the electorate of the community, and both plaintiffs and defendants could challenge the selection of individual jurors. Jurors could deliberate together, and reach general, special, or partial verdicts, but only "clearly and safely" from the evidence presented. Parties could appear pro se, or through (non-compensated) representatives. They could sue for legal damages or equitable relief. Defendants could counterclaim as apt. Parties could be compelled to testify in these civil cases, at the judge's discretion. Plaintiffs could withdraw their suits anytime before the verdict, after paying the defendant's fees in the first case. Cases could be dismissed and the plaintiff fined for barratry, however, if the plaintiff was unduly litigious or sought simply to harass the defendant or harm his reputation. Defendants could plead contributory negligence by the plaintiff in cases of trespass or damage. Defendants were prohibited from feigning poverty to discourage lawsuits or collection of judgments against them. They could not be imprisoned for private debts, except in cases of extreme profligacy. They could claim something of a "homestead exemption" with no taking of a defendant's "corn nor hay that is in the field or upon the cart, nor his garden stuff, nor anything subject to present decay." In all cases, parties could appeal adverse orders or judgments.

The *Body of Liberties* included strong guarantees of private property rights and private contracts based on the same. All competent males, twenty-one or older, had the right to hold, alienate, devise, and inherit private properties without fees, taxes, or government interference. Married women, minors, and the mentally incompetent could do the same "if it be passed and ratified by the consent of a General Court." Forced or "fraudulent conveyances" and alienations of any sort, however, would be reversed and the perpetrators punished upon petition by the injured party. Private landowners had fishing and hunting rights on public lands. While everyone was expected to assist in the public work of the community, nobody could bear a disproportionate burden, and exemptions were to be granted to the aged and the disabled. While all persons were expected to pitch in what they could in cases of emergency, they could not be compelled to military service in offensive wars, and any of their private property taken for public use would need be replaced or its costs reimbursed. The law banned monopolies in general, but granted short-term exclusive patents for new inventions. The law also banned usury and price gouging, but did allow interest charges on loans.

The *Body of Liberties* included special liberties and protections for women, children, and servants, bracketing the traditional common law rules about the right of the paterfamilias to rule the home with little state interference. "Every married woman shall be free from bodily correction or stripes by her husband," and had special procedural protections to bring complaints. A widow could also seek redress from her late husband's estate if her legacy proved inadequate. Children were to be free from any "unnatural severity" from their parents and had special procedures to seek redress in such cases as well as in cases where parents "willfully and unreasonably" withheld their consent to their "timely or convenient marriage." Servants, too, were to be free from "the tyranny and cruelty of their masters" and were to be given sanctuary with other freemen if they escaped. While corporal discipline of servants was presupposed, they were to be freed if their masters injured them severely, and no indentured servitude could last more than seven years. Even domestic animals received some protection: "No man shall exercise any tyranny or cruelty towards any brute creature which are usually kept for man's use."

The *Body of Liberties* set forth a number of public or civil rights. All "freemen" (male church members, twenty-one or older) had the right to vote in political election, to stand for political office, and to participate in popular referenda on fundamental issues of law and morality – and in all such contexts had the right to speak or to be silent and to vote or not to vote in accordance with their conscience. All competent adult males had the right and duty to serve on a jury when selected, though no more than twice a year. All adults, regardless of gender or status, had the right to appear and speak at regular town meetings, provided they were not disruptive or offensive. They had the further "liberty to come to any public court, council, or town meeting, and either by speech or writing to move any lawful, seasonable, and material question, or to present any necessary motion, complaint, petition, bill or information." They also had "free liberty to search" and make copies of public records. The *Body of Liberties* provided a right to sanctuary for anyone "professing the true Christian Religion" who fled to the colony to escape tyranny, oppression, war, famine or shipwreck. It also included a general prohibition against "bond slavery," save where "lawful captives taken in just wars, and such strangers as willingly sell themselves or are sold to us. And these shall have all the liberties and Christian usages which the law of God established in Israel concerning such persons doth morally require."

This last admonition to the colonists to adhere to the law of God in their administration of state law underscored that the *Body of Liberties* was a self-consciously Christian recitation of rights and liberties. "No custom or prescription shall ever prevail amongst us in any moral cause," the law provided, "that can be proved to be morally sinful by the word of God." This overt Christian commitment was further underscored by the detailed provisions on religious liberty for true believers:

1. All the people of God within this jurisdiction who are not in a church way, and be orthodox in judgment, and not scandalous in life, shall have full liberty to gather themselves into a church estate. Provided they do it in a Christian way, with due observation of the rules of Christ revealed in his word.
2. Every church hath full liberty to exercise all the ordinances of God, according to the rules of scripture.
3. Every church hath free liberty of election and ordination of all their officers from time to time, provided they be able, pious and orthodox.
4. Every church hath free liberty of admission, recommendation, dismissal, and expulsion, or disposal of their officers, and members, upon due cause, with free exercise of the discipline and censures of Christ according to the rules of his word.

5. No injunctions are to be put upon any church, church officers or member in point of doctrine, worship, or discipline, whether for substance or circumstance besides the institutions of the Lord.

6. Every church of Christ hath freedom to celebrate days of fasting and prayer, and of thanksgiving according to the word of God.

7. The elders of churches have free liberty to meet monthly, quarterly, or otherwise, in convenient numbers and places, for conferences, and consultations about Christian and church questions and occasions.

8. All churches have liberty to deal with any of their members in a church way that are in the hand of justice. So it be not to retard or hinder the course thereof.

9. Every church hath liberty to deal with any magistrate, deputy of court or other officer whatsoever that is a member in a church way in case of apparent and just offence given in their places, so it be done with due observance and respect.

10. We allow private meetings for edification in religion amongst Christians of all sorts of people. So it be without just offence for number, time, place, and other circumstances.

Earlier the document had set out three provisions that ensured a basic separation of the offices and activities of church and state:

Civil authority hath power and liberty to see the peace, ordinances and rules of Christ observed in every church according to his word so [long as] it be done in a civil and not in an ecclesiastical way.

Civil authority hath power and liberty to deal with any church member in a way of civil justice, notwithstanding any church relation, office, or interest.

No church censure shall degrade or depose any man from any civil dignity, office, or authority he shall have in the Commonwealth.

The 1641 *Body of Liberties* was a remarkably detailed list of public, private, and procedural rights and liberties. It was all the more remarkable in that it was drawn up for a young scattered community of some 15,000 souls, for whom mere survival for a second decade was still the most pressing concern. The *Body of Liberties* was duplicated in whole or in part in a number of other New England colonies, and it became something of an anchor text for New England constitutionalism.[13] Indeed, John Adams and the constitutional conventioneers drew directly on this text in crafting and ratifying many of the substantive and procedural rights provisions of the 1780 Massachusetts Constitution.[14] The main author of the 1641

---

[13] In Massachusetts, many of its provisions were echoed – and some qualified – in *The Laws and Liberties of Massachusetts Bay* (1648), ed. Max Farrand (Cambridge, MA, 1929). For other documents and discussion, see W. Keith Kavenagh, *Foundations of Colonial America: A Documentary History*, 3 vols. (New York, 1973); Donald S. Lutz, *Colonial Origins of the American Constitution* (Indianapolis, IN, 1998); Lutz, *The Origins of American Constitutionalism*.

[14] See sources in note 34 below.

Body of Liberties, Nathaniel Ward, later argued that this was something of a compilation of the rights and liberties of the English common law tradition in which he had been trained, many of them anchored in the Magna Carta and in later medieval cases interpreting its provisions.[15] Ward was deprecating both the novelty and the sweep of his formulations – as Governor Winthrop and the General Council made clear a few years later in comparing the Massachusetts and English formulations.[16] But Ward's argument underscored the reality that the New England Puritans, like the European Calvinists before them, inherited many more rights and liberties than they invented.

What was new in colonial New England was to have these widely scattered traditional common law rights (and many new rights besides) compiled in a single source, generally available to all subjects of the community regardless of the court in which they appeared, and generally binding on all officials and citizens at once. Nothing like that existed in the English common law of the day, with its byzantine complex of courts, writs, and procedures. The one recent attempt by Parliament to compile a few of the more important rights of the people, namely the Petition of Right of 1628, had been cavalierly ignored by the Crown.

What was also new in colonial New England, compared to old England, was to have this *Body of Liberties* serve as something of a written constitutional text that gave preemptory instruction to government authorities on the limits of the law and that gave permanent standing to colonial citizens to press claims to vindicate rights abuses. The Massachusetts colonists understood the novelty of this approach, and took pains to underscore it in the concluding paragraphs of the document:

Howsoever these above specified rights, freedoms, immunities, authorities and privileges, both civil and ecclesiastical, are expressed only under the name and title of liberties, and not in the exact form of laws or statutes, yet we do with one consent fully authorize, and earnestly entreat all that are and shall be in authority to consider them as laws, and not to fail to inflict condign and proportional punishments upon every man impartially that shall infringe or violate any of them.

We likewise give full power and liberty to any person that shall at any time be denied or deprived of any of them, to commence and prosecute their suit, complaint or action against any man that shall so do in any court that hath proper cognizance or judicature thereof.

---

[15] Ward, *Simple Cobler*, 40–61.

[16] See *John Winthrop's Discourse on Arbitrary Government* (1644), in *Winthrop Papers*, 5 vols. (Boston, 1944), IV:468–488; and materials analyzed in Francis C. Gray, *Remarks on the Early Laws of Massachusetts Bay* (Boston, 1843).

Lastly because our duty and desire is to do nothing suddenly which fundamentally concern us, we decree that these rights and liberties shall be audibly read and deliberately weighed at every General Court that shall be held, within three years next ensuing, and such of them as shall not be altered or repealed they shall stand so ratified, that no man shall infringe them without due punishment.

The *Body of Liberties* was intended to serve as a constitutional bill of rights for the Massachusetts Bay colony, and studies of later colonial case law make clear that it was so used – although inevitably, like every law in action, it was also blatantly breached, especially in the hands of some early leaders with oligarchic and theocratic pretensions.[17]

What was most novel of all was the ability of the Massachusetts and other New England colonists to develop a new theological construction of rights and liberties based on the doctrine of covenant. The link between covenant and liberty was, of course, not new in the Calvinist tradition – or indeed in other traditions before and with Calvinism.[18] Calvin and his Zurich counterpart, Heinrich Bullinger, had already tied the biblical teachings on covenant to their theories of spiritual liberty, and these views came to powerful expression in later sixteenth-century Reformed communities on the Continent and in England.[19] Beza and various French and Scottish Calvinist writers with and after him, as we have seen, had already developed covenantal theories of society and politics to justify their theories of resistance and revolt. Althusius and various Dutch and English Calvinists with and after him had also worked out a covenantal theory of family, church, and state to defend their organic theory of the commonwealth. And just as the second generation of New England Puritans was leaving for the new world, the Scots issued the famous *Solemn League and Covenant for Reformation and Defence of Religion, the Honor and Happiness of the King, and the Peace and Safety of the Three Kingdoms of Scotland, England, and Ireland* (1643). Citing the biblical teachings of covenant in 2 Chronicles 15:15, Proverbs 25:5, Jeremiah 50:5, and Galatians 3:15, this new Scottish

---

[17] George L. Haskins, *Law and Authority in Early Massachusetts: A Study in Tradition and Design* (New York, 1960); Richard B. Morris, *Studies in the History of American Law with Special Reference to the Seventeenth and Eighteenth Centuries* (New York, 1930), 46–48; Zechariah Chaffee, "Colonial Courts and the Common Law," in *Essays in the History of Early American Law*, ed. David H. Flaherty (Chapel Hill, NC, 1969), 53–82. For a negative assessment, see Elizabeth Dale, *Debating – and Creating – Authority: The Failure of a Constitutional Ideal in Massachusetts Bay, 1629–1649* (Aldershot, 2001).

[18] See David Novak, *Covenantal Rights: A Study in Jewish Political Theory* (Princeton, 2000); John Witte, Jr. and Eliza Ellison, eds., *Covenant Marriage in Comparative Perspective* (Grand Rapids, MI, 2005).

[19] David A. Weir, *The Origins of Federal Theology in Sixteenth-Century Reformation Thought* (Oxford and New York, 1990); J. Wayne Baker and Charles S. McCoy, *Fountainhead of Federalism: Heinrich Bullinger and the Covenantal Tradition* (Louisville, KY, 1991).

covenant called on the rulers and the people to protect "the true public liberty, safety, and peace of the kingdom, wherein every one's private condition is included" and "to preserve the rights and privileges of the Parliaments, and the liberties of the kingdoms; and to preserve and defend the king's majesty's person and authority, in the preservation and defense of the true religion and liberties of the kingdoms."[20]

The New England Puritans drew directly on these various Calvinist teachings about covenant and liberty in developing their own theories both of liberty of covenant and covenants of liberty. Their idea of a liberty of covenant, while initially exclusivist, eventually became the basis for a robust theory of confessional pluralism. Their idea of covenants of liberty, while initially conservative, eventually became the basis for a robust theory of structural pluralism that protected the rights and liberties of various groups and their members, not least churches.

LIBERTY OF COVENANT

The idea of a divine covenant between God and humanity was part of Western Christian theology from the very beginning. The Bible referred to this covenant 310 times – 286 times in the Hebrew Bible (as *b'rit*), 24 more times in the New Testament (as *foedus*). Classically, Western Christian theologians distinguished two biblical covenants: (1) the covenant of works whereby the chosen people of Israel, through obedience to God's law, are promised eternal salvation and blessing; and (2) the covenant of grace whereby the elect, through faith in Christ's incarnation and atonement, are promised eternal salvation and beatitude. The covenant of works was created in Abraham, confirmed in Moses, and consummated with the promulgation and acceptance of the Torah. The covenant of grace was promised to Abraham, created in Christ, confirmed in the Gospel, and consummated with the confession and conversion of the Christian. A few earlier Christian writers had also described the church as a "covenant community" and the Christian sacraments as "signs" and "symbols" of the covenant of grace. On the whole, however, discussions of covenant in the Christian theological tradition were only incidental and isolated, comprising little more than a footnote to the great doctrines of God and humanity, sin and salvation, law and Gospel.[21]

---

[20] In Stephenson and Markham, 504–505.
[21] See detailed sources in Daniel J. Elazar, *Covenant & Commonwealth: From Christian Separation Through the Protestant Reformation* (New Brunswick, N.J., 1996); Elazar, *Covenant and Civil Society: The Constitutional Matrix of Modern Democracy* (Brunswick, N.J., 1998).

Calvinist writers, first in Europe and then in New England, transformed the covenant into one of the cardinal doctrines of their theology. "The whole of God's word," wrote one Calvinist theologian already in 1597, "has to do with some covenant."[22] "All that we teach you from day to day," another informed his students, "are but conclusions drawn from the covenant."[23] The doctrine of covenant, wrote another leading divine, "embraces the whole of the catechism . . . [N]o context of Holy Scripture can be explained solidly, no doctrine of theology can be treated properly, no controversy can be decided accurately" without reference to this doctrine.[24]

The New England Puritans, and some of their English co-religionists, made two innovations to traditional understandings of God's covenant relationships with persons. First, the Puritans developed a more participatory theory of the covenant of works. Traditionally, the covenant of works was treated as God's special relation with the chosen people of Israel and their representatives, Abraham, Moses, and David. It designated the Israelites as God's elect nation and called them to serve as special agents in God's kingdom. It divulged to them in detail the requirements of God's law – their obligations toward God, neighbor, and self. It demanded of them perfect obedience of God's law, and perfect fulfillment of their divine callings. It promised them, in return, eternal prosperity, blessing, and salvation.

For many Puritan writers, the covenant of works was not so limited in participation or purpose. The covenant of works was not created in Abraham, the representative of the Jews, but in Adam, the representative of all humanity. It was not a privileged relation in which only elect persons participated, but a natural relation, in which all persons participated. For the covenant of works was established at the creation of the world, before the fall into sin, the Puritans argued. Through Adam, the "federal head of the human race," all persons were parties to this covenant. Through Adam, all persons received its promises and blessings as well as its threats and curses.[25]

This pre-fall covenant of works, the Puritans believed, was "God's special constitution for mankind," God's "providential plan for creation."[26]

[22] Robert Rollock, *Tractatus de Vocatione Efficaci* (1597), in *Selected Works of Robert Rollock*, ed. W. Gunn, 2 vols. (Edinburgh, 1849), 1:15.

[23] John Preston, *The New Covenant or the Saints Portion* (London, 1629), 351; see David Zaret, *The Heavenly Contract: Ideology and Organization in Pre-Revolutionary Puritanism* (Chicago, 1985), 151.

[24] Johann Heinrich Alsted, *Catechetical Theology* (1619), quoted by Jaroslav Pelikan, *Reformation of Church and Dogma, 1300–1700* (Chicago, 1984), 367.

[25] See detailed sources in my "Blest be the Ties that Bind: Covenant and Community in Puritan Thought," *Emory Law Journal* 36 (1987): 579.

[26] William Ames, *Medulla Sacrae Theologiae Pertita*, 8 vols. (Frankener, 1623), 1.10; John Norton, *Orthodox Evangelist* (London, 1654), 102ff.

The covenant of works defined each person's telos or purpose in life, each person's role in the unfolding of God's providential plan. It instituted basic human relationships of friendship and kinship, authority and submission. It established basic principles of social, political, familial, and moral life and thought. It created the conditions for perfect communion with God, and perfect community among persons. To abide by this divine covenant, in every particular, was to earn eternal life and salvation; to breach the covenant was to receive eternal death and damnation.[27]

Adam and Eve's fall into sin did not abrogate this covenant of works, the Puritans argued. It only altered humanity's relation to it. The created norms set out in this covenant for the ordering and governing of human life remained in effect. All persons still stood in covenant relationship with God. Because of their sin, however, all persons had lost their view of the norms of creation and lost their capacity to earn their salvation. Thus, after the fall, God sent his son, Jesus Christ, as humanity's guarantor and representative. As guarantor, Christ satisfied each person's debt under the covenant of works and absorbed the punishment that he or she deserved because of their sin. As representative, as the "second Adam," Christ negotiated a second covenant with God, the covenant of grace whereby the elect, despite their sin, could still inherit salvation.[28] This new covenant of grace repeated the terms of the old covenant of works. But, unlike the old covenant, it conditioned a person's salvation on faith in Christ, not on the works demanded by the covenant of works. And this new covenant of grace revealed the terms of the covenant not only in the hearts and consciences of persons, but also in the pages of Scripture.

Second, the Puritans reconfigured not only the traditional covenant of works, but also the traditional covenant of grace. Traditionally, the covenant of grace was treated primarily as God's merciful gift to his elect. God set the terms and obligations of the covenant and determined its parties and their participation. Persons, in their sin, could not demand God's gracious covenant gift or bind God by it once it was conferred. Persons could simply accept the covenant in gratitude. A number of seventeenth-century Puritan writers, by contrast, came to describe the covenant of grace as something of a contractual bargain negotiated between God and each person. Acts of divine will and human will were required to form this covenant. Through "voluntary condescension" (as the Westminster Confession put it), God offered the terms of salvation and promised to abide by the offer. Through

---

[27] *Norton, Orthodox Evangelist*, 14–15; *The Works of Thomas Shepard*, 3 vols. (Boston, 1853), 1:17ff., 90ff.
[28] Richard Alleine, *Heaven Opened: Or the Riches of God's Covenant of Grace* (London, 1665), 29ff.

a voluntary act of faith, a person accepted God's offer. Once God and the person had accepted the terms, both parties were contractually bound to the covenant. Each party could insist upon the faithful compliance of the other. God could demand faithful devotion and service from the person; if the person refused it, God was released from the covenant and free to consign the person to hell. But the person could also demand that God should abide by his promise of salvation. "You may sue [God] of his bond written and sealed," wrote the English Puritan John Preston, "and he cannot deny it." "Take no denial, though the Lord may defer long, yet he will do it, he cannot choose; for it is part of his covenant."[29] What traditionally had been treated as God's gift of faith and salvation to the elect became, in some formulations of later Puritanism, a bargained contract. What traditionally had been understood as God's covenant faithfulness to his people became God's contractual obligation to them. What traditionally had been a person's faithful acceptance of God's irresistible call to grace became a person's voluntary formation of a covenant relationship with God.

Both the expansion of the parties and the contractualization of the terms of the covenant of salvation helped to expand Puritan understandings of religious liberty and religious pluralism. Initially, seventeenth-century New England Puritans were notorious for their religious rigidity and illiberality, and banished any and all who deviated even slightly from the orthodox way. The most famous exiles were Anne Hutchinson and Roger Williams, who were dismissed in the 1630s after sensational trials, but many others were banished as well and with far less ceremony.[30] For, in this early period, the Puritans still treated the covenant of salvation as something of a "divine adhesion contract."[31] God set the covenantal terms for salvation in the Bible that the community had come to interpret in a distinct way. A person had only the freedom to accept or reject these covenantal terms of salvation. Such sentiments can be seen in a lengthy 1682 tract on "covenant liberty" by Samuel Willard, the great systematizer of New England Puritan doctrine. Willard argued that every person had the "equal right," "title," "claim," "liberty" and "prerogative" "to enter and to enjoy every blessing of the covenant." But, by the time Willard finished spelling out all the standard

---

[29] Preston, quoted by Hill, *Puritanism and Revolution*, 246.
[30] See David D. Hall, *The Antinomian Controversy: A Documentary History*, 2nd edn. (Durham, NC, 1990); Stephen Foster, "New England and the Challenge of Heresy, 1630 to 1660: The Puritan Crisis in Transatlantic Perspective," *William & Mary Quarterly* (3rd ser.) 2 (1981): 624–660.
[31] The term is from Paul Ramsey, *Basic Christian Ethics* (New York 1950), 371.

terms and conditions of the covenant, there seemed to be few at liberty to enter the covenant, and little liberty left for those few who could.[32]

By the eighteenth century, however, some Puritan writers began to view this covenantal relationship between God and persons in more open and voluntarist terms. Not only was the covenant made more accessible to parties of various Christian faiths. The terms of the divine covenant itself were made more open to personal deliberation and innovation. Elisha Williams, the great-grandson of early Puritan stalwart John Cotton, put the matter thus in a critical tract on *The Essential Rights and Liberties of Protestants* (1744):

Every man has an equal right to follow the dictates of his own conscience in the affairs of religion. Every one is under an indispensable obligation to search the Scriptures for himself . . . and to make the best use of it he can for his own information in the will of God, the nature and duties of Christianity. And as every Christian is so bound; so he has the inalienable right to judge of the sense and meaning of it, and to follow his judgment wherever it leads him; even an equal right with any rulers be they civil or ecclesiastical.[33]

Such formulations became increasingly common among Puritan writers in the later eighteenth century. These sentiments helped lead the New England leaders to greater open toleration of Baptists, Anglicans, Methodists, and other Christians who abided by the basic terms of the biblical covenants.

It was only a short step from this formulation to the more generic and generous religious liberty guarantee of the 1780 Massachusetts Constitution that John Adams drafted.[34] Freedom of religion was among the first rights that the Massachusetts Constitution protected. We must begin "by setting the conscience free," Adams wrote in presenting his draft Constitution, for the rights of conscience and religion are "indisputable, unalienable, indefeasible, [and] divine."[35] Accordingly, Article II of the "Declaration of Rights" in the Constitution provided:

---

[32] Samuel Willard, *A Compleat Body of Divinity* (Boston, 1726); Willard, *Covenant-Keeping the Way to Blessedness* (Boston, 1682). See further Willard, *Morality not be Relied on for Life* (Boston, 1700); Willard, *Walking with God, The Great Duty and Privilege of True Christians* (Boston, 1701) and T. H. Breen, *The Character of the Good Ruler 1630–1730* (New Haven, 1970), 37–44.

[33] Elisha Williams, *The Essential Rights and Liberties of Protestants* (Boston, 1744), 3, 7–8. On Williams, see Francis Parsons, *Six Men of Yale* (New Haven, 1939).

[34] In Thorpe, III:1888ff. with analysis in my "'A Most Mild and Equitable Establishment of Religion': John Adams and the Massachusetts Experiment," *Journal of Church and State* 41 (1999): 213–252, building on Robert J. Taylor, *Construction of the Massachusetts Constitution* (Worcester, MA, 1980); Samuel Eliot Morison, *A History of the Constitution of Massachusetts* (Boston, 1917); Oscar and Mary Handlin, eds., *The Popular Sources of Political Authority: Documents on The Massachusetts Constitution of 1780* (Cambridge, MA, 1966); Robert J. Taylor, ed., *Massachusetts, Colony to Commonwealth: Documents on the Formation of its Constitution* (Chapel Hill, NC, 1961).

[35] Adams, III:452–456.

It is the right as well as the duty of all men in society, publicly, and at stated seasons to worship the Supreme Being, the great creator and preserver of the universe. No subject shall be hurt, molested, or restrained, in his person, liberty, or estate, for worshipping God in the manner and season most agreeable to the dictates of his own conscience, or for his religious profession or sentiments; provided he doth not disturb the public peace, or obstruct others in their religious worship.[36]

Article III, at least tacitly, recognized the right to form religious associations, to select one's own minister and to pay tithes directly to him. Chapter VI of the "Frame of Government" section of the Constitution included within the ambit of religious freedom the right of Quakers to claim an exemption from the swearing of oaths to which they were "conscientiously opposed."[37]

Adams regarded the protection of religious pluralism as essential for the protection of religious and other forms of liberty. As he later put it in a letter to Thomas Jefferson: "Roman Catholics, English Episcopalians, Scotch and American Presbyterians, Methodists, Moravians, Anbaptists, German Lutherans, German Calvinists, Universalists, Arians, Priestlyians, Socinians, Independents, Congregationalists, Horse Protestants and House Protestants, Deists and Atheists and Protestants *qui ne croyent rien* [who believe nothing] are . . . [n]evertheless all educated in the general principles of Christianity: and the general principles of English and American liberty."[38] "Checks and balances, Jefferson," in the political as well as the religious sphere,

are our only security, for the progress of mind, as well as the security of body. Every species of these Christians would persecute Deists, as [much] as either sect would persecute another, if it had unchecked and unbalanced power. Nay, the Deists would persecute Christians, and Atheists would persecute Deists, with as unrelenting cruelty as any Christians would persecute them or one another. Know thyself, human nature!"[39]

Covenant theology was certainly not the only argument available for the constitutional guarantee of religious liberty of various peaceable theistic religions. But, for the New England Puritans, particularly in Massachusetts, covenant theology provided a sturdy foundation for a theory of ordered religious liberty and orderly religious pluralism. By expanding the ambit of the covenant of works, the Puritans expanded the realm of religious liberty to all persons, not just the elect. By contractualizing the terms of the

[36] Thorpe, III: 1889. [37] Thorpe, III: 1908–1910.
[38] Letter to Thomas Jefferson (June 28, 1813), in *The Adams–Jefferson Letters*, ed. Lester J. Cappon, 2 vols. (Chapel Hill, NC: University of North Carolina Press, 1959), I:339–340.
[39] Letter to Thomas Jefferson (June 25, 1813), in *ibid.*, I:334.

covenant of grace, the Puritans expanded the range of religious exercises, no longer privileging state-established forms. But not all claims of religious liberty could be accepted. Legitimate claims to religious liberty protection had to be anchored in some semblance of a covenant with God, however each person chose to define this God and covenant. Legitimate claimants had to abide by the natural duties of love of God, neighbor, and self taught by the covenant of works, however each community chose to delineate these duties.

COVENANTS OF LIBERTY

The Puritans regarded themselves not only as covenant persons in their relationship to God, but also as covenant people bound together by covenants with each other. Each of these covenants, they believed, though formed by voluntary human acts, was ultimately founded on the norms and principles set forth in the covenant of works. Each of these covenants had a place in God's providential plan, a purpose for which it existed.

Building on their innovations to traditional covenant theology, the New England Puritans distinguished three such covenants: (1) a social or communal covenant; (2) an ecclesiastical or church covenant; and (3) a political or governmental covenant. The social covenant created the society or commonwealth as a whole. The political and ecclesiastical covenants created the two chief seats of authority within that society, the church and the state, whose authority was both separated and pluralized.[40] The social, ecclesiastical, and political covenants confirmed and coordinated the natural, religious, and political liberties of the members of these covenant communities.

Natural liberty and the social covenant

At the creation of the world, the Puritans believed, God had vested all persons with "a natural liberty" and subjected them to "a natural law." The natural person, John Winthrop declared, "stands in relation to [his fellow] man simply, [and] hath liberty to do what he lists; it is a liberty to [do]

---

[40] The New England Puritans also regarded the Christian household as an important institution of authority, but their formulations differed little from conventional Calvinist formulations, analyzed above pages 130–132 and 183–186, and I have thus omitted the discussion here. For details see John Demos, *A Little Commonwealth: Family Life in Plymouth Colony*, 2d ed. (New York and Oxford, 2000); Edmund S. Morgan, *The Puritan Family: Religion and Domestic Relations in Seventeenth-Century New England*, rev. edn. (Westport, CT, 1980); George Elliott Howard, *A History of Matrimonial Institutions, Chiefly in England and the United States*, 3 vols. (Chicago, 1904).

evil as well as to [do] good."[41] The vice or virtue of a person's actions is determined by the natural law, which God has written into the covenant of works that is binding on all.[42]

The Puritans believed, however, that "the voice of nature plainly declares that mankind" join together in social covenant and "dwell together in societies."[43] This calling from a natural state to a social state was born of both human necessity and divine destiny. On the one hand, God had called all persons to form societies in order to provide the order and stability and structures of authority needed to maintain the natural liberty and natural law that God had created. "The exercise and maintaining of [natural] liberty," without social and legal constraints, wrote Winthrop, echoing traditional Calvinist teachings on the civil use of the law, "makes men grow more evil, and in time to be worse than brute beasts."[44] Persons "prey" upon each other, placing the natural liberty of all into jeopardy. Society helps guarantee such liberty. Moreover, in a natural state, persons suffer from "weakness, impotency and insufficiency" both in the apprehension of and the obedience to the natural law.[45] Society helps reconfirm and reinforce these natural law principles. It moves persons from their "natural corrupt liberties" to a "civil or federal liberty . . . in reference to the covenant between God and man, in the moral law, and the politic covenants and constitutions amongst men themselves."[46]

On the other hand, God had called the Puritans, in particular, to form their society to help fulfill his providential plan in the new world. The Puritans believed that God had entered into a special covenant relationship with them to be his "surrogate Israel," his newly elect nation, his newly chosen people.[47] By this covenant, they were called to be a "city on the hill," a

---

[41] John Winthrop, "On Liberty" (1645), in *Winthrop's Journal*, ed. James K. Hosmer, 2 vols. (New York, 1908), II:238. Among numerous studies of Winthrop, see Bremer, *John Winthrop* and Edmund S. Morgan, *The Puritan Dilemma: The Story of John Winthrop* (Boston, 1958). For more, see Geoffrey P. Carpenter, *A Secondary Annotated Bibliography of John Winthrop, 1588–1649* (New York, 1999).

[42] John D. Eusden, "Natural Law and Covenant Theology in New England, 1620–1670," *Natural Law Forum* 5 (1960): 1. For a more rationalist formulation, see John Wise, *A Vindication of the Government of New-England Churches (1717)*, repr. edn. (Gainesville, FL, 1958), 30–45.

[43] John Barnard, *The Throne Established By Righteousness* (1734), in Perry Miller and Thomas Johnson, ed., *The Puritans* (New York, 1938), 270–271.

[44] *Winthrop's Journal*, II:238.

[45] Thomas Hooker, *The Application of Redemption by the Effectual Work of the Word, and Spirit of Christ, for the Bringing Home of Lost Sinners to God* (London, 1659), 43.

[46] *Winthrop's Journal*, II:238–239.

[47] Cotton Mather, *The Serviceable Man* (1690), in Morgan, *Puritan Political Ideas*, 233. See also J. Higginson, *The Cause of God and His People in New England* (Cambridge, MA, 1663), 18.

"light to the nations," "a model of Christ's kingdom among the heathens."[48] They were commanded to preserve and propagate godly beliefs and values, to adopt and advocate godly morals and mores, to arouse themselves and all those around them to Godly obedience. Just as God promised the ancient Israelites (in Deuteronomy 4–6) so he promised the modern-day Puritans peace and prosperity if they succeeded in their covenantal task, but death and damnation if they failed.

The Puritan colonists swore allegiance to such social covenants before God and each other when forming their new communities. "We whose names are underwritten," reads the famous Mayflower Compact of 1620,

[h]aving undertaken for the glory of God, and advancement of the Christian faith . . . a voyage to plant the first colony . . . do by these presents, solemnly and mutually in the presence of God and one of another, covenant, and combine ourselves together into a civil body politic, for our better ordering and preservation, and furtherance of the ends aforesaid.[49]

The citizens of the new town of Salem convened in 1629 to swear: "We covenant with the Lord and one with another; and do bind ourselves in the presence of God, to walk together in all his ways, according as he is pleased to reveal himself unto us in his blessed word of truth."[50] The following year John Winthrop declared in his famous sermon to the colonists about to leave for Massachusetts Bay abroad the good ship, *Arabella*: "Thus stands the cause between God and us, we are entered into Covenant with him for this work, we have taken out a commission, [and He] will expect a strict performance of the articles contained in it."[51] The Watertown Covenant (1630) was even more emphatic and expansive:

We whose names are hereto subscribed, having through God's mercy escaped out of pollutions of the world, and been taken into the society of his people, with all thankfulness do hereby both with heart and hand acknowledge his gracious goodness and fatherly care towards us: And for further and more full declaration thereof, to the present and future ages, have undertaken (for the promoting of his glory and the church's good, and the honor of our blessed Jesus, in our more full and free subjecting of ourselves and ours, under his gracious government, in the practice of, and obedience unto all his holy ordinances and orders, which he hath pleased to prescribe and impose upon us) a long and hazardous voyage from east

---

[48] Winthrop, *Christian Charity*, in Morgan, *Puritan Political Ideas*, 93. J. Scottow, "Narrative of the Planting of Massachusetts (1694)," in *Collections of the Massachusetts Historical Society* (4th ser.), 52 vols. (1871), IV:279.

[49] "The Agreement Between the Settlers of New Plymouth (1620)," in Walker, *Creeds and Platforms*, 92.

[50] "The Covenant of 1629," in Walker, *Creeds and Platforms*, 116.

[51] Winthrop, *Christian Charity*, in Morgan, *Puritan Political Ideas*, 92.

to west, from Old England in Europe to New England in America that we may walk before him, and serve him, without fear in holiness and righteousness, all the days of our lives: And being safely arrived here, and thus far onwards peaceably preserved by his special providence, that we bring forth our intentions into actions, and perfect our resolutions, in the beginnings of some just and meet executions; We have separated the day above written from all other services, and dedicated it wholly to the Lord in divine employments, for a day of afflicting our souls, and humbling ourselves before the Lord, to seek him, and at his hands, a way to walk in, by fasting and prayer, that we might know what was good in his sight: And the Lord was entreated of us.

For in the end of the day, after the finishing of our public duties, we do all, before we depart, solemnly and with all our hearts, personally, man by man for ourselves and others (charging them before Christ and his elect angels, even them that are not here with us this day, or are yet unborn, that they keep the promise unblameably and faithfully unto the coming of our Lord Jesus) promise, and enter into a sure covenant with the Lord our God, and before him with one another, by oath and serious protestation made, to renounce all idolatry and superstition, will-worship, all human traditions and inventions whatsoever, in the worship of God; and forsaking all evil ways, do give ourselves wholly unto the Lord Jesus, to do him faithful service, observing and keeping all his statutes, commands, and ordinances, in all matters concerning our Reformation; his worship, administrations, ministry, and government; and in the carriage of ourselves among ourselves, and one another towards another, as he hath prescribed in his Holy Word. Further swearing to cleave unto that alone, and the true sense and meaning thereof to the utmost of our power, as unto the most clear light and infallible rule, and all-sufficient canon, in all things that concern us in this our way.[52]

More than a hundred such social covenants are sprinkled throughout the seventeenth-century New England archives – variously named as compacts, combinations, charters, or patents.[53] In the second generation of colonization, in Massachusetts and beyond, these covenants become longer and more detailed, and often merged into civil covenants that defined the mechanics of government that followed. The Fundamental Orders of Connecticut (1638/9) was a good example.

For as much as it hath pleased Almighty God by the wise disposition of his divine providence so to order and dispose of things that we the inhabitants and residents of Windsor, Hartford and Wethersfield are now cohabiting and dwelling in and upon the river of Connecticut and the lands thereunto adjoining; and well knowing where a people are gathered together the word of God requires that to maintain the peace and union of such a people there should be an orderly and decent government

---

[52] On http://personal.pitnet.net/primarysources/covenants.html#watertown/ (visited January 5, 2007).

[53] See samples in Lutz, *Colonial Origins* and analysis in Weir, *Early New England*, 75–133, 243–297.

established according to God, to order and dispose of the affairs of the people at all seasons as occasion shall require; do therefore associate and conjoin ourselves to be as one public state or commonwealth; and do for ourselves and our successors and such as shall be adjoined to us at any time hereafter, enter into combination and confederation together, to maintain and preserve the liberty and purity of the Gospel of our Lord Jesus which we now profess, as also, the discipline of the churches, which according to the truth of the said Gospel is now practiced amongst us; as also in our civil affairs to be guided and governed according to such laws, rules, orders and decrees as shall be made, ordered, and decreed.[54]

There followed eleven paragraphs with detailed enumeration of the forms and functions of government in the new colony.

The Covenant of Exeter, New Hampshire (1639) provided similarly:

Whereas it hath pleased the Lord to move the heart of our dread sovereign Charles, by the grace of God, King of England, Scotland, France and Ireland, to grant license and liberty to sundry of his subjects to plant themselves in the western parts of America: we, his loyal subjects, brethren of the church of Exeter, situate and lying upon Piscataquacke, with other inhabitants there, considering with ourselves the holy will of God and our own necessity, that we should not live without wholesome laws and government amongst us, of which we are altogether destitute; do in the name of Christ and in the sight of God combine ourselves together, to erect and set up amongst us such government as shall be to our best discerning, agreeable to the will of [God], professing ourselves subjects to our Sovereign Lord King Charles, according to the [Body of] Liberties of our English Colony of the Massachusetts and binding ourselves solemnly by the grace and help of Christ and in his name and fear to submit ourselves to such godly and Christian laws as are established in the realm of England to our best knowledge, and to all other such laws which shall upon good grounds, be made and enacted amongst us according to God, that we may live quietly and peaceably together in all godliness and honesty.

The Exeter Covenant then called for successive oaths by their rulers and the people. The rulers were to swear by

the great and dreadful name of the high God, maker and governor of heaven and earth and by the Lord Jesus Christ, the prince of the kings and rulers of the earth, that in his name and fear you will rule and govern his people according to the righteous will of God, ministering justice and judgment on the workers of iniquity, and ministering due encouragement and countenance to well doers, protecting of the people so far as in you lieth, by the help of God from foreign annoyance and inward disturbance, that they may live a quiet and peaceable life in all godliness and honesty.

The people, in turn, were to swear that

---

[54] Thorpe, 1:519.

we will submit ourselves to be ruled and governed according to the will and word of God, and such wholesome laws and ordinances as shall be derived therefrom by our honored rulers and the lawful assistants, with the consent of the people, and that we will be ready to assist them by the help of God, in the administration of justice and preservation of the peace, with our bodies and goods and best endeavors according to God. So God protect and save us and ours in Jesus Christ.[55]

Participation in these social covenants had to be wholly voluntary and consensual. "There can be no necessary tie of mutual accord and fellowship come, but by free engagement," wrote Thomas Hooker, the founder of New Haven and author of an important tract on church discipline. "[H]e that will enter must also willingly bind and engage himself to each member of that society . . . or else a member actually he is not."[56] The voluntary participation of both the entering individual and the existing community was essential. No person could be forced to join the community whose covenant and culture he or she found objectionable. No community could be forced to accept or retain a person whose convictions or conduct it found objectionable.[57]

Those who voluntarily joined this covenant were subject to both the benevolence and the discipline of the community. The Puritans attached great importance to public benevolence. Charity and public-spiritedness were prized. Churlishness and private sumptuousness were scorned. "[W]e must entertain each other in brotherly affection," declared Winthrop, sounding the familiar Protestant accent on the priesthood of all believers. "[W]e must delight in each other, make others' conditions our own, rejoice together, mourn together, labor and suffer together, always having before our eyes our commission and community in the work, our community as members of the same body."[58] These were not just homiletic platitudes. The New England Puritans prescribed and practiced Good Samaritanism. They punished citizens who failed to aid their neighbors in need or peril. They set up public trusts, community chests, and work programs for indigents and immigrants. They developed systems of relief for the poor, the

[55] *Ibid.*, IV:2445.
[56] Thomas Hooker, *A Survey of the Summe of Church-Discipline*, 2 vols. (London, 1648), 1:47–50. On Hooker, see Frank Shuffelton, *Thomas Hooker, 1586–1647* (Princeton, 1977); Sargent Bush, Jr., *The Writings of Thomas Hooker: Spiritual Adventure in Two Worlds* (Madison, WI, 1980).
[57] John Winthrop, "A Defense of an Order of Court Made in the Year 1637," in Miller and Johnson, *The Puritans*, 200–201.
[58] Winthrop, *Christian Charity*, in Morgan, *Puritan Political Ideas*, 92; Increase Mather, *The Excellency of a Publick Spirit* (Boston, 1702).

elderly, and the handicapped. They established systems of academic and vocational education.[59]

The Puritans attached even greater importance to social discipline and public virtue. The social covenant, the Puritans believed, placed each covenant community "under a solemn divine Probation" and under threat of "eminent [divine] trial."[60] This belief translated the most mundane of human affairs into cosmic terms. The Puritans stressed ambition, austerity, frugality, and other virtues in their lives in part because the social covenant rendered them agents of God, instruments of God's providential plan in the New World. For them to be lax in zeal, loose in discipline, or sumptuous in living would be a disservice to God, a breach of the social covenant. Such a breach would inevitably bring divine condemnation on the community in the form of war, pestilence, poverty, and other forms of *force majeure*. God had punished his covenant people of Israel when they disobeyed him, and threatened to do the same to the New England Puritans if they betrayed the social covenant.

This belief that the covenant society lived perennially under "solemn divine Probation" is reflected in sundry legal and theological texts alike. A 1675 Massachusetts statute, for example, prefaced its rigid new disciplinary code with these words:

Whereas the most wise and holy God, for several years past, hath not only warned us in his word, but chastised us with his rods, inflicting upon us many general (though lesser) judgments, but we have neither heard the word nor rod as we ought, so as to be effectually humbled for our sins, to repent of them, reform and amend our ways . . .[61]

The Reforming Synod of 1679 wrote similarly in its report on *The Necessity of Reformation*. Lamenting and documenting at length the widespread laxity in religion and morality that prevailed in New England, the synod delegates charged that these "evils have provoked the Lord to bring his judgments on New England."

That the Lord hath a controversy with his New England people is undeniable, the Lord having written his displeasure in dismal characters against us. Though

---

[59] Robert W. Kelso, *The History of Public Poor Relief in Massachusetts, 1620–1920* (Boston and New York, 1922); T. H. Breen and Stephen Foster, "The Puritans' Greatest Achievement: A Study of Social Cohesion in Seventeenth-Century Massachusetts," *Journal of American History* 60 (1973): 5–22.

[60] W. Stoughton, *New Englands True Interest: Not to Lie* (1670), in Miller and Johnson, *The Puritans*, 243.

[61] *Records of the Governor and Company of the Massachusetts Bay in New England*, ed. N. Shurtleff, 5 vols. (Boston, 1853–1854), v:59; *Election Day Sermons: Plymouth and Connecticut*, facs. edn. (New York, 1983).

personal afflictions do oftentimes come only or chiefly for probation, yet as to public judgments it is not wont to be so; especially when by a continued series of providence, the Lord doth appear and plead against his people. 2 Sam. 21.1. As with us, it hath been from year to year. Would the Lord have whetted his glittering sword, and his hand have taken hold on judgment? Would he have sent such a mortal contagion like a besom of destruction in the midst of us? Would he have said, Sword! go through the land and cut off man and beast. Or would he have kindled such devouring fires and made such fearful desolations if he had not been angry.

The synod then called for a "solemn and explicit renewal of the covenant" and a "thorough and hearty reformation" of church, state, family, and society, whose necessary steps it documented in some detail.[62] This call for reformation and renewal of the social covenant was a perennial Puritan theme. "Reform all places, all persons and all callings. Reform the benches of judgment, the inferior magistrates . . . Reform the universities, reform the cities, reform the counties, reform inferior schools of learning, reform the Sabbath, reform the ordinances, the worship of God. Every plant which my Father hath not planted shall be rooted up."[63]

John Adams wrote a good deal of this traditional theory of the social covenant into the 1780 Massachusetts Constitution. The preamble refers to the constitution repeatedly as "a covenant" or "compact" between the people and God: "[T]he whole people covenants with each citizen, and each citizen with the whole people, that all shall be governed by certain laws for the common good." And again,

the people of Massachusetts, acknowledging, with grateful hearts, the goodness of the Great Legislator of the universe, in affording us, in the course of his providence, an opportunity, deliberately and peaceably, without fraud, violence, or surprise, of entering into an original, explicit, and solemn compact with each other; and of forming a new constitution of civil government for ourselves and posterity; and devoutly imploring His direction in so interesting a design, do agree upon, ordain and establish the following Declaration of Rights and Frame of Government.

A variant of this covenant ceremony was the oath-swearing ritual required of state officials. Adams wrote into Chapter VI of the "Frame of Government" the requirement that all state officials must swear a full oath to the constitution and the commonwealth – not just privately, but before the people and their representatives in full assembly. "I, A. B. do declare, that I believe the

---

[62] In Walker, *Creeds and Platforms*, 423–437.

[63] Quoted in Harold J. Berman, "Religious Foundations of Law in the West: An Historical Perspective," *Journal of Law and Religion* 1 (1983): 3, 30. See further, Ward, *Simple Cobler*, 32–42; Increase Mather, *The Necessity of Reformation With the Expedients Thereunto Asserted* (Boston, 1679).

Christian religion, and have a firm persuasion of its truth. . . and I do swear, that I will bear true faith and allegiance to the said Commonwealth . . . so help me God." Adams's insistence on such oaths reflected the conventional Puritan view that the oath was "a cement of society" and "one of the principal instruments of government," for it invoked and induced "the fear and reverence of God, and the terrors of eternity."[64] This provision also reflected Adams's view that the oath of office was a public confirmation of the covenant among God, the people, and their rulers. These preamble and oath-swearing provisions were not merely a bit of hortatory throat-clearing that preceded the real business of constitutional government. They established traditional ceremonies of the social covenant.

Adams also wrote the traditional morality of the social covenant into the 1780 Constitution. Article II stipulated that it was not only the right, but also "the duty of all men in society, publicly, and at stated seasons to worship the Supreme Being, the great creator and preserver of the universe." Article III set out the reason for this duty:

the happiness of a people, and good order and preservation of civil government, essentially depend upon piety, religion, and morality; and . . . these cannot be generally diffused through a community, but by the institution of public worship of God, and of public instructions in piety, religion, and morality.[65]

Article XVIII rendered adherence to these moral duties integral to the character of public offices and public officials:

A frequent recurrence to the fundamental principles of the constitution, and a constant adherence to those of piety, justice, moderation, temperance, industry, and frugality, are absolutely necessary to preserve the advantages of liberty, and to maintain a free government. The people ought, consequently, to have a particular attention to all those principles, in the choice of their officers and representatives, and they have a right to require of their lawgivers and magistrates, an exact and constant observance of them, in the formation and execution of the laws necessary for the good administration of the Commonwealth.[66]

For, as Article VII put it: "Government is instituted for the common good; for the protection, safety, prosperity, and happiness of the people." And, as Chapter V of the "Frame of Government" provided: "Wisdom, and knowledge, as well as virtue, diffused generally among the body of the people, [is] necessary for the preservation of their rights and liberties."[67]

---

[64] Thorpe, III: 1908; see Phillips Payson, "Election Sermon of 1778," in *American Political Writing During the Founding Era, 1760–1805*, ed. Charles S. Hynemann and Donald S. Lutz, 2 vols. (Indianapolis, IN, 1983), 1:529.
[65] Thorpe, III: 1889–1890.   [66] Thorpe, III: 1892.   [67] Thorpe, III: 1906–1908.

These twin goals of the social covenant – to maintain natural law and natural liberty and to attain the ideal community of benevolence and discipline – could not be realized without institutions of law and authority. The church and the state were the two chief instruments of law and authority, the Puritans believed. God had laid the foundations for both these in the covenant of works of creation, on which natural foundation the new covenants of church and state had to be built.

Religious liberty and the church covenant

Following Calvinist commonplaces, the Puritans believed that God had vested in the church the spiritual power of the Word. The church had the power to preach the Gospel, to administer the sacraments, to teach the young, to prophesy against injustice, and to care for the poor and the needy. By such activities, the church would lead all members of the community to a greater understanding of their covenantal responsibilities of piety, benevolence, and love. The church also had the power to devise its own polity, to define its own doctrine, and to discipline its own members who had sinned – using the spiritual means of admonition, the ban, and if necessary excommunication. By such activities, the church would confirm and reinforce the natural law and the divine authority that commanded it.[68]

Most seventeenth-century New England Puritans had a congregationalist understanding of the church, with each church regarded as a self-sufficient community and with several churches gathered in each individual township or county.[69] Each congregational church was constituted by a voluntary covenant between God and like-minded believers. By this covenant, these believers swore to God and to each other to uphold God's ordinances, to discharge the special calling of the church, and to be subject to those whom they elected into authority within the church. "Saints by calling," reads the famous *Cambridge Synod and Platform* (1648), "must have a visible-political-union amongst themselves." They must form a "company of professed believers ecclesiastically confederate."[70] "This form is the visible covenant, agreement, consent whereby they give up themselves unto the Lord, to the observing of the ordinances of Christ together in the same society, which is

---

[68] *The Cambridge Synod and Platform* (1648), chs. 1–3, 5, in Walker, *Creeds and Platforms*, 203–210. See also Richard Mather, *Church Government and Church-Covenant Discussed* (London, 1643), reprinted in R. Robey, ed., *Church Covenant: Two Tracts* (New York, 1972), 217.

[69] See Wise, *Vindication*, 29 and discussion in Perry Miller "Introduction," to *ibid.*, v–xvii.

[70] *Cambridge Synod and Platform*, chs. 4–10, in Walker, *Creeds and Platforms*, 207–220.

usually called the church covenant; for we see not otherwise how members can have church power one over another mutually."[71]

The church covenant was the legal structure used both to define and delimit the religious liberty of each church community and of each member who voluntarily joined this church community. Many seventeenth-century New England Puritan churches were formed by such covenants – sworn to by their founding members, and then confirmed by oaths taken from later members who chose to join the church. The Covenant of the Charles-Boston Church (1630), formed by the Massachusetts Bay founder John Winthrop and others, provided:

In the name of our Lord Jesus Christ, and in obedience to his holy will and divine ordinance, we whose names are here underwritten, being by his most wise and good providence brought together into this part of America in the Bay of Massachusetts, and desirous to unite ourselves into one congregation or church under the Lord Jesus Christ our head, in such sort as becometh all those whom he hath redeemed, and sanctified to himself, do hereby solemnly and religiously (as in his most holy presence) promise and bind ourselves, to walk in all our ways according to the rule of the Gospel, and in all sincere conformity to his holy ordinances, and in mutual love and respect each to other, so near as God shall give us grace.[72]

The Watertown Covenant-Creed of 1647 had more expansive language:

We believe that God's people, besides their general covenant with God . . . ought also to join themselves into a church covenant one with another, and to enter into a particular combination together with some of his people to erect a particular ecclesiastical body, and kingdom, and visible family and household of God, for the managing of discipline and public ordinances of Christ in one place in a dutiful way, there to worship God and Christ, as his visible kingdom and subjects, in that place waiting on him for that blessing of his ordinances and promises of his covenant, by holding communion with him and his people, in the doctrine and discipline of that visible kingdom . . . We . . . do here bind ourselves, in the presence of men and angels, by his grace assisting us, to choose the Lord, to serve him, and to walk in all his ways, and to keep all his commandments and ordinances.[73]

The Dorchester First Church Covenant of 1636, prepared by the distinguished covenant theologian, Richard Mather, was more detailed still:

We whose names are subscribed being called of God to join ourselves together in church communion, from our hearts acknowledging our own unworthiness of such a privilege or of the least of God's mercies, and likewise acknowledging our disability to keep covenant with God or to perform any spiritual duty which he

---

[71] Ibid., ch. 4, 207–209.   [72] *Ibid.*, 131.
[73] Watertown Covenant-Creed (1647), in Miller and Johnson, *The Puritans*, 149, 155–156.

calleth us unto, unless the Lord Jesus do enable us thereunto by his spirit dwelling in us, do in the name of Christ Jesus our Lord and in trust and confidence of his free grace assisting us freely covenant and bind ourselves solemnly in the presence of God himself, his holy angels and all his servants here present that we will by his grace assisting us endeavor constantly to walk together as a right ordered congregation of Christ according to all the holy rules of a church-body rightly established, so far as we do already now it to be our duty or shall further understand it out of God's holy Word:

Promising first and above all to cleave unto him as our chief and only good, and to our Lord Jesus Christ as our only spiritual husband and Lord, and our only high priest and prophet and king. And for the further of us keep this blessed communion with God and with his son Jesus Christ and to grow up more fully therein, we do likewise promise by his grace assisting us, to endeavor the establishing amongst ourselves of all his holy ordinances which he hath appointed for his churches here on earth, and to observe all and every of them in such sort as shall be most agreeable to his will; opposing to the utmost of our power whatsoever is contrary thereunto and bewailing from our hearts our own neglect thereof in former time, and our polluting ourselves therein with any sinful inventions of men.

And lastly we do hereby covenant and promise to further to our utmost power, the best . . . spiritual good of each other, and of all and every one that may become members of this congregation, by mutual instruction, reprehension, exhortation, consolation, and spiritual watchfulness over another for good; and to be subject in and for the Lord to all the administrations and censures of the congregation, so far as the same shall be guided according to the rules of God's most holy word.

Of the integrity of our hearts herein we call God the searcher of all hearts to witness; beseeching him so to bless us in this and all our enterprises, as we shall sincerely endeavor by the assistance of his grace to observe this holy covenant and all the branches of it inviolably forever; and where we shall fail there to wait upon the Lord Jesus for pardon and for acceptance and healing for his name's sake.[74]

The seven males who first joined together to form the Dorchester church signed their name to the covenant. (Other church covenants included female signatories as well.[75]) Members who joined the church later were expected to swear to this covenant, and their names would then be added to the roll. As David Weir has shown, the Dorchester church covenant included all the typical provisions of seventeenth-century Congregationalist church covenants that have survived. The preamble set out the main purposes of the covenant – with God, his angels, and his people invoked as witnesses. The covenant community then submitted to God the Father as their founder and to God the Son as their chief prophet, priest, and king.

---

[74] *Records of the First Church at Dorchester in New England, 1636–1734* (Boston, 1891), 1–2, quoted and analyzed in Weir, *Early New England*, 152–162.

[75] See, e.g., the Charlestown, Massachusetts Bay, First Church (1632), quoted and analyzed in Weir, *Early New England*, 150–152.

They agreed to walk together as brothers and sisters in Christ, exercising the offices of prophet, priest, and king toward each other, and submitting to the government and discipline of the faith and faith community.[76]

Most of these Puritan church covenants contemplated an intensely democratic form of church government and discipline. Full church members participated in the election of ministers and other church officers, in various aspects of corporate worship, education, catechesis, and discipline, and in periodic congregational meetings with the church leadership.[77] By 1662, most Congregationalist churches had clearly differentiated two levels of democratic church participants – "baptized" members of the church, who were not yet of age or character to become full communicant members, and fully "confirmed" or "professed" members. Baptized-only members were viewed to be in a "half way covenant" with the church; they could participate in the worship, baptism, catechesis, and charity of the congregation, but they could not participate in holy communion (the Eucharist) or in congregational meetings or elections. These latter rights were reserved to confirmed believers who were in "full covenant" communion and remained in good religious and moral standing.[78]

Those baptized or confirmed members and church officers who strayed from the beliefs and practices stipulated in the founding church covenant, most notably if they breached the word and law of God, were subject to the discipline of the congregation. Building on traditional Calvinist distinctions, New England Congregationalists distinguished between private or light sins and public or grave sins. Private sins were those immoral thoughts or private acts that caused no tangible harm to others or open scandal – greed, sumptuousness, lust, masturbation, hatred, jealousy, envy, and similar vices. Public sins were those crimes or shameful acts that caused either tangible harm to others or open scandal within the church – "swearing, cursing, Sabbath-breaking, drunkenness, fighting, defamation, fornication, unchastity, cheating, stealing, idleness, lying, and 'such heresies as manifestly overturn the foundations of the Christian religion, and of all piety'."[79] Private sinners were punished by the private admonitions of the

---

[76] *Ibid.*, 136–171.

[77] Joshua Miller, "Direct Democracy and the Puritan Theory of Membership," *The Journal of Politics* 53 (1991): 57–74.

[78] See "The Half-Way Covenant Decisions of 1657 and 1662," in Walker, *Creeds and Platforms*, 238–339 and discussion in E. Brooks Holifield, *The Covenant Sealed: The Development of Puritan Sacramental Theology in Old and New England, 1570–1720* (New Haven, 1974); Robert G. Pope, *The Half-Way Covenant: Church Membership in Puritan New England* (Princeton, 1969).

[79] Emil Oberholzer, *Delinquent Saints: Disciplinary Action in the Early Congregationalist Churches of Massachusetts* (New York, 1956), 31, quoting, in part, Cotton Mather, *Ratio Disciplinae Fratrum*

minister or a church elder. Public sinners were required to confess their sins publicly within the church and faced appropriate sanctions, whether admonition, temporary bans from Holy Communion, or in extreme cases of recalcitrance or recidivism, by excommunication. The goal of this ecclesiastical discipline, as the leading third-generation Puritan, Cotton Mather, put it, was to induce "humility, modesty, patience, petition, tears, with reformation" in sinners in order to welcome them anew into the covenant church community.[80]

The ecclesiastical discipline maintained by the churches was designed to complement not to compete with the civil or criminal discipline maintained by the state. The New England Congregationalist churches did not use formal tribunals and detailed rules of evidence and procedure as the state authorities did. Indeed, by the later seventeenth century, most did not even use formal consistories, as earlier Calvinist churches had done; the whole congregation of communicant members was expected to hear and adjudicate such cases. Offending parties could accordingly be subject to both church discipline and state sanction, and they found no sympathy for their claims of double jeopardy. At least in theory, these church and state cases were to remain separate, and the judgment of each tribunal was to have no bearing on the other. Inevitably, however, in small communities, particularly when jury trials were used by the state, the cases would bleed together, and offending parties, even after serving their full punishment, could well find themselves shunned. Their right to exit the community, without encumbrance, and to start life anew elsewhere, often became an attractive option.[81]

Political liberty and the political covenant

While God vested in the church the spiritual power of the Word, God vested in the state the temporal power of the sword. "Civil rulers," the Puritans believed following traditional Calvinist lore, were "Gods vicegerents here upon earth."[82] They were called to reflect and represent God's majesty

Nov–Anglicorum (Boston, 1726), 43. See similarly Hooker, *Church-Discipline*; John Cotton, *The Keys of the Kingdom of Heaven [1644]* (Boston, 1852); Mather, *Church-Government*, in Robey, *Church Covenant*.

[80] Mather, *Ratio Disciplinae*, 156.

[81] Oberholzer, *Delinquent Saints*, esp. 200–226; David Flaherty, "Law and the Enforcement of Morals in Early America," in *American Law and the Constitutional Order: Historical Perspectives*, ed. Lawrence M. Friedman and Harry N. Scheiber (Cambridge, MA, 1978), 53–66.

[82] Samuel Willard, *The Character of a Good Ruler* (1694), in Miller and Johnson, *The Puritans*, 253; Jonathan Todd, *Civil Rulers the Ministers of God for Good to Men* (London, 1749).

and authority. They were to exemplify godly justice, mercy, discipline and benevolence. They were vested in their offices by a three-party covenant among God, the people, and themselves. By this covenant, the rulers accepted the divine mandate for their political office. The people, in turn, vowed to God and to the rulers to oblige and submit to this rule, to accept and respect the law and authority of the state, so long as the state adhered to the terms of the social and political covenants, and so long as it respected natural law and natural rights.[83]

Accordingly, political officials took on three specific responsibilities under this political covenant, beyond simply confirming the general goals of the social and church covenants that we have already seen. First, the Puritans believed, political officials were required to appropriate and apply natural law in the positive law of the state. The Puritans, following Calvinist commonplaces, often equated this natural law with the Decalogue and thus described the magistrate as a custodian of both tables of the Decalogue.[84] The positive law of the state was thus to govern both the relationship between persons and God, based on the First Table of the Decalogue, and the multiple relationships among persons, based on the Second Table. On the authority of the First Table, political officials were to punish all forms of idolatry, witchcraft, blasphemy, false swearing, and Sabbath Day violations.[85] On the authority of the Second Table, they were to punish all forms of disobedience of authorities, all violations of the person or property of the other, all adultery, prostitution, and other sexual misconduct, all dishonesty, false testimony, and other fraud against another.[86] Only those positive laws that were ultimately rooted in and reflected the natural law, and especially the Decalogue, the Puritans believed, had legitimacy and authority.

Second, political officials were required to protect and promote the rights and liberties of their subjects. "A people are not made for rulers, but rulers for a people," wrote Samuel Willard, echoing Theodore Beza. God has set the rulers in authority, and the people have submitted to that authority, in order to gain a "civil felicity" not available to them in the "natural state." Such "felicity" can exist only "[w]hen men can enjoy their liberties and rights without molestation or oppression," "when they are secured

---

[83] John Winthrop, *On Arbitrary Government*, in Morgan, *Puritan Political Ideas*, 152; Cotton Mather, *Bonifacious: An Essay Upon The Good*, ed. David Levin (Cambridge, MA, 1966), 91, 94.

[84] *Cambridge Synod and Platform*, ch 17, in Walker, *Creeds and Paltforms*, 234–237.

[85] *Ibid.*

[86] Letter from John Cotton to Lord Say (1636), in Miller and Johnson, *The Puritans*, 209–212; Willard, *The Character of a Good Ruler*, in Miller and Johnson, *The Puritans*, 250–256.

against violence, and may be righted against them that offer them any injury, without fraud; and are encouraged to serve God in their own way."[87] Accordingly, many New England Puritan communities developed detailed bills of rights, echoing and emulating in part the detailed 1641 *Body of Liberties* of Massachusetts.

Third, political officials were to be the catalysts and champions of the perpetual reformation mandated by the social covenant. "[A] work of reformation," wrote Samuel Willard, "is set about in vain, and to no purpose, if rulers do not lead in it."[88] Officials were required to compel the community by their example, by their authority, and by their law to reach and retain the covenantal ideals to which the community had subscribed in the social covenant. This mandate often required that the law itself be perpetually emended and amended. "The reformation of the law, and more law for the reformation of the world, is what is mightily called for."[89]

Separation and cooperation of church and state

The theological doctrine of separation of church and state went hand-in-hand with the doctrine of ecclesiastical and political covenants. The Puritans conceived the church and the state as two separate covenantal associations, two coordinate seats of godly authority and power in society. Each institution had a distinct calling and responsibility. Each had a distinct polity and practice. "[O]ur churches and civil state have been planted, and grown up (like two twins)," reads the preamble to the 1648 *Laws and Liberties of Massachusetts*. To conflate these two institutions would be to the "misery (if not ruin) of both."[90]

The Puritans adopted a variety of safeguards to ensure this basic separation of the associations and activities of church and state – or more precisely, of the various church congregations in each township and the political officials who served in the town and provincial governments. Church officials were prohibited from holding political office, from serving on civil or criminal juries, from interfering in governmental affairs, from endorsing political candidates, or from ecclesiastically censuring the official conduct of a statesman who was also a parishioner in the church. Political officials, in turn, were prohibited from holding ministerial office, from interfering

---

[87] Willard, *The Character of a Good Ruler*, 254–255. See Beza above, page 128.
[88] Samuel Willard, *A Sermon Upon the Death of John Leverett, Esq.* (Boston, 1679), 6; see also Mather, *The Necessity of Reformation*, iii–iv.
[89] Mather, *Bonifacious*, 130.   [90] *Laws and Liberties of Massachusetts*, A2.

in internal ecclesiastical government, from performing sacerdotal functions of clergy, or from censuring the official conduct of a cleric who was also a citizen of the commonwealth.[91] To permit any such officiousness on the part of the church or the state, Winthrop averred, "would confound those jurisdictions, which Christ hath made distinct."[92]

Although church and state were not to be confounded, they were still to be "close and compact."[93] For, to the Puritans, these two institutions were inextricably linked in nature and in function. Each was an instrument of godly authority. Each did its part to establish and maintain the covenantal ideals of the community. "I look upon this as a little model of the glorious kingdom of Christ on earth," wrote the Puritan educator, Urian Oakes. "Christ reigns among us in the commonwealth as well as in the church, and hath his glorious Interest involved and wrapped up in the good of both societies respectively." Thus "the Interest of righteousness in the commonwealth, and holiness in the churches are inseparable. The prosperity of church and commonwealth are twisted together. Break one cord, you weaken and break the other also."[94]

It was on the strength of such arguments that various laws and policies were enacted to facilitate the coordination and cooperation of church and state in seventeenth-century Puritan New England. Even though these institutions remained separate from each other in their core form and function, the state provided various forms of material aid to Congregationalist churches and officials. Public lands were donated to church groups for the construction of meetinghouses, parsonages, day schools, orphanages, and other structures used in the church's ministry. Tithes and church taxes were collected to support Congregationalist ministers and teachers. Tax exemptions and immunities were accorded to some of the religious, educational, and charitable organizations that they operated. Special subsidies and military protections were provided for Congregationalist missionaries.

The state also provided various forms of moral support to ensure that "the people be fed with wholesome and sound doctrine" and to preserve the "order and communion of churches."[95] Sabbath-day laws prohibited

---

[91] *Ibid.*, 18–20; *Cambridge Synod and Platform*, ch. 17, in Walker, *Creeds and Platforms*, 234–237. See also the provisions of the 1641 *Body of Liberties* analyzed above pages 281–288, and later formulations discussed in Breen, *The Character of the Good Ruler*, 37–44.

[92] Breen, *The Character of the Good Ruler*, 42.

[93] Letter from John Cotton to Lord Say (1636), in Morgan, *Puritan Political Ideas*, 209.

[94] Urian Oakes, *New England Pleaded With, and Pressed to Consider the Things Which Concern Her* (Cambridge, MA, 1673), 49.

[95] *Records of Massachusetts Bay*, v:328.

all forms of unnecessary labor and uncouth leisure on Sundays and holy days; they also required faithful attendance at services. Blasphemy laws prohibited all forms of false swearing, foul language, and irreverence either "toward the Word preached or the messengers thereof." Idolatry laws sanctioned various forms of sacrilege, witchcraft, sorcery, magic, alchemy, and other invocations of "false gods." Religious incorporation laws required all new churches to secure "the approbation of the magistrates," and required all "schismatic" churches to submit to the "coercive power" of the magistrates.[96]

Churches, in turn, provided various forms of material aid and accommodation to the state. Church meetinghouses and chapels were used not only to conduct religious services but also to host town assemblies, political rallies, and public auctions, to hold educational and vocational classes, to house the community library, to maintain census rolls as well as birth, marriage, and death certificates. Parsonages were used not only to house the minister and his family, but also to harbor orphans and widows, the sick and the aged, victims of abuse and disaster, and other wards of the state. Churches also afforded various forms of moral support to the state. They preached obedience to the authorities and disciplined by spiritual means those parishioners found guilty of "serious" crimes. They encouraged their parishioners to be active in political affairs and each year offered "election day sermons" on Christian political principles, as well as "execution sermons" when local felons were hung. These ministers also offered learned advice on the requirements of God's law, and were often asked to advise during the drafting of new legislation and the resolution of cases that raised particularly trying moral issues.[97]

This system of church–state relations became harder to maintain in the eighteenth century as Massachusetts and other New England colonies became more religiously heterogeneous. Particularly vexing was the role of the state in collecting tithes and furnishing other forms of material support to the churches. This was the subject of a long and controversial law of 1692 in Massachusetts, which was amended several times thereafter and

---

[96] *Ibid.*; *Laws and Liberties of Massachusetts*, 18–20; *Cambridge Synod and Platform*, ch. 17, in Walker, *Creeds and Paltforms*, 234–237.

[97] See, among many others, Richard J. Hoskins, "The Original Separation of Church and State in America," *Journal of Law and Religion* 2 (1984): 221; J. M. Bumsted, "A Well-Bounded Toleration: Church and State in the Plymouth Colony," *Journal of Church and State* 10 (1968): 265; Ronald A. Bosco, "Lectures at the Pillory: The Early American Execution Sermon," *American Quarterly* 30 (1978): 156–176; Increase Mather, *The Wicked Mans Portion, or A Sermon Preached at the Lecture in Boston in New England . . . 1674* (Boston, 1675); Increase Mather, *A Sermon Occasioned by the Execution of a Man Found Guilty of Murder* (Boston, 1687).

had parallels in other New England states.[98] This law effectively blended church and state for purposes of taxation. It designated one territory as both a "parish" and a "township" under the authority of one city council. (In large townships that had more than one church congregation, the multiple "parishes" were called "precincts," and each of these likewise was subject to the same council's authority.) To be a member of the township was automatically to be a member of a parish (or precinct). Each of the 290 odd parishes/townships in Massachusetts in place by 1776 was required to have at least one Congregationalist minister. The community was required to provide him with a salary, sanctuary, and parsonage. Funds for this came from special religious taxes (usually called tithes, sometimes called church, parish, or religious rates) collected by town officials from all subjects in the township, who were by statutory definition also members of the parish.

This tithing system worked well enough when all subjects within the same township were also active members of the same church. It did not work so well for persons who were religiously inactive, or were members of a non-Congregationalist church, whether Baptist, Quaker, Anglican (or in a few distant rural townships, Catholic). As the number of such dissenting churches grew within the townships of Massachusetts, so did the protests to paying these mandatory taxes in support of the Congregationalist ministers and churches alone. During the eighteenth century, colonial courts eventually carved out exceptions for some religious dissenters, allowing them to pay their tithes to support their own dissenting ministers and churches. Such dissenters, however, were required to register each church as a separate religious society, and to demonstrate their own faithful attendance at the same. Not all dissenting churches were able or willing to meet the registration requirements, and not all townships cooperated in granting the registrations or tithe exemptions.[99] If the dissenting church was too small to have its own full-time minister, registration was routinely denied or rescinded. If the dissenting church was conscientiously opposed to legal incorporation and registration, as were New England Baptists after 1773, their members could not be exempt from taxation. If a member of a registered dissenting church was too lax in his attendance of public worship, he could still be denied exemption from the Congregationalist tithe. And if a town treasurer was too pressed for revenue, or too prejudiced against a certain group, he could refuse to give dissenting ministers their share of

---

[98] *Acts and Resolves, Public and Private, of the Province of Massachusetts Bay*, 21 vols. (Boston, 1869), 1:62–63.

[99] Samuel Eliot Morison, "The Struggle over the Adoption of the Constitution of Massachusetts, 1780," *Massachusetts Historical Society Proceedings* 50 (1916–1917): 353, 370ff.

the tithes. In many of these cases, the Massachusetts courts proved notably churlish in granting standing, let alone relief, to groups or individuals who protested such inequities.[100]

This traditional system of state-collected tithes for the established Congregationalist churches found its way into the 1780 Massachusetts Constitution, despite heated protests against it during the drafting of the constitutional convention and ratification debates.[101] Article III provided:

As the happiness of a people, and good order and preservation of civil government, essentially depend upon piety, religion, and morality; and as these cannot be generally diffused through a community, but by the institution of public worship of God, and of public instructions in piety, religion, and morality: Therefore, to promote the happiness and to secure the good order and preservation of their government, the people of this Commonwealth have a right to invest their legislature with power to authorize and require . . . the several towns, parishes precincts and other bodies politic, or religious societies, to make suitable provision, at their own expense, for the institution of the public worship of God, and for the support and maintenance of public Protestant teachers of piety, religion and morality, in all causes which provision shall not be made voluntarily.– And the people of this Commonwealth have also a right to, and do, invest their legislature with authority to enjoin upon all the subjects an attendance upon the instructions of the public teachers aforesaid, at stated times and seasons, if there be any on whose instructions they can conscientiously and conveniently attend – Provided, notwithstanding, that the several towns, parishes, precincts, and other bodies politic, or religious societies, shall, at times, have the exclusive right of electing their public teachers, and of contracting with them for their support and maintenance.– And all monies, paid by the subject of the support of the public teacher or teachers of his own religious sect or denomination, provided there be any on whose institution he attends; otherwise it may be paid towards the support of the teacher or teachers of the parish or precinct in which the said monies are raised– And every denomination of Christians, demeaning themselves peaceably, and as good subjects of the Commonwealth, shall be equally under the protection of the law: And no subordination of any one sect or denomination to another shall ever be established by law.[102]

This final text routinized, and raised to constitutional status, the traditional tithing system, and outlawed some of the hard-fought concessions that Baptists, Anglicans, and other dissenters had secured through litigation in the prior two decades. As Samuel Eliot Morison wrote in a definitive early study on point:

---

[100] John D. Cushing, "Notes on Disestablishment in Massachusetts, 1780–1833," *William & Mary Quarterly* (3rd ser.) 26 (1969): 169–190; see Jacob C. Meyer, *Church and State in Massachusetts From 1740–1833*, repr. edn. (New York, 1968), 32–89; William C. McLoughlin, *New England Dissent 1630–1833*, 2 vols. (Cambridge, MA, 1971), 1:547–565.

[101] See analysis in Witte, "'A Most Mild and Equitable Establishment,'" 225–232, 242–244.

[102] Thorpe, III:1888–1889.

Article III was even less liberal than [the colonial] system, for instead of exempting members of dissenting sects from religious taxation, it merely gave them the privilege of paying their taxes to their own pastors. Unbelievers, non-church goers, and dissenting minorities too small to maintain a minister had to contribute to Congregational worship. The whole Article was so loosely worded as to defeat the purpose of the fifth paragraph [guaranteeing the equality of all sects and denominations]. Every new denomination that entered the Commonwealth after 1780, notably the Universalists and Methodists, had to wage a long and expensive lawsuit to obtain recognition as a religious sect . . . [A] subordination of sects existed in fact.[103]

After ratification of the 1780 Massachusetts Constitution, Article III proved unworkable in practice, and "fruitful in lawsuits, bad feeling, and petty prosecution."[104] Both the casuistry and the clumsiness of the tithing and registration system were exposed in litigation. Resentment at Article III only increased as the religions of Massachusetts liberalized and pluralized – and the former Congregationalist churches were splintered into an array of Trinitarian and Unitarian forms.[105] Eventually, detractors so outnumbered proponents that the Massachusetts Constitution was amended. In 1833, Amendment, Article XI outlawed this traditional tithing system for good in Massachusetts, as it had already been outlawed in other New England states.[106]

Checks and balances

Beyond insisting on this balance of separation and cooperation of church and state, the New England Puritans were rather pragmatic in developing the appropriate forms of government for each. They made little pretense that their government structures were biblically commanded or divinely inspired. John Adams wrote that those "employed in the service of forming a constitution" cannot pretend that they "had interviews with the gods, or were in any degree under the inspiration of Heaven." "[G]overnments [are] contrived merely by the use of reason and the senses." Constitutions "are merely experiments made on human life and manners, society and government."[107] There will always be "a glorious uncertainty in the law."[108]

[103] Morison, "The Struggle," 371.   [104] Morison, *History of the Constitution of Massachusetts*, 24–25.

[105] See McLoughlin, *New England Dissent*, 2:636–659, 1084–1106, 1189–1284; McLoughlin, "The Balkcom Case (1782) and the Pietist Theory of Separation of Church and State," *William & Mary Quarterly*, (3rd ser.) 24 (1967): 267–283.

[106] See details in Sanford H. Cobb, *The Rise of Religious Liberty in America* (New York, 1902); Chester J. Antieau, Phillip M. Carroll, and Thomas C. Burke, *Religion Under the State Constitutions* (Brooklyn, NY, 1965).

[107] Adams, 4:297.   [108] Letter to Josiah Quincy (February 9, 1811), in *ibid.*, IX:629–632, at 630.

"I know of no particular Form of . . . Government," wrote another Puritan leader,

that God Himself has directly and immediately appointed by any clear revelation of his mind and will, to any people whatever . . . God Almighty has left it to the natural reason of mankind, in every nation and country, to set up that form, which, upon a thorough consideration of the nature, temper, inclinations, customs, manners, business, and other circumstances of a people, may be thought best for them.[109]

One constant element in the "nature, temper, and inclinations" of persons, however, was their sinfulness. Each person, by his or her very nature, the Puritans believed, is a fallen, sinful, and depraved creature. Each person is inherently tempted by egoism, greed, and corruption. "Sin has . . . vitiated the human nature," wrote one New England leader, and driven persons to "unruly lusts," "rampant passions," and "a constant endeavor . . . to promote his own, and gratify self."[110]

This temptation toward self-indulgence and self-gain was particularly strong and dangerous among officials in church and state. "Power is too intoxicating and liable to abuse," wrote one Puritan leader.[111] Many officials succumb to their corrupt natures and "make no other use of their higher station, than to swagger over their neighbors, and command their obsequious flatteries, and enrich themselves with the spoils of which they are able to pillage them."[112] Such official arbitrariness and tyrannical abuse would inevitably lead to both popular insurrection and divine sanction. The New England Puritans therefore advocated and adopted a variety of safeguards against tyranny for the state as well as the church.

First, the Puritans insisted that all officials have as "godly a character" as possible, notwithstanding their inherent sinfulness. Officials were to be models of spirituality and morality for the community. They were to be professing members of a local Congregationalist church and to swear oaths of allegiance to God upon assuming their office. They were also to be diligent, upright, respectful, authoritative, and free from guile and graft. "Their very example," wrote Samuel Willard, "will have the force of a law in it, and win many by a powerful attraction, to the avoiding of sin, and practicing of righteousness . . . [T]heir faithful administrations will

---

[109] Barnard, *The Throne Established*, in Miller and Johnson, *The Puritans*, 273.   [110] *Ibid.*, 272.

[111] Peter Whitney, *The Transgression of a Land Punished by a Multitude of Rulers* (Boston, 1774), 21; John Cotton, *An Exposition on the Thirteenth Chapter of the Revelation* (1655), in Morgan, *Puritan Political Ideas*, 175.

[112] Mather, *Bonifacious*, 92.

render them a terror to evil doers, and an encouragement to them that do well."[113]

Second, the Puritans insisted that both state and church officials occupy their offices only for limited tenures. Life tenures were too dangerous, the Puritans believed, for they afforded the official the opportunity slowly to convert his office into an instrument of self-gain and self-aggrandizement. It was safer to limit the official's tenure and require periodic rotation of officers.[114]

Third, the Puritans advocated the development of what they called self-limiting "republican" forms of government for both the church and the state. Rather than consolidate all forms of authority in one person or one office, they insisted on separate forms or branches of authority, each empowered to check the excesses of the other. Without such division and diffusion of authority, one preacher put it, "we shall ultimately find papacy in the church and monarchy in the state."[115] Church government was thus divided among the offices of minister, elder, and deacon. Each office held a distinct responsibility in the congregation, and each wielded a measure of authority over the others.[116] Political government was divided into executive (administrative), legislative, and judicial offices. Each office had a distinct responsibility in the commonwealth. Each wielded a measure of authority over the others.

Fourth, the Puritans advocated the development of legal codes and clear statutes so that "magistrates might not proceed according to their discretions."[117] Early colonial leaders, such as John Winthrop and John Cotton, had resisted such codification. Codified law was, for them, inequitable because it deprived the magistrate of following "the wisdom and mercy of God as well as his justice: as occasion shall require."[118] Early opponents to discretion, such as Thomas Hooker, found this "a course which wants both safety and warrant, [for] it is a way which leads to tyranny, and so to confusion."[119] Proponents of codification prevailed. Rather early in their

---

[113] Willard, *The Character of a Good Ruler*, in Miller and Johnson, *The Puritans*, 250–254.

[114] Breen, *The Character of the Good Ruler*, 74–75.

[115] Willard, *The Character of a Good Ruler*, in Miller and Johnson, *The Puritans*, 251–252; Hooker, *Summe of Church-Discipline*, 3–5.

[116] *Cambridge Synod and Platform*, chs. 5–7, in Walker, *Creeds and Platforms*, 209–215.

[117] *Winthrop's Journal*, II:191.

[118] Quoted by Breen, *The Character of the Good Ruler*, 60. See further on Cotton's views Everett Emerson, *John Cotton*, rev. edn. (Boston, 1990).

[119] *Collections of the Connecticut Historical Society*, 31 vols. (Hartford, CT, 1860–1967): I:11; see Perry Miller, "Thomas Hooker and the Democracy of Early Connecticut," *New England Quarterly* 4 (1931): 663.

development, the New England Puritans devised elaborate legal codes and subjected the most minute of daily affairs to close statutory regulation.

Fifth, the Puritans adopted what they came to call a "federalist" structure of government (from *foedus*, the Latin word for covenant) for both the church and the state. The church was divided into semi-autonomous congregations, each with their own internal structures of pastoral, pedagogical, and diaconal authority and discipline but each loosely conjoined by democratically elected synods and assemblies. The state was divided into semi-autonomous town governments, each with their own internal structures of executive, legislative, and judicial authority, but conjoined in a broader colonial and later state government.[120]

Finally, the Puritans advocated the democratic election of both church and state officials, and periodical congregational and town meetings in between. Winthrop and Cotton opposed democracy as vehemently as they opposed codification. "A democracy is . . . accounted the meanest and worst of all forms of government," Winthrop declared.[121] Democracy is not "a fit government either for church or commonwealth," Cotton argued. "If a people be governors, who shall be governed."[122] Other colonial leaders, however, adducing traditional Calvinist sources, insisted that "election is the foundation of our government."[123] On the one hand, God uses democratic elections to select those officials who will best maintain the covenantal ideal of the community. Thus "the privilege of election, which belongs to the people," wrote Thomas Hooker, "must not be exercised according to their humors, but according to the blessed will and law of God."[124] On the other hand, the people use elections to protect themselves against autocratic, arbitrary, and avaricious rulers. "They who have the power to appoint [or elect] officers and magistrates, it is in their power, also, to set the bounds and limitations of the power and place unto which they call them."[125]

Both church and state officials came to be democratically elected in the colony. Communicant members of the congregation voted by simple majority rule on the pastors, elders, and deacons who served in the church.[126] Citizens of the townships and commonwealth voted by simple majority rule

[120] See, e.g., New England Articles of Confederation (1643) in Thorpe, 1:77–81, and texts and analysis of the Savoy Declaration (1658), the Reforming Synod (1679–1680), the Heads of Agreement (1681), and the Saybrook Platform (1708), in Walker, *Creeds and Platforms*, 301–506.

[121] *Life and Letters of John Winthrop*, ed. R. Winthrop, 2 vols., repr. edn. (New York, 1971), II:430.

[122] Quoted by Clinton Rossiter, *The First American Revolution: The American Colonies on the Eve of Revolution* (New York, 1956), 90.

[123] William Hubbard, *The Benefit of a Well-Ordered Conversation* (Boston, 1684), 25.

[124] *Connecticut Collections*, 1:20; Hooker, *Summe of Church-Discipline*, 8–13.

[125] *Connecticut Collections*, 1:20.

[126] *Cambridge Synod and Platform*, ch. 8, in Walker, *Creeds and Plarforms*, 214–215.

for their respective executive, legislative, and judicial officials.[127] Between such democratic elections, the Puritans held periodic popular meetings. Town meetings were convened for officials to give account of their conduct and citizens to give air to their concerns. Congregational meetings were convened for the purpose of "discussing and resolving of any such doubts and cases of conscience concerning matter of doctrine, or worship, or government of the church."[128]

A PURITAN SEEDBED OF AMERICAN CONSTITUTIONALISM AND RELIGIOUS LIBERTY

These Puritan teachings on liberties of covenant and covenants of liberty were one fertile seedbed out of which later American constitutionalism grew. Many of the basic constitutional ideas and institutions developed by the Puritans in the seventeenth century remained in place in the eighteenth century. These ideas and institutions were advocated and adopted not only in their original forms by Puritan sermonizers and political conservatives, but also in vestigial forms by those who had claimed no adherence to Puritan beliefs.

Puritan constitutional ideas lived on among various Enlightenment Liberal and Civic Republican schools of American political thought in the later eighteenth and nineteenth centuries. Enlightenment liberals of various sorts found in the Puritan ideas of natural man and natural law important sources and analogies for their ideas of the state of nature and natural liberty. They found in the Puritan ideas of a social covenant and a political covenant prototypes for their theories of a social contract and a governmental contract. They found in the doctrine of separation of church and state a foundation for their ideas of disestablishment and free exercise of religion.[129] In turn, Civic Republican writers of various sorts transformed the Puritan idea of the elect nation under "solemn divine probation" into a revolutionary theory of American nationalism under divine inspiration. They recast the Puritan ideal of the covenant community into a theory of public virtue, discipline, and order. They translated the Puritans' insistence on spiritual rebirth and reformation into a general call for "moral reformation" and "republican regeneration."[130]

---

[127] *Laws and Liberties of Massachusetts*, 20–21, 50–51.   [128] *Ibid.*, 19.
[129] Bailyn, *Ideological Origins*, 32–34, 161–229, 246–272.
[130] Gordon S. Wood, *The Creation of the American Republic, 1776–1787* (Chapel Hill, NC, 1969), 107–124.

Some Puritan constitutional institutions likewise survived within the new federal and state constitutions of the later eighteenth and early nineteenth centuries – and not just in Massachusetts and other New England states where Puritan Congregationalists dominated the constitutional conventions. In many state constitutions, political rulers were still required to manifest a moral, virtuous, and godly character, and to swear oaths attesting to their theistic, if not Christian, beliefs. Most officials were required to stand for democratic elections to their offices. Political offices had limited tenures of office in many states. Political authority was distributed among executive, legislative, and judicial branches, each with authority to check the others. Liberties of citizens were copiously enumerated. Church and state were separated in their basic forms, yet allowed to cooperate in their many functions.

In his landmark study on *The American Commonwealth*, James Bryce wrote:

Someone has said that the American government and constitution are based on the theology of Calvin and the philosophy of Hobbes. This at least is true, that there is a hearty Puritanism in the view of human nature which pervades the instrument of 1787. It is the work of men who believed in original sin, and were resolved to leave open for transgressors no door which they could possibly shut. Compare this spirit with the enthusiastic optimism of the Frenchman of 1789. It is not merely a difference of race temperaments; it is a difference of fundamental ideas.[131]

The "fundamental ideas" of Puritan Calvinism did, indeed, contribute to the genesis and genius of the American experiment in ordered liberty and orderly pluralism. American religious, ecclesiastical, associational, and political liberty were grounded in fundamental Puritan ideas of conscience, confession, community, and commonwealth. American religious, confessional, social, and political pluralism, in turn, were bounded by fundamental Puritan ideas of divine sovereignty and created order.

---

[131] James Bryce, *The American Commonwealth* (1941), 2 vols., ed. Gary L. McDowell (Indianapolis, IN, 1995), 1:271. See also *ibid.*, 1:380n.

LIBERTY.   CONCORD.

PRO ARIS ET FOCIS

RECONCILIATION.   THE END.

7. William Pinnock, *Iconology, or Emblematic Figures Explained* (London, 1830)

CHAPTER 6

Concluding reflections: The biography and biology of liberty in early modern Calvinism

The tree [of liberty has] blossomed and yielded its fruit, but without any one having made a botanic study of its nature and growth. Calvinism, in its rise, rather acted than argued [in cultivating this tree]. But now this study may no longer be delayed. Both the biography and the biology of Calvinism must be thoroughly investigated and thought through, or, with our lack of self-knowledge, we shall be side-tracked into a world of ideas that is more at discord than in consonance with the life of our Christian democracy, and cut loose from the root on which we once blossomed so vigorously.

Abraham Kuyper (1898)[1]

Herbert Butterfield once wrote of the habit of his fellow English Protestants "to hold some German up their sleeves . . . and at appropriate moments to strike the unwary Philistine on the head with this secret weapon, the German scholar having decided in a final manner whatever point may have been at issue."[2] Some Anglo-American Protestants today have a similar habit of holding a secret Dutchman up their sleeves, and woe to that Philistine suddenly confronted with this formidable weapon. The secret Dutchman is Abraham Kuyper (1837–1920), one of the great polymaths in the history of the Netherlands – a theologian and philosopher, journalist and educator, churchman and statesman of astonishing accomplishment. He was the author of more than forty books and untold hundreds of articles. He served for nearly half a century as editor-in-chief of both the Dutch daily *Standaard* and the weekly *Hearaut*. He founded the Free University of Amsterdam. He was leader of the Protestant Anti-Revolutionary Party in the Netherlands, and served as Member of Parliament, Minister of Justice, and then Prime Minister of the Netherlands from 1901 to 1905.[3]

---

[1] Abraham Kuyper, *Lectures on Calvinism* 194 (hereafter *Stone Lectures*).
[2] Herbert Butterfield, *Christianity and History* (New York, 1949), 1.
[3] See John Hendrik de Vries, "Biographical Note," in *Stone Lectures*, ii. See P. A. Diepenhorst, *Dr. A. Kuyper* (Haarlem, 1931); G. Puchinger, *Gesprek over de Onbekende Kuyper* (Kampen, 1971). See samples

Abraham Kuyper was also one of the great Tocquevilles in the history of America – a keen European observer of American law, religion, and politics in the tradition of Alexis de Tocqueville, Philip Schaff, Lord Acton, and many others. To be sure, Kuyper wrote no famous *Democracy in America*, like Tocqueville, nor even a popular *American Journal*, like Acton.[4] But Kuyper's *Lectures on Calvinism*, delivered at Princeton Theological Seminary in 1898, together with several of his other writings, held up a comparable mirror in which America could reflect on itself.

Kuyper's mirror offered a rather flattering impression of the American constitutional experiment, which he considered to be the best expression in his day of classic Calvinist understandings of law, religion, and human rights. "America lacks no single liberty for which in Europe we struggle," Kuyper wrote. "In America, modern liberties flourish without reservation." The robust exercise of these liberties has led America neither to an atomistic individualism nor to a monopolistic constitutionalism. Instead, it has led to an orderly pluralism that has become the envy of the world. In America, liberty and pluralism cohere in a "lively correspondence" – liberty serving as the source of pluralism, and pluralism as the condition for liberty.[5]

Kuyper singled out for special praise four types of liberty and pluralism that American law had cultivated to an enviable degree by the later nineteenth century. First, Kuyper praised the American principle of religious liberty and religious pluralism. "In America there is absolute liberty of conscience," he wrote, with attendant rights of "liberty of organization; liberty of the press; liberty of public worship; liberty of thought." "Conscience is the source of human personality, the root of civil rights, and the source of national identity." America was "the first country fully to develop the principle" that conscience is "the palladium of all personal liberty" and to construct its bill of rights on the foundation of its absolute guarantee. Liberty of conscience means, *inter alia*, that each citizen has the liberty to

of his writings in James W. Skillen and Rockne M. McCarthy, eds., *Political Order and the Plural Structure of Society* (Atlanta, GA, 1991), 229–264, 397–418; James D. Bratt, ed., *Abraham Kuyper: A Centennial Reader* (Grand Rapids, MI, 1998).

4 John Bolt, *A Free Church, A Holy Nation: Abraham Kuyper's American Public Theology* (Grand Rapids, MI, 2000). The closest Kuyper came was his *Varia Americana* (Amsterdam and Pretoria, 1899), but much of this volume was focused on sociological anecdotes and the presence of Dutch people, institutions, and practices in the United States. His critical insights in this volume are referenced hereafter.

5 Abraham Kuyper, "The Origin and Safeguard of our Constitutional Liberties," *Bibliotheca Sacra* 52 (1895): 391; Kuyper, *Ons Program*, 4th edn. (Amsterdam and Pretoria, 1897), 80. See further Kuyper, *Encyclopaedie der heilige Godgeleerdheid*, 4 vols. (Kampen, 1909), III:614–624; Kuyper, *Vrijheid. Rede ter Bevestiging van Dr. Ph. S. Ronkel* (Amsterdam, 1873). For context, see Peter Heslam, "Abraham Kuyper's Lectures on Calvinism: An Historical Study" (D.Phil., Oxford, 1993).

form and to reform religious opinions, to enter and to exit religious organizations, without jeopardizing other civil liberties. A plurality of religious opinions and organizations is available from which to choose. "[N]o citizen of the State may be compelled to remain in a church which his conscience forces him to leave."[6]

Second, Kuyper praised the related American principle of ecclesiastical liberty and confessional pluralism. The American doctrine of "separation of church and state," Kuyper wrote, is a "better guarantee [of] . . . ecclesiastical liberty than anything that now prevails in Europe." In America, separation of church and state does not mean the separation of religion and politics. "Magistrates are God-fearing, by proclaiming days of public thanksgiving, honoring public prayer, observing the Sabbath Day – indeed, declaring in the preamble of their Constitution that it was from God that they received the laws by which they are ruled." Separation of church and state means, instead, that "churches are entirely free" from state interference in their doctrines and liturgies, in their polities and properties, in their education and catechization. The state does not prescribe the religious texts, beliefs, and practices of any religious group. The state "does not subsidize the churches" through the donation of property or the collection of tithes. The state does not interfere in the church's organization and order, discipline and discipleship. "In America, Catholics, Lutherans, Calvinists, Baptists, and Methodists are equally respected," despite the plurality of confessions, canons, and cults among them. It is "a fundamental rule that the government must honor the complex of Christian churches as the multiform manifestation of the Church of Christ on earth . . ." America has adopted this rule "not from the desire to be released from church duties" but "from the consciousness that the welfare of the church and the progress of Christianity demand this freedom and independence."[7]

Third, Kuyper praised the American principle of associational liberty and social pluralism. The American tradition of voluntarism and fraternity, Kuyper wrote, has led to ample legal protection not only of churches and religious organizations but also of a plurality of other "social spheres" – families, schools, unions, guilds, plantations, clubs, convents, and corporations.

---

[6] Kuyper, *Stone Lectures*, 108–109; Kuyper, "Constitutional Liberties," 391; Kuyper, *Ons Program*, 93.

[7] Abraham Kuyper, *Dictaten Dogmatiek*, 2d edn., 6 vols. (Kampen, n.d.), v/1:387–388, 444–445; id., *Ons Program*, 382–394; Kuyper, "Constitutional Liberties," 396–397; Kuyper, *Varia Americana*, 18–22, 52–54, 151–162. Elsewhere, Kuyper insisted on the inclusion of Jews within the ambit of religious liberty. Kuyper, *Liberalisten en Joden* (Amsterdam, 1878). At another point, he stretched even further: "[A]ll things within the forum of conscience and on domestic and private life must be free – for the atheist as much as for the fully devout . . . indeed, for all sects." Kuyper, *Dictaten Dogmatiek*, v/1:415. See more generally Kuyper, *Encyclopaedie*, iii:328; Kuyper, *Vrijmaking der Kerk* (Amsterdam, 1869).

Each of these social spheres is amply protected by the provisions of state criminal law. Each is amply facilitated by the procedures of state private law. But none of these social spheres is ultimately dependent upon the state for its existence or for its competence. The formation and maintenance of each social sphere depend upon the voluntary association and activity of private parties. The competence and authority of each social sphere depend upon "its innate norms," its "God-given liberty" – its "inherent sphere sovereignty," in Kuyper's famous phrase. "Sphere sovereignty" does not render a social sphere "a law unto itself" – just as personal sovereignty does not make each person a law unto himself or herself. Instead, sphere sovereignty entails that each of these social spheres has the liberty to operate independently of the state in accordance with its own God-given norms, and in deference to the liberty interests of other social spheres and of all individuals. "[T]here exists side-by-side with the personal sovereignty [of the individual conscience], the sovereignty of the [social] sphere."[8]

Fourth, Kuyper praised the American principle of political liberty and political pluralism. The American constitutional doctrine of a "federalist political unity" within a "republican form of democracy," Kuyper argued, sagely balances the demands of liberty and order, local rule and national unity.[9] On the one hand, political authority in America is divided among federal, state, and local governments. America does have a strong federal government that tends to the nation's common economic, administrative, military, and diplomatic needs. America does have a strong civic faith that manifests itself in Presidential prayers and proclamations, Congressional support for basic religious education, federal judicial protections of cardinal moral and cultural values. But America also recognizes that, historically, "constitutional rights and freedoms first came within local communities," and that these local roots must be retained. It further recognizes that, practically, the protection of liberty and the cultivation of virtue must begin at the local level – through local elections of officials, local town meetings, local participation in juries, local administration of justice, local education in schools and churches. The American constitution thus guarantees each state its own republican form of government and reserves to it all powers not directly delegated to the federal government. The constitution further assures "the decentralized and autonomous character of . . . local

---

[8] Kuyper, *Stone Lectures*, 90–99; Kuyper, *Varia Americana*, 38–49; Kuyper, *Souvereiniteit in eigen Kring* (Amsterdam, 1880), 19ff.; Kuyper, *Dictaten Dogmatiek*, v/1:73–186; id., *Encyclopaedie*, iii:322–330; Kuyper, *Ons Program*, 114–123, 237–254. See also James W. Skillen and W. Carlson Thies, "Religion and Political Development in Nineteenth Century Holland," *Publius* (Summer, 1982): 43–64.

[9] Kuyper, *Dictaten Dogmatiek*, v/1:289–296; Kuyper, *Stone Lectures*, 79–90.

governments." On the other hand, political power at each level is separated among executive, legislative, and judicial branches. Each of these branches of government checks and balances the power of the other – through executive vetoes, legislative impeachments, and judicial review. This separation of powers, Kuyper believed, ensures that the offices of the state are protected against the sinfulness of their officials. It further ensures that the powers of government are sufficiently nuanced to provide ample protection to the liberties of persons, churches, and other social spheres.[10]

Kuyper's robust reflections on the success of the American experiment in ordered liberty and orderly pluralism – though strangely silent on its many failings for women, children, blacks, Indians, abused workers, the poor, and various minorities of the day[11] – were flattering enough to his American audience. Even more flattering were his robust projections of the place and promise of the American experiment in the world in the twentieth century. In his Princeton Lectures of 1898, Kuyper predicted that America would soon inherit from Europe the leadership of the Western world: "Old Europe remains even now the bearer of a longer historical past, and therefore stands before us as a tree rooted more deeply, hiding between its leaves some matured fruits of life. You are yet in your Springtide – we are passing through our Fall."[12] In a follow-up lecture, Kuyper made an even grander prediction: "America is destined in the providence of God to become the most glorious and noble nation the world has ever seen. Some day its renown will eclipse the renown and splendor of Rome, Greece, and older races."[13]

Kuyper did not wax so grandly simply to flatter his American audience. He attached strong theological conditions both to his reflections of the past and to his projections of the future of the American experiment. This move was considerably more controversial – in his day and in our own.

First, Kuyper argued that the source and strength of the American constitutional experiment in rights and liberties was Calvinist theology, not Enlightenment liberalism, classical republicanism, or any other ideology.

[10] Kuyper, *Varia Americana*, 21–24; Kuyper, "Constitutional Liberties," 394–397; Kuyper, *Ons Program*, 82–83, 96–108, 158–212; Kuyper, *Dictaten Dogmatiek*, v/1:289–308; Kuyper, *Varia Americana*, 28–33, 181–184; Kuyper, *Stone Lectures*, 86–88, 191–192; Kuyper, *Souvereiniteit in eigen Kring*, 19–25; Kuyper, *Ons Program*, 63–68, 109–123, 213–236, 268–301, 382–394, 411–476.

[11] I say "strangely" because Kuyper was hardly blind to these problems at home. See, e.g., his *The Problem of Poverty*, trans. and ed. James W. Skillen (Grand Rapids, MI, 1991). In *Varia Americana*, 3–5, 9–12, Kuyper did criticize briefly the impoverishment and lynching of blacks, and the problems of alcoholism and poverty among the working classes.

[12] Kuyper, *Stone Lectures*, 9–10.

[13] Lecture on October 26, 1898, quoted in John Bolt, "The Holland-American Line of Liberty," *Morality and Markets* 1 (1998): 1.

Calvinism, Kuyper wrote, was not only a spiritual movement but also "a political movement which has guaranteed the liberty of nations in constitutional statesmanship; first in Holland, then in England, and since the close of the last century in the United States." The American experiment in liberty and pluralism "points back directly to its puritanical origin, to the invincible spirit of the Pilgrim Fathers and to the spiritual descent from Calvin." "If with us [in Europe today] it has every appearance that the liberty of the people must be purchased at the sacrifice of the faith, there [in America] it is Calvinism which, according to the general conviction, offers the surest safeguards for the continued presence of those liberties." "America is wholly different [from Europe]. The state machinery still, for the most part, answers to the Calvinist fundamentals laid down by the Puritans and Pilgrim fathers. Religion still lives in the public realm. And in social life, Calvinism still finds an open door."[14]

It was Calvinists, Kuyper repeatedly argued, who first "lifted up freedom of conscience" and insisted that "the magistrate has nothing to do with a person's innermost beliefs . . . or with a person's domestic life or friendships." It was Calvinists who first "reached the conclusions that follow from this liberty of conscience, for the liberty of speech, and the liberty of worship . . . and the free expression of thought . . . and ideas." It was Calvinists who "first developed the principle of separation of church and state," and the constitutional recognition that "the church derives its authority directly from God, not mediately through the state or through the community." It was Calvinists who first effectively "protest[ed] against State-omnicompetence; against the horrible conception that no right exists above and beyond existing [positive] laws; and against the pride of absolutism [which is] death to our civil liberties." It was Calvinists who first pressed classical theories of mixed government into constitutional principles of federalism and republicanism.[15]

Though, historically, Calvinists often betrayed their own political principles, Kuyper argued, their views ultimately prevailed in America because of their firm theological mooring. American Calvinists derived their claims of liberty

not by appealing to popular force, nor to the hallucinations of human greatness, but by deducing those rights and liberties of social life from the same source from which the high authority of government flows – even the absolute sovereignty of

---

[14] Kuyper, *Stone Lectures*, 14–17, 78; Kuyper, "Constitutional Liberties," 396–397; Kuyper, *Varia Americana*, 86–87, 119.
[15] Kuyper, *Dictaten Dogmatiek*, v/1:386–387, 415; Kuyper, *Stone Lectures*, 98, 105, 108–109.

God. From this one source, in God, sovereignty in the individual sphere, in the family, and in every social circle, is just as directly derived as the supremacy of state authority.[16]

A plurality of spheres of personal, ecclesiastical, social, and political liberty thus stand alongside each other – each created by God, each governed by God, each accountable to God. A plurality of offices and activities within each sphere of liberty also stand alongside each other – each designed to discharge some portion of God's special calling for that sphere.

But, Kuyper argued, while eighteenth- and nineteenth-century America offered the world the best and fullest example of what Calvinist theories of law, religion, and human rights had built, these Calvinist foundations were cracking in America, having already crumbled in much of Europe after the French Revolution. These Calvinist foundations needed to be shored up if America was to live up to its high promise. Kuyper's concluding lecture at Princeton in 1898 had the tone of a wizened Dutch uncle gently admonishing his young American relatives to live up to their pedigree:

[L]o and behold, while you are thus enjoying the fruits of Calvinism, and while even outside of your borders the constitutional system of government as an outcome of Calvinist warfare, upholds the national honor, it is whispered abroad that all these [fruits] are to be accounted blessings of Humanism, and scarcely anyone still thinks of honoring in them the after-effects of Calvinism, the latter believed to lead a lingering life only in a few dogmatically petrified circles. What I demand . . . is that this ungrateful ignoring of Calvinism shall come to an end . . . I contend in the second place, for an historical study of the principles of Calvinism . . . [that cultivated] the tree of liberty . . . I [demand] in the third place the development of the principles of Calvinism in accordance with the needs of modern consciousness and their application to every department of life . . . Finally, I would add . . . that those Churches which lay claim to professing the Reformed faith, shall cease being ashamed of this confession . . . I exalt multiformity and hail it in a higher stage of development. Even for the Church that has the purest confession, I would not dispense with the aid of other Churches in order that its inevitable one-sidedness may thus be complemented. But what . . . one confesses to be the truth, one must also dare to practice in word, deed, and [the] whole manner of life.[17]

Kuyper's four "demands," while controversial, have not gone unanswered in America during the past century and more – or indeed in many other parts of the world. Calvinism is certainly not ignored today, either in various Christian institutions or in the broader secular world. The historical contributions of Calvinism to Western law, politics, and culture are coming under increasingly close study. The expansion and adaptation of these

---

[16] Kuyper, *Stone Lectures*, 105.   [17] *Ibid.*, 194–195.

contributions to modern American life have continued apace. Calvinism is proudly confessed in a number of churches today both in America and abroad, albeit not always free from the "dogmatic petrification" against which Kuyper warned.[18]

Since Kuyper threw down his avuncular gauntlet in 1898, a number of Calvinist scholars have also emerged to meet his third demand: to work for "the development of the principles of Calvinism in accordance with the needs of modern consciousness and their application to every department of life" – not least in the "department" of human rights and liberties. In the past century, scores of sturdy Calvinists have developed important new theories and themes of law, religion, and human rights, building in part on the insights of the Calvinist tradition, among several others. These include major scholars and activists like Emil Brunner, Jonathan Chaplin, Herman Dooyweerd, Bas de Gaay-Fortman, Charles Glenn, Hendrick van Eikema Hommes, David Little, Paul Marshall, Richard Mouw, Reinhold Niebuhr, Lourens du Plessis, James Skillen, H. G. Stoker, Danie Strauss, Alan Storkey, Helmut Thielecke, Johan van der Vyver, Hendrik Vroom, Henk Woldering, Nicholas Wolterstorff, Bernard Zylstra, and scores of students and colleagues whom they have inspired. Together, these Calvinist scholars have made major contributions, especially to our understanding of modern international, constitutional, and social rights, and with a special accent on the institutional rights of churches, schools, and families, and on the individual rights of the poor, the prisoner, and the racial minority.

Much of this volume on the reformation of rights has been an answer to Kuyper's second demand – the need for closer "historical study of the biography and biology of Calvinism" and its influence on law, religion, and human rights. While these chapters have underscored the value of Kuyper's insights into the influence of these historical Calvinist teachings on rights and liberties, they have also raised two critical caveats to his brief historical sketches on point. First, while historical Calvinist teachings on law, religion, and human rights have been influential, their influence should not be overstated. In the development of rights and liberties in America, sundry other intellectual sources besides Calvinism were also at work: natural law traditions from classical Greece and Rome and from various schools of early

---

[18] See, e.g., James D. Bratt, *Dutch Calvinism in North America: A History of a Conservative Subculture* (Grand Rapids, MI, 1984); George Harinck and Hans Krabbendam, eds., *Breaches and Bridges: Reformed Subcultures in the Netherlands, Germany, and the United States* (Amsterdam, 2000); George Harinck and Hans Krabbendam, eds., *Sharing the Reformed Tradition: The Dutch–North American Exchange, 1846–1996* (Amsterdam, 1996); Luis E. Lugo, ed., *Religion, Pluralism, and Public Life: Abraham Kuyper's Legacy for the Twenty-First Century* (Grand Rapids, MI, 2000); David F. Wells, ed., *Reformed Theology in America: A History of its Modern Development* (Grand Rapids, MI, 1985).

modern Continental jurisprudence; legal and political positivist traditions from Machiavelli to Thomas Hobbes; common law traditions celebrated by everyone from Edward Coke to Edmund Burke; various traditions of constitutionalism among Native Americans; English Whig writings from the early seventeenth century forward; Free Church traditions grounded in the theology of Anabaptism and energized by the Great Awakening; and a host of intellectual movements associated with the English, French, and Scottish Enlightenments. Many of these same groups were also influential on the development of rights in Western Europe, with further strong influences from the civil law and canon law traditions, from various schools of Pietism, and from numerous neo-Thomist and other forms of Catholic natural law theory and moral philosophy.

Moreover, the Calvinist political ideas that were influential on the development of rights in Europe and later in America were not all of the same Genevan color. Kuyper tended to draw easy lines from Geneva to Scotland to Holland to England to America – often thereby deprecating the conceptual variations and expansions of basic Calvinist themes that occurred over time and across cultures. Moreover, he tended to have a flat view of Calvinist political teachings that imputed astonishing foresight to Calvin. "The 20th chapter of the fourth book of Calvin's *Institutes* ["On Civil Government"] is the starting point," Kuyper wrote in his survey of Western political theory. "Everything that later came forth in Reformed theology is nothing but a repetition of foundational insights of Calvin's work."[19] This volume has shown that this is simply not so. Not only is this chapter of the *Institutes* underdeveloped compared to much of Calvin's other thought, but later Calvinists, following Calvin's own ethic of *semper reformanda*, have perennially reformed and transformed his original legal and political teachings to absorb new insights from Scripture and tradition and to accommodate new challenges of their day. Calvinist rights reformers, like Catholic rights reformers, have long understood the need for the "development of doctrine," particularly on fundamental matters of law, religion, and human rights. And the "growing ends" of this tradition (in John Courtney Murray's apt phrase) have moved a long way away from the rudimentary legal and political reflections of Calvin's *Institutes* or the narrow construction of rights and liberties in Calvin's Geneva.[20]

---

[19] Kuyper, *Dictaten Dogmatiek*, v/1:7.
[20] See Russell Hittinger, "Introduction to Modern Catholicism," in Witte and Alexander, *The Teachings of Modern Christianity*, 1:3–38 and the defense of the development-of-doctrine thesis in John T. Noonan, *A Church That Can and Cannot Change: The Development of Catholic Moral Teaching* (Notre Dame, IN, 2005).

It is worth taking a moment to compare the development of rights doctrine in the Catholic and Calvinist traditions. In his magisterial history of rights in the Catholic tradition in the second millennium CE, Brian Tierney writes: "Nowadays it has become fashionable to maintain, as Pope John Paul II recently asserted, that religious rights are the 'cornerstone' of all other rights. But, viewed in historical perspective, religious rights came last; these rights were the most difficult to conceive of, let alone put into practice."[21] Tierney has shown better than anyone that all manner of subjective rights and liberties were created already by medieval Catholic canonists and theologians, and that these rights were further expanded and refined by early modern Spanish and Portuguese Catholic philosophers and moralists. But it was only in the Second Vatican Council's great Declaration of Religious Freedom (*Dignitatis Humanae*) of 1965, Tierney writes, that the Catholic Church came to embrace fully the doctrine of religious rights for individuals and groups, and to rework its vast rights structures with religious rights at their foundation.

The exact opposite pattern of development prevails in the history of Calvinism. In the Calvinist tradition, religious rights came first, for they were the easiest to conceive; other rights developed gradually and sporadically over the next centuries, and with varying intellectual foundations and institutional force. From the start, religious rights were the cornerstones of Calvinist rights theories – freedom of conscience, freedom of exercise, and freedom of the church. Only over time did early modern Calvinists develop systematically the attendant individual freedoms of speech, press, and assembly, rights to petition, dissent, and revolt, rights to marry, divorce, and associate, rights to evangelize, educate, and parent, rights to emigrate, travel, and evangelize, and more. Only over time did they develop corporate rights to chapels, schools, and charities, freedoms of doctrine, liturgy, and worship, rights to catechize, educate, and discipline, freedoms of press, contract, and association. Only over time did they begin to press more generically for various rights to life, liberty, and property, due process and equal protection, and sundry civil and criminal procedural rights. And even when they attained a measure of rights, Robert Bellah recently said to me, Calvinists "wavered when they enjoyed the luxury of hegemony."

A number of these later rights developments were products of immediate challenge and tragedy, more than of deliberate planning or pre-designed logic. Among the most important catalysts of rights development in early

---

[21] Brian Tierney, "Religious Rights in Historical Perspective," in *Religious Human Rights* in *Global Perspective: Religious Perspectives*, ed. John Witte Jr., and Johan D. van der Vyver (The Hague, 1996), 17–18. See further sources by Tierney cited above page 25.

modern Calvinism were the bloody massacres of Calvinists in France and the Netherlands, the severe persecution of Calvinists in Scotland and England, the open wilderness that faced New England Puritans, the new constitutions demanded by the American Revolution. Calvinists responded to these challenges both with sharp swords and with strong words. Out of the hot pamphlets and fiery sermons issued in the heat of revolutionary battle and in justification of their violence, came more systematic tracts and treatises a generation or two later that furnished enduring lessons for the Calvinist tradition, and for the broader Western tradition as well.

Many of these enduring lessons about rights and liberties eventually gravitated toward familiar doctrinal heads of Calvinist theology. The first rights of religion, for example, fell neatly under the first doctrine of Calvinism, namely, the doctrine of God. The religious rights of the individual are in part temporal expressions of what Calvin already called the "eternal rights of God." These are the rights of God the Father, who created humans in his own image and commanded them to worship him properly and to obey his Commandments fully. They are the rights of God the Son, who embodied himself in the church and demanded the free and full exercise of this body upon earth. And they are the rights of God the Holy Spirit, who is "poured out upon all flesh" (Joel 2:28) and governs the consciences of all persons in their pursuit of happiness and holiness. Religious rights are in no small part the right of persons to do their duties as image bearers of the Father, as prophets, priests, and kings of Christ, as agents, apostles, and ambassadors of the Holy Spirit. As image bearers of God, persons are given natural law, reason, and will to operate as responsible creatures with choices and accountability. They are given the natural duty and right to reflect God's glory and majesty in the world, to represent God's sovereign interests in church, state, and society alike. As prophets, priests, and kings of God, persons have the spiritual duty and right to speak and to prophesy, to worship and to pastor, to rule and to govern on God's behalf. As apostles and ambassadors of God, persons have the Christian duty and right to "make disciples of all nations" (Matthew 28:19) by word and sacrament, by instruction and example, by charity and discipline.

Further rights and rights structures fall under the familiar doctrinal heads of creation, fall, and redemption. For historical Calvinists, the "order of creation" often played a role akin to that played by the law of nature in Catholicism. Calvinists saw in the story of God's creation and division of each creature "after its own kind," an original warrant for pluralism. This was not just the plurality of responsibilities that God gave Adam and Eve to name the many creatures, to eat of some trees but not others, to "be fruitful and multiply" themselves into new forms, to dress and keep the Garden of Paradise in various ways. Calvinists eventually imputed to the order of creation structural or social pluralism – the basic division of divine authority and responsibility in the structures of family, church, and state. They also imputed to the order of creation a legal or normative pluralism – the basic division of laws and orders governing each person's relationships to God above them, to persons beside them, and to nature below them. They even imputed to the order of creation a confessional or religious pluralism – the reality that God in his sovereignty can "walk and talk" with each and every human being as he once did with Adam and Eve in Paradise, and that each person draws his or her own conclusions of faith from these divine encounters. It was the need to respect and protect God's sovereign relationships with each and every other human being that eventually led Calvinists to embrace the religious freedom of every peaceable believer in God.

Calvinists would eventually find an additional doctrinal foundation for a specifically Christian pluralism in the story of the resurrection – and more particularly in the Bible's account of how differently Christ appeared to his followers in the forty days after his resurrection, and how differently his followers apprehended him. Mary Magdalene, weeping inconsolably outside the newly discovered empty tomb, had to be called by name before she recognized Christ. Before that, she thought he was the gardener. The ten disciples, gathered in the room in sorrow and fear after the burial of Christ, needed to have Christ breathe his peace on them before they recognized him. Before that, they thought he was a ghost. The two travelers from Emmaus who walked and talked with Christ about salvation history all the way to their city recognized Christ only in the Eucharist, when he held up the bread and blessed it. Before that, they thought he was just a learned traveler. Thomas, the great doubter, wanted to put his fingers in the nail holes of the cross, and his hand in the pierced side of Christ, before he recognized him. Before that, he thought he was a fraud. And Peter, that enigmatic rock of the church, recognized Christ only after he performed the miracle of again filling his nets with fish – and then had to sit through a threefold cross-examination as to whether he really believed in the resurrected Lord: "Simon, Barjona, do you love me?"

These biblical stories force us to appreciate the diversity of ways in which a Christian might experience Christ, and might celebrate that experience in Christian communion with others. Some are called by name. Some are touched by God. Some receive the breath of the Spirit. Some see God in the sacraments. Some experience miracles. And each of these ways of divine encounter and experience can draw to itself its own liturgies, its own communities, its own traditions of cult, confession, creed, and catechism. Some churches emphasize a personal calling, a moment of rebirth before membership is sealed. Some churches are focused on an event, an icon, a site or rite of divine vision. Some churches emphasize the pulpit, the homiletic exposition of God's Word. Some churches emphasize the altar, the Eucharistic celebration of the death and resurrection of Christ. All of these, Calvinists have come to realize, are legitimate ways to serve and to celebrate Christ, to ritualize, canonize, and confess the Christian faith. All of these deserve rights protection.

Early modern Calvinists gathered around the doctrine of sin additional insights into the nature of rights and their protection. It was their doctrine of sin that led Calvinists from the start to emphasize the need both for individual discipline and for structural safeguards on offices of authority. Individual discipline came in part through regular catechesis and education, through regular corporate worship and communal living. But the foundation of individual discipline was the law of God and nature, particularly as distilled in the Ten Commandments. Its two tables prescribed the duties of love that a disciplined believer owed to God and to neighbors respectively. Within a generation after Calvin, his followers had flipped these Decalogue duties into Decalogue-based rights. Nothing that God requires in the Decalogue may the magistrate forbid, they argued. Nothing that God forbids in the Decalogue may the magistrate require. A person thus has the right to "observe the Sabbath Day and keep it holy" and "to labor six days and to rest on the Sabbath." A person has the right to "honor [his or her] father and mother so that [their] days may be long in the land which the Lord your God has given [them]." A person has the right to proper religious worship and speech – to be free from laws commanding them to worship false gods, to maintain graven images, to swear false oaths, or otherwise take the name of God in vain. A person has the right to life (freedom from killing), to property (freedom from stealing), to marital integrity (freedom from adultery), and to reputation and fair process (freedom from false testimony). A person has the right to be free from having his or her family, household, and possessions coveted by others. If the magistrate requires or condones conduct contrary to this divine formula, the magistrate is violating each subject's fundamental rights and liberties. To do so is to practice tyranny and to invite resistance and revolt.

The doctrine of sin also led Calvinists to emphasize strongly the need for constitutional safeguards on authorities within church and state. While the offices of church and state were ordained by God and represent God's authority on earth, the officers who occupy these offices are sinful human creatures. Calvinists thus worked hard to ensure that these offices were not converted into instruments of self-gain and self-promotion. By the seventeenth century, Calvinists emphasized the need for popular election of ministers and magistrates, limited tenures and rotations of ecclesiastical and political office, separation of church and state, separation of powers within church and state, checks and balances between and amongst each of these powers, federalist layers of authority with shared and severable sovereignty, open meetings in congregations and towns, codified canons and laws, transparent proceedings and records within consistories, courts, and councils. All these safeguards and more were designed to protect the offices of church and state from their own officers, but even more to protect the rights and liberties of parishioners and citizens who were subject to these authorities. It was through the doctrine of covenants, modeled in part on the biblical covenants of ancient Israel, that early modern Calvinists were able to constitutionalize these many safeguards.

LAW, RELIGION, AND HUMAN RIGHTS TODAY

To tell this historical story of rights in early modern Calvinism is not to wax nostalgic about a purported golden age of human rights, nor is it to suggest that all the particular rights premises and precepts of early modern Calvinists be accepted in our day – by contemporary Calvinists, let alone by everyone else. To adduce these early teachings is instead to point to a rich understanding of rights that is too little known and too little used today, even by many Protestant insiders. The distinguished Protestant theologian, Don Browning, who does know this rights tradition very well, explains why understanding the historical foundation of rights is important:

Today, modern human rights thought . . . largely stands devoid of critical grounding. The historically most influential traditions conveying human rights to the modern world – the natural rights and natural law traditions of Aristotelian and Stoic philosophy, Roman law, and the early Roman Catholic canonists – have been, for the most part, publicly rejected, although their influence unconsciously lingers on. In a similar way, the grand theological narratives of the Protestant Reformation are also invisible in human rights declarations and conventions of the last several decades. What remains is a list of subjective natural rights that are asserted more or less independently of any theory of objective natural rights. They function as an unchecked wish list, in which these rights increasingly seem to contradict each other, sow seeds of distrust and disregard among the nations of the world, and get used as tools of manipulation by various interest groups around the world to accomplish their own particular political and legal goals. A new critical grounding for human rights is required if the entire tradition is not to explode into scores of conflicting subjective wants that have no real authority and, in reality can never be implemented.[22]

One lesson in this is that today, as much as in the past, human rights norms need religious narratives to ground them critically. There is, of course, some value in simply declaring human rights norms of "liberty, equality, and fraternity" or "life, liberty, and property" – if for no other reason than to pose an ideal against which a person or community might measure itself, to preserve a normative totem for later generations to make real. But, ultimately, these abstract human rights ideals of the good life and the good society depend on the visions and values of human communities and institutions to give them content and coherence – to provide what Jacques Maritain once called "the scale of values governing [their] exercise and concrete manifestation."[23] It is here that religion in all its forms, including Calvinism, must play a vital role. Religion is an ineradicable condition of human lives and human communities. Religions invariably provide many of the sources and "scales of values" by which many persons and communities govern themselves. Religions inevitably help to define the meanings and measures of shame and regret, restraint and respect, responsibility and restitution that a human rights regime presupposes. Religions must thus be seen as indispensable allies in the modern struggle for human rights. To exclude them from the struggle is impossible, indeed catastrophic. To include them, by enlisting their unique resources and protecting their unique rights, is vital to enhancing the regime of human rights.

Conversely, religious narratives need human rights norms both to protect them and to challenge them. There is, of course, some value in religions simply accepting the current protections of a human rights regime – the guarantees of liberty of conscience, free exercise, religious group autonomy, and the like. But passive acquiescence in a secular scheme of human rights will not prove effective in the long term. Religious communities must reclaim their own voices within the secular human rights dialogue that dominates today, and reclaim the human rights voices within their own internal religious dialogues. Contrary to conventional wisdom, the theory and law of human rights are neither new nor secular in origin. Human rights are, in no small part, the modern political fruits of ancient religious beliefs

---

[22] Don S. Browning, "The United Nations Convention on the Rights of the Child: Should it be Ratified and Why?" *Emory International Law Review* 20 (2006): 157, 172–173.

[23] Jacques Maritain, "Introduction," in UNESCO, *Human Rights: Comments and Interpretations* (New York, 1949).

and practices – ancient Jewish constructions of covenant and *mitzvot*,[24] original Qur'anic texts on peace and the common good,[25] classic Christian concepts of *ius* and *libertas*, calling and covenant.

Both these theses – about the place of religion in human rights and about the place of human rights in religion – are highly controversial. By way of conclusion, I offer a few brief reflections on each, saving to a sequel volume a fuller exposition.

Religion and human rights

Many of my friends in the human rights world today think it fundamentally wrong to invite religion to play a more active role in the cultivation and implementation of human rights. Even the great Religions of the Book, they point out to me, do not speak unequivocally about human rights, and none has amassed an exemplary human rights record over the centuries. Their sacred texts and canons say much more about commandments and obligations than about liberties and rights. Their theologians and jurists have resisted the importation of human rights as much as they have helped in their cultivation. Their internal policies and external advocacy have helped to perpetuate bigotry, chauvinism, and violence as much as they have served to propagate equality, liberty, and fraternity. The blood of thousands is at the doors of our churches, temples, and mosques. The bludgeons of pogroms, crusades, jihads, inquisitions, and ostracisms have been used to devastating effect within and among these faiths.

Moreover, the modern cultivation of human rights in the West began in the 1940s when both Christianity and the Enlightenment seemed incapable of delivering on their promises. In the middle of the twentieth century, there was no second coming of Christ promised by Christians, no heavenly city of reason promised by enlightened libertarians, no withering away of the state promised by enlightened socialists. Instead, there was world war, gulags, and the Holocaust – a vile and evil fascism and irrationalism to which Christianity and the Enlightenment seemed to have no cogent response or effective deterrent.

The modern human rights movement was thus born out of desperation in the aftermath of World War II. It was an earnest attempt to find a world faith to fill a spiritual void. It was an attempt to harvest from the traditions of Christianity and the Enlightenment the rudimentary elements

[24] Novak, *Covenantal Rights.*
[25] Abdullahi Ahmed An-Na'im, *Toward an Islamic Reformation: Civil Liberties, Human Rights, and International Law* (Syracuse, NY, 1990).

of a new faith and a new law that would unite a badly broken world order. The proud claims of Article 1 of the 1948 Universal Declaration of Human Rights – "That all men are born free and equal in rights and dignity [and] are endowed with reason and conscience"[26] – expounded the primitive truths of Christianity and the Enlightenment with little basis in postwar world reality. Freedom and equality were hard to find anywhere. Reason and conscience had just blatantly betrayed themselves in the gulags, battlefields, and death camps.

Though desperate in origin, the human rights movement grew precociously in the decades following World War II. The United Nations issued a number of landmark documents on human rights in the 1960s. Foremost among these were the two great international covenants promulgated by the United Nations in 1966 – The International Covenant on Economic, Social, and Cultural Rights (1966) and The International Covenant on Civil and Political Rights (1966). Other international and domestic instruments issued in the later 1960s took particular aim at racial, religious, and gender discrimination in education, employment, social welfare programs, and other forms and forums of public life. Various nations pressed their own human rights movements. In America, the rights revolution yielded a powerful grassroots civil rights movement and a welter of landmark cases and statutes implementing the Bill of Rights and Fourteenth Amendment. In Africa and Latin America, it produced agitation, and eventually revolt, against colonial and autocratic rule. Academics throughout the world produced a prodigious new literature urging constant reform and expansion of the human rights regime. Within a generation, human rights had become the "new civic faith" of the postwar world order.

Christian and other communities participated actively as midwives in the birth of this modern rights revolution, and special religious rights protections were at first actively pursued. Individual religious groups issued bold confessional statements and manifestoes on human rights shortly after World War II. Several denominations and budding ecumenical bodies joined Jewish non-governmental organizations (NGOs) in cultivating human rights at the international level. The Free Church tradition played a critical role in the civil rights movement in America and beyond, as did the Social Gospel and Christian Democratic Party movements in Europe and Latin America.[27]

---

[26] In Brownlie, *Basic Documents on Human Rights*, 57.

[27] John Nurser, *For All Peoples and All Nations: Christian Churches and Human Rights* (Geneva, 2005); Robert Traer, *Faith in Human Rights: Support in Religious Traditions for a Global Struggle* (Washington, DC, 1991).

After expressing some initial interest, however, leaders of the rights revolution consigned religious groups and their particular religious rights to a low priority. Freedom of speech and press, parity of race and gender, provision of work and welfare captured most of the energy and emoluments of the rights revolution. After the 1960s, academic inquiries and activist interventions into religious rights and their abuses became increasingly intermittent and isolated, inspired as much by parochial self-interest as by universal golden rules. The rights revolution seemed to be passing religion by.

This deprecation of the special roles and rights of religions from the later 1960s onward has introduced several distortions into the common theories and laws of human rights in vogue today. First, without religion, many rights are cut from their roots. The right to religion, Calvinists and others discovered, is "the mother of many other rights."[28] For the religious individual, the right to believe leads ineluctably to the rights to assemble, speak, worship, proselytize, educate, parent, travel, or to abstain from the same on the basis of one's beliefs. For the religious association, the right to exist invariably involves rights to corporate property, collective worship, organized charity, parochial education, freedom of press, and autonomy of governance. To ignore religious rights is to overlook the conceptual, and historical, source of many other individual and group rights.

Second, without religion, the regime of human rights becomes infinitely expandable. The classic Religions of the Book adopt and advocate human rights in order to protect religious duties. A religious individual or association has rights to exist and act not in the abstract but in order to discharge discrete religious duties.[29] Religious rights provide the best example of the organic linkage between rights and duties, between subjective and objective rights. Without these linkages, rights become abstract, with no obvious limit on their exercise or their expansion – moral trumps frayed by heavy use and made less valuable with each new use.

Third, without religion, the state is given an exaggerated role to play as the guarantor of human rights. The simple state versus individual dialectic of many modern human rights theories leaves it to the state to protect and provide rights of all sorts. In reality, the state is not, and cannot be, so omnicompetent. Numerous "mediating structures" stand between the state and the individual, religious institutions prominently among them.

---

[28] Jellinek, *Die Erklärung*, 42.
[29] An-Na'im, *Toward an Islamic Reformation*, 1–10; Novak, *Covenantal Rights*, 3–12; World Council of Churches, *Human Rights and Christian Responsibility*, 3 vols. (Geneva, 1975); Wolfgang Huber and Heinz Eduard Tödt, *Menschenrechte: Perspektiven einer menschlichen Welt* (Stuttgart, 1977).

Religious institutions, among others, play a vital role in the cultivation and realization of rights. They can create the conditions (sometimes the prototypes) for the realization of first generation civil and political rights. They can provide a critical (sometimes the principal) means to meet second generation rights of education, health care, child care, labor organizations, employment, artistic opportunities, among others. They can offer some of the deepest insights into norms of creation, stewardship, and servanthood that lie at the heart of third generation rights.

The challenge of this next century is to transform religious communities from midwives to mothers of human rights – from agents that assist in the birth of rights norms conceived elsewhere, to associations that give birth to and nurture their own unique contributions to human rights norms and practices. The ancient teachings and practices of Judaism, Christianity, and Islam, at least have much to commend themselves to the human rights regime. Each of these traditions is a religion of revelation, founded on the eternal command to love one God, oneself, and all neighbors. Each tradition recognizes a canonical text as its highest authority – the Torah, the Bible, and the Qur'an, respectively. Each tradition designates a class of officials to preserve and propagate its faith, and embraces an expanding body of authoritative interpretations and applications of its canons. Each tradition has a refined legal structure – the Halacha, the canon law, and the Shari'a – that has translated its enduring principles of faith into evolving precepts of works. Each tradition has sought to imbue its religious, ethical, and legal norms into the daily lives of individuals and communities. Each tradition has produced a number of the basic building blocks of a comprehensive theory and law of religious rights – conscience, dignity, reason, liberty, equality, tolerance, love, openness, responsibility, justice, mercy, righteousness, accountability, covenant, and community, among other cardinal concepts. Each tradition has developed its own internal system of legal procedures and structures for the protection of rights, which historically have and still can serve as both prototypes and complements for secular legal systems. Each tradition has its own advocates and prophets, ancient and modern, who have worked to achieve a closer approximation of human rights ideals.

Human rights and religion

This leads to my second thesis: that human rights must have a more prominent place in the theological discourse of modern religions. Many of my friends in the religious world consider this second thesis to be as misguided as the first. It is one thing for religious bodies to accept the freedom and autonomy that a human rights regime allows. This at least gives them unencumbered space to pursue their divine callings. It is quite another thing for religious bodies to import human rights within their own polities and theologies. This exposes them to all manner of unseemly challenges.

Human rights norms, religious skeptics argue, challenge the structure of religious bodies. While human rights norms teach liberty and equality, most religious bodies teach authority and hierarchy. While human rights norms encourage pluralism and diversity, many religious bodies require orthodoxy and uniformity. While human rights norms teach freedoms of speech and petition, several religions teach duties of silence and submission. To draw human rights norms into the structures of religion would only seem to embolden members to demand greater access to religious governance, greater freedom from religious discipline, greater latitude in the definition of religious doctrine and liturgy. So why import them?

Moreover, human rights norms challenge the spirit of religious bodies. Human rights norms, religious skeptics argue, are the creed of a secular faith born of Enlightenment liberalism, humanism, and rationalism. Human rights advocates regularly describe these norms as our new "civic faith," "our new world religion," "our new global moral language."[30] The influential French jurist Karel Vasak has pressed these sentiments into a full confession of the secular spirit of the modern human rights movement:

The Universal Declaration of Human Rights [of 1948], like the French Declaration of the Rights of Man and Citizen in 1789, has had an immense impact throughout the world. It has been called a modern edition of the New Testament, and the Magna Carta of humanity, and has become a constant source of inspiration for governments, for judges, and for national and international legislators . . . [B]y recognizing the Universal Declaration as a *living* document . . . one can proclaim one's faith in the future of mankind.[31]

In demonstration of this new faith, Vasak converted the "old trinity" of "*liberté, equalité, et fraternité*" taught by the French Revolution into a "new trinity" of "three generations of rights" for all humanity.[32] The first generation of civil and political rights elaborates the meaning of liberty. The

---

[30] Johan D. van der Vyver, "Universality and Relativism of Human Rights: American Relativism," *Buffalo Human Rights Law Review* 4 (1998): 43–78.

[31] Karel Vasak, "A 30-Year Struggle," *UNESCO Courier* (November 1977): 29; see also Vasak, "Foreword," in *The International Dimensions of Human Rights*, ed. Karel Vasak (Westport, CT, 1982), xv; Vasak, "*Pour une troisième génération des droits de l'homme*," in *Études et essais sur le droit international humanitaire et sur les principes de la Croix-Rouge en l'honneur de Jean Pictet*, ed. Christophe Swinarski (The Hague, 1984), 837–845.

[32] Vasak, "Pour une troisième génération," 837.

second generation of social, cultural, and economic rights elaborates the meaning of equality. The third generation of solidarity rights to development, peace, health, the environment, and open communication elaborates the meaning of fraternity. Such language has become not only the *lingua franca* but also something of the *lingua sacra* of the modern human rights movement. In the face of such an overt confession of secular liberalism, religious skeptics conclude, a religious body would do well to resist the ideas and institutions of human rights.

Both these skeptical arguments, however, presuppose that human rights norms constitute a static belief system born of Enlightenment liberalism. But the human rights regime is not static. It is fluid, elastic, and open to challenge and change. The human rights regime is not a fundamental belief system. It is a relative system of ideas and ideals that presupposes the existence of fundamental beliefs and values that will constantly shape and reshape it. The human rights regime is not the child of Enlightenment liberalism, nor a ward under its exclusive guardianship. It is the *ius gentium* of our times, the common law of nations, which a variety of Hebrew, Greek, Roman, Christian, and Enlightenment movements have historically nurtured in the West and which today still needs the constant nurture of multiple communities, in the West and well beyond. It is beyond doubt that many current formulations of human rights are suffused with fundamental libertarian beliefs and values, some of which run counter to the cardinal beliefs of various religious traditions. But libertarianism does not and should not have a monopoly on the nurture of human rights; indeed, a human rights regime cannot long survive under its exclusive patronage.

I use the antique term *ius gentium* advisedly – to signal the place of human rights as "middle axioms" in our moral and political discourse.[33] Historically, Western writers spoke of a hierarchy of laws – from natural law (*ius naturale*), to common law (*ius gentium*), to civil law (*ius civile*). The natural law was the set of immutable principles of reason and conscience, which are supreme in authority and divinity and must always prevail in instances of dispute. The civil law was the set of enacted laws and procedures of local political communities, reflecting their immediate policies and procedures. Between these two sets of norms was the *ius gentium*, the set of principles and customs common to several communities and often the basis for treaties and other diplomatic conventions. The contents of

---

[33] Abdullahi Ahmed An-Na'im, "Towards an Islamic Hermeneutics for Human Rights," in *Human Rights and Religious Values: An Uneasy Relationship?* ed. Abdullahi Ahmed An-Na'im, *et al.* (Grand Rapids, MI, 1995), 229–242; Robert P. George, "Response," in *A Preserving Grace: Protestants, Catholics, and Natural Law*, ed. Michael Cromartie (Grand Rapids, MI, 1997), 157–161.

the *ius gentium* did gradually change over time and across cultures as new interpretations of the natural law were offered, and as new formulations of the positive law became increasingly conventional. But the *ius gentium* was a relatively consistent body of principles by which a person and a people could govern themselves.

This antique typology helps us to understand the intermediate place of human rights in our hierarchy of legal and cultural norms today. Human rights are the *ius gentium* of our time, the middle axioms of our discourse. They are derived from and dependent upon the transcendent principles that religious traditions (more than any other group) continue to cultivate. They also inform, and are informed by, shifts in the customs and conventions of sundry state law systems. These human rights norms do gradually change over time: just compare the international human rights instruments of 1948 with those of today. But human rights norms are a relatively stable set of ideals by which a person and community might be guided and judged.

This antique typology also helps us to understand the place of human rights within religion. My argument that human rights must have a more prominent place within religions today is not an attempt to import libertarian ideals into their theologies and polities. It is not an attempt to herd Trojan horses into churches, synagogues, mosques, and temples to assail secretly their spirit and structure. My argument is, rather, that religious bodies must again assume their traditional patronage and protection of human rights, bringing to this regime their full doctrinal vigor, liturgical healing, and moral suasion. Using our antique typology, religious bodies must again nurture and challenge the middle axioms of the *ius gentium* using the transcendent principles of the *ius naturale*. This must not be an effort to monopolize the discourse, nor to establish by positive law a particular religious construction of human rights. Such an effort must be part of a collective discourse of competing understandings of the *ius naturale* – of competing theological views of the divine and the human, of good and evil, of individuality and community – that will serve constantly to inform and reform, to develop and deepen, the human rights ideals now in place.[34]

A number of religious traditions of late have begun the process of reengaging the regime of human rights, of returning to their traditional roots and routes of nurturing and challenging the human rights regime. This process has been incremental, clumsy, controversial, and at times even fatal

---

[34] Wolfgang Huber, *Gerechtigkeit und Recht: Grundlinien Christlicher Rechtsethik* (Gütersloh, 1996), 252ff., 366ff., 446ff.; Jerome J. Shestack, "The Jurisprudence of Human Rights," in *Human Rights in International Law: Legal and Policy Issues*, ed. Theodor Meron (Oxford, 1984), 75; David Tracy, "Religion and Human Rights in the Public Realm," *Daedalus* 112 (4) (1983): 237–254.

for its proponents. But the process of religious engagement of human rights is now under way in Christian, Islamic, Judaic, Buddhist, Hindu, and traditional communities alike. Something of a new "human rights hermeneutic" is slowly beginning to emerge among modern religions.[35]

This is, in part, a "hermeneutic of confession." Given their checkered human rights records over the centuries, religious bodies have begun to acknowledge their departures from the cardinal teachings of peace and love that are the heart of their sacred texts and traditions. Christian churches have taken the lead in this process – from the Second Vatican Council's confession of prior complicity in authoritarianism, to the contemporary church's repeated confessions of prior support for apartheid, communism, racism, sexism, fascism, and anti-Semitism.[36] Other communities have also begun this process – from recent Muslim academics' condemnations of the politicization of "jihad" to the Dalai Lama's recent lamentations over the "sometimes sorry human rights record" of both his own and rival traditions.[37]

This is, in part, a "hermeneutic of suspicion," in Paul Ricoeur's famous phrase. Given the pronounced libertarian tone of many recent human rights formulations, it is imperative that we do not idolize or idealize these formulations. We need not be bound by current taxonomies of "three generations of rights" rooted in liberty, equality, and fraternity. Common law formulations of "life, liberty, or property," canon law formulations of "natural, ecclesiastical, and civil rights," or Protestant formulations of "civil, theological, and pedagogical uses" of rights might well be more apt classification schemes. We need not accept the seemingly infinite expansion of human rights discourse and demands. Rights bound by moral duties, by natural capacities, or by covenantal relationships might well provide better boundaries to the legitimate expression and extension of rights. We also need not be bound only to a centralized legal methodology of articulating

---

[35] See, e.g., An-Na'im, *Toward an Islamic Reformation*; Huber and Tödt, *Menschenrechte*; Novak, *Covenantal Rights*; Max L. Stackhouse, *Creeds, Society, and Human Rights* (Grand Rapids, MI, 1984); William Theodore de Bary, *Asian Values and Human Rights: A Confucian Communitarian Perspective* (Cambridge, MA, 1998); William Theodore de Bary and Tu Weiming, eds., *Confucianism and Human Rights* (New York, 1998); Irene Bloom *et al.*, eds., *Religious Diversity and Human Rights* (New York, 1996); Joanne R. Bauer and Daniel A. Bell, eds., *The East Asian Challenge for Human Rights* (Cambridge, 1999); Arvind Sharma, *Hinduism and Human Rights: A Conceptual Approach* (New Delhi, 2004).

[36] See Luke Timothy Johnson, "Religious Rights and Christian Texts," in Witte and van der Vyver, *Religious Human Rights*, 70–73; Charles Villa-Vicencio, *A Theology of Reconstruction: Nation-Building and Human Rights* (Cambridge, 1992).

[37] An-Na'im, *Toward an Islamic Reformation*, 171–172; Farid Esack, "Muslims Engaging the Other and the Humanum," in Witte and Martin, *Sharing the Book*, 119–120; Dalai Lama, *Commencement Address of the Dalai Lama at Emory University*, May 11, 1998.

and enforcing rights. We might also consider a more pluralistic model of interpretation that respects "the right of the [local] community to be the living frame of interpretation for [its] own religion and its normative regime."[38]

This is, in part, a "hermeneutic of history," that has been the burden of this book. While acknowledging the fundamental contributions of Enlightenment liberalism to the modern rights regime, we must also see the deeper genesis and genius of many modern rights norms in religious texts and traditions that antedate the Enlightenment by centuries, even by millennia. We must return to our religious sources. In part, this is a return to ancient sacred texts freed from the casuistic accretions of generations of jurists and freed from the cultural trappings of the communities in which these traditions were born. In part, this is a return to slender streams of theological jurisprudence that have not been part of the mainstream of the religious traditions, or have become diluted by too great a commingling with it. In part, this is a return to prophetic voices of dissent, long purged from traditional religious canons, but, in retrospect, prescient of some of the rights roles that the tradition might play today.

[38] An-Na'im, *Toward an Islamic Reformation*, 235.

Bibliography

Achinstein, Sharon, *Milton and the Revolutionary Reader* (Princeton, 1994)

Acts and Resolves, Public and Private, of the Province of Massachusetts Bay, 21 vols. (Boston, 1869)

Adams, John, *Papers of John Adams*, eds. R. Taylor, M. Kline and G. Lint, 2 vols. (Cambridge, MA, 1977)

    The Works of John Adams, Second President of the United States, with a Life of the Author, Notes, and Illustrations, ed. C. F. Adams, 10 vols. (Boston, 1850–1856)

Ahlstrom, Sidney "The Puritan Ethic and the Spirit of American Democracy," in Hunt, ed., *Calvinism and the Political Order*, 88

Alleine, Richard, *Heaven Opened: Or the Riches of God's Covenant of Grace* (London, 1665)

Althusius, Johannes, *Assertiones juridicae* (Herborn, 1604)

    Centuria conclusionum de pignoribus et hypothecis (Herborn, 1591)

    Civilis conversationis libri duo recogniti et aucti. Methodice digesti et exemplis sacris et profanis passim illustrati (Hanover, 1601, 1611)

    De injuriis et famosis libellis (Basel, 1601)

    De matrimonio contrahendo et dissolvendo (Basel, 1593)

    Dicaeologicae libri tres, totum et universum jus, quo utimur, methodice complectentes (Herborn, 1617; Frankfurt, 1618)

    Jo. Althusius aphorismi universi juris civilis vel repertorium (Basel, 1630)

    Jurisprudentiae Romanae libri duo ad leges methodi Rameae conformati et tabellis illustrati (Basel, 1586)

    Politica Johannes Althusius, ed. and trans. F. S. Carney (Indianapolis, IN, 1995)

    Politica methodice digesta atque exemplis sacris & profanis illustrata, 3rd edn. (Herborn, 1614), reprinted as *Politica Methodice Digesta of Johannes Althusius (Althaus)*, ed. Carl J. Friedrich (Cambridge, MA, 1932)

    Politik, trans. Heinrich Janssen, ed. Dieter Wyduckel (Berlin, 2003)

    Theses miscellaneae (Herborn, 1604)

    Tractatus tres de poenis, de rebus fungibilibus ac de jure retentionis (Kassel, 1611)

Ames, William, *Medulla Sacrae Theologiae Pertita*, 8 vols. (Frankener, 1623)

Amussen, Susan Dwyer, *An Ordered Society: Gender and Class in Early Modern England* (Oxford, 1988)

An-Na'im, Abdullahi Ahmed, *Toward an Islamic Reformation: Civil Liberties, Human Rights, and International Law* (Syracuse, NY, 1990)

"Towards an Islamic Hermeneutics for Human Rights," in *Human Rights and Religious Values: An Uneasy Relationship?* ed. Abdullahi Ahmed An-Na'im, *et al.* (Grand Rapids, MI, 1995), 229

Antholz, Heinz, *Die politische Wirksamkeit des Johannes Althusius in Emden* (Aurich, 1955)

Antieau, Chester J., Phillip M. Carroll, and Thomas C. Burke, *Religion Under the State Constitutions* (Brooklyn, NY, 1965)

Aristotle, *The Basic Works of Aristotle*, ed. Richard Mckeon (New York, 1941)

Armitage, David, Armand Himy and Quentin Skinner, eds., *Milton and Republicanism* (Cambridge, 1995)

Bailyn, Bernard, *The Ideological Origins of the American Revolution* (Cambridge, MA, 1967)

Bainton, Roland H., *Bernardino Ochino* (Florence, 1941)
　　Concerning Heretics. . . . An Anonymous Work Attributed to Sebastian Castellio (New York, 1935)
　　"Documenta Servetiana," *AFR* 44 (1953): 223; *ibid.*, 45 (1954): 99
　　Hunted Heretic: The Life and Death of Michael Servetus (Boston, 1953)
　　Sebastian Castellio: Champion of Religious Liberty (New York, 1951)
　　"The Struggle for Religious Liberty," *Church History* 10 (1941): 96
　　The Travail of Religious Liberty (London, 1953)

Baird, Henry Martin, *Theodore Beza: The Counselor of the French Reformation, 1519–1605* (New York, 1899)

Baker, J. Wayne and Charles S. McCoy, *Fountainhead of Federalism: Heinrich Bullinger and the Covenantal Tradition* (Louisville, KY, 1991)

Balke, Willem, *Calvin and the Anabaptist Radicals*, trans. William Heynen (Grand Rapids, MI, 1981)

Bancroft, George, *History of the United States of America*, 15th edn., 2 vols. (Boston, 1853)

Baron, Hans, "Calvinist Republicanism and its Historical Roots," *Church History* 8 (1939): 30

Bauer, Joanne R. and Daniel A. Bell, eds., *The East Asian Challenge for Human Rights* (Cambridge, 1999)

Baur, Jürgen, *Gott, Recht und weltliches Regiment im Werke Calvins* (Bonn, 1965)

Beeke, Joel R. and Sinclair B. Ferguson, *Reformed Confessions Harmonized* (Grand Rapids, MI, 1999)

Beer, Barrett L., "John Ponet's Short Treatise of Politike Power Reassessed," *Sixteenth Century Journal* 21 (1990): 373

Benedict, Philip, *Christ's Churches Purely Reformed: A Social History of Calvinism* (New Haven and London, 2002)

Bennett, Joan S., *Reviving Liberty: Radical Christian Humanism in Milton's Great Poems* (Cambridge, MA, 1989)

Béranger, Jean, *Nathaniel Ward (ca. 1578–1652)* (Bordeaux, 1969)

Berkvens-Stevelink, C., J. Israel, and G. H. M. Posthumus Meyjes, eds., *The Emergence of Tolerance in the Dutch Republic* (Leiden, 1997)

Berman, Harold J., *Faith and Order: The Reconciliation of Law and Religion* (Atlanta, GA, 1993)

Law and Revolution: The Formation of the Western Legal Tradition (Cambridge, MA, 1983)

Law and Revolution II: The Impact of the Protestant Reformations on the Western Legal Tradition (Cambridge, MA, 2003)

"Religious Foundations of Law in the West: An Historical Perspective," *Journal of Law and Religion* 1 (1983): 3

Beyerhaus, Gisbert, *Studien zur Staatsanschauung Calvins mit besonderer Berücksichtigung seines Souveränitätsbegriffs*, repr. edn. (Aalen, 1973)

Beza, Theodore, *Concerning the Rights of Rulers Over Their Subjects and the Duties of Subjects Toward Their Rulers*, trans. Henri-Louis Gonin (Cape Town and Pretoria, 1956)

Correspondance de Théodore de Bèze, ed. Hippolyte Aubert, *et al.*, 21 vols. (Geneva, 1960–1999)

De repudiis et divortiis (Geneva, 1569), reprinted in Beza, TT 2:50ff

Du Droit des Magistrats, ed. Robert M. Kingdon (Geneva, 1970)

Iesu Christi D. N. Novum Testamentum, sive novum foedus, 2 vols. (Geneva, 1565)

Lex dei, moralis, ceremonialis et civilis (Geneva, 1577)

Propositions and Principles of Divinity, Propounded and Disputed in the University of Geneva, trans. Robert Waldegrave (Edinburgh, 1591)

Psalmorum davidis et aliorum prophetarum libri quinque (London, 1580)

Sermons sur les trois premiers chapitres du cantique des Cantiques de Salomon (Geneva, 1586)

Sermons sur l'histoire de la passion et sepulture de nostre Seigneur Iesus Christ, descrite par les quatre Evangelistes (Geneva, 1592)

Tractatus pius et moderatus de vera excommunicatione et christiano presybterio (Geneva, 1590)

Tractationum Theologicarum, 3 vols., 2nd edn. (Geneva, 1582)

Traicté des vrayes essencielles et visibiles marques de la vraye Eglise Catholique (Geneva, 1592)

Bloom, Irene, *et al.*, eds., *Religious Diversity and Human Rights* (New York, 1996)

Bodian, Miriam, "The Biblical 'Jewish Republic' and the Dutch 'New Israel' in Seventeenth-Century Dutch Thought," *Hebraic Political Studies* 1 (2006): 186

Bohatec, Josef, *Budé, und Calvin: Studien zur Gedankenwelt des französischen Frühhumanismus* (Graz, 1950)

Calvin und das Recht (Graz, 1934)

Calvins Lehre von Staat und Kirche mit besonderer Berücksichtigung des Organismusgedankens, repr. edn. (Aalen, 1961)

"Das Territorial- und Kollegialsystem in der holländischen Publizistik des XVII. Jahrhunderts," *ZSS (KA)* 66 (1948):1

England und die Geschichte der Menschen-und Bürgerrecht, 3rd edn., edn., Otto Weber (Graz, 1956)

Bolt, John, *A Free Church, A Holy Nation: Abraham Kuyper's American Public Theology* (Grand Rapids, MI, 2000)

"The Holland-American Line of Liberty," *Morality and Markets* 1 (1998): 1

Bosco, Ronald A., "Lectures at the Pillory: The Early American Execution Sermon," *American Quarterly* 30 (1978):156

Bouwsma, William J., *John Calvin: A Sixteenth Century Portrait* (New York and Oxford, 1988)

Bowen, Catherine Drinker, *John Adams and the American Revolution* (Boston, 1950)

Brailsford, H. N., *The Levellers of the English Revolution*, ed. Christopher Hill (London, 1961)

Bratt, James D., *Dutch Calvinism in North America: A History of a Conservative Subculture* (Grand Rapids, MI, 1984)

Bratt, James D., ed., *Abraham Kuyper: A Centennial Reader* (Grand Rapids, MI, 1998)

Bratt, John H., ed., *The Heritage of John Calvin* (Grand Rapids, MI, 1973)

Breen, Quirinius, "John Calvin and the Rhetorical Tradition," *Church History* 26 (1957): 14

John Calvin: A Study in French Humanism (Grand Rapids, MI, 1931)

Breen, T. H., *Puritans and Adventurers: Change and Persistence in Early America* (New York and Oxford, 1980)

The Character of the Good Ruler 1630–1730 (New Haven, 1970)

Breen, T. H. and Stephen Foster, "The Puritans' Greatest Achievement: A Study of Social Cohesion in Seventeenth-Century Massachusetts," *Journal of American History* 60 (1973): 5

Bremer, Francis J., *John Winthrop: America's Forgotten Founding Father* (Oxford, 2003)

Brett, Annabel S., *Liberty, Right, and Nature: Individual Rights in Late Scholastic Thought* (Cambridge and New York, 1997)

Bromley, J. S. and E. H. Kossman, eds., *Britain and the Netherlands* (The Hague, 1971)

Browning, Don S., "The United Nations Convention on the Rights of the Child: Should it be Ratified and Why?" *Emory International Law Review* 20 (2006): 157

Brownlie, Ian, ed., *Basic Documents on Human Rights*, 3rd edn. (Oxford, 1992)

Brunner, Emil, *Justice and the Social Order*, trans. Mary Hottinger (New York, 1945)

Bryce, James, *The American Commonwealth* (1941), 2 vols., ed. Gary L. McDowell (Indianapolis, IN, 1995)

Bumsted, J. M., "A Well-Bounded Toleration: Church and State in the Plymouth Colony," *Journal of Church and State* 10 (1968): 265

Burns, J. H., ed., *The Cambridge History of Political Thought, 1450–1700* (Cambridge, 1991)

Bush, Sargent, Jr., *The Writings of Thomas Hooker: Spiritual Adventure in Two Worlds* (Madison, WI, 1980)

Butterfield, Herbert, *Christianity and History* (New York, 1949)

"Toleration in Early Modern Times," *Journal of the History of Ideas* 38 (1977): 573

Calvin, John, *Calvin's Commentary on Seneca's De Clementia*, trans. Ford Lewis Battles and A. M. Hugo (Leiden, 1969)

Institution of the Christian Religion (1536), trans. Ford Lewis Battles (Atlanta, GA, 1975)

Institutes of the Christian Religion (1559), ed. John T. McNeill, trans. Ford Lewis Battles (Philadelphia, 1960)

Ioannis Calvini opera quae supersunt omnia, ed. G. Baum, *et al.*, 59 vols. (Brunswick, 1863–1900) (Corpus Reformatorum Series, vols. XXIX–LXXXVII)

Joannis Calvini opera selecta, ed. Peter Barth, Wilhelm Niesel, and Dora Scheuner, 5 vols. (Munich, 1926–52)

Supplementa Calvinia: Sermons inédits, ed. Erwin Mülhaupt, *et al.* (Neukirchen-Vluyn, 1936–)

Tracts and Treaties in Defense of the Reformed Faith, trans. Henry Beveridge, ed. T. F. Torrance, 3 vols. (Grand Rapids, MI, 1958)

Cappon, Lester J., ed., *The Adams–Jefferson Letters*, 2 vols. (Chapel Hill, NC: University of North Carolina Press, 1959)

Carney, Frederick S., Heinz Schilling and Dieter Wyduckel, eds., *Jurisprudenz, Politische Theorie und Politische Theologie* (Berlin, 2004)

Carpenter, Geoffrey P., *A Secondary Annotated Bibliography of John Winthrop, 1588–1649* (New York, 1999)

Case, Thomas, *Spiritual Whoredom Discovered* (London, 1647)

Castellio, Sebastian, *Concerning Heretics* (1554), ed. Roland H. Bainton (New York, 1935)

De haereticis an sint persequendi (1553; facs. edn. Geneva, 1954)

Catalogue of the Thomason Tracts in the British Museum (London, 1906)

Chaffee, Zechariah "Colonial Courts and the Common Law," in *Essays in the History of Early American Law*, ed. David H. Flaherty (Chapel Hill, NC, 1969), 53

Chenevière, M. E., *La pensée politique de Calvin*, repr. edn. (Geneva, 1970)

Choisy, Eugène, *L'État chrétien calviniste a Genève au temps de Théodore de Bèze* (Geneva, 1902)

Chupp, Jesse and Cary J. Nederman, "The Calvinist Background to Johannes Althusius's Idea of Religious Toleration," in *Jurisprudenz, Politische Theorie*, 243

Clarke, J. C. D., *The Language of Liberty 1660–1832: Political Discourse and Social Dynamics in the Anglo-American World* (Cambridge, 1994)

Cleaver, Robert, *A Godly Form of Householde Gouernment* (London, 1598)

Clegg, C. S., *Censorship in Jacobean England* (Cambridge, 2001)

Press Censorship in Elizabethan England (Cambridge, 1997)

Cobb, Sanford H., *The Rise of Religious Liberty in America* (New York, 1902)

Cochrane, Arthur C. ed., *Reformed Confessions of the Sixteenth Century* (Philadelphia, 1966; repr. edn., Louisville, 2003)

Coffey, John, *Politics, Religion, and the British Revolutions: The Mind of Samuel Rutherford* (Cambridge, 1997)

Cohen, Morris, "Legal Literature in Colonial Massachusetts," in *Law in Colonial Massachusetts 1630–1800*, ed. Daniel Coquillete (Boston and Charlottesville, VA, 1984), 243

Coke, Edward, *The Selected Writings of Sir Edward Coke*, ed. Steve Sheppard, 3 vols. (Indianapolis, IN 2003)

Colclough, David, *Freedom of Speech in Early Stuart England* (Cambridge, 2005)

Collections of the Connecticut Historical Society, 31 vols. (Hartford, CT, 1860–1967)

Confessio et apologia pastorum & reliquorum ministrorum Ecclesiae Magdeburgensis (Magdeburg, 1550)

Conring, Emil, *Kirche und Staat nach der Lehre der niederländischen Calvinisten in der ersten Hälfte des 17. Jahrhundert* (Berlin, 1965)

Cotton, John, *The Keys of the Kingdom of Heaven [1644]* (Boston, 1852)

Cottret, Bernard, *Calvin: A Biography*, trans. M. Wallace McDonald (Grand Rapids, MI, 2000)

Cushing, John D., "Notes on Disestablishment in Massachusetts, 1780–1833," *William & Mary Quarterly* (3rd ser.) 26 (1969): 169

Dahm, Karl-Wilhelm, Werner Krawietz and Dieter Wyduckdel, eds., *Politische Theorie des Johannes Althusius* (Berlin, 1988)

Dale, Elizabeth, *Debating – and Creating – Authority: The Failure of a Constitutional Ideal in Massachusetts Bay, 1629–1649* (Aldershot, 2001)

Danner, Dan G., "Christopher Goodman and the English Protestant Tradition of Civil Disobedience," *Sixteenth Century Journal* 8 (1977): 60

Davies, Tony, "Borrowed Language: Milton, Jefferson, Mirabeau," in Armitage, Himy and Skinner, eds., *Milton and Republicanism*, 254

Davis, J. C., *Oliver Cromwell* (Oxford, 2001)

Davis, R. W., ed., *The Origins of Modern Freedom in the West* (Stanford, CA, 1995)

Dawson, Hugh J., " 'Christian Charitie' as Colonial Discourse: Rereading Winthrop's Sermon in its English Context," *Early American Literature* 33 (1998): 117

de Bary, William Theodore, *Asian Values and Human Rights: A Confucian Communitarian Perspective* (Cambridge, MA, 1998)

de Bary, William Theodore and Tu Weiming, eds., *Confucianism and Human Rights* (New York, 1998)

De Blecourt, Anne S. and Nicolaas Japiske, eds., *Klein plakkaatboek van Nederland. Verzameling van ordonnantien en plakkaten betreffende regeeringsvorm, kerk en rechtsspraak (14e eeuw tot 1749)* (Groningen, 1919)

De Jong, O. J., "Unie en Religie," in *De Unie van Utrecht. Wording en werking van een verbond en van een verbondsacte*, eds. S. Groenveld and H. L. Ph. Leeuwenberg (The Hague, 1979), 155

de Klerk, Peter, ed., *Calvin and the State* (Grand Rapids, MI, 1993)

Demos, John, *A Little Commonwealth: Family Life in Plymouth Colony*, 2nd edn. (New York and Oxford, 2000)

Denis, Philippe, and Jean Rott, *Jean Morély (ca. 1524 – ca. 1594) et l'utopie d'une démocratie dans l'eglise* (Geneva, 1993)

Diefendorf, Barbara, *Beneath the Cross: Catholics and Huguenots in Sixteenth-Century Paris* (New York and Oxford, 1991)

Diepenhorst, P. A., *Dr. A. Kuyper* (Haarlem, 1931)

Dierickx, M., "De lijst der veroordeelden door de Raad van Beroerten," *Revue belge de philologie et d'histoire* 60 (1962): 415

   De oprichting der nieuwe bisdommen in de Nederlanden onder Filips II, 1559–1570 (Antwerp, 1950)

Donahue, Charles A., "*Ius* in the Subjective Sense in Roman Law: Reflections on Villey and Tierney," in *A Ennio Cortese*, ed. D. Maffei, 2 vols. (Rome, 2001), 1:506

Dorff, Elliot N., and Arthur Rossett, *The Living Tree: The Roots and Growth of Jewish Law* (Albany, NY, 1988)

Doumergue, Emile, *Jean Calvin. Les hommes et les choses de son temps*, 7 vols. (Lausanne, 1899–1927)

Duguit, Léon, *Les Constitutions et les principales lois politiques de la France depuis 1789* (Paris, 1952)

Ehler, Sidney Z. and John B. Morrall, eds., *Church and State Through the Centuries: A Collection of Historic Documents with Commentaries* (Newman, MD, 1954)

Elazar, Daniel J., *Covenant & Commonwealth: From Christian Separation Through the Protestant Reformation* (New Brunswick, NJ, 1996)

   Covenant and Civil Society: The Constitutional Matrix of Modern Democracy (Brunswick, NJ, 1998)

Election Day Sermons: Plymouth and Connecticut, facs. edn. (New York, 1983)

Ellis, Joseph J., *Passionate Sage: The Character and Legacy of John Adams*, 2nd edn. (New York and London, 2001)

Emerson, Everett, *John Cotton*, rev. edn. (Boston, 1990)

Esmein, Adhemar, *A History of Continental Criminal Procedure with Special Reference to France*, repr. edn. (South Hackensack, NJ, 1968)

Eusden, John D., "Natural Law and Covenant Theology in New England, 1620–1670," *Natural Law Forum* 5 (1960): 1

Evans, J. Martin ed., *John Milton: Twentieth-Century Perspectives, Volume 4: Paradise Lost* (New York, 2003)

Fallon, Robert T., *Divided Empire: Milton's Political Imagery* (University Park, PA, 1995)

   Milton in Government (University Park, PA, 1993)

Feenstra, Robert, "A quelle époque les Provinces-Unies sont-elles devenues indépendantes en droit l'égard du Saint-Empire," *Tijdschrift voor Rechtsgeschiedenis* 20 (1952): 30–63, 182–218

Feinberg, Joel, *Rights, Justice, and the Bounds of Liberty* (Princeton, 1980)

Fell, A. London, *Origins of Legislative Sovereignty and the Legislative State*, 6 vols. (Königstein and Cambridge, MA, 1983–)

Flaherty, David, "Law and the Enforcement of Morals in Early America," in *American Law and the Constitutional Order: Historical Perspectives*, ed. Lawrence M. Friedman and Harry N. Scheiber (Cambridge, MA, 1978), 53

Flaherty, David H., ed., *Essays in the History of Early American Law*, (Chapel Hill, NC, 1969)

Fontaine, P. F. M., *De raad van state. Zijn taak, organisatie en werkzaamheden in de jaren 1588–1590* (Groningen, 1954)

Foster, Herbert D., *Collected Papers of Herbert Darling Foster* (n.p., 1927)

Foster, Stephen, "New England and the Challenge of Heresy, 1630 to 1660: The Puritan Crisis in Transatlantic Perspective," *William & Mary Quarterly* (3rd ser.) (1981): 624

Frank, Joseph, *The Levellers: A History of the Writings of Three Seventeenth-Century Social Democrats, John Lilburne, Richard Overton, and William Walwyn* (New York, 1969)

Franklin, Julian H., *Constitutionalism and Resistance in the Sixteenth Century: Three Treatises by Hotman, Beza, and Mornay* (New York, 1969)

Friedman, Jerome, *Michael Servetus: A Case Study in Total Heresy* (Geneva, 1978)

Friedman, Lawrence M. and Harry N. Scheiber, eds., *American Law and the Constitutional Order: Historical Perspectives* (Cambridge, MA, 1978)

Friedrich, Carl J. and Robert G. McCloskey, eds., *From the Declaration to the Constitution: The Roots of American Constitutionalism* (New York, 1954)

Fukuda, Arihiro, *Sovereignty and the Sword: Harrington, Hobbes, and Mixed Government in the English Civil Wars* (Oxford, 1997)

Ganoczy, A., *Le jeune Calvin. Genése et evolution de la vocation réformatrice* (Wiesbaden, 1966)

Gardiner, S. R., *History of the Commonwealth and Protectorate, 1649–1656*, 4 vols., repr. edn. (Adelstrop, Gloucestershire, 1988–1989)

The Constitutional Documents of the Puritan Revolution, 1625–1660, 3d rev. ed. (Oxford, 1906)

Garrison-Estèbe, Janine, *Tocsin pour un massacre, la saison des Saint-Barthélemy* (Paris, 1968)

Gaustad, Edwin S., *Liberty of Conscience: Roger Williams in America* (Grand Rapids, MI, 1991)

Geisendorf, Paul, *Théodore de Bèze* (Geneva, 1967)

Geisst, Charles R., *The Political Thought of John Milton* (New York, 1984)

Geurts, P. A. M., *De Nederlandse Opstand in de Pamfletten, 1566–1584* (Nijmegen and Utrecht, 1956)

Geyl, Pieter, *The Revolt of the Netherlands, 1555–1609*, 2nd edn. (London, 1958)

Gierke, Otto von, *The Development of Political Theory*, trans. Bernard Freyd (New York, 1966)

Gilbert, Neal W., *Renaissance Concepts of Method* (New York, 1960)

Gillett, Charles R., *Catalogue of the McAlpin Collection of British History and Theology: Index* (New York, 1930)

Glendon, Mary Ann, *Rights Talk: The Impoverishment of Political Discourse* (New York, 1991)

Gooch, G. P., *English Democratic Ideas in the 17th Century*, 2nd edn. (New York, 1959)

Goodman, Christopher, *How Superior Powers Ought to be Obeyd* (1558), fasc. edn., ed. Charles H. McIlwain (New York, 1931)

Gorski, Philip S., *The Disciplinary Revolution: Calvinism and the Rise of the State in Early Modern Europe* (Chicago, 2003)

Gouge, William, *Of Domestical Duties: Eight Treatises* (London, 1622)

Gough, J. W., *The Social Contract: A Critical Study of its Development*, 2nd edn. (Oxford, 1957)

Grabill, Stephen J., *Rediscovering the Natural Law in Reformed Theological Ethics* (Grand Rapids, MI, 2006)

Gray, Francis C., *Remarks on the Early Laws of Massachusetts Bay* (Boston, 1843)

Gregg, Pauline, *Free-Born John: The Biography of John Lilburne*, repr. edn. (London, 2000)

Groenveld, S. and H. L. Ph. Leeuwenberg, eds., *De Unie van Utrecht. Wording en werking van een verbond en van een verbondsacte* (The Hague, 1979)

Haas, Günther, *The Concept of Equity in John Calvin's Ethics* (Waterloo, Ontario, 1997)

Hall, David D., "On Common Ground: The Coherence of American Puritan Studies," *William & Mary Quarterly* (3rd ser.) 44 (1987): 193

The Antinomian Controversy: A Documentary History, 2nd edn. (Durham, NC, 1990)

Hall, David W., *The Genevan Reformation and the American Founding* (Lexington, MA 2003)

Haller, William R., *Liberty and the Reformation in the Puritan Revolution* (New York, 1955)

The Rise of Puritanism, Or, the Way to the New Jerusalem as Set Forth in Pulpit and Press from Thomas Cartwright to John Lilburne and John Milton, 1570–1643, 4th printing (New York, 1965)

Haller, William, ed., *Tracts on Liberty in the Puritan Revolution, 1638–1647*, 3 vols. (New York, 1934)

Handlin, Oscar and Mary Handlin, eds., *The Popular Sources of Political Authority: Documents on The Massachusetts Constitution of 1780* (Cambridge, MA, 1966)

Harinck, George, and Hans Krabbendam, eds., *Breaches and Bridges: Reformed Subcultures in the Netherlands, Germany, and the United States* (Amsterdam, 2000)

Sharing the Reformed Tradition: The Dutch–North American Exchange, 1846–1996 (Amsterdam, 1996)

Haskins, George L., *Law and Authority in Early Massachusetts: A Study in Tradition and Design* (New York, 1960)

Heise, Volker, *Der calvinistische Einfluss auf das humanistische Rechtsdenken exemplarisch dargestellt an den "Commentarii de iure civili" von Hugo Donellus (1527–1591)* (Göttingen, 2004)

Heller, Henry, *The Conquest of Poverty: The Calvinist Revolt in Sixteenth-Century France* (Leiden, 1986)

Helmholz, R. H., ed., *Canon Law in Protestant Lands* (Berlin, 1992)

Hemming, Nicolas, *De lege naturae apodicta methodus* (Wittenberg, 1563)

Henkin, Louis, *et al.*, *Human Rights* (New York, 1999)

Henty, George A., *By Pike and Dyke: A Tale of the Rise of the Dutch Republic* (New York, 1894)

Hertzke, Allen D., *Freeing God's Children: The Unlikely Alliance for Global Human Rights* (Lanham, MD, 2004)

Heslam, Peter, "Abraham Kuyper's Lectures on Calvinism: An Historical Study" (D. Phil., Oxford, 1993)

Hesselink, I. John, *Calvin's Concept of the Law* (Allison Park, PA, 1992)

Higginson, J. *The Cause of God and His People in New England* (Cambridge, MA, 1663)

Hill, Christopher, *God's Englishman: Oliver Cromwell and the English Revolution* (New York, 1970)

   Milton and the English Revolution (New York, 1977)

   Puritanism and Revolution: Studies in Interpretation of the English Revolution of the Seventeenth Century (London, 1965)

   The Century of Revolution, 1603–1714 (London, 1974)

   The World Turned Upside Down: Radical Ideas During the English Revolution, repr. edn. (New York, 1988)

Hill, Christopher and Edmund Dell, eds., *The Good Old Cause: The English Revolution of 1640–1660, Its Causes, Course, and Consequences. Extracts from Contemporary Sources* (London, 1940)

Hittinger, Russell, "Introduction to Modern Catholicism," in *The Teachings of Modern Christianity on Law, Politics, and Human Nature*, eds. John Witte, Jr. and Frank S. Alexander, 2 vols. (New York and London, 2005), 1:3

Hohfeld, W. N., *Fundamental Legal Conceptions* (New Haven, 1919)

Holifield, E. Brooks, *The Covenant Sealed: The Development of Puritan Sacramental Theology in Old and New England, 1570–1720* (New Haven, 1974)

   Theology in America: Christian Thought from the Age of the Puritans to the Civil War (New Haven and London, 2003)

Honoré, Tony, *Ulpian: Pioneer of Human Rights*, 2nd edn. (Oxford, 2002)

Hooker, Thomas, *A Survey of the Summe of Church-Discipline*, 2 vols. (London, 1648)

   The Application of Redemption by the Effectual Work of the Word, and Spirit of Christ, for the Bringing Home of Lost Sinners to God (London, 1659)

Höpfl, Harro, *The Christian Polity of John Calvin* (Cambridge, 1982)

Hoskins, Richard J., "The Original Separation of Church and State in America," *Journal of Law and Religion* 2 (1984): 221

Hotman, François, "Francogallia," in *Constitutionalism and Resistance in the Sixteenth Century: Three Treatises by Hotman, Beza, and Mornay*, ed. Julian Franklin (New York, 1969), 55

Howard, George Elliott, *A History of Matrimonial Institutions, Chiefly in England and the United States*, 3 vols. (Chicago, 1904)

Hubbard, William, *The Benefit of a Well-Ordered Conversation* (Boston, 1684)

Huber, Wolfgang, *Gerechtigkeit und Recht: Grundlinien Christlicher Rechtsethik* (Gütersloh, 1996)

Huber, Wolfgang and Heinz Eduard Tödt, *Menschenrechte: Perspektiven einer menschlichen Welt* (Stuttgart, 1977)

Hudson, Winthrop S., "John Locke: Heir of Puritan Political Theorists," in *Calvinism and the Political Order*, ed. George L. Hunt (Philadelphia, 1960), 108

John Ponet (1515?–1556): Advocate of Limited Monarchy (Chicago, 1942)

Hueglin, Thomas O., *Early Modern Concepts for a Late Modern World: Althusius on Community and Federalism* (Waterloo, Ontario, 1999)

Hughes, Merritt Y., "Milton's Treatment of Reformation History in *The Tenure of Kings and Magistrates*," *The Seventeenth Century: Studies in the History of English Thought and Literature from Bacon to Pope*, ed. Richard F. Jones *et al.* (Stanford, 1951), 247

Ten Perspectives on Milton (New Haven, CT, 1965)

Hunsinger, George, "Karl Barth," in *Modern Christian Teachings on Law, Politics, and Human Nature*, ed. John Witte, Jr. and Frank S. Alexander 2 vols. (New York, 2005), I:352, II:280

Hunt, George L., ed., *Calvinism and the Political Order* (Philadelphia, PA, 1965),

Hynemann, Charles S. and Donald S. Lutz, eds., *American Political Writing During the Founding Era, 1760–1805*, 2 vols. (Indianapolis, IN, 1983)

Innes, William C., *Social Concern in Calvin's Geneva* (Allison Park, PA: Pickwick Publications, 1983)

Israel, Jonathan, *The Dutch Republic: Its Rise, Greatness, and Fall, 1477–1806*, repr. edn. (Oxford, 1998)

Janssen, Heinrich, *Die Bibel als Grundlage der politischen Theorie des Johannes Althusius* (Frankfurt am Main, 1992)

Jászi, Oscar and John D. Lewis, *Against the Tyrant: The Tradition and Theory of Tyrannicide* (Glencoe, IL, 1957)

Jellinek, Georg, *Die Erklärung der Menschen- und Bürgerrechte: Ein Beitrag zur modernen Verfassungsgeschichte* (Leipzig, 1895)

Johnson, Herbert A., *Imported Eighteenth Century Law Treatises in American Libraries, 1700–1799* (Knoxville, TN, 1978)

Jones, Richard F., *et al.*, eds., *The Seventeenth Century: Studies in the History of English Thought and Literature from Bacon to Pope* (Stanford, CA, 1951)

Jordan, W. K., *The Development of Religious Toleration in England*, 4 vols. (Cambridge, MA, 1938)

Justinian, *The Institutes of Justinian: Text, Translation, and Commentary*, ed. and trans. J. A. C. Thomas (Cape Town, 1975)

Kahn, Victoria, "Early Modern Rights Talk," *Yale Journal of Law and the Humanities* 13 (2001): 391

"The Metaphorical Contract in Milton's *Tenure of Kings and Magistrates*," in Armitage, Himy and Skinner, eds., *Milton and Republicanism*, 82–105

Wayward Contracts: The Crisis of Political Obligation in England, 1640–1674 (Princeton, 2004)

Kaplan, Benjamin J., *Calvinists and Libertines: Confession and Community in Utrecht, 1578–1620* (Oxford, 1995)

Kaser, Max, *Ausgewählte Schriften*, 2 vols. (Naples, 1976–1977)

Ius Gentium (Cologne, 1993)

Kavenagh, W. Keith, ed., *Foundations of Colonial America: A Documentary History*, 3 vols. (New York, 1973)

Kelley, Donald R., *François Hotman: A Revolutionary's Ideal* (Princeton, 1973)

Kelso, Robert W., *The History of Public Poor Relief in Massachusetts, 1620–1920* (Boston and New York, 1922)

Kenyon, J. P., ed., *The Stuart Constitution* (Cambridge, 1986)

Kessler, Sanford, "Locke's Influence on Jefferson's 'Bill for Establishing Religious Freedom'," *Journal of Church and State* 25 (1983): 231

Kingdon, Robert M., *Adultery and Divorce in Calvin's Geneva* (Cambridge, MA and London, 1995)

"Althusius' Use of Calvinist Sources," *Rechtstheorie* 16 (1997): 19

"Beza's Political Ideas as Expressed in His Sermons on the Passion" (unpub. ms.)

"Calvinism and Democracy," in *The Heritage of John Calvin*, ed. John H. Bratt (Grand Rapids, MI, 1973), 177

"Calvinism and Resistance Theory, 1550–1580," in *The Cambridge History of Political Thought, 1450–1700*, ed. J. H. Burns (Cambridge, 1991), 193

Geneva and the Coming of the Wars of Religion in France 1555–1563 (Geneva, 1956)

Geneva and the Consolidation of the French Protestant Movement 1564–1572: A Contribution to the History of Congregationalism, Presbyterianism and Calvinist Resistance Theory (Madison, WI, 1967)

Myths About the St. Bartholomew's Day Massacres, 1572–1576 (Cambridge, MA, 1988)

"The First Expression of Theodore Beza's Political Ideas," *AFR* 46 (1955): 88

Kingdon, Robert M. and Robert D. Linder, *Calvin and Calvinism: Sources of Democracy?* (Lexington, MA, 1970)

Klingenheben, Werner, "Der demokratisierte Staat und die herrschaftsfreie Kirche bei Theodor Beza" (Ph.D. Diss. Göttingen, 1974)

Knoppers, Laura Lunger, "*Paradise Regained* and the Politics of Martyrdom," *Modern Philology* 90 (1992): 200

Knox, John, *The Works of John Knox*, ed. David Laing, 6 vols. (Edinburgh, 1846; repr. edn., New York, 1966)

Knuttel, Willem P. C., *Catalogus van de pamflettenverzameling berustende in de Koninkje Bibliothek*, 9 vols. (The Hague, 1889–1920)

De toestand der nederlandsche katholieken ten tijde der republiek, 2 vols. (The Hague, 1892–1894)

Köhler, Walter, "Book Review," *Theologische Jahrbericht* 24 (1904): 579

Zürcher Ehegericht und Genfer Konsistorium, 2 vols. (Leipzig, 1942)

Kossman, E. H., *Political Thought in the Dutch Republic: Three Studies* (Amsterdam, 2000)

"Popular Sovereignty at the Beginning of the Dutch Ancien Regime," *The Low Countries History Yearbook* 14 (1981): 1

Kossman, E. H. and A. Mellink, eds., *Texts Concerning the Revolt of the Netherlands* (Cambridge, 1974)

Kuehne, Dale S. *Massachusetts Congregationalist Political Thought, 1760–1790* (Columbia, MO, 1996)

Kurland, Philip B. and Ralph S. Lerner, eds., *The Founders' Constitution*, 5 vols. (Chicago, 1987)

Kuyper, Abraham, *Dictaten Dogmatiek*, 2nd edn., 6 vols. (Kampen, n.d.)

Encyclopaedie der heilige Godgeleerdheid, 4 vols. (Kampen, 1909)

Lectures on Calvinism [1898], repr. edn. (Grand Rapids, MI, 1981)

Liberalisten en Joden (Amsterdam, 1878)

Ons Program, 4th edn. (Amsterdam and Pretoria, 1897)

Souvereiniteit in eigen Kring (Amsterdam, 1880)

"The Origin and Safeguard of our Constitutional Liberties," *Bibliotheca Sacra* 52 (1895): 391

The Problem of Poverty, trans. and ed. James W. Skillen (Grand Rapids, MI, 1991)

Varia Americana (Amsterdam and Pretoria, 1899)

Vrijheid. Rede ter Bevestiging van Dr. Ph. S. Ronkel (Amsterdam, 1873)

Vrijmaking der Kerk (Amsterdam, 1869)

Lactantius, *De Mortibus Persecutorum* [*c.* 315], ed. and trans. J. L. Creed (Oxford, 1984)

Lambert, Thomas A., "Preaching, Praying, and Policing in Sixteenth-Century Geneva" (Ph.D. Diss. Wisconsin, 1998)

Landau, Peter, "Zum Ursprung des 'Ius ad Rem' in der Kanonistik," in *Proceedings of the Third International Congress of Medieval Canon Law* (1971): 81

Langbein, John H., *Prosecuting Crime in the Renaissance: England, Germany, France* (Cambridge, MA, 1974)

Laursen, John Christian, ed., *New Essays on the Political Thought of the Huguenots of the Refuge* (Leiden, 1995)

Laws and Liberties of Massachusetts Bay (1648), ed. Max Farrand (Cambridge, MA, 1929)

Lecler, Josef, *Toleration and the Reformation*, 3 vols. (London, 1960)

Lerner, Natan, *Religion, Secular Beliefs, and Human Rights: 25 Years After the 1981 Declaration* (Leiden, 2006)

Lewalski, Barbara Kiefer, "*Paradise Lost* and Milton's Politics," in *John Milton: Twentieth-Century Perspectives, Volume 4: Paradise Lost*, ed. J. Martin Evans (New York, 2003), 213

"'To try and teach the erring Soul': Milton's Last Seven Years," in *Milton and the Terms of Liberty*, ed. Graham Parry and Joad Raymond (Cambridge, 2002), 175

Little, David, *Protestantism and World Order* (forthcoming)

"Reformed Faith and Religious Liberty," in *Major Themes in the Reformed Tradition* ed. Donald R. McKim (Grand Rapids, MI 1992), 196

"Roger Williams and the Separation of Church and State," in *Religion and the State: Essays in Honor of Leo Pfeffer*, ed. James E. Wood, Jr. (Waco, TX, 1985), 1

Loades, David, *Politics, Censorship and the English Reformation* (London, 1991)

Locke, John, *The Works of John Locke*, 12th edn., 9 vols. (London, 1824)

Two Treatises of Government, ed. Peter Laslett (Cambridge, 1960)

Lomonaco, Fabrizio, "Huguenot Critical Theory and 'Ius Maiestatis' in Huber and Althusius," in Laursen, ed., *New Essays*, 171

Lugo, Luis E., ed., *Religion, Pluralism, and Public Life: Abraham Kuyper's Legacy for the Twenty-First Century* (Grand Rapids, MI, 2000)

Lutz, Donald S., *Colonial Origins of the American Constitution: A Documentary History* (Indianapolis, IN, 1998)

The Origins of American Constitutionalism (Baton Rouge, LA, 1988)

Maffei, D., ed., *A Ennio Cortese*, 2 vols. (Rome, 2001)

Malcolm, Joyce Lee, ed., *The Struggle for Sovereignty: Seventeenth-Century English Political Tracts*, 2 vols. (Indianapolis, IN, 1999)

Mäkinen, Virpi and Petter Korkman, eds., *Transformations in Medieval and Early-Modern Rights Discourse* (Dordrecht, 2006)

Manetsch, Scott M., *Theodore Beza and the Quest for Peace in France, 1572–1598* (Leiden, 2000)

Maritain, Jacques, "Introduction," in UNESCO, *Human Rights: Comments and Interpretations* (New York, 1949)

Maruyama, Tadataka, *The Ecclesiology of Theodore Beza: The Reform of the True Church* (Geneva, 1978)

Mather, Cotton, *Bonifacious: An Essay Upon The Good*, ed. David Levin (Cambridge, MA, 1966)

Ratio Disciplinae Fratrum Nov-Anglicorum (Boston, 1726)

Mather, Increase, *A Sermon Occasioned by the Execution of a Man Found Guilty of Murder* (Boston, 1687)

The Excellency of a Publick Spirit (Boston, 1702)

The Necessity of Reformation With the Expedients Thereunto Asserted (Boston, 1679)

The Wicked Mans Portion, or A Sermon Preached at the Lecture in Boston in New England . . . 1674 (Boston, 1675)

Mather, Richard, *Church Government and Church-Covenant Discussed* (London, 1643)

McCullough, David, *John Adams* (New York, 2001)

McDowell, Nicholas, *The English Radical Imagination: Culture, Religion, and Revolution, 1630–1660* (Oxford, 2003)

McGiffert, Michael, "American Puritan Studies in the 1960's," *William & Mary Quarterly* (3rd ser.) 27 (1970): 36

McKim, Donald R., *Introducing the Reformed Faith* (Louisville, KY, 2001)
Major Themes in the Reformed Tradition (Grand Rapids, MI, 1992)

McLoughlin, William G., *New England Dissent, 1630–1833: The Baptists and the Separation of Church and State*, 2 vols. (Cambridge, MA, 1971)
"The Balkcom Case (1782) and the Pietist Theory of Separation of Church and State," *William & Mary Quarterly* (3rd ser.) 24 (1967): 267

McMichael, Jack R., and Barbara Taft, eds., *The Writings of William Walwyn* (Athens, GA, 1989)

McNeill, John T., "John Calvin on Civil Government," in *Calvinism and Political Order*, ed. George L. Hunt (Philadelphia, 1965), 30
"Natural Law and the Teaching of the Reformers," *Journal of Religion* 26 (1946): 168
"The Democratic Element in Calvin's Thought," *Church History* 18 (1949): 153
The History and Character of Calvinism (Oxford and New York, 1954)

Meland, Bernard E., "John Milton: Puritan or Liberal?" *Encounter* 33 (1972): 129

Menk, Gerhard, "Johannes Althusius und die Reichsstaatsrechtslehre," in *Politische Theorie des Johannes Althusius*, ed. Werner Krawietz and Dieter Wyduckdel (Berlin, 1988) 255

Meron, Theodore, ed., *Human Rights in International Law: Legal and Policy Issues* (Oxford, 1984)

Meyer, Jacob C., *Church and State in Massachusetts From 1740–1833*, repr. edn. (New York, 1968)

Miller, Joshua, "Direct Democracy and the Puritan Theory of Membership," *The Journal of Politics* 53 (1991): 57

Miller, Perry, *Orthodoxy in Massachusetts 1630–1650: A Genetic Study* (Cambridge, MA, 1933)
"Thomas Hooker and the Democracy of Early Connecticut," *New England Quarterly* 4 (1931): 663

Miller, Perry and Thomas Johnson eds., *The Puritans* (New York, 1938)

Milton, John, *Areopagatica and Other Political Writings of John Milton* (Indianapolish, IN, 1999)
Complete Prose Works of John Milton, 8 vols., gen. ed. Don M. Wolfe (New Haven, 1953–)

Monter, E. W., "Crime and Punishment in Calvin's Geneva, 1562," *AFR* 64 (1973): 281

Morély, Jean, *Traicté de la discipline & police Chrestienne* (Lyon, 1562), facs. ed. (Geneva, 1968)

Morgan, Edmund S., *Roger Williams: The Church and State* (New York, 1967)
The Puritan Dilemma: The Story of John Winthrop (Boston, 1958)
The Puritan Family: Religion and Domestic Relations in Seventeenth-Century New England, rev. edn. (Westport, CT, 1980)

Morgan, Edmund S., ed., *Puritan Political Ideas 1558–1794*, repr. edn. (Indianapolis, IN and Cambridge, 2003)

Morison, Samuel Eliot, *A History of the Constitution of Massachusetts* (Boston, 1917)
  Builders of the Bay Colony (Boston, 1930)
  "The Struggle over the Adoption of the Constitution of Massachusetts, 1780," *Massachusetts Historical Society Proceedings* 50 (1916–1917): 353

Morris, Richard B., *Studies in the History of American Law with Special Reference to the Seventeenth and Eighteenth Centuries* (New York, 1930)

Motley, John Lothrop, *The Rise of the Dutch Republic: A History*, 3 vols. (New York, 1877)

Muldoon, James, "The Great Commission and the Canon Law," in *Sharing the Book: Religious Perspectives on the Rights and Wrongs of Proselytism*, ed. John Witte, Jr. and Richard C. Martin (Maryknoll, NY, 1999), 158

Muller, Richard A., *After Calvin: Studies in the Development of a Theological Tradition* (Oxford, 2003)

Nobbs, Douglas, *Theocracy and Toleration: A Study of the Disputes in Dutch Calvinism from 1600–1650* (Cambridge, 1938)

Noll, Mark A., *America's God: From Jonathan Edwards to Abraham Lincoln* (Oxford and New York, 2002)

Noonan, John T., *A Church That Can and Cannot Change: The Development of Catholic Moral Teaching* (Notre Dame, IN, 2005)

Norton, John, *Orthodox Evangelist* (London, 1654)

Novak, David, *Covenantal Rights: A Study in Jewish Political Theory* (Princeton, 2000)

Nürnberger, Richard, "Calvin und Servet: Eine Begegnung zwischen reformatorischem Glauben und modernem Unglauben im 16. Jahrhundert," AFR 49 (1958): 196

Nurser, John, *For All Peoples and All Nations: Christian Churches and Human Rights* (Geneva, 2005)

Oakes, Urian, *New England Pleaded With, and Pressed to Consider the Things Which Concern Her* (Cambridge, MA, 1673)

Oberholzer, Emil, *Delinquent Saints: Disciplinary Action in the Early Congregationalist Churches of Massachusetts* (New York, 1956)

Ong, Walter, *Ramus and the Decay of Dialogue: From the Art of Discourse to the Art of Reason* (Chicago, 2004)

Palmer, R. R., *The Age of the Democratic Revolution*, 2 vols. (Princeton, 1959–1964)

Parker, Geoffrey, *The Dutch Revolt* (Ithaca, NY, 1977)

Parker, William R., *Milton's Contemporary Reputation* (Columbus, OH, 1940)

Parry, Graham and Joad Raymond, eds., *Milton and the Terms of Liberty* (Cambridge, 2002)

Parsons, Francis, *Six Men of Yale* (New Haven, 1939)

Pelikan, Jaroslav, *Reformation of Church and Dogma, 1300–1700* (Chicago, 1984)

Perkins, William, *The Work of William Perkins*, ed. Ian Breward, 3 vols. (Abingdon, Berks, 1970)

Perry, Michael J., *The Idea of Human Rights: Four Inquiries* (New York and Oxford, 1998)
  Toward a Theory of Human Rights: Religion, Law, Courts (Cambridge, 2007)
Phillipson, Nicholas, and Quentin Skinner, eds., *Political Discourse in Early Modern Britain* (Cambridge, 1993)
Po-Chia Hsai, R. and Henk van Nierop, *Calvinism and Religious Toleration in the Dutch Golden Age* (Cambridge, 2002)
Ponet, John, *A Shorte Treatise of Politike Power* (1556), facs. ed. appended to Winthrop S. Hudson, *John Ponet (1516?–1556): Advocate of Limited Monarchy* (Chicago, 1942)
Pope, Robert G. *The Half-Way Covenant: Church Membership in Puritan New England* (Princeton, 1969)
Preston, John, *The New Covenant or the Saints Portion* (London, 1629)
Puchinger, G., *Gesprek over de Onbekende Kuyper* (Kampen, 1971)
Ramsey, Paul, *Basic Christian Ethics* (New York, 1950)
Rauschenbusch, Walter, *Selected Writings*, ed. Winthrop S. Hudson (New York, 1984)
Reardon, Barbara, "The Politics of Polemic: John Ponet's Short Treatise on Politic Power and Contemporary Circumstances, 1553–1556," *The Journal of British Studies* 22 (1982): 35
Records of the First Church at Dorchester in New England, 1636–1734 (Boston, 1891)
Records of the Governor and Company of the Massachusetts Bay in New England, ed. N. Shurtleff, 5 vols. (Boston, 1853–1854)
The Register of the Company of Pastors of Geneva in the Time of Calvin, trans. Philip E. Hughes (Grand Rapids, MI 1966)
Registers of the Consistory of Geneva in the Time of Calvin, gen. ed. Robert M. Kingdon, trans. M. Wallace McDonald, 21 vols. (Grand Rapids, MI 2000–)
Registres de la compagnie des pasteurs de Genève au temps de Calvin, ed. Jean-Francois Bergier and Robert M. Kingdon, 2 vols. (Geneva, 1964)
Reibstein, Ernst, *Johannes Althusius als Fortsetzer der Schule von Salamanca* (Karlsruhe, 1955)
Reicke, Bo, *Die zehn Worte in Geschichte und Gegenwart* (Tübingen, 1973)
Reid, Charles J., Jr., *Power Over the Body, Equality in the Family: Rights and Domestic Relations in Medieval Canon Law* (Grand Rapids, MI, 2004)
  "Rights in Thirteenth Century Canon Law: An Historical Investigation" (Ph.D. Diss. Cornell, 1994)
  "Roots of a Democratic Church Polity in the History of the Canon Law," *Canon Law Society of America Proceedings* 60 (1998): 150
  "Thirteenth Century Canon Law and Rights: The Word *ius* and its Range of Subjective Meanings," *Studia Canonica* 30 (1996): 295
Reid, W. Stanford, "John Knox's Theology of Political Government," *Sixteenth Century Journal* 19 (1988): 529
Ridley, Jasper G., *John Knox* (Oxford, 1968)

Riker, William H., "Dutch and American Federalism," *Journal of History of Ideas* 18 (1957): 495

Federalism: Origin, Operation, Significance (Boston, 1964)

Rivoire, Emile and Victor van Berchem, eds., *Les Registres du Conseil de Genève*, 13 vols. (Geneva, 1900–1940)

Les Sources du droit du canton de Genève, 4 vols. (Aarau, 1927–1935)

Robertson, D. B., *The Religious Foundations of Leveller Democracy* (New York, 1951)

Robey, R., ed., *Church Covenant: Two Tracts* (New York, 1972)

Rogers, Thorold, "Review of William E. Griffis, *Brave Little Holland*," *The New England Magazine* (n.s.) 10 (1894): 517

Rogier, L., *Geschiedenis van het katholicisme in Noord-Nederland in de zestiende en zeventiende eeuw*, 3 vols. (Amsterdam, 1945–1947)

Rollock, Robert, *Selected Works of Robert Rollock*, ed. W. Gunn, 2 vols. (Edinburgh, 1849)

Rossiter, Clinton, *The First American Revolution: The American Colonies on the Eve of Revolution* (New York, 1956)

The Political Thought of the American Revolution (New York, 1963)

Rousseau, Jean-Jacques, *The Social Contract and the Discourse on the Origin of Inequality*, ed. Lester G. Crocker (New York, 1967)

Rowen, Herbert H., ed., *The Low Countries in Early Modern Times: A Documentary History* (New York, 1972)

Russell-Smith, H. F., *Harrington and his Oceana: A Study of a 17th Century Utopia and its Influence in America* (Cambridge, 1914)

Rutherford, Samuel, *A Free Disputation Against Pretended Liberty of Conscience Tending to Resolve Doubts Moved by Mr. John Goodwin, Dr. Jeremy Taylor . . . Arminians, Socinians . . . Contending for Lawless Liberty, or Licentious Toleration of Sects and Heresies* (London, 1649)

Lex, Rex, or the Law and the Prince (1644), facs. edn. (Harrisonburg, VA, 1982)

The Divine Right of Church-Government and Excommunication (London, 1646)

Rutman, Darrett B., "God's Bridge Falling Down": Another Approach to New England Studies Assayed," *William & Mary Quarterly* (3rd ser.) 19 (1962): 408

Sap, John W., *Paving the Way for Revolution: Calvinism and the Struggle for a Democratic Constitutional State* (Amsterdam, 2001)

Saurat, Denis, *Milton: Man and Thinker* (London, 1944)

Scheible, Heinz, *Das Widerstandsrecht als Problem der deutsche Protestanten 1523–1546* (Gütersloh, 1969)

Schulte, J. W. Nordholt, *The Dutch Republic and American Independence*, trans. H. H. Rowen (Chapel Hill, NC, 1982)

Scott, Jonathan, *Commonwealth Principles: Republican Writing of the English Revolution* (Cambridge, 2004)

Scottow, J. "Narrative of the Planting of Massachusetts (1694)," in *Collections of the Massachusetts Historical Society* (4th ser.), 52 vols. (1871), IV:279

Scupin, Hans Ulrich *et al.*, eds., *Althusius-Bibliographie. Bibliographie zur politischen Ideengeschichte und Staatslehre, zum Staatsrecht und zur Verfassungsgeschichte des 16. bis 18. Jahrhundert* (Berlin, 1973)

Selden, John, *De iure naturali et gentium, juxta disciplinam Ebraeorum libri septem* (London, 1640)

Opera Omnia tam edita quam inedita in tribus voluminibus, 3 vols. (London, 1726)

Servetus, Michael, *De haereticis an sint persequendi* (1553), fasc. edn. (Geneva, 1954)

Shanley, Mary Lynn, "Marriage Contract and Social Contract in Seventeenth Century English Political Thought," *Western Political Quarterly* 32 (1979): 79

Sharma, Arvind, *Hinduism and Human Rights: A Conceptual Approach* (New Delhi, 2004)

Shepard, Thomas, *The Works of Thomas Shepard*, 3 vols. (Boston, 1853)

Shestack, Jerome J., "The Jurisprudence of Human Rights," in *Human Rights in International Law: Legal and Policy Issues*, ed. Theodor Meron (Oxford, 1984), 75

Shuffelton, Frank, *Thomas Hooker, 1586–1647* (Princeton, 1977)

Shuffelton, Frank, ed., *The American Enlightenment* (Rochester, NY, 1993)

Skillen, James W., and Rockne M. McCarthy, eds., *Political Order and the Plural Structure of Society* (Atlanta, GA, 1991)

Skillen, James W., and W. Carlson Thies, "Religion and Political Development in Nineteenth Century Holland," *Publius* (Summer, 1982): 43

Skinner, Quentin, *Foundations of Modern Political Thought*, 2 vols. (Cambridge, 1978)

Liberty Before Liberalism (Cambridge, 1998)

Stackhouse, Max L., *Creeds, Society, and Human Rights* (Grand Rapids, MI, 1984)

Stewart, Randall, "Puritan Literature and the Flowering of New England," *William & Mary Quarterly* (3rd ser.) 3 (1946): 319

Stokes, Anson P., *Church and State in the United States*, 3 vols. (New York, 1950)

Stone, Lawrence, *Road to Divorce: England 1530–1987* (Oxford, 1990)

The Causes of the English Revolution, 1629–1642 (San Francisco, 1972)

Stolleis, Michael, ed. *Recht, Verfassung und Verwaltung in der frühneuzeitlichen Stadt* (Böhlau, 1991)

Strauss, Gerald, *Law, Resistance and the State: The Opposition to Roman Law in Reformation Germany* (Princeton, 1986)

Strauss, Leo, *Jewish Philosophy and the Crisis of Modernity: Essays and Lectures in Modern Jewish Thought*, ed. Kenneth H. Green (Albany, NY, 1997)

Natural Right and History (Chicago, 1953)

The Political Philosophy of Hobbes: Its Basis and its Genesis, trans. Elsa Sinclair (Chicago, 1952)

What is Political Philosophy? And Other Studies (Glencoe, IL, 1959)

Strohm, Christoph, "Althusius' Rechtslehre im Kontext des reformierten Protestantismus," in *Juriprudenz, Politische Theorie, Politische Theologie*, 71

Ethik im frühen Calvinismus (Berlin and New York, 1996)

"Recht und Jurisprudenz im reformierten Protestantismus 1550–1650," *ZSS (KA)* 123 (2006): 453

Talmon, Jacob Leib, *The Origins of Totalitarian Democracy* (Boston, 1952)

Taylor, Robert J., *Construction of the Massachusetts Constitution* (Worcester, MA, 1980)

Taylor, Robert J., ed., *Massachusetts, Colony to Commonwealth: Documents on the Formation of its Constitution* (Chapel Hill, NC, 1961)

Thompson, C. Bradley, *John Adams and the Spirit of Liberty* (Lincoln, NE, 1998)

Thompson, John Lee, *John Calvin and the Daughters of Sarah* (Geneva, 1992)

Thorpe, Francis, ed., *The Federal and State Constitutions, Colonial Charters, and Other Organic Laws*, 7 vols. (Washington, DC, 1909)

Tierney, Brian, *Religion, Law, and the Growth of Constitutional Thought, 1150–1650* (Cambridge, 1982)

    "Religious Rights in Historical Perspective," in *Religious Human Rights in Global Perspective: Religious Perspectives* ed. John Witte, Jr. and Johan D. van der Vyer (The Hague, 1996), 17

    Rights, Law, and Infallibility in Medieval Thought (Aldershot, Hampshire, 1997)

    The Idea of Natural Rights: Studies on Natural Rights, Natural Law, and Church Law, 1150–1625 (Grand Rapids, MI, 1997)

    "Villey, Ockham, and the Origin of Individual Rights," in *The Weightier Matters of the Law: Essays on Law and Religion*, ed. John Witte, Jr. and Frank S. Alexander, GA (Atlanta, 1988), 1

Tillyard, E. M. W., *The Miltonic Setting Past and Present* (Cambridge, 1938)

Todd, Jonathan, *Civil Rulers the Ministers of God for Good to Men* (London, 1749)

Towers, S. Mutchow, *Control of Religious Printing in Early Stuart England* (Woodbridge, Suffolk, 2003)

Tracy, David, "Religion and Human Rights in the Public Realm," *Daedalus* 112 (4) (1983): 237

Traer, Robert, *Faith in Human Rights: Support in Religious Traditions for a Global Struggle* (Washington, DC, 1991)

Troeltsch, Ernst, *The Social Teaching of the Churches*, trans. O. Wyon, 2nd. impr., 2 vols. (London, 1949)

Trusen, Winfried, "Forum internum und gelehrtes Recht im Spätmittelalter," *ZSS (KA)* 57 (1971): 83

Tuck, Richard, *Natural Rights Theories: Their Origins and Development* (Cambridge and New York, 1979)

Tuttle, Elizabeth, "Biblical References in the Political Pamphlets of the Levellers and Milton," in *Milton and Republicanism*, ed. David Armitage, Armand Himy and Quentin Skinner, (Cambridge, 1995), 63–81.

Ullmann, Walter, *Medieval Political Thought*, rev. edn. (Harmondworth, 1975)

    Principles of Government and Politics in the Middle Ages, 3rd edn. (London, 1974)

van der Berg, J. and P. G. Hoftijzer, eds., *Church Change and Revolution* (Leiden, 1991)

van der Vyver, Johan D., *Leuven Lectures on Religious Institutions, Religious Communities and Rights* (Leuven, 2004)

Seven Lectures on Human Rights (Cape Town, Wynberg, Johannesburg, 1976)
"The Doctrine of Private-Law Rights," in *Huldigingsbundel vir W. A. Joubert*, ed. S. Strauss (Durban, 1988), 201
"Universality and Relativism of Human Rights: American Relativism," *Buffalo Human Rights Law Review* 4 (1998): 43
VanDrunen, David, "The Two Kingdoms: A Reassessment of the Transformationist Calvin," *Calvin Theological Journal* 40 (2005): 248
van Gelderen, Martin, *The Political Thought of the Dutch Revolt, 1555–1590* (Cambridge, 1992)
van Heijsbergen, P., *Geschiedenis der Rechtswetenschap in Nederland* (Amsterdam, 1925)
van Kappen, O. Moorman, "Die Niederlande in der 'Politica' des Johannes Althusius," in *Politische Theorie des Johannes Althusius*, ed. Werner Krawietz and Dieter Wyduckdel (Berlin, 1988), 123
van Kley, Dale, *The Religious Origins of the French Revolution: From Calvin to the Civil Constitution, 1560–1791* (New Haven, 1996)
van Meteren, E., *Historien de Nederlanden* VIII (Amsterdam, 1647)
van 't Spijker, Willem, "The Kingdom of Christ According to Bucer and Calvin," in *Calvin and the State*, ed. Peter de Klerk (Grand Rapids, MI, 1993), 121
van Toorenenbergen, J. J., *Gheschiedenissen ende Handelingen die voornemelick aengaen de nederduystche natie ende gemeynten wonende in Engelant ende uit bysonder tot Londen* (Amsterdam, 1873)
Vasak, Karel, "A 30-Year Struggle," *UNESCO Courier* (November 1977): 29
"Foreword," in *The International Dimensions of Human Rights*, ed. Karel Vasak (Westport, CT, 1982)
"Pour une troisième génération des droits de l'homme," in *Études et Essais sur le Droit International Humanitaire et sur les Principes de la Croix-Rouge en l'Honneur de Jean Pictet*, ed. Christophe Swinarksi (The Hague, 1984), 837
Villey, Michel, *La Formation de la pensée juridique moderne* (Paris, 1968)
Le Droit et les droits de l'homme (Paris, 1983)
Leçons d'histoire de la philosophie du droit, new edn. (Paris, 1977).
Voetius, Gisbertus, *Politica Ecclesiastica*, 4 vols. (Leiden, 1663–1676)
Tractatus selecti de Politica Ecclesiastica, ed. F. L. Rutgers (Amsterdam, 1885)
Waldron, Jeremy, *God, Locke, and Equality: Christian Foundations of John Locke's Political Thought* (Cambridge, 2002)
Walker, Williston, ed., *The Creeds and Platforms of Congregationalism* (New York, 1960)
Walzer, Michael, "Revolutionary Ideology: The Case of the Marian Exiles," *The American Political Science Review* 57 (1963): 643
Spheres of Justice: A Defense of Pluralism and Equality (New York, Basic Books, 1983)
The Revolution of the Saints: A Study in the Origins of Radical Politics (Cambridge, MA, 1965)
Ward, Nathaniel, [Theodore de la Gaurd], *The Simple Cobler of Aggawam in America* (1646/7), ed. P. M. Zall (Lincoln, NE, 1969)

Weir, David A., *Early New England: A Covenanted Society* (Grand Rapids, MI, 2005)

    The Origins of Federal Theology in Sixteenth-Century Reformation Thought (Oxford and New York, 1990)

Wellman, Carl, *An Approach to Rights* (The Hague and Boston, 1997)

Wells, David F., ed., *Reformed Theology in America: A History of its Modern Development* (Grand Rapids, MI, 1985)

Wessels, J., *History of Roman Dutch Law* (Cape Town, 1908)

Whitford, David M., *Tyranny and Resistance: The Magdeburg Confession and the Lutheran Tradition* (St. Louis, MO, 2001)

Whitney, Peter, *The Transgression of a Land Punished by a Multitude of Rulers* (Boston, 1774)

Willard, Samuel, *A Compleat Body of Divinity* (Boston, 1726)

    A Sermon Upon the Death of John Leverett, Esq. (Boston, 1679)

    Covenant-Keeping the Way to Blessedness (Boston, 1682)

    Morality not be Relied on for Life (Boston, 1700)

    Walking with God, The Great Duty and Privilege of True Christians (Boston, 1701)

Williams, Elisha, *The Essential Rights and Liberties of Protestants* (Boston, 1744)

Williams, Roger, *The Complete Writings of Roger Williams*, 7 vols. (New York, 1963)

Winters, Peter J., "Das Widerstandrecht bei Althusius," in *Politische Theorie des Johannes Althusius*, ed. Werner Krawietz and Dieter Wyduckdel (Berlin, 1988), 543

Winthrop, John, *Life and Letters of John Winthrop*, ed. R. Winthrop, 2 vols., repr. edn. (New York, 1971)

    Winthrop's Journal, ed. James K. Hosmer, 2 vols. (New York, 1908)

    Winthrop Papers, 5 vols. (Boston, 1944)

Wirszubski, C., *Libertas as a Political Idea at Rome During the Late Republic and Early Principate* (Cambridge, 1950)

Wise, John, *A Vindication of the Government of New-England Churches (1717)*, repr. edn. (Gainesville, FL, 1958)

Witte, John, Jr., "A Dickensian Era of Religious Rights," *William and Mary Law Review* 42 (2000): 707

    " 'A Most Mild and Equitable Establishment of Religion': John Adams and the Massachusetts Experiment," *Journal of Church and State 41* (1999): 213

    "Blest be the Ties that Bind: Covenant and Community in Puritan Thought," *Emory Law Journal* 36 (1987): 579

    From Sacrament to Contract: Marriage, Religion, and Law in the Western Tradition (Louisville, KY, 1997)

    God's Joust, God's Justice: Law and Religion in the Western Legal Tradition (Grand Rapids, MI, 2006)

    Law and Protestantism: The Legal Teachings of the Lutheran Reformation (Cambridge and New York, 2002)

    Religion and the American Constititutional Experiment, 2nd edn. (Boulder, CO and London, 2005)

"The Development of Herman Dooyeweerd's Concept of Rights," *South African Law Journal* 110 (1993): 543

"The Plight of Canon Law in the Dutch Republic," in *Canon Law in Protestant Lands*, ed. R. H. Helmholz (Berlin, 1992), 135

Witte, John, Jr., and Frank S. Alexander, eds., *The Teachings of Modern Christianity on Law, Politics, and Human Nature*, 2 vols. (New York and London, 2005)

The Weightier Matters of the Law: Essays on Law and Religion (Atlanta, GA, 1988)

Witte, John, Jr., and Eliza Ellison, eds., *Covenant Marriage in Comparative Perspective* (Grand Rapids, MI, 2005)

Witte, John, Jr., and Robert M. Kingdon, *Sex, Marriage and Family in John Calvin's Geneva*, 3 vols. (Grand Rapids, MI, 2005–)

Witte, John, Jr., and Richard C. Martin, eds., *Sharing the Book: Religious Perspectives on the Rights and Wrongs of Proselytism* (Maryknoll, NY, 1999)

Witte, John, Jr., and Johan D. van der Vyver, eds., *Religious Human Rights in Global Perspective: Religious Perspectives* (The Hague, 1996)

Wolf, Erik, *Grosse Rechtsdenker der deutschen Geistesgeschichte*, 4th edn. (Tübingen, 1963)

Rechtstheologische Studien (Frankfurt am Main, 1972)

"Theologie und Sozialordnung bei Calvin," in Erik Wolf, *Rechtstheologische Studien* (Frankfurt am Main, 1972), 3

Wolf, Erik, ed., *Quellenbuch zur Geschichte der deutschen Rechtswissenschaft* (Frankfurt am Main, 1949)

Wolfe, Don M., *Milton in the Puritan Revolution* (New York, 1941)

Wolfe, Don M., ed., *Leveller Manifestoes of the Puritan Revolution* (New York, 1944)

Wolfe, Michael, *The Conversion of Henry IV: Politics, Power, and Religious Beliefs in Early Modern France* (Cambridge, MA, 1993)

Wolgast, Eike, *Die Religionsfrage als Problem des Widerstandsrechts im 16. Jahrhundert* (Heidelberg, 1980)

Wollebius, John, *Compendium Theologiae Christiniae: The Abridgement of Christian Divinity* (London, 1650)

Wollman, David H., "The Biblical Justification for Resistance to Authority in Ponet's and Goodman's Polemics," *Sixteenth Century Journal* 13 (1982): 29

Wolter, Udo, "Amt und Officium in mittelalterlichen Quellen vom 13. bis 15. Jahrhundert: Ein begriffsgeschichtliche Untersuchung," *ZSS KA* 78 (1988): 246

Wolterstorff, Nicholas P., *Until Justice and Peace Embrace* (Grand Rapids, MI, 1983)

Woltjer, J. J., "Dutch Privileges: Real or Imaginary," in *Britain and the Netherlands*, ed. J. S. Bromley and E. H. Kossman (London, 1975), 19

Wood, Gordon S., "Struggle over the Puritans," *New York Review of Books* 36 (1989): 26

The Creation of the American Republic, 1776–1787 (Chapel Hill, NC, 1969)

Woodhouse, A. S. P., *Puritanism and Liberty Being the Army Debates (1647–9)*, 2nd edn. (Chicago, 1951)

Wooton, David, "Leveller Democracy and the Puritan Revolution," in *The Cambridge History of Political Thought, 1450–1700*, ed. J. H. Burns (Cambridge, 1991), 412

Worden, Blair, *The Rump Parliament 1648–1653* (Cambridge, 1974)

World Council of Churches, *Human Rights and Christian Responsibility*, 3 vols. (Geneva, 1975)

Yule, George, *Independents in the English Civil War* (Cambridge, 1958)

Zagorin, Perez, *How the Idea of Religious Toleration Came to the West* (Princeton, 2003)

Zaret, David, *The Heavenly Contract: Ideology and Organization in Pre-Revolutionary Puritanism* (Chicago, 1985)

Zuckert, Catherine H., and Michael P. Zuckert, *The Truth About Leo Strauss: Political Philosophy and American Democracy* (Chicago, 2006)

Zuckert, Michael P., *Launching Liberalism: On Lockean Political Philosophy* (Lawrence, KS, 2002)

  Natural Rights and the New Republicanism (Princeton, 1994)

  The Natural Rights Republic: Studies in the Foundation of the American Political Tradition (Notre Dame, IN, 1996)

Zweig, Stefan, *Strijd rond een brandstapel. Castellio tegen Calvijn* (Amsterdam, 1936)

Zwierlein, Cornel, "The Importance of 'Confessio' in Magdebourg (1550) for Calvinism: A Historiographical Myth," *Bibliothèque d'humanisme et renaissance* 68 (2005): 27

Index to biblical sources

Index

Calvin, John, and foundations Calvinist (*cont.*)
  on God's rights, 65, 116–117
  on heretics and heresy
    Servetus and other open heretics,
      prosecution of, 67
    spiritual liberty accorded to, 46
  historical views of, 39–42
  on law
    abusive authority, litigation as means of
      dealing with, 52
    on canon law, 45–47, 72
    on church law, 70–76
    church respect for rule of law, 78
    education of, 42–43
    equity, concept of, 48, 67
    on moral law, 59–62, 78
    natural law and natural rights, 59
    prominence of law and order in mature
      writings of, 58
    property rights, concern with, 57
    on state law, 62–70
  litigation as means of dealing with abusive
    authority, 52
  Magdeburg Confession, response to, 114–117
  magistrates and ministers, political
    responsibilities of, 52
  mature formulations of, 56–76
  Milton influenced by, 245, 265, 272
  moderation, importance of, 42, 51, 52, 57, 60,
    67
  on moral law, 59–62, 78
  natural law and natural rights, 59
  New England Puritans influenced by, 280,
    319
  persecution of church by state, no provision
    for, 6, 85
  on political liberty of individuals, 44, 47–56
  on political suffrage, 56
  on positive law, 62–70
  on religious liberty, 3
    of church, 56, 75
    church law and individual liberty, 74–75
    differing views on Calvin's contributions
      to, 39–42
    moral law theory and, 62
    Servetus and other open heretics,
      prosecution of, 67
    spiritual liberty or liberty of conscience of
      individuals, 44, 45–47, 74–75, 79
    state law and, 62–70
  on resistance theory, 50–54, 65–66, 87, 114–117
  Servetus, prosecution of, 67
  significance of, 77–80
  single faith in each community, assumption
    of, 6, 85

  on state law, 62–70
  subjective rights talk used by, 57, 61
  theological nature of writings, 40
  two kingdoms theory of, 43–45, 55, 58, 59, 62,
    76
  two-track system of morality in, 78
Calvinism
  Althusius on state establishment of, 173, 175,
    196–199
  in Dutch republic
    control assumed by, 147
    increasing role in revolt, 145–146
    ministerial denunciation of Spanish
      spiritual reforms, 144
  totalitarian aspects of, 1
  use of term, 18
Calvinist rights doctrine, xi–xii, 1–3
  alternative influences on development of
    rights, 328
  in America, 31, 325–334 (*See also* Puritan
    New England)
  Catholic rights doctrine development
    compared to, 330
  constitutional rights and documents
    developed from, 2–3
  doctrinal theology and, 331–334
  Dutch revolt and republic and (*See* Althusius,
    Johannes; Dutch revolt and republic)
  in England (*see* English revolutions; Milton,
    John)
  foundations of (*See* Calvin, John, and
    foundations of Calvinist rights theory)
  influence and significance of, 325–334
  Kuyper on, 325–334
  methodology of study, 18–20
  modern rights classifications and, 34–37
  religious rights as basis for, 2
  resistance, right of (*See* Beza, Theodore, and
    right of resistance)
  resistance theory as critical development in,
    86–87
Cambridge Synod and Platform, 303
canon law, 26, 45–47, 72, 329
capital crime in Puritan New England, 278, 282
Castellio, Sebastian, 47, 69, 89, 94, 97
Catholicism (*See* Roman Catholicism)
censorship, Milton on, 260–268
Chandieu, Antoine de, 89
Chaplin, Jonathan, 328
charity and benevolence, Puritan valuation of,
  299
Charles-Boston Church, Covenant of, 304
Charles I of England, 11, 209–212, 213, 214, 219,
  223–224, 251, 261, 262
Charles II of England, 11, 213, 279